For Ellen

SUMMARY OF CONTENTS

CONTENTS

1   THE CONTEXT OF CONSTITUTIONAL LAW   1

2   JUDICIAL REVIEW AND ITS LIMITS

4   THE FEDERAL COMMERCE POWER   81

5   BEYOND COMMERCE: THE OTHER NATIONAL LEGISLATIVE POWERS

7   SEPARATION OF POWERS   159

8 THE DUE PROCESS CLAUSES — 193

10 STATE ACTION AND CONGRESSIONAL ENFORCEMENT OF CIVIL RIGHTS

11   FREE EXPRESSION OF IDEAS   387

COMMON ABBREVIATIONS IN THE TEXT

Gunther—Gerald Gunther and Kathleen Sullivan, Constitutional Law (14th ed., Foundation Press 2001).

Lockhart, American Constitution—William B. Lockhart, Yale Kamisar, Jesse H. Choper, Steven H. Shiffrin, Richard H. Fallon, The American Constitution (8th ed., West 1996).

Lockhart, Constitutional Rights—William B. Lockhart, Yale Kamisar, Jesse H. Choper, Steven H. Shiffrin, Richard H. Fallon, Constitutional Rights and Liberties (8th ed., West 1996).

Nowak & Rotunda—John E. Nowak, Ronald D. Rotunda, Nowak and Rotunda's Hornbook on Constitutional Law (5th ed., West 1995).

Tribe—Laurence H. Tribe, American Constitutional Law (2d ed., Foundation Press 1988).

Stone, et al.—Geoffrey R. Stone, Louis M. Seidman, Cass R. Sunstein, Mark V. Tushnet, Constitutional Law (4th ed., Aspen Law & Business 2001).

CASEBOOK CORRELATION

Aspen RoadMap	Brest, Levinson, Balkin & Amar, Processes of Constitutional Decisionmaking: Cases and Materials (4th ed. 2000)	Chemerinsky, Constitutional Law (1st ed. 2001)	Farber, Eskridge & Frickey, Constitutional Law: Themes for the Constitution's Third Century (2d ed. 1998)	Gunther & Sullivan, Constitutional Law (13th ed. 1997) References are to chapters (c) and to sections (s)	Lockhart, Kamisar et al., Constitutional Law (8th ed. 1996)	Massey, American Constitutional Law: Powers and Liberties (1st ed. 2000)	Rotunda, Rotunda's Modern Constitutional Law: Cases and Notes (6th ed. 2000)	Stone, Seidman, Sunstein & Tushnet, Constitutional Law (4th ed. 2001)
1. THE CONTEXT OF CONSTITUTIONAL LAW								
A. Introduction	1		1-2	c1, intro		1		
B. Historical Context	1-17	10-21	1-23	c1, s1; c2; c3, s2; c7, intro, s1		3-6		1-22
C. Methods of Constitutional Interpretation	33-44, 137-146		85-131			42-49		55-72, 685-692, 949-951
D. Techniques and Puzzles in Constitutional Adjudication	99-100, 428-435, 464-476	527-533	21-23		17-25	49-51		474-475
2. JUDICIAL REVIEW AND ITS LIMITS								
A. *Marbury v. Madison* and the Theory of Judicial Review	71-103	1-10	33-85	c1, s1	1-21	6-42	1-14, suppl. 1-2	22-45
B. *Martin v. Hunter's Lessee* and the Power to Review State Court Judgments	66-70, 77-79, 143, 731-732	9-10	9, 1023-1025	c1, s3	21-25	26-35	14-28	45-49
C. Congressional Power to Control the Jurisdiction of Federal Courts	730-732	21-28	1017-1025	c1, s4	43-51	59-72	28-37	51-55, 72-84
D. The Eleventh Amendment: A Constitutional Limit to Federal Jurisdiction	71-72, 611-613	201-230	851-856	c3, s4		121-124	43-45	49-51, 230-231
E. The Concept of Justiciability	730-735	28-89	1052-1054	c1, s2	51-55	72-73	46-51, 1460-1473	85-86
F. Standing to Sue	732-733	32-66	1054, 1059-1082	c1, s2	1511-1537	76-92	1423-1473, suppl. 101-102	87-112
G. No Advisory Opinions	639, 733-734	29-32, 71-72	63, 1010	c1, s2	1505-1511	72-75	37-45	86-87

Aspen RoadMap	Brest, Levinson, Balkin & Amar	Chemerinsky	Farber, Eskridge & Frickey	Gunther & Sullivan	Lockhart, Kamisar et al.	Massey	Rotunda	Stone, Seidman, Sunstein & Tushnet
H. Ripeness and Mootness	899, 1172	66-76	1054-1059	c1, s2	1537-1549	94-95	1412-1423, suppl. 101	133-135
I. Political Questions	613-614, 733-735	76-89	129-131, 761-766, 1030-1052	c1, s2	25-43, 1530-1537	96-117	45-69	112-133
J. Declining to Exercise Jurisdiction: Abstention and Other "Passive Virtues"	415-463		851-856			117-121		135-136
3. FEDERALISM, THE SUPREMACY CLAUSE, AND THE "NECESSARY AND PROPER" CLAUSE								
A. What Federalism Means	1-6, 60-70, 415-463, 565-620	1-2, 99-102	749-750	c2		125-131	10-14	137-160, 199-203, 182-183, 252-253, 327, 1418-1419, 1502-1506
B. The Supremacy Clause	168-214	303-317	900-904	c5, s3	281-287	34-35, 342-353	147-154, suppl 3-4	252, 324-328
C. The Scope of the "Necessary and Proper" Clause	17-33	91-102	750-766	c2	60-67	133-158	70-81	65-69
4. THE FEDERAL COMMERCE POWER								
A. The Commerce Clause	117-121	102-180	766, 769, 903-904	c3, s1		158		160-161
B. Doctrine Before 1937	126-143, 355-378	102-119	769-808, 857-862	c3, s2	67-80, 221-234	183-194	82-97, 165-189	143-149, 160-175
C. Franklin Roosevelt versus The Nine Old Men	463-465	119-123	781-785, 793-795	c3, s2	80-100	194-199	188-189	174-179
D. Modern Doctrine	465-476, 511-533	119-159	789-808	c3, s1; c3, s3	112-120	158-183	189-200, 217-235, suppl. 5-18	149-160, 179-203
E. State Autonomy as a Limit on the Federal Commerce Power	148-181, 551-613	91-102, 133-180	820-851, 900-903	c3, ss4, 5	145-158	207-238	236-270, suppl. 18-19	230-256

Aspen RoadMap	Brest, Levinson, Balkin & Amar	Chemerinsky	Farber, Eskridge & Frickey	Gunther & Sullivan	Lockhart, Kamisar et al.	Massey	Rotunda	Stone, Seidman, Sunstein & Tushnet
C. Content-Based Regulation of Speech	378-387	903-919, 968-1128	566-655	c11, ss2-6	614-760	855-978	931-944, 1034-1058, 1103-1171, 1245-1294, suppl. 75-77	1005-1091, 112-1234
D. Content-Neutral Regulations of Speech	1450-1475	903-919, 1137-1143	564-566, 575-577, 635-672	c12, ss1-2; c13, s3	761-808, 875-909, 1011-1038	979-1008	1206-1225	1234-1365
E. Government as Sovereign and Proprietor	1427-1450	1129-1180	672-685	c12, s2C; c13, s2C	992-1010	1008-1042	961-1034, suppl. 44-64	1044-1051, 1086-1088, 1246-1301, 1346-1350
F. Implicit Expression Rights	768-772, 1101-1102, 1135, 1249, 1419-1427, 1452-1457, 1481-1492	953-961, 1180-1200	177-193, 632-634, 652-672, 685-691, 705-710, 709-710	c12, s2B	910-937	1058-1083	1171-1206, suppl. 64-74	1256-1257, 1266-1268, 1359-1364
G. Free Expression and the Political Process		1113-1128, 1184-1185		c12, s2A4; c13, s1B; c13, s4D	898-910, 937-963	1083-1106	1225-1244, suppl. 74-75	1286-1288, 1323-1350, 1352-1359
H. Freedom of the Press	60-70	1201-1236	591-603, 632-635, 652-655, 693, 694	c13, s4	937-963	1106-1118	1058-1103	1365-1409
12. THE RELIGION CLAUSES								
A. Introduction and Overview	1587-1593	1237-1246	710-711	c14, intro & s1		1119-1124		1411-1426
B. The Establishment Clause	1571-1604	1266-1324	724-748	c14, s3	1039-1105	1146-1161	1295-1381, suppl. 78-100	1426-1469, 1486-1500
C. The Free Exercise Clause	309-314, 1475-1481	1246-1266	415, 711-724	c14, s2	1105-1127	1124-1146	1381-1411	1469-1500
13. ECONOMIC RIGHTS: THE TAKINGS CLAUSE AND THE CONTRACTS CLAUSE								
A. Introduction and Overview	445-463	449-482	418-431	c8, s2A (intro); s2B (intro)		605		942
B. The Takings Clause	405, 446-463, 104-117, 146-147, 415-445	497-526	429-448	c8, s2A	338-363	605-606	524-541	957-992
C. The Contracts Clause		482-497	418-420	c8, s2B	363-369	638-653	513-524	942-957

CAPSULE SUMMARY

Don't use this summary instead of the outline itself. Use it for review.

 ## THE CONTEXT OF CONSTITUTIONAL LAW

A. HISTORY AND STRUCTURE

The Constitution's meaning has changed over time, partly by amendment but mostly by judicial interpretation. The original design of a central government of a few defined powers of national consequence and autonomous states exercising domestic policy choices independent of the central government has been transformed into a central government of vast power, with the states exercising sharply limited independent policy choices. Recently, however, the Court has begun to exercise meaningful review of the extent of the federal government's powers.

1. Extent of Federal Power

While the national government created by the Constitution possesses an enormous range of powers it is not, however, all-powerful. The Constitution gives the national government only certain enumerated powers, and limits the exercise of even those powers by the various individual rights provisions of the Constitution—primarily but not exclusively the Bill of Rights. Courts generally exercise very deferential review over the scope of the national government's powers. As a consequence, federalism—the allocation of governmental power between states and the central government—has become primarily **politically enforceable** rather than **judicially enforceable**. This state of affairs is changing as the Court steadily exercises meaningful judicial review.

2. Limits on State Power

There are express and implied limits on state power. Various clauses in Article I, the supremacy clause of Article VI, the privileges and immunities clause of Article IV, and the 13th, 14th, and 15th Amendments are the principal express limitations. By judicial interpretation, most of the Bill of Rights is enforceable against the states through the due process clause of the 14th Amendment. Through the supremacy clause Congress may preempt state law by ordinary legislation that is otherwise legitimate. States, of course, are also limited by the independent provisions of their state constitutions.

B. METHODS OF CONSTITUTIONAL INTERPRETATION

There are five major ways of interpreting the Constitution. The best constitutional arguments are persuasive in each of these five modes. The weakest arguments fail to persuade in any of these modes. The toughest cases require the interpreter to choose which mode is most relevant to the problem at hand.

1. Textual

Meaning is to be derived from the present sense of the words in the Constitution. This isn't much help if the words are themselves open-ended, like ''equal protection.''

2. Historical

Meaning is to be derived from the original intentions of the draftsmen, if known, and the subsequent historical sense of the provision in question.

3. Structural

Meaning is to be derived from the relationships among governments, and between governments and people, created by the Constitution. For example, since the constitutional structure presumes a central government of limited power (but supreme within its sphere of power) and autonomous state governments (supreme within their sphere of power) it is a reasonable structural implication to confine federal power to ensure autonomous state governance.

4. Doctrinal

Meaning is to be derived from past judicial precedents on the Constitution. This is the common law method of reasoning from prior decisions, treated as binding under the doctrine of *stare decisis*.

5. Prudential

Meaning is to be derived from practical realities. This form of reasoning is especially common in separation of powers problems involving the proper role of President and Congress with respect to foreign affairs.

C. LEVELS OF JUDICIAL REVIEW

So far as the courts are concerned, constitutional law boils down to what level of judicial review applies to challenged actions of government. Laws are presumed to be valid, and so most governmental actions are subjected to **minimal scrutiny,** or **deferential review.** But some laws or actions are so facially suspicious that they are presumed to be invalid and are subjected to **strict scrutiny.** A variety of issues are subjected to **intermediate scrutiny.** And some issues are evaluated under custom formulae that are, nevertheless, variations on this theme of three levels of review.

1. Minimal Scrutiny

Sometimes called *rational basis review,* this deferential scrutiny places the burden of proof on the challenger to prove that the law has **no** *rational relationship* to a *legitimate state interest.* A legitimate state interest is any interest that is not otherwise unlawful. A rational relationship to that interest simply means that the connection is plausible and not bizarre or surreal. In most applications, the courts will accept purely hypothetical state interests, even if there is no evidence that the state actually had the hypothesized interest as its objective.

2. Strict Scrutiny

Some laws or actions openly appear to violate our understanding of the Constitution, such as a law that forbids political speeches or one that forbids interracial marriages. When the challenged law or action comes with an indicator of invalidity it is presumed to be invalid and the government has the burden of proving that the law is *necessary* to accomplishing a *compelling government objective.* Necessary means essential. Usually the government must prove that the law is the most narrowly tailored, or least restrictive, way of achieving the compelling objective. It is not enough to show that the law is rationally related to the objective. A compelling objective is one that is of critical importance, not just legitimate. It must be something of overwhelming social importance, such as the elimination of racial distinctions.

3. Intermediate Review

Intermediate review can take a variety of forms. It is triggered if a law or action displays some qualified, or tentative, indicator of invalidity, such as distinctions based on sex. The government must prove that the law is *substantially related* to an *important government objective.* This formulation attempts to split the difference between strict scrutiny and minimal scrutiny. "Substantially related" means that the law has to be more than rational but not necessarily the least restrictive way of achieving the government's goal. An important objective is more than merely legitimate but not so pressing or critical as a compelling objective. This is a highly subjective standard.

4. Other Standards of Review

A number of issues have specialized, custom-built standards of review, but these are really just specialized applications of minimal scrutiny, strict scrutiny, or intermediate scrutiny.

Example: Most dormant commerce clause issues are evaluated under a balancing test that presumes the validity of the state law unless it is proven that the burdens it places on interstate commerce substantially outweigh the legitimate local benefits of the law. This is a unique standard but it is really just a specific application of deferential review.

Example: State laws that burden the ability of out-of-state residents to earn a living are presumed to violate Article IV's privileges and immunities clause unless the state can prove that there is some good reason, apart from being out of staters, for the discrimination. This unique test is really just a specific application of intermediate scrutiny.

 ## 2   JUDICIAL REVIEW AND ITS LIMITS

A.   JUDICIAL REVIEW

Federal courts have the power to decide if government conduct is in violation of the Constitution. The Supreme Court may review the final judgments of the highest courts of the states, but *only as to matters of federal law.* Judicial review is implied by the Constitution's structure, has a sound basis in history and the intentions of the Framers, and is a practical necessity to make the Constitution supreme law. But the fact that unelected and politically unaccountable judges exercise a veto power over the actions of democratically elected lawmakers is inconsistent with democratic self-governance. Accordingly, the courts recognize that the scope of judicial review is not (and should not be) unlimited.

1. Scope of Judicial Review

A number of doctrines confine the scope of judicial review. Some are constitutionally required; some are created by the Court for prudent reasons but are not constitutionally mandated.

    a.   Constitutionally required limits.   The Constitution limits judicial review in the following ways.

        i.   Article III heads of jurisdiction.   Federal courts may only exercise jurisdiction permitted under Article III of the Constitution.

(a) **Adequate and independent state grounds.** Even if federal law is involved in a case decided by a state court, if the state court decision is explicitly based on state law that is adequate for the decision and independent of federal law, the Supreme Court lacks power to review the case.

ii. **Separation of powers and the "case or controversy" requirement.** The Constitution's structure prevents the judiciary from exercising legislative or executive power. Article III limits the federal courts to adjudication of "cases or controversies." The Court has used these principles to limit judicial review in several important ways.

   (a) **No advisory opinions.** Judicial review cannot be exercised in the abstract. Courts will not decide cases unless the decision will finally end a real dispute between adverse parties.

   (b) **Standing.** A plaintiff must have a real stake in the controversy in order to have "standing" to assert the claim. The Constitution requires a litigant to have suffered (1) *personal injury in fact*, (2) *caused by the action complained of*, which is (3) *redressable by courts*. Associations may assert the claims of their members if the member could have sued, the association's purposes are germane to the claim, and the member's participation is not necessary to resolution of the claim. Litigants may also assert the claims of third parties where (1) the plaintiff's claim is inextricably linked with the third party's or (2) where the third party is unable to assert his own claim, risks losing the claim unless asserted by another, and the plaintiff is a reliable conduit for the third party claim.

   (c) **Ripeness and mootness.** Federal courts will not decide unripe or moot issues. An issue is not ripe if future events may render decision unnecessary and moot if past events have rendered decision unnecessary. Ripeness focuses on whether the issue has crystallized into a concrete dispute. Mootness is "standing in a time frame"—it focuses on whether the litigant has lost his personal stake in the claim.

iii. **Political questions.** Federal courts will not decide political questions. Among other reasons, a political question exists if the Constitution commits resolution of the issue to another branch of government. But courts decide if there is such a constitutional commitment. Judicial review ends with this threshold question if the courts conclude that the underlying issue is committed to another branch for decision.

    iv. **Eleventh Amendment.** Under the Eleventh Amendment, states, but not local governments, are immune from suit in federal court unless they have consented to such suit or Congress has clearly abrogated their immunity. Congress has power to abrogate the states' Eleventh Amendment immunity only under section 5 of the 14th Amendment. Suits against state officials seeking equitable relief only are permitted.

  b. **Nonconstitutional "prudential" limits.** The Court has also created a number of self-imposed limits on judicial review that it deems to be prudent, rather than required by the Constitution.

    i. **Political questions.** Most of the indicators of what constitutes a political question are not necessarily required by the Constitution. Those prudential factors include the following: (1) the lack of judicially cognizable standards by which the issue can be resolved, (2) the fact that judicial decision requires a judicially inappropriate policy choice, (3) the existence of a pressing need to adhere to a decision already made by Congress or the President, or (4) a risk that a judicial decision would embarrass the nation. Courts decide whether these factors are present. When the courts conclude that an issue is a political question they avoid deciding the issue on the merits, although the decision that the issue is a political question inevitably leaves some government action undisturbed.

    ii. **Abstention.** Federal courts will abstain from exercising their jurisdiction when necessary to do so in order to avoid interfering with ongoing state judicial proceedings in which a state has a significant interest (*Younger* abstention) or to permit state courts to decide unsettled issues of state law that may dispose of the case (*Pullman* abstention). The rationale for these doctrines is that the constitutional structure of federalism requires that state courts should be given room to decide the issues that are properly brought before them and which are part of the process of independent governance of the states. This logic suggests that these abstention doctrines are constitutionally required but the Court has never so held. Rather, the Court says that these doctrines are *not* constitutionally required.

    iii. **Some aspects of standing.** Some parts of the standing doctrine are not constitutionally required. For example, courts typically require that a plaintiff demonstrate that he is within the "zone of interests" protected by a law in order to have standing to invoke the law.

  c. **Congressionally imposed limits.** Article III gives Congress power to make "exceptions and regulations" to the judicial power. Congress may restrict (but not expand) the jurisdiction granted the Supreme Court under Article III, so long as the congressional restrictions do not violate some other constitutionally guaranteed right. It has never been decided whether the structural role of the federal courts in interpreting the Constitution also limits congressional power to eliminate the power of federal courts to decide constitutional issues.

3 FEDERALISM, THE SUPREMACY CLAUSE, AND THE "NECESSARY AND PROPER" CLAUSE

A. FEDERALISM: A BASIC CONSTITUTIONAL PRINCIPLE

The United States is a federal system. Governmental power is divided between the national government and the state governments.

1. Powers of the National Government

The federal government has only the powers enumerated in the Constitution (the "power-granting" provisions), limited by specific constitutional prohibitions upon the exercise of those powers (the "rights-protecting" provisions). For example, the interstate commerce clause grants Congress power to regulate the interstate shipment of books, but the First Amendment protects the people's right to speak freely by limiting the way in which Congress could regulate interstate book shipments. Thus, Congress could not prohibit the interstate shipment of books advocating tobacco use but could require that all books shipped interstate be shipped in federally prescribed containers.

2. Powers of the State Governments

Unlike the federal government, states have the power to do anything reasonably related to the general welfare of the state ("police power"), except as limited by the Constitution, valid federal law, or the state constitution. These three limits are each of considerable scope.

3. Concurrent or Exclusive Power

Some powers belong exclusively to the national government (e.g., the power to declare war); others may also be exercised by the states (e.g., the power to tax). Some exclusive powers of the federal government are implied; others are explicitly given by the Constitution.

B. THE SUPREMACY CLAUSE

The supremacy clause of Article VI provides that federal statutory and constitutional law is supreme and binds the states, regardless of anything to the contrary in a state's common, statutory, or constitutional law.

1. Preemption

A principal effect of the supremacy clause is the **preemption** doctrine. Federal statutory law displaces state statutory or constitutional law whenever Congress so intends. Congress may expressly state its intention to displace state law, or such intention may be inferred from the federal legislation. That intention is inferred when there is an **actual conflict** between federal and state law or when the nature and extent of the federal law implies a congressional intent to **occupy the field** exclusively.

C. THE "NECESSARY AND PROPER" CLAUSE

The final clause of Article I, §8 gives Congress the power to use all **necessary and proper** *means* to execute the powers of the federal government. Courts defer to Congress' judgment of the necessity and propriety of the means it selects. So long as the means employed by Congress are **rationally related** to an enumerated power of the federal government the courts will not invalidate the legislation as unnecessary or improper.

1. Not a Separate Source of Authority

The necessary and proper clause is *not* a separate and independent source of authority for congressional action. It serves only to permit Congress to use any rational means to *implement some other authorized power.*

2. "Pretext" Limits Effectively Abandoned

In *McCulloch v. Maryland* John Marshall cautioned that if Congress enacted legislation on the pretext that it was rationally related to one of its authorized powers the Court would not hesitate to strike it down. Though Marshall's statement has never been repudiated, in practice the Court does not second-guess congressional motive for its legislation.

4   THE FEDERAL COMMERCE POWER

A. THE SCOPE OF CONGRESSIONAL POWER TO REGULATE COMMERCE

1. Source of Authority

Article I, §8 grants to Congress power to regulate **interstate, foreign, and Indian** commerce. Even though no other commerce is subject to congressional regulation, Congress's power to regulate "interstate, foreign, and

Indian commerce" is commonly called the "commerce power." The Court has construed the term "interstate commerce" to include a wide variety of *intrastate* and *noncommercial* activities that Congress has rationally concluded have a substantial effect upon interstate commerce. As a result the "commerce power" is the single largest source of federal regulatory authority.

2. **Judicial Test for the Scope of the Commerce Power**

   Congress may use its commerce power to enact legislation if all three of the following criteria are satisfied.

   a. **Congressional determination.** Congress must determine factually that the activity regulated is actually **in commerce,** or *substantially affects commerce.*

      i. **In commerce.** An activity is "in commerce" if it is an "instrumentality" of interstate commerce (e.g., communications and transportation), or if it involves the interstate movement of an article of commerce. An article of commerce is anything that is the subject of market exchange.

      ii. **Activities that substantially affect commerce.** Congress may regulate purely **intrastate** commerce if it *substantially affects interstate commerce* and Congress makes a specific factual finding of the manner in which the regulated activity substantially affects interstate commerce. Without such a congressional finding the courts will exercise their independent judgment concerning the substantiality of the effect on intrastate commerce. Also, when Congress regulates a purely **intrastate** and **noncommercial** activity, the courts will not defer to congressional findings of fact that the regulated activity substantially affects interstate commerce, but will decide that issue independently.

   b. **Rational judgment.** The congressional determination must be **rational**—Congress must have some plausible basis to believe that the activity it regulates is in commerce or substantially effects commerce.

   c. **Reasonable means.** The means chosen by Congress must be **reasonably related** to its regulatory objective. This element is the Court's test, derived from *McCulloch v. Maryland,* for whether Congress has selected a "necessary" or "proper" means to regulate commerce.

3. **State Autonomy as a Limit on the Federal Commerce Power**

   Principles of state autonomy derived partly from the **Tenth Amendment** limit the way Congress may use its commerce power to regulate the states. The following principles apply.

a.   Laws of general application.   There is no judicially enforceable state autonomy limit on federal legislation (otherwise valid under the commerce power) that applies equally to the states and private persons.

Example: Suppose Congress enacts a minimum wage law that applies to *all* employers, whether private businesses or state governments. Assuming that Congress has rationally concluded that employment is an activity that substantially affects interstate commerce, the law is valid. It applies *equally* to governments and private persons.

This element is based on the idea that state autonomy is generally protected by the political process of Congress, a body of elected representatives of the states.

b.   Laws that apply only to states.   When Congress uses its commerce power to regulate **only** the states, it **must** do the following.

i.   Unmistakable clarity.   The legislation must regulate the states with ***unmistakable clarity,*** in order to be sure that Congress really intended to regulate states.

ii.   General application to the states.   Congress may not unfairly **single out a state** for regulation.

iii.   Full participation by the states in the political process.   Congress may not deny a state full **participation in the national political process** by excluding its representatives from the deliberative process.

iv.   No compulsion of state lawmaking.   Congress may not **interfere with a state's lawmaking process,** as, e.g., by compelling a state to enact federally prescribed legislation.

v.   No compulsion of state administration of federal programs.   Congress may not force state executive officials to administer federal programs.

 5   BEYOND COMMERCE: THE OTHER NATIONAL LEGISLATIVE POWERS

A.   SOURCE OF NATIONAL LEGISLATIVE POWERS

The Constitution expressly gives Congress a number of important powers. Most are set forth in Article I, §8, but some are found in other constitutional provisions, including the amendments. Congress also enjoys an unenumerated power over some aspects of foreign affairs.

1. Express Powers

The principal express powers include **taxation, spending, implementing treaties, declaring war, controlling patents, copyrights, bankruptcy, federal property, and immigration and naturalization, regulating the armed forces, regulating federal elections, and implementing the Reconstruction Amendments (13th, 14th, and 15th).** The judicial tests for determining the outer boundaries of these powers vary; in general the Court upholds legislation that is plausibly related to any express power of Congress.

2. Implied Powers

The Court recognizes that Congress has implied power to control some aspects of foreign affairs. Some foreign affairs powers are entirely Congress's—such as the power to declare war; other foreign affairs powers belong entirely to the President—such as the power to extend diplomatic recognition; and some are shared with the President.

B. TAXATION

Congress may impose taxes for **any purpose** so long as the tax *produces some revenue* and the *regulations* accompanying the tax are *reasonably related to enforcement of the tax*. In the unlikely event that a tax is found to be a regulation, rather than a *bona fide* tax, it is valid only if supported by some other power of Congress.

C. SPENDING

1. Scope of the Power

Congress *may spend*, but **may not regulate,** for the *general welfare* of the nation. So long as Congress acts rationally, it is up to Congress to decide what constitutes the general welfare. The line between spending and regulation is none too clear. Congress may **not coerce compliance** with regulations, but may **condition the receipt of federal funds** upon the recipient's behaving in the same way.

2. Conditional Spending

Congress may attach conditions to the receipt of federal funds by states, so long as the conditions meet the following criteria.

    a. "Clear and unambiguous." The conditions imposed must be plain and obvious, so that the state knows what it must do to get money.

    b. Conditions related to a "particular federal interest." Any condition to a state's receipt of federal money must relate to the federal interest in the particular national project or program embodied in the spending itself. In practice, the Court defers to "rational" or "reasonable" congressional judgments concerning the relationship between the national interest in the spending and the condition imposed upon its receipt.

c. **Otherwise constitutionally valid.** It is axiomatic that any condition imposed upon the receipt of federal money is void if it violates some other constitutional provision, such as equal protection.

d. **Not coercive.** The Court has stated that conditions that impose enough financial pressure on the states to constitute "compulsion" are invalid. But the Court has not struck down any conditions as coercive, and has upheld a condition that withdrew five percent of a state's federal highway money from noncomplying states.

D. TREATIES

Congress may implement treaties without the necessity of using one of its enumerated legislative powers, but Congress may not violate any other constitutional rights in doing so.

1. Power to Implement Treaties

Congress has power to enact any necessary or proper means to implement treaties negotiated by the President and ratified by the Senate. It is not limited to the use of its other regulatory powers (e.g., taxation, commerce, or spending). The Court has intimated that this power might be limited to treaties whose subject matter is of "national interest," but that is apt to be true of all treaties.

2. Congress Can't Use Unconstitutional Means

Of course, the congressional means chosen to implement treaties must not violate other **independent constitutional rights.**

Example: Congress may not implement a treaty obligating the United States to deny legal counsel to accused international drug smugglers.

E. WAR AND FOREIGN AFFAIRS

The federal government as a whole has *exclusive power* over foreign affairs. Congress has the sole power to *declare war* and may enact reasonable measures to effectuate its power to provide the means for conducting war.

F. RECONSTRUCTION AMENDMENTS (13th, 14th, and 15th)

1. Source and Nature of Congressional Power

Each of these amendments gives Congress power to **enforce the rights guaranteed by the amendment.** Defining the outer boundaries of this power has required the Court to struggle with the proper balance between congressional and judicial power to define the content of these rights.

2. **Scope of Congressional Power**

    Congress may provide reasonable remedies for past or prospective violations of the Reconstruction Amendments but Congress has no power to redefine the substance of these constitutional rights.

    a. **Fourteenth and Fifteenth Amendments.** Congress may provide remedies for adjudicated violations of these amendments and can act to prevent possible future violations if it finds facts sufficient to support its reasonable judgment that the specific remedy has a plausible connection to a possible violation of these amendments.

        Example: Congress had power to bar New York's constitutionally valid English literacy requirement for voting because it found that the remedy—forcing New York to extend the franchise to certain Spanish-literate citizens—was reasonably designed to enable New Yorkers from Puerto Rico to remedy at the polls possible unconstitutional discrimination against them in the provision of public services.

        But Congress **has no power to define the substance** of 14th or 15th Amendment rights independently of the courts. The difference between forbidden substantive legislation and permitted remedial legislation is that the scope of remedial legislation must be **congruent** with the constitutional injury addressed by the legislation and **proportional** to that injury. To assess congruence and proportionality a court must first determine the scope of the constitutional right and then determine whether Congress made specific findings of fact of state violations of the constitutional right at issue. The scope of the constitutional right is defined by the level of review applied to such claims (e.g., minimal, intermediate, or strict scrutiny) and the congressional findings of fact must be based on specific evidence of state violation of the constitutional right rather than on evidence of general societal discrimination.

        Example: Congress lacked power to make states civilly liable to private citizens for their discrimination against the disabled because (1) such discrimination by states is constitutionally permissible so long as it is rationally related to a legitimate state interest, and (2) Congress based its ostensibly remedial legislation mostly upon evidence of discriminatory treatment of the disabled by society in general.

    b. **The Thirteenth Amendment.** The Court has concluded that Congress's power to enforce the abolition of slavery enables it to enact legislation that is rationally related to elimination of the "badges or incidents" of slavery.

6   LIMITATIONS UPON STATE POWER TO REGULATE INTERSTATE COMMERCE

A.   CONSTITUTIONAL SOURCE OF LIMITS ON STATE POWER TO REGULATE INTERSTATE COMMERCE

There are three principal constitutional limits on state power to regulate interstate commerce. The first is Congress's power, via the supremacy clause and the commerce clause, to preempt state law pertaining to interstate commerce. The second is implied from the commerce clause. The third is Article IV's privileges and immunities clause.

1.   Preemption

Within the scope of its authority, Congress always may preempt or displace state law by expressly doing so, or by implication when federal and state law conflict or federal law so fully occupies a field that it may be inferred that Congress intended to oust state law from the field.

2.   The Dormant, or Negative, Commerce Clause

The Constitution does not explicitly forbid the states from regulating interstate commerce, but the Court has implied some limits upon state power over interstate commerce from the constitutional grant of power to Congress to regulate interstate commerce. Because Congress preempts state law regulating interstate commerce when it acts on the same subject, the dormant commerce clause only operates when Congress has **failed to act.** When Congress has acted—either by preempting state law or by explicitly consenting to state laws that regulate interstate commerce—the dormant commerce clause is not relevant. Instead, Congress has simply exercised its own power over interstate commerce.

3.   Article IV's Privileges and Immunities Clause

The privileges and immunities clause of Article IV bars states from denying to nonresident natural persons the same privileges and immunities it affords its own citizens. The clause prevents discrimination against outsiders in more than commercial exchanges, but is an effective tool against state discrimination in interstate commerce.

B.   THE DORMANT, OR NEGATIVE, COMMERCE CLAUSE

1.   Overview

The power to regulate interstate commerce is shared concurrently by the states and the federal government. But when Congress exercises its power it displaces contrary state law through the force of the supremacy clause. Effectively, the states may regulate interstate commerce if Congress has

failed to act or if Congress has exercised its commerce power to permit the states to regulate. When Congress has failed to act the issue is whether state regulation of interstate commerce violates any implied barriers in the commerce clause. Even if the courts strike down state regulation of interstate commerce, Congress remains free to exercise its commerce power to permit the states to do what the courts said they could not. Court rulings under the dormant commerce clause are thus reversible by Congress, which may exercise its legitimate commerce power as it pleases.

2. **The Judicial Limits on State Regulation of Interstate Commerce**

   Courts apply four principal doctrines to state laws impinging on interstate commerce.

   a. **Rationally related to a legitimate state purpose.** All state laws must be **rationally related to a *legitimate* state purpose.** Economic protection, by itself, is an illegitimate purpose.

      Example: A Hawaii law that exempted local wine and liquor from otherwise applicable liquor taxes was rationally related to the objective of protecting Hawaii's infant wine and liquor industry, but that objective was illegitimate since it was naked economic protectionism.

   b. **Laws that facially discriminate against interstate commerce.** State laws that **facially discriminate** against interstate commerce are *invalid* unless the state proves that it has a *legitimate objective that cannot be accomplished by any less discriminatory alternative.*

      Example: Maine barred the importation of non-native baitfish. Although facially discriminatory, Maine proved that its legitimate objective—protecting native fish from disease and non-native predator fish—could only be accomplished by its import ban.

   c. **Laws that regulate interstate commerce evenhandedly.** Nondiscriminatory state laws that incidentally regulate interstate commerce are *valid* unless the challenger to the law can show that the **burdens placed on interstate commerce** by the law are **clearly excessive** in relation to the **putative local benefits** of the law. This requires courts to compare the *quantity* and *quality* of burdens imposed on commerce with the local benefits delivered. Burdens and benefits are not easily compared. Unless the challenger can prove that burdens *clearly outweigh* the local benefits the law is valid.

      Example: Ostensibly for safety reasons, Arizona limited the length of interstate trains traveling through Arizona. Because the law imposed significant financial costs on the railroads and was proven to deliver negligible safety benefits it was voided.

   d. **The market participation doctrine.** When states act as *market partici-*

pants, rather than market regulators, they are exempt from the dormant commerce clause. States are market participants when they are engaging in, or creating, commerce rather than simply controlling other people's commerce. The Court is apt to define the relevant "market" in which a state participates narrowly, in order to avoid wholesale undermining of the dormant commerce clause doctrine.

Example: If Alaska refused to sell the standing timber it owns to non-Alaskans, the refusal would be facially discriminatory but exempt from dormant commerce clause review because Alaska would be a participant in the market for timber. But because Alaska stipulated that anyone who bought standing timber from Alaska must also process it in Alaska the requirement was not exempt from dormant commerce clause scrutiny because Alaska was not a participant in the timber processing market.

C. ARTICLE IV'S PRIVILEGES AND IMMUNITIES CLAUSE

Under Article IV's *privileges and immunities* clause, states may not, without a **substantial reason,** discriminate against nonresidents with respect to matters that are **fundamental** to interstate harmony and national union. This doctrine applies to state actions that are exempt from the dormant commerce clause because the state is a market participant. The privileges and immunities clause protects only natural persons, however, not corporations.

1. Fundamental Interests

The principal fundamental interest protected by the privileges and immunities clause is the right to pursue a livelihood, or the "privileges of trade and commerce." Other fundamental interests include access to the judicial system.

2. Justified Discrimination

In order validly to discriminate on fundamental matters, states must prove three items. Only if a state proves all three may it discriminate against nonresidents.

   a. Outsiders are the problem.   A state must show that nonresidents are a **peculiar source of the problem** the state is trying to solve. The problem must be something more than their status as outsiders.

   b. The discrimination is *substantially related* to the problem.   A state must prove that the particular discriminatory practice it has chosen is **substantially related** to the problem the state seeks to address.

   c. No less discriminatory alternatives.   A state must prove that there are no practical less discriminatory alternatives available to the state to solve the problem.

7 SEPARATION OF POWERS

A. OVERVIEW

The Constitution is designed to separate the executive, legislative, and judicial powers of the federal government. The mechanisms for doing so are not always obvious. Two principles guide decision here: (1) **prevent any one branch from dominating,** and (2) **prevent the fusion of powers.** Resolution of these issues often turns on prudential considerations or settled historical precedent. Some of these issues may not be justiciable.

B. PRESIDENTIAL POWERS

Article II stipulates that "[t]he executive Power shall be vested in a President" but does not specify precisely what those powers are. In general, the President **executes Law,** but does *not make law.* From this axiom it might be thought that the President is powerless to act except when legislation authorizes or requires him to do so, but that is not correct. The President has a number of powers that he or she may exercise unilaterally. The President:

- Has the **exclusive power to appoint** *principal* **federal officers,** subject to Senate confirmation.

- Has the unilateral power to **remove** principal executive officers.

- Has the power to **veto bills** or **sign them into law.**

- May extend or withdraw **diplomatic recognition** of other nations.

- May grant **pardons.**

- Negotiate **treaties,** subject to Senate confirmation.

- Is the **Commander in Chief** of the armed services, and may unilaterally commit armed forces to repel sudden attacks on the nation or to protect American lives and interests in times of sudden emergency.

C. CONGRESS AND THE PRESIDENT

Congress's function is to make law. By making law, Congress may increase or restrict the President's powers, so long as the legislation does not violate some other constitutional principle.

1. Appointments and Removal Power

The President has the power to appoint principal officers, subject to Senate confirmation, but Congress may specify whether inferior officers may be appointed by the President alone, the heads of executive departments, or the courts. Similarly, while the President has the unilateral power to remove principal executive officers, Congress may restrict the President's power to remove inferior officers, so long as the limitations do not impede the President's performance of his core duties. Congress itself may neither appoint no remove executive officers.

2. Legislative Authority for Presidential Action

Within its own sphere of power, Congress may authorize the President to take action or to bar the President from acting. The Court may infer congressional authorization or prohibition from congressional acquiescence to presidential action, historical precedent, or other significant forms of congressional silence. Of course, Congress may not bar the President from exercising powers given to him by the Constitution, nor may Congress authorize the President to take actions prohibited by the Constitution.

3. Foreign Affairs Power

Congress and the President share an exclusively federal **"unenumerated foreign affairs power."** Some aspects of this power belong entirely to the President (e.g., the power to extend diplomatic recognition) and some belong exclusively to Congress (e.g., the power to declare war). Most foreign affairs actions fall into a shadowy zone of authority held concurrently by the President and Congress. In general, the courts recognize that the President has more freedom of unilateral action in foreign than domestic affairs.

a. **War.** The power to make war is a particularly nettlesome issue, made even more troublesome by the awful (and often unintended) consequences of war. Congress has the power to **declare war.** Increasingly, this seems to mean some formal congressional authorization of presidential commitment of American troops to warfare, though that is probably not what was meant by the Framers. The President has the power to **conduct warfare,** once it has been declared. Even so, the President may commit the armed services to combat without a congressional declaration of war when the nation has been attacked, or when American citizens or property are subject to immediate armed threat. Beyond this, the President's unilateral authority to commit American troops to hostilities is questionable. The 1973 War Powers Resolution is Congress's attempt to define the circumstances under which the President may use armed force unilaterally and temporarily.

D. CONGRESS AND THE ADMINISTRATIVE STATE

1. The Nondelegation Doctrine

A corollary to the principle that Congress **makes law** is the doctrine that Congress **may *not* delegate its legislative power.** But every law necessarily gives to the executive some discretion in how to execute the law. To draw the line, the Court's test is that Congress has **not** delegated its legislative power *if* Congress declares an **intelligible principle** that both **declares a policy** and **defines "the circumstances in that its command is to be effective."**

Example: A statute that authorizes the President "to issue regulations to prevent contamination of drinking water whenever the President has determined that there is a reasonable risk to the health and safety of the public from contaminated drinking water" both declares an intelligible principle—prevent contaminated drinking water—and defines the circumstances when the President may act—whenever there is a "reasonable risk to the health and safety of the public from contaminated drinking water."

2. Unorthodox Governmental Arrangements

Congress may create entirely new governmental arrangements so long as they pose no danger of either **aggrandizement** of a single branch or **encroachment** upon the powers of any branch.

Example: Congress created a Sentencing Commission, composed of judges, academics, and other presidential appointees, and empowered it to fashion binding federal "sentencing guidelines." Even though the Commission was neither executive, legislative, or judicial, but an ungainly amalgamation of all three, the Court upheld its validity as posing neither threat.

3. No Legislative Veto

As Congress effectively delegated ever more of its legislative power to administrative agencies it began to devise new ways of controlling agency discretion. One such device was the legislative veto—the reservation by one or both houses of Congress of a power to nullify agency action. The Court held that Congress may *not* exercise a **legislative veto.**

E. IMMUNITIES AND PRIVILEGES

1. Legislative Immunity

Members of Congress are absolutely immune from suits or grand jury probes premised upon their **legislative acts,** and are temporarily immune from civil suits while Congress is in session. Legislative action consists of acts or omissions in the course of the entire legislative deliberative process. This immunity extends to legislative aides engaged in legislative acts.

2. Executive Immunity

The President is **absolutely immune** from civil suits for damages based on his **official acts,** has **no immunity** from civil suits based on his **unofficial acts,** and **probably is not immune** from criminal prosecution. Executive officials other than the President enjoy a **qualified immunity** for their official acts taken in **good faith.**

3. Executive Privilege

The President possesses a qualified evidentiary privilege—**executive privilege**—to preserve the confidentiality of presidential communications and documents. To determine whether executive privilege may be invoked, courts must *balance* the *need for the information* sought and the *reasons asserted for confidentiality*.

8 THE DUE PROCESS CLAUSES

A. OVERVIEW OF DUE PROCESS

1. Two Due Process Clauses

There are two due process clauses. Both require governments to give people "due process" before depriving them of life, liberty, or property. The Fifth Amendment applies to the federal government; the 14th Amendment applies to states and their political subdivisions.

2. Two Functions to Due Process

Although the phrase "due *process*" implies a guarantee of procedural regularity, and its historical origin supports that view, due process has acquired a larger and more controversial role. The due process clauses protect certain **substantive rights** and deliver certain **procedural rights.**

a. **Substantive due process.**   Courts use the due process clauses to protect **substantive rights** as follows:

   i. **Fundamental rights: Strict scrutiny.**   If a claimed interest in life, liberty, or property has been found to be **fundamental** it may only be infringed if it passes **strict scrutiny.** To satisfy strict scrutiny the **government must prove** that the infringement is **necessary** to achieve a **compelling state objective.**

      (a) **What's fundamental?**   A claimed interest in life, liberty, or property is **fundamental** if it is "*implicit in the concept of ordered liberty*" or is "*deeply rooted in this Nation's history and tradition.*" That is a highly subjective measure. Accordingly, the issue of what is "fundamental" is eminently contestable. To the extent the Court treats as "fundamental" rights that have no textual connection to the Constitution, it invites criticism that it is substituting its judicial veto for the judgment of the people's elected representatives.

(b) Changing fashions in fundamental rights. From the late 19th century until the 1930s economic rights—e.g., liberty of contract—were regarded as fundamental rights protected by substantive due process. Franklin Roosevelt's New Deal Justices rejected that view and, ever since, economic rights have not been regarded as fundamental despite the fact that the Constitution was drafted in part to secure economic rights more effectively. Today, the fundamental rights protected by substantive due process consist entirely of certain noneconomic personal rights where government intrusion is thought to be especially suspect.

ii. **Nonfundamental rights: Minimal scrutiny.** If a claimed interest in life, liberty, or property is **not fundamental** it may be infringed unless the **challenger proves** that the infringement fails **minimal scrutiny.** Under minimal scrutiny the infringement is invalid if it is *not* **rationally related to a legitimate state interest.**

B. **FUNDAMENTAL RIGHTS PROTECTED BY SUBSTANTIVE DUE PROCESS**

The major fundamental rights protected by substantive due process follow.

1. **The Incorporation Doctrine**

Most of the rights guaranteed by the Bill of Rights are "incorporated" into the 14th Amendment's due process clause, thus making them applicable to the states in the *same form* as they apply to the federal government. This effectively makes the content of these rights uniform across the country. The incorporation doctrine treats state infringements of the Bill of Rights as a question of whether the state has afforded the individual "due process."

Example: If a state prohibits all public political speech it has denied its residents due process by interfering with their right to free speech protected by the First Amendment. We often speak of such cases as "First Amendment" cases. Technically, they are 14th Amendment due process cases, although the substance of the controversy is indeed the First Amendment guarantee of free speech.

2. **Contraceptives**

All adults, single or married, have a fundamental liberty interest in obtaining and using contraceptives free of state interference.

3. **Abortion**

Until viability of the fetus, a woman has a fundamental liberty interest to be free of "undue burdens" placed by the state on her decision to terminate her pregnancy. An "undue burden" is anything intended to create or that has the effect of creating a substantial obstacle to an abortion. Unemancipated minors may be required either to notify their parents or obtain judicial permission prior to obtaining an abortion. In general, it is not an undue burden on the abortion right for governments to refuse to fund abortions.

4. Family Relationships

People have a fundamental liberty interest in living with their extended family members as a family unit. In general, there is a fundamental right on the part of parents to rear their children as they see fit and to maintain their relationship with their children, but this latter aspect of the right exists more to preserve existing parent-child relationships than it does to create them on the basis of genetic relations alone.

5. Right to Marry

In general, the right to marry is a fundamental liberty interest. Laws that significantly interfere with the decision to marry are valid only if they withstand strict scrutiny. Laws that only incidentally interfere with the decision to marry are subjected to minimal scrutiny.

Example: A law that forbids welfare recipients to marry significantly interferes with the fundamental right to marry and is valid only if the state can prove the elements of strict scrutiny. A law that terminates welfare benefits upon marriage incidentally interferes with the fundamental right to marry and is valid unless the challenger can prove it is not rationally related to a legitimate state interest. The former law determines who may lawfully marry; the latter conditions a public benefit on marital status.

C. "FUNDAMENTAL" OR NOT? OTHER CLAIMED RIGHTS

Only a few asserted rights are fundamental liberty interests. Some claimed liberties have been found not to be fundamental; others may be fundamental, but the Court has not so held. A brief catalog follows.

1. Right to Die

The Court has not yet resolved whether there is such a fundamental right, much less determined its scope. The Court has hinted, but not held, that competent adults have a fundamental right to reject government mandated life-prolonging medical treatment. As the result, the following debatable issues are very much in flux.

   a. **Suicide.**   The Court has not yet determined whether there is a fundamental right to commit suicide but has rejected the claim that there is a fundamental liberty interest in obtaining assistance in suicide.

   b. **Incompetent patients.**   The Court has held that states may insist on clear and convincing evidence that an incompetent patient, while competent, desired to reject life-prolonging medical treatment. The Court has not determined whether states may prohibit competent patients from giving binding instructions concerning their medical care after incompetency or whether states may bar competent patients from delegating another person to make all medical decisions for them.

2. Right to Consensual Sex

Outside of marriage, there is no such fundamental liberty. The Court has specifically rejected a right to homosexual sex, and while a heterosexual version of this right seems implicit in the contraceptive and abortion cases, the Court has never so held. This right could be claimed in several different contexts—incest, adultery, or fornication—and the Court's response might vary with the context, but at present there is no constitutionally fundamental right to sex outside marriage.

3. Right to Personal Appearance

When asserted by police officers and schoolchildren the Court has rejected such a fundamental right. It has never decided whether such a right exists in favor of the general population.

4. Right of ''Anonymity''

The "right" to be free of government collection and storage of personal information is not fundamental.

D. PROCEDURAL DUE PROCESS

The due process clauses compel governments to observe certain **procedures** when they deprive people of their **life, liberty, or property.**

1. No General Right to Regular Procedures

There is *no* **general** *right* to *procedural regularity*. Procedural due process attaches only when the government is about to deprive a person of **life, liberty,** or **property.** When those interests are not implicated by government action, governments are free to use any procedure they desire.

2. Analytical Approach to Procedural Due Process

To analyze a procedural due process question you must do two things.

a. **Life, liberty, or property at stake?** First determine whether a life, liberty, or property interest has been or is about to be infringed by the government. If not, there is no procedural due process issue.

b. **Procedures required by due process.** Second, if a life, liberty, or property interest is infringed by government, determine what procedures are required—what sort of "process" is "due" to the affected individual? The minimum procedures required by due process will vary with the affected interest and the government's reason for acting, but will always require notice and an opportunity to be heard.

3. When Is a "Liberty" or "Property" Interest Affected?

The answers to these questions are neither self-evident nor entirely a matter of constitutional law.

a. **Property.** Some government actions obviously affect property interests, as when a city proposes to rezone your residence so that you can no longer live in it. Others are less evident. When *government benefits* are being terminated, the question of whether the benefits are a *property interest*, sufficient to require procedural due process, is a *matter of state law* (or federal law, if the benefits are federal). The government action must interfere with a property interest recognized by the applicable state or federal law. If state or federal law does not treat the affected benefit as a property interest the government may terminate the benefit by any procedure.

b. **Liberty.** In general, government action that does *not* alter one's *legal status under applicable law* is no infringement of liberty for due process purposes. But government actions that invade liberty interests recognized as such in other constitutional contexts require due process, regardless of other law.

Example: Suppose a state makes no legal distinction between imprisonment in a penitentiary or a mental hospital, and permits the state to decide unilaterally whether any particular convicted criminal should be confined in a penal or a mental institution. Although due process attaches to the initial criminal trial in which liberty is at issue, there would be no liberty interest raised **under state law** by the separate question of whether the inmate should be in a prison or a mental hospital. But forced confinement in a mental hospital is recognized as such a loss of liberty under **federal constitutional law** that procedural due process would attach to this separate question.

4. What Process Is Due?

If a liberty or property interest has been infringed, the government must provide, at minimum, **notice of the charges** and **an opportunity to be heard.**

a. **Major deprivations.** For deprivations of life and major deprivations of liberty, as is the case in criminal prosecutions, nothing short of a trial will provide due process.

b. **Minor deprivations.** For minor deprivations of liberty and of property, the procedures required will vary with the circumstances. Courts weigh three factors.

    i. **The private interest affected.** Courts examine the significance or importance to the affected individual of the particular private interest affected by the alleged denial of due process. The formality and scope of the procedures required will vary in rough proportion with the significance of the affected interest.

ii. **Risk of error of current procedures v. probable value of other procedures.** If the risk of error on the underlying substantive issue is low it is likely that the existing procedures conform to due process. This is even more probable if alternative procedures are not likely to increase the accuracy of the underlying decision. On the other hand, existing procedures that carry a high, or even moderate, risk of error are vulnerable to due process challenges, especially if there are reasonable alternatives that would likely reduce the risk of error.

iii. **Public interest.** In deciding whether existing procedures conform to due process courts must determine whether the public interest is served by those procedures or by some alternative ones. "Public interest" refers to the **administrative burden** and **additional cost** of alternative procedures as well as the fact that resources devoted to more elaborate procedures will likely result in fewer resources being distributed to deserving beneficiaries, because resources are not infinitely expandable. In applying this test courts must give *substantial weight* to the *good-faith judgments* of the relevant government officials. This produces a very flexible and context-oriented assessment of the procedures required by due process.

c. **Post-deprivation hearings.** Due process is satisfied by post-deprivation hearings in two general circumstances: (1) when governments temporarily deprive people of liberty or property to prevent imminent public harm, or (2) when permanent deprivations are minor and a pre-deprivation hearing is impractical.

9   EQUAL PROTECTION

A. OVERVIEW

The 14th Amendment provides that "No State shall . . . deny to any person within its jurisdiction the equal protection of the laws." The Court has applied the same principle to the federal government via the due process clause of the Fifth Amendment. Equal protection applies when *any* government (state or federal) treats *entire groups of people* differently. It does *not* apply to the question of whether a particular individual is within or without a specified group.

Example: If the government permits only licensed drivers without traffic convictions to operate autos it has divided the people into two classes. Equal protection applies, though the classification is almost certainly valid. The question of whether Amy is a licensed driver without any traffic convictions is *not* an equal protection issue. The question of whether the government may restrict auto operation to licensed drivers without any traffic convictions *is* an equal protection issue.

B.   THREE LEVELS OF JUDICIAL SCRUTINY

When equal protection applies, whether through the 14th Amendment or the Fifth Amendment, courts use three increasingly demanding levels of review to determine whether the classification at issue is valid. The basic, or "default," level of review is **minimal scrutiny.** More rigorous scrutiny applies only when the classification has something constitutionally disfavored associated with it. In analyzing equal protection problems, start from the presumption that minimal scrutiny applies, but check for the indicators of more rigorous scrutiny.

1.   Minimal Scrutiny

When minimal scrutiny applies the challenger has the burden of proving that the classification is *not* rationally related to any conceivable legitimate state interest, however hypothetical that state interest may be. Legitimate state interests consist of any purpose not prohibited by the Constitution. Minimal scrutiny is often called "*rationality*" review or "*rational basis*" review.

2.   Strict Scrutiny

This is the toughest level of review. Under strict scrutiny the classification at issue is presumed to be invalid. To sustain the law the government must prove that the law is **necessary to accomplish a compelling governmental interest.** This generally means that the law must be the least restrictive way in which the government's extremely important objective can be achieved. This is a very difficult burden of proof to overcome. Strict scrutiny applies whenever a law employs a **suspect classification** or **substantially infringes upon a fundamental right.**

3.   Intermediate Scrutiny

Intermediate scrutiny is a middle level of review created primarily to deal with sex-based classifications. When intermediate scrutiny applies the law is presumed invalid and will be upheld only if the government can prove that the classification at issue is **substantially related to an important government interest.** This burden of proof is of moderate difficulty to overcome. In assessing the relationship of the law to the government's purposes the courts insist upon using the **actual purposes** for the law. Unlike minimal scrutiny, hypothetical purposes are not sufficient. Intermediate scrutiny is applied to classifications on the basis of *sex* or *illegitimate birth*.

4. "Enhanced" Minimal Scrutiny

Occasionally the Court applies an "enhanced" version of minimal scrutiny. It will either insist upon using the actual purpose for the classification or reverse the burden of proof (making the state prove the rational relationship of a classification to a legitimate purpose), or view rationality and legitimacy more skeptically. The trigger for this "enhanced" review is not clear—it often appears to be based on the Court's "gestalt" reaction to specific facts that do not warrant the application of either strict or intermediate scrutiny but that nevertheless strike a majority of the Court as involving "quasi-suspect" classifications or "quasi-fundamental" rights.

D. STRICT SCRUTINY: SUSPECT CLASSIFICATIONS

Suspect classifications are those statutory classifications that appear to be the product of irrational prejudice against a discrete and insular minority, such that the normal functions of representative government are unlikely to redress the situation. In practice, only **race, national origin,** and **alienage (in** *some* **circumstances)** are suspect classifications. A suspect classification must be apparent on the *face of the law* or, if not, the challenger must prove that the law was *intended to be discriminatory in the suspect manner* in order for strict scrutiny to be applied. Then, the burden shifts to the government to prove that the classification is necessary to achieve a compelling purpose.

1. Race and National Origin

When governments divide people into groups on the basis of *race* or *national origin* for the purpose of discriminating on that basis they have used a suspect classification—subject to strict scrutiny.

    a. Intentional or purposeful discrimination. Only those classifications that **intentionally** discriminate on racial or national origin grounds are suspect. Intentional discrimination is established if any of the following are present.

        i. Facial discrimination. If the racial or national origin classification is explicit it is conclusively presumed to be intentional. Examples include racial segregation, racial preferences, or any other open racial distinction.

        ii. Discriminatory application and motivation. When a facially neutral law is *applied* on the basis of racial or national origin it is presumed to be intentionally discriminatory. The challenger must prove that the government has acted *intentionally* to apply a neutral law only to members of a racial group. To do so the challenger must rely on more than statistical evidence of a disparate racial impact. If a facially neutral law that produces results identifiable by race or national origin was adopted **solely** for the purpose of discriminating on the basis of race or national origin the law is intentionally discriminatory. The challenger must prove the existence of this discriminatory motivation, not an easy thing to do. Even if there is evidence of racially discriminatory motivation the government may *rebut* this showing by proving that it would have adopted the law anyway. If the government is unable to rebut the presumption of intentional discrimination the classification is suspect and strict scrutiny applies.

Example: Suppose a city requires all job applicants to achieve a minimum score on a exam testing basic literacy and mathematical skills. Assume that members of one racial group fail the exam three times more frequently than any other racial group. Absent *some other proof* of purposeful discrimination the racially disparate impact of the race-neutral exam is not enough to prove intentional discrimination.

iii. **No special rules for racial preferences.** Strict scrutiny applies to racial classifications that are intended to benefit racial minorities as well as to racial classifications designed to disadvantage racial minorities. Thus, racially preferential hiring programs or school admission programs are subject to strict scrutiny. Some racial preferences (but not many) will satisfy strict scrutiny. Racial preferences undertaken to remedy specific unlawful racial discrimination may satisfy strict scrutiny.

2. **Alienage**

Drawing lines on the basis of alienage, at least with respect to *lawful residents* of the nation, is suspect *unless* one of the following conditions is present.

a. **Political functions.** If a *state* classifies on the basis of alienage in order to confine the performance of *political functions* to citizens the classification is **not subject to strict scrutiny** and is valid if rationally related to the legitimate interest of confining political functions to citizens. The category of political functions is surprisingly broad, including not only elected officials but police officers, schoolteachers, and probation officers.

b. **Federal classifications.** The federal government has more freedom than the states to employ alienage classifications without triggering strict scrutiny because the federal government has exclusive authority to regulate immigration and naturalization. The federal government must act either through **Congress** or the **President;** the courts are not willing to defer to agency classifications on the basis of alienage.

c. **Illegal aliens.** State or federal laws that classify on the basis of aliens' **illegal presence** in the country are not suspect and are not subject to strict scrutiny. But the Court occasionally applies "enhanced" minimal scrutiny to some *state* classifications based on illegal alienage.

E. STRICT SCRUTINY: FUNDAMENTAL RIGHTS

When governments classify people in a way that impinges upon a constitutionally fundamental right, strict scrutiny applies. Constitutionally fundamental rights are those rights *explicitly* or *implicitly* guaranteed by the Constitution. In theory, this means that almost any classification that infringes another constitutional right (e.g., free speech) is subject to strict scrutiny as a matter of equal protection. In practice, the level of review that applies to the infringement of, say, free speech is identical to the review that would be applied under equal protection so there is little reason to frame such cases as equal protection violations. Most of the equal protection law concerning fundamental rights involves rights that the Court concludes are implicitly guaranteed by the Constitution. The principal categories of fundamental rights that trigger strict scrutiny under equal protection follow.

1. Voting

The right to vote is *implicit* in the Constitution. Substantial impairments of the right to vote trigger strict scrutiny. Important examples are the poll tax and malapportioned electoral districts. But there are a number of exceptions to this rule.

a. Limited purpose governmental units. When governments limit voting for "limited purpose" governmental units (e.g., an agricultural irrigation district) to those primarily affected, only minimal scrutiny applies. This is a *very narrow* exception.

b. Barring felons from voting. Because the 14th Amendment expressly recognizes this practice, strict scrutiny does not apply.

c. Write-in and absentee votes. Governments may ban write-in votes because there is no constitutionally fundamental right to write in your choice. Reasonable limits on absentee voting are subject to minimal scrutiny.

d. Ballot access restrictions. So long as governmental restrictions on access to the ballot are reasonable and do not severely impair the right of minor parties or candidates to get on the ballot, strict scrutiny will *not* apply.

2. Access to the Judicial Process

Strict scrutiny is largely confined to state laws that, as a practical matter, place an indigent at a strong disadvantage in attempting directly to appeal a criminal conviction or vindicate some especially important civil interest. There is no **general** fundamental right of access to the judicial process.

3. **Right of Interstate Mobility**

State laws or policies that impose permanent denials of some benefit to some residents of a state based on their recent arrival in the state, or which erect major obstacles to interstate movement, are subject to strict scrutiny. Congress, however, has substantially greater freedom to impose such barriers.

4. **"Societally Important" Rights are *Not* Fundamental**

Just because something is "societally important"—such as education or housing, or the "general necessities" of life—does *not* make it a constitutionally fundamental right. Provision of socially important needs is the function of the market economy and the democratic political process.

F. INTERMEDIATE SCRUTINY: SEX AND ILLEGITIMATE BIRTH

When governments divide people into groups on the basis of their sex or illegitimate birth for purposes of discriminating on that basis, *intermediate scrutiny* is triggered. The classification is presumed to be invalid and is upheld only if the government can prove that the law **is substantially related to an important actual government objective.**

1. **Sex Classifications**

Sex, like race, is often a basis for prejudicial stereotypes but, unlike race, sex is sometimes relevant to legitimate government objectives. Thus, intermediate scrutiny applies to sex classifications.

a. **Intentional discrimination.** As with race, only those sex classifications that intentionally discriminate by sex trigger intermediate scrutiny.

b. **No special rules for sexual preferences.** As with race, sex-based "affirmative action" programs are subjected to the same scrutiny as other forms of sex discrimination. But since the intermediate standard is more easily met than strict scrutiny, sex-based affirmative action plans are more easily justified than race-based plans.

c. **The importance of "real" sex differences.** When a classification reflects a "real" sex difference (e.g., only women become pregnant) the intermediate standard is easily met. But when the classification reflects stereotypical assumptions about sex roles it will be hard to justify.

d. **Only *actual purposes* count.** Unlike minimal scrutiny, where the government's objective may be *any conceivable* legitimate objective, no matter how hypothetical, intermediate scrutiny requires governments to prove the substantial relationship of the classification to the *actual purposes* of the classification.

2. Illegitimacy

Intermediate scrutiny also applies to classifications by illegitimacy. This problem has usually arisen in the context of intestacy statutes restricting the inheritance rights of illegitimate children. It could come up in other contexts—e.g., a law denying child welfare benefits to illegitimate children, or a law denying to adopted children (mostly, but not entirely, born outside marriage) the right to learn the identities of their mothers.

 10 STATE ACTION AND CONGRESSIONAL ENFORCEMENT OF CIVIL RIGHTS

A. STATE ACTION

1. Overview

The **state action doctrine** pervades constitutional law. With very few exceptions the Constitution limits *governments* only, and does *not* ordinarily limit *private action.*

Example: A question of constitutional law is presented if a government bans political speech. State action is present. No question of constitutional law is presented if a private person ejects from his home a guest who talks about politics. There is no state action.

State action refers to **any government action,** not just the actions of the member states of the United States. State action may be *express* or *implied.* Express state action is usually obvious; implied state action almost always involves *nominal private action* in which the state is so involved that it is treated as state action.

2. Nominally Private Actors as State Actors

This is the usual problem of implied state action. There are five variations on this theme.

    a. **Public function.** State action is present when governments **delegate** to private persons functions that traditionally have belonged **exclusively to government.**

    Example: If a state permits a political party, a private organization, to decide who is eligible to vote, it has delegated the traditionally governmental function of controlling the franchise to a private party. The acts of the private party are treated as those of the government.

b. Inextricable entanglement.   State action is present if the connection between the government and the private actor involves an **extraordinary degree of interdependence** or **intervention by the government in the specific action** in question.

Example: A government's lease of space in a public parking garage to a restaurant that openly practiced racial discrimination, under an arrangement that made the state the financial beneficiary of the restaurant's profitable racism, was sufficiently "symbiotic" to make the private discrimination state action.

c. State coercion or encouragement of private conduct.   State action is present when governments either **coerce** or **provide extraordinary encouragement to** private persons to take particular actions.

Example: After the California legislature enacted a law forbidding private racial discrimination in housing, California voters amended the state constitution to guarantee the right of private persons to rent or sell their real property to whoever they desired. The Court ruled that this action provided extraordinary encouragement to private persons to practice private racial discrimination, thus making the private discrimination state action.

d. Joint action.   State action is present when the challenged private action could not have been effective without joint participation by the government.

Example: In litigation between private parties one party seeks to attach the assets of the other party before judgment. The attachment cannot occur until and unless a state court official issues a writ of attachment. The joint participation by the state in the attachment proceedings turns the private action of seeking attachment into state action.

e. State ratification of the private action.   State action is present when the government has ratified, or adopted as its own act, the challenged private actions.

f. Government licensing or regulation *not* enough.   By itself, mere licensing or regulation of private action by government is not sufficient to create state action. Government regulation must amount to explicit approval of the private act at issue.

B. CONGRESSIONAL ENFORCEMENT OF CIVIL RIGHTS

Congress may protect Americans from invidious private acts of discrimination under many of its regulatory powers, such as the commerce clause. The Reconstruction Amendments—the 13th, 14th, and 15th—each give Congress power to enforce its substantive provisions. Through these enforcement powers Congress may regulate the states and, to a limited extent, may regulate some private conduct.

1. The 13th Amendment

Congress may regulate *private or public conduct* that it rationally determines is a *badge or incident* of slavery, but that power is probably limited to instances of invidious racial discrimination. Although the 13th Amendment is also *self-executing*, its scope is *very narrow* unless Congress enacts legislation to enforce it. Without congressional action the 13th Amendment probably only bars *actual slavery* or its near-equivalent, *peonage.*

2. The 14th and 15th Amendments

Congress may regulate *state action* that interferes with rights secured by the 14th and 15th Amendments, but it is not clear whether Congress can regulate any private invidious discrimination. Though not entirely free from doubt, Congress is **probably** able to use its enforcement power to punish private action directed *at state officials and designed to interfere with their obligation to comply with the 14th or 15th Amendments.* Congress may act to provide remedies for violation of 14th and 15th Amendment rights but may **not** alter their substance.

11 FREE EXPRESSION OF IDEAS

A. OVERVIEW

The First Amendment protects the **free expression of ideas**—freedom of speech, association, the press, assembly, and the right to petition the government for redress of grievances. The First Amendment applies directly to the federal government and, via the incorporation doctrine, applies to the states as well.

1. Content-Based or Content-Neutral Regulations

The level of judicial scrutiny applied to speech regulations by government depends on whether they are *content based* or *content neutral.*

a. Content-based regulations. Laws aimed at the *communicative impact of speech* are content based. A law forbidding political speech is content based.

    i. Viewpoint-based. Some content-based speech regulations are viewpoint discriminatory. A law forbidding Marxist speech is viewpoint based. Viewpoint-based speech regulations trigger the strictest scrutiny of all.

b.   **Content-neutral regulations.**   Laws aimed at some aspect of speech other than its communicative impact are content neutral. A law banning public speech at night is content neutral.

2.   **Judicial Review of Content-Based Regulations**

With one major exception, content-based regulations are *presumptively invalid.* They are upheld only if the government can prove that the regulation is *narrowly drawn* to accomplish a *compelling government interest.*

a.   **Exception: "categorical balancing."**   Some speech categories, defined by their content, are so unrelated to the purposes of free speech that they are either constitutionally unprotected or receive a lesser degree of protection. Governments may regulate speech freely within these unprotected categories, so long as the regulation is **viewpoint neutral,** that is, it does *not suppress one particular viewpoint.*

Example: A government may prohibit obscene speech but may not prohibit only obscene speech that is critical of the government.

To determine whether a category of speech is unprotected, courts balance the governmental interest in regulating the category and the value of the speech category in terms of the purposes of free speech. The principal purpose of free speech is to enable us to govern ourselves as a representative democracy. But free speech is also important to discover truth, develop civic and moral virtue, enhance societal tolerance and self-restraint, and to enable dissidents to "let off steam."

3.   **Judicial Review of Content-Neutral Regulations**

Content-neutral speech restrictions are valid if they are **reasonable, narrowly tailored to serve a significant government interest,** and **leave open ample alternative channels of communication.** When governments use content-neutral regulations to restrict speech on government property that is not a **public forum**—a place traditionally open for public speech or voluntarily dedicated to that purpose—the regulations are valid if they are **reasonable** and **viewpoint-neutral.**

B.   **UNPROTECTED CATEGORIES OF SPEECH**

The Court has concluded that the following categories of speech are constitutionally unprotected. But remember that even with respect to these categories governments may not regulate on a viewpoint-specific basis.

1.   **Incitement of Crime**

Speech that is intended to **incite "imminent lawless action"** and that is **"likely to incite or produce such action"** is not protected. The speaker must **intend** to produce an immediate crime and the speech must be uttered under circumstances where it is very likely to incite immediate commission of crime.

Example: Suppose a mob has just broken into a jail and seized a prisoner suspected of a notorious and loathsome crime. If a speaker urges the mob to "lynch him now!" and points to a nearby tree, from which dangles a stout rope, his speech is surely unprotected.

2. Obscenity

Obscene speech is unprotected. Obscenity consists of speech that the average person, applying contemporary community standards, would find appeals to the prurient interest in sex and that depicts or describes sex in a patently offensive way, so long as a reasonable person would conclude that the speech, taken as a whole, lacks serious literary, artistic, political, or scientific value.

3. Child Pornography

Even "nonobscene" pornography that depicts children in well-defined sexual conduct is unprotected. There need not be proof of prurience or patent offensiveness, and it is possible that child pornography with serious value is unprotected. Pornography that depicts adults is protected so long as it is not obscene, but in practice the courts provide rather limited protection to adult pornography.

4. "Fighting Words"

So-called fighting words—face-to-face abuse likely to cause violence—are unprotected. Unpleasant speech that is emotionally disturbing but that does not constitute "fighting words" receives limited constitutional protection.

Example: If a person accosts another on the street and addresses him with a string of abusive and profane epithets the speech is likely unprotected. If, on the other hand, a person tacks up a poster on the town bulletin board containing the same abusive and profane epithets describing an entire group of people the speech is not unprotected on the ground that it is fighting words.

C. "LIMITED PROTECTION" CATEGORIES OF SPEECH

Some categories of speech receive only limited protection. Each of these categories has its own special rules for determining the validity of speech regulations within the category. In general, the standard of validity is more easily met than if the usual rule of strict scrutiny of content-based regulations applied. The following speech categories receive limited protection.

1. Offensive Speech and the Hostile Audience

Offensive speech is generally protected. However, speech that offends a hostile audience may be punished when four factors are present.

    a. **Imminent threat of violence.** The mood of the audience must be sufficiently ugly to threaten immediate violence.

    b. **Reasonable efforts to protect the speaker.** The police must have made "all reasonable efforts" to protect the speaker.

    c. **Police request to cease speaking.** After having failed in all reasonable efforts to protect the speaker, the police must request the speaker to cease and explain the reason for the request.

    d. **Refusal to cease speaking.** If the previous three conditions have been met and the speaker refuses to stop speaking, then and only then may the speech be punished.

2. Speech That Offends Captive or Sensitive Audiences

Indecent speech—lewd but not obscene—may be punished if it is delivered to an audience that cannot escape or that is especially sensitive to the speech. This is a highly fact-specific doctrine.

Example: The FAA may discipline a commercial airline pilot who uses the cabin public address system to tell lewd jokes to the passengers. The passengers cannot escape. On the other hand, a city may not ban the exhibition of nude scenes at drive-in movie theaters because passers-by may avert their gaze. They are not captive. Similarly, the FCC may reprimand a radio station for airing a lewd monologue during hours in which children might reasonably be expected among the audience but could not reprimand the station if the monologue were aired at 3 A.M.

3. Defamation

Until 1964 defamation was an entirely unprotected category of speech. Since then, defamation has acquired substantial constitutional protection.

    a. **Public figures.** Defamation of a **public figure** is protected unless the false statement of fact was made with **actual malice**—either *knowledge of its falsity* or *reckless indifference to its truth or falsity.* Public officials and famous or notorious people involved in public affairs are "public figures" for all purposes. People who have voluntarily entered a public controversy or, very rarely, people who have been involuntarily thrust into such a controversy by the actions of public officials (e.g., a criminal defendant) are "public figures" only for purposes of the specific public issue.

    b. **Private figures.** When a private figure is defamed as to a matter of "public interest" the First Amendment requires proof of *negligence* in order to recover actual damages, and *actual malice* must be proven in order to recover punitive damages. When a private figure is defamed as to a matter of *no public interest*, there is no First Amendment barrier to the recovery of either actual or punitive damages.

4. **Infliction of Emotional Distress**

Speech that inflicts emotional injury is protected if it is visited upon a public figure. Private figures may be able to maintain suit on such speech, but probably only if the speech lacks any connection to the underlying purposes of the free speech guarantee.

Example: A political parody of Bill Clinton that depicts residents of Arkansas as randy buffoons may inflict emotional injury on private figures, but the speech is protected because of its connection to the central purposes of the free speech guarantee.

5. **Invasion of Privacy**

Individual privacy may be tortiously invaded by casting a person in a false and offensive light or by disclosing true but highly personal information. Both forms of privacy invasion receive limited constitutional protection.

   a. **False light.** If privacy is invaded by casting a person in a false light with respect to **matters of public concern,** the invasive falsehood is constitutionally protected unless it is uttered with **actual malice.**

   b. **Disclosure of true but highly personal information.** When such information is obtained from public court records or proceedings its disclosure is constitutionally protected. The Court has not decided whether the Constitution protects disclosure of such information obtained in other ways.

6. **Invasion of Economic Interests**

Speech that infringes another's copyright is not constitutionally protected. Commercial defamation **may** be protected unless the speaker has acted with **actual malice,** but the Court has never so held.

7. **Commercial Speech**

Commercial speech receives limited constitutional protection. Governments may freely regulate commercial speech that is either *misleading* or concerns *unlawful activity.* Governments may regulate truthful, accurate commercial speech concerning lawful activity only if the government has a *substantial interest* in such regulation, the regulation *directly advances* that substantial governmental interest, and the regulation is *reasonably narrowly tailored* to achieve the objective.

D. **JUDICIAL REVIEW OF CONTENT-NEUTRAL REGULATIONS**

1. **In General**

Content-neutral regulations of speech are valid if *narrowly tailored* to serve a *significant government interest* **and** *leave open ample alternative channels of communication.*

2. **Place of Expression—Public Forum or Not**

Content-neutral regulations of speech in **a public forum** must be *narrowly tailored* to serve a *significant government interest* **and** *leave open ample alternative channels of communication*. Content-neutral flat bans on speech in a **public forum** must be *narrowly drawn* to accomplish a *compelling government interest*.

a. **Public fora.**   Public fora are government property that are *either* traditionally open for speech (e.g., parks, streets and sidewalks) or voluntarily dedicated to all speech purposes (e.g., a community billboard created for the public to post notices). Public fora may not be closed to speech so long as they remain public fora.

   i. **Limited public fora.**   A "limited public forum" is government property voluntarily dedicated to **specific speech purposes.**

   Example: A public school opened after-hours for *student* speech purposes only is a limited public forum. Nonstudent speakers could be excluded from the school.

   Limited public fora are open to speech only for their limited purpose, but that purpose may not be defined in a viewpoint-specific fashion.

b. **Severity of the restriction.**   Content-neutral speech restrictions in a **nonpublic forum** depend on the severity of the restriction.

   i. **Severe restrictions.**   When such speech restrictions are *so severe as to leave no alternative way to speak* they are *presumed invalid* and subjected to *strict scrutiny.*

   ii. **Nonsevere restrictions.**   Insubstantial content-neutral speech restrictions need only be *rationally related* to a *legitimate government objective.*

E. **SYMBOLIC CONDUCT**

Nonverbal conduct that *intends to convey an idea* and that is *reasonably understood to convey that idea* is symbolic conduct that is protected speech. Governments may restrict symbolic conduct only if the restriction furthers an *important* or *substantial* government interest, that government interest is *unrelated to the suppression of ideas*, and the speech restriction is *no greater than necessary* to further the government interest. If the government interest is related to suppression of ideas the law still might be valid if it can pass *strict scrutiny.*

F. **MONEY AS SPEECH—POLITICAL CONTRIBUTIONS AND EXPENDITURES**

Money is necessary to speak effectively for political purposes. Thus, the Court treats the expenditure of money on speech as the equivalent of speech itself. Contribution of money to enable others to speak is given less protection.

1. Expenditures

Governments may not limit expenditures by political candidates from their own funds, or expenditures by individuals or organizations independent from a candidate. In order to receive public funds, political candidates may be required to limit their total campaign expenditures. Although corporations are generally treated like individuals with respect to spending on speech, governments may limit speech expenditures by business corporations made from their general treasury.

2. Contributions

Governments may limit contributions to political candidates or organizations but contributions made in connection with ballot measures may not be limited because there is less risk of corruption.

G. RESTRICTIONS ON THE SPEECH OF PUBLIC EMPLOYEES

Governments may restrict the speech of public employees to the extent justified by the government interest in efficiently delivering public services.

1. Partisan Political Activity

In order to maintain the unbiased delivery of government services and to reduce coercive partisan pressures upon civil servants, governments may regulate political activities by public employees.

2. Criticism of Government

While private employers generally may punish employee speech critical of their employer, governments are required to display more patience. Critical speech by public employees that relates to a matter of **public concern** may be regulated only to the extent necessary to maintain an efficient work place. Governments may freely regulate public employees' speech that does **not** relate to a matter of public concern.

3. Patronage

Patronage—the practice of hiring, firing, and promoting public employees on the basis of their political loyalties—is an old American tradition. But the Court has concluded that the First Amendment permits patronage hiring, firing, or promotion **only** with respect to jobs for which party affiliation is an *appropriate* criterion to ensure *effective job performance*.

4. Loyalty Oaths

Governments may require that their employees proclaim their loyalty by oath or affirmation so long as the oath is **not vague,** does **not** require the **disclaimer of constitutionally protected speech,** does **not** require the **disclaimer of past or present political views,** and does **not** require the

CAPSULE SUMMARY

disclaimer of past or present associations except with respect to **knowing participation in illegal acts** or purposes.

5. Confidential Information

Governments may restrict employee speech to protect confidential information entrusted to government employees.

6. Government Licensees or Contractors

The rules governing restriction of employee speech also apply to government licensees and independent contractors.

H. REGULATION OF SPEECH IN CONTROLLED ENVIRONMENTS

Certain settings augment governmental power to control speech because the governmental interest in controlling speech is thought to be especially strong.

1. Prisons and Military

Regulation of the speech of prison inmates or military personnel is permissible so long as the regulation is an appropriate device to secure some legitimate state objective. This is a very deferential standard of review. Such regulations will be struck down only if the challenger can prove by clear and convincing evidence that the speech restriction is inappropriate to the accomplishment of some legitimate state objective.

2. Schools

Speech of elementary and secondary school students may be regulated to **avoid disruption to school business** and to the extent **student speech is related to the curriculum.** Speech of university students may be regulated only to the extent it is related to the curriculum.

I. FREE EXPRESSION RIGHTS OF ACCESS TO PRIVATE PROPERTY

In general, there is no right of access to private property for free expression purposes. State constitutions may differ, and when private property is voluntarily devoted to public purposes, free speech access rights generally follow.

J. FREEDOM OF ASSOCIATION

Although the First Amendment does not mention freedom of association the Court has implied such a right from the right to speak freely and the right to assemble peaceably. This **expressive association** differs from **intimate association,** which is generally protected by substantive due process.

1. Standard of Review

When governments *substantially* restrict freedom of association the restriction is *presumptively void*. The restriction is valid *only* if the government can prove that it is the *least restrictive means* to accomplish a *compelling* government interest that is *unrelated to the suppression of ideas.*

K. FREEDOM FROM *COMPELLED* SPEECH OR ASSOCIATION

There is just as much right *not* to express ideas as there is a right to expression. Governmental attempts to compel speech or association are *presumptively invalid* and will be upheld only if the government can prove that the compulsion is the *least restrictive means* of accomplishing some *compelling governmental interest* that is unrelated to the forced expression of ideas.

1. Freedom from Compelled Disclosure

A close relative of the freedom from compelled speech or association is freedom from compelled disclosure of private information. Whenever forced disclosure of such information substantially restrains freedom of association or speech the First Amendment is presumed to be violated. The forced disclosure is valid only if the government can prove that compelled disclosure is necessary to the accomplishment of some compelling government objective.

L. FREEDOM OF THE PRESS

The press enjoys all the usual protection of free speech and one special right. **The press may not be subjected to laws that apply only to the press on the basis of the content of speech.** The press also enjoys a right of access to criminal trials and related proceedings that is coextensive with that of the public.

M. OVERBREADTH, VAGUENESS, AND PRIOR RESTRAINTS

These three doctrines cut across free speech.

1. Overbreadth

When laws *on their face* are *substantially overbroad*—most of their possible applications are invalid—they are facially invalid. This principle permits a litigant to whom a law is **validly** applied to challenge it, on the theory that law-abiding citizens will curb their protected speech to conform to the invalid law and thus never violate the unconstitutional law.

2. Vagueness

As a matter of due process, if a law is so vague that ordinary people cannot know in advance what conduct or speech is forbidden, the law is invalid.

3. Prior Restraints

Restraining speech before it occurs—even speech that might lawfully be punished—is especially suspect, on the ground that such restraints operate to chill speakers who might utter protected speech. Only the most *compelling government interests*—such as an unimpeachable assertion of national security interests—support prior restraints. The classic example is a restraint on disclosure of a troopship departure in time of war.

THE RELIGION CLAUSES

A. OVERVIEW

The First Amendment contains two **religion clauses.** The **establishment clause** prevents governments from establishing religions. The **free exercise clause** prevents governments from interfering with religious beliefs. Both clauses are intended to secure freedom of religion by separating religion and government from each other. The religion clauses apply directly to the federal government and are incorporated into the due process clause of the 14th Amendment, thus making them applicable to the states.

1. Core Purposes of the Religion Clauses

   a. Establishment clause.   Governments may not create an *official state church*, a *de facto state church* (through excessive government support), *endorse* or *coerce* either religion or non-belief, or *prefer one religion to another.*

   b. Free exercise clause.   Governments may not interfere in any way with *religious belief*, and must provide *limited accommodation to religious practices.*

2. Conflict Between the Clauses

Some accommodations of religion undertaken to foster free exercise (but not required by it) may violate the establishment clause, but free exercise requires some accommodations. The Court attempts to keep the clauses in dynamic balance.

B. THE ESTABLISHMENT CLAUSE

There are two approaches to the establishment clause: **neutrality** and **accommodation.**

1. Neutrality

The neutrality approach relies primarily upon the three part test first developed in *Lemon v. Kurtzman.* Under the *Lemon* test, government assistance to religion violates the establishment clause if *any* of the following elements are not satisfied.

   a. Secular purpose.   The purpose of the governmental action must be to further a *secular objective*. This element is satisfied so long as there is **any** actual secular objective that can plausibly be served by the governmental action.

Example: Providing free public bus transport to and from school for students in religious schools (on the same basis that such transport is provided students in the public schools) serves the secular objectives of encouraging education and enhancing the safety of schoolchildren.

b. **Neutral effect.**   The primary effect of the governmental action must *neither advance nor inhibit religion.* This does **not** mean that the government action must have no positive or negative effect on religion whatever. So long as the government action is facially neutral and the religious effect is "remote, indirect, or incidental" this element is satisfied. If a facially neutral government action produces religious effects because of intervening choices of private persons, the government action is still considered to be neutral.

Example: Minnesota granted a tax credit for expenditures on education. Over 90% of the credits were claimed by parents of children attending private religious schools. The Court upheld the credits against an establishment clause challenge, reasoning that it was the individual choice of private persons that produced the religious effect. The tax credit was facially neutral—equally available to parents of children in public and private schools, whether religious or not.

c. **Excessive entanglement.**   The governmental action must not *excessively entangle* government and religion. The most important factor in determining whether the entanglement between government and religion is excessive is governmental aid that requires continual government monitoring of religion or religious accounting to government. This element is now only a factor in determining whether or not the government's action has a neutral effect.

2. **Accommodation**

The accommodation approach rejects *Lemon.* Under accommodation, government involvement with religion violates the establishment clause if any of the following three factors are present.

a. **Discrimination among religions.**   Government aid to religion that discriminates among religious groups is a *de facto* establishment, on the theory that the essence of "establishment" is official government favoritism of one sect.

b. **Endorsement of religion.**   For the same reason, the accommodation approach forbids any government action that amounts to an endorsement of a particular religious view, or that amounts to an endorsement of hostility to religion. But some adherents to accommodation reject endorsement as an independent element.

c. **Coercion of religious belief.**   Accommodationists argue that governments must refrain from any actions that amount to a coercion of religious belief or nonbelief.

3. **Which Approach?**

Establishment clause law is unstable because the Court is badly divided over the proper approach to employ. In theory, the *Lemon* test still dominates. In practice, the accommodation approach has both influenced *Lemon* (especially its neutral effects prong) and supplanted *Lemon* in some areas (particularly public displays of religious imagery).

4. **Applications of the Establishment Clause**

Establishment clause problems crop up in a variety of contexts.

a. **Financial aid.**   The *Lemon* test is used to evaluate the validity of financial aid to religious institutions. *Direct aid* to religious institutions is generally void, the principal exception being aid to religious colleges to finance construction of secular buildings. *Indirect aid* to religious institutions is generally valid when it is part of a general, secular aid plan to private persons.

b. **Religion and the public schools.**   A combination of the *Lemon*, endorsement, and coercion tests is used to evaluate religion in the public schools. Religious instruction and school-sponsored prayer are not permitted, but truly spontaneous student-initiated prayer is probably permissible. The establishment clause does not bar governments from providing equal access to religious users of public facilities.

c. **No preferences.**   Governments may not prefer one religion to any other, whether they do so openly or through a religious gerrymander.

d. **Religious-based exemptions from law.**   Religious institutions may be included in general exemptions given generally to secular institutions (e.g., charities) but exemptions designed solely to aid religion (and not required by the free exercise clause) are invalid.

    Example: A property tax exemption afforded all charitable organizations (including churches) furthers a secular purpose of promoting charity and does not have the principal effect of promoting religion. But a law exempting only religious publications from an otherwise generally applicable sales tax is void because its sole purpose is to aid religion.

e. **Delegations of public power to religious institutions.**   Whether through application of *Lemon* or the endorsement test, such delegations of public power to religion are invalid.

f. **Government ceremonies or displays of religious imagery.**   Governments may participate in ceremonies invoking religion or display religious imagery so long as their action does not endorse or coerce religious belief. This is a very fine line and the distinctions made in this area are quite fact specific.

Example: The federal government may imprint "In God We Trust" on the coinage because it is a "ceremonial deism"—drained of all effective content. A government may display religious images in December so long as the display is combined with enough nonreligious images to make the entire message incoherent. A government may not sponsor a ritual benediction at a public school graduation because it would subtly coerce nonbelievers into religious observance. But a state legislature may open each session with a nondenominational prayer because it is partly a ceremonial deism, and partly because adult legislators are thought unlikely to be coerced into religious belief.

g. **No government inquiry into religious belief.** Governments may not inquire into religious beliefs but may assess whether such beliefs are sincerely held. This rule owes as much to the free exercise clause as to the establishment clause.

Example: Courts will not adjudicate controversies that require them to decide points of religious doctrine, as when contests arise over title to church property that is held "so long as the XYZ Church subscribes to the true principles of the XYZ religion."

This rule does not prevent governments from inquiring into the "sincerity" with which a claimed religious belief is held, but it does prevent governments from deciding whether the belief is really religious or not.

C. THE FREE EXERCISE CLAUSE

The free exercise clause absolutely bars governments from interfering with *religious belief* but does not prevent governments from interfering with *religious conduct*.

1. **Standards of Review**

    a. **Minimal scrutiny.** Governmental interference with *religious conduct* that is produced by a law *generally applicable to everyone* is presumptively valid and is upheld unless the challenger can prove that it is not rationally related to a legitimate government objective.

    b. **Strict scrutiny.** Strict scrutiny applies to governmental interference with religious conduct that is *deliberately intended to suppress only religious conduct*, or when coupled with an *infringement of another constitutional right*, or when government benefits are denied on an individualized basis.

        i. **Purposeful interference with religious practice.** Strict scrutiny applies when governments single out religious practice for disfavored treatment.

Example: A law that prohibits the use of wine for sacramental purposes only is subject to strict scrutiny because it singles out religious conduct. By contrast, a law that prohibits *anyone* from consuming alcoholic beverages is subject to minimal scrutiny because it is a law generally applicable to everyone.

ii. **Denials of public benefits on an individualized basis.** Strict scrutiny applies when governments employ an individualized assessment to deny public benefits and the denial is based on reasons of religious practice that are not in conflict with general criminal law.

iii. **Simultaneous burdens on religious conduct and other constitutional right.** Strict scrutiny applies when governments take action that burdens *both* religious conduct and another constitutional right.

Example: Wisconsin required children to attend school until age fourteen. The Old Order Amish contended that the requirement abridged both their due process right to control the upbringing of their children and their right to free exercise of their religious belief that education beyond elementary school was sinful. The Court struck down the Wisconsin law as violative of both claimed rights. If a litigant can plausibly assert that a given government action offends both free exercise and another independent constitutional right strict scrutiny will apply.

2. **The Religious Freedom Restoration Act**

   A federal statute, the Religious Freedom Restoration Act, prohibits any government from imposing *substantial burdens* on religious conduct unless the government can prove that the burdens imposed are the least restrictive means of achieving a compelling government objective. RFRA has been invalidated as applied to the states. Its validity as applied to the federal government is an open question.

 ECONOMIC RIGHTS: THE TAKINGS CLAUSE
AND THE CONTRACTS CLAUSE

A. **OVERVIEW**

One of the objectives of the Constitution's framers was to protect significant economic rights. Two of the most important such protective devices are the takings clause and the contracts clause. Prior to the New Deal revolution of the

1930s the substantive component of due process was also a major device for protection of economic rights.

B. TAKINGS CLAUSE

1. Scope

The Fifth Amendment's takings clause ("nor shall private property be taken for public use without just compensation") prohibits the federal and state governments from taking private property *except for **public use,*** and then only if *just compensation* is paid. The takings clause applies directly to the federal government and applies to the state governments because it is incorporated into the 14th Amendment's due process clause. The takings clause applies to both tangible and intangible property and to any governmental action, whether legislative, executive, or judicial.

2. Public Use

So long as a taking of private property is *rationally related* to **any conceivable** *public purpose* the public use requirement is satisfied.

Example: A Hawaii law that condemned landlords' private property in order to transfer it to the tenants upon payment of just compensation to the landlords was found by the Court to further the public purpose of reducing oligarchy in land ownership in Hawaii.

3. Regulatory Takings

Most takings are straightforward—the government simply declares its intent to take ("condemn") the property and the only issues presented are the amount of compensation and whether the taking is for a public use. But governments can take property even when they deny any intention to do so. Government regulations may be a *de facto* taking if the regulations are sufficiently destructive of property rights. Courts use three *per se* rules and a multifactor balancing test to determine if a regulation is a taking. If it is a taking, the government may proceed with the regulation only if it pays affected property owners just compensation.

a. **Nuisance regulations are *not* takings.** If a regulation simply abates a common law nuisance it is not a taking, regardless of what other effects it may have. It is a *per se* "nontaking." The question of what constitutes a common law nuisance is a question of underlying state law. The rationale for this rule is that the property owner never possessed a legal right to use his property in a fashion that constitutes a nuisance, so the government has not taken any property right.

b. **Permanent dispossession of private property is a *per se* taking.** Regulations that permanently dispossess an owner from his property are *per se* takings. This rule has most frequently been applied to real property. The government regulation must effect a permanent physical occupation of any portion of the real property in order to be a *per se* taking. But the Court has applied this rule to regulations that seized intangible property as well.

    c. Destruction of all economically viable uses of property. Regulations that bar the property owner from all economically viable uses of the property are *per se* takings. In essence, the Court regards such regulations as functionally identical to a permanent dispossession.

    d. Balancing. If government regulations do not fit within any of the *per se* rules the courts will apply a balancing test to evaluate whether the regulations constitute a taking. Regulations that interfere with property rights must **substantially advance a legitimate state interest** in order not to be treated as a taking. In assessing this relationship, courts examine three factors.

        i. Public benefits v. private costs. The more the private costs imposed by the regulation outweigh the public benefits produced the more likely that the regulation will be treated as a taking. The more the public benefits outweigh the private costs the less likely the regulation will be a taking.

        ii. Reasonable return. If a regulation leaves the property owner with a "reasonable return" on his "investment-backed expectations" it is not likely to be treated as a taking.

        iii. Arbitrary regulations. Government regulations that are arbitrary are surely takings. This has little practical significance since arbitrary regulations probably violate due process and fail minimal scrutiny as well.

4. Regulatory *Conditions* as Takings

An important subset of regulatory takings involves the conditioning of some governmental license or benefit upon a property owner's waiver of some aspect of his bundle of property rights. This problem is also part of the larger issue of "unconstitutional conditions"—conditioning receipt of a government benefit upon the recipient's waiver of a constitutional right. In regulatory takings the problem usually surfaces as a condition attached to the issuance of a building permit.

    a. Standard of review. Governments may **not** attach conditions to building permits that would be takings if imposed in isolation, unless the government proves two conditions.

        i. Essential nexus. The condition imposed must advance the government's legitimate reason for restricting the owner's development in the first place. The Court labels this relationship the "essential nexus."

Example: Suppose Ciudad restricts development in order to conserve its scarce water supply. If Ciudad then conditions receipt of a building permit upon the property owner's "donation" of a portion of her property to Ciudad for public parking, the condition is a taking because it lacks the required essential nexus. The condition imposed—creating more public parking—bears no relationship to Ciudad's reason for restricting development in the first place—preserving Ciudad's scarce water supply.

  ii. Rough proportionality. The extent of the conditions imposed must be "roughly proportional" to the impact of the proposed development.

Example: Refer to the prior example. Suppose Ciudad conditions a building permit upon the property owner's installation of a cistern of specified size to collect rain water for household use. This condition will satisfy the essential nexus test. It will satisfy the rough proportionality test if the water captured by the cistern is "roughly proportional" to the increased demand on Ciudad's water supply that would otherwise occur because of the development.

C. CONTRACTS CLAUSE

1. Scope

The contracts clause bars states from enacting any "Law impairing the Obligation of Contracts." While this appears to be an absolute bar, the Court construes the contracts clause to prohibit states from *unreasonable* impairments of contractual obligations.

2. Standard of Review

Sliding scale scrutiny applies—the *more severe* the impairment the *closer the scrutiny.* Different rules apply to impairments of *public* and *private* contracts.

  a. Private contracts. Impairments of private contracts—those in which the parties are all private persons—may be analyzed as follows.

    i. Substantial (but *not* severe) impairment. Is there a "*substantial impairment* of some contractual relationship? If not, the contracts clause is not violated. If so, but the impairment is not **severe,** *the state must justify the impairment* by showing all of the following elements. But courts will defer to legislative judgment as to the necessity and reasonableness of the law.

      (a) Significant public purpose. The reason for the impairment must be some public purpose that is not only *legitimate* but of some practical *significance* to the community. It need not be a compelling public purpose.

    (b) Appropriate character. The impairment's *character* must be appropriate to the public purpose. It must be rationally related to accomplishment of the public purpose.

    (c) Reasonable. The extent of the impairment (even though substantial) must be reasonable under the circumstances in which it is adopted.

  ii. Severe impairments of private contracts. When governments *severely impair* private contracts courts will *carefully examine* the *nature and purpose* of the law. Severe impairments occur when *express terms* of a private contract are *nullified* and an *unexpected and potentially disabling* liability is imposed.

    (a) Standard of review. Severe impairments are *presumed invalid*. To be upheld, the state must prove that the impairment is **necessary to meet an important social objective.** This proof is made easier if the state can show that the impairment is **temporary, reasonable in scope,** and **directly related** to a **compelling** or **emergency** objective of the state. Laws that permanently impair contracts in order to benefit a ''narrow class'' rather than ''to protect a broad societal interest'' are especially suspect.

b. Public contracts. When states unilaterally modify their own contracts courts will *not defer* to the legislative assessment of reasonableness and necessity. The state must prove that the impairment was *necessary* and *reasonable.*

  i. Necessity. To be necessary, the impairment must be *essential*—there must be *no less impairing alternative* available to the state to achieve its public objectives.

  ii. Reasonable. The impairment must be prompted by radically altered circumstances of an unforeseeable nature at the time the contract was made.

THE CONTEXT OF CONSTITUTIONAL LAW

CHAPTER OVERVIEW

This chapter provides context—history, interpretational methods, and some important doctrinal techniques. **Go straight to Chapter 2 if you don't want context in advance of substance.** The most important points in this chapter are:

History

- Colonial Americans thought that governments should have only those powers given to them by the people.

- The Constitution was a reaction to the weak national government created under the Articles of Confederation.

- The Constitution sought to limit the national government's powers to specified (or **enumerated**) powers and to divide those enumerated powers among the three branches of government: executive, legislative, and judicial.

- Anti-Federalist opponents of the Constitution thought it gave too much power to the national government and failed to state (or enumerate) the important rights of the people in a Bill of Rights. The Bill of Rights was the reaction to these charges.

- The Civil War and the 13th, 14th, and 15th Amendments profoundly limited the scope of state power.

- During the economic depression of the late 1930s the Court all but abandoned judicial review of the scope of congressional power, leaving that issue to the national political process. The result has been to transform a government of limited, enumerated powers into one with virtually general power, limited only by rights-protecting constitutional provisions.

Methods of Constitutional Interpretation

- **Textual.** Meaning is to be derived from the present sense of the words in the Constitution.

- **Historical.** Meaning is to be derived from the original intentions of the drafts-men and the subsequent historical sense of the provision in question.

- **Structural.** Meaning is to be derived from the relationships among govern-ments, and between governments and people, created by the Constitution.

- **Doctrinal.** Meaning is to be derived from past judicial precedents on the Constitution.

- **Prudential.** Meaning is to be derived from practical realities.

Levels of Judicial Scrutiny

- **Minimal Scrutiny** is applied to most laws, which are presumed valid unless the challenger can prove they are not rationally related to a legitimate state interest.

- **Strict Scrutiny** is applied to laws that possess some indicator of likely invalidity. Such laws are presumed void unless the government can prove that they are necessary to accomplish a compelling government interest. Necessity is often shown by proving that there is no less restrictive or burdensome alternative open to the government to achieve its objective.

- **Intermediate Scrutiny** applies to laws with characteristics that raise doubts about their validity. Such laws are presumed void unless the government can prove that they are substantially related to an important state interest.

A.   INTRODUCTION

This chapter puts the study of Constitutional Law in a larger context. Part B is a brief history of major "constitutional events"—from the American Revolution to the New Deal. Part C sets forth the principal well-accepted modes of reasoning about the Constitution's meaning. Part D describes some of the pervasive tech-niques employed by courts deciding constitutional law issues. If you need histori-cal context, read Part B. If not, skip it. If you find it helpful to know abstractly the way judges reason about the Constitution, read Part C. Otherwise, refer back to it when it becomes helpful. If you desire an abstracted preview of major doctrinal techniques, read Part D. Otherwise, skip it. Most Constitutional Law courses start with the material in Chapter 2.

B.   HISTORICAL CONTEXT

1.   The Political Justifications for Rebellion

Politically speaking, the United States is a descendant of the British legal tradition and European liberalism of the 17th and 18th centuries. Colonial Americans considered themselves owners of all the rights of Englishmen, even though they were separated by a vast and dangerous ocean. One of those rights was that taxes could not be imposed on the people by the Crown but, rather, were the free gift of the people to the Crown. In practice this meant that taxes could only be imposed by Parliament, in which body the people acted through their representatives. Americans were outraged when in 1763, after the end of the Seven Years War (or French and Indian War, as it was more commonly called in America), the British Parliament began to impose a variety of taxes on Americans in order to make them pay for the considerable costs of defending their frontier from Indian raids and foreign incursions. Americans had no representation in Parliament, and so Parliament could not lawfully impose taxes on them. Not so, said the British government, since Americans were "virtually" represented in Parliament. Virtual representation meant that a member of Parliament, though elected only by voters in Britain, was a representative for all Englishmen, no matter where in the far-flung Empire they might be located. Americans sneered at this fiction and demanded the right to have their own elected representatives make the decisions that affected them.

The British contributed to this situation by permitting the American colonies to have their own legislative assemblies, albeit with minimal and curtailed powers. But the experiment in home rule only provided proof to American colonists that they could make their own way. "Virtual representation" in a distant Parliament was hardly an equivalent to the familiar legislative assemblies convening in Boston or Williamsburg.

Perhaps revolt was only a matter of time, since by 1776 Americans had more than 150 years of practical self-government, albeit under the ultimate rule of royal governors or proprietors chartered by the Crown. During that time, Americans had discovered that their local institutions, including courts, could check the power of that far-off Parliament. In 1760, in the famous *Writs of Assistance Case*, Americans had argued successfully that courts could invalidate acts of Parliament, relying upon a cryptic dictum of the famous English jurist, Lord Coke, that the law could control Parliament. John Adams later wrote that "then and there the child Independence was born." Adams may have overstated the case a bit, but there is no doubt that Americans turned venerable English institutions to their own purposes.

Equally important was the incendiary political thought of such philosophers as John Locke, who argued that *governments possessed only the power that the people ceded to them.* Even in the political context of a liberal constitutional monarchy (George III was no tyrant, whatever the revolutionary generation said) this was extravagant doctrine. But Americans took it to heart and Locke's writings became a political gospel of sorts. So it was that a justifiable attempt by Parliament to make the American colonists pay for their own military protection turned into an armed revolution that led to a new nation.

2.   **The Awkward Relationship of the States Under the Articles of Confederation**

With independence virtually achieved by the surrender of Cornwallis in 1781 Americans needed to establish new national institutions. During the revolutionary period the states had cooperated with one another through the mechanism of the Continental Congress, a body of delegates from each of the various American colonies that formulated a "national" policy on the momentous events of armed rebellion. The Articles of Confederation, our first constitution, was an attempt to perpetuate that arrangement.

The Articles created a rough confederation of equal sovereigns. The Articles expressly stipulated that each state retained its "sovereignty, freedom, and independence," except as to those powers expressly delegated to "the United States, in Congress assembled." The powers of national government were held entirely by Congress, and those powers were extremely limited. Although Congress was given the "sole and exclusive" power to make war it had no power to tax or regulate interstate commerce.

Predictably, the new nation experienced great difficulty. States with harbors gouged their neighbors by imposing import and export tariffs. Interstate transactions were hampered by fluctuating rates of exchange between the currencies of the various states. The national debt incurred to finance the revolution went unpaid because Congress could not levy taxes to raise funds for its payment. Instead of a nation developing from the successful revolution, the United States consisted of a family of selfish, squabbling, irresponsible siblings.

It could not continue. By 1786, representatives of several Chesapeake Bay states met in Annapolis to consider amendment to the Articles. The best thing they did was to resolve that a general convention be held in Philadelphia the following year to address the problems. In the summer of 1787 fifty-five delegates from the states met in Philadelphia in answer to the call for a convention.

3.   **The Ambitions of the 1787 Convention**

The authority of the Constitutional Convention of 1787 was quite narrow. The delegates were instructed to consider such changes to the Articles "as shall appear to them necessary to render the constitution of the federal government adequate to the exigencies of the Union." The delegates interpreted that charge liberally and set about designing an entirely new charter of government. From the beginning they were committed to two radical principles.

One was the idea of a **central government endowed with only limited, specified (or enumerated) powers.** The usual assumption was that a government possessed every conceivable power except those denied to them by the people when constituting the government. The Constitution's framers stood that idea on its head by investing the central government with only enumerated powers. Of course, the powers so enumerated were considerably broader than those given to the Congress under the Articles of Confederation.

The other radical idea was separation of powers. Borrowing from Montesquieu, the Framers created a central government with its powers divided among the three branches of government: executive, legislative, and judicial. By contrast, the British parliamentary system combines the executive and legislative powers and does not endow the judiciary with the power of constitutional judicial review.

The Framers did not specifically provide that the courts could exercise the power of judicial review. In all probability they expected courts to assume that role and saw no need to explicitly say so. Judicial review had an established, if contested, history in America. It is entirely possible that the Framers wished to dodge the issue by failing explicitly to provide for judicial review.

4. The Fears of the Anti-Federalist Opponents of the Constitution

Opponents of ratification of the Constitution—the so-called Anti-Federalists—were bound together by a variety of common beliefs. They contended that republican government worked best when it was decentralized. The smallest scale of government possible was generally preferable, because it was closer to the people affected and thus better able to detect and address public needs.

Anti-Federalists pointed to the lack of a Bill of Rights to argue that the embryonic national government was not prevented from invading the rights of the people. Federalists responded that a Bill of Rights was unnecessary, since the federal government only possessed limited powers. Indeed, said Federalists, enumeration of individual rights was dangerous for two reasons. First, it would imply that the enumerated rights were all the rights individuals possessed. Second, it would imply that the federal government must possess some implied powers, for what was the reason for prohibiting Congress from abridging freedom of speech if Congress did not have some power to do so? If Congress possessed one implied power, how many more might there be found to be? Anti-Federalists retorted that the proposed national government's powers were already too extensive. Against this background the states ratified the proposed Constitution, although many did so subject to a proviso that the first Congress propose specific amendments in the form of a Bill of Rights.

5. The Bill of Rights: The First Ten Amendments

The implicit bargain of ratification was carried out by the First Congress, which proposed twelve amendments. Ten of those were promptly ratified and became the first ten amendments. Another was ratified by five states, but two centuries later was ratified by the then requisite thirty-eight states and has become the 27th Amendment (barring congressional pay raises until an election has intervened).

The substantive content of the Bill of Rights occupies a great deal of modern constitutional law. For the moment, note the political compromise embedded in the Ninth and Tenth Amendments. The Ninth Amendment provides that "[t]he enumeration in the Constitution of certain rights shall not be construed to deny or disparage others retained by the people." Here can be seen the response to the Federalist concern of danger in enumerating rights, for it seeks to negate the inference that the enumerated rights are all there are and to prevent the argument that, because of an enumeration of rights, the federal government must possess implied powers. The Tenth Amendment, on the other hand, seeks to restate the fundamental constitutional principle that the national government possesses only those powers that the Constitution gives to it, leaving the states with all residual power (subject to the Constitution and the directives of the people of each state). It is noteworthy that such power-limiting devices would be inserted into a Bill of Rights. The explanation is that the founding generation conceived of rights as beginning where governmental power ended, a point of view that confirms the founding generation's belief that liberty inhered in freedom from governmental control.

6. The Civil War: A Revolution in Federal-State Relations

The Civil War altered forever the relationship of the federal and state governments. Prior to the war the national government took a relatively small role in regulating the economic and social life of the nation. States were the principal regulators of the domestic affairs of the country. The war changed that. The 13th Amendment, abolishing slavery, removed at one stroke an odious institution that had been almost entirely subject to state authority. The 14th Amendment specifically obligated the states to afford due process and the equal protection of law to all their residents. These broad guarantees would, in time, be transformed into potent limitations upon state power. Finally, the 15th Amendment stripped states of the power to deny the vote to people on account of their race. Until this amendment, the franchise had been almost entirely within state regulatory power.

Of equal importance was the lesson, confirmed in blood, that the Union was indissoluble, and that the states had no unilateral power to secede. Out of this came a truly national consciousness, symbolized by a change in the language. The "United States" became a singular noun. Prior to the war, people would say, "the United States *are* . . . ." After the war, people began to say "the United States *is* . . . ." That change symbolized a new acceptance of national power, manifested by congressional initiatives and changes in constitutional law during the latter part of the 19th century.

7. Franklin Roosevelt's New Deal

The great economic and social crisis of the 1930s caused yet another transformation in constitutional law. Prior to 1937 the Court often invalidated federal legislation as *ultra vires*—beyond the enumerated constitutional powers of Congress. The Court regarded federalism—the allocation of power between the national government and the states—as judicially enforceable. In the exercise of its duty to review legislation, the Court struck down a fair amount of Roosevelt's New Deal legislation. Angered, and emboldened by his mammoth electoral triumph in 1936, Roosevelt proposed an alteration of the Court, one that would permit him to appoint six new Justices, bringing the total to fifteen. This "Court-packing" plan, for that is what it was, met with opposition even from some of Roosevelt's political kin. In the end it was narrowly averted but the Supreme Court evidently got the message. The Court reversed itself in 1937 and began to find New Deal legislation valid. Within a few years, and aided by a squad of Roosevelt appointees, the Court revolutionized federalism. While continuing to state that it held the power to invalidate legislation as *ultra vires*, the Court shifted to a standard of evaluation so deferential to Congress that, between 1937 and the 1990s no federal laws were struck down on these grounds. The Court essentially abandoned judicial review of the scope of congressional power and left that issue to be decided by the national political process. But in recent years the Court has begun to assert a new brand of judicially enforceable federalism. Even so, this shift from a judicially enforceable federalism to a politically enforceable federalism is one that has, in practice, altered the fundamental structure of the Constitution. In two centuries, we have moved from a national government of limited powers to a national government of almost unlimited power—checked mostly by individual rights guarantees. The constitutional checks on governmental power were once the scope of the enumerated *powers*; now they are primarily the scope of the enumerated *rights*.

C. METHODS OF CONSTITUTIONAL INTERPRETATION

A constant problem with any written constitution is reaching agreement on how it should be interpreted. How do we know what it means? To students of philosophy, this will be quickly recognized as just another problem in epistemology—how do we know anything? There are at least five methods commonly employed to decide upon the meaning of the Constitution. They are not mutually exclusive. Often they are combined in the same argument or opinion. From case to case, lawyers and judges accentuate these methods differently. The best constitutional argument is one that can employ each one of these methods convincingly. As you read constitutional opinions and commentary you will become aware of the ubiquity of these methods. Philip Bobbitt, Constitutional

Fate (1982), explores these modes of argument in detail. Each will be briefly considered below.

1. Textual

After all, it is a *written* Constitution. Textual argument "is drawn from a present sense of the words of the provision." Bobbitt, at 7. Some might object that it is impossible to know authoritatively the meaning of any text. There may (or may not) be an authorial intention, which may (or may not) coincide with the reader's understanding. Granted that words are not crystals, but the skins of living thoughts, to paraphrase Justice Holmes, it may still be possible to reach some common agreement on the meaning of ordinary thoughts residing within word-skins. Fervent believers in the indeterminacy of language may contend that the Constitution's requirement that the President "shall . . . have attained to the Age of thirty five years" be read as a requirement of maturity, but less rarefied thinkers are probably content to treat this as a simple arithmetic calculation. On the other hand, text may not be of much help in deciphering the meaning of "cruel or unusual," "due process," or "equal protection of the laws."

2. Historical

Historical argument may be broken down into three varieties. One is commonly described as the "original intentions" of the constitutional framers. Another is the original meaning of their words. The third is an attempt to derive historical meaning from the "vectors" of history, the way in which constitutional understanding has changed over time.

a. Original intentions. This is an attempt to discover the authorial intentions behind any constitutional provision. It is often said that the original intention should govern because it was the extraordinary action of the national polity at enactment that is binding upon us now. In other words, it was Americans in 1791, or 1868, who proposed and ratified the Bill of Rights, or the 14th Amendment, not us, so we should divine their intent, since that is what was placed into the Constitution. Even if that premise is granted (and it may be questioned, since the Constitution contains their *words* rather than their *intentions*) there are daunting obstacles to ascertaining intent. Whose intent counts? What about those excluded then, but included now, like women and blacks? What is the best evidence of intent? What happens when the draftsmen disagree? Even if we solve these considerable problems, does original intention matter when the application of the constitutional provision in question is to some problem utterly outside of the Framers' knowledge? Nevertheless, despite these vexing issues, there is value to be gained from delving into the intentions of those who framed our Constitution.

b. Original meaning. Whatever their original intentions may have been the words used by the Framers had a meaning commonly understood in their time. Divining that meaning may at times be difficult because of the problem of transporting ourselves into past and different cultural circumstances. Reliance on original meaning, however, freezes in place a cultural understanding of a past time and raises the question of whether the Constitution incorporates those bygone cultural values.

c. **The "vectors" of history.** History may be conceived of as a snapshot, a faded sepia photograph in the national photo album, or it may be thought of as a video, continuously running and always recording new scenes. The former view is static, the latter is dynamic. History as "original intentions" or "original meaning" is static; history as "vectors" is dynamic. Thus, in attaching meaning to "cruel or unusual punishment" one might wish to ascertain the direction of movement on this issue. The pillory was certainly not unusual in the late 18th century, but surely it is now. Of course, over-reliance on the "vectors" of history results in a methodology that is as much fortune-telling as constitutional interpretation. As with all constitutional interpretation, good sense is at a premium.

3. Structural

Structural arguments involve "claims that a particular principle or practical result is implicit in the structures of government and the relationships that are created by the Constitution among citizens and governments." Bobbitt, at 7. The argument that Congress may not use its power to regulate the jurisdiction of the federal courts virtually to eliminate federal court jurisdiction of constitutional claims is one that is rooted in the claim that the structure of the Constitution implies an active role for the federal courts in deciding constitutional law. These claims are not capable of scientific proof. Structural arguments are postulates about the type of governance created by the Constitution. They are constitutional interpolations; they compose an interstitial constitution—one that fills the gaps left by the governmental structures created by the Constitution.

4. Doctrinal

Doctrinal arguments are familiar to common lawyers, for they are the essence of the common law method. Doctrinal argument "asserts principles derived from precedent" and sometimes "judicial or academic commentary on precedent." Bobbitt, at 7. Stare decisis, or the rule of precedent, is a cornerstone principle in our common law method. Yet, as applied to constitutional law, the Court has repeatedly said that stare decisis is at its weakest. This is because of the extreme difficulty of correcting constitutional decisions of the Court. But even with a relatively weak principle of stare decisis in constitutional law the Court adheres to past decisions with uncommon frequency. There is virtue in legal stability, for as Justice Brandeis once put it, "in most matters it is more important that the applicable rule of law be settled than it be settled right." *Burnet v. Coronado Oil & Gas Co.*, 285 U.S. 393, 406 (1932) (Brandeis, J., dissenting).

5. Prudential

Prudential arguments boil down to "advancing particular doctrines according to the practical wisdom of using the courts in a particular way." Bobbitt, at 7. In short, these arguments are the most removed from the more traditional sources of constitutional law. Nevertheless, they are important and, at times, so persuasive as to be dispositive. For example, the contention that courts should not review the grounds for impeachment of the President relies almost entirely on the powerful prudential argument that such judicial review would have a potentially catastrophic destabilizing effect on the national government. Many arguments surrounding the proper separation of powers are prudential arguments.

D. TECHNIQUES AND PUZZLES IN CONSTITUTIONAL ADJUDICATION

1. Tiered Scrutiny

The most important technique of constitutional adjudication is "tiered" scrutiny. Tiered scrutiny involves different levels of judicial review of legislation.

   a. Minimal scrutiny. Normally, legislation is presumed to be valid and the challenger is required to prove its unconstitutionality. Legislation is constitutionally valid if it is **rationally related** to a **legitimate state interest.** Sometimes this standard is phrased as **reasonably related** to a legitimate state interest or just **reasonable.** In any case this level of judicial review is very deferential to legislative judgment. Almost all legislation subjected to this level of review is found valid.

   b. Strict scrutiny. At the opposite end of the spectrum, some legislation is presumptively invalid. The trigger of presumptive invalidity may vary. For example, laws that classify on the basis of race are presumed invalid, and laws that regulate speech according to its content are generally presumed invalid. The state must prove that such laws are **necessary** or **essential** to accomplish some **compelling governmental interest.** The proof of necessity is often the lack of any less restrictive or burdensome alternative. Sometimes it is said that the law must be **narrowly tailored** to serve the **compelling interest.** Most often, laws subject to strict scrutiny are invalidated. One of the great problems with tiered review is justifying why some legislation is subjected to deferential review and other legislation is subjected to strict scrutiny. This problem is perhaps most acute in equal protection, but it pervades constitutional law. The classic explanation is contained in Justice Stone's footnote 4 to *United States v. Carolene Products Co.,* 304 U.S. 144 (1938):

There may be narrower scope for operation of the presumption of constitutionality when legislation appears on its face to be within a specific prohibition of the Constitution, such as those of the first ten Amendments . . . [or] which restricts those political processes which can ordinarily be expected to bring about repeal of undesirable legislation . . . [or] statutes directed at particular religious, . . . or national, . . . or racial minorities, . . . [or] whether prejudice against discrete and insular minorities may be a special condition, which tends seriously to curtail the operation of those political processes ordinarily to be relied upon to protect minorities. . . .

From this acorn a vast oak of constitutional doctrine has emerged.

c. **Intermediate scrutiny.** Tiered scrutiny also includes an intermediate category. Some laws are presumed invalid unless the state proves that the law is **substantially related** to an **important state interest.** Laws that classify on the basis of sex are subjected to intermediate scrutiny, but a few other categories are included as well. In essence, the Court has determined that some classifications deserve higher scrutiny but ought not be subjected to the strong presumption of invalidity that accompanies strict scrutiny.

2. Hard Facts and Soft Facts

As you study constitutional law be aware of how the Supreme Court uses facts. The Court relies on "hard facts"—phenomena that are empirically proven or legally proven in a trial court—but also employs "soft facts"— hypothetical facts, fictional facts, and judicial assumptions about the society of which it is a part. The assumption that hard facts can be proven may be one reason that the Court creates doctrinal rules that require the evaluation of several factors.

 EXAMPLE AND ANALYSIS

State laws that regulate interstate commerce are presumed valid unless the burdens the law places on interstate commerce are "clearly excessive" in relation to the "putative local benefits" of the law. See Chapter 6. This test assumes that a trial court can measure the burden upon interstate commerce of any given law (possibly a "hard fact"), the "putative" or "supposed" local benefits of the law (surely a "soft fact"), and then compare these two items (an even softer fact). If you doubt that this can be done (accurately or at all) you may wish to criticize doctrine. But if your professor wants you only to apply doctrine, you need to sift his or her question for the hard facts, your own imagination and accumulated knowledge for the soft facts, and your common sense for the comparison. This isn't much different from what the Court does. The Justices rely on the record for the hard facts, lawyers' conjecture and various sources of culturally received wisdom for the soft facts, and their common sense for the comparison.

When the Court is extremely deferential to legislatures, upholding laws if they are rationally related to some legitimate purpose, the Court is quite willing to rely almost entirely on soft facts. But this can also be true of strict scrutiny—the presumption of invalidity unless the state can show that the law is essential to accomplishment of a compelling purpose.

3. Legislative Motive

Be aware of the way the Court evaluates legislative motives for challenged laws.

a. Second-guessing Congress. The Court often says of Congress that it will not second-guess its motive for legislation.

Example: In *United States v. Darby,* discussed in Chapter 4, the Court said that Congress acts within its commerce power when it regulates the interstate movement of articles of commerce, even if Congress's motive for the law was to accomplish an objective outside of its powers. In doing so, the Court overturned *Hammer v. Dagenhart,* a case in which the Court had struck down a statute because the motive for the law was to accomplish an objective beyond the powers of Congress.

Yet, the modern Court makes some of its doctrine depend on a judicial assessment of motivation.

Example: Laws that are not racially discriminatory on their face are subjected to deferential scrutiny unless it can be shown that the law was produced from an intentional racially discriminatory motive. See Chapter 9, infra.

The Court thus defers more to Congress on matters like the scope of the commerce power than it does to Congress on whether its racially neutral legislation was the product of an intentionally discriminatory motive. In essence, the latter scrutiny (which employs motive assessment) is less deferential than the former (which eschews motive assessment). Not all minimal scrutiny is equal.

b. Second-guessing the states. The Court is more willing to assess motivations for state legislation. Where a state law has the effect of discriminating against out of staters, thus raising some question about the motives behind the law, motive assessment is a device to subject the law to a deserved higher scrutiny. Where a state law impinges upon a constitutional right the Court is also willing to guess about legislative motive.

Example: Louisiana enacted legislation that required public school teachers who taught the theory of evolution also to teach "creation science." Although the legislative history suggested that the legislature's motive was simply to ensure academic freedom and diversity, the Court divined an impermissible motive of establishing a particular religious viewpoint in the schools and so struck down the law. *Edwards v. Aguillard,* 482 U.S. 578 (1987).

EXAM TIP

- **Not Tested Directly.** These matters are almost never tested *directly.* Rather, the historical overview provides contextual background for all of constitutional law. The methods of constitutional interpretation provide you with tools to think about the Constitution's meaning. These materials are contextual and most professors test your doctrinal understanding.

JUDICIAL REVIEW AND ITS LIMITS

CHAPTER OVERVIEW

This chapter examines the role of all federal courts, but particularly the Supreme Court, in enforcing the Constitution. The key points in this chapter are:

Judicial Review: Federal courts, and ultimately the Supreme Court, have the power (and perhaps the obligation) to decide if laws enacted by Congress or actions of the executive branch are in violation of the Constitution.

Supreme Court Review of State Court Decisions on Matters of Federal Law: The Supreme Court has the authority to review the final judgments of the highest courts of the states, but *only as to matters of federal law.*

- **Adequate and Independent State Grounds Doctrine:** Even if federal law is involved in a case, if the state court decision is based on adequate grounds in state law, independent of the federal law involved, and the state basis for decision is clearly stated, the Supreme Court lacks power to review the case.

The Scope of Judicial Review Is Limited:

- **Expressly by the Constitution:**

  — **Article III:** Federal courts may only exercise the jurisdiction permitted under Article III, which principally consists of federal questions (cases arising under the Constitution or federal statute), cases between two states, admiralty, cases between citizens of different states, and cases with either foreign nations or citizens as a party.

— **Eleventh Amendment:** States, but not local governments, are immune from suit in federal court unless they have consented or Congress has clearly abrogated immunity. Suits against state officials seeking equitable relief are generally permitted.

- **By Congressional Action:** Congress may restrict the appellate jurisdiction granted the Supreme Court under Article III (but may not expand it), so long as that restriction does not violate some other constitutionally guaranteed right. Congress may eliminate the lower federal courts entirely, and may thus eliminate or restrict the jurisdiction of the lower federal courts.

- **By Judicial Self-Restraint:** The Supreme Court has devised a number of "justiciability" doctrines to limit the scope of federal court review:

  — **Standing:** The Constitution requires a litigant to have suffered (1) **personal injury in fact,** (2) **caused by the action complained of,** which is (3) **redressable by courts.**

  — **No Advisory Opinions:** Courts will not hear cases lacking truly adverse parties with a real dispute.

  — **Ripeness and Mootness:** Federal courts will not decide unripe or moot issues. An issue is not ripe if future events may render decision unnecessary and moot if past events have rendered decision unnecessary.

  — **Political Questions:** Federal courts will not decide political questions. A political question exists if: (1) the Constitution commits resolution of the issue to another branch of government (but courts decide if there is such a commitment), or (2) there are no judicially cognizable standards by which the issue can be resolved, or (3) decision requires a judicially inappropriate policy choice, or (4) there is a pressing need to adhere to a decision already made by Congress or the President, or (5) there is a risk that a judicial decision would embarrass the nation.

  — **Abstention:** Federal courts will abstain from exercising their jurisdiction when necessary to do so in order to avoid interfering with ongoing state judicial proceedings or to permit state courts to decide dispositive state law issues.

A. *MARBURY v. MADISON* AND THE THEORY OF JUDICIAL REVIEW

Judicial review—the power of courts to declare legislation or executive acts invalid as unconstitutional—is the keystone principle of American constitutional law. That authority is not expressly given to the federal courts under the Constitution, but has been treated as an implied power of courts almost from the beginnings of the nation. While judicial review is an established fact, the implications of this power continue to shape the way the courts interpret the Constitution. It is thus important to understand the arguments concerning the justifications for, utility, and consequences of judicial review.

1. *Marbury v. Madison,* 5 U.S. 137 (1803)

Marbury definitively established the judiciary's power to declare federal legislation unconstitutional. Outgoing President Adams had appointed Marbury a justice of the peace for the District of Columbia but the commission had not been delivered to him. Incoming President Jefferson's Secretary of State, Madison, refused to deliver the commission and Marbury filed suit directly in the Supreme Court under §13 of the 1789 Judiciary Act, seeking a writ of mandamus to compel Madison to deliver his commission.

a. **The Court opinion.** For a unanimous Court, Chief Justice John Marshall posed and answered three principal questions:

   i. **Did Marbury have a right to his commission?** Yes. Even though delivery is often required for effectiveness in other areas of law (e.g., deeds) Marshall concluded that Marbury's commission was complete upon its signing by the President.

   ii. **Did Marbury have a judicially enforceable remedy?** Yes. Invoking common law maxims and revolutionary democratic theory, Marshall concluded that the very essence of civil liberty was for courts to provide a remedy for every wrong. Marshall then admitted that the political acts of the President and his cabinet within their lawful discretion are not reviewable by courts.

   iii. **Was Marbury entitled to mandamus from the Supreme Court?** No. Marshall read §13 of the Judiciary Act to give the Court original jurisdiction of any case in which mandamus against a federal officer was sought. But Article III only gives the Court original jurisdiction of cases involving foreign diplomats or between two states. Marshall resolved the conflict by concluding that when a statute and the Constitution conflict, (1) the Constitution, as a higher law, prevails, and (2) "it is emphatically the province and duty of the judiciary to say what the law is." The Court held that Congress could not expand the jurisdiction created under Article III and, therefore, the Supreme Court lacked jurisdiction over Marbury's suit.

      (a) **Justifications for judicial review.** Marshall offered five justifications for judicial review: (1) it is a necessary inference from a written Constitution, for otherwise "written constitutions are absurd attempts, on the part of the people, to limit a power in its own nature illimitable"; (2) it is a necessary aspect to the judicial role of interpreting law; (3) it is implied from the command of the Supremacy Clause (Art. VI, cl. 2) that the Constitution is the "supreme law of the Land" and is to be binding on state courts; (4) it is implied from the fact that Article III gives the federal courts jurisdiction over all cases arising under the Constitution; and (5) it is implied in the fact that judges take an oath to support and uphold the Constitution.

b. Criticisms of the Court opinion. Two general criticisms of Marshall's opinion are often made. First, Marshall is attacked for even reaching the question of judicial review. Second, Marshall's justifications for judicial review are said to be inadequate, more assertion than justification of the power.

    i. Marshall shouldn't have decided the issue. These critics contend that: (1) section 13 should not have been read as conferring original jurisdiction on the Court in all cases involving mandamus against federal officers, (2) delivery should have been required for Marbury's commission to be effective, or (3) Marbury's remedy should have been limited to the political process. By any one of these means Marshall could have avoided the momentous question of judicial review. Those who argue that the Court should avoid constitutional decisions unless absolutely necessary are most fond of these criticisms.

    ii. Marshall's justifications for judicial review are inadequate. These critics contend that the fact that the Constitution is supreme law does not compel the conclusion that the Court is the final interpreter of the Constitution. Since the Constitution does not explicitly give the courts judicial review, the critics contend that each branch of government is equally entitled to determine for itself the meaning of the Constitution. None of Marshall's justifications entirely dispose of this objection, although taken together they form a convincing argument.

2. Judicial Exclusivity in Constitutional Interpretation?

Marbury v. Madison did not decide the related question of whether the courts have the exclusive power to interpret the Constitution. *Cooper v. Aaron,* 358 U.S. 1 (1958), which involved Arkansas's refusal to desegregate its schools in compliance with *Brown v. Board of Education,* 347 U.S. 483 (1954), confirmed that the Court's power is exclusive when the other contender is a state. But that conclusion is less firm when the other contender is Congress or the President. Although outright defiance of Court decrees would involve a real constitutional crisis, Presidents especially enjoy a practical discretion in enforcing many constitutional decisions of the Court.

3. Arguments for the Utility of Judicial Review

Judicial review is often asserted to be desirable for the following reasons:

a. Countermajoritarian role. Congress will manifest the will of the majority, which may (perhaps often) be intolerant of unpopular political minorities. But constitutional rights are intended to protect political minorities, so Congress cannot be thus trusted. Federal judges, appointed for life, are relatively immune from majoritarian pressure, so they are better equipped to decide whether legislation is constitutional.

b. Stability. If each branch of the federal government is equally free to determine the meaning of the Constitution there will never be any settled meaning. Court decisions would bind the particular litigants but would have no broader effect. Congress might choose to overturn those court decisions, even as to the particular litigants. The possibility of this constitutional chaos is avoided by acceptance of judicial review.

4. Arguments Against the Utility of Judicial Review

Judicial review is often asserted to be pernicious for the following reasons:

a. Antidemocratic. Federal judges are unelected and are not politically accountable. To vest final authority over the meaning of the Constitution in such people is a repudiation of the principle of democratic self-governance. Instead of the people interpreting their own Constitution, that power is performed by a judicial politburo.

b. Entrenched error. Judicial review means that it is very difficult to correct mistaken judicial interpretations of the Constitution. Neither Congress nor the President may ignore Court decisions with impunity. The only avenues for correction are (1) persuasion of the Court to change its mind (often requiring new Justices as a prerequisite), (2) impeachment, or (3) constitutional amendment. None of these are easy. Judicial review means that when the Court gets the Constitution wrong it stays wrong.

5. Practical Consequences of Judicial Review

These conflicting positions about the desirability of judicial review have produced a variety of doctrines (some as constitutional interpretations, some not) that have as their practical objective an accommodation of both points of view by preserving judicial review yet restricting the opportunity for its exercise. The principal such doctrines are discussed in the remainder of this chapter. In addition, the Court claims to observe some rules that limit constitutional decisions even in cases clearly within the Court's jurisdiction: (1) the Court will not formulate a rule of constitutional law broader than necessary by the facts of the case, (2) the Court will not decide the constitutional issue if the case can be decided on some other ground, (3) the Court will not decide constitutional challenges to statutes brought by people who have taken advantage of the statutory benefits, and (4) the Court will attempt to construe statutes, if possible, to avoid a conflict with the Constitution. See *Ashwander v. TVA*, 297 U.S. 288, 346 (1936); *Rescue Army v. Municipal Court*, 331 U.S. 549 (1947). But the Court does not always adhere to its own rules. Note that Marshall violated some of these principles in *Marbury*.

B. *MARTIN v. HUNTER'S LESSEE* AND THE POWER TO REVIEW STATE COURT JUDGMENTS

Issues of federal constitutional law often arise in cases brought in state courts. *Martin v. Hunter's Lessee* held that the Supreme Court may review the decisions of the highest state courts on matters of federal law. This appellate jurisdiction does not extend to review of state court decisions on matters of *state law*. No federal court, including the Supreme Court, has any power to review state court decisions that are entirely about state law.

1. *Martin v. Hunter's Lessee,* 14 U.S. 304 (1816)

Title to a vast tract of northern Virginia was at stake in this case. Hunter derived his title from Virginia, which had seized the property from Martin, who remained loyal to George III, under a Virginia statute confiscating the property of loyalists. But the Virginia statute was arguably in conflict with the 1783 peace treaty between Britain and the United States. Martin asserted that Supreme Court review of this issue was authorized by §25 of the 1789 Judiciary Act. Hunter claimed that the decision of Virginia's highest court was final and dispositive, and that §25 was an unconstitutional attempt by Congress to give the Court jurisdiction beyond Article III. The Court held that §25 was valid and that the Court could review the federal constitutional decisions of a state's highest court.

a. Rationales. The Court's opinion, by Justice Joseph Story, was grounded in three rationales.

i. Article III. Since Article III grants the Court appellate jurisdiction over *all* cases arising under the Constitution that grant must include those that arise from the state courts. The supremacy clause plainly implies that state courts will decide federal constitutional issues. The failure of Article III to distinguish between constitutional cases originating in federal court or state court indicates that the Court has appellate review over constitutional cases coming from state courts.

ii. No state sovereignty over constitutional interpretation. The Union, said Story, is not a compact between independent nations, but a charter of government for a single nation. The Constitution abrogates state sovereignty in a number of important ways and the supremacy clause clearly indicates that state judges are bound by the Constitution.

iii. Need for uniformity. As a practical matter, a system in which each state's highest court could interpret the Constitution differently would produce fifty different Constitutions. Supreme Court review of state constitutional decisions was necessary "to control these jarring and discordant judgments, and harmonize them into uniformity."

2. The Adequate and Independent State Grounds Doctrine

From "the time of its foundation" the Supreme Court "has adhered to the principle that it will not review judgments of state courts that rest on adequate and independent federal state grounds." *Herb v. Pitcairn,* 324 U.S. 117 (1945).

a. **Operation of the doctrine.** Under *Michigan v. Long,* 463 U.S. 1032 (1983), the Court presumes that, in state court cases presenting *both* federal and state law issues, the state court relied on federal law for its decision **unless the state court includes in its opinion a plain statement of its reliance on state law as the sole ground for its decision.** As a practical matter, a state court may interpret its own constitution more expansively than the analogous federal guarantee.

EXAMPLES AND ANALYSIS

Example: The Supreme Court has held that warrantless searches of garbage left for curbside pickup are a valid search under the federal Constitution, but if a state supreme court plainly rules that such searches are a violation of the search and seizure provision of the state constitution, the adequate and independent grounds doctrine prevents the Supreme Court from reviewing the case.

Even if a state court plainly states its reliance solely upon state law the Supreme Court might conclude that the state law basis for decision is not **independent** of federal law or is not an **adequate** basis for decision.

Example (Not Independent): If a state court finds a state law violates the state constitution but treats the substantive content of the state constitution as defined by the federal Constitution the Court will conclude that there is no independent state law basis for decision. See *Standard Oil Co. of California v. Johnson,* 316 U.S. 481 (1942), in which the Court reviewed and reversed a California determination of state tax liability because the state court used a federal standard to measure the state claim.

Example (Not Adequate): If a state court finds that a state procedural rule bars consideration of a federal claim the state law ground for decision is inadequate if it was created with the specific intent of barring the federal claim or is an unreasonable interference with the assertion of federal rights. See *Williams v. Georgia,* 349 U.S. 375 (1955); *Ford v. Georgia,* 498 U.S. 411 (1991). But these circumstances will almost never occur, so long as the state procedural rule is of general applicability to all litigants and not imposed peculiarly on those asserting federal claims.

b. **Source of the doctrine.** The Court has never squarely held that the adequate and independent state grounds doctrine is constitutionally mandated. The Court dodged the issue in *Murdock v. Memphis,* 87 U.S. 590 (1874), holding instead that Congress had not clearly enough granted the Court jurisdiction to review state law issues, though it intimated that the Constitution forbade such review. If Congress were to attempt to confer upon the Court power to review state law issues it is likely that the "Court would declare such an extension of its jurisdiction to be unconstitutional" as an effective denial of the states' lawmaking autonomy. See Tribe, at 163.

C. CONGRESSIONAL POWER TO CONTROL THE JURISDICTION OF FEDERAL COURTS

1. Overview

Two provisions of Article III give Congress considerable authority to restrict the jurisdiction of all federal courts, including the Supreme Court. But this authority is not unlimited.

a. **Power to establish federal courts.** Article III, section 1 locates the federal judicial power in one Supreme Court and "in such inferior Courts as the Congress may from time to time ordain and establish." This provision probably permits Congress to eliminate all inferior federal courts. (Cf. *Stuart v. Laird,* 5 U.S. 299 (1803), implicitly upholding the elimination of the entire federal court of appeals.) Subject to the general limits discussed below, this provision certainly permits Congress to curtail at its pleasure the jurisdiction of the inferior federal courts. See *Sheldon v. Sill,* 49 U.S. 441 (1850).

b. **Exceptions to and regulations of Supreme Court appellate jurisdiction.** Article III, section 2 gives the Supreme Court appellate review of all cases within the federal judicial power (except those in which the Court has original jurisdiction) **"with such Exceptions, and under such Regulations as the Congress shall make."**

c. **Significance of the issues.** Taken together, these provisions raise important questions. Could Congress eliminate all inferior federal courts and eliminate all of the Supreme Court's appellate jurisdiction, leaving the Court a trial court hearing cases between states and cases involving foreign diplomats and citizens? Or, could Congress eliminate all federal jurisdiction over cases challenging the constitutional validity of state laws regulating a particular subject, e.g., abortions? Some answers follow.

2. *Ex parte McCardle,* 74 U.S. 506 (1869)

In the only case in which it has squarely confronted the issue, the Court held in *Ex parte McCardle* that Congress could strip the Court of its appellate jurisdiction, even as to an argued case pending final decision by the Court.

McCardle was a newspaper editor imprisoned by the military governor of Mississippi under the post-Civil War Reconstruction Acts. Under an 1867 federal statute he sought habeas corpus in federal circuit court, charging that the Reconstruction Acts were unconstitutional. When he lost there McCardle appealed to the Supreme Court under the same 1867 law. After argument in the Court and fearing a Court decision invalidating the Reconstruction Acts Congress repealed (over President Johnson's veto) the portions of the 1867 act that gave the Court jurisdiction. The Court upheld the repeal, relying on Article III, §2, the exceptions and regulations clause.

   a. **Scope of *McCardle*.** Though it upheld congressional repeal of its jurisdiction the Court noted that McCardle had other avenues by which he could bring a habeas petition before the federal courts, including the Supreme Court. The hint was that if Congress had attempted to eliminate *all* federal habeas jurisdiction it might have exceeded its authority. From this nugget later thinkers have refined the following series of possible limits on the congressional power to restrict the jurisdiction of the federal courts.

3. Limits on Congressional Power to Curtail Federal Court Jurisdiction

There are two types of limitations: "internal" and "external." **Internal limits** are connected to Article III and the structural relationship of the federal courts and Congress. They are "internal" limits because they are part of, or inside, the grant of judicial power in Article III. **External limits** are constitutional limits that have nothing to do with Article III. Congress may not curtail jurisdiction in a way that violates some other constitutional guarantee, such as equal protection or due process. They are called "external" limits because they are outside of Article III. Some of these limits are firmly established by precedent, and others lie in the realm of custom and theory.

   a. ***United States v. Klein* and attempts to dictate the outcome of pending cases.** *United States v. Klein,* 80 U.S. 128 (1872), involved a claim for compensation from the federal government for property destroyed by the Union army during the Civil War. By law compensation was due only to people who were loyal to the United States during the Civil War. Klein, who had accepted President Johnson's general presidential pardon following the war, had proven his loyalty in the lower federal courts by relying upon a line of cases that held that recipients of such pardons were conclusively presumed to be loyal. While the government's appeal of Klein's compensation award was pending Congress enacted legislation that provided that recipients of Johnson's general pardon were conclusively deemed to be *disloyal,* and directing federal courts to dismiss for want of jurisdiction any compensation case brought by such a person. The Supreme Court held the legislation to be unconstitutional as applied to *Klein.*

i. **Rationale and scope of *Klein*.** The Court relied primarily on separation of powers—the idea that no branch of the federal government may usurp the essential functions of any other branch—to strike down the act at issue in *Klein*. Congress may alter the substantive law to be enforced by federal courts, and may specify the rules of evidence or procedure to be applied by those courts, but Congress **may not direct the courts how to decide.** If Congress wants to change the rules it must do so generally, by a law that applies with neutral force to all litigants. The vice in *Klein* was Congress's attempt to leave undisturbed the governing substantive and procedural law but to command the courts what inference to draw from the evidence before them.

 ## EXAMPLE AND ANALYSIS

In 1988 environmentalists brought two suits challenging the legality of logging in old-growth forests. Congress responded with legislation that temporarily altered the rules governing such logging, and that "determine[d] and direct[ed]" that the logging challenged in the two suits, which were mentioned by name and docket number in the statute, was now legal. In *Robertson v. Seattle Audubon Society,* 503 U.S. 429 (1992), the Court upheld this law because it mandated a "change in law, not specific results under old law."

But in *Plaut v. Spendthrift Farm,* 514 U.S. 211 (1995), the Court voided an amendment to federal law that not only changed the limitations period for certain securities fraud suits but also commanded federal courts to reopen cases dismissed as untimely under the prior law. This latter command offended the implicit Art. III principle that courts decide cases, not Congress.

b. **Jurisdictional alterations that destroy the Supreme Court's "essential role."** This limit is one advanced by respected scholars, originating with Professor Henry Hart in a famous law review article, 66 Harv. L. Rev. 1365: "[T]he exceptions must not be such as will destroy the essential role of the Supreme Court in the constitutional plan." Hart's limit invites the question: What *is* the Court's **essential role**? The answer to that depends on whether judicial review makes the Court the special guardian of the Constitution or whether it merely obliges the Court to decide only the unavoidable constitutional questions it encounters in its prosaic business as a law court. Some argue that elimination of *all* the Court's appellate jurisdiction would be inconsistent with its essential function as a creator of a uniform body of federal constitutional law. Others argue that the Court's "essential role" in the exercise of appellate jurisdiction is whatever Congress says it is. The holding of *McCardle* lends support to the latter view; the Court's dicta in *McCardle* about the availability of other appellate avenues lends support to the former view. This debate, albeit academic, is important; the Court has not had occasion to deliver its view since Congress has never been willing to so completely destroy the Court's appellate jurisdiction.

   i.   **A note on Supreme Court jurisdiction.** Other than the Court's original jurisdiction, specified by Article III, the Court's jurisdiction is controlled by statute. A tiny fraction of the Court's appellate docket consists of **appeals,** which are cases the Court *must* hear. The remainder of the docket is entirely within the Court's discretion. Litigants seeking Supreme Court review file petitions seeking a **writ of certiorari.** These "cert petitions" are granted if four justices agree to do so. Denials of certiorari are of no precedential value, as they are not decisions on the merits. The Court's rules indicate that the Court will be more inclined to grant review of cases (1) involving a conflict between two different federal appeals courts, (2) in which the highest courts of two states disagree on a matter of federal law, or (3) involving important questions not yet settled by the Court.

   c.   **Jurisdictional alterations that destroy the "essential role" of lower federal courts.** Even though Article III gives Congress the power to eliminate the lower federal courts and to curtail their jurisdiction, it is possible that this power may be exercised in a way that is constitutionally impermissible. The Court has never decided whether Congress could eliminate the Supreme Court's appellate jurisdiction and all federal lower court jurisdiction over constitutional cases. This "neutron bomb" approach is considered invalid by some, who argue that Article III commands that the federal judicial power *shall* extend to constitutional cases. See Amar, 65 B.U. L. Rev. 205. But a strict reading of the scant precedent supports its validity.

   d.   **Jurisdictional alterations that violate other parts of the Constitution.** No matter whether Congress is otherwise entitled to restrict federal court jurisdiction, it may not do so in a manner that violates some other constitutional guarantee.

   Example: Suppose Congress enacts legislation providing that the Supreme Court may not review cases where the petitioner is a woman. This sex-based disability would certainly be violative of the equal protection component of the Fifth Amendment's due process clause.

   More troublesome are cases where Congress eliminates federal jurisdiction over an entire class of cases. Congress did just that in the 1932

Norris-LaGuardia Act, which stripped all federal courts of power to issue injunctions in labor disputes. The Court upheld the validity of the Act in *Lauf v. E.G. Shinner & Co.,* 303 U.S. 323 (1938). But the nature of the subject matter upon which a jurisdiction repealer is based might be significant.

Example: Suppose Congress enacts legislation providing that the Court may not exercise appellate review over cases calling into question the constitutional validity of any state or federal statute regulating abortions. Is it possible that this would not violate any constitutional right, since some court (either a federal appeals court or the highest court of a state) would ultimately make the final review?

The last example, while troubling in its possible result, has two practical restraints upon its adoption. First, such withdrawals of jurisdiction tend to freeze in place the Court decision that Congress dislikes and to which it is reacting. Second, although Congress has considered a number of selective jurisdiction-stripping proposals it rarely, if ever, has adopted them, leading to the conclusion that Congress recognizes the uncertain validity of jurisdiction-stripping for the purpose of undercutting the Court's constitutional decisions. Moreover, the Norris-LaGuardia Act's jurisdiction-stripping aspect proved unworkable over time and was effectively repealed by judicial construction. See *Boys Markets, Inc. v. Retail Clerks Local 770,* 398 U.S. 235 (1970).

D. THE ELEVENTH AMENDMENT: A CONSTITUTIONAL LIMIT TO FEDERAL JURISDICTION

Article III, section 2 confers federal judicial power over cases between a state and the citizens of another state and cases between a state and foreign citizens. In *Chisholm v. Georgia,* 2 U.S. 419 (1793), the Court ruled that states were amenable to suit in federal court by foreigners. The Eleventh Amendment was promptly adopted in 1798 to overturn *Chisholm.* It declares that the federal judicial power shall not extend to suits brought against states "by Citizens of another State, or by Citizens or Subjects of any Foreign State."

1. *Hans v. Louisiana* and the Current Doctrine

Over a century elapsed before the Court delivered the current interpretation of the Eleventh Amendment. In *Hans v. Louisiana,* 134 U.S. 1 (1890), the Court concluded that the amendment was intended to confer sovereign immunity upon the states from suit in federal court by citizens of the defendant state, even when the claim is premised upon federal law or the Constitution. The states may voluntarily waive that immunity, or it may be abrogated by Congress using its powers under the 14th Amendment. *Fitzpatrick v. Bitzer,* 427 U.S. 445 (1976). But Congress can only do so by a "clear statement" of its intention to abrogate the states' Eleventh Amendment immunity. *Atascadero State Hospital v. Scanlon,* 473 U.S. 234 (1985). Congress may not use its Article

I powers to abrogate state sovereign immunity. *Seminole Tribe v. Florida*, 517 U.S. 44 (1996).

a. **The officer-suit fiction.** Eleventh Amendment immunity does not attach when suit is brought against an official of the state, rather than the state itself, at least so long as only prospective injunctive relief is sought. *Ex parte Young*, 209 U.S. 123 (1908). But when equitable relief is sought against a state official that would cause the state to pay compensation for past actions, Eleventh Amendment immunity does attach. *Edelman v. Jordan*, 415 U.S. 651 (1974). In short, if a plaintiff wants damages from the state (even for constitutional violations) the federal courts are closed (absent waiver or congressional abrogation), but if the plaintiff wants an injunction to prevent a state official from continuing his unconstitutional behavior he may obtain such an order in federal court so long as it is a state official that is enjoined.

2. **Beyond Doctrine: The Debatable Meaning of the Eleventh Amendment**

Three competing conceptions of the Eleventh Amendment have been offered and debated among judges and academics.

a. **The sovereign immunity view.** The prevailing wisdom, embodied in *Hans v. Louisiana* and the reigning doctrine, is that the amendment was intended to preserve state sovereign immunity. The text of the amendment, however, plainly exempts claims made against a state by its own citizens. *Hans* corrected that oversight. This view is premised upon an assumption that a broad state sovereign immunity was part of the founding generation's conception of federalism. The historical record provides some, but not dispositive, support for that view.

b. **The diversity jurisdiction repealer view.** Justice Brennan, supported by a variety of academics, took the position that the Eleventh Amendment simply operated to repeal two **diverse party-based** heads of Article III jurisdiction, but did not disturb suits against states based upon federal law. In this view, suits against states based upon **state law**—and in federal court only because of diverse citizenship—are the only ones affected by the Eleventh Amendment. Suits founded on *federal law*, no matter what the party alignment, would not be barred by the Eleventh Amendment. The principal problem with this view is again the text of the amendment, which plainly seems to bar *all* suits against states by those with the disfavored citizenship. See *Atascadero State Hospital*, supra, Brennan, J., dissenting; Fletcher, 35 Stan. L. Rev. 1033.

c. **The diverse party-based ouster of jurisdiction view.** A final view is that the text of the amendment is to be taken at face value. The amendment is said to oust the federal courts of jurisdiction over **all cases**—whether founded on state or federal law—that present the party alignments described in the amendment. This view disagrees with *Hans* by asserting that suits against states in federal court by citizens of the defendant state ought to be permitted. This view disagrees with the diversity theorists by making no exception for suits based upon federal law. This view holds that the *general* issue of state sovereign immunity has nothing to do with the Eleventh Amendment but ought properly be considered as an aspect of the Tenth Amendment. See Massey, 56 U. Chi. L. Rev. 61; W. Marshall, 102 Harv. L. Rev. 1372; L. Marshall, 102 Harv. L. Rev. 1342.

E. THE CONCEPT OF JUSTICIABILITY

The "justiciability" doctrines are the subject of the remainder of this chapter.

1. Overview

Justiciability consists of a congeries of rules created by the Court that limit the ability of federal courts to exercise the power of judicial review. Some of these rules are rooted in the Constitution, others are a product of the discretionary prudential judgment of the Court as to what cases within federal jurisdiction ought to be heard by federal courts. Some justiciability doctrines are intended to ensure that at the outset of the litigation the matter is indeed an actual dispute between rival rights-holders. The political question doctrine is intended to eschew judicial review when its assertion would create constitutional difficulties with other branches of the federal government. The abstention doctrines are largely intended to restrain federal judicial interference in the operation of state courts because state courts are partners in the administration of federal law, including constitutional law. Recall that judicial review is itself contestable, and that its assertion (especially in constitutional cases) produces rulings that are hard to modify. The justiciability doctrines operate to temper the judicial aggression that is latent in the entire concept of judicial review.

2. Justiciability Distinguished from Jurisdiction

Justiciability differs from jurisdiction as follows. A court may have **jurisdiction** of the case (the Constitution and statutory law endows it with power to hear the case) but if the matter is not **justiciable** (e.g., it is a feigned, nonadversarial case, or it raises a political question, or the plaintiff lacks standing) it will not be heard by the courts. Justiciability would be easier if all the justiciability doctrines were nonconstitutional exercises of the Court's discretionary power to refrain from employing its jurisdiction, but some of the justiciability doctrines are constitutionally compelled. In the following discussion, the constitutional or discretionary nature of each doctrine (or aspect thereof) will be noted.

F. STANDING TO SUE

Federal courts may not hear a case unless the plaintiff has **standing** to bring the claim. A plaintiff has standing if he has such a significant stake in the controversy that he ought to be recognized as the proper party to bring the claim. Standing doctrine is an attempt to eliminate those cases that are brought by officious bystanders, professional litigants who wish to use the courts to alter public policy rather than to vindicate a personalized grievance. Standing, like many justiciability principles, is partly intended to ensure vigorous advocacy by the parties so that the issues will be sharply drawn for judicial decision. Standing has a constitutional core to it and a variety of peripheral doctrines that are not compelled by the Constitution, but that have been devised by courts in the exercise of their prudential discretion. The focus in standing law is upon the plaintiff and his connection to the claim, rather than upon the merits of the claim itself: Is this litigant the proper party to raise these issues?

1.   The Constitutional Core of Standing

The Court has created a **three-part test of standing** that must be met in order to satisfy the Constitution. A plaintiff must allege and prove (1) **personal and actual or imminent injury in fact,** (2) **caused by or fairly traceable to the defendant's action complained of,** which is (3) **redressable by the courts.** Two parts of the Constitution mandate these requirements. First, Article III limits federal judicial power to "cases or controversies." The Court regards that limit as one that disables the federal judiciary from hearing cases that are not truly adversarial. A litigant lacking the constitutional elements of standing is thought to be so unrelated to the controversy that he lacks adversarialness. Second, and more importantly, the doctrine of separation of powers (see Chapter 7, infra) requires that courts refrain from adjudicating disembodied policy questions. Setting public policy is the principal job of Congress; if a litigant lacks the standing criteria the courts are being asked to formulate public policy in the guise of a lawsuit. To do so would impermissibly infringe upon the powers of Congress. The significance of the constitutional core to standing is that Congress may not confer standing upon litigants who lack the core requirements by simply declaring that they have a right to sue in federal court.

a.   Personal, actual or imminent injury in fact. This element involves several disparate factors.

i.   Injury in fact. The plaintiff must have suffered some injury in fact. Plaintiffs with no injuries probably have no case on the merits but surely lack standing to sue. If a person who never buys lottery tickets sues the state lottery claiming that the lottery draw is rigged he has suffered no injury in fact sufficient to create standing to litigate the claim.

A litigant's injury in fact need not be economic or tangible. Other injuries, including aesthetic, emotional, and environmental, are sufficient to confer standing if the remaining elements of standing are present.

EXAMPLE AND ANALYSIS

Users of a national forest bring suit to block the Interior Department from permitting a ski development in a mountain valley the plaintiffs frequent. The asserted injury is a loss of aesthetic and recreational pleasure and environmental well-being. Injury in fact is satisfied. See *Sierra Club v. Morton,* 405 U.S. 727 (1972), involving substantially these facts. In *Sierra Club* the Court regarded these injuries as sufficient to satisfy the injury in fact requirement but plaintiffs were held to lack standing because there was no showing that the Sierra Club nor any of its members actually suffered these injuries.

> ii. **Actual or imminent injury.** The injury in fact must be actual or imminent. It must be one that has already been suffered or, if threatened, will occur immediately. Injuries that are speculative, or too far in the future, fail to qualify.

 ## EXAMPLES AND ANALYSIS

Example: A wildlife conservation organization and two of its members sue a federal agency, charging that the agency's actions violate the Endangered Species Act and that thereby their opportunities to observe elephants and crocodiles, two endangered species, in the wild have been and will be diminished. Plaintiffs have visited the habitat of the two species and assert an intention to do so again at some unspecified future time. Held: no standing, as the threatened injury is too remote in time and too speculative to constitute an actual and imminent injury in fact. Such " 'some day' intentions—without any description of concrete plans, or . . . any specification of when the some day will be—do not support" actual or imminent injury. *Lujan v. Defenders of Wildlife,* 504 U.S. 555 (1992).

Similarly, indisputable injuries that have occurred, but may never reoccur, do not support standing to seek injunctive relief to prevent their future occurrence.

Example: Lyons, a motorist with a burned out taillight, was stopped by the Los Angeles police. Despite his acquiescence to a police search he was subjected to a "choke-hold"—extreme pressure to the larynx—with such force that he lost consciousness and suffered damage to his larynx. Although the Court recognized Lyons's standing to seek damages, the Court denied Lyons's standing to seek injunctive relief without proof that he would again be choked without reason. *Los Angeles v. Lyons,* 461 U.S. 95 (1983).

iii. **Personalized injury.** The injury in fact must be suffered personally. Two somewhat conflicting rules flow from this proposition. First, abstract and generalized injuries suffered by everyone are probably insufficient to meet the personal injury in fact requirement. Second, if the litigant is personally injured it does not matter how many other people suffer the same injury.

(a) **Abstract or generalized injuries.** There is no personal injury in fact, and thus no standing, when *everyone* suffers the same *abstract* injury.

 # EXAMPLES AND ANALYSIS

Example: Plaintiffs claimed that the incompatibility clause (Art. I, sec. 6), which bars members of Congress from holding simultaneously any other federal office, prohibited members of Congress from holding commissions as reserve officers in the armed services. Held: no standing, since the injury alleged, the lack of constitutional governance, was one suffered by all Americans. There was nothing personalized or particularized about the injury these plaintiffs had suffered. *Schlesinger v. Reservists to Stop the War,* 418 U.S. 208 (1974). Accord *United States v. Richardson,* 418 U.S. 166 (1974) (involving a challenge to secret expenditures of the CIA as violative of the public accounting clause, Art. I, sec. 9, cl. 7).

The *Schlesinger* and *Richardson* cases are sometimes read as satisfying the injury-in-fact requirement but failing to meet a nonconstitutional prudential limit upon standing imposed by the Court. See subsection 3, supra. The better reading is that a generalized abstract grievance fails to satisfy the personalized injury component of the constitutional injury-in-fact requirement.

Example: Louisiana voters attacked the constitutionality of Louisiana's congressional districts as constituting a "racial gerrymander" in violation of the equal protection clause. The plaintiffs did not live in the district that was the principal focus of their claim. The Court concluded that the plaintiffs lacked standing. "In light of [the constitutional core elements of standing] we have repeatedly refused to recognize a generalized grievance against allegedly illegal governmental conduct as sufficient for standing to invoke the federal judicial power." *United States v. Hays,* 515 U.S. 737 (1995).

Even injuries that are not suffered by everyone, but that are abstract, generalized, and diffused over a very large body of people with a common interest, are insufficient to support injury in fact.

Example: Black parents of schoolchildren in Memphis contended in part that the IRS practice of granting tax-exempt charitable status to racially segregated private schools injured them by inflicting the stigma of supposed racial inferiority upon them.

Held: the alleged injury is too abstract and generalized, for it would permit any black American, wherever situated, to challenge IRS rulings that affect the racial composition of public schools far removed from the complainant. Recognition of such injury as sufficient to support standing would turn the federal courts into "no more than a vehicle for the vindication of value interests of concerned bystanders." *Allen v. Wright,* 468 U.S. 737 (1984), discussed below.

(b)   Personal, even though general, injury. If a litigant is personally injured in fact it does not matter how many other people suffer the same injury.

 ## EXAMPLE AND ANALYSIS

A student environmental group, users of forests, parks and other natural places in the Washington, D.C., area, challenged the publicly regulated railroad freight rate structure, alleging that high freight rates increased the use of nonrecyclable goods, which would spur resource extraction in the natural areas used, and which would result in more litter in the areas used by plaintiffs. Despite the fact that these areas are public commons, open to everyone, the Court found standing. The plaintiffs had suffered a personalized injury; the fact that others suffered it as well was irrelevant. *United States v. SCRAP,* 412 U.S. 669 (1973). *Caution:* Most commentators believe that *SCRAP* would not be followed by the Court today, in part because it predates the constitutionalization of standing.

The rules may be harmonized. If an abstract injury affects all Americans equally, simply by virtue of their citizenship, it is too generalized to be asserted by anyone on the basis of her citizenship. Plaintiffs suffering injuries in common with large numbers of other people must allege and prove at least some marginally particularized harm to satisfy the injury-in-fact requirement.

Example: If the plaintiffs in *Reservists to Stop the War* had alleged that they were more likely to be forced to serve in an allegedly illegal war because members of Congress unlawfully served as reserve officers, they would almost certainly have met the injury-in-fact requirement. But note that such an injury might not be sufficient to satisfy the causation requirement, discussed below.

Example: The plaintiffs in *Allen v. Wright* also alleged that IRS failure to deny tax-exempt status to the racially segregated

academies deprived them of the opportunity to send their
children to a truly racially integrated public school. This injury,
though general, was held to be sufficient to constitute injury
in fact.

b.   Causation. This element of standing requires that the injury in fact be
caused by, or fairly traceable to, the defendant's conduct about which
plaintiff complains. Despite the Court's use of the phrase "fairly traceable
to," the causal connection required is a close one, approaching but not
quite reaching a "but for" standard; i.e., the injury would not have
occurred but for the defendant's action. The required causal connection
is a *"substantial likelihood"* that the injury suffered would not have occurred but for the defendant's actions.

   i.   *Allen v. Wright,* 468 U.S. 737 (1984). Black parents of schoolchildren in Memphis contended that the IRS practice of granting
tax-exempt charitable status to racially segregated private schools
injured them by depriving them of the opportunity to send their
children to a truly racially integrated public school. The deprivation
occurred, said the plaintiffs, because the tax exemption made it
financially easier for white parents to shift from the public to these
private schools, thus leaving the public schools disproportionately
black. While this met the injury-in-fact test it failed the causation
test, because the injury complained of—lessened opportunity to
attend a fully integrated public school—resulted "from the independent action of some third party not before the court," namely the
white parents who chose to avoid the public schools. The Court
(5-3) ruled that to establish causation the plaintiffs must prove:
(1) there were enough segregated private academies to make a
meaningful difference in the racial composition of the public
schools, (2) the loss of the exemption would cause a significant
number of the private schools to change their policies, and (3) that
if the exemption was withdrawn a significant number of white
parents would send their children to the public schools. While this
is not quite a "but for" standard it is certainly a rule requiring proof
of a fairly direct form of causation. Justice Stevens, dissenting,
argued that a subsidy in the form of a tax exemption was sufficient
causation because it effectively provides some financial encouragement to the independent third parties to alter their behavior.

   ii.   *Warth v. Seldin,* 422 U.S. 490 (1975). Plaintiffs claimed that the
zoning laws of Penfield, New York, a relatively affluent suburb of
Rochester, injured them by effectively preventing the construction
of low income housing. Plaintiffs consisted of: (1) low income
people who claimed to have unsuccessfully sought housing in Penfield, (2) a civic group, some of whose members lived in Penfield
and who claimed to be injured by the lack of economic diversity

within the community, (3) Rochester taxpayers who contended that the failure of Penfield to permit low income housing caused Rochester taxes to be higher in order to construct such housing within Rochester, and (4) several real estate developers who asserted that they would have built low income housing in Penfield if the zoning laws permitted. The Court (5-4) found that none of these plaintiffs possessed standing, because of the absence of either or both of causation or redressability.

(a) **Rationale.** The low income claimants lacked standing because they had not alleged, and apparently could not prove, that even if the zoning restrictions were removed there was a "substantial probability" they would actually reside in Penfield. Without proof that a third party would build housing the claimants could afford and would desire, the requisite "substantial probability" was missing. The developers lacked standing because there was no specific project that had been prohibited by Penfield's zoning. As in *Allen,* the Rochester taxpayers lacked standing because their taxes were a function of independent decisions made by Rochester. The civic group lacked standing because the asserted harm—the lack of economic diversity due to the exclusion of others—was essentially an impermissible attempt to assert the rights of third parties (see discussion of third party standing, below).

iii. *Duke Power.* In *Duke Power Co. v. Carolina Environmental Study Group,* 438 U.S. 59 (1978), the Court permitted plaintiffs who resided near a nuclear power plant to challenge the validity of a federal statute limiting liability for nuclear accidents on the grounds that the plaintiffs had demonstrated a **"substantial likelihood"** that the power plant near them would not have been constructed **but for** the liability limitations established by Congress.

c. **Redressability.** This last prong of the constitutional core of standing consists of a requirement that the injury suffered can actually be redressed by some remedy within the court's power. If the court lacks the ability to assuage the injury by an award of damages, and can do nothing to enjoin continuation of the injuries, the element of redressability is missing.

 # EXAMPLES AND ANALYSIS

Example: Welfare recipients sued the IRS, challenging the validity of its policy of granting tax-exempt status to hospitals who refused to provide free nonemergency services to indigents. Though the court concluded that the injury asserted—less access to medical care—was not caused by the IRS, it also opined that, even if the IRS caused the injury, the courts had no power to redress the injury. The courts could order the IRS to alter its policy, but that change would not necessarily result in greater medical care to indigents. *Simon v. EKWRO,* 426 U.S. 26 (1976).

Example: The *Lujan* plaintiffs asserted that their injury—diminished opportunity to view endangered species in the wild—was caused by the Interior Secretary's interpretation of the Endangered Species Act permitting American aid to foreign development projects that would destroy wildlife habitat. The Court noted that the plaintiffs' "most obvious problem . . . is redressability." First, the American agencies supplying foreign aid were not defendants; second, the American aid supplied to the foreign developments was a minimal portion of their cost. The courts could order the Secretary to interpret the Endangered Species Act differently, but there was no certainty that any such court order would actually cure the injury complained of. *Lujan v. Defenders of Wildlife,* supra.

Redressability and causation are linked concepts. It is highly likely that in most cases both will either be present or absent.

    d. The significance of the constitutional core of standing. Congress may desire to provide certain persons a forum in the federal courts for vindication of their injuries. It cannot do so by simply declaring that the federal courts have jurisdiction if the plaintiffs lack the constitutional requirements for standing.

 # EXAMPLES AND ANALYSIS

Example: In *Simon,* the plaintiffs relied on a federal law that gives a right to judicial review to any person "adversely affected or aggrieved by agency action." Despite that law the Court held that the plaintiffs lacked standing because they had failed to allege and prove both causation and redressability. If these elements were not constitutionally compelled, but merely discretionary rules applied by the Court for its convenience, Congress could override them.

Example: In *Lujan* the Court invalidated an attempt by Congress to authorize "any person" to file suit to enforce the Endangered Species Act. (See subsection 3, infra.)

    However, Congress may alter the substantive law by creating new legally cognizable injuries, and thus new chains of causation that may be redressed by courts. In that manner, Congress can confer standing where it did not exist before, but only by altering the substantive law. In a sense, the congressional role regarding standing is similar to the congressional role in mandating rules of decision for the courts (see *United States v. Klein, Robertson,* and *Plaut,* supra).

 # EXAMPLES AND ANALYSIS

Example: If Congress enacted legislation that prohibited the IRS from granting tax-exempt status to hospitals that deny free nonemergency services to indigents, and provided that any indigent denied such services by a tax-exempt hospital would be entitled to damages of $10,000 from the IRS for each such occurrence, the indigent plaintiffs in *Simon* would have standing to pursue their newly created right.

Congress probably may not accomplish this objective simply by declaring that causation exists where the Court says it does not.

Example: If Congress enacted legislation declaring that the denial of free nonemergency services by tax-exempt hospitals to indigents was "directly caused" by the IRS decision to grant the tax exemption, the Court would likely ignore the congressional declaration.

On this point, consider Justice Kennedy's concurrence in *Lujan:* "Congress has the power to define injuries and articulate chains of causation that will give rise to a case or controversy where a none existed before. . . . In exercising this power, however, Congress must at the very least identify the injury it seeks to vindicate and relate the injury to the class of persons entitled to bring suit." The first example above does that; the last example arguably does not.

2. **Taxpayer Standing**

The preceding rules regarding the constitutional core of standing are generally applicable to all cases. However, prior to the constitutionalization of standing in the 1970s the Court fashioned some peculiar standing rules for cases in which a taxpayer challenges some governmental expenditure. These cases have never been repudiated and thus govern instances in which a taxpayer seeks to challenge the validity of a federal expenditure.

   a. *Frothingham v. Mellon,* 262 U.S. 447 (1923). Frothingham, a federal taxpayer, alleged that federal expenditures to reduce maternal and infant mortality were beyond the enumerated powers of Congress. She claimed injury in that her taxes would be increased by the expenditure and asserted that the increase was a taking of her property in violation of due process. The Court unanimously agreed that Frothingham lacked standing. Her financial interest in the expenditures was "shared with millions of others; is comparatively minute and indeterminable." The effect of the expenditures "upon future taxation [is] . . . so remote, fluctuating, and uncertain" as to preclude standing. In modern parlance, she lacked the requisite injury in fact—her injury was either too speculative or too universal to support standing. Recognizing such standing would permit any taxpayer to challenge any expenditure on any constitutional grounds, thus transforming the courts into umpires of constitutional abstractions.

b. *Flast v. Cohen,* 392 U.S. 83 (1968). Federal taxpayers challenged the validity of federal financial aid to religious schools as a violation of the First Amendment's ban of governmental establishments of religion. The Court (8-1) ruled that taxpayer standing rules should be relaxed where a federal taxpayer challenges federal spending as violative of the religion clauses. In place of the normal rules of injury in fact and causation the Court substituted an opaque "double-nexus" test.

   i. The "double-nexus" test

- "First, the taxpayer must establish a logical link between that status and the type of legislative enactment attacked." Boiled down to plain English, taxpayers must show that it is a federal expenditure they are attacking.

- Second, "the taxpayer must establish a nexus between that status and the precise nature of the constitutional infringement alleged." This means that the only taxpayer challenge to expenditures permitted are those that contend that the expenditure violates a specific limit on congressional power (like the establishment clause) rather than being *ultra vires*. The creation of this prong enabled the Court to distinguish *Flast* from *Frothingham*.

   ii. Harlan's dissent. Justice Harlan charged that the Court's objective—measuring the plaintiff's personal stake in the controversy—was not satisfied by the double-nexus test, since the test does not even purport to measure that quality. Harlan urged that the Court not act on its own to grant standing to litigants with only a public, rather than private, interest in the case, but to await congressional authorization to hear such suits. Harlan's view would permit Congress virtually unlimited latitude to create such "public interest" standing; the modern constitutional rules greatly shrink congressional power to do so.

c. ***Valley Forge College v. Americans United for Separation of Church and State,*** 454 U.S. 464 (1982). Federal taxpayers sought to overturn the transfer of surplus federal property to a religious college on the grounds that the transfer violated the establishment clause. The Court (6-3) found that the plaintiffs lacked standing. They failed the first prong of the *Flast* test because (1) *Valley Forge* did not involve an expenditure but, rather, a disposal of federal property, and (2) the transfer was an administrative rather than legislative act. The Court took the opportunity to emphasize the constitutional nature of standing, and to reiterate the core elements. Probably *Flast* now applies only to the fairly rare case of a taxpayer challenging federal spending in aid or suppression of religion.

3. Citizen Standing

People sometimes allege that, simply by virtue of being citizens, they are injured by some unconstitutional government practice. They allege that their injury consists of enduring the unconstitutional governance, and they seek an injunction to stop the practice and thereby stop the injury.

Example: *United States v. Richardson* was a citizen claim that secret CIA expenditures violated the public accounting clause of Article I, section 9. *Schlesinger v. Reservists to Stop the War* was a citizen claim that the incompatibility clause, which bars members of Congress from holding any other federal office, prohibited members of Congress from holding reserve commissions in the armed forces. Both are examples of claimed citizen standing; the Court denied standing in each case.

These cases were considered in subsection 1.a.3, supra, as an aspect of the constitutionally mandated injury-in-fact requirement, although both cases precede the Court's enthusiastic embrace of a constitutional core to standing. However, in *Lujan* the Court invalidated a citizen-suit provision in the Endangered Species Act, upon which plaintiffs relied, which authorized "any person" to sue in federal court to enjoin the government from violating the Act. "To permit Congress to convert the undifferentiated public interest in executive officers' compliance with the law into an 'individual right' vindicable in the courts is to permit Congress to transfer from the President to the courts the Chief Executive's most important constitutional duty, to 'take Care that the Laws be faithfully executed,' Art. II, sec. 3." If denial of citizen standing was simply an exercise of prudential discretion on the Court's part Congress would be free to overrule the Court by enactment of citizen-suit provisions of the sort invalidated in *Lujan*. After *Lujan,* citizen standing is dead, an unconstitutional notion.

a. **The significance of the death of citizen standing.** Without citizen standing there are potentially a large number of unconstitutional practices that will escape judicial review. Few, if any, people will be so directly and uniquely injured by the allegedly unconstitutional practices posed by *Richardson* and *Schlesinger* to possess the constitutional prerequisites for standing to litigate their validity. Thus, accountability for these arguably invalid governance practices is left entirely to the political realm.

4. Legislator Standing

The increasingly common practice of challenges to the constitutional validity of federal legislation by individual members of Congress was sharply curtailed in *Raines v. Byrd*, 521 U.S. 811 (1997). Six members of Congress who voted against the Line Item Veto Act challenged its validity, but lacked standing because they did not possess the requisite "personal stake" in the controversy. The legislators claimed that their personal injury inhered in a diminished "effectiveness of their votes." The Court rejected that contention and distinguished the case from *Coleman v. Miller*, 307 U.S. 433 (1939), where legislator standing was found since the votes of the legislator-plaintiffs had been "completely nullified." In *Raines*, the votes of the legislator-plaintiffs "were given full effect. They simply lost that vote." The injury alleged, a relative transfer of power from Congress to the President, was not individual but institutional, wholly abstract, and widely dispersed.

5. Nonconstitutional Standing Rules

In addition to the constitutional elements of standing, the Court has devised a series of principles that deny standing to litigants when the Court has determined that it is prudent to do so. These rules are considered in this subsection.

a. Jus Tertii: Asserting the rights of third parties. The general rule is that a person must assert his own rights, not someone else's rights. The rule is justified by (1) *restraint*—the desire to avoid unnecessary or premature decisions, (2) *respect*—the desire to respect the apparent decision of third parties **not** to assert their rights, and (3) *autonomy*—the belief that third parties can best represent themselves. While the rule seems implicit in the constitutional injury-in-fact requirement, the Court has nonetheless regarded it as an exercise of its prudential discretion, not as part of the constitutional core of standing. For that reason, the Court has freely deviated from the rule, creating so many exceptions to the rule that influential commentators believe its significance is doubtful (see, e.g., Tribe, at 136). Some commentators believe that the exceptions are best explained "as *sub silentio* recognitions of *first-party* rights—of the interests of the *litigant*." Tribe, at 136; Monaghan, 84 Colum. L. Rev. 297-316; Sedler, 70 Cal. L. Rev. 1322-1344. Whatever the theory, the Court articulates three factors as key justifications for endorsing an exception to the rule: (1) a **substantial or special relationship between the claimant and the third parties,** (2) the **impossibility or impracticality of the third parties asserting their own interests,** and (3) the **risk that the rights of the third parties will be diluted or lost unless the claimant is allowed to assert their claims.** The second and third factors are in fact but two facets of a single consideration—the threatened impairment of third party rights unless the claimant is permitted to assert the third party's rights. Both of these factors are considered below.

i. **Substantial or special relationship.** The requisite relationship may be established by showing that vindication of the third party's rights is so inextricably connected to vindication of the claimant's rights that the claimant is necessarily simultaneously asserting its own and the third party's rights. This symbiotic connection between the claimant and the third party assures that the claimant is an authentic advocate for the third party rights, alleviating any concern that the third party would be a better champion of his own rights.

Example: A vendor of beer challenged the validity of an Oklahoma law that permitted women to buy beer at age eighteen but required men to be twenty-one. The vendor had standing to assert the rights of third parties—eighteen- to twenty-one-year-old men—because the vendor's right to sell beer to these men was inextricably connected with their right to purchase beer. To assert his right to sell beer to eighteen-year-old men the vendor necessarily asserted the men's right to purchase beer. See *Craig v. Boren,* discussed in Chapter 9, infra.

ii. **Threatened impairment of third party rights.** There may be instances where legal or practical obstacles to the third party's assertion of his own rights are overwhelming. So long as the claimant has some demonstrable reason to state the third party's case with the zeal of his own, third party standing is recognized. The second and third justifications for denying third party standing—respect and autonomy—are completely irrelevant to these cases.

(a) **Legal obstacles.** Threatened impairment of third party rights is clearly satisfied whenever *the litigant is legally obliged to take or refrain from action that prevents the third party from asserting his own rights.*

Example: White, owner of real property burdened by a racially restrictive "whites only" servitude, sells his property to Black. Bigot, owner of property "benefited" by the servitude, sues White for damages due to White's breach of the servitude. White may defend on the ground that enforcement of the servitude violates the equal protection rights of Black. If White were not permitted to do so he could not sell to Black without incurring liability to Bigot since he is legally obligated to abide by the servitude. White would not likely sell to Black under these conditions and there would never be an occasion for Black to assert his own rights. See *Barrows v. Jackson,* discussed in Chapter 10, infra.

(b) **Practical obstacles.** Even if the claimant is not legally obligated to take or refrain from action that prevents the third party from asserting his rights, the practical obstacles to the third party's assertion of his own rights may be so large as to permit the claimant to assert the third party's rights. But the claimant must have an interest in the controversy that is sufficiently congruent with the third party to assure zealous advocacy of the third party's rights.

EXAMPLE AND ANALYSIS

Oregon enacted a law imposing criminal penalties on parents who failed to send their children to public school. A religious school challenged the validity of the law as a violation of the substantive due process rights of the parents and their children. The religious school was permitted to assert third party rights because of the presence of two practical obstacles to the assertion by the parents and children of their own rights. First, most parents would be sufficiently cowed by the criminal sanctions that they would comply with the law, rather than assert their own constitutional rights as a defense in a criminal prosecution. Second, if the school could not assert the rights of the parents and children, the strong possibility would exist that the school would close for lack of students before the parents and children could in fact vindicate their own rights. See *Pierce v. Society of Sisters,* discussed in Chapter 8, infra.

b. **The ''zone-of-interests'' requirement.** This nonconstitutional rule requires ''that a plaintiff's complaint fall within the zone of interests protected by the law invoked.'' *Allen v. Wright,* 468 U.S. at 751. This means that unless the plaintiff's injury is of a type that the law invoked was meant to protect against the plaintiff lacks standing.

    Example: A federal agency permitted national banks to offer data processing services to other banks, in competition with data processing companies. The data processing companies challenged the agency action as violative of a bank regulatory statute. The data processing companies were found to have met the zone-of-interests test because their injury—increased competition from banks—was an injury of the type that the bank regulatory statute was intended to address. *Assoc. of Data Processing Service Organizations v. Camp,* 397 U.S. 150 (1970).

c. **Organizational standing.** Organizations pose some special standing problems. When organizations assert their own rights, the applicable standing rules are no different from those previously considered. But organizations often assert the interests of people whom they claim to represent.

i.   Associational standing

(a)   Direct claims. For associations to assert their *own* interests they must meet the usual requirements. The sticking point is often injury in fact; an association must show "a concrete and demonstrable injury" to its own activities; a mere "setback to [its] abstract social interests" will not suffice. *Havens Realty Corp. v. Coleman,* 455 U.S. 363, 379 (1982). If the injury is noneconomic it must be at least an interference with the *active pursuit* of some noneconomic objective rather than simply an interference with its desired public policy objectives.

(b)   Indirect claims. When associates assert their **members' interests** they must establish three points: (1) the **members would have standing to sue independently,** (2) the **interests asserted are germane to the association's purpose,** and (3) **neither the claim asserted nor the relief requested requires the members' participation in the suit.**

Example: A Washington State agency created to promote and protect the state's apple industry challenged North Carolina's apple-marketing regulations as violative of the commerce clause. The agency, which alleged no injury to itself, was permitted to assert the claims of Washington apple growers and vendors. *Hunt v. Washington State Apple Advertising Commission,* 432 U.S. 333 (1977), discussed in Chapter 6, infra.

The third prong of this test is often critical. Courts usually deny standing to associations seeking money damages for their members since the question of damage almost always requires individualized inquiry.

ii.   Standing of states. The usual standing rules apply when the state litigates its own claims, but special rules govern a state's assertion of its citizens' claims. It is sometimes difficult to tell when a state is asserting its own interests, rather than those of its citizens. If the state's injury is to its sovereignty—its ability validly to exercise regulatory power over individuals and entities—or to its proprietary interests, the state will be seen to be pressing its own claims.

EXAMPLES AND ANALYSIS

Example: New York challenged the constitutionality of federal legislation that required states either to assume all liability for radioactive waste generated within their borders or to adopt specific federally prescribed standards for its disposal. New York was asserting its own claim, and had standing, because the injury asserted was a diminution of New York's power to decide upon its own legislation, whether with respect to disposal of waste or assumption of liability. *New York v. United States,* 505 U.S. 144 (1992), discussed in Chapter 6, infra.

Example: Georgia owned and operated a railroad in competition with the Pennsylvania Railway, a private corporation. Georgia brought suit against the Penn. Ry. under the federal antitrust laws and was held to have standing to assert its own claims, as the owner of the railroad. *Georgia v. Pennsylvania Ry.,* 324 U.S. 439 (1945).

A state may assert the claims of its citizens in order to promote quasi-sovereign interests—concrete, specific interests in the well-being of its citizens.

 # EXAMPLE AND ANALYSIS

Example: Georgia brought suit against the Tennessee Copper Co., seeking to enjoin it from emitting noxious gases that crossed the Tennessee border into Georgia. Georgia had standing to do so, even though the injury was not so much to Georgia but to the well-being of its residents. But the injury was one which Georgia would be likely to address legislatively. *Georgia v. Tennessee Copper Co.,* 206 U.S. 230 (1907).

---

6. Standing in State Courts and Supreme Court Review

States can and do have their own rules concerning standing. Even if a federal substantive claim is pressed in state court the state courts are free to apply their own rules of standing. If a case comes to the Supreme Court from the state courts, federal standing will be determined when the case arrives in the Supreme Court. See *Asarco, Inc. v. Kadish,* 490 U.S. 605 (1989).

G. NO ADVISORY OPINIONS

Article III, section 2 limits the federal judicial power to "cases" or "controversies." During President Washington's first term the question arose whether the Court had the authority to opine upon abstract, hypothetical questions. The Court disclaimed that power; thus, federal courts may not render advisory opinions. Policy justifications for the rule include the need to keep judicial and executive power separated and the importance of deciding only cases that have concrete adversaries in sharp conflict over real disputes. The danger of deciding abstractions is thought to be (1) the lack of zealous advocacy for both sides of the question, and (2) the possibility of overbroad decision produced by the absence of a real-world application of the issue that narrows the conflict.

1. *The Correspondence of the Justices*

In July 1793, President Washington, through his Secretary of State Thomas Jefferson, asked the Justices of the Court if they were at liberty to deliver their opinion on a variety of legal questions pertinent to preservation of American neutrality in the war between Britain and France. Three weeks later the Justices replied, by letter, that "the lines of separation drawn by the Constitution between the three departments of the government . . . afford strong arguments against the propriety of" advisory opinions, especially since Article II expressly empowers the President to ask for opinions from the heads of his executive departments. The inference the Court drew from the existence of this Article II power was that the judiciary was precluded from rendering extrajudicial opinions to the President.

2. *Hayburn's Case:* **The Need for Judicial Finality**

A federal law assigned to the Justices of the Supreme Court the obligation to certify persons as Revolutionary War veterans eligible for receipt of a pension. In *Hayburn's Case,* 2 U.S. 408 (1792), the Justices, sitting on circuit, refused to do so since the statute assigned nonjudicial duties to the Court. The duties were nonjudicial in part because the Court's judgment was subject to modification by the Secretary of War. This principle is still adhered to. In *C. & S. Airlines v. Waterman Corp.,* 333 U.S. 103 (1948), the Court held that Congress had impermissibly demanded advisory opinions from the federal courts by directing courts to review the award of international air routes, because their decisions were subject to presidential modification.

3. **Declaratory Judgments**

Courts are sometimes asked to decide or declare the legal consequences of the litigant's conduct rather than to award damages or injunctive relief. Such judgments are **declaratory judgments.** Declaratory judgments are not advisory opinions so long as the controversy is sufficiently concrete to make the court's judgment a final disposition of the matter.

 # EXAMPLES AND ANALYSIS

Example: Railroad was about to become liable for a state tax that Railroad contended was an unconstitutional burden on interstate commerce. In state court Railroad sought a declaratory judgment that the tax was unconstitutional. The Supreme Court reviewed the state court decision because the controversy was real and not hypothetical, presented sharply adverse positions, and the court's judgment was dispositive. Under these conditions, the form of the relief sought did not matter. *Nashville, C. & St. L. Ry. v. Wallace,* 288 U.S. 249 (1933).

But where the controversy is still abstracted and hypothetical, a declaratory judgment would be an advisory opinion.

Example: Lessee desired to demolish the leased premises and construct a new building. One of the Lessors informally opined that the lease probably required Lessee to obtain the consent of all Lessors and Lessor's bondholders. Lessee sought a declaratory judgment in federal court that it could demolish the building without obtaining the consents. The Court held that the case presented no case or controversy because there was "neither hostile act nor a threat." *Willig v. Chicago Auditorium Ass'n,* 277 U.S. 274 (1928). Dicta in the case suggesting that declaratory judgments are beyond the power of federal courts has been rejected by *Wallace,* supra, and *Aetna Life Ins. Co. v. Haworth,* 300 U.S. 227 (1937), upholding the power of Congress to authorize federal courts to issue declaratory judgments in cases of "actual controversy."

H. RIPENESS AND MOOTNESS

These problems are opposite sides of a single coin. Both doctrines ask whether the issues raised in the suit are raised at the right time. An issue is not ripe, and therefore not justiciable, if future events may render decision unnecessary. It is moot if past events have rendered a decision unnecessary.

1. Ripeness

The essential problem of an unripe controversy is that the lines of conflict have not yet sufficiently hardened. The plaintiff may not have yet acted in a way that has lasting legal consequences or the defendant may not yet have acted to injure the plaintiff. This doctrine is related to the advisory opinion doctrine; both doctrines seek to preclude decision of cases that are ethereal, abstract, and not yet charged with actions that produce consequences. Ripeness involves "the **fitness of the issues for judicial decision**" and consideration of "the **hardship to the parties of withholding court consideration.**" The first issue is required by the Constitution's case or controversy requirement. The second proposition is within the discretionary prudence of the Court. Most of ripeness involves the constitutional problem.

    a. **Specific harm.** For a case to be ripe the plaintiff must show that he has either (1) **already suffered harm,** (2) is faced with a **"specific present objective harm,"** or (3) is under a **"threat of specific future harm."**

 EXAMPLES AND ANALYSIS

Example: Congress enacted the Hatch Act, which barred public employees from "any active part in political management or in political campaigns." Public employees and their union sought to enjoin the Civil Service Commission from enforcing the Hatch

Act and obtain a judicial declaration of its unconstitutionality. With one exception, the plaintiffs admitted that they had not violated the Act but asserted only that they desired to do so. The Court found the controversy unripe because their assertions of their future intentions were vague, nonspecific, and general. The Court characterized their grievances as more of "an attack on the political expediency" of the Hatch Act than as an attempt to vindicate personal injuries. *United Public Workers v. Mitchell,* 330 U.S. 75 (1947).

Example: During the Vietnam War the U.S. Army collected information about people and organizations it thought had a potential for "civil disorder." Plaintiffs attacked the scheme as a violation of their free expression rights, claiming that it had a "present inhibiting effect" on them. The Court (5-4) held that allegations of a present subjective chill on speech were too vague, and nonspecific, to present a ripe controversy. Plaintiffs must show either specific present objective harm or a threat of specific future harm. *Laird v. Tatum,* 408 U.S. 1 (1972).

> **b. Anticipatory review.** Ripeness prevents a litigant faced with compliance with an arguably invalid law from obtaining review of the law before its effective date.

 # EXAMPLES AND ANALYSIS

Example: A federal agency issues new regulations, effective in the future, that will force Corporation to incur major costs to change its business practices. Corporation believes the regulations are unlawful. Corporation may comply and incur the considerable costs of compliance, or it may refuse to comply and incur criminal prosecution and terrible publicity, but it may not seek review of the validity of the regulations in advance of their effective date. The dispute is concrete enough to be a constitutional case or controversy, but the Court thought that there was insufficient hardship to the parties in withholding its consideration. *Abbott Laboratories v. Gardner,* 387 U.S. 136 (1967).

The same problem of anticipatory review is presented when the President threatens to take unlawful action.

Example: In November 1990, prior to the Persian Gulf War of January and February 1991, and while American forces were building up in Saudi Arabia, President Bush the elder announced his intention to secure an offensive capability for Allied forces in the Persian Gulf. Fifty-four members of Congress sought to enjoin the President from commencing hostilities without "genuine approval" from Congress. A federal district judge denied a preliminary injunction on the ground that the controversy was not yet ripe, since President Bush had not yet taken that action. *Dellums v. Bush,* 752 F. Supp. 1141 (D.D.C. 1990).

---

    c. Unenforced criminal laws. Ripeness may prevent a litigant from attacking the validity of a criminal statute that the litigant admits violating but that is not enforced. When a married couple and a physician challenged a long unenforced law making contraceptive use a crime their claim was unripe because there was no actual threat of enforcement against them. *Poe v. Ullman,* 367 U.S. 497 (1961).

    This rule is not ironclad. Even though Arkansas had not enforced its statute prohibiting the teaching of evolution for over forty years, and there was no actual present threat of enforcement, in *Epperson v. Arkansas,* 393 U.S. 97 (1968), the Court treated a challenge to the law as ripe and reached a decision on the merits. Because the Court felt free to treat *Epperson* as presenting a ripe controversy it apparently does not regard this aspect of the doctrine to be constitutionally compelled.

2. Mootness

A moot case is not justiciable. A case is rendered moot if events occur after the case is begun that eliminate the plaintiff's stake in the controversy. Mootness is thus first cousin to standing. It is "the doctrine of standing set in a time frame: The requisite personal interest that must exist at the commencement of the litigation (standing) must continue throughout its existence (mootness)." Monaghan, 82 Yale L.J. at 1384. See also Tribe, at 83 n.3. Mootness is constitutionally required, an aspect of the "case or controversy" requirement. See, e.g., *U.S. Parole Commission v. Geraghty,* 445 U.S. 388, 395-397 (1980); *Liner v. Jafco, Inc.,* 375 U.S. 301, 306 n.3 (1964). See also Tribe, at 82 n.1.

Example: On his own behalf and not as a class action, Marco DeFunis sued the University of Washington, claiming that its law school's admission practices were racially discriminatory. A trial court ordered his admission pending appellate review. When the Supreme Court heard the case, DeFunis was in his final quarter of study and the school agreed that he would be allowed to complete his studies. The Court found the case moot; DeFunis no longer had any personal stake in the matter and decision was both unnecessary and precluded by the lack of a real case or controversy. *DeFunis v. Odegaard,* 416 U.S. 312 (1974).

Even though mootness is a constitutional doctrine the Court has fashioned a number of exceptions to the doctrine, leading some commentators to question whether the doctrine is really as constitutionally rooted as the Court says.

See Lee, 105 Harv. L. Rev. 603. In any case, the principal exceptions are considered below.

a. Exception: "Capable of repetition, yet evading review." If a problem is **capable of repetition, yet evading review** courts will ignore otherwise applicable problems of mootness and decide the issue on the merits. The exception originated in *Southern Pacific Terminal Co. v. ICC,* 219 U.S. 498 (1911), well before the Court's 1964 confirmation that mootness is constitutionally compelled, but has continued to be a part of the constitutional law of mootness. The exception requires a showing that (1) the **life of the controversy is too short to be fully litigated prior to its termination,** and (2) that there is a **reasonable expectation that the plaintiff will again be subjected to the same problem.**

 ## EXAMPLE AND ANALYSIS

Norma McCorvey, a pregnant woman, challenged the constitutional validity of Texas laws prohibiting abortions in most circumstances. By the time her case was heard by the Court she was no longer pregnant. Nevertheless, the Court reached the merits of the case having concluded that, given the relative speed of courts and gestation, a challenge to abortion laws by a pregnant woman was a classic instance of a case capable of repetition, yet evading review. The case could not be fully litigated in nine months and there was a reasonable expectation that McCorvey might be pregnant again. On this last point, the Court seemingly broadened the exception, by noting that "pregnancy . . . will always be with us." *Roe v. Wade,* 410 U.S. 113 (1975).

Marco DeFunis's challenge to the University of Washington's law school admission practices was not treated the same way because it was entirely possible that the case could have been fully litigated in three years (it almost was) and there was a virtual certainty that DeFunis would never again be subject to the same problem.

b. Exception: Voluntary cessation by the defendant. If the defendant voluntarily ceases the challenged conduct the case is not thereby rendered moot. There is still a live controversy if the plaintiff seeks damages, and if the plaintiff desires only injunctive relief the controversy is alive if there is any reasonable expectation that the alleged violation will recur. See *City of Erie v. Pap's A.M.,* 120 S. Ct. 1382 (2000); *County of Los Angeles v. Davis,* 440 U.S. 625, 631 (1979). Marco DeFunis's case did not fall within this exception because the University of Washington had not voluntarily ceased its allegedly discriminatory law admission practices.

c. Exception: Collateral consequences to the plaintiff. A case is not moot even though the challenged action is completed if there are adverse collateral consequences to the plaintiff. The existence of adverse collateral consequences constitutes a continuing injury to the plaintiff.

Example: Plaintiff, convicted of a felony, has served his entire sentence by the time the Court hears his challenge to the constitutional validity of the conviction. The case is not moot because the plaintiff faces a number of adverse collateral consequences, such as loss of voting rights, possible increased sentences for future crimes, and loss of employment opportunities. Cf. *Sibron v. New York,* 392 U.S. 40 (1968).

This exception is almost always limited to challenges of criminal convictions after sentence has been served.

I. POLITICAL QUESTIONS

This doctrine treats certain kinds of cases as nonjusticiable "political questions." The label is unfortunate since the doctrine does *not* mean that cases involving political parties or political issues are nonjusticiable. Like standing, the political question doctrine has a constitutional core and a prudential periphery. The constitutional core consists of those issues that courts may not decide because the Constitution mandates that they be finally decided by other branches of the federal government. The prudential periphery consists of those issues that the Court thinks are best left undecided by courts, because there is insufficient information upon which to decide, or judicial decision would undermine the courts or compromise some other important principle of democratic governance.

1. *Baker v. Carr:* The Reigning Doctrine

In *Baker v. Carr,* 369 U.S. 186 (1962), the Court delivered a "definitive" statement of the political question doctrine. Plaintiffs in *Baker* contended that the failure of the Tennessee legislature to reapportion itself for more than sixty years, as required by the Tennessee constitution, was also a violation of the 14th Amendment's equal protection clause. The Court concluded that the claim did not present a political question.

  a. Factors identifying a political question. The Court recited six factors that identify political questions. If *any one* of these factors is present in a case, it is a nonjusticiable political question. None were held to be present in *Baker.*

   i. Constitutional commitment of decision of the issue to another branch: A "textually demonstrable commitment" in the Constitution of decision of the issue "to a coordinate political department" (Congress or the President).

   ii. Lack of standards for decision: No "judicially discoverable and manageable standards for resolving" the issue.

   iii. Decision requires a judicially inappropriate policy choice: The case presents "the impossibility of deciding without an initial policy determination of a kind clearly for nonjudicial discretion."

    iv. **Decision would lack respect for Congress or the President:** A court cannot decide the case without "expressing lack of respect due coordinate branches of government."

    v. **Political decision already made:** There exists "an unusual need for unquestioning adherence to a political decision already made."

    vi. **Potential for embarrassment:** A judicial decision would create "the potentiality of embarrassment from multifarious pronouncements by various departments on one question."

b. **Source of the *Baker* factors.** The first factor—constitutional commitment of decision of the issue to another branch—is most clearly constitutionally mandated. The second factor is partly the product of constitutional concerns, but also admits of purely prudential concerns. Although the Court in *Baker* suggested that all of these factors might be related to separation of powers principles, the remaining four factors are mostly if not entirely within the Court's prudential discretion.

c. **Use of the *Baker* factors.** Although the presence of a single factor is sufficient to create a political question, rarely is one single factor present in a case. This lends some confusion to the political question doctrine as it is not often clear whether it is the combination of factors, or one particular factor, that impels the decision to regard an issue as a political question.

2. **Issues Constitutionally Committed for Decision to Congress or the President**

If some part of the Constitution vests Congress or the President with the sole authority to decide a particular issue, it is a nonjusticiable political question. This does not apply to claims that the Constitution gives the states sole authority over an issue.

    a. **Impeachment.** Two issues are presented, only one of which has been decided by the Court. First, are the *reasons* for impeachment and conviction reviewable? Second, is the *type of trial* afforded by the Senate reviewable?

        i. **Grounds for impeachment.** Though the issue has never been decided, it is likely that the grounds chosen by the House of Representatives to impeach the President or other federal officials, and the Senate's decision to convict on those grounds, are nonjusticiable political questions. The Constitution permits the House to impeach for "high Crimes and Misdemeanors" and obligates the Senate to try impeachments. Is this a sufficiently "textually demonstrable constitutional commitment" of these issues to the House and Senate? When President Ford was minority leader of the House he stated that "an impeachable offense is whatever a majority of the House says it is." Whether Ford was correct may be debatable but there is little debating the confusion that would arise in the wake of a successful judicial challenge by an impeached President to his impeachment. Which President is commander-in-chief? Which President may sign and veto legislation? The reason the grounds for impeachment are nonjusticiable political questions is as much due to an "unusual need for unquestioning adherence to a political decision already made"—impeachment and conviction—as it is the product of a constitutional commitment of these issues to Congress.

ii. **Type of trial afforded.** The type of trial an impeached official is given by the Senate is constitutionally committed to the Senate and is a nonjusticiable political question.

 # EXAMPLE AND ANALYSIS

Walter Nixon, a federal judge, was convicted of bribery, then impeached, convicted, and removed from office on those grounds. The Senate delegated a committee of twelve Senators to hear evidence. The committee gave the entire Senate a copy of the transcript and the Senate convicted on that basis. Nixon argued that the Senate had not complied with Article I, §3, cl. 6, which requires the Senate to "try all impeachments." The Court concluded that the type of trial is for the Senate to decide, since the full clause states that "the Senate shall have *sole Power* to try all Impeachments." As well, the Court identified the lack of finality problem as an additional basis for its ruling. See *Nixon v. United States,* 506 U.S. 224 (1993).

b. **The process of constitutional amendment.** The validity of the process by which a constitutional amendment is proposed and adopted is probably also constitutionally committed to Congress. In *Coleman v. Miller,* 307 U.S. 433 (1939), a plurality of the Court agreed it was for Congress alone to decide whether Kansas had ratified a proposed constitutional amendment: "Congress has sole and complete control over the amending process, subject to no judicial review. . . ." But no majority coalesced around that position and some commentators believe that "an absolute bar on judicial review of the amendment process is doubtful." Tribe, at 101.

Example: In 1992 Michigan ratified the 27th Amendment, which bars congressional pay raises from taking effect until after an intervening election. The amendment had been among the first twelve amendments proposed by the First Congress. Five states ratified it in 1789-1791, another in 1873, and thirty-two acted from 1978-1992, Michigan being the requisite 38th. Not happy with its content, some members of Congress toyed with the idea of declaring it improperly ratified for lack of a "contemporaneous ratification." Congress did not do so.

c. **Qualifications of members of Congress.** The issue of whether a member of Congress is qualified to hold the office was found to be judicially reviewable, and not a political question, in *Powell v. McCormack,* 395 U.S. 486 (1969). The House refused to seat Adam Clayton Powell because he had allegedly embezzled House funds and lied to the House. Powell sought a judicial declaration that he was entitled to take his seat. Although Article I, §5, provides that "[e]ach House shall be the Judge of the . . . Qualifications of its own Members" the Court ruled that the issue was reviewable by the courts and not a political question. The Court's rationale was that since Article I, §2, specifies three qualifications—age, citizenship, and residency—that implies that there can be no more qualifications added by Congress. The Court in *Powell* did not decide whether the Constitution commits to the House and Senate the sole power to determine whether the three constitutional qualifications are satisfied. The *Powell* Court also did not address the question of whether it could review the validity of expulsion of a member of Congress.

i. **State-imposed qualifications.** *Powell* did not address the question of whether a state may impose its own qualifications for its federal congressional delegation. In *United States Term Limits v. Thornton,* 514 U.S. 779 (1995), the Court ruled on the merits that a state may not do so, thus also removing any doubt that this issue might be a nonjusticiable political question.

d. **Control of the National Guard.** When four college students protesting the Vietnam War were killed by Ohio National Guardsmen, the federal courts were asked to determine whether the Ohio National Guard was sufficiently well trained to comport with the 14th Amendment's due process clause. In *Gilligan v. Morgan,* 413 U.S. 1 (1973), the Court treated this as a political question and denied the federal courts authority to decide on the merits. The Court relied in part on Article I, §8, which gives Congress power to organize and discipline the Militia (today, the National Guard) and to delegate to the states "the Authority of training the Militia according to the discipline prescribed by Congress." But in addition to this apparent constitutional commitment of the issue to Congress, the Court also relied on the "lack of judicially discoverable and manageable standards for resolving" the issue: "[I]t is difficult to conceive of an area of governmental activity in which the courts have less competence. The complex, subtle, and professional decisions as to the composition, training, equipping, and control of a military force are essentially professional military judgments, subject *always* to civilian control of the Legislative and Executive Branches."

3. Issues Lacking Judicially Discoverable and Manageable Standards for Decision

This *Baker* factor responds in part to constitutional limits on judicial review and in part to prudential concerns of the Court. If the standards for decision are inscrutable and unusable, the exercise of judicial power might be a gratuitous interference with other lawful decision-makers, as well as being so arbitrary as to constitute a denial of due process. In applying this factor the Court has been opaque as to when it is using it as a constitutional rule, and when as a prudential rule.

a. *Coleman v. Miller,* 307 U.S. 433 (1939). This case raised two questions: (1) whether a state could ratify a constitutional amendment it had once rejected, and (2) whether a proposed amendment has become a dead letter if not ratified within a reasonable period of time. The Court found both questions to be nonjusticiable. On the first question, a plurality ruled there was "no basis in either Constitution or statute for . . . judicial action." This enigmatic conclusion hardly advances understanding. It could mean that resolution of the issue has been constitutionally committed to the other branches, or it could mean that there were no judicially discoverable standards for decision. On the second issue, the Court was more direct. "Where are to be found the criteria for such a judicial determination?" asked the Court. Not in the Constitution, but only in "political, social, and economic" factors outside "the appropriate range of evidence receivable in a court."

b. **Political gerrymanders.** In *Davis v. Bandemer,* 478 U.S. 109 (1986), the Court concluded that there were judicially discoverable standards by which to evaluate whether a political gerrymander of a state's congressional districts violated the equal protection clause. The standard, said a plurality of the Court, was whether "the electoral system is arranged in a manner that will consistently degrade a voter's or a group of voters' influence on the political process as a whole." Justice O'Connor, dissenting, charged that this was no standard at all, that it would "prove unmanageable and arbitrary" and "make adjudication of political gerrymandering claims impossible." She charged that the Court had given to the federal courts the impossible task of "reconcil[ing] the competing claims of political, religious, ethnic, racial, occupational, and socio-economic groups."

4. The Need to Adhere to Political Decisions Already Made and the Potential for Embarrassment from Multiple Voices

Several types of political question cases fall into this category, which is almost certainly an exercise in the prudential discretion of the Court.

a. **The power to make war.** Article I, §8 vests in Congress the power to "declare War," while Article II, §2 designates the President as "Commander in Chief" of the armed services. Questions periodically arise whether the President has acted illegally by committing American forces to combat without a formal declaration of war. If those questions were presented to a court it is likely that they would not present a justiciable controversy, partly because it may be necessary to adhere to the political decision already made.

 # EXAMPLE AND ANALYSIS

Throughout the Vietnam War a number of challenges were brought to the constitutional validity of that conflict, since the only congressional authorization was the Gulf of Tonkin resolution and the continuing appropriation of funds for the war. One such challenge was brought by a soldier who claimed that his orders to serve in Vietnam were illegal because the war was unconstitutional. Like all the other challenges, the Court refused to hear the claim. What made this one noteworthy was Justice Stewart's dissent from denial of certiorari, calling into question the apparent nonjusticiability of the issue. *Mora v. McNamara,* 389 U.S. 934 (1967) (Stewart, J., dissenting from denial of certiorari).

However, when fifty-four members of Congress sought to enjoin the elder President Bush from commencing hostilities in the Persian Gulf without "genuine approval" from Congress, a federal district judge indicated in dicta he thought the claim was justiciable, although he denied a preliminary injunction on the ground that the controversy was not yet ripe. *Dellums v. Bush,* supra. Nevertheless, it is probable that, as in the case of the Vietnam War, the Court would treat challenges to presidential commitment of troops to combat as nonjusticiable, given the domestic and international turmoil that would result from a judicial decision that an ongoing conflict was illegal. Could American judges have *effectively* enjoined the war in Vietnam?

b. **Foreign affairs short of war.** Challenges to acts that "involve[] the authority of the President in the conduct of our country's foreign relations" are nearly always political questions, because of the strong need for the nation to speak with a single voice in foreign affairs. This reason implicates the last two *Baker* factors: the unusual need to adhere to past political decisions and the pressing need to avoid multiple pronouncements.

Example: Senator Goldwater challenged the validity of President Carter's unilateral abrogation of a defense treaty with Taiwan. The Court decided that the issue was a nonjusticiable political question, but couldn't muster a majority for a single rationale. A four-Justice plurality thought the case was a political question because of the desirability of speaking with one voice on foreign affairs. *Goldwater v. Carter,* 444 U.S. 996 (1979).

5. The Guarantee Clause

Article IV, §2 obligates the United States to "guarantee to every State . . . a Republican Form of Government." There is no textual indication which organ of the United States government is entrusted with this responsibility. Nevertheless, when the Court first encountered a claim involving the guarantee clause it ruled it nonjusticiable. The rationale for this view is grounded in so many *Baker* factors that the guarantee clause deserves *sui generis* treatment.

a. ***Luther v. Borden,*** 48 U.S. 1 (1849). In the 1840s Rhode Islanders lacking the vote under the colonial charter still in effect formed a new and more democratic government, which was not recognized by the charter government. Each government insisted it was the lawful government of Rhode Island. Officials of the charter government entered the home of an official of the insurgent government and arrested him. He brought suit, claiming that the entry was an unlawful trespass. To resolve the issue on the merits the Court would be required to decide which was the lawful government. That, in turn, depended partly on which government was republican. The Court ruled that a federal court could not by itself decide which of two rival state governments was the lawful one.

   i. **The Court's rationales.** The Court relied on a number of factors. (1) It thought that there was no meaningful way for judges to measure which government was republican, a precursor to the "lack of judicially discoverable standards." (2) Related to the first point, the entire enterprise of evaluating two ostensibly democratic governments for the purpose of ascertaining their republican nature carried with it the grave risk that any decision would be permeated with an initial policy choice beyond the range of judicial competence. (3) Congress had already acted, by delegating to the President the task of deciding which was the lawful Rhode Island government. Congress's exercise of this power suggested to the Court that the power to resolve the controversy was constitutionally committed to Congress. (4) President Tyler had used the authority bestowed upon him by Congress to recognize the charter government as the lawful one. The Court seemed to treat this action as a political *fait accompli,* presenting an unusual need for adherence by the judiciary. Long before *Baker, Luther v. Borden* is a prime example of the interweaving of *Baker* factors to describe a political question.

   ii. ***Pacific States Tel. & Tel. Co. v. Oregon,*** 223 U.S. 118 (1912). A public utility claimed that Oregon's use of the direct legislative initiative was a violation of the guarantee clause because it was democratic, rather than republican. The Court held that the question of whether a state's government was republican was beyond judicial competence to answer.

iii. **Modern hints of a new direction.** In recent years Justice O'Connor has suggested that the guarantee clause might not invariably be nonjusticiable. She has hinted at the possibility that the guarantee clause might be judicially enforceable by *states* in order to prevent the federal government from interfering in a "state's most fundamental structural choices"—"how its people are to participate in their own governance." Tribe, at 398. Justice O'Connor's views are best set out in *New York v. United States,* 505 U.S. 144 (1992). See also Merritt, 88 Colum. L. Rev. 1.

J. DECLINING TO EXERCISE JURISDICTION: ABSTENTION AND OTHER "PASSIVE VIRTUES"

Judicial review places the courts in conflict with other political branches. Some of the devices to limit judicial review are constitutionally required, but some are products of the Court's prudential discretion to decline to exercise its jurisdiction. When the latter occurs, there is a constitutional conundrum to be considered. Chief Justice Marshall, in *Cohens v. Virginia,* declared that courts *must decide* the cases properly brought before them: "We have no more right to decline the exercise of jurisdiction which is given, than to usurp that which is not given. The one or the other would be treason to the Constitution." Is the Court committing treason to the Constitution when it declines to exercise its jurisdiction out of prudential, nonconstitutional concerns? Or are those supposedly prudential grounds really constitutionally mandated? Or has Marshall simply been repudiated? While the answers to those questions are debatable, a reasonable set of answers are: "No," "some are and some aren't," and "yes." One area that especially attracts consideration of this conundrum is abstention.

1. The Concept of Abstention

Federal courts abstain from exercising their jurisdiction when one of a number of factors is present. A common thread among the various abstention doctrines is the need for the federal courts to refrain from interfering in the ongoing judicial processes of the state courts. However, with dual court systems—federal and state—a certain amount of intercourt conflict is inevitable. Abstention seeks to dampen, not totally eliminate, this conflict. Two of the most important abstention doctrines, *Younger* abstention and *Pullman* abstention, are discussed below.

2. *Younger* Abstention

Sometimes litigants in state court ask the federal courts to enjoin the state proceedings on some constitutional ground, or declare the constitutional rights of the litigants in the state proceeding. *Younger* abstention forbids the federal courts from exercising jurisdiction and requires them to dismiss the case. The reason for the doctrine is to respect the integrity of each state's judicial system, recognizing that state courts, just like federal courts, are obligated to apply the Constitution faithfully to preserve the rights of litigants before them. The Court has stated that *Younger* abstention is not constitutionally mandated, but in its objective to respect the autonomous governance process of a state it seems to be applying constitutional values that will be discussed more fully in Chapter 4, infra. *Younger* abstention takes its name from *Younger v. Harris,* 401 U.S. 37 (1971).

a. ***Younger v. Harris* and pending criminal prosecutions.** In *Younger* itself the Court ruled that a federal court could not grant an injunction of allegedly unconstitutional state behavior sought by a defendant in a state criminal prosecution, so long as the defendant has an opportunity to litigate the constitutional claim in the pending state criminal prosecution. A companion case to *Younger, Samuels v. Mackell,* 401 U.S. 66 (1971), ruled that, in the same circumstances, federal courts may not grant a declaratory judgment as to the constitutionality of the state basis for the pending criminal prosecution. An exception to the *Younger* doctrine is the special case where the state defendant and federal plaintiff can establish that the state criminal proceeding is wholly meritless, and simply the result of bad faith or harassment.

b. **Pending civil cases.** Two cases, *Middlesex County Ethics Commission v. Garden State Bar Ass'n,* 457 U.S. 423 (1982), and *Pennzoil Co. v. Texaco, Inc.,* 481 U.S. 1 (1987), combine to extend *Younger* abstention to state civil proceedings, so long as important state interests are involved in the state civil proceeding.

 # EXAMPLE AND ANALYSIS

In a Texas state court, Pennzoil won a $10.5 *billion* verdict against Texaco for tortious interference with Pennzoil's agreement with Getty Oil to acquire Getty. In order to appeal the verdict, Texaco was required to post a bond of some *$13 billion,* a practical impossibility even for a giant corporation such as Texaco. Texaco asked a federal court to enjoin the Texas appeal bond requirement on the grounds that its imposition would deprive Texaco of its constitutional rights. The Court held that *Younger* abstention applied, inasmuch as Texas had an important interest in imposing a generally applicable appeals bond requirement. *Pennzoil v. Texaco,* supra.

c. **Meaning of ''pending proceedings.''** A federal litigant may obtain injunctive or declaratory relief against a threatened, but not yet instituted, state prosecution. *Steffel v. Thompson,* 415 U.S. 452 (1974). But this conclusion must be qualified at least twice. First, the federal Anti-Injunction Act (28 U.S.C. §2283), which has unbroken antecedents from 1793, bars federal courts from enjoining "proceedings in a State court except as expressly authorized by Act of Congress." In *Mitchum v. Foster,* 407 U.S. 225 (1972), the Court concluded that claims brought under 42 U.S.C. §1983, which permits the federal courts to hear "suit[s] in equity" to redress the loss of constitutional rights occurring under color of state law, were "expressly authorized" under the Anti-Injunction Act. Second, even if the state proceedings have not begun when the federal complaint is filed, if the state proceedings commence before "any proceedings of substance on the merits have taken place in the federal court" *Younger* abstention applies. *Hicks v. Miranda,* 422 U.S. 332 (1975). In short, only constitutional claims may support an injunction of threatened state proceedings, and, as a practical matter, the federal claim must begin well in advance of the state proceeding.

3. *Pullman* Abstention

Pullman abstention requires a federal court to abstain from exercising its jurisdiction whenever "a federal constitutional claim is premised on an unsettled question of state law, . . . in order to provide the state courts an opportunity to settle the underlying state law question and thus avoid the possibility of unnecessarily deciding a constitutional question." *Harris Cty. Commissioners' Court v. Moore,* 420 U.S. 77, 83 (1975). The doctrine is primarily rooted in the desire to avoid rendering advisory opinions. The Court has described the "*Pullman* concern" as follows: "[A] federal court will be forced to interpret state law without the benefit of state-court consideration and therefore under circumstances where a constitutional determination is predicated on a reading of the [state] statute that is not binding on state courts and may be discredited at any time—thus essentially rendering the federal-court decision advisory and the litigation underlying it meaningless." *Moore v. Sims,* 442 U.S. 415 (1979). While this might suggest that *Pullman* abstention is required by Article III, the Court has never so held.

a.   The *Pullman* case. The doctrine takes its name from *Railroad Commission of Texas v. Pullman Co.,* 312 U.S. 496 (1941). The Texas Railroad Commission, a state agency, ruled that railroads must have their sleeping cars under the control of a conductor rather than a porter. At that time, conductors were uniformly white men and porters were uniformly black men. The affected railroads, the Pullman Co., and the Pullman porters sought and obtained an injunction in federal court against enforcement of the commission's order on the grounds that it was unconstitutional. But there was also some question whether, under Texas law, the Texas Railroad Commission was empowered to issue the order. The Supreme Court reversed and remanded to the federal district court, with orders to stay its jurisdiction pending a decision of the Texas courts whether Texas law authorized the Commission to act.

b. **Application of *Pullman*.** A federal court abstaining under *Pullman* does not dismiss the case, but merely stays its jurisdiction. But *Government Employees v. Windsor,* 353 U.S. 364 (1957), requires that all claims—federal and state—be submitted to the state court. That would ordinarily mean that the state court's decision on the federal claims would be *res judicata,* thus precluding a return to federal court.

However, the Court in *England v. Louisiana State Board of Medical Examiners,* 375 U.S. 411 (1964), ruled that a litigant could bring his federal claims back to federal court for final disposition if, on the record of the state case, the litigant reserves his right to try his federal claims in federal court. Some commentators think that *Pullman* abstention is far too byzantine and that the entire enterprise should be scrapped. See Weinberg, Federal Courts, at 607. Perhaps it persists because it is constitutionally required, even though the Court has never said so.

REVIEW QUESTIONS AND ANSWERS

Question: The state of Orange's constitution provides that the state "may not prohibit the free exercise of religion." Mark, an Orange resident, practices an exotic religion whose central sacramental rite involves ingesting hallucinogenic mushrooms. The state of Orange has made possession of any hallucinogen a felony. Mark was convicted in an Orange court of possession of an hallucinogen. He appealed his conviction to the Orange Supreme Court on the ground that the law, as applied to his possession of hallucinogens for religious purposes, violated the Orange constitution. The Orange Supreme Court agreed with Mark and set aside his conviction. The State of Orange has filed a petition for writ of certiorari in the United States Supreme Court. May the Supreme Court hear the case?

Answer: No. The only issue raised by Mark in his appeal to the Orange Supreme Court was the validity of the criminal statute under the Orange constitution. That question was answered by the Orange Supreme Court in Mark's favor. There is no issue of federal law presented and thus the United States Supreme Court has no basis for asserting jurisdiction.

Question: Same facts as the previous question, except that Mark appeals his conviction on the ground that the Orange criminal law violates both the Orange constitution and the United States Constitution. The Orange Supreme Court concluded that the law violated both constitutions and thus set aside Mark's conviction. In considering the Orange constitution, the Orange Supreme Court relied exclusively upon Orange precedents, and expressly disavowed any reliance upon federal precedents. May the United States Supreme Court grant Orange's petition for certiorari?

Answer: No. The decision of the Orange Supreme Court is founded upon an *adequate and independent state ground*—the Orange constitution. If the Orange criminal law violates the Orange constitution there is *no need to consider the federal Constitution*—the Orange Supreme Court's discussion of federal constitutional law and conclusion that the Orange statute also violates the United States Constitution is simply dicta, or an advisory opinion. The federal constitutional issue would be dispositive only if the Orange statute did *not* violate the Orange constitution.

Question: Same facts as the first question, except that the Orange constitution contains the following provision: "This constitution's guarantee of free exercise of religion shall not be construed more broadly than the United States Supreme Court construes the guarantee of free exercise of religion in the United States Constitution." May the United States Supreme Court grant Orange's cert petition?

Answer: Yes. By making the substance of its own constitution depend on federal law, Orange has abandoned its constitutional independence. There is no longer any *independent state law grounds* for the Orange Supreme Court's decision. Even though the Orange Supreme Court was purportedly deciding an Orange constitutional issue, under the Orange constitution it could only do so by reference to federal constitutional law.

Question: Suppose Congress eliminates all civil federal question jurisdiction for the federal trial courts. At the same time Congress enacts an omnibus statute providing that any civil claim founded on federal law may be brought in a state court. The law makes no change to the United States Supreme Court's appellate jurisdiction. Is the legislation constitutional?

Answer: Yes. Congress has virtually complete control over the scope of the jurisdiction of the lower federal courts. Some academics might argue that this elimination violates a structural premise of the Constitution that an Article III court be available to hear federal claims, but that argument has never been accepted by the Court. Indeed, it seems pretty clearly rejected by *Sheldon v. Sill,* 49 U.S. 441 (1850). Note that there was no general grant of federal question jurisdiction for nearly the first century of the nation.

Question: Marvin, a citizen of the state of Arapahoe, applies for a job as a prison guard at the state prison. He is *rejected solely* because of his race. He brings suit in federal district court against the state of Arapahoe and its Director of Corrections, charging that his 14th Amendment equal protection rights have been violated. He seeks damages and an injunction requiring the State to consider his application for employment as a prison guard without considering his race. Arapahoe moves to dismiss the claim as barred by the Eleventh Amendment. What result?

Answer: The claim against the state of Arapahoe is barred by the Eleventh Amendment. *Hans v. Louisiana* construed the Eleventh Amendment bar to extend to suits brought by citizens of a state against their own state. The claim against the Director of Corrections is not barred, insofar as it seeks the described injunctive relief (which will not require a monetary payment by the state). The claim for damages against the Director of Corrections is barred to the extent that any money damages would be satisfied out of the state treasury.

Question: Wanda, a social worker, is deeply distressed by the plight of homeless people she sees daily. She learns that a federal agency statutorily charged with the responsibility of providing meals to homeless people has refused to provide meals to homeless people. Relying on a federal law that grants to "any person the right to sue a federal agency for its violations of federal law" Wanda sues the federal agency, seeking an injunction requiring the agency to comply with its statutory obligations and provide meals to homeless people. The agency moves to dismiss her complaint on the ground that she lacks standing. What result?

Answer: Wanda lacks standing; her complaint will be dismissed. She has suffered no personal injury in fact—her injury consists of observing other people's distress, or, alternatively, suffering the knowledge that the agency is acting illegally. Both conditions are insufficient to establish personal injury in fact—the first because it is so gossamer as not to constitute injury, the second because it is so general that it is not a *personal* injury. Even if the first of these "injuries" sufficed it would not likely be regarded as fairly traceable to the agency action, since Wanda's discomfort at the plight of homeless people would likely remain even after the agency had supplied meals. Third party standing will not suffice—the rights of the homeless are not so inextricably linked to Wanda that she is simultaneously asserting her rights and their rights, nor are the homeless persons' rights so impaired that they cannot assert them independently. The federal law purporting to grant standing is unconstitutional as applied here because the core elements of standing—injury in fact, causation, and redressability—are constitutionally required as a predicate for federal court jurisdiction.

Question: The state of Mandala has enacted a statute prohibiting the possession or use of tobacco. The National Association for Smokers' Rights, an unincorporated association of tobacco smokers dedicated to preserving the rights of smokers, sues Mandala state officials in federal court to enjoin enforcement of the law on the grounds that it is a denial of substantive due process. Does the Association have standing to bring this claim?

Answer: The Association has no standing in its own right, since it has suffered no injury to itself, only to its "abstract social interests." But the Association may assert its members' interests since they would have standing independently, the members' interests asserted are germane to the Association's purpose, and neither the claim nor the requested relief requires the members' participation in the suit.

Question: Congress is debating a bill prohibiting anyone who has been a United States citizen for less than ten years from holding office in or employment by the federal government. While the bill is pending in Congress, Representative Phlegm, who has been a United States citizen for seven years, files suit in federal court against the Speaker of the House, seeking a declaration that the bill is unconstitutional. The Speaker moves to dismiss. What result?

Answer: The suit will be dismissed. It seeks an advisory opinion because the issue is abstract and hypothetical. In addition, Representative Phlegm's claim is not yet ripe. He has not yet suffered harm, is not faced with a specific present objective harm, and is not even under a threat of specific future harm until the bill becomes law.

Question: As in years past, on December 15 the City of Gotham erects a large illuminated Latin cross on its city hall. The next day, on behalf of its members, the Association for Separation of Church and State sues the city in federal court on the ground that the display violates the First Amendment's clause prohibiting governmental establishments of religion. The Association seeks to enjoin the city from further display of the cross. The cross is removed promptly on New Year's Eve. On January 2, the city moves to dismiss the complaint on grounds of mootness. What result?

Answer: Although the plaintiff's stake in the controversy has ended because the injury has ceased, the problem is capable of repetition, yet evading review. The two-week display is too short a period for full litigation of the merits of the dispute and, since the display seems to be a regular practice of the city, there is a reasonable expectation that the plaintiff will again be subjected to the same problem.

Question: A President is elected and takes office. The President was born in Iran to an American mother. Her father is unknown. The President signs into law a new income tax statute. A taxpayer refuses to pay his taxes due under the new law and defends the resulting prosecution on the ground that the law is invalid because the President is not constitutionally eligible to hold the office of President, since she is not a "natural born Citizen" of the United States. What result?

Answer: The taxpayer's contention almost certainly raises a nonjusticiable political question. While resolution of the issue of whether the President is a "natural born Citizen" is not demonstrably textually committed by the Constitution to another branch for decision, and while there may be judicially cognizable standards for decision of the question, the effect of a judicial declaration that an incumbent President is not entitled to be President is so destabilizing that the case presents "an unusual need for unquestioning adherence to a political decision already made" and would create "the potentiality of embarrassment from multifarious pronouncements by various departments" on the issue.

EXAM TIPS

- **Pervasive Issues.** Issues of the scope of judicial review pervade constitutional law but are not usually tested in isolation. *Be alert:* Many of these issues can occur in almost any question.

- **Adequate and Independent State Grounds.** Though not frequently tested, watch out for this if the exam problem poses a constitutional issue coming to the Supreme Court from a *state's highest court.* If the state court decided the issue on adequate and independent state grounds (and that disposition does not itself raise a separate federal constitutional issue) the Supreme Court has no business reviewing the matter.

- **Eleventh Amendment.** These issues of state immunity from suit in federal court are usually covered in the course on Federal Courts. If relevant to your course, check to see if the case is against the state itself (barred by the Eleventh Amendment) or against a state official seeking injunctive relief (permitted by the Eleventh Amendment). If the case is against the state, check to see if Congress has validly abrogated the state's Eleventh Amendment immunity or if the state has waived its immunity.

- **Congressional Restriction of Federal Court Jurisdiction.** Congress may restrict or eliminate the jurisdiction of the lower federal courts. To an uncertain extent Congress may restrict the appellate jurisdiction of the Supreme Court (but may not expand it beyond the limits of Article III). A common exam question is to pose a federal statute that restricts the Supreme Court's appellate jurisdiction over a specified subject; e.g., abortion.

- **Standing.** Every question has a *potential* standing issue. Make sure the plaintiff has suffered actual or immediately threatened personal injury in fact caused by the action complained of, and that can be redressed by courts.

- **Advisory Opinions.** Make sure that the controversy itself is real, concrete, involves true adversaries, and is not just a feigned case to pose a hypothetical question.

- **Ripeness and Mootness.** Make sure the case needs to be decided—future events will not make decision unnecessary, nor have past events made decision unnecessary.

- **Political Questions.** Make sure the issue presented is not a political question. Most issues aren't. A political question is most likely to occur when the issue is the proper separation of powers among the three federal branches.

- **Abstention.** Abstention is rarely covered in Constitutional Law. If relevant to your course, check to be sure there is no issue of *Younger* abstention—federal court interference in ongoing state criminal proceedings or civil matters involving an important state interest—or *Pullman* abstention—the answer to a federal constitutional issue raised in federal court depends upon resolution of an unsettled point of state law.

3

FEDERALISM, THE SUPREMACY CLAUSE, AND THE "NECESSARY AND PROPER" CLAUSE

CHAPTER OVERVIEW

This chapter examines the nature of federalism, constitutional sources of and limits upon the powers of the national and state governments, the relationship between federal and state law, and the broad power of Congress to select the means to execute its powers. The key points in this chapter are:

- **Federalism:** The United States is a federal system, with powers divided between the national government and the state governments.

    — **Powers of the National Government:** The federal government has only the powers enumerated in the Constitution (the "power-granting" provisions), limited by specific constitutional prohibitions upon the exercise of those powers (the "rights-protecting" provisions).

    — **Powers of the State Governments:** States possess a general "police power" (the power to act for public welfare), except as limited by the Constitution, valid federal law, or the state constitution.

    — **Concurrent or Exclusive Power:** Some federal powers may be exercised also by the states but some belong exclusively to the national government.

- **The Supremacy Clause:** Federal statutory and constitutional law is supreme and binds the states.

    — **Preemption:** Federal law displaces state statutory or constitutional law whenever Congress so intends. Congress may expressly state its intention to displace state law or such intention may be inferred from the federal legislation. That intention is inferred when there is an **actual conflict** between federal and state law or when the nature and extent of the federal law implies a congressional intent to **occupy the field** exclusively.

— **The "Necessary and Proper" Clause:** Congress has the power to use all necessary and proper means to execute the powers of the federal government. So long as the means employed by Congress are **rationally related** to an enumerated power of the federal government the courts will not invalidate the legislation as unnecessary or improper.

A.   WHAT FEDERALISM MEANS

1.   Dual Governments: One National Government, Many States

The United States is a **federal** government. People often refer to the national government, seated in Washington, D.C., as the "federal government." Strictly speaking, that is a bit of a misnomer. A federal government consists of both a national government and some number of regional, state, or provincial governments. In a federal system, the total permissible powers of government are divided between the national government and the regional governments. The Constitution allocates the respective powers of our national government and the state governments by enumerating a limited set of powers that the national, or federal, government may exercise, and prohibiting the states from exercising some powers. All other powers are left to the states, subject to how much power the people of each state are willing to give their state governments. That basic structural point is explicitly reinforced by the Tenth Amendment, which declares that the powers neither given to the federal government nor barred from the states are reserved for the states. Many of the powers of the federal government may also be exercised **concurrently** by the states. Other federal systems divide powers differently.

a.   **The problem of enforcing federalism.** Because the national (federal) government has only its constitutionally enumerated powers the question of when the federal government has exceeded its powers is necessarily a question of constitutional law. Building on *Marbury,* the Court considered and decided these issues virtually from the beginning of the nation. Beginning in 1937, however, the Court began to adopt standards of review that are very deferential to Congress's judgment about the scope of its constitutionally assigned powers. The result is that, until recently, the Court has all but abandoned meaningful judicial review over federalism. Some applaud this change on the grounds that the question of the proper allocation of powers ought to be left to the national political process. See Choper, Judicial Review and the National Political Process (1980). An ever-present tension thus pervades the question of the constitutional allocation of power between the national governments and the states. Is the proper allocation to be resolved judicially, as with all other matters of constitutional law, or is it to be resolved politically?

b. Should federalism be judicially or politically enforceable? The principal value of federalism is that it enhances liberty and autonomy, by permitting state-by-state experimentation with government, thus enabling public policy to be tailored to local needs. The question is whether federalism is better preserved by courts or the political process.

i. Politically enforceable. Those who argue that federalism should be politically enforceable usually cite Federalist No. 46, in which Madison argued that if the people should eventually prefer the federal government to exercise power "the people ought not surely to be precluded from giving most of their confidence where they may discover it to be due." They argue that the preferences of the people, expressed in their congressional representatives, ought to govern power allocations between Congress and the States. Some also claim that the Court's negation of congressionally ordered power arrangements puts the Court in opposition to the democratic will in a way that is untenable, and thus saps the Court of its practical power to preserve individual rights through judicial review.

ii. Judicially enforceable. Those who argue for judicially enforceable federalism point to the present powers of the federal government and contend that the resulting picture is a bloated caricature of the original scheme. They contend that the Court has simply abandoned judicial review of federalism, thus permitting Congress to decide the scope of its own power. Because Congress rarely curbs itself federal power has ballooned, thus stifling innovative state governance and depriving people of the opportunity to choose differing legal regimes.

2. Powers of the National Government

a. Limited to enumerated powers. The national, or federal, government is a government of limited powers. It may only exercise those powers specifically given to it under the Constitution. Those enumerated powers may be thought of as "power-granting" provisions of the Constitution, since without them the national government would lack power to do anything. Congress has no power to legislate simply because it perceives a problem that it thinks needs to be fixed. Congress may not simply legislate for the general well-being of the country, no matter how important the issue. Instead, the federal government may act *only* if each statute or regulation comes within the scope of a specific, enumerated power of the national government.

Example: Congress decides that a national minimum wage is a good idea. Congress may not enact such a law simply because it thinks it will be for the general welfare of the nation. It must justify the law as a legitimate use of its power to regulate interstate commerce. See *United States v. Darby,* discussed infra. See also discussion of general welfare in relation to the taxing and spending powers, infra.

b. **Limited by constitutional prohibitions on governmental power.** The powers of the national government are also curbed by a number of specific prohibitions that the Constitution places upon the use of otherwise legitimate power, most of which are contained in the Bill of Rights and other constitutional amendments.

Example: Suppose Congress enacts legislation that bans the interstate shipment of books for resale. While this is surely a regulation of interstate commerce (and thus apparently within the power of Congress) the First Amendment prohibits Congress from making any law "abridging the freedom of speech, or of the press."

These specific prohibitions upon governmental power may usefully be thought of as the "rights-protecting" provisions of the Constitution. Both the "rights-protecting" and "power-granting" provisions of the Constitution preserve personal liberty by restricting the scope of government action upon the people.

c. **Specific powers of the federal government**

i. **Congress.** The powers of Congress are mostly in Article I, §8, which enumerates a long list of specific powers. Among them are the following important powers:

- lay and collect **taxes**

- **spend** for the general welfare

- **borrow** money

- provide for **national defense**

- **declare war**

- regulate **interstate and foreign commerce**

- **coin money** and regulate the money supply

- establish a **uniform system of weights and measures**

- regulate **immigration**

- regulate **bankruptcy**

- establish and maintain a **postal service**

- regulate the issuance of **patents and copyrights**

- **establish federal courts**

- regulate federal **military reservations** and the **District of Columbia.**

Another very important power given Congress is the power to use any means **"necessary and proper"** for executing its enumerated powers and the other powers of the federal government. This is a key power, though *by itself it gives Congress no power.* It is simply a **"means-enabling"** power, useless without the specified **ends** toward which Congress may act. Congress also has some powers that come from other parts of the Constitution, e.g., the exceptions and regulations power of Article III (which enables Congress to control the jurisdiction of federal courts), the power to regulate territories and other federal property (Art. IV, §3), and various power-granting provisions contained in the amendments. The most important of the latter are §§2 of the 13th and 15th Amendments, and §5 of the 14th Amendment, each of which gives Congress power to enforce, by appropriate legislation, the provisions of the relevant amendment. Most of these powers will be discussed in detail in Chapters 4-6, infra.

ii. **President.** The President's powers are mostly collected in Article II. The principal powers include:

- the power to **veto** or **sign bills** into law

- **executing the laws**

- **appointing** judges, diplomats, and other principal federal officers

- acting as **Commander-in-Chief** of the armed services

- granting **pardons**

- **extending diplomatic recognition** to foreign nations.

iii. **The judiciary.** Virtually all of the judicial power of the United States is specified by Article III, which enumerates a number of heads of jurisdiction. Chapter 2 discusses judicial review and the various constitutional and prudential limits upon that keystone power of the courts.

d. **Implied powers of the federal government.** In theory, there should be *no* implied powers of the national government. Nevertheless, one very important power—the power to control **foreign relations**—has been implied from the structure of the Constitution to belong exclusively to the federal government. See Chapter 5, infra.

e. **Concurrent and exclusive powers.** Some of the powers of the federal government belong exclusively to the federal government and may not be exercised by states. Some examples of exclusively federal powers are the power to coin money or to declare war. Other powers are shared *concurrently* with the states, meaning that both the national government and the states may exercise these powers. Examples include the imposition of taxes, the power to spend for the general welfare, and regulation of interstate commerce. Of course, when federal law and state law conflict in an area of concurrent power federal law displaces the state law. This is the product of the supremacy clause, discussed in section B of this chapter, infra.

3. **Powers of the State Governments**

Unlike the national government, state governments possess a general **''police power''**—the power to do anything related to public health, safety, welfare, or morals, limited only by the following sources:

- the *federal Constitution,*

- *valid federal legislation* enacted pursuant to constitutional authority, and

- the *state's own constitution*.

These limitations will be considered in turn.

a. **Limitations imposed directly by the Constitution.** There are two main sources of direct constitutional limits imposed upon the states.

  i. **Article I, §10.** Article I, §10 contains a list of sovereign powers that the states are specifically prohibited from exercising. States may not engage in war, enter into treaties, coin money, grant titles of nobility, enact bills of attainder, ex post facto laws, or laws impairing contractual obligations. Without the consent of Congress, states may not enter into interstate compacts, maintain military forces, or impose tariffs.

  ii. **Rights-protecting provisions.** States are also forbidden from using their otherwise legitimate power to infringe most of the individual rights guaranteed by the Constitution. This is the product of **''in-corporation,''** a Court-created doctrine that interprets the 14th Amendment's due process clause as ''incorporating'' most of the rights-protecting provisions of the Bill of Rights. Incorporation is discussed in detail in Chapter 8, infra.

b. **Limitations imposed by federal law.** When Congress validly enacts legislation that conflicts with state law, or is intended to displace state law, the supremacy clause of Article VI, cl. 2, mandates that federal law govern. The displacement of state law does not occur directly by the Constitution without congressional action. Once Congress has acted the supremacy clause dictates that federal law displaces state law. See section B of this chapter, infra.

c. **Limitations imposed by state constitutions.** The people of each state remain free to decide how much power, and of what kind, to delegate to their state governments. Their device for doing so is the state constitution. If the state constitution contains no restrictions upon the power of the state government, the only limits will be those imposed by federal statutory and constitutional law. However, every state's constitution contains a set of rights-protecting provisions, some more expansive than the rights-protecting provisions of the federal Constitution. Thus, the powers of every state government are also limited by its state constitution.

B. THE SUPREMACY CLAUSE

1. Overview

Article VI, cl. 2, provides that the "Constitution, and the Laws of the United States which shall be made in Pursuance thereof, and all treaties made, or which shall be made under the Authority of the United States, shall be the Supreme Law of the Land; and the Judges in every State shall be bound thereby, any Thing in the Constitution or Laws of any State to the Contrary notwithstanding." This compound sentence packs a lot of legal punch. It makes federal constitutional law the highest trump of all law, enables Congress to displace state statutory and constitutional law, and makes explicit that state judges are bound by paramount federal law. The President and the Senate, by negotiation and ratification of treaties, also may displace state statutory and constitutional law. A number of important conclusions flow from these propositions.

2. Preemption of State Laws

Congress may displace, or **preempt,** state law whenever it intends to and is acting within the scope of its constitutionally enumerated powers.

a. **Intent of Congress controlling.** The Court repeatedly states that the "question whether a certain state action is pre-empted by federal law is one of congressional intent." See, e.g., *Gade v. National Solid Waste Management Ass'n,* 505 U.S. 88 (1992), quoting *Allis-Chalmers Corp. v. Lueck,* 471 U.S. 202, 208 (1985). That intent may be stated expressly in the statute or may be implied from "the structure and purpose of the statute." Id. However, since the Court consistently presumes that "Congress did not intend to displace state law," proof of congressional intent to preempt state law must be "clear and manifest." *Maryland v. Louisiana,* 451 U.S. 725, 746 (1981); *Rice v. Santa Fe Elevator Corp.,* 331 U.S. 218 (1947).

    b. Express preemption. Even when Congress has clearly declared its intent to preempt state law, problems may arise in deciding whether a particular state law is one that Congress intended to preempt.

 # EXAMPLE AND ANALYSIS

Congress enacted ERISA, a comprehensive statute regulating employee benefits. ERISA expressly preempts all state laws insofar as they relate to any employee benefit plan covered by ERISA. ERISA also explicitly states that by preempting state law it does not intend to impair any federal law. In Title VII of the 1964 Civil Rights Act Congress barred sex discrimination in employment and created an enforcement scheme that relies heavily upon state courts and complementary state law. New York's Human Rights law prohibits, as a form of sex discrimination in employment, employers treating pregnancy differently from other occupational disabilities under an employee benefits plan. In *Shaw v. Delta Air Lines,* 463 U.S. 85 (1983), the Court held that New York's law was one relating to covered employee benefits plans, but that the New York law was saved because of ERISA's exception to prevent impairment of other federal law.

"Such cases may pose complex questions of statutory construction but raise no controversial issues of power." Tribe, at 479.

    c. Implied preemption. Courts look primarily to the structure and purpose of the statute to determine whether Congress impliedly intended to preempt state law. Courts will find implied preemption under two circumstances, known as **field preemption** and **conflict preemption.**

        i. Conflict preemption. Conflict preemption occurs when courts determine that there is an *actual conflict* between state and federal law. An actual conflict is seen to be present whenever it is **impossible to comply with both federal and state law** or the state law "**stands as an obstacle** to the accomplishment and execution of the full purposes and objectives of Congress." *Hines v. Davidowitz,* 312 U.S. 52 (1941). Conflict preemption also occurs when the actual conflict is between state law and federal agency regulations. *Hillsborough County v. Automated Medical Laboratories,* 471 U.S. 707, 713 (1985).

            (a) Impossibility of dual compliance. As the test indicates, these cases are fairly straightforward. When it is impossible to comply with both state and federal law, state law is implicitly preempted by federal law. See *McDermott v. Wisconsin,* 228 U.S. 115 (1913).

   (b) State law as an obstacle. When state law is in conflict with
   the specific objectives underlying the federal law it will be
   treated as an "obstacle" to the federal objectives and
   preempted.

 # EXAMPLES AND ANALYSIS

Example: Florida law denied unemployment benefits to any person unemployed as a result of a labor dispute. That provision was relied on by a Florida agency to deny benefits to an applicant fired because she had filed unfair labor practice charges with the NLRB. The Court concluded that, as applied, the Florida law was an obstacle to the federal objectives of encouraging compliance with and ensuring enforcement of federal labor laws. *Nash v. Florida Industrial Comm'n,* 389 U.S. 235 (1967).

"Obstacle" conflict preemption may also be found even when both federal and state law share a common goal, if the state law "interferes with the methods by which the federal statute was designed to reach that goal."

Example: After Massachusetts enacted a law generally barring state agencies from purchasing goods or services from companies doing business with Burma, Congress enacted a statute that authorized the President to impose similar economic sanctions against Burma and to lift those sanctions if Burma should substantially improve its human rights practices and commitment to democratic governance, or if American national security should so dictate. In *Crosby v. National Foreign Trade Council,* 120 S. Ct. 2288 (2000), the Court ruled that the Massachusetts law was impliedly preempted since the state law was an obstacle to the accomplishment of the intended purpose and natural effect of the federal law in three ways: (1) the state law undermined presidential discretion to lift sanctions, (2) interfered with the congressional decision to limit economic pressure against Burma to a specific range, and (3) was at odds with the President's authority to speak for the nation in formulating an international strategy to deal with Burma.

But "obstacle" conflict preemption will not be found because state law is simply in "general tension with broad or abstract goals that may be attributed to various federal laws or programs." Tribe, at 487.

Example: Montana imposed a severance tax on coal removed from the ground. Montana coal miners claimed that the tax was in actual conflict with federal objectives to encourage the production and use of coal, because the tax made coal more costly. The Court rejected this argument. The Court agreed that several federal statutes expressed a general congressional purpose to encourage coal use, but concluded that state laws that are relatively mild and indirect impediments to "general expressions of 'national policy'" are not, for that reason alone, in sufficient conflict with federal law to warrant a finding of "obstacle" conflict preemption. *Commonwealth Edison Co. v. Montana,* 453 U.S. 609 (1981).

---

ii. **Field preemption.** Field preemption occurs when courts determine that Congress impliedly intended to "occupy the field" so fully that it "left no room for the States to supplement it." This unexpressed intent of Congress can be detected in several differing ways: (1) when federal regulation of a field is "so **pervasive** as to make reasonable the inference that Congress" intended to displace state regulatory authority, (2) when the federal law "touch[es] a field in which the **federal interest is so dominant** that the federal system will be assumed to preclude enforcement of state laws on the same subject," and (3) when "the **object sought to be obtained** by the federal law and the **character of obligations imposed** by it may reveal" a congressional intent fully to occupy the field. *Rice v. Santa Fe Elevator Corp.,* 331 U.S. 218 (1947). The effect of field preemption is to disable the states from *any* regulation of the field, even if the state law is consistent with and supplementary to the federal law. If an activity within the field is unregulated by Congress it may not be regulated by the states, thus creating a "regulatory vacuum."

(a) **Pervasive federal regulation.** Where the federal regulatory scheme consists of multiple and comprehensive laws governing virtually every activity within a given field, courts are likely to find field preemption.

Example: Congress has repeatedly regulated the field of unionized labor relations. When a discharged union worker claimed that his discharge was wrongful under state law, and that claim depended on the worker's interpretation of the labor contract's union security clause, the Court concluded that federal statutory regulation of collective bargaining was so pervasive that Congress had occupied the field, thus ousting state law. *Amalgamated Assoc. of Street, Elec. Ry. & Motor Coach Employees v. Lockridge,* 403 U.S. 274, 296 (1971).

Courts are far less likely to find field preemption when the "pervasive regulation" is created not by statute but by rules adopted by a federal agency, since such preemption would be "virtually tantamount to saying that whenever a federal agency decides to step into a field, its regulations will be exclusive." *Hillsborough County v. Automated Medical Laboratories,* 471 U.S. 707, 717 (1985). Remember, it's the *congressional* intention that counts. Because field preemption creates a regulatory vacuum—activities within the field unregulated by Congress may not be regulated by the states—courts are apt to define the field to correspond with the extent of actual federal regulation.

 ## EXAMPLE AND ANALYSIS

California refused to permit new nuclear power generation plants until a state agency had determined that the United States has approved and there existed a demonstrated method for the disposal of nuclear waste produced by power generation. PG & E, a power utility, challenged the validity of the condition as impliedly preempted by the federal Atomic Energy Act. The Court concluded that Congress intended to occupy the field of the "safety aspects involved in the construction and operation of a nuclear plant," but also concluded that Congress had done nothing to regulate the economic questions of nuclear power. "It is almost inconceivable that Congress would have left a regulatory vacuum." Thus, the Court read the field of nuclear power plant safety so narrowly that it excluded California's condition, which the Court regarded as an attempt by California to regulate the economic rather than safety aspects of nuclear power generation. *PG & E v. State Energy Resources Cons. & Dev. Commn.*, 461 U.S. 190 (1983).

(b) **Dominant federal interest.** Where the federal interest in regulation is "dominant" courts will also find field preemption.

 ## EXAMPLES AND ANALYSIS

Example: Pennsylvania enacted an Alien Registration Law that required all aliens resident in Pennsylvania to register with the state. A year later Congress enacted the Alien Registration Act of 1940, requiring all aliens in the country to register with the federal government. Relying on the strong federal interest in immigration and naturalization the Court barred enforcement of the Pennsylvania law, finding the field preempted by federal law. *Hines v. Davidowitz*, 312 U.S. 52 (1941).

But there is an established presumption against any such finding when Congress legislates "in a field which the States have traditionally occupied."

Example: Recall that the Court in *PG & E* concluded that through the Atomic Energy Act Congress intended fully to occupy the field of nuclear power safety. Karen Silkwood, an employee at a nuclear power plant operating in compliance with federal nuclear safety regulations, was seriously injured by escaping plutonium radiation. She brought a state law tort claim against the power plant operator and obtained compensatory and punitive damages. The Court rejected the contention that state tort law was preempted with respect to injuries suffered in connection with nuclear power generation, confining the occupied field to the substantive issues of nuclear safety rather than including tort remedies for injuries attributable to nuclear power generation. *Silkwood v. Kerr-McGee Corp.,* 464 U.S. 238 (1984).

3. Other Aspects of the Supremacy Clause

The supremacy clause also imposes other duties upon states. State courts must provide access to litigants with federal claims, to the extent the state permits analogous state claims to be heard in state court and the federal courts have not been given exclusive jurisdiction. See *Testa v. Katt,* 330 U.S. 386 (1947). State judges are also obligated to apply federal law when it is properly raised.

C. THE SCOPE OF THE "NECESSARY AND PROPER" CLAUSE

Article I, §8, which enumerates the principal powers of Congress, gives Congress the power "[t]o make all Laws which shall be necessary and proper for carrying into Execution the foregoing powers, and all other Powers vested by this Constitution in the Government of the United States, or in any Department or Officer thereof." This clause gives Congress considerable power to select the *means* by which to accomplish the legitimate *ends* of the national government. It does *not* confer independent power on Congress to enact legislation it thinks is "necessary and proper."

1. *McCulloch v. Maryland,* 17 U.S. 316 (1819)

The meaning of the "necessary and proper" clause was settled by this famous case. The Bank of the United States was a national bank created by the United States. Although its purpose was laudable—to regulate the money supply—it was feared and loathed by state bankers and their allied politicians who claimed, with some justification, that the Bank's administration was corrupt. Maryland enacted a tax upon all banks in the state that were not chartered by the state. Although couched in general terms the law applied only to the Bank of the United States. The Bank refused to pay the tax and Maryland sued in state court to collect it. The Court ruled that Maryland's tax was unconstitutional.

a. The key questions. In striking down Maryland's tax Chief Justice Marshall, writing for the Court, answered two key questions.

- First, did Congress have the constitutional authority to create a national bank? Marshall concluded that Congress did possess that authority.

- Second, was Maryland constitutionally prohibited from taxing the Bank, an instrument of the national government? Marshall determined that it was prohibited from doing so.

The first issue raises the question of the scope of the means Congress may employ to execute its powers. The second question raises the problem of the existence and scope of implied constitutional prohibitions upon state power. That general issue pervades Chapter 6.

b. **Congressional authority to charter the Bank.** Marshall reasoned as follows to conclude that Congress possessed the power to charter a national bank. It is the nature of a constitution, suggested Marshall, that it will not "contain an accurate detail of all the subdivisions of . . . its great powers . . . , and of all the means by which they may be carried into execution. . . ." In an enigmatic truism that has assumed legendary status in American constitutional law, Marshall declared that "we must never forget that it is a constitution we are expounding." By this, Marshall presumably meant to imply that in interpreting the Constitution the Court should recognize the reasonable implications of the constitutional structure. Less abstractly, and as applied to *McCulloch,* Marshall thought the Court should validate the reasonable means chosen by Congress to execute its powers.

    i. **The meaning of "necessary."** Marshall did not have to rely on pithy aphorism alone; he also grounded his argument in the necessary and proper clause. He rejected Maryland's contention that "necessary" meant "absolutely necessary" or "indispensable" to the enumerated power. Rather, said Marshall: "Let the end be legitimate, let it be within the scope of the constitution, and all means which are appropriate, which are plainly adapted to that end, which are not prohibited, but consist with the letter and spirit of the constitution, are constitutional."

   ii. **Application of the necessary and proper clause.** Marshall then applied his interpretation of "necessary" by noting the various ways in which a nationally chartered bank could be of service to the legitimate ends of taxation, spending, borrowing, and maintaining the national defense. He illustrated other instances of means used by Congress to execute its enumerated powers. In execution of its power to establish a post office Congress could and did punish mail theft. To aid execution of all its legitimate powers Congress could and did impose criminal penalties for violation of valid federal laws. Finally, Marshall suggested that judicial scrutiny of the **degree of necessity** for legislation would violate separation of powers by inserting the courts into an area reserved for legislative discretion.

iii. **The "pretext" qualifier.** Although Marshall seemingly left the choice of legislative means almost entirely to Congress he qualified that discretion: "Should Congress, **under the pretext of executing its powers,** pass laws for the accomplishments of objects not entrusted to the government" the Court would be under a "painful duty . . . to say that such an act was not the law of the land." To apply this "pretext" qualifier requires some inquiry into congressional motive. The Court has spasmodically applied this pretext qualifier, but since 1937 it has fallen into disuse. See Chapter 4, infra.

c. **Federal immunity from Maryland's tax.** The Court then ruled that Maryland could not tax the Bank, a federal institution. It reasoned that taxation carried with it the power to destroy, that if states could exercise this power on the federal government they could effectively thwart valid federal powers, and that the supremacy clause implies sufficient immunity from state power to enable the federal government to exercise its legitimate powers. On a more theoretical level, the Court reasoned that because states represent only their own residents they may not tax the entire nation in the form of the federal government. Otherwise, a state would be tempted to tax others (the federal government) in order to confer benefits to itself. The Court's reasoning here is a source of the modern "representation-reinforcement" theory—the idea that the Court should interpret the Constitution to correct imperfections in representative government so that the outcomes from our political institutions will better reflect the people's preferences.

2.   Importance of *McCulloch*

McCulloch continues to be of enormous importance. So long as Congress employs a **means** that is **rationally related** to an **enumerated power of Congress** the Court will defer to the congressional judgment of the necessity and propriety of the means. In making this assessment, the Court will not generally inquire into the motives of Congress. Even if the congressional motive is to accomplish a constitutionally forbidden end the Court will not usually invalidate the legislation so long as the legislation is rationally related to a legitimate, albeit unintended, end. These propositions cannot be stated dogmatically because the "pretext" qualifier continues to lie dormant, almost never used but exuding a latent potential for judicial scrutiny of congressional motive. In general, only if Congress has selected some utterly fantastic, bizarre, or arbitrary means to execute its legitimate powers will the Court strike down legislation under the necessary and proper clause. As a consequence, there is virtually no meaningful judicial review of legislation under the necessary and proper clause.

REVIEW QUESTIONS AND ANSWERS

Question: Congress enacts a statute prohibiting all smoking of tobacco on any vehicle engaged in interstate transportation. Joe, a smoker, is prosecuted for violating the law and defends on the ground that the law exceeds Congress's powers. What result?

Answer: Joe loses. Congress has the power to regulate interstate commerce. Congressional power under the necessary and proper clause is limited to means that are rationally related to the accomplishment of legitimate ends. Because Congress may regulate interstate commerce its ban on smoking in vehicles engaged in interstate transport is surely rationally related to that legitimate federal power.

Question: Congress enacts a new antismoking statute—one that prohibits all smoking of tobacco anywhere, anytime. The law recites that a nationwide smoking ban is a "necessary and appropriate measure to achieve the general health and welfare of the nation." Joe, an unrepentant smoker, is again prosecuted for violating the law and defends on the ground that the law exceeds Congress's powers. What result?

Answer: Joe might prevail. Congress has no general power to legislate for the general health and welfare. Congressional power under the necessary and proper clause is limited to means that are rationally related to the accomplishment of legitimate ends. If this total smoking ban related *only* to a perceived need to improve health and welfare the necessary and proper clause would not help, since the means selected (the smoking ban) are not rationally related to a *legitimate* end.

Question: Congress has enacted an Immigration and Nationality Act that extensively regulates the conditions for entry into the United States, temporarily and permanently, and governs the conditions for obtaining and losing American citizenship. The State of Parsnip enacts a law that limits the issuance of drivers' licenses to legal residents of Parsnip and the United States. The Parsnip Department of Motor Vehicles is required to determine independently whether applicants for drivers' licenses are lawfully admitted to the United States and, if in the judgment of the Parsnip DMV, an applicant is not lawfully admitted to the United States, a report to that effect must be made to the United States Immigration and Naturalization Service. An applicant for a Parsnip drivers' license seeks an injunction of enforcement of the law on the ground that the Parsnip statute is preempted by federal law. What result?

Answer: The injunction will be granted in part and denied in part. The portion of the law that limits drivers' licenses to legal residents of both Parsnip and the

United States is not preempted by federal law. The INS statute does not expressly preempt the issuance of drivers' licenses, and there is neither conflict or field preemption. There is no impossibility of dual compliance, and the Parsnip limitation upon driver eligibility does not frustrate any specific policy of the federal government. The field that Congress has preempted is immigration and citizenship, not the use of those federally determined factors for determining driver eligibility. See, e.g., *DeCanas v. Bica,* 424 U.S. 351 (1976) (finding no preemption of a state law limiting unemployment compensation to lawful entrants into the United States).

However, the portion of the law that requires Parsnip officials to make their own independent determination of a drivers' license applicant's immigration status is preempted. Congress has preempted the field of immigration regulation because its regulation of that field is pervasive and the federal interest in immigration is dominant. Field preemption leaves no room for state action in the field.

EXAM TIPS

- **Federalism.** Federalism issues are tested by posing questions about specific allocations of power between the states and the federal government, usually ones that probe the outer limits of federal power. But you can't answer those questions with any sophistication unless you understand that the powers of the federal government are limited to those enumerated.

- **The Supremacy Clause.** This keystone principle undergirds constitutional law: **Validly enacted federal law is supreme and displaces conflicting state law.** The supremacy clause is the constitutional foundation for **preemption,** a doctrine sometimes tested in constitutional law. If the fact pattern presents a federal statute and a state law on the same general subject, you have a potential preemption issue. The issue in preemption is always **congressional intention.** Congress may expressly state its intent to preempt state law, or that intent may be inferred. This inference is drawn if there is an unavoidable conflict, if the state law is an obstacle to the accomplishment of a specific federal objective, or the federal regulation is so pervasive that Congress has "occupied the field."

- **The Necessary and Proper Clause.** A common error is to assert that Congress can enact some law under its "necessary and proper" power. ***Don't make this error!*** The necessary and proper clause gives Congress great discretion in selecting the **means** to achieve one of the specified **powers** of the federal government. That's all it does. It isn't an independent power—it only enables Congress to choose how to achieve some *other* federal power.

THE FEDERAL COMMERCE POWER

CHAPTER OVERVIEW

This chapter examines the scope of the congressional power to regulate **interstate, foreign, and Indian** commerce. This is the federal commerce power. For precision and to avoid the notion that Congress may regulate *all* commerce, it might usefully be thought of as the "IF&I" commerce power, but that usage is uncommon. The "IF&I" commerce power is usually called the **commerce power.** "Commerce" means "IF&I Commerce." The most important points in this chapter are:

- **Judicial Test for the Scope of the Commerce Power:** In general, Congress may validly regulate under its commerce power if all three of the following criteria are satisfied:

  — **Congressional Determination:** Congress has determined that the activity regulated is **in commerce,** or *substantially* affects commerce, and

  — **Rational Judgment:** The congressional determination is **rational,** and

  — **Reasonable Means:** The means chosen by Congress are **reasonably related** to its regulatory objective.

- **Practical Impact of the Judicial Test:** The test gives Congress extremely broad authority to decide for itself the extent of its commerce power. However, the Court will not defer to a congressional determination that an *intrastate noncommercial* activity substantially affects commerce. The Court will decide for itself whether such activities substantially affect commerce.

- **State Autonomy as a Limit on the Federal Commerce Power:** When Congress seeks to use the commerce power to **regulate the states,** principles of state autonomy, derived in part from the **Tenth Amendment,** limit the way Congress may use the commerce power.

— **Laws of General Application:** So long as Congress enacts legislation, otherwise valid under the commerce power, that applies equally to the states and private persons, courts will intervene to protect state autonomy only when there is an "extraordinary failure" of the national political process.

— **Laws That Apply Only to States:** When Congress uses its commerce power to regulate only the states, it **must:**

(1)   Do so with **unmistakable clarity**

(2)   Refrain from **unfairly singling out a state**

(3)   Not **deny a state participation in the national political process**

(4)   Not **interfere with a state's lawmaking process,** as, e.g., by compelling a state to enact federally prescribed legislation

(5)   Not **compel a state to administer a federal program.**

A.   THE COMMERCE CLAUSE

1.   Source of Federal Legislative Power

Article I, §8 provides that "Congress shall have Power . . . To regulate Commerce with foreign Nations, and among the several States, and with the Indian Tribes." Congress is given no power to regulate *commerce* as such; its power is limited to three distinct types of commerce. Nevertheless, for the sake of convenience, it is often said that Congress may regulate commerce. Foreign, interstate, or Indian commerce constitute all the commerce that Congress may regulate.

a.   Foreign commerce. This branch of the commerce power has been generously construed to include "transactions which either immediately, or at some stage of their progress, must be extraterritorial." *Veazie v. Moor,* 55 U.S. 568, 573 (1852). The power to regulate foreign commerce is not exclusively federal, even though foreign commerce has been described as "necessarily national" in character. *Lord v. Goodall Steamship Co.,* 102 U.S. 541, 544 (1880). The ability of states to regulate foreign commerce is, however, tightly constrained. See Chapter 6, Section G, infra.

b.   Indian commerce. The power to regulate commerce with Indians has been rendered largely redundant by judicial decisions expanding other sources of federal authority over Indian tribes. *Worcester v. Georgia,* 31 U.S. 515 (1832) (federal treaty power includes treaties with Indian tribes); *United States v. Kagama,* 118 U.S. 375 (1886) (inherent implied federal power exists to govern Indian affairs). The result is that Congress need not rely on its power over Indian commerce to regulate Indian affairs and relations with Indians. See Newton, 132 U. Pa. L. Rev. 195.

c.   **Interstate commerce.** The power to regulate interstate commerce is of central importance. It is the source of authority for most congressional legislation and, by implication, also a restriction upon state power to regulate interstate commerce. This chapter considers the commerce clause as an affirmative source of congressional authority. Chapter 6 considers the "negative implications" of the commerce clause—its role in limiting state power to regulate interstate commerce.

2.   Historical Note on the Development of the Commerce Power

Commerce clause doctrine is often divided into two distinct phases: before and after 1937. Prior to 1937 the Court exercised judicial review to strike down federal laws that were beyond the scope of the commerce power. After 1937, the Court continued to claim that it had the power to review the legitimacy of congressional regulation under the commerce clause, but employed standards for doing so that were so deferential to Congress's judgment of the scope of its own power that, in practice, it has amounted to an abandonment of judicial review. Since *United States v. Lopez* the Court has begun to revive pre-1937 doctrine. Thus, it is important to trace the development of commerce clause doctrine from *Gibbons v. Ogden,* the beginning, to its current state.

B.   DOCTRINE BEFORE 1937

1.   *Gibbons v. Ogden,* 22 U.S. 1 (1824)

Gibbons v. Ogden is the effective beginning of the constitutional law of the commerce clause.

a.   **Facts.** New York had granted to Fulton and Livingston a monopoly on steamboat navigation in New York waters. Fulton & Livingston granted Ogden a license to operate a steamboat between New York and New Jersey. Gibbons held a license from the United States to navigate a steamboat in "coastal trade" and was operating a steamboat between New York and New Jersey, in competition with Ogden. Ogden obtained an injunction in the New York courts restraining Gibbons from further operation of his steamboat in New York waters. Gibbons sought and obtained review in the Supreme Court.

b.   **Holding.** In an opinion by Chief Justice Marshall the Court reversed the New York courts, concluding that the federal statute under which Gibbons held his license was a valid exercise of the commerce power, and thus it preempted the conflicting New York monopoly statute upon which Ogden relied.

c. **Rationale.** The Court could have based its conclusion on a finding that the commerce clause gave to Congress **exclusive power** over commerce, but **it did not.** Marshall conceded that there "is great force in this argument" but did not adopt that reading of the commerce power. Instead, Marshall based the decision upon two conclusions: (1) **Congress could regulate navigation on New York waters to the extent that such navigation was part of interstate commerce,** and (2) **because Congress had so acted, its law displaced the conflicting New York monopoly law.**

   i. **Congress could regulate navigation.** In this part of his opinion, Marshall explained the scope of congressional power to regulate interstate commerce.

      (a) **Commerce defined.** Marshall first sought to define "commerce" and then to define "commerce among the several states." Commerce, said Marshall, "is traffic [—buying and selling—], but it is something more: it is . . . commercial intercourse." All of "America understands . . . the word 'commerce' to comprehend navigation." The Framers so understood it because the "power over commerce, including navigation, was one of the primary objects for which the people of America adopted their government."

      (b) **Commerce among the states.** Marshall then turned to the meaning of "commerce among the states," in order to determine whether Congress had the power to license vessels operating in New York waters. "Among the states," said Marshall, means "intermingled with." But this does not mean that the commerce power stops at state boundaries, for interstate commerce "may be introduced into the interior" of a state. So long as the intrastate activity is part of a commercial transaction involving another state, it is within interstate commerce. Marshall did not spell out in more detail how these transactions are to be identified and separated from purely intrastate ones. That task was deferred for later cases.

      (c) **Purely intrastate commerce.** Marshall recognized that commercial activity that is both "completely internal" to a single state and that does not "affect other states" is outside the scope of Congress's power to regulate commerce. The Constitution's "enumeration of the particular classes of commerce to which the power was to be extended presupposes something not enumerated, and that . . . is the exclusively internal commerce of a state."

   ii. **Federal law displaced conflicting New York law.** Having concluded that Congress could regulate interstate navigation occurring within New York, Marshall considered whether the federal law operated to displace New York law. First, he reiterated the supremacy of federal law. The power of Congress, "though limited to specified objects, is plenary as to those objects." Thus, the commerce power "is complete in itself, may be exercised to its utmost extent, and acknowledges no limitations, other than are prescribed by the constitution." To the extent that New York's law was in conflict with the federal licensing statute, the federal law must prevail. Marshall then concluded that New York's law was indeed in conflict with the federal law. Because Ogden's injunction of Gibbons was based on invalid New York law it was overturned and Gibbons was free to steam between New York and New Jersey.

iii.   **The "wisdom" and "discretion" of Congress.** In an oft-cited passage of his opinion, Marshall observed that, *within the legitimate scope of the commerce power,* "[t]he wisdom and the discretion of congress, their identity with the people, and the influence which their constituents possess at elections, are . . . the sole restraints on which they have relied, to secure them from . . . abuse" of the commerce power. Justice Thomas, in *United States v. Lopez,* argued that this means only that, so long as Congress is validly exercising its commerce power, the choice of how it may be exercised is entirely up to Congress. Justice Jackson, in *Wickard v. Filburn,* argued that Marshall's statement means that "effective restraints on [the] exercise [of the commerce power] must proceed from political rather than from judicial processes."

2.   Commerce and "Not Commerce"

In the years following *Gibbons* the Court often distinguished between activity that was commerce and that which was not commerce. The distinction was important because Congress may only regulate *commerce.* In a series of post-Civil War cases, the cases drew a clear distinction between manufacturing and commerce. "Manufacture is transformation—the fashioning of raw materials into a change of form for use. The functions of commerce are different. The buying and selling and the transportation incidental thereto constitute commerce." *Kidd v. Pearson,* 128 U.S. 1 (1888). In *United States v. E.C. Knight Co.,* 156 U.S. 1 (1895), the Court held that a monopoly of sugar *manufacture* did not constitute a monopoly of *commerce* in sugar. Congress, said the Court, could not regulate manufacturing monopolies because "[c]ommerce succeeds to manufacture, and is not a part of it."

Much the same view was taken of agriculture, mining, insurance, and other "precommercial" activity. Adopting a formal category of "commerce," however artificial, meant that entire categories of human industry were outside of the commerce power. This view ensured that congressional regulatory power over commerce did not become transmuted into a general legislative power. The categorical doctrine had some flexibility. Noncommercial acts that were **intended to affect commerce,** and that would **necessarily and immediately do so,** sufficiently affected commerce to be part of commerce, and thus subject to federal regulation. Thus, the Court applied federal anti-trust law to a local work stoppage because the strike was taken with intent "to restrain interstate commerce . . . and the restraint of such commerce was the necessary consequence of the acts and the immediate end in view." *Coronado Coal Co. v. United Mine Workers,* 268 U.S. 295 (1925). The Court eventually declared the entire "manufacturing/commerce" distinction un-sound, *Standard Oil v. United States,* 221 U.S. 1 (1911), but the concept continued to resonate.

3. **Interstate and Intrastate Commerce**

Even more important than the categorical distinction between commerce and noncommerce were the Court's various doctrines to distinguish when the regulation touched upon interstate commerce (and was valid) or reached only intrastate commerce (and so was invalid). The Court developed the five following approaches to this problem.

a. **Interstate movement of articles of commerce: The "commerce-prohibiting" technique of regulation.** In the late 19th and early 20th century, various political interest groups persuaded Congress to use its commerce power to accomplish a wide variety of regulatory objectives. Many of these objectives had little to do with commerce, as the Court understood the term, but much to do with regulating behavior in the interest of the health, welfare, or morals of the nation. Congress invoked its commerce power by simply **prohibiting the interstate movement** of specified items or persons.

   i. *Champion v. Ames (The Lottery Case),* 188 U.S. 321 (1903). Congress prohibited the interstate shipment of lottery tickets. The avowed purpose of the law was to suppress lotteries in order to maintain public morality. Champion was indicted for shipping a box of Paraguayan lottery tickets from Texas to California. He challenged the constitutional power of Congress to enact the law. The Court rejected his challenge, finding the law within Congress's power to regulate interstate commerce.

      (a) **Rationale.** Justice Harlan, writing for the Court, concluded first that lottery tickets were articles of commerce. Four Jus-tices, led by Chief Justice Fuller, dissented on this point. Then Harlan rejected the idea that the power to regulate did not extend to complete prohibition. But he did so by suggesting that Congress's power to prohibit interstate commerce might be tied to "the nature of the interstate traffic which [Congress sought] to suppress." Congress possessed the power to **pro-**

hibit "that which will harm the public morals," but Harlan reserved judgment as to whether Congress had the power to prohibit articles of commerce that were "useful or valuable." In short, Harlan held that the power to **regulate** commerce did not *invariably* include the power to *prohibit* commerce; only that the regulatory power over commerce included a power to prohibit interstate shipment of items harmful to public morals.

ii. **Valid applications of *The Lottery Case*.** Congress used its "commerce-prohibiting" technique to address a variety of perceived public harms. The Mann Act, which prohibits the interstate transport of women for immoral purposes, was upheld in *Hoke v. United States*, 227 U.S. 308 (1913). The Court also permitted the seizure of banned articles of commerce *after they had moved interstate*, as a necessary aid to the power to prohibit the movement in commerce of harmful articles of commerce.

 # EXAMPLE AND ANALYSIS

The Pure Food and Drugs Act prohibited the interstate shipment of impure food. A shipment of impure preserved eggs was seized after it had moved in interstate commerce, and the seizure was challenged on the ground that the shipment had passed out of interstate commerce. A unanimous Court rejected the argument, noting that the adulterated eggs were "outlaws of commerce," which "may be seized wherever found." The seizure "complete[d] the purpose" of the Act, which was "to prevent trade in [impure food] between the States by denying to them the facilities of interstate commerce." *Hipolite Egg Co. v. United States*, 220 U.S. 45 (1911).

iii. ***Hammer v. Dagenhart (The Child Labor Case)*,** 247 U.S. 251 (1918). Reacting to public clamor about the practice of child labor, Congress prohibited the interstate shipment of goods produced by children. The Supreme Court (5-4) held that Congress lacked power to enact the Child Labor Act. The Court distinguished the prior commerce-prohibiting cases by noting that in those cases (1) the articles of commerce prohibited were themselves noxious evils, and (2) the interstate shipment itself had been part of the evil Congress sought to suppress. Neither condition was true in *Dagenhart*. The articles of commerce—textiles—were themselves "useful or valuable" and the problem was not the interstate shipment of the textiles but the conditions of their production which, according to *E.C. Knight,* was manufacturing, not commerce. Accordingly, the Court concluded that Congress had no power to prohibit the interstate shipment of these articles of commerce.

(a) Judicial assessment of motive. In striking down the Child Labor Act, the Court assessed the motive of Congress in prohibiting interstate shipment of manufactured goods and concluded that Congress was motivated by an impermissible regulatory objective—controlling local conditions of manufacture. The Court did not explain why a congressional purpose to suppress lotteries was permissible while eliminating child labor was not. The Court did state that, if Congress could use the commerce-prohibiting technique to regulate intrastate, noncommercial activities, it would have the power to regulate anything in the name of commerce. That result, said the Court, was inconsistent with the constitutional plan of a federal government wielding only its limited, enumerated powers.

(b) Holmes's dissent. Justice Holmes's dissent has proven to be the more enduring, as his logic was later endorsed by the Court in *United States v. Darby,* infra, the case that overruled *Hammer v. Dagenhart.* Holmes argued that, so long as Congress did just what the Constitution permitted it to do, its actions ought be valid regardless of the indirect effect the legislation might have upon activities within the power of states to regulate. Holmes contended that Congress had simply regulated interstate commerce by prohibiting from interstate commerce designated articles of commerce. "The act does not meddle with anything belonging to the States. They may regulate their internal affairs and their domestic commerce as they like. But when they seek to send their products across the state line they are no longer within their rights." To Holmes, congressional motive was irrelevant, so long as the regulatory technique employed by Congress involved interstate commerce.

b. Regulation of activities "directly connected" to interstate commerce. Another doctrinal issue was the degree to which Congress could regulate local economic activities in order to achieve its undisputed power to regulate interstate commerce. The problem could be conceived in two ways.

- Was regulation of local economic activity a reasonable "means" to accomplishment of the "end" of regulating interstate commerce, and thus permitted under the necessary and proper clause?

- Or, was regulation of local economic activity permissible when the local activity was so "intermingled with" interstate commerce as to be part of the "deep streams" of interstate commerce? *Gibbons,* supra.

The Court developed two answers to these questions. One was practical and relied on economic realities: Congress could regulate local economic activity in order to **protect interstate commerce.** That answer is addressed in subsection c, infra. The other answer was formal and categorical: Only local activities that **directly affected** interstate commerce could be regulated by Congress. This subsection b deals with that answer.

 ## EXAMPLES AND ANALYSIS

Example: In *E.C. Knight* the Court rejected the contention that Congress could regulate a monopoly of sugar production, a local activity, because the production monopoly would inevitably produce a monopoly upon commerce in sugar. "Doubtless the power to control the manufacture of a given thing involves . . . the control of its disposition, but this is a secondary and not the primary" effect. "[A]lthough the exercise of [monopoly] power [over manufacturing sugar] may result in bringing the operation of commerce into play, it . . . affects it only incidentally and indirectly." *United States v. E.C. Knight Co.,* supra.

The Court's focus was upon a formal and logical connection between the regulated local activity and interstate commerce. The local activity must lead ineluctably to interstate commerce, in some lineal cause and effect manner, to support congressional regulatory power over the local activity.

Example: During the Great Depression Congress sought to impose minimum wages and prices upon a number of industries. Schechter, a poultry wholesaler in Brooklyn, contested the validity of these regulations as applied to him, because he bought poultry in New York City and sold only to New York City retailers. Although most of the poultry sold in New York City came from other states, and Schechter's wages and prices might have had an impact on interstate competitors, the Court thought these effects on interstate commerce were indirect, and thus beyond congressional power to regulate. *Schechter Poultry Corp. v. United States,* 295 U.S. 495 (1935).

Example: Another New Deal statute imposed maximum hours and minimum wages for coal miners. Even though nearly all the coal produced would be sold in interstate commerce, and the production of coal was vital to nearly all economic activity in the country, the Court struck down the act. The activity regulated—wages and hours in coal mining—was a local, precommerce, activity. Even though the **magnitude** of the effect of coal mining upon interstate commerce was enormous, there was no **direct, logical, and linear link** between the specific thing regulated—wages and hours in local coal production—and interstate commerce. *Carter v. Carter Coal Co.,* 298 U.S. 238 (1936).

---

c. **The "protective principle": The power to regulate local activities of instrumentalities of interstate commerce in order to protect interstate commerce itself.** Simultaneously with the development of the "commerce-prohibiting" technique and the "direct-indirect" distinction, the Court created a third doctrinal strand. The Court upheld congressional regulation of the *intrastate* activities of railroads and other "*instruments of interstate commerce*" in circumstances where the local actions had substantial physical or economic effects upon interstate commerce. The doctrine originated in *The Daniel Ball,* 77 U.S. 557 (1871), where the Court upheld the power of Congress to license ships operating exclusively within one state but engaged in transporting cargoes that had moved or would move across state lines. The exemplar of this approach is *The Shreveport Rate Case.*

   i. *The Shreveport Rate Case (Houston E. & W. Texas Ry. v. United States),* 234 U.S. 342 (1914). The Interstate Commerce Commission set maximum railroad freight rates for interstate shipment between Shreveport, Louisiana, and Texas cities. The Texas Railroad Commission established maximum railroad freight rates for traffic *entirely within Texas* that were lower than the interstate rates set by the ICC. Reasoning that the lower Texas rates discouraged interstate shipping the ICC ordered that this "price discrimination" against interstate commerce cease. The railroads argued that Congress lacked authority to regulate intrastate freight rates. The Court upheld the ICC order.

      (a) **Rationale.** Congress could regulate the "instruments of interstate commerce," and railroads were certainly such an instrument. As part of that power, Congress could regulate the *intrastate activities* of "instruments of commerce" so long as those activities had a **"close and substantial relation to interstate traffic."** Congress could regulate the intrastate activities of instruments of commerce whenever it was "necessary or appropriate" to do so in order to **protect interstate commerce.** This, in time, came to be known as the **"protective principle."** See also *Railroad Commission of Wisconsin v. Chicago, Burlington, & Quincy Railroad,* 257 U.S. 563 (1922) (upholding an ICC order requiring *all* Wisconsin freight rates be raised to conform to the interstate rates).

ii. **Other applications of the protective principle.** *The Shreveport Rate Case* relied upon an earlier line of cases upholding the power of Congress to regulate various intrastate activities of railroads engaged in interstate commerce. In *Southern Ry. v. United States*, 222 U.S. 20 (1911), the Court upheld a federal law requiring that all rail cars "used on any railroad engaged in interstate commerce" be equipped with various safety devices. Congress had the power to protect the physical safety of trainmen working in interstate commerce by requiring that even strictly local railcars of an interstate railroad have safety devices.

d. **The "stream of commerce" metaphor.** The Court also employed a metaphor as an aid in determining the scope of the commerce power. The Court described interstate commerce as a stream, or current. Once the stream of commerce had begun to flow, Congress could regulate it at any point, including intrastate eddies within that current. This was because the intrastate actions were **part of the stream of interstate commerce,** rather than simply affecting such commerce.

 EXAMPLES AND ANALYSIS

Example: Relying on the Sherman Antitrust Act, a trial court enjoined local meat dealers from fixing prices at the stockyards. The meat dealers contended that Congress could not validly regulate their price fixing, which took place entirely within a single state. The Court, per Justice Holmes, rejected the argument, noting that there was a constant stream of cattle between the states, and that "the purchase of the cattle [at a local stockyard] is a part . . . of such commerce." *Swift & Co. v. United States*, 196 U.S. 375 (1905).

Example: The federal Packers and Stockyards Act regulated the business practices of brokers and dealers at stockyards. The Court upheld the Act, noting that "stockyards are not a place of rest or final destination . . . but [are] a throat through which the current [of interstate commerce] flows." The actions of the brokers and dealers were found to be "essential," "necessary," and "indispensable" to the flow of interstate commerce. *Stafford v. Wallace*, 258 U.S. 495 (1922).

e. **The "dual sovereignty" doctrine.** Finally, the Court employed the "dual sovereignty" doctrine to confine the commerce power by describing a zone of state regulatory authority with which Congress could not interfere. The idea was simple: two sovereignties—federal and state—existed, and the federal power could not impinge upon the zone of state power. Because Congress only possesses limited powers, any construction of the commerce power that would transform it into a general legislative power is constitutional error. Thus, Congress may not use its commerce power to displace state authority over matters of purely local concern.

EXAMPLE AND ANALYSIS

Congress prohibited all sales of naphtha and illuminating oils that would ignite at less than 110 degrees F. A unanimous Court struck down the law on the ground that it was a "police regulation, relating exclusively to the internal trade of the States." *United States v. DeWitt,* 76 U.S. 41 (1870).

Note that *The Lottery Case* upheld "police regulations" that employed the commerce-prohibiting technique to suppress moral evils. The interstate shipment was a national, not a local, concern. But the "dual sovereignty" principle prevented Congress from using the commerce-prohibiting technique to regulate matters entirely of local concern.

EXAMPLE AND ANALYSIS

In *Hammer v. Dagenhart* the Court struck down a use of the commerce-prohibiting technique to suppress child labor because the purpose of the law was to regulate production of goods. "[T]he production of articles, intended for interstate commerce, is a matter of local regulation. [If] it were otherwise, all manufacture intended for interstate shipment would be brought under federal control to the practical exclusion of the authority of the States. . . . The maintenance of the authority of the States over matters purely local is as essential to the preservation of our institutions as is the conservation of the supremacy of the federal power in all matters entrusted to the Nation." *Hammer v. Dagenhart,* 247 U.S. 251 (1918).

C.   FRANKLIN ROOSEVELT VERSUS THE NINE OLD MEN

1.   The Threat to FDR's New Deal

The Roosevelt administration sought to counter economic depression by a variety of major governmental initiatives regulating economic activity. The principal source of federal power relied on to enact these laws was the commerce power. Roosevelt's lawyers argued that the "protective principle" of *The Shreveport Rate Case* was broad enough to support FDR's regulatory initiatives, contending that **any activity** that had a **close and substantial relationship to interstate commerce** could be regulated. They also urged that the stream of interstate commerce be conceived broadly, so that much local economic activity would be seen as attached to that current. The Court rejected these arguments in striking down key New Deal statutes.

 ## EXAMPLES AND ANALYSIS

Example: In *Schechter Poultry* the Court struck down the National Industrial Recovery Act, a comprehensive statute that effectively imposed price and wage controls on most American industries. Schechter, a Brooklyn poultry wholesaler who sold only to New York City retailers, bought all his poultry from a New York City market. But nearly all the poultry had come from other states. The Court held that Schechter's activities were not within the "stream of commerce" because that stream had come to an end when the poultry arrived in New York for its final destination. The Court also rejected the argument that Schechter's activities, while local, had a "close and substantial" relation to interstate commerce. There was no **direct relationship** between Schechter's wages and prices and interstate commerce. The protective principle remained confined to local actions of instruments of commerce. *Schechter Poultry Corp. v. United States,* 295 U.S. 495 (1935).

Example: In *Carter Coal* the Court struck down the Bituminous Coal Conservation Act, which set maximum hours and minimum wages for coal miners on the grounds that there was no direct, logical relationship between the hours and wages of coal miners (a local activity falling outside commerce) and interstate commerce in coal. *Carter v. Carter Coal Co.,* 298 U.S. 238 (1936).

The Court also invoked the "dual sovereignty" approach to strike down New Deal legislation.

Example: The Railroad Retirement Act of 1934 mandated that railroads engaged in interstate commerce establish retirement and pension plans for their workers. Despite the safety appliance cases the Court refused to use the "protective principle" to uphold the Act. Instead, the Court brushed aside the argument that pensions were "related to efficiency of transportation" and stated that since the purpose of the Act was to secure "the social welfare of the worker" it was "remote from any regulation of commerce." *Railroad Retirement Bd. v. Alton Railroad Co.,* 295 U.S. 330 (1935).

2. The Court-Packing Plan

After a landslide re-election triumph, FDR set about to "fix" the Court. He proposed legislation that would permit the President to appoint one new

Justice for each Justice over age seventy who had not resigned or retired, up to a maximum of fifteen Justices in all. Applied to the Court at the time, FDR would have had six new appointments, more than enough to tip the Court's decisions his way. At first, Roosevelt pretended that the reason for the proposal was to alleviate the burden of the workload. Nonsense, said Chief Justice Hughes, we're not overworked. FDR then admitted that the proposal was really intended to force changes in constitutional law, and that the amending process was just too cumbersome to serve his purposes. The proposal was widely condemned as a crass political expedient designed to alter the Constitution to serve FDR's political ends. When Roosevelt's Senate manager of the bill, Arkansas Senator Joseph Robinson, whom FDR had promised to appoint to the Court, died of a sudden heart attack the steam went out of the proposal and it was rejected. The battle for a compliant Court was lost, but Roosevelt won the war.

3. *NLRB v. Jones & Laughlin Steel Corp.:* **The ''Switch in Time That Saved Nine''**

While the Court-packing plan was still under debate, the Court decided the validity of the National Labor Relations Act (NLRA). The NLRA prohibited certain ''unfair labor practices,'' one of which was firing employees because of their union activity. The NLRB (created by the NLRA) sought an injunction against Jones & Laughlin to prevent it from continuing to fire union organizers. In *NLRB v. Jones & Laughlin Steel Corp.,* 301 U.S. 1 (1937), the Court (5-4), upheld the validity of the Act. Justice Roberts, author of the Court's restrictive opinion in *Alton Railroad,* supplied the crucial fifth vote, perhaps the ''switch in time that saved nine,'' as the wags of the day put it.

a. **Rationale.** The Court expanded the protective principle. Previously confined to those intrastate activities of ''instruments of commerce'' that bore a close and substantial relation to interstate commerce, the Court broadened its reach to include any intrastate activity that exerted a **substantial effect on interstate commerce.** The Court found such an effect due to the far-flung commercial activities of Jones & Laughlin. While it produced steel only in Pennsylvania, it employed great numbers of people in several different states, mined iron ore in Minnesota and Michigan, owned a shipping line to transport ore to Pennsylvania, maintained a nationwide distribution system, and shipped 75% of its manufactured steel outside of Pennsylvania. A work stoppage, said the Court, ''would have a most serious effect on interstate commerce.''

b. **Effect.** One immediate effect of *Jones & Laughlin* was to render useless the ''stream of commerce'' metaphor. No longer would the Court need to ponder the somewhat metaphysical question of when streams of commerce began and ended. That question was subsumed under the new **substantial economic effect** approach. The decision also raised the possibility that the ''dual sovereignty'' limit, reserving ''local concerns'' for exclusive regulation by states, might be ripe for abandonment. Politically, it signalled that Roosevelt had won in his contest of wills with the Court. His victory was cemented when shortly after the decision Justice Van Devanter, a dissenter in *Jones & Laughlin,* retired and was replaced by an ardent New Dealer, Senator Hugo Black of Alabama.

D. MODERN DOCTRINE

1. In General

The Court is generally extremely deferential to congressional judgment about the scope of the commerce power. But *United States v. Lopez* and *United States v. Morrison* signal a more active judicial role in defining the scope of the commerce power. The Court created one new doctrine and remodeled two old ones to support expanded review of congressional regulation under the commerce clause.

- In place of the old "protective principle" the Court created a **"substantial economic effects"** test.

- The Court abandoned the "dual sovereignty" limitation, thus freeing the **"commerce-prohibiting technique"** to serve any purpose.

- The Court also created a new doctrine, permitting Congress to regulate economic activities so long as their **"cumulative effect"** upon interstate commerce was substantial.

These doctrinal alterations will be considered in subsection 2.

a. The modern test: Deference to congressional rationality. Under the highly deferential modern judicial test Congress has validly used its commerce power if

- Congress has **determined** that the **regulated activity** either

    (1) **substantially affects commerce,** or

    (2) is actually **part of commerce,**

  and

- The congressional determination is **rational,**

  and

- The chosen means are **reasonably adapted** to reach the end.

  i. Congressional determination. "Congress normally is not required to make formal findings" concerning the connection between the activity regulated and commerce in order to invoke its commerce power. *United States v. Lopez,* 514 U.S. 549 (1995); *Perez v. United States,* 402 U.S. 146, 156 (1971). But when Congress fails to do so there is little basis apart from conjecture to evaluate the rationality of the congressional determination. The Court is then free to make its own determination, independent of Congress, whether the regulated activity substantially affects commerce.

ii. **"Part of" or "substantial effect" on commerce.** Activities are "part of" interstate commerce if Congress regulates or protects (1) the movement of people or things in interstate commerce (the "channels of interstate commerce," or (2) the instrumentalities of interstate commerce. Congress may regulate **intrastate activities** that have a **substantial effect** on interstate commerce, but Congress's judgment about the substantiality of the effect is not always controlling.

iii. **Rationality.** If Congress has made a determination that the regulated activity is part of or substantially affects interstate commerce the Court will defer to that judgment "if there is any rational basis for such a finding." *Hodel v. Virginia Surface Mining & Reclamation Ass'n,* 452 U.S. 264, 276 (1981). This means that if Congress acts on testimony or other factual understanding that provides rational support for Congress's judgment about the requisite connection between the regulated activity and commerce, the Court will find the legislation to be within the commerce power. But the Court will give no deference to Congress when it regulates noncommercial intrastate activities or fails to make factual findings supporting the substantial effect of regulated intrastate commercial activities on interstate commerce.

iv. **Means "reasonably adapted" to the end.** This element is a restatement of the *McCulloch* test of the scope of the necessary and proper clause. There is nothing unique about its application to the commerce clause.

b. **Limits to judicial deference.** There are three areas where the Court is less deferential to Congress in assessing the scope of the commerce power.

i. **State autonomy.** When Congress uses its commerce power to regulate the states, and only the states, the Court will examine more carefully the manner in which Congress has exercised that power. The Court insists that Congress state clearly its intention to use the commerce power to regulate the states and forbids Congress from using that power to compel the states to legislate in a prescribed fashion. See section E for extended discussion.

    ii. **Regulation of commercial intrastate activities.** Congress must make findings of fact to support its judgment that such activities substantially affect interstate commerce. Otherwise, the Court will decide this question on its own. See *United States v. Lopez.*

    iii. **Regulation of noncommercial intrastate activities.** When Congress regulates noncommercial intrastate activities the Court will determine the substantiality of the effect on interstate commerce, regardless of congressional fact-finding. See *United States v. Morrison.*

2. Activities That Have a "Cumulative Effect" on Interstate Commerce

Following the New Deal revolution the Court developed a new doctrine that greatly expanded the scope of the commerce power. So long as the *class* of activities regulated by Congress has a **substantial effect on interstate commerce** the law may be applied validly to a person whose **individual activities** have almost no impact on interstate commerce. This doctrine originated in *Wickard v. Filburn,* 317 U.S. 111 (1942).

    a. **The *Wickard* case.** Congress authorized a federal agency to impose limits on the amount of wheat that farmers could plant. Filburn, a farmer in Ohio, planted twelve more acres to wheat than he was permitted, harvesting 239 "excess" bushels of wheat, thereby incurring a "marketing penalty" of $117.11. Filburn attacked the validity of the enabling statute, contending that his activity—growing wheat primarily for use on his farm—was neither interstate nor commercial. The Court disagreed, upholding the legislation. The question, said the Court, was whether Filburn's activity, even if local and noncommercial, "exert[ed] a substantial economic effect on interstate commerce." It did. Even though the effect of Filburn's wheat on interstate commerce was trivial, the effect of Filburn's acts, "taken together with that of many others similarly situated, is far from trivial." Thus was born the idea that only the **cumulative effects** of individual actions will be used to assess the substantial effect of any activity upon interstate commerce. The cumulative effects doctrine simply means that the critical effect on interstate commerce is that of the **entire regulated activity,** not just the impact of one member of the regulated class on interstate commerce.

    b. **The *Perez* case.** When Congress enacted the Consumer Credit Protection Act, which prohibited "loan sharking," the practice of extending credit as a device to extort money by violence or threatened violence, it concluded that loan sharking "directly affect[ed] interstate and foreign commerce" and that loan sharking produced a "substantial part of the income of organized crime," an interstate activity. In *Perez v. United States,* 402 U.S. 146 (1971), the Court found the law to be within Congress's commerce power, resting its decision on two principles:

- Congress can regulate a **class of activities** that substantially affects interstate commerce "without proof that the particular intrastate activity against which a sanction was laid had an effect on commerce."

- Where the **class of activities** regulated is "within the reach of federal power, the courts have no power 'to excise, as trivial, individual instances' of the class." (quoting *Maryland v. Wirtz,* 392 U.S. 183 (1968)).

3. Activities That "Substantially Affect" Interstate Commerce

Title II of the 1964 Civil Rights Act prohibits racial discrimination by private persons offering public accommodations to interstate travelers or, in the case of restaurants, if a significant portion of the food served has moved in interstate commerce. These provisions were challenged and upheld in two landmark cases.

a. *Heart of Atlanta Motel v. United States,* 379 U.S. 241 (1964). A large motel in central Atlanta that catered to interstate guests (75% of its trade), located near two major interstate highways and that solicited guests nationwide, sought to invalidate Title II on the grounds that it exceeded the congressional power to regulate commerce. The Court upheld the Act, relying on congressional findings that local racial discrimination inhibited interstate travel by black Americans. Congress could regulate local racial discrimination in public accommodations because of its *substantial effect* on interstate travel and commerce. In an echo of the old "protective principle" the Court quoted *United States v. Women's Sportswear Mfrs. Assn.,* 336 U.S. 460 (1949): "[I]f it is interstate commerce that feels the pinch, it does not matter how local the operation that applies the squeeze."

b. *Katzenbach v. McClung (Ollie's Barbecue),* 379 U.S. 294 (1964). Ollie's Barbecue, a restaurant in Birmingham, Alabama, catered to a local trade, but because 46% of the meat it purchased had moved in interstate commerce it was subject to Title II. When Congress enacted the law it relied upon testimony that provided a rational basis for believing that racial discrimination by the class of actors of which Ollie's Barbecue was a part—restaurants who purchased a significant portion of their supplies from interstate sources—had a substantial effect on interstate commerce. Even though Congress made no such explicit finding, the testimony adduced in the deliberative process provided a "rational basis for [Congress to find] a chosen regulatory scheme necessary to the protection of commerce." At that point, said the Court, "our investigation is at an end."

c. **The outer limits of "affecting commerce."** The furthest the Court has pushed the logic of permitting Congress to regulate acts that "substantially affect'' interstate commerce occurred in dicta in *United States v. Darby,* infra. Congress required that all employees producing goods for interstate commerce be employed at prescribed minimum wages and for maximum hours. The Court upheld the validity of the law. As an alternative holding it reasoned that there was a substantial relationship between the requirement of minimum wages/maximum hours and a congressional objective of closing off interstate commerce to articles of commerce produced by workers under ''substandard'' conditions. In this holding, the Court did *not* find that the employment of workers at substandard wages and hours substantially affected interstate commerce; rather, it was enough that the employment restrictions substantially affected another valid commerce-based regulation—prohibition of the interstate shipment of goods produced by ''substandard'' working conditions. Congress could first use the ''commerce prohibiting technique'' as a **means** to the **end** of **regulating interstate commerce,** then regulate wholly local activities on the grounds that **such regulation** is a **means** to the **''end''** of **accomplishing the prior means**—prohibiting the interstate movement of specified articles of commerce.

Example: Suppose Congress first bans the interstate shipment of meat products. Then it bans the slaughter of any animal for purposes of food consumption. The first regulation is a valid use of the commerce-prohibiting technique. The ''means affecting means'' principle would justify the second regulation as substantially related to the first *regulation,* rather than as a regulation of an activity substantially affecting interstate commerce.

This possible sweeping commerce power has probably (but not definitely) been eliminated by *United States v. Lopez* and *United States v. Morrison.*

4. **Regulation of the ''Channels'' and ''Instrumentalities'' of Interstate Commerce**

Even before the New Deal revolution Congress had considerable leeway to regulate the instrumentalities of interstate commerce—transportation and communication. But its power to regulate the channels of interstate commerce—the interstate movement of articles of commerce and people engaged in commerce—was more problematic. *Hammer v. Dagenhart* ruled that Congress could not regulate the channels of commerce if its purpose for so doing was to accomplish an *ultra vires* objective. The New Deal Justices obliterated that limit in *United States v. Darby,* effectively giving Congress free rein to regulate the channels of commerce.

a. *United States v. Darby,* 312 U.S. 100 (1941). The federal Fair Labor Standards Act (1) barred the interstate shipment of goods produced other than in conformity with its minimum wage and maximum hour rules and (2) prohibited employment of people producing goods ''for interstate commerce'' except at the prescribed wage and hour conditions.

Darby alleged that the Act was outside the commerce power. The Court disagreed, upholding both aspects of the law.

    i. **Closing the channels of interstate commerce.** The Court overturned *Hammer v. Dagenhart,* ruling that Congress could regulate or close the channels of interstate commerce no matter what its motive or purpose might be. Congress's "motive and purpose" for regulating the channels of interstate commerce "are matters for the legislative judgment upon the exercise of which the Constitution places no restriction and over which the courts are given no control." So long as Congress regulates the movement of people or goods in interstate commerce it is free to do so for any reason whatever.

    ii. **Prohibiting employment at "substandard" conditions.** The Court upheld the ban on employment of workers making goods for interstate commerce on two theories. First, the Court concluded that the employment ban was a substantially related means to the valid end of closing interstate commerce to the products of substandard labor conditions. Second, the Court concluded that "substandard" labor conditions affected interstate commerce by giving the products of such labor a competitive advantage in the interstate marketplace.

  b. **Instrumentalities of interstate commerce.** Congress may freely protect the instrumentalities of interstate commerce.

5. *Lopez* **and** *Morrison:* **"Dual Sovereignty" Revived**

United States v. Lopez, 514 U.S. 549 (1995), and *United States v. Morrison,* 120 S. Ct. 1740 (2000), represent a partial revival of the dual sovereignty principle, by reducing the deference the Court gives to Congress concerning the scope of the commerce power.

  a. *Lopez.* When Congress enacted the Gun Free School Zones Act, which made the possession of a gun in or near a school a crime, it never considered the impact of the regulated activity on interstate commerce. Lopez, a high school senior in San Antonio, Texas, was convicted of possession of a loaded hand gun in his school and appealed on the ground that Congress lacked the power to enact the law. In *United States v. Lopez,* 514 U.S. 549 (1995), the Court voided the law as beyond Congress's commerce power. Writing for a 5-4 majority, Chief Justice Rehnquist emphasized two points:

      • When Congress invokes its commerce power to regulate activities affecting interstate commerce, **the effect on interstate commerce must be substantial.**

- If Congress adduces no evidence supporting the substantial effect on interstate commerce of the regulated activity the **Court will not defer to Congress's judgment** because it is impossible to know whether Congress had any rational basis for its judgment. The Court will not hypothesize a rational basis for the substantial effect on interstate commerce of the regulated activity.

Justices Kennedy and O'Connor concurred because the law "upsets the federal balance to a degree that renders it an unconstitutional assertion of the commerce power." This was deduced from three factors: (1) "neither the actors nor their conduct have a commercial character," (2) "neither the purposes nor the design of the statute have an evident commercial nexus," and (3) the law "seeks to intrude upon an area of traditional state concern." Justice Thomas also concurred, arguing that commerce ought to be given a more limited meaning and questioning the validity of the "substantial effects" test. Part of the problem with the "substantial effects" test, said Thomas, was the cumulative effects doctrine, which "has no stopping point. . . . [O]ne *always* can draw the circle broadly enough to cover an activity that, when taken in isolation, would not have substantial effects on commerce. . . ." Four Justices dissented on the grounds that the effects of guns in or near schools on interstate commerce was in fact substantial and that so long as Congress *could have made that finding* the Court should defer to Congress.

b. *Morrison.* In *United States v. Morrison,* 120 S. Ct. 1740 (2000), the Court ruled (5-4, with the same voting alignment as in *Lopez*), that the commerce power did not authorize Congress to enact the civil remedy provision of the Violence Against Women Act, 42 U.S.C. §13981, which creates a civil cause of action against "a person who commits a crime of violence motivated by gender." Congress had explicitly determined that gender-motivated violence had a substantial effect on interstate commerce but the Court did not defer to these findings by asking simply whether they were rational. Instead, the Court declared that these "findings are substantially weakened by the fact that they rely so heavily on a method of reasoning that we have already rejected as unworkable if we are to maintain the Constitution's enumeration of powers." The inherent weakness was the length of the causal chain—from the violent crime to "every attenuated effect upon interstate commerce." The Court rejected the idea that Congress could "regulate any crime as long as the nationwide, aggregated impact of that crime has substantial effects on employment, production, transit, or consumption. [Congress may not] use the Commerce Clause to completely obliterate the distinction between national and local authority. [The] Constitution requires a distinction between what is truly national and truly local." The Court also noted that the Act struck down in *Lopez* had "nothing to do with 'commerce' or any sort of economic enterprise, however broadly one might define those terms. . . . While we need not adopt a categorical rule against aggregating the effects of any non-economic activity . . . , thus far in our nation's history our cases have upheld Commerce Clause regulation of intrastate activity only where that activity is economic in nature."

c. **Post-*Lopez* and *Morrison* questions.** Here are some open questions produced by *Lopez* and *Morrison*.

- Will the Court defer to congressional judgment concerning the substantial effect on interstate commerce if Congress regulates a *commercial* intrastate activity but *makes no findings of fact concerning the activity's effect on interstate commerce*?

- What criteria will the Court use to distinguish commercial from noncommercial activities?

- What is the role for the cumulative effects or aggregation principle?

 # EXAMPLE AND ANALYSIS

Congress has made criminal both the destruction of an aircraft and theft from interstate shipments. See 18 U.S.C. §§32 and 659. In the former case Congress has validly acted to protect an instrumentality of interstate commerce. In the latter case Congress has validly protected both an instrumentality of interstate commerce and the channels of such commerce. 18 U.S.C. §844 makes criminal the simple possession of marijuana, presumably an intrastate noncommercial activity. Does possession of marijuana have a substantial effect on interstate commerce? Is the effect greater or lesser than the effect of guns in schools or sex-motivated violence on interstate commerce? How will (should) the Court assess this?

E.   STATE AUTONOMY AS A LIMIT ON THE FEDERAL COMMERCE POWER

1.   In General

When Congress seeks to use the commerce power to **regulate only the states,** principles of state autonomy derived in part from the **Tenth Amendment** limit the way Congress may use the commerce power. This does *not* mean that Congress is unable to use the commerce power to regulate the states; rather, Congress is constrained in the *manner* it uses its commerce power to regulate the states.

a. **The Tenth Amendment.** The Tenth Amendment provides: "The powers not delegated to the United States by the Constitution, nor prohibited by it to the States, are reserved to the States respectively, or to the people." The Tenth Amendment simply restates the constitutional structure: States retain all government powers not exercised by the federal government or prohibited to the states by the Constitution, subject to whatever limits the people of any state may impose through their state constitution. The Tenth Amendment is a truism, but the structural principle that it restates supports some limits on the way Congress may exercise its commerce power.

2. **Judicially Enforceable Federalism Limits: The Ten Year Reign of *National League of Cities v. Usery***

The first case since the New Deal revolution to void a federal law based on the commerce power was *National League of Cities v. Usery,* 426 U.S. 833 (1976). In 1974, Congress extended the Fair Labor Standards Act (mandating minimum wages and maximum hours) to include all employees of states and their political subdivisions. The Court (5-4) invalidated the extension of the law, concluding that Congress could not validly employ its commerce power to (1) **impinge on essential attributes of state sovereignty** or (2) **"directly impair State ability to structure integral operations in areas of traditional governmental functions,"** unless the **nature of the federal interest justified state submission to the federal regulation.** The test led to much litigation about which governmental functions were "traditionally governmental" (and thus within the immunity zone created by *Usery*) and which were "proprietary," or "nongovernmental" (and thus subject to congressional regulation via the commerce power). This litigation produced such varied and unpredictable results that Justice Blackmun changed his mind nine years later, joining a new 5 to 4 majority that overturned *National League of Cities v. Usery.*

3. **Politically Enforceable Federalism Limits**

a. ***Garcia v. San Antonio Metropolitan Transit Authority,*** 469 U.S. 528 (1985). Justice Blackmun, for a five-Justice majority, overruled *National League of Cities.* Rather than fashion a new test that would keep the Court as a guardian of federalism Blackmun abandoned the attempt. He contended that the states' "residuary and inviolable sovereignty" was entrusted exclusively to Congress for safekeeping, since "the built-in restraints that our system provides through state participation in federal governmental action" was sufficient to protect the states' autonomy.

b. **The judicial role after *Garcia*.** The *Garcia* opinion left one role for the courts to play in enforcing federalism-based limits on the commerce power. Said Blackmun, "any substantive restraint on the exercise of [the commerce power] must find its justification in the procedural nature of [the political process], and it must be **tailored to compensate for possible failings in the national political process** rather than to dictate a 'sacred province of state autonomy.' " The post-*Garcia* role of the Court is to invalidate legislation that stems from an **extraordinary defect in the national political process.**

4.   The Rise of Process Federalism

Since *Garcia* the Court has created a "process federalism" doctrine that polices the political process in the name of preserving state autonomy.

   a.   ***South Carolina v. Baker,*** 485 U.S. 505 (1988). Interest from state bonds is exempt from federal income tax. Congress amended the law to impose the income tax on interest from bearer bonds issued by states, thus requiring states to issue their bonds in the name of the purchaser in order to avoid the loss of the federal tax exemption. South Carolina claimed that the amendment was the product of an extraordinarily defective political process because the law was "imposed by a vote of an uninformed Congress relying upon incomplete information." The Court rejected the challenge. In dicta, the Court suggested two possible extraordinary defects that would warrant judicial intervention: (1) **deprivation of a state's right to participate in the national political process,** and (2) **legislation that singles a state out in a way that leaves it "politically isolated and powerless."** Congress may not exclude a state's congressional delegation, or perhaps even a meaningful portion of it, and then proceed to regulate the excluded state. This is unlikely to occur; the only instance in American history of its occurrence was after the Civil War, when Congress ousted the congressional delegations of the former Confederate states until they had ratified the 14th Amendment. Nor may Congress regulate one single state in a way that suggests that it was singled out for unfair treatment.

   Example: Suppose Congress enacted a law requiring that all nuclear waste must be deposited in Nevada. Suppose that the legislative history strongly suggests a desire on the part of all other legislators to avoid nuclear waste being deposited in their states. Against this background it might be plausible for the Court to conclude that Nevada was "unfairly" singled out in a way that left it politically isolated and powerless.

   b.   ***Gregory v. Ashcroft,*** 501 U.S. 452 (1991). The Court held that the Age Discrimination in Employment Act did not apply to a state's mandatory retirement age for its judges. The Court interpreted the ADEA to exempt judges from the statute's ban of mandatory retirement, whether imposed by private or public employers. The Court, per Justice O'Connor, concluded that Congress may use the commerce power to "impose its will on the States . . . in areas traditionally regulated by the States" but only if Congress makes **a plain statement of its intent to do so.** Congressional displacement of state authority is "an extraordinary power . . . , a power that we must assume Congress does not exercise lightly." The plain statement rule effectively guards against unconsidered congressional infringement of state autonomy. The plain statement rule applies, however, only when Congress has used its commerce power to invade the **essential sovereign or political functions of a state.**

c. *New York v. United States,* 505 U.S. 144 (1992). The Low-Level Radioactive Waste Policy Act was designed to facilitate disposal of waste by inducing states to form compacts for disposal of such waste or to dispose of their own waste. The 1985 amendments to the Act created monetary incentives for creation of in-state disposal sites, permitted sited states or members of sited compacts to exclude waste from nonmembers, and required nonsited and noncompact states to take title to all waste generated within their state after January 1, 1996, and to assume all liability stemming therefrom. The Court upheld the validity of the first two provisions but struck down the "take title" provision.

   i. **The Court's rationale.** The legislation essentially commanded states either (1) to assume all liability for low-level nuclear waste generated within their borders or (2) establish a waste disposal facility in accordance with specific federal standards. The law did not regulate the conduct of anyone other than states. Congress could not simply order the states to assume unknown liabilities or to legislate as Congress directs. "Congress may not simply 'commandeer the legislative processes of the States by directly compelling them to enact and enforce a federal regulatory program.'" (quoting *Hodel v. Virginia Surface Mining,* 452 U.S. 264 (1981)). The Court reasoned that a federal command to states to legislate in a certain fashion undermined political accountability, since Congress could thereby avoid direct accountability for its actions. Note that the *New York* principle—**Congress may not "commandeer" state legislative processes**—confines only the **method** of regulation open to Congress. Congress remains free to use its commerce power to regulate the field and displace the states from regulation; it just may not require the states to do Congress's work for it. The *New York* rule is a rule of *procedure,* not of substance. It does not confer any substantive zone of immunity from federal regulation on the states; it does protect the states from federal interference in the process of autonomous state governance.

 EXAMPLES AND ANALYSIS

Example: Suppose Congress determines, on the basis of ample factual support, that the generation and disposal of low-level nuclear waste has a substantial effect on interstate commerce. Congress then enacts legislation that forbids the generation of any such waste until and unless the generator has irrevocably arranged for its disposal in a site meeting federally specified standards. The same legislation expressly preempts any state legislation bearing on the same subject. The law is valid. Its effect may well be to compel the construction of disposal sites meeting federal standards or to inhibit the generation of low-level waste. But the federal goals are not achieved by the forbidden method of conscripting the state as a foot soldier in the army of federal regulation.

Note that the *New York* limit will only come into play when Congress chooses to regulate *only the states*. If a law regulates states and private persons alike it is virtually impossible that it could commandeer a state's legislative process.

Example: The federal Fair Labor Standards Act compels all employers, public or private, to comply with minimum wage and maximum hour regulations. The law does not force states to legislate in a certain way. Along with all other employers the state's freedom to enter into employment arrangements is restricted, but the state's legislative process remains unimpeded and autonomous.

---

    d. *Printz v. United States,* 521 U.S. 898 (1997). The federal Brady Handgun Control Act compelled the "chief law enforcement officer" of each local jurisdiction to conduct background checks on prospective handgun purchasers. The Court invalidated this conscription of state executive officials into "the administration of a federally enacted regulatory scheme." The Court offered three principal reasons for finding that Congress lacked power "to impress the state executive into its service."

         • *History*: Our constitutional practice "suggests an assumed *absence* of such power."

         • *Structure*: The federal government operates upon the people, not the states. Conscripting the states into the army of federal administrators would violate the states' "residuary and inviolable sovereignty" and subvert Art. II's command that the *President* execute federal law.

         • *Policy*: The Brady Act's directive to local police chiefs and sheriffs distorted the political accountability of both federal and state officials and compromised the independence and autonomy that states retain "within their proper sphere of authority." After *Printz* Congress may not force state executive officials to administer federal laws. Congress can, of course, impose that task on the federal executive.

    e. *Alden v. Maine,* 527 U.S. 706 (1999). Maine probation officers filed suit in a Maine court, seeking damages for Maine's alleged failure to pay them proper overtime pay as required by the federal Fair Labor Standards Act. The Court held that Congress lacked power to subject a state to suit brought against it by private citizens in its own state courts. The decision was partly based on the principle of state sovereign immunity imbedded in the Eleventh Amendment, but the Court also noted that "power to press a State's own courts into federal service to coerce the other branches of the State [is] the power first to turn the State against itself and ultimately to commandeer the entire political machinery of the State against its will and at the behest of individuals. Such plenary federal control of state governmental processes denigrates the separate sovereignty of the States" by threatening state "financial integrity," state "autonomy," state "decisionmaking ability," and "political accountability." While "Congress may declare federal law binding and enforceable in state courts" it may not force state courts to entertain claims that cannot be heard in federal courts. Such a power is inconsistent with the "history, practice, precedent, and the structure of the Constitution."

5.   Restatement of the Current Law

Congress may use its commerce power to regulate the states themselves if Congress complies with the following rules.

a.   Laws of general application. So long as Congress enacts otherwise valid legislation that applies equally to the states and private persons, there is virtually no state autonomy limit that is judicially enforceable. This means that state autonomy limits apply when Congress regulates the states and not other people.

b.   Laws that apply only to states. When Congress uses its commerce power to regulate only the states, it **must:**

- Do so with **unmistakable clarity**

- Refrain from **unfairly singling out a state**

- Not **deny a state participation in the national political process**

- Not **interfere with a state's lawmaking process,** as, e.g., by compelling a state to enact federally prescribed legislation

- Not **compel a state to administer a federal program.**

REVIEW QUESTIONS AND ANSWERS

Question: Congress engages in fact-finding hearings that produce some evidence that treatment of frostbitten ears entails medical expenses of several million dollars annually, imposed primarily on interstate medical insurers. Acting on this belief, and in an attempt to prevent these costs, Congress enacts a law making it a federal misdemeanor for anyone to be outdoors in temperatures of less than 0 degrees Celsius without wearing a federally approved garment fully covering the ears. Max goes outside in subzero weather with no ear protection, suffers frostbitten ears, and is prosecuted under the law. He asserts that Congress has no enumerated power that enables it to enact the law. Is the statute constitutional?

Answer: Possibly. Congress was relying upon its power to regulate interstate commerce to enact this law. It would contend that the intrastate noncommercial activity of being outside in cold weather without ear protection substantially affects interstate commerce through the medical costs resulting from frostbite. After *Morrison* the Court will not defer to congressional judgments about the substantial effect on interstate commerce of noncommercial intrastate activities.

Question: Congress enacts a minimum wage law that applies to all employers, public and private. A state argues that Congress can not validly apply the law to it. Will the state succeed?

Answer: No. Congress may use its commerce power to enact a minimum wage law, since wages paid to workers, in the aggregate, have a substantial effect on interstate commerce. The state will be unable to assert immunity from the law because it applies equally to states and private persons.

Question: Congress believes that the award of punitive damages in civil cases increases the cost of business operation, making products more costly to consumers and decreasing the competitiveness of American industry in the world market. Accordingly, Congress enacts legislation that provides that states must either (1) forbid the award of punitive damages in civil cases or (2) pay to the federal government annually a sum of money equal to the total of all punitive damage awards under that state's law for that year, for the purpose of supporting efforts to enhance global competitiveness of American industry. A state contests the validity of this law. Is the law constitutional?

Answer: No. Congress has ordered the states either to change their law or to pay a "tax" or "fine" for the privilege of continuing to make their own law on the subject of punitive damages. Neither prong of the command is permissible.

Question: Even though the Constitution does not give Congress exclusive authority over interstate commerce, why does Congress in practice possess inchoate exclusive power over interstate commerce?

Answer: Congress may preempt contrary state law by exercising its regulatory power under the commerce clause. The courts have become extremely deferential to Congress's judgment about the scope of its own regulatory power, and so Congress may, in practice, displace state law at its virtual pleasure.

Question: Why does the Supreme Court insist that Congress make a rational determination that an activity has a "substantial effect" on interstate commerce?

Answer: By deferring to rational congressional judgment about the effect any activity might have on interstate commerce, the Supreme Court was indicating its faith that Congress would make a considered judgment about the substantiality of an activity's effect on interstate commerce. The Court seemed to think that if Congress made a considered judgment, that would be an adequate way of protecting the constitutional concept of limited power in the federal government. But if Congress no longer considers the issue at all there is no longer any guarantee that any limits at all are applied to congressional power. Thus, at the very least, Congress must consider in some rational way the limits of its own power.

Question: Why are states given a limited exemption from the scope of the commerce power?

Answer: Congress may regulate everyone—states and ordinary people—so long as it does so validly and evenhandedly. But when Congress seeks to regulate *only* the states, it runs into a structural obstacle. The Constitution was designed to cause two governments—the central government and the states—to share power. If Congress can dictate to the state governments how they must govern, the state governments no longer share in power but have become wholly subservient tools of the federal government. The limited (and entirely procedural) exemption from Congress's commerce power that states enjoy is designed to ensure their continued governmental autonomy.

EXAM TIPS

- **The Commerce Power Is Very Broad, but Not Unlimited.** The modern scope of the commerce power has become so vast it sometimes seems unlimited. It is not. Congress may validly regulate using its commerce power if **Congress determines that the regulated activity is** *in commerce* or *substantially affects commerce,* the congressional judgment is **rational,** and the **means chosen by Congress are** *reasonably related* to its regulatory objective. This standard is very deferential to Congress. Check to see if Congress has made the requisite factual determination. If it has, and that finding is not outlandish, the congressional action is probably valid. A federal statute with an attenutated connection to interstate commerce raises these issues. **Caveat:** The Court will not defer to a congressional determination that an **intrastate, noncommercial** activity substantially affects interstate commerce, but will decide on its own whether that activity is connected closely enough to interstate commerce to enable Congress to regulate the activity.

- **State Autonomy Limits on the Federal Commerce Power.** This is another likely area for testing. If Congress uses its commerce power to regulate the states and private citizens alike there are no special judicially enforced limits on the commerce power—the only limits are those inherent in the national political process. But Congress has less freedom to employ its commerce power to regulate only the states. Congressional regulation of the states via the commerce power must be **clear and unambiguous,** may **not single out a state,** may **not deny a state its participation in the national political process,** may **not compel a state to legislate in a prescribed manner,** and may **not compel a state to administer a federal program.**

BEYOND COMMERCE: THE OTHER NATIONAL LEGISLATIVE POWERS

 CHAPTER OVERVIEW

This chapter examines the source and scope of some of the more important congressional powers. The power to tax, spend, implement treaties, legislate in aid of the war power, regulate foreign affairs, and enforce the Reconstruction amendments are considered in detail. Other federal powers are mentioned. The most important points in this chapter follow.

- **Taxation:** Congress may impose taxes for any purpose so long as the tax **produces some revenue** and the **regulations** accompanying it are **reasonably related to enforcement of the tax.**

- **Spending:** Congress **may spend,** but **may _not_ regulate,** for the **general welfare** of the nation. Congress may attach **conditions** to the receipt of federal funds by states, so long as the conditions are:

  — **Clear** and **unambiguous,**

  — Related to the **federal interest in particular national projects or programs,**

  — Not violative of **other constitutional provisions,** such as the Bill of Rights,

  — Not **coercive.**

- **Treaties:** Congress may implement treaties without the necessity of using one of its enumerated legislative powers, but Congress may not violate constitutional rights in doing so.

- **War:** Congress has the sole power to **declare war** and may enact reasonable measures to effectuate its power to provide the means for conducting war.

- **Foreign Affairs:** The federal government has **exclusive power** over foreign affairs. The division of that power between the President and Congress is discussed in Chapter 7.

- **Reconstruction Amendments (13th, 14th, and 15th):** Congress may **enforce** the rights guaranteed by these amendments in the following manner:

  — By providing **remedies for violations determined by courts,**

  — By providing **remedies for future violations,** so long as those remedies are *congruent* with the constitutional injury remedied and *proportional* to that injury.

  — For the 13th Amendment *only,* by providing remedies to eliminate the "badges or incidents" of slavery.

A.   TAXATION

Several provisions of the Constitution govern the taxing power of the United States and the state governments. The first section of this chapter deals with the power of Congress to tax.

1.   Sources of Authority for Federal Taxation

Article I, §8 provides that "Congress shall have Power to lay and collect Taxes, Duties, Imposts and Excises. . . ." This power is independent of the other powers of Congress. In other words, Congress may tax things that it may not have power to regulate. **Example:** Congress may levy a tax upon the possession of household pets. Absent some substantial connection to interstate commerce Congress has no power to regulate the possession of household pets, but Congress has an independent power to tax.

2.   Specific Constitutional Limits on Congressional Power to Tax

Congress's general power of taxation is limited by several other provisions of the Constitution.

   a.   **No taxes on exports.** Article I, §9 prohibits any duties on exports.

   b.   **Uniform indirect taxation.** Article I, §8 specifies that "all Duties, Imposts and Excises shall be uniform throughout the United States. . . ." This means that "indirect" taxes—those levied upon an *activity* rather than upon *property*—may not discriminate among the states. It does not mean that taxation of all affected individuals must be uniform.

   c.   **Apportioned direct taxes.** Article I, §2 provides that "direct Taxes shall be apportioned among the several States . . . according to their respective Numbers. . . ." This means that taxes imposed directly upon property must be levied in such a way that each state's proportion of the total revenue produced by the tax is the same as each state's proportion of the total population of the nation. This rule applies only to **direct taxes**—taxes levied upon real or personal property. In *Pollock v. Farmers' Loan & Trust Co.,* 157 U.S. 429 (1895), the Supreme Court ruled that a national income tax was a direct tax and subject to this limit. That ruling was overturned by the 16th Amendment, ratified in 1913, which provides that "Congress shall have power to lay and collect taxes on incomes, from whatever source derived, without apportionment among the several States. . . ."

3. Implied Constitutional Limits on Congressional Power to Tax

In addition to the specific constitutional limits on federal taxation, the Supreme Court has established some implied limits.

a. **Disguised regulation.** Because taxes alter human behavior (people tend to change their actions in order to avoid taxes) *any tax will have some regulatory effect.* **Example:** If Congress imposes a tax on liquor some people will be deterred from consuming as much liquor as they would have in the absence of taxation. The tax has a regulatory effect by deterring liquor consumption.

A regulatory effect is not necessarily forbidden. If Congress has the **independent** power to regulate, the regulatory effect of a tax is of no consequence. **Example:** If Congress imposes a tax on the interstate shipment of cigarettes, the regulatory effect of the tax (deterring consumption of cigarettes) is of no constitutional significance. Congress has the independent power to regulate interstate commerce, and the interstate shipment of cigarettes is part of interstate commerce. But if the regulatory effect of a tax is one which Congress could not have accomplished using one of its limited and enumerated powers the tax may be invalid. The validity of such a tax depends on whether it is truly **a revenue-raising measure** or whether it is **disguised regulation.**

i. **The *Child Labor Tax Case.*** In *Bailey v. Drexel Furniture Co. (The Child Labor Tax Case),* 259 U.S. 20 (1922), the Court invalidated the Child Labor Tax Law of 1919, which imposed a tax of 10% of the annual net profits on any business that employed children as laborers. The Court reasoned that this tax was not so much a tax as a penalty. It deduced its character as a penalty from the fact that (1) only employers who *knew* they were employing children were liable for the tax (a characteristic of penal laws), (2) the amount of the tax was not proportional to the amount of child labor employed by the business, and (3) enforcement of the tax was in the hands of the Labor Department rather than the Internal Revenue Service. *The Child Labor Tax Case* is of little importance today. First, because the scope of the commerce power is so much broader now, there is less likelihood that any given tax will exert a regulatory effect that is outside of Congress's independent power to regulate. Second, the Court has refined its criteria by which it distinguishes between legitimate taxes and disguised regulations. The modern criteria are discussed below.

b. **Modern criteria: ''Tax'' or ''regulation''?** The Supreme Court today has developed a number of criteria to determine whether a ''tax'' is really a tax or, instead, a disguised regulation.

   i. **No motive inquiry.** The Court states it will not inquire ''into the hidden motives which may move Congress'' to tax. *Sonzinsky v. United States,* 300 U.S. 506 (1937). Thus, Congress may tax for purely regulatory objectives, so long as the form of the ''regulation'' is a tax.

   ii. **Productive of revenue.** If a tax produces ''*some revenue*'' it is likely to be treated as a legitimate tax. Thus, the Court has upheld taxes upon firearms dealers, gambling, and marijuana, even though the revenue raised by the taxes was relatively small. See *Sonzinsky, United States v. Sanchez,* 340 U.S. 42 (1950), *United States v. Kahriger,* 345 U.S. 22 (1953).

   iii. **''Regulatory'' tax rates permitted.** Taxes that ''regulate'' by means of their rate structure are permissible and valid taxes. **Example:** Congress levied a tax on yellow oleomargarine of ten cents per pound and levied a tax on white oleomargarine of one quarter cent per pound. Even though the rate structure operated to deter the manufacture and sale of yellow oleomargarine, the tax was upheld. *McCray v. United States,* 195 U.S. 27 (1904).

   iv. **Regulations ''reasonably related'' to tax enforcement.** Congress may impose regulations as part of a tax so long as those regulations are **reasonably related** to enforcement of the tax. **Example:** Congress levied a tax on ''bookies'' that also required them to file a tax return, including their name and address. Although the registration requirement was no doubt intended to facilitate criminal prosecution of illegal gambling the Court upheld the registration requirement on the ground that it was ''adapted to the collection of a valid tax.'' *United States v. Kahriger,* 345 U.S. 22 (1953).

B. SPENDING

The other side of taxation is spending, but the power to tax is not the source of the power to spend. Article I, §8 gives Congress separate authority to spend. The principal issue regarding the spending power is the scope of congressional power to attach conditions to the receipt of federal expenditures, particularly when those conditions oblige the states to alter their constitutions or laws.

1. Source of Authority to Spend

Article I, §8 gives Congress power "to pay the Debts and provide for the common Defence and general Welfare of the United States."

2. Scope of the Spending Authority

Two issues are important. First, what is the general welfare for which Congress may spend? Second, may Congress attach conditions to the receipt of federal funds and, if so, are there any limits to such conditions?

a. *United States v. Butler,* 291 U.S. 1 (1936). Through the Agricultural Adjustment Act ("AAA") Congress sought to raise farm prices by limiting production. A tax was levied on the first processor of each farm commodity and those tax revenues were used to pay farmers who entered into contracts to limit production of farm commodities. Butler, on behalf of a cotton processor, attacked the validity of the processing tax. The Court struck it down as part of a spending program that was beyond Congress's power to spend.

  i. **The Court's rationale.** First, the Court decided that the phrase "general welfare" did not limit Congress's spending power to spending that was necessary or proper to effectuate some *other* enumerated power of the federal government. James Madison had argued for that position in the early years of the nation; his political foe Alexander Hamilton asserted that Congress could spend for any purpose necessary or proper to the general welfare, regardless of whether it was in aid of some other enumerated federal power. But, said the Court, Congress had *not* simply *spent* for the general welfare; it had *regulated* for the general welfare. **While Congress may spend for the general welfare, it may not regulate for the general welfare.** The Court concluded that Congress could not validly regulate agricultural production, a local and "pre-commercial" activity. The Court concluded that Congress had regulated because the AAA coerced farmers into compliance with the acreage reduction scheme. Farmers who didn't enter into contracts to limit production suffered severe economic loss; Congress could not "purchase" compliance with a regulatory scheme that it could not otherwise constitutionally enact.

  ii. **Stone's dissent.** Justice Stone dissented, arguing that it was oxymoronic to "to say that there is a power to spend for the national welfare, while rejecting any power to impose conditions reasonably adapted to the attainment of the end which alone would justify the expenditure."

b. *Steward Machine Co. v. Davis,* 301 U.S. 548 (1937). The Court upheld a provision of the Social Security Act that granted a credit against federal payroll taxes for payments made by employers to state unemployment compensation schemes, so long as those state plans complied with minimum federal requirements. The Court concluded that the federal payroll tax and accompanying credit were not "weapons of coercion, destroying or impairing the autonomy of the states." The credit against the federal payroll tax was merely a condition imposed on a federal expenditure that did not coerce the states because the states remained free to decide whether they wished to enact an unemployment compensation scheme complying with the federal standards necessary to trigger the federal tax credit. But, said Justice Cardozo, "we leave many questions open." The Court hinted that a tax "laid upon the condition that a state may escape its operation through the adoption of a statute unrelated in subject matter to activities fairly within the scope of national . . . power" was invalid. As well, the Court intimated that taxes and expenditures that "call for a surrender by the states of powers essential to their quasi-sovereign existence" would be invalid.

c. Conditional spending: *South Dakota v. Dole,* 483 U.S. 203 (1987). By statute, Congress directed the Secretary of Transportation to withhold 5% of the federal highway funds otherwise due under other federal laws from any state that permitted persons under age twenty-one to purchase and possess alcoholic beverages. South Dakota, which permitted nineteen year olds to buy 3.2% beer, sought a declaration that the law was beyond Congress's spending power. The Court upheld the law. In doing so it outlined the constitutional limits upon the practice of conditioning state receipt of federal funds on compliance with federally specified standards. For conditional spending to be valid it must comply with the following criteria:

- Conditions on spending must be in **pursuit of the general welfare,** but courts will "defer substantially to the judgment of Congress" as to what is in aid of the general welfare of the nation.

- Conditions on spending must be **unambiguous,** to enable the states to exercise a knowing choice.

- Conditions on spending **must be related to the "federal interest in particular national projects or programs,"** a requirement that means that the condition must reasonably further some **particular** national project or program otherwise within federal power. Congress has no power to use conditions upon receipt of federal funds to purchase state compliance with something far removed from the subject of the spending. This requirement imposes a rule of "reasonable proximity" between the means (the condition) and the end (the "particular federal project or program").

Example: Suppose Congress limits receipt of federal funds for highway construction to those states that prohibit anyone under the age of eighteen from marriage. It is unlikely that the condition—a minimum age for marriage—reasonably furthers the *particular* federal interest in highway construction—transportation safety or efficiency.

- Conditions on spending **must not violate "other constitutional provisions"** that "provide an independent bar to the conditional grant of federal funds." This requirement simply means that Congress may not condition receipt of federal funds on a state's violation of the Constitution.

Example: Suppose Congress offers money to states for public health purposes, but withholds receipt of federal funds from those states that permit abortions. The condition is invalid because it obligates states to violate an independent constitutional provision—the substantive due process right of a woman to terminate her pregnancy before viability without undue burdens being imposed upon its exercise.

- Conditions on spending must **not be coercive.** When "pressure turns into compulsion" a condition becomes coercive. In *Dole* the Court thought that because noncompliance with the drinking age condition would cost a state only "a relatively small percentage of . . . federal highway funds" the condition was not coercive. Instead, the Court characterized the condition as a congressional offer of "relatively mild encouragement to the States to enact higher minimum drinking ages than they would otherwise choose." The Court gave no hint as to the point at which the withholding of federal funds might become coercive. *Dole* leaves an opportunity for states to argue that conditions imposing more severe cutbacks are coercive, but *Dole* offers no guidance as to the point at which coercion begins.

  i. **O'Connor's dissent.** Justice O'Connor dissented, arguing that the condition—a twenty-one-year-old drinking age—was not reasonably related to the expenditure of federal funds on highways. O'Connor agreed that Congress could impose conditions on its spending but contended that **such conditions could extend no further than to specify how federal money is to be spent.** Any other condition "is not a condition, but a regulation, which is valid only if it falls within one of Congress' delegated regulatory powers."

C. INTERNATIONAL TREATIES

1. Source of Authority to Make Treaties

Article II, §2 empowers the President to make treaties, but a treaty is not effective until two-thirds of the Senate has ratified it.

2. Relation of Treaties to Statutes

The supremacy clause provides that treaties, by themselves and independent of congressional action, are the law of the land. Nevertheless, there are two reasons why some treaties require legislative implementation to be effective within the United States. First, some treaties are drafted to require legislative implementation. Such treaties are effective as a matter of international law but without congressional action have no effect at home. The failure to implement such a treaty might be a violation of international law. Second, the Constitution may require congressional implementation of some treaties.

Example: A treaty requiring the appropriation and expenditure of funds cannot be self-executing. Article I requires congressional appropriation of funds. See *Turner v. American Baptist Missionary Union,* 24 F. Cas. 344 (No. 14251) (C.C. Mich. 1852).

Since treaties and statutes are legal equivalents the Court regards the latest action—whether a treaty or statute—as controlling in the event of a conflict. Of course, a treaty that is not self-executing cannot supersede prior conflicting law; only new legislation can do that.

3. Scope of Congressional Power to Implement Treaties

Two questions of congressional power are raised by treaties.

- First, does Congress have power to implement treaties by any "necessary and proper" legislation, or may Congress only implement treaties by employing some other enumerated power of Congress? The Court answered this question in *Missouri v. Holland,* 252 U.S. 416 (1920).

- Second, is Congress free to implement treaties without regard to any constitutional limits other than the necessary and proper clause? A plurality of the Court answered this question in *Reid v. Covert,* 354 U.S. 1 (1957).

a. *Missouri v. Holland,* 252 U.S. 416 (1920). Missouri challenged the constitutionality of federal legislation implementing a migratory bird treaty between Canada and the United States. The federal legislation preempted Missouri's regulation of gamebirds, preventing Missouri hunters from killing as many birds as Missouri law permitted. Missouri contended that Congress could regulate the hunting of gamebirds only if some enumerated power (e.g., the commerce power) authorized Congress to do so. The Court upheld the law, ruling that Congress could use any means necessary and proper to implement treaties and that Congress need not rely upon its other enumerated powers to do so. Put another way, the power to implement treaties is not bounded by the specifically enumerated heads of congressional authority. Recall that the necessary and proper clause empowers Congress to adopt any means "necessary and proper for carrying into execution . . . *all* . . . powers vested by this Constitution in the Government of the United States." One of those powers is the power to make and ratify treaties. Justice Holmes, for the Court, did note that "[t]he treaty in question does not contravene any prohibitory words to be found in the Constitution," thus implying that Congress might lack the power to implement treaties the terms of which offend the Constitution.

Example: Suppose the United States made and ratified a treaty with Colombia obligating the United States to execute all presently convicted drug dealers who had received a lesser sentence. Congress could not implement the treaty because the imposition of a new sentence for past crimes would offend the ex post facto clause.

Holland erases any federalism-based limits on the power of Congress to implement treaties. So long as a treaty deals with issues "properly the subject of negotiation with a foreign country," *DeGeofroy v. Riggs,* 133 U.S. 258 (1890), Congress has the power to implement the treaty by legislation.

b. ***Reid v. Covert,*** 354 U.S. 1 (1957). Following World War II, the United States entered into agreements with other nations that gave to American military courts exclusive jurisdiction over offenses committed by American servicemembers or their dependents on foreign soil. Congress implemented the agreements with legislation vesting the military courts with such exclusive jurisdiction. A civilian dependent of an American military member was convicted of murder by a military court. She appealed, contending that Congress had no power to deprive her of a jury trial in a civilian court. The government invoked *Missouri v. Holland,* arguing that the statute was "necessary and proper to carry out the United States' obligations under the international agreements." A plurality of the Court struck down the law, noting that "no agreement with a foreign nation can confer power on the Congress, or on any other branch of Government, which is free from the restraints of the Constitution." Seizing on Justice Holmes's observation in *Holland* that the treaty there did not violate any "prohibitory words" of the Constitution, Justice Black concluded that Congress was free to implement treaties without regard to federalism restraints but could not do so in violation of constitutionally guaranteed individual rights.

Example: In an effort to suppress the worldwide demand for pornography, suppose the United States enters into a treaty to prohibit the possession of nonobscene pornography. Congress may not validly implement the treaty since it violates the free speech guarantee.

4.   Executive Agreements Distinguished From Treaties

Executive agreements are international agreements made by the President alone without Senate ratification. See Chapter 7, section B(4)(c). Unlike treaties, executive agreements do not override prior acts of Congress. *United States v. Guy W. Capps, Inc.,* 204 F.2d 655 (4th Cir. 1953); Tribe, at 229. But, as with treaties, executive agreements do override conflicting state law, because foreign affairs is an exclusively federal concern. *United States v. Belmont,* 301 U.S. 324, 331 (1937).

D.   WAR AND FOREIGN AFFAIRS

1.   War Power

Article I, §8 gives Congress the power to **declare war,** to **raise and support Armies,** to **provide and maintain a Navy,** to **regulate the armed services,** and to **tax and spend for the national defense.** Article II, §2, gives the President as Commander-in-Chief the authority to conduct war. This division of the power to wage war produces several important issues, considered below and also in Chapter 7.

a.   Declaring and waging war. Congress has the power to declare war and to provide for the means to wage war, but once war has been initiated by Congress the conduct of war itself is constitutionally entrusted to the President. (1) To what extent may the President use armed force without a congressional declaration of war? (2) May Congress declare war implicitly, by authorizing the President to conduct war in the absence of a formal declaration of war? (3) May Congress control the President's conduct of war, with or without a prior declaration of war? These important issues will be explored in more detail in Chapter 7, dealing with the separation of powers.

b.   Legislative power to regulate in order to facilitate waging war. Through the "necessary and proper" clause Congress has the power to enact reasonable measures to effectuate its power to provide the means for conducting war.

    i.   *Woods v. Cloyd W. Miller Co.,* 333 U.S. 138 (1948). In 1947 Congress enacted the Housing and Rent Act, which froze rents at their wartime levels. The Court rejected a challenge to Congress's power to enact the law, ruling that "the war power sustains this legislation." The means-enabling power of the necessary and proper clause supported congressional power to regulate an economic condition—housing shortages—partly produced by the intense national war effort of World War II. In a concurrence, Justice Jackson expressed "misgivings" about "this vague, undefined and indefinable 'war power,'" noting its tendency to be "invoked in haste and excitement" without deliberation, amidst a "patriotic fervor that makes moderation unpopular, . . . interpreted by judges under the influence of the same passions and pressures. . . . Particularly when the war power is invoked to [impose liberty or property restrictions] that only indirectly affect conduct of the war and do not relate to the management of the war itself, the constitutional basis [of laws based on the 'war power'] should be scrutinized with care."

2. Foreign Affairs

Power over foreign affairs resides in a constitutional netherworld.

a. **Source of authority.** The Constitution does not explicitly vest in Congress or the President a general power over foreign affairs. Some aspects of foreign affairs are entrusted to the President alone (e.g., diplomatic recognition of foreign governments), some are given to the President subject to Senate approval (e.g., treaties), some are given to Congress (e.g., the power to define and punish piracy, felonies on the high seas, and "offenses against the law of nations").

b. **Exclusive federal power.** However divided between President and Congress, the Court has consistently declared that **only the federal government has power to conduct foreign affairs.** This is partly the product of impeccable prudential logic, partly rooted in the historical intentions of the founders, and partly inferred from constitutional structure, particularly the provisions of Article I, §10 that disable states from making treaties, engaging in war, or entering into agreements with foreign nations without congressional consent. As the Court in *Perez v. Brownell*, 356 U.S. 44, 57 (1958), phrased it: "The States that joined together to form a single Nation and to create, through the Constitution, a Federal Government to conduct the affairs of that Nation must be held to have granted that Government the powers indispensable to its functioning effectively in the company of sovereign nations."

c. **Implied federal legislative power.** In *Perez v. Brownell* the Court upheld a federal law that stripped Americans of their citizenship if they voted in foreign elections. Even though the Constitution contains "no specific grant to Congress of power to enact legislation for the effective regulation of foreign affairs" the Court concluded that Congress impliedly had such power. Legislation that is rationally related to regulation of foreign affairs is valid.

E. POWER TO ENFORCE THE RECONSTRUCTION AMENDMENTS

1. Introduction and Overview

The Reconstruction Amendments—the 13th, 14th, and 15th—each contain a grant of power to Congress to enforce its provisions by "appropriate legislation." The relevant portion is §2 of the 13th and 15th Amendments and §5 of the 14th Amendment. The 13th Amendment bars anyone—government or private citizen alike—from practicing slavery. The 14th and 15th Amendments, by contrast, forbid certain government conduct but have no effect on private conduct. The content and scope of these guarantees is, of course, subject to judicial interpretation. To what extent may Congress enforce these guarantees independently from the Court's interpretations? Other aspects of the enforcement power, particularly the extent to which it enables Congress to regulate *private* conduct, are discussed in Chapter 10, section B, infra.

2. The Scope of Congressional Power to Enforce the Rights Guaranteed by the Reconstruction Amendments

a. The 13th Amendment: *Jones v. Alfred H. Mayer Co.,* 392 U.S. 409 (1968). A Reconstruction statute codified at 42 U.S.C. §1982 prohibits private and public racial discrimination in the sale or rental of property. In *Mayer* the Court upheld Congress's power to reach private racial discrimination "as a valid exercise of the power of Congress to enforce the 13th Amendment." The *Civil Rights Cases,* 109 U.S. 3 (1883), had established that under the 13th Amendment Congress could regulate private racial discrimination only to the extent necessary and proper to abolish the "badges and incidents of slavery," as the Court defined those terms. In *Mayer* the Court rejected that idea: "Congress has the power under the Thirteenth Amendment rationally to determine what are the badges and incidents of slavery, and the authority to translate that determination into effective legislation." This is a virtually unbounded power. "Seemingly, Congress is free, within the broad limits of reason, to recognize whatever rights it wishes, define the infringement of those rights as a form of domination and thus an aspect of slavery, and proscribe such infringements as a violation of the thirteenth amendment." Tribe, at 332-333. Yet, for all its apparent broad scope *Mayer* may not mean quite what it says. Cases arising under the 13th Amendment enforcement power all involve race, and it is unlikely that congressional power to enforce the abolition of America's long dead race-based system of slavery empowers Congress to enforce a panoply of human rights having little if anything to do with race, much less slavery. See also Chapter 10, section B, infra.

b. The 15th Amendment: Voting Rights. The 15th Amendment's guarantee of racially unrestricted voting is self-executing, requiring no congressional legislation to be enforceable against the states. *Guinn v. United*

States, 238 U.S. 347 (1915). In the absence of legislation, the substance of the 15th Amendment is what the courts say it is. But when Congress does act the scope of congressional authority to augment judicial interpretation of the amendment is at issue. The most significant federal legislation enacted under the 15th Amendment's enforcement power is the Voting Rights Act of 1965, "probably the most radical piece of civil rights legislation since Reconstruction." Tribe, at 336. Among other things the Voting Rights Act suspended literacy tests in jurisdictions where fewer than 50% of the voting age residents were registered voters, and subjected the election laws of those jurisdictions to approval by the U.S. Attorney General. The courts had ruled that literacy tests were not illegal on their face, but only if applied in a racially discriminatory fashion.

i.   *South Carolina v. Katzenbach,* 383 U.S. 301 (1966). The Court upheld the validity of the Voting Rights Act, ruling that the 15th Amendment left "Congress . . . chiefly responsible for implementing the rights created." The Court rejected South Carolina's argument that "Congress may do no more than to forbid violations of the Fifteenth Amendment in general terms—that the task of fashioning specific remedies or of applying them to particular localities must necessarily be left entirely to the courts." Instead, the Court said that so long as Congress had acted rationally in enacting legislation necessary and proper to securing racially nondiscriminatory voting the Court would defer to the congressional judgment. The Court concluded that if Congress found facts sufficient to establish a violation of the 15th Amendment as interpreted by courts, it was within Congress's enforcement power to remedy those violations by appropriate legislation. Courts determine the substance of the 15th Amendment but Congress may ascertain facts that establish substantive violations and then act to remedy those violations.

ii.   **The *Rome* and *Mobile* cases.** The Court decided *City of Rome v. United States,* 446 U.S. 156 (1980), and *Mobile v. Bolden,* 446 U.S. 55 (1980), on the same day. Each case involved at-large elections that were claimed to reduce the chances of electoral success for black candidates. Rome's electoral system was covered by the Voting Rights Act; Mobile's was not covered. Mobile's system was upheld as comporting with both the 14th and 15th Amendments because there was not enough evidence to prove that the electoral system was adopted or maintained with the *intent* to discriminate racially. In *City of Rome* there was no evidence that Rome's identical system was adopted or maintained with the intent to discriminate racially, but the Court found that it violated the Voting Rights Act because the Act prohibits electoral systems that have either the purpose or *effect* of diluting black voting strength. Thus, the Court was forced to consider whether Congress had enforcement power under the 15th Amendment to ban a practice valid under that amendment.

The Court concluded that Congress could do so. "[B]ecause electoral changes by jurisdictions with a demonstrable history of intentional racial discrimination in voting create the risk of purposeful discrimination, . . . [Congress could] prohibit changes that have a discriminatory impact." Congress had the power to head off *future* violations of the 15th Amendment by barring actions that Congress has reason to believe are commonly motivated by racial discrimination.

c.   **The 14th Amendment.** Congress's enforcement power under the 14th Amendment (and implicitly under the 15th as well) is **remedial only.** Although *Katzenbach v. Morgan,* infra, suggested that Congress might have power to define for itself the substance of such rights as equal protection or due process that is no longer the case. After *City of Boerne v. Flores,* infra, congressional enforcement of these rights must be *congruent* with the constitutional right enforced and the remedy afforded must be *proportional* to the scope of the constitutional injury addressed.

  i.   *Katzenbach v. Morgan,* 384 U.S. 641 (1966). Section 4(e) of the Voting Rights Act provided that persons who had completed the sixth grade in Puerto Rico, where Spanish is the language of instruction, could not be required to demonstrate English literacy in order to vote. *Lassiter v. Northampton Election Board,* 360 U.S. 45 (1959), had held that English literacy requirements did not violate either the 14th or 15th Amendments. New York voters challenged §4(e) as outside of the congressional enforcement power under either the 14th or 15th Amendments. The Court upheld the section, relying on two different theories. First, the Court reasoned that Congress could reasonably conclude that elimination of a barrier to Puerto Rican voting would enable Puerto Ricans to secure equal treatment in the provision of public services, and was a remedy for unconstitutional acts unrelated to voting. This stretches the "remedial powers" of Congress to their limits, for the remedy adopted by Congress had only the most remote connection to the constitutional violations being remedied. Second, the Court thought that Congress had power to determine for itself that an English literacy requirement violated equal protection. This view rejects the *Marbury* principle of judicial primacy in constitutional interpretation by permitting Congress to ignore or even reverse the Court's constitutional judgments concerning the substance of the

14th or 15th Amendments. Justice Harlan, a dissenter in *Morgan,* expressed the problem best in his opinion in *Oregon v. Mitchell,* 400 U.S. 112, 204-205 (1970): "Congress's expression of [its] view . . . cannot displace the duty of this Court to make an independent determination whether Congress has exceeded its powers. . . . Congress is . . . controlled only by the political process. In Article V, the Framers expressed the view that the political restraints on Congress alone were an insufficient control over the process of constitution making. The concurrence of two-thirds of each House and of three-fourths of the States was needed for the political check to be adequate. To allow a simple majority of Congress to have final say on matters of constitutional interpretation is therefore fundamentally out of keeping with the constitutional structure." Justice Brennan, writing for the Court in *Morgan,* replied that Congress has "no power to restrict, abrogate, or dilute [14th Amendment] guarantees." Brennan did not explain why Congress lacks this power if it otherwise has power to ignore the Court's substantive interpretations of the 14th Amendment, nor did he suggest any way to determine when a congressional initiative dilutes 14th Amendment guarantees. The view that Congress has such a substantive power was overruled by *City of Boerne v. Flores.*

ii. *City of Boerne v. Flores,* 521 U.S. 507 (1997). Congress enacted the Religious Freedom Restoration Act (RFRA) to overturn *Employment Division v. Smith,* 494 U.S. 872 (1990) (see Chapter 12 section C, infra), by prohibiting governments from imposing substantial burdens on religious conduct unless such burdens were the least restrictive means of furthering a compelling governmental interest. *Smith* held that substantial burdens on religious conduct did not violate the free exercise clause, as applied to the states, so long as the burdens were generally applicable to everyone. RFRA was ostensibly an exercise of congressional power to enforce the 14th Amendment, but the Court voided RFRA as exceeding Congress's power. The Court partially overruled *Morgan,* making it clear that Congress has only a remedial power: "Congress does not enforce a constitutional right by changing what the right is. It has been given the power 'to enforce,' not the power to determine what constitutes a constitutional violation."

For congressional action to be remedial "[t]here must be a congruence and proportionality between the injury to be prevented or remedied and the means adapted to that end." There should be some empirical evidence of a real problem and remedial legislation "should be adapted to the mischief and wrong which the Fourteenth Amendment was intended to prevent." RFRA was "so out of proportion to a supposed remedial or preventive object that it cannot be understood as responsive to, or designed to prevent, unconstitutional behavior."

iii.   Developments since *Flores*. The requirement of empirical proof of a real problem was driven home in *Florida Prepaid Postsecondary Education Expense Bd. v. College Savings Bank,* 527 U.S. 627 (1999), in which the Court found that Congress had exceeded its 14th Amendment enforcement powers by enacting a law subjecting states to suit in federal court for their patent violations. Though such patent violations might constitute due process violations the Court concluded that there was almost no history of such violations, and thus the invocation of Congress's enforcement powers under the 14th Amendment was entirely out of proportion to the supposed remedial object of the legislation.

In *Kimel v. Florida Bd. of Regents,* 120 S. Ct. 631 (2000), the Court held that Congress had exceeded its enforcement powers under §5 of the 14th Amendment by including in the Age Discrimination in Employment Act (ADEA) provisions that subjected states to damage suits in federal court for age discrimination with respect to their employees. The issue arose in the context of whether Congress had validly used its §5 power to abrogate the states' Eleventh Amendment sovereign immunity. Because age discrimination does not violate the equal protection guarantee if it is rationally related to a legitimate governmental purpose, the Court concluded that the ADEA provisions in question were " 'so out of proportion to a supposed remedial or preventive object that [they] cannot be understood as responsive to, or designed to prevent, unconstitutional behavior.' " The ADEA provisions, which made *all* age discrimination unlawful, prohibited "substantially more state employment decisions and practices than would likely be held unconstitutional under the applicable . . . rational basis standard. . . . Congress never identified any pattern of age discrimination by the States, much less any [unconstitutional] discrimination." Congress exceeded its §5 enforcement power because of "the indiscriminate scope of the [ADEA's] substantive requirements and the lack of evidence of widespread and unconstitutional age discrimination by the States."

In *United States v. Morrison,* 120 S. Ct. 1740 (2000), the Court ruled that a federal civil remedy for victims of gender-motivated violence exceeded the scope of the §5 enforcement power. Congress had enacted the law after concluding that "there is pervasive bias in various state justice systems against victims of gender-motivated violence," and that such bias "denies victims of gender-motivated violence the equal protection of the laws." The Court concluded that the law was "simply not 'corrective in its character' " because it lacked "congruence and proportionality between the injury to be prevented or remedied and the means adopted to that end." First, the law was "directed not at any State or state actor, but at individuals who have committed criminal acts motivated by gender bias. [The law] visits no consequence whatever on any Virginia public official involved in investigating or prosecuting" the rape that produced the civil claim at issue in *Morrison*. Second, the remedy adopted by Congress was national in scope but Congress had acted on evidence of unconstitutional sex-based discrimination in only 21 states. In dissent, Justice Breyer noted that in *Flores* the Court had stated that Congress "sometimes can enact remedial 'legislation . . . [that] prohibits conduct which is not itself unconstitutional,' " and observed that the civil remedy at issue in *Morrison* "may lead state actors to improve their own remedial systems [and] restricts private actors only by imposing liability for private conduct that is, in the main, already forbidden by state law. Why is the remedy 'disproportionate'?" Justice Breyer also wondered why Congress could "not take the evidence before it as evidence of a national problem," noting that the Court has never "held that Congress must document the existence of a problem in every State prior to proposing a national solution."

In *Board of Trustees of the University of Alabama v. Garrett*, 121 S. Ct. 955 (2001), the Court held that Congress lacked power under §5 to make states civilly liable to private citizens for their discrimination against the disabled because (1) such discrimination by states is constitutionally permissible so long as it is rationally related to a legitimate state interest, and (2) Congress based its ostensibly remedial legislation mostly upon evidence of discriminatory treatment of the disabled by society in general. *Garrett* requires Congress to identify and prove specific government unconstitutional action in order to invoke its §5 enforcement power.

F. OTHER NATIONAL POWERS

There are many other national powers, some of which are the foundation upon which substantial bodies of law have been created. A brief listing follows.

1. Principal Remaining Legislative Powers

Under Article I, §8, Congress has the following additional powers:

- To **borrow** and **coin money,** to regulate its value, and to punish counterfeiting,

- To regulate **immigration and naturalization,**

- To establish a uniform **bankruptcy law,**

- To fix **standard weights and measures,**

- To establish **postal service,**

- To protect **copyrights, patents, and trademarks,**

- To govern the **District of Columbia.**

Article IV, §3 empowers Congress to control **federal property.** Article V gives to Congress the power to **propose constitutional amendments** by a vote of two-thirds of each house, subject to ratification by three-fourths of the states.

2.   Executive Powers

The powers of the President will be discussed in Chapter 7.

3.   Judicial Power

The powers of the federal courts are examined in detail in the Federal Courts course. Chapter 2 examined some of the limitations upon the exercise of those powers. The heads of jurisdiction of the federal courts are specified in Article III, §2. Recall that Congress may regulate and restrict the exercise of these heads of jurisdiction.

REVIEW QUESTIONS AND ANSWERS

Question: Congress decides that cosmetic surgery is generally medically unnecessary and wasteful of resources. It enacts a tax of $10,000 on each cosmetic surgery, payable by the surgeon. The legislative history is replete with evidence that Congress has enacted the tax solely because it wishes to discourage cosmetic surgery. The tax produces revenue of about $500,000 annually. Dr. Facelift, a cosmetic surgeon, sues to obtain a judicial declaration that the Act is invalid because it is beyond the power of Congress. Will his suit succeed? Why or why not?

Answer: His suit is unlikely to succeed. The courts will not inquire into the congressional motives in enacting the statute. The tax has a regulatory impact but it produces a nontrivial amount of revenue.

Question: Congress amends the statute described in the question above to impose the tax only on those cosmetic surgeries that have *not* been approved by the federal Department of Health and Human Services as medically necessary. Otherwise the facts are as in the first question. Will Dr. Facelift's suit succeed now?

Answer: His suit has a better chance of success. The tax only applies as a result of a regulation—the failure of the Department of Health and Human Services to approve the surgery as medically necessary—and that regulation, viewed *independently* from the tax, must be within Congress's power in order for the tax to be valid. The regulation will be valid if cosmetic surgery substantially affects interstate commerce. Otherwise, it is probably outside of congressional power.

Question: Congress decides to provide welfare assistance to families with dependent children by granting sums of money to the states to be spent only for that purpose. However, no state is eligible to receive any money unless it has enacted legislation that suspends the driving privileges of any person who is in arrears in child support payments for which they are legally obligated. The State of Fox challenges the validity of this condition to the expenditure, seeking a declaration that the condition is invalid. What result?

Answer: The first condition—that the money be spent on AFDC—is valid. The second condition—that the state suspend driving privileges of deadbeat parents—is probably valid. The federal expenditure itself is surely for the general welfare. The condition at issue is unambiguous and not violative of other constitutional provisions. Fox has two plausible arguments:

1. First, the condition—state action to deny drivers' licenses to deadbeat parents—is peripherally related to the federal interest in granting money to the states to assist needy families with children. The condition is designed to spur deadbeat parents to comply with their child support obligations, but their failure to do so will not alter the amount of *federal* money available to needy families. Of course, parental compliance will presumably reduce the demand on the funds made available, thus enabling the actual assistance to needy families to be slightly more generous. The relationship is probably sufficient to establish validity.

2. Second, the condition *may* be coercive since it is an "all-or-nothing" condition—if Fox complies it gets the money to spend on assistance to needy families; if Fox does not comply the entire burden of such assistance is deposited on Fox's doorstep. If there is any bite to the coercion element this ought to be such a case, but it is not at all clear what constitutes sufficient pressure to produce coercion.

Question: In reliance solely upon §5 of the 14th Amendment Congress enacts legislation that forbids states from discriminating on the basis of sexual orientation. The State of Oriole contends that Congress lacks the power to enact the legislation. What result?

Answer: The law is almost certainly invalid. After *Flores,* Congress may only remedy or prevent unconstitutional action. There is no judicially established equal protection right to be free of official discrimination on account of sexual orientation. Unlike *Morgan,* where the *specific practice* attacked by Congress was valid, but the elimination of that practice could reasonably be thought to remedy *other* actions violative of equal protection, this statute does not have any remedial connection to existing equal protection rights.

EXAM TIPS

- **Taxation.** This is not usually tested in isolation because the Court is extremely deferential to congressional discretion concerning the mode of taxation. But if the tax is imposed only upon taxpayers who fail to comply with a regulation that is itself independently beyond congressional power, the tax is likely invalid. This means that taxation issues can easily be combined with the commerce clause; e.g., a federal tax imposed only on people who fail to cut their grass once a week.

- **Spending.** Don't forget that while Congress may *spend* for the **general welfare,** it may *not* **regulate for the general welfare.** This distinction is important mostly when Congress attaches conditions to its expenditures. Coercive conditions are regulations. When Congress attaches conditions to the receipt of federal money by states, the conditions must be **clear and unambiguous,** related to the **federal interest in specific national programs,** not violate some other constitutional provision, and not coercive. Conditional spending is the issue commonly tested.

- **Treaties.** Congress has power to implement treaties by legislation without reference to its usual heads of legislative authority, so long as it doesn't violate some constitutional liberty. This is not tested much because its importance has diminished with the expansion of other sources of legislative power, particularly the commerce power.

- **War.** Congress has sole power to declare war but it also has power to legislate to aid wartime objectives. This is a potentially vast power that has not been used much because of the easy availability of the commerce power. Remember its existence. Don't confuse this with the analytically separate issue of whether the President has unilateral power to commit American troops to combat without a congressional declaration of war.

- **Foreign Affairs.** Congress and the President share an unenumerated power over foreign affairs. The states have no power over foreign affairs.

- **Power to Implement the Reconstruction Amendments.** Congress may enforce the rights guaranteed under the 13th, 14th, and 15th Amendments by providing remedies for violations of those rights. Congress may define the substance of 13th Amendment rights independently of the courts. The 13th Amendment bars private conduct as well as state action. The 14th and 15th

Amendments apply only to state action. It is now definitively settled that congressional enforcement of the 14th (and, probably, the 15th) Amendments only extends to state action and that congressional enforcement must be *congruent* with constitutional injuries and *proportional* to those injuries. This is a fertile exam topic. Don't overlook these considerable powers.

LIMITATIONS ON STATE POWER TO REGULATE INTERSTATE COMMERCE

CHAPTER OVERVIEW

This chapter examines an implied aspect of the commerce clause, often called the **dormant commerce clause** or the **negative commerce clause,** which limits the power of the states to regulate interstate or foreign commerce. A functionally related provision, the privileges and immunities clause of Article IV, §2, is also examined. The most important points in this chapter follow.

- The Constitution limits state power expressly, by permitting Congress to pre-empt state law, and by implication.

- The commerce clause impliedly limits state power to regulate interstate or foreign commerce. Its implied limits are called the **dormant commerce clause** or **negative commerce clause.**

  — The dormant commerce clause only operates when Congress has *failed to act*. When Congress has acted (either by preempting state law or by explicitly consenting to state laws that regulate interstate commerce) the dormant commerce clause is not relevant.

    — Court rulings under the dormant commerce clause are thus reversible by Congress as it exercises its legitimate commerce power.

  — Courts apply the following doctrines to state laws impinging on interstate commerce:

    — All state laws must be **rationally related to a** *legitimate* state purpose. Economic protection, by itself, is an illegitimate purpose.

— State laws that **facially discriminate** against interstate commerce are *invalid* unless the state proves that it has a **legitimate objective that cannot be accomplished by any less discriminatory alternative.**

— Nondiscriminatory state laws that incidentally regulate interstate commerce are *valid* unless the challenger to the law can show that the **burdens placed on interstate commerce** by the law are **clearly excessive** in relation to the **putative local benefits** of the law.

— When states act as *market participants,* rather than market regulators, they are exempt from the dormant commerce clause.

— States are market participants when they are engaging in, or creating, commerce rather than simply controlling other people's commerce.

— Under Article IV's *privileges and immunities* clause, states may not, without a **substantial reason,** discriminate against nonresidents with respect to matters that are **fundamental** to interstate harmony and national union.

— The *fundamental* interest protected by the privileges and immunities clause is mostly the right to pursue a livelihood.

— In order to discriminate on fundamental matters, states must prove that

(1) Nonresidents are a **peculiar source of the problem** the state is trying to solve,

(2) The discriminatory practice is **substantially related** to solution of the problem, and

(3) There are **no practical less discriminatory alternatives available to the state** to solve the problem.

— There is **no market participant exemption** from the privileges and immunities clause.

— Corporations are **not protected** by the privileges and immunities clause.

A.   CONSTITUTIONAL LIMITS ON STATE POWER

The Constitution limits state power expressly and impliedly. The principal express limits are reviewed below. One of the most important implied limits is the judicially created doctrine known as the **dormant** or **negative commerce clause.** This chapter is devoted to it and its doctrinal kin—the "market-participant doctrine" and Article IV's "privileges and immunities" clause.

1. **Express Limits**

   The Constitution sets out a number of express limits on state power.

   a. **Article I, §10 declares that states may not:**

   - Enter into any **"Treaty, Alliance, or Confederation."**

   - Grant **"Letters of Marque and Reprisal."** In the 18th century, a recognized power of sovereign governments was issuance of such letters to private vessels, authorizing them to wage war on behalf of the nation against foreign enemies specified in the letter of authorization. Negation of this sovereign power to wage naval warfare necessarily implies a general prohibition upon the power to declare war.

   - **Coin Money** or issue **Bills of Credit** (modern currency).

   - "[M]ake any Thing but gold and silver Coin a Tender in Payment of Debts."

   - Enact any **bill of attainder** or **ex post facto law.**

   - Enact any law **impairing the obligation of contracts.**

   - Grant any title of nobility.

   Except with congressional consent, Article I, §10 forbids states from

   - Imposing any **import or export taxes.**

   - Making **war** or maintaining **a standing army or navy.**

   - Entering into **interstate or foreign compacts.**

   b. **Article IV** contains several provisions that restrict state power.

   - Section 1 requires each state to give **"Full Faith and Credit"** to the public acts, records, and judicial proceedings of every other state.

   - Section 2 ensures that the "Citizens of each State shall be entitled to all **Privileges and Immunities** of Citizens in the several States." See section I, infra.

   - Section 2 requires states to extradite upon request fugitives from justice in another state.

   c. **The supremacy clause** of Article VI ensures that constitutionally valid federal law displaces conflicting state law. See Chapter 3, supra. Congress may displace state regulation by enacting law under any of its enumerated powers.

d. Individual rights guarantees. The Constitution's guarantees of individual rights also impinge upon state power. The most important provision is the 14th Amendment, which obligates each state to afford equal protection of the law to all persons, and to refrain from taking life, liberty, or property without due process of law. As will be discussed in Chapter 8, section B, the 14th Amendment's due process clause "incorporates" the specific individual rights guarantees of the Bill of Rights, thus making them applicable to the states.

2. Implied Limits

Some limits on state power have been implied from the Constitution. The most important implied limits are those designed to ensure a cohesive, unified national marketplace, free of internal trade restrictions. The principal source of these implied limits is the commerce clause.

B. THE DORMANT COMMERCE CLAUSE: AN OVERVIEW

1. In General

The commerce clause does not expressly prohibit the states from regulating interstate commerce; rather, it is a grant of power to Congress to regulate the specified types of commerce. Nevertheless, there are two ways the states can be barred from the subject.

- First, Congress may simply exercise its own regulatory power over interstate commerce to preempt state laws.

- Second, *even in the absence of any federal legislation,* certain types of state regulation are presumed by courts to be invalid. This latter doctrine is known as the **dormant commerce clause,** sometimes called the **negative commerce clause.**

a. Role of Congress. Even when a court has declared a state law void as in violation of the dormant commerce clause Congress remains free to use its own power over interstate commerce to validate such a law. Within its legitimate scope Congress controls the commerce power. Congress **may act to regulate commerce itself** (and preempt conflicting state laws), or it **may act to consent to state regulation of commerce that would otherwise be impermissible.** *Only when Congress has **not** so acted* will courts void a state law on the grounds that the law violates the dormant commerce clause.

b. A theoretical conundrum. The fact that courts void state regulations of commerce that are not in conflict with federal law raises a theoretical problem. If Congress controls the commerce power through its power of **preemption** or **consent,** why does the Court have any authority to strike down state laws regulating commerce when Congress has not acted? There are two answers, which are not mutually exclusive.

- First, some aspects of commerce may be reserved for federal regulation—there may be a zone within the larger set of "commerce" that is off-limits to any state regulation unless Congress acts specifically to permit it.

- Second, since the Court acts only when Congress has *not* acted the Court may be doing nothing more than presuming a congressional negative "against state action which in its effect constitutes an unreasonable interference with national interests, the presumption being rebuttable at the pleasure of Congress." Dowling, 27 Va. L. Rev. 1.

2.   The Foundations of Modern Doctrine

Nineteenth century justices were preoccupied with identifying which aspects of the commerce power were exclusively federal and which were subject to concurrent regulation by the states and the federal government.

Example: Imagine a sphere that represents the total possible commerce power. All of the sphere is subject to congressional control. Inside the sphere is a smaller sphere—the core—that is subject *only* to federal control. Nineteenth century judges tried hard to define the boundary between the core and the larger sphere. Today, we would say that the core is exclusively federal unless Congress acts specifically to permit the states to enter the core.

The reason for this concern was general agreement that the Framers had intended the commerce power to be a key part of the larger constitutional structure that ensured an internal common market—a single national marketplace, free from state-imposed barriers to national commerce. To achieve this goal it was necessary to identify which state laws interfered with this constitutional objective, even if they did not collide with federal statutory law.

a.   *Gibbons v. Ogden* **and exclusive federal power.** In the early years of the nation some contended that Congress possessed the *exclusive power* to regulate commerce. Recall that in *Gibbons v. Ogden,* John Marshall observed that "[t]here is great force in this argument, and the court is not satisfied that it has been refuted." But the Court in *Gibbons* did *not rely* upon the idea of *exclusive federal power* over commerce to strike down New York's steamboat monopoly law. Only Justice William Johnson thought that the power to regulate commerce was exclusively federal. But both Justice Johnson and the majority agreed that even if the commerce power was exclusively federal states could regulate interstate commerce *incidentally,* so long as their purpose in legislating was not to regulate interstate commerce.

b. ***Willson v. Black Bird Creek Marsh Co.,*** 27 U.S. 245 (1829). Delaware law authorized the Company to dam a navigable creek and to fill part of the marsh. Willson, owner of a vessel licensed under federal navigation laws, broke the dam to pass through. The Company sued for damages and Willson defended on the ground that the Delaware enabling law violated the commerce clause. The Court, per Chief Justice Marshall, upheld the law. Delaware's *purpose* was not to regulate interstate commerce but to improve the health and safety of its citizens and there was no actual conflict between the Delaware law and any federal law. By contrast, the New York monopoly law at issue in *Gibbons* was designed to regulate interstate commerce and was in actual conflict with federal law.

   i.   Importance. After *Willson* the Court began to distinguish between state laws intended to regulate or impede interstate commerce (generally void) and those intended to accomplish some legitimate local purpose (generally valid).

c. ***Cooley v. Board of Wardens,*** 53 U.S. 299 (1851). The validity of a Pennsylvania law requiring ships to take on pilots to enter or leave Philadelphia was at issue. A 1789 federal law authorized states to regulate pilotage. The Court held that the scope of the dormant commerce clause was defined by the nature of the regulated activity. If the subject was **inherently national**—its "nature" required nationally uniform rules—it was off limits to the States. Congress had *exclusive power* to regulate inherently national activities. If the subject was **inherently local**—its nature admitted of a welter of local rules—the States were free to act until and unless Congress acted to preempt them. The states and Congress shared *concurrent power* to regulate inherently local activities. Over time, the Court found it difficult to distinguish between the local and the national. It tried to do so by assessing whether the state law placed a **direct** or **indirect** burden on interstate commerce, but this test proved to be of little help.

3.   The Triad of Modern Doctrines: Illegitimate Economic Protectionism, Discrimination Against and Burdens on Interstate Commerce

The Court has effectively abandoned the *Cooley* doctrine in favor of three other doctrines.

   • The first is a simple requirement that all state laws be **rationally related to a *legitimate* state purpose.**

   • The second is a **discrimination** doctrine: **State laws that *unjustifiably discriminate* against interstate commerce are prohibited by the dormant commerce clause *until and unless* Congress permits the states to discriminate.**

- The third is a **burden** doctrine: Nondiscriminatory **state laws that *unduly burden* interstate commerce are prohibited by the dormant commerce clause *until and unless* Congress permits the states to impose the burden.**

Not surprisingly, the problem with these doctrines is the difficulty of assessing discrimination or undue burden. The following sections examine these three doctrines.

C. RATIONAL RELATIONSHIP TO LEGITIMATE STATE PURPOSES

1. Rational Relationship

Almost any state law will be treated as rationally related to some state goal. When applying a rational relationship test courts are extremely deferential to the legislative judgment. If there are any facts that establish any plausible connection between the law and some state goal the rationality of the relationship is proven.

2. Legitimate and Illegitimate State Purposes

While virtually any state law is rationally related to *some* state goal, if the purpose is **not legitimate** the law is automatically invalid. One illegitimate state purpose is economic protectionism. The Constitution was intended to create a common market within the nation, free of internal trade restrictions, and the commerce clause was part of that design. Attempts by states to wall themselves off from interstate commerce are repugnant to that principle. Thus, laws that are purposefully or openly protectionist are invalid per se, since deliberate protectionism is an *illegitimate* state objective. Very few statutes are so brazenly protectionist.

 # EXAMPLE AND ANALYSIS

Example: Oklahoma required electric generation plants using coal as a fuel to devote at least 10% of their fuel consumption to Oklahoma-mined coal. Even though this law did not produce very much economic protection it was openly and purposefully protectionist and so struck down on that ground without further inquiry. *Wyoming v. Oklahoma*, 502 U.S. 437 (1992).

D. THE DISCRIMINATION DOCTRINE

1. Assessing Discrimination

There are several ways by which the Court finds sufficient discrimination against interstate commerce presumptively to void state laws and one test by which a state may justify such discrimination.

a. **Facial discrimination.** When a state law **discriminates on its face** against interstate commerce it is *invalid* unless the state proves that it has a *legitimate objective that cannot be accomplished by any less discriminatory alternative.*

 # EXAMPLES AND ANALYSIS

Example: In order to protect its environment and the health of its citizens, New Jersey banned out-of-state garbage from New Jersey dumps. The Court ruled that New Jersey's ban was facially discriminatory and that New Jersey had failed to prove its legitimate purposes could not be achieved by less discriminatory alternatives. For example, New Jersey could limit the amount of garbage from anywhere (including New Jersey) that could be deposited in New Jersey. *Philadelphia v. New Jersey,* 437 U.S. 617 (1978).

Example: Clarkstown, New York built a facility to sort, for a fee, recyclable materials from garbage. To assure the financial success of the facility Clarkstown required that all solid waste in the town be deposited at the facility. Carbone, a private recycler, contended that the "flow control" ordinance was invalid. The Court agreed, treating the law as almost a mirror image to *Philadelphia v. New Jersey.* The ordinance squelched outside competition and was facially a form of "[d]iscrimination against interstate commerce in favor of local business." Clarkstown was unable to show that it lacked less discriminatory alternatives to achieve its legitimate local objectives. *C & A Carbone, Inc. v. Clarkstown,* 511 U.S. 383 (1994).

When a state law is discriminatory on its face the Court will not inquire into the question of whether, in actual practice, the law has a discriminatory effect on interstate commerce. It only examines the justifications offered by the state.

 # EXAMPLES AND ANALYSIS

Example: To protect its native fish species Maine prohibited the importation of non-native baitfish. Though the law was facially discriminatory Maine was able to demonstrate that its legitimate goal of preserving native fish species from destruction due to inadvertent introduction of non-native predators and disease could not be accomplished by anything less than an outright ban. Maine proved that testing or screening of imported baitfish (less discriminatory alternatives) were not effective and would not accomplish Maine's legitimate objective. *Maine v. Taylor,* 477 U.S. 131 (1986).

Example: To conserve its native minnow population, Oklahoma prohibited the export of minnows taken from Oklahoma waters. The law was facially discriminatory and although Oklahoma's objective—wildlife conservation—was legitimate there were other less discriminatory alternatives available to accomplish that objective. Oklahoma could have simply imposed limits on the number of minnows taken for any purpose. *Hughes v. Oklahoma*, 441 U.S. 322 (1979).

When a state law is discriminatory on its face the Court will take into account other state laws that have the effect of neutralizing the apparently facially discriminatory statute.

 # EXAMPLES AND ANALYSIS

Example: Washington imposed a sales tax on goods sold in the state and a "use tax" on goods purchased outside Washington for use within the state. The sales and use taxes were set at the same rate. Although the use tax discriminated against out-of-state purchases it was upheld because it was an attempt to equalize tax burdens by taxing substantially equivalent events in like manner. Had Washington imposed only a use tax and no sales tax, or imposed higher rates on use, it would likely have been struck down. *Henneford v. Silas Mason Co.,* 300 U.S. 577 (1937).

Example: Oregon charged 85 cents per ton for disposal of solid waste generated in Oregon and $2.25 per ton for disposal of out-of-state waste. The difference was facially discriminatory but Oregon argued that the fee differential was a valid "compensatory" use tax or fee, because a portion of the actual cost of disposal of Oregon-generated waste was paid through collection of Oregon income taxes. The Court rejected the argument, invalidating the differential fees. The compensatory nature of a tax, said the Court, is "merely a specific way of justifying a facially discriminatory tax." To be compensatory, the differential fees or taxes must be imposed on "substantially equivalent taxable events." The fee imposed on dumping waste was held not to be substantially equivalent to income taxes, even though some portion of the income tax might be used to defray the cost of solid waste disposal. *Oregon Waste Systems, Inc. v. Department of Environmental Quality,* 511 U.S. 93 (1994).

---

    b.   Economic protectionism. The Court always sees discrimination against interstate commerce in a state law that is **economically protectionist.** Laws that are openly and purposefully protectionist are automatically void. But laws that are protectionist in their effect and have no apparent purpose apart from local economic protection are equally infirm.

 # EXAMPLE AND ANALYSIS

Example: Hawaii imposed an excise tax on all liquor sales but exempted pineapple wine and brandy from the tax. The scheme, though facially neutral, had both the purpose and effect of local economic protection and was invalidated. *Bacchus Imports, Ltd. v. Dias*, 468 U.S. 263 (1984).

   c. **Discriminatory application of neutral laws.** A state may enact a law that is perfectly neutral toward interstate commerce but if the law, *as applied,* discriminates against interstate commerce it will be **void unless the state proves that it has a legitimate objective that cannot be accomplished by any less discriminatory alternative.**

 # EXAMPLE AND ANALYSIS

A state requires all trucks operating in the state to pass an annual safety inspection. The law is neutral since it applies to in-state trucks just as much as it does to interstate trucks. But if the state routinely passes unsafe in-state trucks and routinely fails safer interstate trucks, the law is discriminatory as applied. The law is void unless the state could show that its discriminatory safety standards are necessary to a legitimate state objective. That is highly unlikely.

A neutral law might be applied in a fashion that is so discriminatory and economically protectionist that the law, as applied, will be automatically invalid.

Example: New York required all milk processors to obtain an operating license but conditioned the issuance of a license upon an administrative finding that the new processing plant was "in the public interest" and "will not tend to a destructive competition in a market already adequately served." New York refused a license to Hood, a Boston milk distributor who wished to purchase New York milk, process it in New York, and transport it to Boston for sale, on the ground that Hood's activities might jeopardize local supplies of milk for retail sale. Although New York's licensing requirement and criteria for issuance were neutral, the Court concluded that New York's refusal was the product of sheer economic protectionism and applied a *per se* rule of invalidity. *H.P. Hood & Sons v. Du Mond*, 336 U.S. 525 (1949).

E.   THE BURDEN DOCTRINE: BALANCING BURDENS AND BENEFITS

1.   The *Pike* Test

A state law that does not discriminate against interstate commerce is presumed to be valid. It is void only if the challenger to the law can show that the **burdens placed on interstate commerce** by the law are **clearly excessive** in relation to the **putative local benefits** of the law.

 EXAMPLE AND ANALYSIS

Example: Arizona required that Arizona-grown cantaloupes be packed in Arizona so that their Arizona origin would be clear and the reputation of Arizona's high quality cantaloupes would be enhanced. The regulation was attacked by an Arizona grower who packed his cantaloupes in California. The Court concluded that Arizona's objective was legitimate but of slight importance, and that the burdens imposed on interstate commerce were substantial. The regulation was struck down. *Pike v. Bruce Church, Inc.,* 397 U.S. 137 (1970).

This inquiry requires courts to *balance* the *benefits to the state* against the *burdens on interstate commerce.* It is difficult if not impossible to measure state benefits and burdens on commerce with the same scale, but the Court tries it anyway. The Court will uphold state laws unless the burdens, however measured, *heavily outweigh* the state benefits, however measured. This entire enterprise has been criticized by Justice Scalia, who has characterized the effort to balance benefits and burden as "more like judging whether a particular line is longer than a particular rock is heavy." *Bendix Autolite Corp. v. Midwesco Enterprises, Inc.,* 486 U.S. 888 (1988).

2.   Balancing Benefits and Burdens

When there is a large disparity between benefits and burdens application of the balancing test is easy. A state law imposing high burdens on commerce and delivering low benefits to the state is the classic example of a law failing the balancing test. When the burdens on commerce are low and the benefits are high the law is easily valid. The harder assessments of benefits and burdens occur when the benefits and burdens are more nearly equal: both are high, or both are low. Because the balancing test presumes the validity of the state law unless the challenger can show that the burdens *heavily outweigh* the benefits one might suppose that these laws would generally be held valid. But the Court does not merely compare the relative *quantity* of benefits and burdens, it also assesses the *nature* or *quality* of the burdens and benefits.

EXAMPLE AND ANALYSIS

Arizona limited railroad train length within the state. Southern Pacific challenged the validity of the statute and showed that the law forced it to break up and remake trains on either side of Arizona, imposed greater labor costs, and added fuel expenses. Though the law was intended to enhance safety in Arizona, Southern Pacific proved that in fact a greater number of short trains traveling through Arizona increased accidents. The law failed the burden doctrine. *Southern Pacific Co. v. Arizona,* 325 U.S. 761 (1945).

  a. **Assessing burdens.** Courts employ a variety of methods to assess the burden a law places on interstate commerce.

   • First, if the burdens on commerce consist of discriminatory effects or are the product of a hidden discriminatory purpose the Court will employ an awkward amalgam of the discrimination doctrine and the burden doctrine to scrutinize the law more closely. See section F, infra.

   • Second, burdens are not assessed in isolation. The burden of a law may depend, in part, on the laws of other states.

 EXAMPLES AND ANALYSIS

Example: Illinois required trucks to have contoured mudflaps. Arkansas required trucks to have straight mudflaps. All other states required either type. A trucking company challenged the Illinois law, arguing that the law burdened interstate commerce because no other state required contour mudflaps and one other state barred them. Since straight mudflaps were the industry norm, the company argued that it was required to alter its interstate trucks to conform to Illinois and that traffic involving both Illinois and Arkansas was especially hampered. The Court found the burdens imposed heavily outweighed any benefits to Illinois. *Bibb v. Navajo Freight Lines, Inc.,* 359 U.S. 520 (1959).

Example: Iowa banned certain truck-trailer combinations from its roads. All its neighboring states permitted the combinations barred from Iowa. The ban was challenged in part because the prohibited combinations were efficient and widely used in the industry, but due to Iowa's ban interstate trucks skirted Iowa and burdened the roads of Iowa's neighbors. These burdens, combined with other factors, voided the law. *Kassel v. Consolidated Freightways Corp.,* 450 U.S. 662 (1981).

- Third, burdens are measured in terms of the law's effect on interstate commerce. Those effects are often economic and quantifiable, but noneconomic effects count as well.

b.   Assessing benefits. The benefits of public policy are always hard to measure but the Court tries to do so in terms of how much the law actually accomplishes its purposes. **Example:** The Arizona train length limit involved in *Southern Pacific v. Arizona* was intended to enhance the safety of Arizona motorists at railroad grade crossings. But the law actually produced more accidents of the very type Arizona sought to prevent, demonstrating that the law not only failed to accomplish its purpose but was perverse.

Like burdens, benefits are not measured in isolation. If a state law purports to deliver benefits, but other laws of the state undermine those benefits, the weight of the benefits is reduced. **Example:** Iowa's ban of certain truck-trailer combinations was ostensibly to improve highway safety, but Iowa provided so many exceptions that it undermined its claimed purposes. *Kassel v. Consolidated Freightways Corp.,* supra.

Similarly, if a state law provides benefits that are already provided by other laws, its marginal benefit is insubstantial. **Example:** Illinois adopted a "business takeover" act, designed to protect Illinois shareholders, among others. The shareholder benefits Illinois sought to confer were already provided by the federal securities laws. The marginal benefit to the state was very slight while the burden on interstate commerce was substantial. *Edgar v. MITE Corp.,* 457 U.S. 624 (1982).

The Court sometimes says that state laws that deliver real, nontrivial health and safety benefits are valid without the necessity of balancing burdens and benefits but even then it often inquires into the purported benefits in order to determine whether or not those benefits are illusory or real. **Example:** Trial courts undertook extensive inquiry into the actual safety benefits produced by Arizona's train length limits and Iowa's ban on certain tractor trailer combinations. In the Arizona case the court found that no safety benefits were produced. In the Iowa case, the courts were satisfied that the safety benefits produced were so slight as to be trivial or illusory. Both laws were invalidated. *Southern Pacific v. Arizona,* supra. *Kassel v. Consolidated Freightways Corp.,* supra.

F.   FACIALLY NEUTRAL LAWS WITH DISCRIMINATORY EFFECTS OR PURPOSES

1.   In General

States sometimes enact laws that are facially nondiscriminatory but that either (1) have a **discriminatory effect** on interstate commerce, or (2) are motivated by a **hidden discriminatory purpose.** The Court treats these cases as hybrids, partaking both of the discrimination doctrine and the burden doctrine.

2. **Discrimination Sufficient to Invalidate State Law**

   a. **The hybrid test of *Hunt*.** Sometimes the Court regards discriminatory effects and the suggestion of economic protectionism as sufficient to invoke a hybrid of the discrimination and burden doctrines.

 ## EXAMPLE AND ANALYSIS

North Carolina required apples sold in the state to be packed in cartons carrying only the United States Department of Agriculture grade or no grade at all. Washington State employed a different grading system that was uniformly regarded by apple dealers as preferable to USDA grades. Although the North Carolina regulation applied equally to all apples, it had the effect of depriving Washington packers of the benefits of their superior grading system. The discriminatory effects were significant and there was some evidence that the law was intended to protect North Carolina's apple producers. That combination of distinct discriminatory effects and hint of a forbidden purpose caused the Court to employ a hybrid standard. "When discrimination against commerce of the type we have found is demonstrated, *the burden falls on the State to justify it **both** in terms of the local benefits flowing from the statute and the unavailability of nondiscriminatory alternatives adequate to preserve the local interests at stake.*" The Court found North Carolina's claimed benefit—preventing consumer deception—to be slight and concluded that less discriminatory alternatives were available to North Carolina to achieve this small benefit. *Hunt v. Washington State Apple Advertising Commission,* 432 U.S. 333 (1977).

If the balancing test of the burden doctrine applied the *challenger* would be forced to prove that the burdens on commerce heavily outweigh the local benefits. But the Court in *Hunt* shifted the burden of proof to North Carolina, requiring it to prove *both* local benefits and lack of nondiscriminatory alternatives. If anything, the hybrid test is even more stringent than the discrimination doctrine.

   b. **Discrimination doctrine applied.** Some combination of discriminatory effects and possible protectionist purpose may trigger application of the discrimination doctrine alone.

 ## EXAMPLE AND ANALYSIS

Madison, Wisconsin barred the sale of milk unless it had been pasteurized within a five-mile radius of Madison. The Court found the discriminatory effect of this law profound, since it completely barred milk from out of state. The Court treated as irrelevant the fact the law also barred most Wisconsin milk. Madison's legislative objective—public health—could readily have been achieved by reliance on federal inspection of remote pasteurization plants. The Court thus applied the discrimination doctrine to strike down Madison's law. *Dean Milk Co. v. Madison,* 340 U.S. 349 (1951).

---

     c.   Illegitimate objective: Economic protectionism. The presence of either or both of discriminatory effects and discriminatory motives may establish, in some cases, an illegitimate objective—economic protectionism—on the part of the state.

 # EXAMPLE AND ANALYSIS

Massachusetts taxed all milk sold in the state, whether produced inside or outside of Massachusetts. The tax revenues were used to pay subsidies to Massachusetts dairy farmers. An out-of-state milk producer challenged the validity of the tax and subsidy program. The Court struck it down, finding that the program in its entirety produced discriminatory effects and was motivated by an illegitimate desire to protect higher cost local dairy farmers from more efficient out-of-state competitors. Although the tax was nondiscriminatory—it applied to all milk sold in the state, whatever its origin—the subsidy program amounted to a rebate to a favored in-state group—dairy farmers. The "purpose and effect" of the program, said the Court, was "to divert market share to Massachusetts dairy farmers. . . . Its avowed purpose and its undisputed effect are to enable higher cost Massachusetts dairy farmers to compete with lower cost dairy farmers in other States. . . . Like an ordinary tariff, the tax is . . . effectively imposed only on out-of-state products." Once perceived as economically protectionist, it was struck down without further discussion. *West Lynn Creamery, Inc. v. Healy,* 512 U.S. 186 (1994).

---

     d.   Burden doctrine applied. Sometimes the Court finds the discriminatory effects insufficient to trigger anything but the burden doctrine's balancing test.

 # EXAMPLES AND ANALYSIS

Example: Minnesota banned the sale of milk in plastic jugs, thus encouraging its sale in paper containers. Minnesota has no manufacturers of plastic jugs but does have a paper industry that makes paper milk cartons. The Court found the discriminatory effects too slight to invoke the discrimination doctrine and upheld the law under the balancing test. *Minnesota v. Clover Leaf Creamery Co.,* 449 U.S. 456 (1981).

Example: Maryland barred refiners of gasoline from the retail sale of gasoline. All refiners of gasoline are located outside Maryland. The Court found no discriminatory effect because the law did not on its face restrict the movement of gasoline across state lines. The Court found no protectionist purpose despite evidence that one legislative motivation was to protect local independent retailers of gasoline. The Court applied balancing and sustained the law. *Exxon Corp. v. Maryland,* 437 U.S. 117 (1978).

---

    e. Summary of the discriminatory effects or motives cases. Two explanations of the Court's mixed signals follow. Each seems reasonably accurate, though neither is a perfect explanation of what is, at bottom, a confused and inconsistent piece of constitutional law.

        i. "Burden doctrine plus." The Court applies the burden doctrine to these cases. If, in the application of the balancing test, the Court finds significant discriminatory effects or hidden discriminatory purposes, it invalidates because the burdens on commerce clearly outweigh the local benefits.

        ii. Triggers for the discrimination doctrine. Discriminatory effects or motives are "triggers" that activate the discrimination doctrine. Thus:

- If the discriminatory effects are sufficiently pronounced their presence triggers the discrimination doctrine.

- If a discriminatory motive is proven, the discrimination doctrine is triggered, although logic suggests that such statutes ought to be void per se as undertaken for an illegitimate purpose.

- If discriminatory motive and effects establish economic protectionism as the purpose of the law, it is invalid *per se.*

- If no discriminatory motive is proven, and the discriminatory effects are slight, the burden doctrine applies.

G. FOREIGN COMMERCE

1. Application

The dormant commerce clause doctrine applies also to state regulation of foreign commerce, but with the following differences.

2.   Greater Federal Power Over Foreign Commerce

The power to regulate foreign commerce is almost an exclusive federal power. The Court has characterized "an essential attribute" of the foreign commerce power to be that "its exercise may not be limited, qualified or impeded to any extent by state action." *Board of Trustees of the Univ. of Illinois v. United States,* 289 U.S. 48, 56 (1933). That overstates the case, but not by much. "It is a well-accepted rule that state restrictions burdening foreign commerce are subjected to a more rigorous and searching scrutiny" than state regulations touching upon interstate commerce. *South-Central Timber Development v. Wunnicke,* 467 U.S. 82 (1984). At the very least, state regulations affecting foreign commerce may not impinge significantly upon national concerns. This is because it "is crucial to the efficient execution of the Nation's foreign policy that 'the Federal Government . . . speak with one voice when regulating commercial relations with foreign governments.' " *Wunnicke,* supra, quoting *Michelin Tire Corp. v. Wages,* 423 U.S. 276, 285 (1976). While dormant commerce clause rules apply, the burden on foreign commerce need not be great to result in invalidation of the state law.

3.   States as Market Participants

The doctrine that states are exempt from the restrictions of the dormant commerce clause when they are acting as market participants (see section H, infra) may not apply to foreign commerce, although the Court has not so ruled. Cf. *Crosby v. National Foreign Trade Council,* 120 S. Ct. 2288 (2000), in which the Court struck down on statutory preemption grounds a Massachusetts law barring state agencies from dealing with companies doing business with Burma.

H.   THE MARKET-PARTICIPATION DOCTRINE

1.   The Concept: *Reeves, Inc. v. Stake,* 447 U.S. 429 (1980)

When a state acts as a **market participant** rather than as a sovereign regulator of markets the limitations of the dormant commerce clause do not apply. When a state is participating in the marketplace rather than regulating it, the state is treated just like a private party. Like private market participants a state, when acting as a market participant, may discriminate against interstate commerce.

 EXAMPLE AND ANALYSIS

South Dakota owned and operated a cement plant. It restricted sales of cement to South Dakota residents. Because South Dakota was participating in the cement market it was free to discriminate against outsiders. By contrast, if South Dakota had simply barred the export of cement from South Dakota its law would certainly have been struck down. *Reeves, Inc. v. Stake*, 447 U.S. 429 (1980).

2. Defining the Market

The key issue in administering the market participation doctrine is defining the market in which the state is a participant. The Court says it will define the market narrowly in order to confine the states' ability to hamper interstate commerce.

 EXAMPLES AND ANALYSIS

Example: Alaska sold its standing timber pursuant to a contract that required purchasers to mill the timber into lumber in Alaska. Alaska claimed that the processing condition was an aspect of its participation in the timber market. The Court rejected that contention, concluding that the condition related to the timber *processing* market, a market in which Alaska did not participate. *South-Central Timber Development, Inc. v. Wunnicke*, 467 U.S. 82 (1984).

But even though the Court says it will define the market narrowly it occasionally fails to do so.

Example: Boston required that all contractors on Boston public construction projects use a workforce on those projects composed of at least 50% Boston residents. Even though the construction workers were not employed by Boston the Court concluded that Boston was participating in the labor market through its construction contracts and upheld the requirement. *White v. Massachusetts Council of Construction Employers, Inc.*, 460 U.S. 204 (1983).

3. Defining Participation

When states *create* commerce rather than simply *regulating existing commerce*, they are participating in a market.

 EXAMPLE AND ANALYSIS

Maryland sought to encourage the destruction of old autos by paying a "bounty" for Maryland-licensed junk cars. If the car came from a Maryland resident or junkyard, few questions were asked. If the car came from an out-of-stater stringent documentary proof of the car's Maryland registration was required. The discrimination was upheld as permissible because Maryland was participating in the market for junked autos by purchasing them. Maryland's action created commerce by increasing demand for auto hulks. *Hughes v. Alexandria Scrap Corp.,* 426 U.S. 794 (1976).

The same economic result could be achieved by a pure subsidy, but economic subsidies delivered through regulation or tax breaks are subjected to dormant commerce clause scrutiny. There are two explanations of this different treatment. It is fair to allow a state to retain public benefits created by public investment. Also, state spending is less coercive than regulation or taxation and thus less hostile to affected outsiders. See Regan, 84 Mich. L. Rev. 1091, 1194.

I. THE PRIVILEGES AND IMMUNITIES CLAUSE OF ARTICLE IV

1. Function and Purpose

Article IV, §2 provides that "[t]he Citizens of each State shall be entitled to all Privileges and Immunities of Citizens in the several States." This prevents states from denying to *all* outsiders (whether they are noncitizens or simply nonresidents) the privileges and immunities enjoyed by insiders. Corporations, however, are not regarded as "citizens" and thus do not enjoy the protection of the clause. "The primary purpose of this clause . . . was to help fuse into one nation a collection of independent, sovereign states. It was designed to insure to a citizen of State A who ventures into State B the same privileges which the citizens of State B enjoy." *Toomer v. Witsell,* 334 U.S. 385, 395 (1948). Article IV's privilege and immunities clause should not be confused with the privileges and immunities clause of the 14th Amendment.

2. The Meaning of Protected Privileges and Immunities

Two problems are raised in interpreting the clause: (1) What are the "privileges and immunities" protected? (2) Are those "privileges and immunities" *absolutely* or *conditionally* protected?

    a. Fundamental rights. Privileges or immunities consist of interests that are *fundamental to the promotion of interstate harmony* or to the *maintenance and well-being of the nation.* In practice the fundamental interest protected is the **pursuit of a livelihood.** The concept of fundamental rights in the context of the privileges and immunities clause differs from fundamental rights in the context of the due process clause or equal protection. See Chapters 8 and 9, infra.

        i. The "natural rights" conception. Early in the nation's history Justice Bushrod Washington (President Washington's nephew) concluded that the privileges and immunities protected are those "which are in their very nature, fundamental." *Corfield v. Coryell,* 6 Fed. Cas. 546 (No. 3230) (C.C.E.D. Pa. 1823) (on circuit). Washington conceived "fundamental rights" to be rooted in principles of natural law—human rights that transcend governmental institutions.

ii. **The modern view: "basic to the maintenance or well-being of the union."** Rather than perceiving "fundamental" rights to be natural rights the modern Court regards the clause as designed to protect "all the privileges of trade and commerce." *Austin v. New Hampshire,* 420 U.S. 656 (1975). This conception is seen by comparing three cases:

 # EXAMPLES AND ANALYSIS

Example: Montana imposed a fee of $225 on outsiders to hunt elk, but imposed a fee of only $30 on Montanans. The Court concluded that hunting elk, a recreational activity, was not "fundamental" to the promotion of interstate harmony or to the "maintenance and well-being of the Union." *Baldwin v. Montana Fish & Game Comm'n,* 436 U.S. 371 (1978).

Example: Alaska enacted a law requiring employers in the oil business to prefer Alaskans to outsiders in hiring for jobs in the oil industry. The Court concluded that the opportunity to seek employment is fundamental to the promotion of interstate harmony. The Court then struck down the law because Alaska's justifications for the discrimination were insufficient. *Hicklin v. Orbeck,* 437 U.S. 518 (1978).

Example: New Hampshire sought to restrict the practice of law to those who resided in New Hampshire. Piper, a resident of Vermont, wished to practice law in both states. The Court concluded that the practice of law was sufficiently fundamental to the national purposes of the clause and struck down the New Hampshire limitation because New Hampshire's justifications were inadequate. *Piper v. New Hampshire,* 470 U.S. 274 (1985).

b. **Justified discrimination.** Even if a state law impinges upon a fundamental interest states may discriminate against outsiders when there is a **"substantial reason"** for differential treatment. "[T]he Privileges and Immunities Clause is not absolute." *Toomer v. Witsell, supra.* States have the burden of proving the existence of a substantial reason. To do so, states must show:

- A *specific connection* between the state goal and the discriminatory practice; i.e., nonresidents must be shown to "constitute a **peculiar source of the evil** at which the statute is aimed." *Toomer v. Witsell*, 334 U.S. at 398.

- A *substantial relationship* between the discriminatory practice and the problem the law addresses.

- A *lack of workable less discriminatory alternatives* to achieve the state's goal.

EXAMPLES AND ANALYSIS

Example: South Carolina imposed a $25 fee for commercial shrimp boats owned by South Carolinians and a $2500 fee for commercial shrimp boats owned by outsiders. South Carolina argued that the differential was justified because it served to conserve shrimp and to defray the cost of South Carolina's additional shrimp conservation measures attributable to outside fishing. The Court struck down the law, finding no evidence in the record "that non-residents use larger boats or different fishing methods than residents, or that any substantial amount of the State's general funds is devoted to shrimp conservation." South Carolina could have charged fees based on boat size or a fee calculated to equalize the burden of conservation between inside and outside users of the fishery. *Toomer v. Witsell*, 334 U.S. 385, 398 (1948).

Example: Camden, New Jersey, enacted a law requiring that at least 40% of all employees of contractors on city construction jobs must be Camden residents. Camden sought to justify the preference on the grounds that it was necessary to redress the extreme economic depression of Camden and provide job opportunities to its large population of unemployed or underemployed minority members. The Court concluded that the law impinged upon the fundamental interest of interstate employment but remanded to the lower court to determine whether there was a substantial reason for the differential treatment. *United Building & Construction Trades Council v. Camden*, 465 U.S. 208 (1984).

3. Relationship to the Market-Participation Doctrine

Recall that states are exempt from dormant commerce clause scrutiny when they are participating in a market. *No such exemption applies to Article IV's privileges and immunities clause.* States can never escape scrutiny of their actions under the privileges and immunities clause. Even when acting as market participants, when a fundamental interest is involved states must prove the *substantial reason* for any discrimination toward outsiders that they practice.

4.   Relationship to Equal Protection

There are two important differences between the privileges and immunities clause and equal protection.

- Corporations are "persons" for purposes of equal protection but not "citizens" for purposes of the privileges and immunities clause.

- Under the privileges and immunities clause discrimination against nonresidents with respect to earning a living must be justified by the state by a more stringent standard than would apply under equal protection. See Chapter 9, infra.

REVIEW QUESTIONS AND ANSWERS

Question: In an attempt to ensure the health and safety of its citizens, the City of Bliss, located in the State of Awate about ten miles from Awate's border with the State of Nogorra, enacts a law that requires that all agricultural produce sold in Bliss be certified by the Bliss Department of Agriculture as free of all pesticides. The Bliss agricultural inspectors regularly inspect farms in Awate, some as far away as 100 miles from Bliss, but never inspect farms in Nogorra. There are several large farms in Nogorra, located within fifteen miles of Bliss, that are completely free of pesticides and that wish to sell their produce in Awate. The Nogorran farms challenge the validity of Bliss's law. Will the challenge succeed?

Answer: Probably. The law is facially neutral with respect to interstate commerce but, as applied, is either actually discriminatory or productive of severe discriminatory effects. Thus, it is likely that the law is void unless Bliss can prove that its legitimate objective of preserving the health and safety of its citizens can only be accomplished by the inspection process as Bliss applied. That is not likely the case. Bliss can easily send its inspectors to Nogorra or rely on other proof of their pesticide free status.

Question: The State of Orixis is home to the last virgin forest of yellow cedar in the United States. Yellow cedar is much prized by users located in other states and in foreign countries. There is almost no demand for yellow cedar in Orixis. In order to preserve the cedar forest, Orixis enacts legislation that forbids the shipment out of state of any yellow cedar from Orixis. A lumber company who owns part of the cedar forest challenges the constitutional validity of the law. What is the basis for the lumber company's challenge and is the challenge likely to succeed?

Answer: The basis of the challenge is the contention that the Orixis law violates the dormant aspect of the commerce clause. The challenge will succeed. The Orixis law is facially discriminatory since it bars all interstate shipment of Orixis yellow cedar. Orixis may contend that the law is intended to accomplish the legitimate objective of preserving the rare yellow cedar forest. That legitimate state objective can be accomplished by less discriminatory means, such as a limit on the amount of yellow cedar that may be cut by anyone. Because Orixis's objective may be accomplished by less discriminatory means the law will be voided.

Question: In order to minimize its road repair and maintenance expenses, the state of Zucchini prohibits trucks from using its highways if they weigh over 5,000 kilograms. Zucchini relied on multiple tests of various weight limits before concluding that a limit of 5,000 kilograms would minimize these expenses. After adopting the law, Zucchini's road repair and maintenance expenses fell by two-thirds. One of its neighboring states has no weight limits, the others all prohibit trucks weighing over 20,000 kilograms. Every other state in the United States imposes weight limits of between 15,000 to 20,000 kilograms. Most interstate trucks weigh between 10,000 and 15,000 kilograms. An interstate trucking company challenges the constitutional validity of Zucchini's limit. Will the challenge succeed? Why or why not?

Answer: The challenge will probably succeed. The statute is evenhanded toward interstate commerce but has a discriminatory effect on interstate commerce since most interstate trucks will be required to avoid the state and interstate shipments into Zucchini must be on small, light trucks. The burden imposed on interstate commerce is substantial, and consists almost entirely of these discriminatory effects. The benefit achieved is legitimate, and is substantial because the statute seems to accomplish its aims quite effectively. The burden on interstate commerce amounts to an almost complete closure of Zucchini's highways to interstate truck traffic. A burden of that size, or discriminatory effects of that sort, will likely result in a finding that the burdens heavily outweigh the benefits.

Question: The state of Wessex owns and operates the University of Wessex. The University of Wessex charges students who are not Wessex residents annual tuition of $20,000, approximately 98% of the cost of their education. Wessex residents are charged $5,000 annually. A University of Wessex student who is not a resident of Wessex challenges the constitutional validity of this practice. What is the best grounds for the challenge and will it succeed?

Answer: The challenge will probably not succeed. The challenge is best made under the privileges and immunities clause of Article IV. To succeed with that argument the challenger must show that university education is fundamental to interstate harmony. That may be difficult, as the Court has effectively limited fundamental interests protected by the privileges and immunities clause to employment. Of course, some university education is a prelude to employment, but some is not. Unless the Court is willing is broaden its concept of fundamentality Wessex may be free to impinge upon out of staters' access to its university education. Even if education is a fundamental interest for these purposes Wessex can probably establish that outsiders seeking an education at the University of Wessex are indeed a peculiar source of the problem differential tuition addresses. Wessex taxpayers fund the University of Wessex and outsiders contribute nothing by taxation to its support. Higher tuition for out of staters is a measure designed to remedy this disparity.

Under the commerce clause, Wessex is probably a participant in the market for university education. There are many institutions that offer university education, both within and without Wessex. Thus, if Wessex is a market participant it is free to discriminate against out of staters. If Wessex is not a market participant the differential tuition is facially discriminatory and is valid only if Wessex can prove that it has no less discriminatory means to achieve its legitimate objective of equalizing the cost of a University of Wessex education between Wessex residents and outsiders. Wessex may well be able to prove this, since there does not seem to be any way other than differential tuition to equalize the cost.

Question: Why has the Supreme Court construed the commerce clause as impliedly limiting state power to regulate interstate commerce?

Answer: One of the intentions of the draftsmen of the Constitution was to create an internal common market within the United States, free of trade restrictions imposed by the states on interstate commerce. If the states were free to frustrate interstate commerce much of that objective would be lost. The commerce clause gives Congress paramount authority over interstate commerce, but the Court thinks that even when that authority is not exercised it should act to curb state regulations unduly restrictive of interstate commerce.

Question: Are the two tests the Supreme Court uses to evaluate state regulation of interstate commerce—the discrimination doctrine and the burden doctrine—really a single test?

Answer: Yes and no.

Yes, in the sense that the indicia of discrimination also describe very severe burdens upon interstate commerce, so severe that they are likely to heavily outweigh whatever legitimate local benefits are produced by the law. Thus, the discrimination doctrine might be thought of as a particularized way of assessing the burdens imposed on interstate commerce.

No, in the sense that the presence of discrimination reverses the burden of proof, placing upon the state the obligation to justify its discrimination. In the burden test, the state never has the burden of proof.

Question: How does the Supreme Court assess burdens and benefits and compare them in applying the burden doctrine?

Answer: It assesses burdens on interstate commerce by measuring the extent of the impediments placed on interstate commerce by the subject law. It assesses benefits by examining the effectiveness of the law in actually achieving its own goals. To some extent, the Court also examines the importance of the state objectives, though that is a very subjective judgment. Comparison of the two is extremely difficult because they are really two different things. As Justice Scalia has said, it is like comparing the length of a line to the weight of a rock. Nevertheless, so long as there are some benefits produced, the law will be upheld unless the burdens are extremely large.

Question: Does the Supreme Court evaluate state laws that are neutral toward interstate commerce, but that produce discriminatory effects, with reference to a single standard?

Answer: No. The Supreme Court first evaluates the severity of the discriminatory effects, then subjects cases of severe effective discrimination to strict judicial scrutiny. If the discriminatory effects on interstate commerce are not severe the law is examined in accordance with the burdens/benefits balancing test.

Question: What is the market-participation doctrine?

Answer: This doctrine is an exemption from the dormant commerce clause for states when they are actually participating in a market, rather than regulating it. It permits states, as market participants, to discriminate against interstate commerce in a way that would not be permissible if they were regulating the market.

Question: What is protected by the privileges and immunities clause of Article IV?

Answer: The right of people to look for work anywhere in the nation on equal terms with those already residing in any locality is what is really protected. As construed, the clause prohibits states from abridging "fundamental" rights unless there is some "substantial reason" for treating outsiders differently. The only "fundamental" right protected by the privileges and immunities clause that is not otherwise afforded constitutional protection is the right to look for work anywhere in the nation.

EXAM TIPS

- **Often Tested.** The dormant aspect of the commerce clause is often tested because it is a lively area of constitutional law with a rich doctrine that is not entirely settled.

- **Dormant Commerce Clause Applies When Congress Has *Not* Acted.** The dormant, or negative, aspect of the commerce clause limits state regulation of interstate commerce. Since this is an **implied** aspect of the commerce clause, and Congress always remains free to regulate interstate commerce as it pleases, the dormant commerce clause applies only when Congress has **failed to regulate interstate commerce.** The states may then regulate commerce, subject to these implied limits.

- ■ **Check to See If Congress Has Acted.**

  - If Congress has acted **by regulating the same subject that the states regulate** you may have a **preemption** issue. Only if there is no presumption will you have a dormant commerce clause issue.

  - If Congress has acted **by explicitly consenting to state laws regulating interstate commerce** there is no dormant commerce clause issue. This is true **even if the Court has already decided that the state regulation violates the commerce clause,** because Congress remains free to regulate interstate commerce at its pleasure, even if that means letting the states regulate in ways that the Court thinks are impliedly barred by the commerce clause.

  - **Market-Participant Exception.** Remember that states are exempt from the dormant commerce clause when they act as **market participants**—engaging in or creating commerce—rather than market regulators—controlling other people's commerce.

  - **Checklist for Applying the Dormant Commerce Clause.**

    — Is the law **rationally related to a** *legitimate* **state purpose?** If not, it's void. If yes, ask the following:

    — Is the law **facially discriminatory** to interstate commerce? If yes, it's void unless the state can prove that it has **no less discriminatory alternative** to achieve a legitimate goal. If not, ask the following:

    — Are the law's **burdens on interstate commerce** *clearly excessive* **when compared to the supposed local benefits** of the law? If so, the law is void. If not, the law is valid.

  - **Privileges and Immunities.** Article IV's privileges and immunities clause prevents states from discriminating against outsiders on matters **fundamental to interstate harmony and union**—mostly earning a living—unless there is **substantial reason**—the outsiders are a **peculiar source of the problem,** the discriminatory practice is **substantially related** to its solution, and there is **no less discriminatory alternative available.**

    — **There is no market-participation exemption.**

    — **Corporations aren't protected—only individuals receive privileges and immunities protection.**

7   SEPARATION OF POWERS

CHAPTER OVERVIEW

This chapter examines the constitutional rules intended to preserve separation between the executive, legislative, and judicial powers of the federal government. The most important points in this chapter follow.

- **Presidential Powers:** The President

  — **Executes law,** but does *not make law.*

  — Has the **exclusive power to appoint** *principal* **federal officers,** subject to Senate confirmation.

  — Has the power to **veto bills** or **sign them into law.**

  — May extend or withdraw **diplomatic recognition** of other nations.

  — May grant **pardons.**

  — May **negotiate treaties,** subject to Senate confirmation.

  — Is the **Commander-in-Chief** of the armed services, and may unilaterally commit armed forces to repel sudden attacks or to protect American interests in times of sudden emergency.

- **Congress and the President:**

  — The *President* may **remove** principal executive officers but *Congress* may **limit** the President's power to remove inferior officers, so long as the limitations do not impede the President's core duties. Congress may neither appoint not remove executive officers.

— Congress may authorize the President to take action or bar the President from acting, but Congress may not prohibit the President from exercising his constitutional powers. The Court may infer congressional authorization or prohibition from congressional acquiescence to presidential action, historical precedent, or other significant forms of congressional silence.

— Congress and the President share an exclusively federal **"unenumerated foreign affairs power."** The President has more power of unilateral action in foreign than domestic affairs.

— Congress has the power to **declare war,** but the President has the power to **conduct warfare.**

- **Congress and the Administrative State:** Congress may

— Create government arrangements that do *not* **aggrandize** a single branch nor **encroach** upon the powers of any branch.

— **Delegate** its legislative power, *if* Congress does so by an **intelligible principle** that both **declares a policy** and **defines when its command is to be effective.**

— *Not* exercise a **legislative veto.**

- **Immunities and Privileges:**

— Members of Congress are absolutely immune from suits based on their **legislative acts** and are temporarily immune from civil suits while Congress is in session.

— The President is **absolutely immune** from civil suits for damages based on his official acts but has **no immunity** from civil suits based on his unofficial conduct. It is uncertain whether the President may be criminally prosecuted before impeachment and conviction.

— Executive officials other than the President enjoy a **qualified immunity** for their official acts taken in **good faith.**

— The President possesses a qualified evidentiary privilege—**executive privilege**—to preserve the confidentiality of presidential communications and documents. To determine whether executive privilege may be invoked, courts must **balance** the **need for the information** sought and the **reasons asserted for confidentiality.**

A. INTRODUCTION: THE REASONS FOR SEPARATED POWERS IN THE FEDERAL GOVERNMENT

1. Original Intentions and Structure

The constitutional plan was to divide and separate government powers in order to enhance liberty by minimizing the possibility of concentrated government power. Federalism, the pervasive theme of Chapters 3 through 6, involves the division of power between the national government and the state governments. The Constitution assigns to each branch of the federal government—executive, legislative, and judicial—some of the powers of the federal government. The doctrine of separation of powers is designed to preserve this separation. It does *not* mean that each branch of the federal government is wholly independent of the others. As James Madison stated in Federalist No. 47, separation of power does "not mean that these departments ought to have no *partial agency* in, or no *control* over, the acts of each other. . . . [It does mean] that where the *whole* power of one department is exercised by the same hands which possess the *whole* power of another department, the fundamental principles of a free constitution are subverted." The point of separated powers is to **prevent domination by one branch** and to **prevent fusion of powers.**

a. **"Checks and balances."** The Constitution separates power by creating a number of explicit "checks and balances"—devices that permit one branch partially to control or monitor the actions of other branches. Other such devices have been created by statute or by judicial implication.

    i. **Explicit checks.** Some important explicit checks are:

    - The President's power to veto legislation

    - The Senate's power to confirm or deny presidential appointments

    - Congressional power to declare war and presidential power to wage war.

    ii. **Implied checks.** Perhaps the most important implied check is the power of judicial review. But Congress creates new checks by legislation, and the validity of those innovations will be considered in the remainder of this chapter.

2. Sources of Authority for Deciding These Issues

Apart from the explicit checks contained in the Constitution there are few constitutional reference points for judicial decision of these issues. More than in other areas of constitutional law decision of these issues stems from prudential reasoning, political realities, and historical practices. The importance of these criteria for decision-making also raise a heightened possibility that some of these issues may well be nonjusticiable political questions. See Chapter 2, supra.

B. EXECUTIVE ACTION

1. Sources of Executive Authority

The President's authority to act comes from two sources—directly from the Constitution and from congressional authorization. Congress, of course, may only act within the scope of its constitutional competence, but when it does so it may authorize the President to take action he might not have authority to undertake absent congressional action.

2. Specific Constitutionally Granted Powers of the President

The Constitution does not itemize the President's powers in as much detail as it does for Congress. The following are the express executive powers:

- **"The executive Power shall be vested in a President . . ."** (Art. II, §1). While this clause does not define the scope of the executive power it makes clear that *it is the President that holds the executive power.*

- "The President shall be **Commander-in-Chief** of the Army and Navy . . ." (Art. II, §2). Not only does this confirm ultimate civilian control of the armed services; it establishes that the President controls the actual conduct of war.

- The President may **"grant Reprieves and Pardons** for Offenses against the United States, except in Cases of Impeachment." (Art. II, §2).

- The President may **negotiate treaties,** effective upon Senate ratification by a two-thirds majority. (Art. II, §2).

- The President has the power to **appoint,** subject to Senate confirmation by majority vote, ambassadors, federal judges, and other principal federal officers, such as cabinet secretaries. (Art. II, §2). The President may also fill vacancies in these offices without Senate confirmation if the Senate is in recess. Such **"recess appointments"** expire at the end of the next Senate session if not sooner confirmed.

- The President has the power to **appoint the Vice President,** subject to confirmation by a majority vote of both houses of Congress, in the event of a vacancy in the office (25th Amendment, §2). This provision has been used twice. Following the resignation of Spiro Agnew as Vice President, President Nixon appointed Gerald Ford. Following President Nixon's resignation, President Ford appointed Nelson Rockefeller.

- The President has the power to "receive Ambassadors and other public Ministers," meaning that the President alone has the power to decide to extend or withdraw **diplomatic recognition** of other nations (Art. II, §3).

- The President has the power to **call Congress into extraordinary session** and, in case of disagreement between the houses as to the time of adjournment, may adjourn Congress to a time set by the President (Art. II, §3).

- The President has the power and duty to **"take Care that the Laws be faithfully executed."** (Art. II, §3).

- The President has the power to **sign bills into law** or to **veto bills** (Art. I, §7).

Controversies surrounding some of the more important of these powers are discussed below.

a. **Presentment of legislation: The veto power.** Article I, §7 requires that every bill passed by both the House and Senate "shall, before it become a Law, be presented to the President." The President has "ten days (Sundays excepted)" to either sign the bill into law or veto it. If unsigned after that period it becomes law unless Congress has adjourned. If vetoed, it is returned to Congress and becomes law only if two-thirds of those present and voting in each house (if a quorum) vote for its passage a second time. See *Missouri Pacific Railway v. Kansas,* 248 U.S. 276 (1919).

   i. **The "pocket veto."** The President enjoys an absolute veto power in one instance. If Congress has adjourned during the ten day period a bill is presented to the President for signature or veto, Article I, §7 provides that the bill "shall not be a Law" unless the President signs it. Thus, the President need not act on bills presented within ten days of congressional adjournment in order to kill them—he can simply veto such bills by "putting them into his pocket." The clause was intended not to enhance presidential power but to prevent Congress from denying to the President his right to ask Congress to reconsider legislation. The term "adjournment" means a prolonged adjournment, consisting of adjournment at the end of either the first or second session of each congress (*The Pocket Veto Case,* 279 U.S. 655 (1929)), or of more than "ten days (Sundays excepted)." *Wright v. United States,* 302 U.S. 583 (1938) (dicta).

   ii. **The "line-item veto."** The veto power applies to "every Bill . . . , Every Order, Resolution, or Vote to which the Concurrence of the Senate and the House of Representatives may be necessary." This means that Congress controls the form and content of the legislation presented to the President. Bills typically contain a variety of provisions; the President may not pick and choose—legislation is a "take it or leave it" proposition. The Line Item Veto Act gave the President power to "cancel in whole" three types of provisions signed into law: (1) any amount of discretionary budget authority, (2) any item of new direct spending, and (3) any "limited" tax benefit. President Clinton used this power to cancel an item of direct spending in favor of New York and a limited tax benefit favoring certain agricultural cooperatives. In *Clinton v. City of New York,* 524 U.S. 417 (1998), the Court invalidated the Act on the ground that cancellation of provisions signed into law amounted to a partial repeal of the law by the President alone, in violation of the bicameralism and presentment requirements of Art. I, §7.

b. **The appointments power and its implied corollary: The removal power.** Subject to Senate confirmation, the President has the power to appoint ambassadors, federal judges, and "all other Officers of the United States, whose Appointments are not herein otherwise provided for, and which shall be established by Law: but the Congress may by Law vest the Appointment of such inferior Officers, as they think proper, in the President alone, in the Courts of Law, or in the Heads of Departments."

   i. **Appointment.** Note that the "other Officers of the United States" consist of **principal** officers (the appointment of which is vested in the President subject to Senate confirmation) and **inferior** officers (the appointment of which Congress can give to the President, the courts, or executive department heads). An "officer of the United States," whether principal or inferior, is "any appointee exercising significant authority pursuant to the laws of the United States." *Buckley v. Valeo,* 424 U.S. 1 (1976).

      (a) **Principal and inferior officers.** Although the Court has never precisely distinguished between principal and inferior offices, principal officers consist of the highest echelon of government—cabinet secretaries and their equivalents. *Any* office less powerful is probably inferior.

 # EXAMPLE AND ANALYSIS

Pursuant to authorizing legislation, a "special division" of the U.S. Court of Appeals appointed an "independent prosecutor" to investigate and prosecute alleged executive wrongdoing. The independent prosecutor had "full power and independent authority to exercise all investigative and prosecutorial functions and powers of the Department of Justice [and] the Attorney General" and could not be removed by the President but only by the Attorney General for "good cause." The independent prosecutor's tenure was indefinite and largely subject to her control. The validity of the independent prosecutor's appointment (by one of the "Courts of Law") was challenged. The Court concluded that the independent prosecutor was an "inferior" officer and upheld her appointment. *Morrison v. Olson,* 487 U.S. 654 (1988).

    (b) **No role for Congress in appointment. Congress may *not* appoint *any* executive officers.** The most that Congress may do is specify qualifications for inferior offices—such as age and experience—so long as the qualifications are reasonably germane to the office. See *Shoemaker v. United States,* 147 U.S. 282 (1893); Nowak & Rotunda, at 265. Congress may appoint legislative subordinates—aides and congressional staff supporting the legislative function—but it may not appoint anyone "exercising significant [executive] authority pursuant to the laws of the United States."

 # EXAMPLE AND ANALYSIS

Congress created a Federal Election Commission to administer and enforce the Federal Election Campaign Act by rulemaking and civil prosecutions. A majority of the members of the Commission were appointed by the President *pro tempore* of the Senate and the Speaker of the House. The Court struck down the Commission as constituted, since the Commission wielded executive powers and Congress had no authority to appoint executive officers. *Buckley v. Valeo,* 424 U.S. 1 (1976).

    ii. **Removal by the President.** Except for impeachment the Constitution is silent about whether Congress, the President, or both, may remove federal officers during their term in office. Federal judges, who are appointed for life, are removable only by impeachment. The Court has filled this gap by creating doctrine that connects the removal power to the appointments power. **Congress may restrict the President's power to remove inferior federal officers, but may neither restrict the President's unilateral power to remove principal officers nor otherwise impose removal restrictions that "impede the President's ability to perform his constitutional duty."**

    (a) *Myers, Humphrey's Executor,* **and** *Wiener.* Congress first tried to restrict presidential removal of executive officers with the Tenure of Office Act, which barred the President from removing cabinet secretaries without Senate consent. President Andrew Johnson promptly fired Secretary of War Edwin Stanton and was impeached as a result. Johnson escaped conviction by a single vote; years later the Court opined that the Tenure of Office Act (though by then repealed) was an unconstitutional attempt to limit the **President's unilateral power to remove principal officers.** *Myers v. United States,* 272 U.S. 52 (1926).

 # EXAMPLE AND ANALYSIS

Congress enacted a statute, similar to the Tenure of Office Act, that provided that certain postmasters, appointed by the President with Senate approval, could be removed by the President only after obtaining Senate consent. The Court, in an opinion by former President and then Chief Justice Taft, held the statute unconstitutional. Taft relied primarily on the record of debates in the First Congress in concluding that the President's removal power is "incident to the power of appointment," and that "the President has the exclusive power of removing executive officers of the United States whom he has appointed" and the Senate has confirmed. Taft's reading of history has been criticized by legal historians (see Corwin, 27 Colum. L. Rev. 360-370; R. Berger, Impeachment, 139-140). *Myers v. United States,* 272 U.S. 52 (1926).

Myers does *not* stand for the proposition that Congress may not place *any* limits on the President's removal of executive officers. The Court quickly modified *Myers* by holding that the *functional character of the office* determined whether or not Congress could restrict the President's removal power. Congress could place no restrictions on the President's power to remove "purely executive officers," said the Court, but Congress *could attach conditions to presidential removal of "quasi-legislative" or "quasi-judicial" officers.*

 # EXAMPLES AND ANALYSIS

Example: Congress created the Federal Trade Commission and, in so doing, sought to create an agency "independent" of the President. Commissioners were appointed by the President for prescribed terms and the President was empowered to dismiss Commissioners only for "inefficiency, neglect of duty, or malfeasance in office." The President sought to remove an incumbent Commissioner for other reasons. The Court upheld the removal restrictions, reasoning that since Congress had power to create "quasi-legislative or quasi-judicial agencies [and] to require them to act . . . independently of executive control" Congress could also, "as an appropriate incident" to that power, impose restrictions on presidential removal of such officials. *Humphrey's Executor v. United States,* 295 U.S. 602 (1935).

Example: Congress created the War Claims Commission to decide the validity of claims made against the federal government. The President attempted to remove a Commissioner and the Court concluded that the President could not do so, reasoning that because the function of a Commissioner was "quasi-judicial"—to make decisions that the President was powerless to alter—he could not be removed by the President unilaterally. *Wiener v. United States,* 357 U.S. 349 (1958).

    (b) *Morrison v. Olson,* 487 U.S. 654 (1988). The Court upheld significant restrictions upon removal of a "purely executive," albeit inferior, federal officer, thus furthering narrowing the scope of *Myers.* Federal law authorized the U.S. Court of Appeals to appoint an independent prosecutor to investigate and prosecute alleged executive crimes. The independent prosecutor, determined by the Court to be an inferior officer, could *not* be removed by the President for any reason, but could be removed by the Attorney General for "good cause." The Court concluded that restrictions on removal of an inferior executive officer "cannot be made to turn on whether or not that official is classified as 'purely executive.' . . . [T]he **real question is whether the removal restrictions are of such a nature that they impede the President's ability to perform his constitutional duty.** . . ." The Court thought that presidential control of the independent prosecutor was not "so central to the functioning of the Executive Branch as to require as a matter of constitutional law that the counsel be terminable at will by the President," but the Court never explained how one can detect those core offices or functions.

  iii. **No removal by Congress.** Congress may *not,* **by itself, remove any executive officers.** Congress may limit the President's removal power, or may expand the President's removal power by explicitly conferring unilateral removal power over inferior executive officers, but Congress may not exercise any removal power over executive officers.

    (a) *Bowsher v. Synar,* 478 U.S. 714 (1986). In 1985 Congress enacted the Gramm-Rudman Act, a comprehensive plan to remedy chronic budget deficits. The Act established budget deficit reduction targets for five succeeding fiscal years and, in the event Congress failed to enact specific spending reductions to meet the targets, vested in the Comptroller General the power to determine the precise programmatic budget cuts necessary to meet the targets. Once the Comptroller General had acted, the President was required to implement the Comptroller General's decisions. The Court invalidated the Act. First, it concluded that the Comptroller General was an executive officer. Second, because the Comptroller General was not removable by the President, but by joint resolution of Congress for specific causes, the Court concluded that "congressional participation in the removal of executive officers is unconstitutional."

(b) Impeachment. Congress may, of course, remove federal officers by impeachment. Article II, §4 provides that "all civil Officers of the United States shall be removed from Office on Impeachment for, and Conviction of, Treason, Bribery, or other high Crimes and Misdemeanors." Impeachment occurs by majority vote of the House and conviction requires a vote of two-thirds of those Senators present and voting.

c. **Extending diplomatic recognition.** Article II, §3, gives the President power to "receive Ambassadors and other public Ministers." Alexander Hamilton argued and it has been accepted that this provision gives the President "power to recognize governments and terminate relations with foreign nations." See Nowak & Rotunda, at 205; Tribe, at 220 n.7.

d. **The Commander-in-Chief.** Article II, §2 makes the President the "Commander in Chief of the Army and Navy." This provision gives the President ultimate responsibility and authority for the conduct of military operations, but it does not give the President unlimited authority to employ the armed forces absent a declaration of war or other congressional authorization. This issue is discussed more fully in subsection 4, infra.

3. General Test for Validity of Executive Action

Given the paucity of specific constitutional enumeration of the President's powers, conflict can and does arise concerning the validity of unilateral presidential actions. At one extreme are those who argue that the President possesses inherent powers nowhere stated in the Constitution. Theodore Roosevelt and Taft both embraced the "stewardship" theory of presidential power: the President *can* and *must* do **anything** necessary for the good of the nation so long as he does not violate some constitutional provision or valid act of Congress. Chief Justice Taft, in *Myers v. United States,* claimed that presidential possession of *all* executive power meant that, within the sphere of "executive power," the President has implied authority to act unless expressly limited elsewhere. Just as the scope of *Myers* has narrowed with respect to removal, so has the *Myers* opinion diminished in force with respect to the general scope of presidential power.

a. ***Youngstown Sheet & Tube Co. v. Sawyer (The Steel Seizure Case),*** 343 U.S. 579 (1952). During the Korean War the steel companies and their unionized employees were unable to agree on a new collective bargaining agreement. The workers announced their intention to strike and, a few hours before the strike was to begin, President Truman ordered the Secretary of Commerce to seize the steel mills and keep them running by agreeing to the union's terms. The Court found the seizure to be unconstitutional. The concurring opinions, especially that of Justice Jackson, are almost as important as the Court's opinion.

   i.   **The Court's opinion.** For the Court, Justice Black reasoned that the "President's power . . . to issue the order must stem either from an act of Congress or from the Constitution itself." Because Congress had not authorized the seizure, Truman defended his action by reciting the indispensability of steel to the war effort, and claiming implied powers as Commander-in-Chief, from his duty to execute the laws, and as the Constitution's holder of all executive power.

      (a) **Commander-in-Chief.** The Court rejected the notion that the Commander-in-Chief has power "to take possession of private property in order to keep labor disputes from stopping production" of needed war materials.

      (b) **The "take care" clause: execution of law.** While the President must *execute law,* the President has no power to *make law.* President Truman's seizure was not a directive "that a congressional policy be executed in a manner prescribed by Congress—[instead] it directs that a presidential policy be executed in a manner prescribed by the President."

      (c) **"Inherent" executive power.** President Truman contended that the President has inherent implied powers. The Court found it unnecessary to reject *Myers's* contention that there are such powers since the Court thought that seizure of private property was legislative, and thus not among any inherent implied powers that might exist.

   ii. **Jackson's concurrence.** Justice Jackson contended that the President's "powers are not fixed but fluctuate, depending on their disjunction or conjunction with those of Congress." He described a tripartite framework:

- Presidential power is at its **maximum** "[w]hen the President **acts pursuant to an express or implied authorization of Congress,**" because the President is then able to exercise all the power "that he possesses in his own right plus all that Congress can delegate."

- Presidential power "is at its **lowest ebb**" when presidential action is "**incompatible with the expressed or implied will of Congress** . . . for then he can rely only upon his own constitutional powers minus any constitutional powers of Congress over the matter."

- Presidential power is in a "**zone of twilight**" when "the President acts in the **absence of either a congressional grant or denial of authority.**" Here, both President and Congress may share power and "*congressional inertia, indifference, or quiescence* may . . . as a practical matter, enable . . . independent presidential" action. In the twilight zone "any actual test of power is likely to depend on the *imperatives of events and contemporary imponderables* rather than on abstract theories of law."

iii. **Frankfurter's concurrence.** Justice Frankfurter made two points. First, Congress had considered and rejected the idea of giving the President seizure authority when it enacted the 1947 Taft-Hartley Act. In this "non-action" Frankfurter found congressional negation of the President's action. Second, and more generally, Frankfurter thought that "a systematic, unbroken, executive practice, long pursued to the knowledge of Congress and never before questioned, engaged in by Presidents who have also sworn to uphold the Constitution, . . . may be treated as a gloss on [the President's] 'executive Power'. . . ."

iv. **The dissenters.** Three Justices dissented, arguing that the President possessed inherent power to act in national emergencies.

b. **What constitutes congressional authorization or congressional prohibition?** Given that the President's power depends in part on whether Congress has authorized or prohibited his actions, it is important to understand what sort of congressional actions constitute authorization or prohibition.

i. **Explicit congressional action.** When Congress has enacted legislation that specifically authorizes or prohibits presidential action the case is easy.

ii. **Implicit congressional action.** Implied congressional authorization or prohibition is more problematic, partly because it is harder to know what meaning, if any, to attach to congressional inaction or silence.

(a) Rejection of legislation. The Court sometimes finds implicit congressional prohibition of presidential action in congressional *rejection* of legislation.

(b) Congressional acquiescence. Sometimes the Court finds implicit authorization of presidential action from congressional acquiescence to the practice. This occurs most commonly in the field of foreign affairs.

 # EXAMPLE AND ANALYSIS

Agee, a former employee of the CIA, engaged in a campaign abroad to reveal the identities of CIA agents. As a result of his activities several CIA agents fell victim to violence. Although no law expressly permitted the State Department to revoke his passport, the State Department did so on the ground that Agee's actions abroad caused "serious damage to the national security." The Court upheld the revocation of Agee's passport. Congress had remained silent over the years while the State Department had revoked passports on national security grounds and promulgated regulations governing this administrative practice. Such silence was acquiescence to executive revocation of passports on national security grounds. "[I]n the areas of foreign policy and national security, . . . congressional silence is not to be equated with congressional disapproval." *Haig v. Agee,* 453 U.S. 280 (1981).

(c) Inferences from legislation: *Dames & Moore v. Regan.* Another kind of congressional silence is that which fills the gaps between existing legislation. In *Dames & Moore v. Regan,* 453 U.S. 654 (1981), the Court found implicit congressional approval in those gaps. Following the Iranian revolution Dames & Moore, an American engineering and construction firm, sued Iran in U.S. district court to recover damages for breach of contract and attached Iranian assets in the United States. Presidents Carter and Reagan then obtained the release of American hostages in Iran and, in exchange, issued a series of executive orders nullifying all such attachments and suspending all claims against Iran pending in U.S. courts. Dames & Moore attacked the validity of the executive orders. The Court unanimously upheld the orders. The Court found sufficient congressional authorization in several vaguely related laws, none of which spoke directly to the issue, but which taken together "indicate [congressional] acceptance of a broad scope for executive action in circumstances such as those presented in this case." The Court's reasoning was heavily influenced by the broad foreign affairs powers acknowledged to be possessed by the President.

4. The Special Case of War and Foreign Affairs

The President has most power to act alone in the field of foreign affairs. Part of this is due to recognition of a broad, and largely implicit, presidential foreign affairs power. Partly this is due to the fact that Congress can authorize the President to act and, in some cases, limit presidential freedom to act. Professor Louis Henkin has concluded that power to conduct foreign affairs is fissured. While all such power is federal, some "powers . . . belong to the President, some to Congress, some to the President-and-Senate; some can be exercised by either the President or Congress, some require the joint authority of both. Irregular, uncertain division renders claims of usurpation more difficult to establish and the courts have not been available to adjudicate them." L. Henkin, Foreign Affairs and the Constitution 32 (1972). Congress and the President share an **unenumerated foreign affairs power.**

a.   Recognition of shared power. The Court has recognized both broad inherent presidential power in foreign affairs and broad congressional power to add to the President's foreign affairs power.

   i.   *United States v. Curtiss-Wright Export Corp.,* 299 U.S. 304 (1936). By joint resolution, Congress authorized the President to proclaim an embargo on shipments of arms to Bolivia or Paraguay, then engaged in a war, and made it a crime to violate any such embargo. President Roosevelt proclaimed an embargo and Curtiss-Wright was indicted for its violation. The Court, in an opinion by Justice George Sutherland, concluded that Congress had power to delegate to the President quasi-legislative power in the foreign affairs field. The "non-delegation" doctrine, barring Congress from delegating its legislative power to others, has since become flaccid (see section C(2) infra), and so the holding of *Curtiss-Wright*—that Congress may delegate legislative power to the President in the foreign affairs field—is of diminished importance. But the three reasons the Court used to justify its holding bear examination:

   • An exclusively federal power over foreign affairs was implied in the Constitution.

   • The President holds "plenary and exclusive power . . . as the sole organ of the federal government in the field of international relations—a power that does not require as a basis for its exercise an act of Congress."

- Congress had "vested in the President" all of its authority on this issue "by an exertion of legislative power."

Although Sutherland's description of the breadth of the President's foreign affairs power is dicta, the opinion has been influential. Everyone agrees that there is in fact an unenumerated foreign relations power; disagreement centers on the degree to which it is shared by President and Congress.

b. **Use of armed force.** Sharp conflicts have arisen with respect to the use of American armed forces. Only Congress may **declare war,** but the President is the **Commander-in-Chief** of the armed forces.

i. **Unilateral presidential action.** The President has some *unilateral power to commit American armed forces to military actions abroad,* without the necessity of a formal declaration of war, but the extent of that power is highly controversial. Courts are apt to refrain from deciding cases posing these issues on the grounds that they raise nonjusticiable political questions. See Chapter 2, supra.

(a) **Repelling sudden attack:** *The Prize Cases.* The President has the power to use armed force to **repel sudden attacks** on the nation. In *The Prize Cases,* 67 U.S. 635 (1863), the Court upheld the validity of President Lincoln's executive order declaring a naval blockade of Southern ports. The Court, 5-4, concluded that Congress had authorized the President's action by two old statutes (1795 and 1807) empowering the President to "use the military and naval forces . . . to suppress insurrection against the . . . United States." The President need not wait for a formal declaration of war, said the Court: "If a war be made by invasion . . . , the President is not only authorized but bound to resist force, by force . . . without waiting for any special legislative authority. . . . President [Lincoln] was bound to meet [the Civil War] in the shape it presented itself, without waiting for Congress to baptize it with a name."

Example: The soldiers, sailors, and marines at Pearl Harbor, subalterns of the President, had the constitutional power to shoot back on the morning of December 7, 1941. No doubt that power extended to sinking the Japanese fleet, had that been possible.

(b) **Actions to protect American citizens and interests.** The President probably has authority to take unilateral armed action to protect American citizens and interests abroad. Scholars have so argued (see Tribe, at 232; Note, 81 Harv.

L. Rev. 1787-1794) and Congress has acquiesced in several such presidential excursions.

Example: President Reagan ordered an armed invasion of the island nation of Grenada to protect American medical students said to be threatened by hostile actions on the part of the Grenada government. Although his decision was controversial, Congress acquiesced in the action.

Example: President Carter ordered a military invasion of Iran to rescue American hostages in 1979. Although the mission was aborted before success, Congress acquiesced.

(c) **Aiding national allies.** It is undecided whether, or in what circumstances, the President may unilaterally use armed force to aid American allies. One influential scholar thinks that "the Constitution might be read as allowing executively initiated military action, without congressional consent, in the event of a surprise attack upon an important ally." Tribe, at 232-233. His view is not gospel.

Example: For a time prior to the Persian Gulf War, President Bush the elder declared his intention to prepare for offensive military operations against Iraq without any congressional approval. Although congressional approval was ultimately obtained, it is an open question whether the President had legitimate power to proceed unilaterally.

(d) **Preemptive strikes.** The President probably lacks power to order a preemptive strike against national enemies. The classic Cold War example to the contrary—a preemptive nuclear attack under circumstances when a massive enemy nuclear attack is imminent—may be the exception. We will probably never know for sure.

ii. **Congressionally authorized presidential action.** The easy case is, of course, when the President acts pursuant to a formal declaration of war. The last time the United States formally declared war was in 1941, entering World War II. Since the end of World War II, over 112,000 Americans have died and another 160,000 have suffered wounds fighting undeclared wars "authorized" by Congress. These authorized but undeclared wars come in several forms.

(a) **Advance authorization.** Congress may authorize the President in advance to use discretion in committing American armed forces to warfare. Congress may convey *de facto* authorization by action short of a formal declaration of war. The Korean, Vietnam, and Persian Gulf Wars are reminders of that fact. But the constitutional validity of those authorizations is more controversial.

 # EXAMPLES AND ANALYSIS

Example: Congress jointly passed the Gulf of Tonkin resolution in 1964, giving President Lyndon Johnson complete discretion "to take all necessary steps, including the use of armed force, to assist" South Vietnam. Some scholars argue that a delegation of warmaking power "unaccompanied by any articulated standards, would be unconstitutional as an overbroad delegation of congressional authority." See Tribe, at 234. Although the Gulf of Tonkin resolution might be unconstitutionally overbroad, the courts refused to decide the legal validity of the Vietnam War. See Chapter 2, on political questions.

Example: In order to suppress the predations of Tripoli against American vessels, in 1802 Congress authorized the President to "equip, man, and supply such . . . armed vessels of the United States as may be [needed] . . . for protecting effectually" American commerce and seamen and to take "such . . . acts of precaution or hostility as the state of war will justify, and may, in his opinion, require." 2 Stat. 130. No one seemed to think a declaration of war was necessary for the President lawfully to proceed to make war on Tripoli. President Jefferson did so, and America applauded the actions of naval heroes like Stephen Decatur.

Some congressional authorizations in advance are more specific. American armed involvement in both the Korean War and the Persian Gulf War was commenced after Congress had, by joint resolution, authorized the President to commit armed forces in support of specific United Nations resolutions acting against the armed aggression of North Korea and Iraq, respectively. See generally, A. Sofaer, War, Foreign Affairs and Constitutional Power.

(b) **Mutual defense treaties.** The United States has entered into a number of mutual defense treaties that may obligate the United States to provide military assistance to any member nation in the event of attack. These treaties might not provide constitutional support for war, partly because they represent the judgment of President and Senate alone, rather than both houses of Congress. Although the issue is not resolved, it is probable that, at most, such treaties support presidentially directed armed force in aid of treaty allies *only until Congress can act.*

iii. The 1973 War Powers Resolution. Congress can also limit the President's power unilaterally to wage undeclared war. The principal modern limitation is the War Powers Resolution, enacted in 1973 over President Nixon's veto. The declared purpose of the Resolution is to "insure that the collective judgment of both the Congress and the President" is brought to bear upon the use of American armed forces.

(a) How it works. The Resolution requires the President to:

- *Consult with Congress* before introducing American forces into hostilities or threatened hostilities.

- *Report* to the Speaker of the House and the President *pro tempore* of the Senate within forty-eight hours after either committing American troops to hostilities or threatened hostilities, deploying combat ready troops in foreign nations, or substantially enlarging the numbers of such deployed troops.

- *Terminate* the use of armed force within sixty days (ninety days if the President certifies in writing that safe withdrawal requires the extra month) unless Congress has declared war, authorized the continuing use of force, or is "unable to meet as a result of an armed attack upon the United States."

- *Terminate* the use of armed force without a declaration of war or specific congressional authorization at any time Congress so directs by joint resolution.

The Resolution also prohibits authority for presidential use of armed force being inferred from congressional appropriations or from treaties but also declares that nothing in it "is intended to alter the constitutional authority of Congress or of the President."

(b) Objections. Presidents from Nixon to Clinton have contended that the Resolution unconstitutionally infringes upon their constitutional powers as Commander-in-Chief. Those objections are probably rooted more in self-interest than reality—the war power is surely a shared power and the Resolution does not impinge upon any power held *solely* by the President. Note also the strong possibility that the provision requiring the President to recall troops unilaterally committed to battle whenever Congress so demands is invalid as a legislative veto. See subsection C(2)(b), infra.

(c) **Utility.** The War Powers Resolution has not proven utile. Presidents have been able to deploy and remove American troops from small scale combat missions within the sixty-day period. Congress is charged with the responsibility to decide upon war. "To do that requires understanding, . . . courage, . . . insight, . . . and . . . fortitude. . . . For a Congress composed of such members, no War Powers Resolution would be necessary; for a Congress without them, no War Powers Resolution would be sufficient." M. Glennon, Constitutional Diplomacy 123 (1990).

c. **Executive agreements.** Executive agreements are international agreements made by the President alone without Senate ratification. See Chapter 5, supra. While the precise dividing line between executive agreements and treaties is unresolved, the President may enter into executive agreements with other nations if the subject of the agreement is within the legitimate scope of enumerated presidential powers.

Example: The President, as Commander-in-Chief, may enter into an executive agreement for an armistice. See L. Henkin, Foreign Affairs and the Constitution 177 (1972).

Example: The President may enter into an executive agreement to extend diplomatic recognition to another country because Article II, §3 empowers the President alone to "receive Ambassadors and other public Ministers." Cf. *United States v. Pink*, 315 U.S. 203 (1942).

Otherwise, the agreement must likely take the form of a treaty. Executive agreements override conflicting state law, since foreign affairs is an exclusively federal concern. *United States v. Belmont*, 301 U.S. 324, 331 (1937) ("complete power over international affairs is in the national government and is not and cannot be subject to any curtailment or interference on the part of the several states"). The power of the President to enter into executive agreements, at least with respect to international claims, has been affirmed by the fact that "Congress has acquiesced in [the] long-standing practice of claims settlement by executive agreements." *Dames & Moore v. Regan*, supra.

C. LEGISLATIVE ACTION AND THE ADMINISTRATIVE STATE

1. The General Test

Congressional action is void as contrary to the principle of separated powers when it creates a "danger of either **aggrandizement** or **encroachment.**" *Mistretta v. United States*, infra.

- **Aggrandizement** occurs when Congress enacts law that "accrete[s] to a single branch powers more appropriately diffused among separate branches," *id.,* or impermissibly enlarges a single branch's powers at the expense of other branches.

- **Encroachment** occurs when Congress enacts law that "undermine[s] the authority and independence of one or another coordinate branch." *Id.*

a. **Scope of the test.** The general test is an all-purpose test. Courts will employ specific, narrower doctrines, if any apply. If not, or if the law meets those specific tests, it is subject to the general test.

 # EXAMPLES AND ANALYSIS

Example: Congress created the Sentencing Commission, "an independent commission in the judicial branch," composed of seven members appointed by the President subject to Senate approval (at least three of which were to be federal judges). Commissioners were removable by the President for "good cause," and empowered to establish mandatory sentencing guidelines for federal judges. The Court upheld the arrangement. Congress had instructed the Commission to create uniform sentences for similarly situated criminals. The Court first determined that the arrangement complied with the narrower doctrine barring excessively broad delegation of legislative power (see subsection C(2), *infra*). Then the Court applied the general test to uphold the Commission against the charge that the law assigned to the judiciary "tasks that are more appropriately accomplished by [other] branches," and "impermissibly threatens the institutional integrity of the Judicial Branch." *Morrison v. Olson*, supra. *Mistretta v. United States,* 488 U.S. 361 (1989).

Example: In *Morrison v. Olson* the Court applied the general test to determine that the appointment and removal arrangements for independent prosecutors neither aggrandized the courts nor encroached upon presidential power. See also subsection B(2)(b), *supra.*

2. **The Specific, Narrow Doctrines**

The Court applies a variety of specific doctrines to test aspects of congressional action for compliance with separation of powers principles. These doctrines follow.

a. **Nondelegation doctrine.** Congress may delegate "authority . . . sufficient to effect its purposes." *Lichter v. United States,* 334 U.S. 742, 778

(1948). This means that Congress can (1) authorize courts, the President, or an administrative agency to make rules in areas specified by Congress and subject to congressionally specified guidelines, or (2) condition legislation upon a finding of fact by the President or an agency. To do either validly, Congress must both **declare a policy** and **define "the circumstances in which its command is to be effective."** *Opp Cotton Mills, Inc. v. Administrator*, 312 U.S. 126, 144 (1941). At the very least, Congress must set forth "by legislative act an **intelligible principle** to which the person or body authorized to take action is directed to conform." *J.W. Hampton, Jr. & Co. v. United States*, 276 U.S. 394, 409 (1928). The primary rationale for limiting delegation is to ensure accountability—unelected administrators are not directly accountable to the electorate.

 # EXAMPLES AND ANALYSIS

Example: Congress enacted the Occupational Safety and Health Act, giving the Labor Secretary power to adopt those standards "reasonably necessary or appropriate to provide safe or healthful employment . . . which most adequately assure[], to the extent feasible, on the basis of the best available evidence, that no employee will suffer material impairment of health." The Court concluded that this was a permissible delegation. Justice Rehnquist thought that it was "difficult to imagine a more obvious example of Congress simply avoiding a choice which was both fundamental for purposes of the statute and . . . [too] politically divisive [to address with specificity]. . . . It is the hard choices, not the filling in of the blanks, which must be made by the elected representatives of the people." *Industrial Union v. American Petroleum Institute*, 448 U.S. 607 (1980).

Example: Congress made the export of arms to Bolivia or Paraguay a crime, conditioned upon a presidential finding that an arms embargo would "contribute to the reestablishment of peace between those countries" and presidential proclamation of the embargo. The Court upheld the delegation. *United States v. Curtiss-Wright Export Corp.*, 299 U.S. 304 (1936).

Example: Congress created the Sentencing Commission and told it to establish sentencing guidelines that would be mandatory on federal judges. The Court upheld the arrangement. Congress had instructed the Commission to create uniform sentences for similarly situated criminals. The Court thought that instruction was an "intelligible principle . . . sufficiently specific and detailed to meet constitutional requirements." Congress could give the Commission "significant discretion in formulating guidelines," and could delegate the power to "exercise judgment on matters of policy." *Mistretta v. United States*, 488 U.S. 361 (1989).

The nondelegation doctrine lacks much bite today, as the Court tolerates broad, general delegations of legislative power to executive
administrators.

b.   Bicameralism and presentment: The legislative veto. Article I, sections
1 and 7 impose a *bicameralism* and a *presentment* requirement on all
legislation.

  - **Bicameralism** means that every bill—every *legislative* act—must
    pass both houses of Congress to become law.

  - **Presentment** means that every bill—every *legislative* act—must
    be presented to the President for signature or veto.

i.   *INS v. Chadha,* 462 U.S. 919 (1983). Pursuant to its exclusive power
over immigration, Congress enacted a comprehensive immigration
statute that defined certain aliens as "deportable." Nevertheless,
Congress frequently permitted deportable aliens to remain, by enacting so-called private bills (bills introduced by a member to provide specific relief to a constituent). To eliminate that cumbersome
procedure, Congress amended the immigration law, by delegating
to the Attorney General the power to suspend the deportation of
any deportable alien if the alien met certain criteria. The Attorney
General was required to report all such suspensions of deportation
to Congress. If either house of Congress passed a resolution disfavoring any such suspension, the alien would again be subject to
deportation. The validity of this **"legislative veto"** was placed at
issue when Chadha, a deportable alien who had his deportation
suspended by the Attorney General, challenged the power of the
House to deport him by passing the prescribed resolution disfavoring suspension. The Court invalidated the legislative veto.

(a)   The Court's rationale. The Court regarded the action of
a single house disfavoring suspension of deportation to be
a legislative act, because by that act "the House took action
that had the purpose and effect of *altering the legal rights,
duties, and relations* of persons . . . outside the legislative
branch." Without the action, Chadha would stay; by the
action, Chadha would go. The Court also thought that the
"legislative character of the one-House veto . . . is confirmed by the character of the Congressional action it
supplants." Before the legislative veto, the only way Congress could alter the deportable status of an alien was for
both houses to pass a bill (bicameralism) that would either
be signed by the President or passed over his veto (presentment). The legislative veto at issue circumvented these

requirements, thus failing to meet either the bicameralism or presentment requirements.

(b) **Justice White's dissent.** Justice White argued that a functional approach should be taken. He contended that it was anomalous to permit Congress to delegate vast rulemaking power to administrative agencies and deny it the more limited power to check the exercise of administrative discretion by legislative veto. White argued that the legislative veto did not violate the principles behind bicameralism and presentment because any change of Chadha's status required the *concurrence* of both houses and the executive branch. For Chadha to change from "deportable" to being permitted to stay required the affirmative conclusion of the Attorney General (the President's deputy) that Chadha's deportation warranted suspension, and the passive "action" of both houses of Congress in the form of failing to disapprove the suspension.

ii. **Significance of *Chadha*.** *Chadha* wiped out an increasingly favored tool of Congress to monitor and check the exercise by agencies of the discretion given them in their enabling legislation. Once the Court all but abandoned the nondelegation doctrine, Congress could and did vest in administrative agencies enormous discretionary policymaking and rulemaking authority. The legislative veto was a quick and reasonably efficient method for monitoring that discretion. With its abolition Congress faced a tough choice at the extremes—either remove much agency discretion, thus forcing Congress to grapple with a myriad specific (and often technical) issues, or trust agencies to exercise their discretion wisely. Of course, Congress can always check agency discretion by legislation satisfying the bicameralism and presentment requirements.

iii. **The two-house veto.** While *Chadha* did not decide the validity of a *two-house* legislative veto, in *U.S. Senate v. FTC*, 463 U.S. 1216 (1983), the Court summarily affirmed invalidation of a two-house veto.

c. **Congressional encroachment on the executive branch.** Congress may not encroach upon the executive branch by wielding executive powers, nor may Congress itself appoint or remove executive officials. See subsection B(2), supra.

i. *Metropolitan Washington Airports Authority v. Citizens for the Abatement of Aircraft Noise,* 501 U.S. 252 (1991). Congress transferred operational authority over Reagan National and Dulles Airports from the federal government to the Metropolitan Washington Airport Authority, a Virginia state authority. Transfer was conditioned upon Virginia's creation of a Board of Review, to be composed of nine members of Congress appointed by the Authority from lists provided by the Speaker of the House and the President *pro tempore* of the Senate, invested with veto power over major decisions of the Authority. The Court invalidated the Board of Review, first finding that the Board, although created by Virginia, was for a federal purpose and thus "exercise[d] sufficient federal power as an agent of Congress to mandate separation-of-powers scrutiny." Congress, said the Court, may not "invest itself or its Members with . . . executive power," and it must exercise its legislative powers in accordance with the bicameralism and presentment procedures of Article I. It was impermissible for the Board to exercise executive power, and if the Board possessed legislative power instead it was not used in a manner complying with the procedural requirements of Article I.

ii.   *Bowsher v. Synar,* 478 U.S. 714 (1986), discussed in subsection B(2), supra. The Court struck down the Gramm-Rudman Deficit Reduction Act because an executive power—the power to make specific program-by-program cuts in federal spending binding on the President—was vested in the Comptroller General, an official removable for cause by Congress.

iii.   *Buckley v. Valeo,* 424 U.S. 1 (1976). The Court held invalid the attempt by Congress to appoint inferior executive officers—members of the Federal Election Commission. See subsection B(2)(b), supra.

d.   **Congressional encroachment on the judicial branch.** Congress may *not* assign the judicial power described in Article III to "legislative" courts—courts lacking the independence (chiefly life tenure of judges) of Article III courts. There are important exceptions to this rule:

- Congress may create non-Article III courts for the territories and the District of Columbia by virtue of its "extraordinary control" over those areas under Articles I and IV.

- Congress may create non-Article III military courts by virtue of its Article I power to regulate the military.

- Congress may create administrative courts—adjudicating public rather than private rights—because Congress has an "exceptional power" to do so stemming from "historical consensus."

Northern Pipeline Construction Co. v. Marathon Pipe Line Co., 458 U.S. 50 (1982).

These exceptions, while substantial, do not swallow the rule.

EXAMPLE AND ANALYSIS

Congress enacted the Bankruptcy Act of 1978, creating a new Bankruptcy Court staffed by judges lacking life tenure and empowered to decide virtually any case that might arise within the context of a bankruptcy proceeding. Northern, a bankrupt, sued Marathon in Bankruptcy Court on state-created contract claims. Marathon contended that the Bankruptcy Court could not validly decide the claim since the Bankruptcy Act was unconstitutional. The Court agreed, reasoning that none of the exceptions, particularly the "public rights" exception, was applicable. *Northern Pipeline Construction Co. v. Marathon Pipe Line Co.*, 458 U.S. 50 (1982).

D. IMMUNITIES AND PRIVILEGES

In order to preserve the autonomy of each branch of government, the Constitution confers certain immunities and privileges upon executive, legislative, and judicial officials.

1. Legislative Immunities

The Constitution explicitly confers a limited immunity from suit on members of Congress.

a. The speech and debate clause. Article I, section 6 provides that members of Congress "shall not be questioned in any other Place . . . for any Speech or Debate in either House." The purpose for such immunity is to foster uninhibited legislative debate and to protect legislators from the distraction of defending suits based on their performance of their duties.

    i. Scope. Members of Congress are absolutely immune from suits (civil or criminal) or grand jury investigations premised upon their **legislative acts.** Members of Congress may also assert their immunity to protect the "legislative acts" of their aides. See *Gravel v. United States*, 408 U.S. 606 (1972).

        (a) Meaning of "legislative acts." Legislative acts comprise everything that is integral to "the deliberative and communicative processes by which members participate" in the official business of Congress. Legislative action includes not just the literal "speeches and debates" of Congress but also voting, committee work, and other official business of Congress. It does not include constituent service or political campaigning.

 EXAMPLES AND ANALYSIS

Example: A member of Congress may not be prosecuted for *voting in a particular manner* because he was bribed to do so, but he may be prosecuted for the nonlegislative act of *taking the bribe.* The resulting bribery prosecution may not, however, introduce evidence of legislative acts on the part of the member of Congress. *United States v. Johnson,* 383 U.S. 169, 184-185 (1966); *United States v. Brewster,* 408 U.S. 501, 526 (1972); *United States v. Helstoski,* 442 U.S. 477, 489 (1979).

Example: With much attendant publicity and fanfare, Senator Proxmire regularly bestowed a "Golden Fleece Award" on a recipient of federal money, illustrating what Proxmire regarded as wasteful, needless government spending. Hutchinson, a professor receiving a federal grant to pay for certain research, sued Proxmire for defamation; the Court concluded that Proxmire was not immune from suit because his actions were not "legislative." *Hutchinson v. Proxmire,* 443 U.S. 111 (1979).

    b. The privilege from arrest. Article I, section 6 also provides that, except for cases of "Treason, Felony and Breach of the Peace," members of Congress are "privileged from Arrest during their Attendance at the Session of their respective Houses, and in going to and returning from the same." In 1787 this effectively conferred an immunity from arrest for nonpayment of debt. Translated into modern parlance, it is best read as a temporary immunity from civil suit during the pendency of congressional sessions.

2. Executive Immunities

The Constitution does not expressly confer any immunity upon the President or other executive branch officials, but the courts have created a limited immunity from suit for both, implied from the Constitution's structure and as part of "federal common law."

    a. Source of immunities

        i. Presidential immunity. The courts have found an implied immunity for the President in the doctrine of separation of powers. The Supreme Court has said that absolute presidential immunity for the President's *official acts* is "a functionally mandated incident of the President's unique office, rooted in the constitutional tradition of separation of powers and supported by our history." *Nixon v. Fitzgerald*, 457 U.S. 731, 749 (1982).

    ii. Other executive officers' immunity. Executive branch officials have long enjoyed a judicially created common law immunity from civil suit for acts performed in the course of their official duties. *Spalding v. Vilas*, 161 U.S. 483, 498 (1896). This immunity is not as extensive as that enjoyed by the President.

  b. Immunity from judicial process. Neither the President nor other executive branch officials are immune from *judicial process*. Thus, they are susceptible to the courts' subpoena power, both with respect to their testimony and documents in their custody. If sufficiently justified, the President may be able to protect the confidentiality of some matters by invoking *executive privilege*. See section 3, infra.

  c. Presidential immunity from civil liability. The President is **absolutely immune** from *civil suits for damages* based on the President's *official acts*.

EXAMPLE AND ANALYSIS

Fitzgerald, a civilian Air Force analyst, was fired after he embarrassed the Nixon Administration by testifying before Congress about cost overruns in Air Force weapons procurement. The evidence suggested that President Nixon may have personally ordered Fitzgerald's discharge. Following a Civil Service Commission ruling that Fitzgerald was entitled to be reinstated and given back pay, he sued Nixon for damages. The Court ruled that President Nixon was absolutely immune, and concluded that such immunity could not be limited to "particular functions" of the Presidency, but extended to all "acts within the 'outer perimeter' of his official responsibility." *Nixon v. Fitzgerald*, 457 U.S. 731 (1982).

Injunctive relief against the President is generally barred by the political question doctrine. See *Mississippi v. Johnson*, 71 U.S. 475, 500 (1867); Chapter 2, supra. The President does not possess any immunity from civil suits based on his nonofficial actions.

EXAMPLE AND ANALYSIS

Paula Jones, a onetime Arkansas state employee, sued President Clinton for sexual harassment, charging that he asked her for sexual favors while he was Governor of Arkansas. President Clinton claimed temporary immunity from suit during his incumbency. The Court disagreed. Presidential immunity, an implied aspect of the separation of powers doctrine, exists only to permit the President to perform his *official actions* without fear of suit. It has no application to the President's *unofficial conduct.* Though not constitutionally required, a trial judge has "broad discretion to stay proceedings" to minimize "interference with the President's duties." *Clinton v. Jones,* 520 U.S. 681 (1997).

---

    d. **Nonpresidential executive immunity from civil liability.** Executive officials subordinate to the President enjoy a **qualified immunity,** limited to actions taken in **good faith** in connection with *official duties.* See *Butz v. Economou,* 438 U.S. 478 (1978); *Scheuer v. Rhodes,* 416 U.S. 232 (1974).

        i. *Harlow v. Fitzgerald,* 457 U.S. 800 (1982). This case and *Nixon v. Fitzgerald,* supra, arose from the same set of facts. Fitzgerald, the Air Force analyst who blew the whistle on cost overruns, also sued Bryce Harlow, one of Nixon's top personal aides. The Court denied Harlow's claim of absolute immunity, observing in dicta that executive branch officials had absolute immunity only when "entrusted with discretionary authority in such sensitive areas as national security or foreign policy." The Court ruled that executive officials had **good faith immunity**—for *official actions taken in good faith*—and that such immunity was proven by showing that the executive officer had a **reasonable basis to believe that his or her action was lawful.**

    e. **Immunity from criminal prosecution.** It is an open question whether the President enjoys any immunity from criminal prosecutions. Some argue that *impeachment is the sole remedy,* others argue that there is *probably no immunity* at all for the President. Compare Tribe, at 268, with A. Bickel, New Republic 14-15, Oct. 6, 1973. History suggests no such immunity exists. Vice President Agnew was indicted for tax evasion before his resignation. President Nixon was not indicted, although he figured prominently as an "unindicted co-conspirator" in the principal Watergate indictments. President Clinton was impeached for perjury and obstruction of justice and then made an immunity bargain with the special prosecutor just prior to leaving office. The issue has never been adjudicated.

3. **Executive Privilege**

Unlike immunity from liability, executive privilege is an **evidentiary privilege** held by the President, **limited in scope,** that can be raised to protect presidential confidentiality in either **judicial** or **legislative proceedings.** The privilege is constitutionally mandated, inferred from Constitutional structure in order to protect the President from "encroachment" by either Congress or the courts. *United States v. Nixon*, 418 U.S. 683 (1974).

a. **The Nixon tapes case: *United States v. Nixon,* 418 U.S. 683 (1974).** President Nixon recorded his Oval Office conversations and stored the tapes for later reference. Nixon himself became the subject of a criminal investigation into a conspiracy to obstruct justice, centering on his involvement in an alleged "cover-up" of the Watergate burglary (in which the Democratic Party headquarters had been burgled by agents of the President's reelection campaign). In the course of criminal proceedings against Nixon's top aides, a federal court issued a subpoena to Nixon to produce certain of his tape recordings. Nixon asserted that the President was immune from all judicial process and that he enjoyed an absolute executive privilege to withhold information he deemed confidential. The Court rejected Nixon's claims.

   i. **No immunity from judicial process.** The Court concluded that courts had the power to order the President to testify or produce documents, but admitted that it was undecided whether a President could be jailed or fined for contempt of a subpoena. The few Presidents who have been subpoenaed have substantially complied with the judicial orders.

   ii. **Qualified executive privilege exists.** The Court rejected Nixon's claim of an absolute privilege but did recognize that separation-of-powers principles compelled judicial recognition of a **qualified privilege.** In any given case the existence of executive privilege will be **decided by courts.** The Court left open the possibility that Congress might have power to set the boundaries of executive privilege, or that the courts might defer to presidential claims of privilege in highly sensitive areas like national security. To decide whether the privilege against disclosure exists, a court must *balance* the *need for the information* sought and the *reasons asserted for confidentiality.* In the *Nixon* case, the Court balanced Nixon's need for executive confidentiality (mostly avoidance of political disaster) versus the criminal justice system's need for probative evidence of crime or exculpation (essential to the guarantee of a fair trial). The Court intimated that a trial judge would need to conclude that the demanded presidential evidence is **"essential to . . . justice,"** implying that an exceptional need must be shown to exist in order to subpoena the President.

   iii. **Scope: open questions.** The precise scope of the qualified executive privilege is undetermined, but at least the following principles apply.

- The privilege is strongest when revelation of a *state secret* (highly sensitive information critical to national security) is sought. The courts will likely inspect the evidence *in camera*—privately—before ruling.

- The privilege is weakest when a criminal defendant seeks information (not a state secret) to bolster his defense.

- The privilege extends to civil cases and it is probable that civil cases are on the same footing as criminal cases. See *Dellums v. Powell*, 561 F.2d 242 (D.C. Cir. 1977), cert. denied, 434 U.S. 880 (1977).

- The President may assert the privilege with respect to presidential communications or documents even after leaving the office. *Nixon v. Administrator of General Services*, 433 U.S. 425 (1977).

- The availability of executive privilege in response to a congressional subpoena is highly controversial, but likely subject to judicial resolution. When Congress and the President are so sharply at swords' points impeachment is also possible.

REVIEW QUESTIONS AND ANSWERS

Question: Congress enacts legislation that provides that, in appointing the Director of the National Park Service, the Secretary of the Interior must select from a list of persons supplied by Congress. Is the legislation valid?

Answer: No. The Director is an inferior officer, so Congress can specify whether the appointment is to be made by the President alone, the courts of law, or an executive department head (like the Secretary of the Interior). However, Congress has attempted to control the appointment by reducing the Secretary's discretion to selecting among people already picked by Congress. See *Metropolitan Washington Airports Authority,* where the Court invalidated a similar scheme.

Question: Congress provides by legislation that the Secretary of the Treasury may not be removed except with the consent of the Senate. Is the legislation valid?

Answer: No. Congress may not restrict the President's unilateral power to remove principal officers. A cabinet secretary is the paradigmatic principal officer. This question presents, in essence, the Tenure in Office Act, the legislation that President Andrew Johnson ignored and for which he was impeached but not convicted. Its invalidity was later confirmed by *Myers v. United States.*

Question: Suppose the President unilaterally ordered American armed forces to attack Cuba by surprise and to invade and occupy that island nation. Would the President's action be valid?

Answer: Probably not. The President has no authority to undertake unilateral military action except to repel sudden attacks, to protect American citizens and interests abroad, and perhaps to aid national allies. None of those factors seem present here. On the other hand, congressional acquiescence to the action probably constitutes *de facto* authorization. In addition, the issue may well escape judicial scrutiny by reason of the political question doctrine.

Question: The President makes a public appearance to promote the reelection chances of the Governor of Olema. After the speech, and in a private hotel room, the President grabs the Governor and demands sex from her. She refuses and sues him in state court for assault and intentional infliction of emotional distress, seeking damages. The President moves to dismiss on grounds that he is immune from civil suits for damages. What result?

Answer: The Governor's suit will probably continue. The President is immune from civil suits for damages only with respect to his *official actions*. He enjoys no absolute immunity from civil suits based on his unofficial actions. The actions complained of are not official actions of the President.

EXAM TIPS

- **Analyzing Separation of Powers Problems.** Courts sometimes apply very prudential reasoning to these problems—epitomized by broad, flexible, balancing tests—and sometimes apply bright-line textual rules. Check to see if the problem presented violates any of the bright-line rules. If not, then determine whether the flexible, prudential, tests are satisfied.
- **Appointment and Removal of Executive Officers.** The President may appoint principal executive officers, subject to Senate confirmation. Congress may direct by law whether the President alone, the heads of executive departments, or the courts may appoint inferior officers of the United States. Congress may restrict the President's ability to remove inferior executive officers but may not restrict the President's ability to remove principal officers. Congress may neither appoint nor remove executive officers.

- **Presidential Power and Congressional Action.** Because the President **executes** law and Congress **makes** law much of the President's power is derived from enabling statutes. Thus:

- Presidential power is at its greatest when the President acts under authority validly granted by Congress.

- Presidential power is at its weakest when the President acts contrary to legislation—valid only if the President has constitutional authority for unilateral action.

- When Congress has not acted on a subject of presidential action, presidential authority is in a "twilight zone," resolved by prudential reasoning about the specific context of the issue.

- **War and Foreign Affairs.** Congress and the President share the nation's exclusive power over foreign affairs. Primarily because of the nation's need to speak with one voice on foreign affairs the President has more freedom to act unilaterally than in domestic affairs. Although only Congress can declare war the President has authority to commit Americans to combat to defend the nation against sudden attacks and possibly other small-scale limited expeditions in defense of threatened American lives or property.

- **Nondelegation.** Congress may delegate its legislative power to administrative agencies if it states an **intelligible principle** that both **declares policy** and **defines the circumstances that activate the policy.** Check whether Congress has acted so vaguely that it has violated this principle; e.g., by a law authorizing the EPA to "do what's right" to "improve the environment."

- **No Legislative Veto.** Congress can't control executive action by a legislative veto.

- **Prudential Assessment.** If the bright-line rules are satisfied, courts still invalidate schemes that give a branch power to do something **incongruous** with its constitutional role or that enable one branch to interfere with another branch's **essential role.** This prudential assessment is applied most commonly to unorthodox governmental devices that combine elements of each branch (e.g., the Sentencing Commission).

- **Remember the Political Question Doctrine.** Courts are more prone to find separation of powers issues to be nonjusticiable political questions than many other areas of constitutional law. If the exam question presents these issues for court decision, consider if the issues are political questions.

- **Immunities and Privileges.** This topic is often left out of constitutional law courses. If it's in your course, remember the following rules:

  - **Legislative Immunity.** Members of Congress and their aides are **absolutely immune** from suit based on their **legislative acts,** and are **temporarily immune** from civil suits while Congress is in session.

- **Executive Immunity.** The President is **absolutely immune** from **civil suits seeking damages** based on the President's **official conduct,** has **no immunity** from such suits based on his **unofficial conduct,** and probably has no immunity from criminal prosecution. Other executive officials are only immune from suit based on their **official actions taken in good faith.**

- **Executive Privilege.** The President has a qualified evidentiary privilege for presidential communications. When it is invoked, courts balance the need for the information sought and the reasons asserted for confidentiality.

THE DUE PROCESS CLAUSES

8

CHAPTER OVERVIEW

This chapter examines the two due process clauses—one contained in the Fifth Amendment and the other in the 14th Amendment. The most important points in this chapter follow.

- **Two Due Process Clauses:** The Fifth Amendment bars the federal government from denying due process. The 14th Amendment applies only to the states and their political subdivisions.

- **Two Functions to Due Process:** The due process clauses protect some **substantive rights** and certain **procedural rights.**

- **Substantive Due Process:**

  - If a claimed right is **fundamental** courts apply **strict scrutiny:** The **government must prove** that any infringement of the right is **necessary** to achieve a **compelling state objective.**

  - A right is **fundamental** if it is *"implicit in the concept of ordered liberty"* or is *"deeply rooted in this Nation's history and tradition."*

  - If a right is **not fundamental** courts apply **minimal scrutiny:** The **challenger must prove** that any infringement is *not* **rationally related to a legitimate state interest.**

  - Since the late 1930s economic rights have been treated as **not fundamental.**

- Substantive due process protects certain noneconomic personal rights where government intrusion is thought to be especially suspect. Here are the major fundamental rights:

  — *Incorporation Doctrine:* The 14th Amendment's due process clause "incorporates" most of the Bill of Rights guarantees, thus making them applicable to the states in the *same form* as they apply to the federal government.

  — *Contraceptives:* All adults, single or married, have a fundamental right to use and obtain contraceptives.

  — *Abortion:* Until viability of the fetus, a woman has the fundamental right to be free of "undue burdens" placed by the state on her decision to terminate her pregnancy. An "undue burden" is anything that is intended to impose or that has the effect of imposing a "substantial obstacle" to an abortion. Unemancipated minors may be required either to notify their parents or obtain judicial permission prior to obtaining an abortion. In general, it is not an undue burden on the abortion right for governments to refuse to fund abortions.

  — *Family Relationships:* There is a fundamental right of extended families to live together as a family unit, an ill-defined fundamental right on the part of parents to rear their children as they see fit, and to maintain existing functional relationships with their children.

  — *Right to Marry.*

- The following claimed rights have not been declared fundamental, and so are *unprotected by substantive due process:*

  — *Right to Die:* The Court has hinted, but not held, that there is such a fundamental right.

  — *Right to Consensual Sex:* There is no such right. The Court has specifically rejected a right to homosexual sex, and while a right to heterosexual sex seems implicit in the contraceptive and abortion cases, the Court has never so held.

  — *Right to Personal Appearance:* The Court has rejected such a right on the part of police officers. It has never addressed the question of whether the general public has such a right.

  — *Right of "Anonymity":* There is no fundamental right to be free of government collection and storage of information about you.

■ **Procedural Due Process:**

- There is *no* **general** right to *procedural regularity.* Procedural due process attaches only when the government is about to deprive a person of **life, liberty,** or **property.**

- *Two Parts to Procedural Due Process:*

    — Due process is required when government action infringes upon a life, liberty, or property interest.

    — Depending on the nature of the infringement, the procedures "due" to the affected individual will vary.

- *Property:* The question of whether *government benefits* are a *property interest* sufficient to require procedural due process is a *matter of state law.*

- *Liberty:* Government action that does *not* alter one's *legal status under state law* does not infringe liberty, but in any case government invasions of liberty recognized as such in other constitutional contexts require due process.

- *What Process Is Due?* The government must provide at least **notice of the charges** and **an opportunity to be heard.** In criminal prosecutions only a trial will do. For minor deprivations of liberty and of property, the procedures required vary with the circumstances. Courts weigh three factors to determine the minimum procedures required:

    — the private interest affected,

    — the risk of error in using the challenged procedures and the "probable value" of other or additional procedures, and

    — the public interest, including costs and burdens to the government.

In applying this test courts must give *substantial weight* to the *good-faith judgments* of the relevant government officials.

A. INTRODUCTION AND OVERVIEW

The due process clauses are the source of a variety of substantive and procedural individual rights judicially enforceable against the federal and state governments.

1. The Fifth Amendment's Due Process Clause

The Fifth Amendment provides that "No person shall . . . be deprived of life, liberty, or property, without due process of law." The clause has ancient origins in Anglo-American law, at least to Magna Carta, which protected free men from government acts unless in accord with "the law of the land." Americans have long treated this guarantee as both procedural and substantive, although its substantive aspects are among the most controversial issues in constitutional law. The Fifth Amendment's due process clause is *enforceable only against the federal government.*

2. The Fourteenth Amendment's Due Process Clause

The 14th Amendment provides that "No State shall . . . deprive any person of life, liberty, or property, without due process of law." Like the Fifth Amendment's due process clause this provision has been read by courts to guarantee important substantive and procedural rights. Though probably not intended to "incorporate" by implication the Bill of Rights, the 14th Amendment due process clause serves that purpose. (See section 2, infra.) It is *enforceable only against the states.*

B. THE BILL OF RIGHTS AND THE INCORPORATION DOCTRINE

1. Original Scope of the Bill of Rights

The first ten amendments—the Bill of Rights—were drafted by the First Congress and ratified in 1791. They were created to alleviate fears of Anti-Federalist opponents of the Constitution that the new federal government had power to invade important individual liberties long cherished by Americans. State constitutions contained similar (often identical) rights guarantees enforceable against state government. Thus, it was widely accepted that the Bill of Rights guarantees applied only to the federal government but the Court did not address that issue until 1833.

    a. *Barron v. Baltimore,* 32 U.S. 243 (1833). In the course of street construction the city of Baltimore diverted several streams, flushing great quantities of silt and sand into Baltimore harbor in the vicinity of Barron's wharf, thus making it impossible for vessels to use the wharf. Barron sued the city, claiming that the city had taken his property for public use without just compensation, as required by the Fifth Amendment. Barron argued that since the "takings" clause is "in favour of the liberty of the citizen, [it] ought to be so construed as to restrain the legislative power of a state, as well as that of the United States." Not so, said Chief Justice Marshall, for the Court. Marshall concluded that the "fifth amendment must be understood as restraining the power of the general government, . . . and is not applicable to the legislation of the states." He reasoned that (1) the Bill of Rights had been intended by its Framers to restrain federal power alone, and (2) when the Constitution restrains state power it does so expressly, thus blunting any argument that the Bill of Rights should be read to restrain state power by implication. *Barron* settled the issue until after the Civil War.

2. The Initial Effect of the 14th Amendment

The 14th Amendment contains three major limits on state power. No state may "abridge the privileges or immunities of citizens of the United States." No state may "deprive any person of life, liberty, or property, without due process of law." No state may "deny to any person within its jurisdiction the equal protection of the laws." The idea that these provisions reversed *Barron v. Baltimore* was soon put to the test.

    a. *The Slaughter-House Cases,* 83 U.S. 36 (1873). Ostensibly as a public health measure Louisiana chartered the Crescent City Company and gave it a twenty-five year monopoly over livestock slaughtering in and around New Orleans. Other butchers were given the right to slaughter animals at the Crescent City Company's abattoir, upon payment of fees fixed by statute. Those butchers contended that the law deprived them of their right to exercise their trade, and that by so doing Louisiana had violated each of the 14th Amendment's due process, equal protection, and privileges and immunities clauses. The Court sustained the law.

i. **The Court's rationale.** The Court used a different rationale to dispose of each of the butchers' 14th Amendment claims.

(a) **Privileges and immunities.** The Court relied upon the 14th Amendment's text to conclude that federal and state citizenship were distinctly different. The privileges and immunities clause of the 14th Amendment bars a state from abridging privileges or immunities incident to **national citizenship,** *not* state citizenship. The Court concluded that Louisiana's interference, if any, with the butchers' right to pursue their trade was an interference with a privilege resulting only from *state citizenship.* Privileges of federal citizenship include such rights as access to the federal government, use of navigable waters, habeas corpus, freedom from slavery, racially nondiscriminatory access to the vote, and equal treatment in a new state of residence.

(b) **Due process.** The Court used prior judicial interpretations of the Fifth Amendment's due process clause and the various state constitutions' due process clauses to reach the conclusion that the butchers had not been deprived of any property "within the meaning of" the due process clause.

(c) **Equal protection.** The Court dismissed the equal protection argument by expressing doubt that the clause covered anything more than state racial discrimination.

ii. **The dissents.** Justices Field and Bradley dissented, arguing that the 14th Amendment's privileges and immunities clause forbade states from violating the unwritten "fundamental rights of the citizen," which surely included "the right to pursue a lawful employment in a lawful manner."

iii. **Significance of *The Slaughter-House Cases.*** The Court's decision drained the 14th Amendment's privileges and immunities clause of any importance. It also defeated for the moment the idea that the 14th Amendment reversed the rule of *Barron v. Baltimore.* In *Saenz v. Roe,* 526 U.S. 489 (1999), the Court relied on the 14th Amendment's privileges and immunities clause to strike down a California law limiting welfare benefits of newly arrived Californians to the levels of their former state of residence for the first year of their residence in California. See Chapter 9 (I)(6), infra. This may signal a revival of sorts of the 14th Amendment's privileges and immunities clause.

3. The Incorporation Doctrine

The Court was eventually faced with the question of what procedures the 14th Amendment's due process clause required of the states in the course of criminal trials. To answer that question, the Court considered whether the 14th Amendment's due process clause **incorporated** the Bill of Rights guarantees, making them applicable to the states.

   a. **Selective incorporation.** The Court has applied a doctrine of **selective incorporation** of the Bill of Rights into the 14th Amendment's due process clause. The test to determine which rights are incorporated has been variously phrased, but boils down to whether the right at issue is a "fundamental principle of liberty and justice which inheres in the very idea of free government." *Twining v. New Jersey,* 211 U.S. 78, 106 (1908). The modern version is whether the right in question is **"fundamental to the American scheme of justice."** *Duncan v. Louisiana,* 391 U.S. 145 (1968).

 EXAMPLES AND ANALYSIS

Example: Connecticut permitted the state to appeal criminal cases, a practice from which the federal government is barred by the double jeopardy clause of the Fifth Amendment. Connecticut appealed Palko's second-degree murder conviction and it was reversed. Palko was then convicted of first-degree murder and he appealed. The Court, per Justice Cardozo, stated that the 14th Amendment's due process clause incorporated those parts of the Bill of Rights that are "the very essence of a scheme of ordered liberty," things " 'so rooted in the traditions and conscience of our people as to be ranked as fundamental,' " or rights such "that neither liberty nor justice would exist if they were sacrificed." Freedom from double jeopardy was not such a right. *Palko v. Connecticut,* 302 U.S. 319 (1937). (*Benton v. Maryland,* 395 U.S. 784 (1969), reversed *Palko* on the precise point, holding protection against double jeopardy to be so fundamental that it must be incorporated.)

Example: Louisiana denied a jury trial for people accused of crimes not punishable by death or imprisonment at hard labor. Duncan was convicted of battery, an offense punishable by a maximum sentence of two years' imprisonment and a $300 fine. He contended that he was convicted unconstitutionally by denial of a jury trial. The Court agreed, finding that the 14th Amendment's due process clause "guarantees a right of jury trial in all criminal cases which—were they to be tried in a federal court—would come within the Sixth Amendment's guarantee" of a jury trial. *Duncan v. Louisiana,* 391 U.S. 145 (1968).

---

    b. Total incorporation. This view, *never accepted by a majority of the Supreme Court,* was that the "original purpose" of the 14th Amendment was "to guarantee that thereafter no state could deprive its citizens of the privileges and protections of the Bill of Rights." *Adamson v. California,* 332 U.S. 46 (1947) (Black, J., dissenting). Justice Black, the principal advocate for this position, based his argument upon a reading of history disputed by historian Charles Fairman, 2 Stan. L. Rev. 5, and the belief that the "fundamental rights" approach of selective incorporation was an indeterminate "natural law" approach inappropriate to the explication of a written Constitution. Justice Frankfurter, concurring in *Adamson,* argued that Black's position would deprive the 14th Amendment's due process clause of any "independent potency" or "independent function," make Fifth and 14th Amendment due process mean two different things, and stifle state innovation in criminal procedure.

    c. The modern state of incorporation. The debate concerning incorporation is largely over. In the course of applying "selective incorporation" the Court has made virtually every Bill of Rights guarantee applicable to the states. The only portions of the first eight amendments not yet held applicable to the states are the Second and Third Amendments, the grand jury indictment requirement of the Fifth Amendment, and the Seventh Amendment's civil jury trial right.

        i. "Jot-for-jot" incorporation. Once a right is incorporated into the 14th Amendment's due process clause and made applicable to the states, its precise meaning is the same as when applied against the federal government. The right is said to be incorporated "jot-for-jot," or "bag and baggage."

        Example: In *Wolf v. Colorado,* 338 U.S. 25 (1949), the Court concluded that the Fourth Amendment's prohibition upon unreasonable searches and seizures was incorporated into the 14th Amendment's due process clause, but ruled that state courts were not required to exclude illegally obtained evidence even though federal courts were so required. In *Mapp v. Ohio,* 367 U.S. 643 (1961), the Court changed its mind, ruling that the contours of the search and seizure guarantee must be the same when applied to the states or the federal government.

        (a) Exception: nonunanimous jury verdicts. The exception to "jot-for-jot" incorporation is with respect to conviction of a criminal offense by less than unanimity of the jurors. Federal juries must reach criminal verdicts unanimously; state juries may convict the defendant by less than unanimity. *Apodaca v. Oregon,* 406 U.S. 404 (1972).

C. SUBSTANTIVE DUE PROCESS

1. Introduction

Substantive due process is a bit of an oxymoron, rather like speaking of "green pastel redness," as John Ely put it in *Democracy and Distrust,* at 18. The due process clauses seemingly refer to *procedures* that must be followed in divesting people of life, liberty, or property. But from the beginning of American constitutional law there has been a doctrinal voice that insists there are unwritten individual rights that should be judicially protected against governmental invasion. The due process clauses, in their "substantive" dimension, are the home of this doctrine. Substantive due process has had two eras: first, an era, now repudiated, in which economic regulations were struck down and, second, an era, still continuing, in which some state regulations of intimate relationships (e.g., human reproduction, family) have been invalidated. The core of substantive due process is the idea that some laws invade life, liberty, or property in such a fashion that they cannot be considered valid law. The *procedures* required by the due process clauses are discussed in section D, infra.

a. **The constitutional context of substantive due process.** Substantive due process is the major doctrinal part of a larger constitutional enterprise—judicial protection of unenumerated rights. The Court has extended constitutional protection, not always using due process, to "such fundamental rights as the right to associate with others, the right to vote, the right to be accorded equal protection of the laws by the federal government, the right to be presumed innocent and to have that presumption overcome only by proof beyond a reasonable doubt, the right to travel, the right to marry or not, the right to have children or not, and the right to enjoy a zone of personal privacy or autonomy into which government may not intrude." Massey, *Silent Rights,* at 3-4. Yet the process of doing so is and always has been highly controversial. At the heart of this controversy is disagreement over the proper scope of judicial review. Is the Court the best mechanism to assure governmental observance of "important" but constitutionally unexpressed rights? The answer may depend on your view of the legitimacy of judicial review. How can courts decide which unwritten rights to recognize without succumbing to personal preferences alone?

b. **Origins of substantive due process.** Two events facilitated development of the doctrine. The first was the belief, now mostly discredited, that *natural law* principles were part of the Constitution. The second was the *economic views and conditions* that predominated in the latter 19th century.

    i. **Natural law.** The classic exchange of views concerning the relevance of natural law to constitutional law occurred in *Calder v. Bull,* 3 U.S. 386 (1798). A law "against all reason and justice" is void, said Justice Samuel Chase, because "[t]here are certain vital principles in our free republican governments which will determine and overrule an apparent and flagrant abuse of legislative power." It did not matter to Chase that these principles were unexpressed in the Constitution—they were binding anyway. Not so, said Chase's colleague James Iredell. Only the written Constitution supplied the boundaries of legislative power. If a legislature enacted a law within its constitutional power, said Iredell, "the court cannot pronounce it void, merely because it is, in their judgment, contrary to the principles of natural justice. The ideas of natural justice are regulated by no fixed standard; the ablest and purest men have differed upon the subject. . . ." The modern doctrine of substantive due process is a fusion of these differing views. It pays homage to Iredell in its reliance on constitutional text—the due process clauses—but defers to Chase in its frank recognition of rights nowhere mentioned in the Constitution and inferred from text in a fashion that Chase would describe as the simple use of natural "reason and justice."

    ii. **Economic events of the late nineteenth century.** As the industrialization of America reached its early maturity in the late 19th century, governments acted to remedy perceived abuses produced by the great disparity in economic power that resulted from industrialization. At the same time, economic theories supporting the inequalities of wealth produced by industrialization began to win favor among those benefited by industrialization. Courts reacted to the latter by treating governmental regulation of business practices with a somewhat jaundiced eye, and to the former by upholding the validity of many such regulations.

 # EXAMPLES AND ANALYSIS

Example: Illinois's regulation of rates charged for grain storage by grain elevators was attacked as violating the 14th Amendment's due process clause. The Court upheld the measure, concluding that governments could regulate private property when it is "affected with a public interest," or "used in a manner to make it of public consequence, and affect[s] the community at large," but hinted that regulations might be unreasonable and void when applied to "mere private contracts, relating to matters in which the public has no interest." *Munn v. Illinois,* 94 U.S. 113 (1877).

Example: Kansas prohibited alcoholic beverages. Mugler, a brewer, contended that the law unconstitutionally deprived him of his property. The Court upheld the law but declared that laws having "no real or substantial relation" to a state's legitimate police powers, or which are "palpable invasion[s] of rights secured by the fundamental law" would be struck down. *Mugler v. Kansas,* 123 U.S. 623 (1887).

Example: Louisiana prohibited insuring any Louisiana property except through an insurer licensed to do business in Louisiana. Allgeyer purchased marine insurance on his goods shipped from New Orleans from a New York insurer not licensed to do business in Louisiana. Allgeyer's conviction under the Louisiana law was unanimously reversed by the Court. The term "liberty" in the due process clauses, said Justice Peckham for the Court, "embrace[s] the right of the citizen to be free in the enjoyment of all his faculties; to be free to use them in all lawful ways; to live and work where he will; to earn his livelihood by any lawful calling; to pursue any livelihood or avocation, and for that purpose to enter into all contracts which may be proper, necessary and essential to his carrying out to a successful conclusion the purposes above mentioned." *Allgeyer v. Louisiana,* 165 U.S. 578 (1897).

---

2. **Economic Regulations and Substantive Due Process**

The era of striking down economic regulations as violative of substantive due process began with *Allgeyer* in 1897 and died in the New Deal revolution. During that period the Court occasionally struck down laws impinging on the individual "liberty of contract" broadly described in *Allgeyer.* This period of substantive due process is often referred to as the "*Lochner* era," after the leading case.

a. **The *Lochner* era**

   i. *Lochner v. New York,* 198 U.S. 45 (1905). New York prohibited bakery workers from working more than ten hours daily or sixty hours per week. Lochner was convicted and fined for employing a baker for more than sixty hours per week. The Court, 5 to 4, reversed his conviction.

   (a) **The Court's opinion.** Justice Peckham, for the Court, acknowledged that states may regulate labor conditions to achieve public health or safety, preserve public morals, or further the general welfare. But in every such case, said Peckham, it must be asked whether the law is "a fair, reasonable and appropriate exercise of [the police power], or is it an unreasonable, unnecessary and arbitrary interference with the right of the individual to his personal liberty or to enter into those [labor] contracts . . . which may seem to him appropriate or necessary for the support of himself and his family?" Peckham answered the question by asserting that there was no "reasonable ground" for the regulation. Bakers were not shown to be in need of public protection. Nor did the law involve public safety, health, or morals, despite New York's contention that it did, because there was no *"direct relation"* between the state's *objective* (preserving the health of bakers) and the *means* of doing so (limiting the working hours of bakers). Instead, the Court characterized laws "limiting the hours in which grown and intelligent men may labor to earn their living" as "mere meddlesome interferences with the rights of the individual," subject to state regulation only when there is a reasonable basis "to say that there is material danger to the public health or to the health of the employees." The "real object and purpose" of the New York law was not health, but "simply to regulate the hours of labor . . . in a private business, not dangerous . . . to morals or . . . health." That objective was illegitimate as an unjustified interference with liberty of contract.

(b) The dissents. Justice Harlan, for himself and two others, cited various medical authorities in arguing that it was reasonable for New York to conclude that there was "material danger" to the health of bakers in working long hours. Justice Holmes, dissenting separately, espoused a hard-edged legal positivism by arguing that "the word liberty in the 14th Amendment is perverted when it is held to prevent the natural outcome of a dominant opinion." States should be free to enact any measure reasonably related to health. Holmes's dissent is most famous for his charge that the majority decided the case "upon an economic theory which a large part of the country does not entertain. . . . The 14th Amendment does not enact Mr. Herbert Spencer's Social Statics." Spencer was a leading advocate of "Social Darwinism," the idea that in human social relationships, as with natural flora and fauna, the fittest will survive.

ii. Criticisms of *Lochner*. *Lochner* has been severely criticized. These criticisms, listed below, all present untidy conundrums in terms of explaining *Lochner's* error while simultaneously justifying the modern version of substantive due process.

- *Lochner* was wrong because the courts have no warrant to invoke due process to invalidate legislation in the name of constitutionally unenumerated rights. If this is correct, can cases such as *Roe v. Wade* (abortion) and *Griswold v. Connecticut* (contraceptives), infra, be rightly decided?

• *Lochner* was wrong because the Court applied too strict a standard of review to the New York law, and should have been more deferential to the state's choice of means to accomplish its legitimate objectives. If this is right, should the Court be equally deferential to state regulations of abortion?

• *Lochner* was wrong because the Court read "liberty" too expansively. Most commonly this view asserts that "liberty" means "fundamental" liberty, and liberty of contract is not a fundamental liberty. Why not? Why is contraception more fundamental?

• *Lochner* was wrong because the Court had too narrow a conception of the legitimate objectives of government. Recall that the Court thought that labor regulations were illegitimate. Why are controversial economic regulations legitimate ends of government but controversial moral regulations not legitimate?

iii.   **Application of *Lochner*.** As the Court applied *Lochner* the force of the doctrine began to erode from within.

• *Adair v. United States,* 208 U.S. 161 (1908), struck down a federal law that prohibited interstate railroads from "yellow dog" contracts—conditioning employment upon an employee promise not to join a labor union.

• *Coppage v. Kansas,* 236 U.S. 1 (1915), struck down a Kansas statute prohibiting all employers from "yellow dog" contracts. The Court found the right to contract rooted in property as well as liberty. *Adair* and *Coppage* were overturned by *Phelps Dodge v. NLRB,* 313 U.S. 177 (1941).

• *Muller v. Oregon,* 208 U.S. 412 (1908), upheld an Oregon law that limited women to no more than ten hours labor in a day. Liberty of contract "is not absolute," said the Court. The opinion reeked of paternalism, as the Court sought to justify a law that would be void as applied to men. The Court cited "inherent difference between the two sexes," the public interest in "healthy mothers," and the need to protect women.

• *Bunting v. Oregon,* 243 U.S. 426 (1917), upheld an Oregon law that required overtime pay after ten hours labor in a

day, and also barred working more than thirteen hours in
a day. Inexplicably, the Court did not mention *Lochner*.
Apparently there was no constitutionally protected liberty
to contract for more than thirteen hours labor daily.

- *Adkins v. Children's Hospital*, 261 U.S. 525 (1923), struck
  down a D.C. law prescribing minimum wages for women.
  The Court seized on the 19th Amendment (guaranteeing
  the vote for women) as proof that women were now equal
  with men and thus no longer warranted special legal treatment. A minimum wage, said the Court, was simply "a
  naked, arbitrary exercise" in power.

b. **The modern era: Repudiation of *Lochner*.** The New Deal revolution
   swept away *Lochner*. The Court seemingly repudiated the entire principle
   of substantive due process, but substantive due process has enjoyed a
   modern revival. (See section C.3, infra.)

   i. **The New Deal shift.** The New Deal Court rejected *Lochner* by
      widening the scope of legitimate governmental objectives and em-
      ploying a more deferential standard of review to measure the con-
      nection between legislative means and ends. Two cases exemplify
      this process.

      (a) *Nebbia v. New York,* 291 U.S. 502 (1934). New York created
          a Milk Control Board to set the retail price of milk. Nebbia,
          a retail grocer in Rochester convicted of selling milk for less
          than the fixed price, appealed on the ground that New York
          could not constitutionally fix milk prices. The Court upheld
          the regulation, 5 to 4. Laws comply with substantive due
          process so long as they are **not "unreasonable, arbitrary or
          capricious"** *and* **"the means selected shall have a real and
          substantial relation to the object sought to be attained."**
          New York sought to stabilize milk prices in order to preserve
          an adequate milk supply in the midst of a ruinous economic
          depression that threatened to drive many dairy farmers into
          extinction. A state, said the Court, "is free to adopt whatever
          economic policy may reasonably be deemed to promote pub-
          lic welfare, and to enforce that policy by legislation adapted
          to its purpose." The Court did not so much reject *Lochner* as
          apply it in a far more deferential fashion.

      (b) *West Coast Hotel Co. v. Parrish,* 300 U.S. 379 (1937). Washing-
          ton enacted a minimum wage law for women. Even though
          the Court had struck down almost identical such laws in
          Adkins v. Children's Hospital and *Morehead v. New York ex rel.
          Tipaldo,* 298 U.S. 587 (1936), the Court (5-4) upheld Washing-

ton's law, overruling *Adkins.* The law was not "arbitrary or capricious" because Washington "was clearly entitled to consider the situation of women in employment, the fact that they are in the class receiving the least pay, that their bargaining power is relatively weak, and that they are the ready victims of those who would take advantage of their necessitous circumstances." Moreover, the law reasonably furthered a legitimate public purpose since "the denial of a living wage is not only detrimental to [worker] health and well being but casts a direct burden for their support upon the community."

ii. **The modern standard of extreme deference.** The Court's position in *Nebbia* and *Parrish* proved to be transitional. Very quickly the Court moved toward a position of *extreme deference* to economic regulatory legislation.

(a) *United States v. Carolene Products,* 304 U.S. 144 (1938). Congress enacted the Filled Milk Act, which banned the interstate shipment of "filled milk"—milk from which the butterfat has been removed and vegetable oils substituted. Congress had concluded that the substitution of vegetable oil for animal fat resulted in "undernourishment." The Court upheld the law against a Fifth Amendment due process challenge. The congressional findings of fact were helpful, but not necessary, since "the existence of facts supporting the legislative judgment is to be presumed." More precisely, "regulatory legislation affecting ordinary commercial transactions" is **constitutional unless proven that there is** *no rational basis* for the legislation.

(b) *Williamson v. Lee Optical Co.,* 348 U.S. 483 (1955). Oklahoma barred opticians from making eyeglasses without a prescription from either an ophthalmologist or optometrist. The Supreme Court reversed a federal trial judge's ruling that the ban was not "reasonably and rationally related to . . . health and welfare." The Court, per Justice Douglas, ruled that so long as there was "an evil at hand for correction," however modest it may be, the law must be upheld if "it *might* be thought that the . . . legislati[on] . . . was a **rational** way to correct it." In essence, the Court ruled that if there was **any conceivable basis** to surmise that a law was **rationally related to a legitimate state goal** the law would be upheld.

(c) *Ferguson v. Skrupa,* 372 U.S. 726 (1963). Kansas made it unlawful for anyone except lawyers to carry on the business of debt adjusting. The Court upheld the law in an opinion by Justice Black that seemed to extirpate any remaining vestiges of substantive due process. "There was a time when the Due Process Clause was used by this Court to strike down laws which were thought unreasonable, . . . unwise or incompatible with some particular economic or social philosophy. [Substantive due process] has long since been discarded." Two years later the Court would revive substantive due process in the name of personal privacy or autonomy.

c. **The contemporary standard.** Today, laws that regulate *commercial, economic, or business relations* are upheld against due process challenges so long as there is some **conceivable basis to conclude that the law bears a rational relationship to a constitutionally permissible objective of the government.**

3. Noneconomic Rights and Substantive Due Process

Even though the Court has totally repudiated the use of the due process clauses to protect unenumerated economic rights it has displayed a willingness, at times an eagerness, to use the due process clauses to strike down laws that impinge on what the Court thinks are important unenumerated noneconomic rights. The all-purpose rubric to describe these rights is **privacy,** but that term is a bit of a misnomer. Rather, the Court uses the due process clauses to protect an ill-defined cluster of noneconomic personal interests which the Court thinks are critical to **human autonomy.**

a. **Overview.** Before looking in detail at the doctrine it is useful to understand both the framework—the judicial tests used to evaluate the validity of governmental action—and the origins of this branch of substantive due process.

   i. **Doctrinal mechanics.** Courts first determine whether the right asserted is a **fundamental right.**

      (a) **Two levels of judicial scrutiny.** Courts apply **strict scrutiny** to laws that impinge upon **fundamental rights,** but only **minimal scrutiny** to laws that impinge upon nonfundamental rights.

   - Under **strict scrutiny** the government must prove that it has a **compelling objective or interest** that *cannot* be accomplished in any **less burdensome way.** Most laws subjected to strict scrutiny will be struck down.

   - Under **minimal scrutiny** the challenger of the law must prove that the law is not **rationally related to a legitimate state interest.** Almost any law subjected to minimal scrutiny will be upheld.

- The level of scrutiny turns on whether the right is *fundamental*, and the **challenger of the law has the burden of proving that the claimed right is fundamental.**

(b) **Fundamental rights.** To determine which rights are fundamental, the Court has borrowed from the jurisprudence of selective incorporation. (See section B.3, supra.) As in *Palko*, the Court has said that fundamental rights are those which are "implicit in the concept of ordered liberty," "so **rooted in the traditions and conscience of our people** as to be ranked as fundamental," or so important "that neither liberty nor justice would exist if they were sacrificed." This is a vague formula, leaving much room for judicial imagination. Some Justices argue that, in determining fundamental liberty, courts should "refer to the most specific level at which a relevant tradition protecting, or denying protection to, the asserted right can be identified." *Michael H. v. Gerald D.,* 491 U.S. 110 (1989) (Scalia, J.). The Court as a whole, however, requires a "careful description" of the claimed right. Justice Harlan, dissenting in *Poe v. Ullman,* 367 U.S. 497 (1961), thought that in determining fundamental rights courts must balance "respect for the liberty of the individual" and "the demands of organized society." They do not do so in a vacuum, however, since "the balance [is] struck by this country, having due regard to what history teaches are the traditions from which it developed as well as the traditions from which it broke. That tradition is a living thing. . . ." Liberty, said Harlan, "is a rational continuum which, broadly speaking, includes a freedom from all substantial arbitrary impositions and purposeless restraints."

As a practical matter the court has recognized fundamental rights in only a few areas, centering on marriage, family, childbearing and rearing, and, perhaps, death.

ii. **Origins of the doctrine.** Modern substantive due process has its origins in the same soil as economic substantive due process.

(a) *Meyer v. Nebraska,* 262 U.S. 390 (1923). Meyer was convicted of teaching German to children, a crime in World War I vintage Nebraska. The Court reversed his conviction, opining that "liberty" included not only the economic rights protected by the *Lochner* Court but also the right "to acquire useful knowledge, to marry, establish a home and bring up children, . . . and generally to enjoy those privileges long recognized at common law as essential to the orderly pursuit of happiness by free men." The Court intimated that the law might have been upheld had Nebraska offered a convincing justification for its necessity.

(b) *Pierce v. Society of Sisters,* 268 U.S. 510 (1925). Oregon enacted a law requiring all children to attend public schools. Parochial and private schools, together with students at such schools and their parents, challenged the validity of the law as a denial of liberty without due process of law. A unanimous Court invalidated the law, finding that Oregon had shown no justification for its interference "with the liberty of parents and guardians to direct the upbringing and education of children under their control."

(c) *Skinner v. Oklahoma,* 316 U.S. 535 (1942). Oklahoma mandated sterilization of people thrice convicted of felonies involving moral turpitude. Skinner, a petty but felonious thief, challenged the validity of the law as applied to him, primarily on equal protection grounds. The Court voided the law as a denial of equal protection, but employed a substantive due process rationale. Strict scrutiny was required, said the Court, because the law "involves one of the basic civil rights of man. Marriage and procreation are fundamental to the very existence and survival of the race." Application of the law would have "forever deprived [Skinner] of a basic liberty."

(d) **The incorporation doctrine.** Selective incorporation of the Bill of Rights into the due process clause of the 14th Amendment (see section B.3, supra) is but another form of substantive due process. Recall that only those rights regarded as "fundamental" are entitled to be incorporated. The major difference between substantive due process and selective incorporation is that selective incorporation is more bounded—only the Bill of Rights guarantees are eligible for inclusion into 14th Amendment due process, while substantive due process opens the door to judicial embrace of all manner of possible fundamental rights.

b. **Contraceptives.** The revival of substantive due process began with judicial recognition of a fundamental right to use contraceptives. *Griswold,* the first case examined, is the cornerstone upon which most of the edifice has been erected.

i. *Griswold v. Connecticut,* 381 U.S. 479 (1965). Connecticut prohibited the use of contraceptives and assisting others to use contraceptives. The law, which had not been enforced for many years, was attacked by two physicians who were convicted as accessories after having goaded the local authorities into prosecution. The Court invalidated the law.

(a)   **The Court's opinion.** Justice Douglas, for the Court, first asserted that it was not reviving substantive due process, then proceeded to do so. The "specific guarantees in the Bill of Rights have penumbras, formed by emanations from those guarantees that help give them life and substance." The Court then found in that uncertain half-shadow of the Constitution a **"zone of privacy"** that forbade governments from preventing married couples from using contraceptives. The Court was careful not to extend this new privacy right beyond its immediate application—married couples using contraceptives—but new law was quickly troweled on to the *Griswold* cornerstone.

(b)   **The dissents.** Justices Stewart and Black called the law "offensive," "silly," and suggested it was "unwise, . . . even asinine." But they refused to call it unconstitutional. Neither Justice could find a privacy right "in any . . . part of the Constitution, or in any case ever before decided by" the Court. Justice Black offered the pointed criticism that "the natural law due process philosophy" was "no less dangerous when used to enforce this Court's views about personal rights than those about economic rights."

ii.   *Eisenstadt v. Baird,* 405 U.S. 438 (1972). Massachusetts prohibited the distribution of contraceptives to unmarried persons. The Court struck down the law, purporting to apply *minimal scrutiny*—rational relationship to a legitimate state objective—under the equal protection clause. But in fact *Eisenstadt* was a significant addition to *Griswold.* Together they formed the foundation for *Roe v. Wade.* Justice Brennan, for the Court, wrote the following influential dictum, commenting on the fact that *Griswold* had confined the privacy right to married couples: "If the right of privacy means anything, it is the right of the *individual,* married or single, to be free from unwarranted governmental intrusion into matters so fundamentally affecting a person as the decision whether to bear or beget a child."

iii. *Carey v. Population Services Intl.* 431 U.S. 678 (1977). New York prohibited anyone but a licensed pharmacist from dispensing contraceptives. The Court invalidated the law, reading *Griswold,* "in light of its progeny," to hold "that the Constitution protects individual decisions in matters of childbearing from unjustified intrusion by the State." Because New York could not show a **compelling** state interest "narrowly drawn to express *only* the legitimate state interests at stake" the law was void.

c. **Abortion: The basic issue.** The right of a woman to terminate her pregnancy, and the power of governments to intrude upon that decision, surely represents the most controversial application of the *Griswold* privacy right.

   i. ***Roe v. Wade,*** 410 U.S. 113 (1973). Texas made it a crime to "procure an abortion" except upon "medical advice for the purpose of saving the life of the mother." Jane Roe, a pregnant young single woman whom we now know to be Norma McCorvey, challenged the validity of the law. The Court struck down the law as a denial of the "personal liberty" protected by the 14th Amendment's due process clause. For the Court, Justice Blackmun relied on *Griswold, Skinner, Eisenstadt, Pierce,* and *Meyer* to declare that the "right to privacy . . . is broad enough to encompass a woman's decision whether or not to terminate her pregnancy." In doing so the Court concluded that a fetus is not a person within the meaning of the 14th Amendment, yet stated that the Court "need not resolve the difficult question of when life begins," a question the Court acknowledged had no definitive answer. Because a woman's right to an abortion was found to be part of the *fundamental right to privacy,* the Court brought **strict scrutiny** to bear upon the Texas law.

      (a) **The trimester framework.** The Court rejected the idea that a woman's right to terminate her pregnancy is absolute. Instead, the Court divided the thirty-six weeks of pregnancy into three twelve-week trimesters and used the trimesters to pinpoint when various state interests would become *compelling,* thus enabling the state validly to restrict abortion.

         • *First Trimester:* During the first trimester the *state has no compelling reason to restrict abortion.*

         • *Second Trimester:* The Court relied on "present medical knowledge" to conclude that the state had a compelling interest—"preserving and protecting the health of the pregnant woman"—to restrict abortion after the first trimester. During the second and third trimesters "a *State may regulate the abortion procedure to the extent that the regulation reasonably relates to the preservation and protection of maternal health.*"

         • *Third Trimester:* After viability—the moment that the fetus has the capacity to live outside the womb—the state's interest in "protecting the potentiality of human life" becomes compelling. When *Roe* was decided viability roughly coincided with the end of the second trimester. Thus, *during the third trimester states could prohibit abortion "except when it is necessary to preserve the life or health of the mother."*

(b)   The dissents. Justices White and Rehnquist dissented. They found "nothing in the language or history of the Constitution to support the Court's judgment," thought that the Texas law ought to be subjected to minimal scrutiny, lamented the Court's exercise in "judicial legislation," and pronounced the decision to be "an exercise of raw judicial power, . . . an improvident and extravagant exercise of the power of" judicial review.

(c)   Criticisms of *Roe*. Criticisms of *Roe* are legion. Here are some of the more significant ones:

- If there is no medical, philosophical, or other agreement upon when life begins, the Court should have deferred to the state's legislative judgment on the issue. As a practical matter, this would have permitted states to reach different judgments on the issue, thus producing easy abortion availability in some states and little access in others. This would have reduced the intense political friction created by a unitary constitutional rule on abortion.

- *Roe* uses the same methodology as *Lochner,* yet the Court says *Lochner* is wrong. Both *Roe* and *Lochner* identify an extraconstitutional value, call it "fundamental," and then assimilate it to the Constitution. The only difference is that *Lochner* called it "liberty of contract" and *Roe* called it "privacy." Both approaches are examples of **noninterpretivist** constitutional decision-making. Since it is a *written* Constitution that the Court interprets, the Court has no authority to import values and rights that have no fair textual connection to the Constitution. Recall the 1798 exchange between Justices Chase and Iredell in *Calder v. Bull,* supra.

- *Roe* is an unwarranted extension of the *Meyer-Pierce-Skinner-Griswold-Eisenstadt* line of cases because the unifying principle of those cases is that the govern-

ment may restrict individual liberty only where necessary to protect others from harm. In those cases the
government was *not* acting to prevent others from
harm.

(d)   **In the wake of *Roe*.** *Roe* produced an intense political reaction.
Several constitutional amendments were proposed to reverse
Roe. The most neutral one would have permitted states to
allow, prohibit, or regulate abortions. The ones most hostile
to abortion would have protected fetuses "from the moment
of conception" and "at every stage of their biological development." None came to fruition. Instead, a variety of legislative
initiatives were undertaken, all designed to inhibit abortions.
Some denied public funding for abortions, others sought to
exploit abortion regulations apparently permitted by *Roe*. The
validity of these regulations is considered in subsections C.3.d
and C.3.e, infra.

ii.   *Akron v. Akron Center for Reproductive Health,* 462 U.S. 416 (1983).
Applying strict scrutiny and *Roe's* trimester framework the Court
struck down a range of abortion regulations, considered more fully
in subsection d, infra. The importance of *Akron* to the basic issue
of abortion lies in Justice O'Connor's dissent, joined by White
and Rehnquist, where she argued that the trimester framework
was too dependent on the shifting state of medical science (the
trimester framework was "clearly on a collision course with itself")
and badly reflected the relative interests of the pregnant woman
and the state throughout pregnancy. O'Connor contended that
abortion regulations ought to be treated as constitutional unless
they **"unduly burden"** the woman's right to terminate her
pregnancy.

iii.   *Planned Parenthood of S.E. Penn. v. Casey,* 505 U.S. 833 (1992). In
the late 1980s the Court was repeatedly urged to overturn *Roe*. In
a series of 5 to 4 decisions *Roe* was upheld, but the majority seemed
exhausted. In *Webster,* infra, Justice Blackmun expressed his fears
about the continuation of *Roe:* "[T]he signs are evident and very
ominous, and a chill wind blows." Whether or not chill, *Casey* was
a new wind. In considering the validity of a series of Pennsylvania
restrictions upon abortion the Court (5-4) restated that "the Constitution protects a woman's right to terminate her pregnancy in its
early stages" but the majority could not agree on the mechanics
of that protection. Justices Stevens and Blackmun would have
continued to apply *Roe's* trimester framework. Justices O'Connor,
Kennedy, and Souter abandoned *Roe's* trimester framework while
purportedly reaffirming "the essential holding of *Roe*." The plural-

ity substituted for the trimester framework a version of Justice O'Conner's **undue burden** test.

(a) The plurality's test. Before *viability* of the fetus, a "woman has a right to choose to terminate her pregnancy" but states may regulate previability abortions. However, if those regulations impose an **undue burden**—"shorthand for the conclusion that a state regulation has the *purpose* or *effect* of placing a *substantial obstacle* in the path of a woman seeking an abortion of a nonviable fetus"—they are *always invalid*. But after viability states are free to regulate or even prohibit abortions except where necessary to save the life of the pregnant woman.

(b) Application of "undue burden" in *Casey*. Pennsylvania's Abortion Control Act imposed the following regulations upon abortion, except in cases of "medical emergency":

- *Informed Consent:* At least twenty-four hours prior to an abortion a woman must be given certain information about the risks of abortion and childbirth, the gestational age of the fetus, the nature of the procedure, and the availability of adoption or child support services. A woman must certify in writing that she has received this information.

- *Parental Consent:* A minor must either obtain the informed consent of one parent or obtain judicial permission in order to terminate her pregnancy.

- *Notice to Husband:* Generally, a married woman must notify her husband of her decision to abort.

- *Records and Reports:* Abortion providers must keep records and make reports on abortions.

The Court applied the undue burden test to conclude that the informed consent, parental consent, and recordkeeping and reporting requirements were all in furtherance of compelling state interests and did not place a substantial obstacle in the path of the woman desiring to end her pregnancy. But the Court concluded that the risk to a married woman of spousal abuse or other retaliation as a result of notification to her husband did pose a substantial obstacle and thus the *spousal notification requirement was held invalid as an undue burden.*

(c) The dissenters. Four Justices—Rehnquist, White, Scalia, and Thomas—dissented. The dissenters denied that there was anything in constitutional text, history, or precedent to support the idea "that the right to terminate one's pregnancy is 'fundamental.'" The dissenters would have applied minimal scrutiny and upheld the Act in its entirety.

iv. *Stenberg v. Carhart,* 120 S. Ct. 2597 (2000). Nebraska sought to outlaw "partial-birth" abortions and so made it a crime to perform an abortion by means of delivering a "substantial portion" of a living fetus into the birth canal, unless necessary to save the life of the pregnant woman. The Court, 5 to 4, affirmed a ruling invalidating the Nebraska law as an "undue burden" on a woman's right to terminate her pregnancy prior to fetal viability. The majority (Breyer, Stevens, O'Connor, Souter, and Ginsburg) explicitly adopted the *Casey* plurality's undue burden test as the operative standard, and then found the Nebraska law invalid under the *Casey* analysis for two reasons. First, the prohibition was so broadly worded that it would cover both "dilation and extraction" ("D&X," the grisly method of dismemberment of a fetus to accomplish abortion) and "dilation and evacuation" ("D&E," a less invasive and much more widely used method of abortion for late second-trimester abortions). Thus, the Nebraska ban had the effect of precluding most second-trimester, previability abortions. Second, even assuming that the law only barred D&X abortions, Nebraska made no exception for those cases where D&X would be necessary to preserve the health of the pregnant woman. The Court confirmed that *Casey* required such an exception whenever there was reasonable medical evidence (as had been presented at trial) that D&X was medically necessary for the woman's health in some uncertain number of cases. Though Justice O'Connor joined the majority, she stated in a concurrence her view that a law prohibiting D&X alone, except where necessary to preserve the woman's life or health, would be valid.

d. **Abortion: The limits of governmental regulation.** In the wake of *Roe* the validity of a wide variety of abortion regulations has been decided by the Court. While many of these decisions predate the Court's effective adoption in *Casey* of the "undue burden" framework they are still generally good law.

   i. **Third party consent requirements.** These requirements condition abortion upon the prior *consent* of either a married woman's husband or, in the case of a minor, one or both of her parents.

      (a) **Husband's consent:** *Planned Parenthood v. Danforth,* 428 U.S. 52 (1976). The Court invalidated a Missouri law requiring a married woman seeking an abortion to provide the prior written consent of her husband, except where abortion was necessary "to preserve the life of the mother." While recognizing the validity of Missouri's objective of fostering marital communication, the Court noted that when husband and wife disagree on abortion the wife's view must prevail legally, since she "is the more directly and immediately affected." Constitutionally speaking, husbands lack a veto power over abortion and a woman need not bring a note from her husband to get an abortion. The same rule undoubtedly would apply were a state to condition an unmarried woman's abortion on the consent of the man who impregnated her.

(b)   Parental consent. A state may condition abortion for an unemancipated minor upon *either:*

- The prior consent of one parent, or

- A "judicial bypass," by which the minor may obtain judicial permission to abort, upon a showing that either (1) she is mature enough to decide for herself or (2) it would be in her best interest to abort.

Bellotti v. Baird (Bellotti II), 443 U.S. 622 (1979), invalidated a Massachusetts requirement that a minor seeking an abortion must obtain either the consent of *both* her parents or a court order. A plurality of the Court indicated the necessity of a judicial bypass as an alternative to parental consent. In *Planned Parenthood v. Ashcroft,* 462 U.S. 476 (1983), and in *Casey* the Court upheld a parental consent requirement that included an adequate judicial bypass, thereby effectively establishing the constitutional necessity of a judicial bypass to a parental consent requirement.

ii.   **Third party notice requirements.** These requirements condition abortion upon prior *notice* to either a married woman's husband or, in the case of a minor, one or both of her parents.

(a)   Notice to husband. A woman need not notify her husband of her abortion. *Casey.*

(b)   Parental notification. States may condition abortions for unemancipated minors upon *either* prior notice to one or both parents *or* a judicial order of approval of the abortion. *Hodgson v. Minnesota,* 497 U.S. 417 (1990), struck down a naked two-parent notification requirement but upheld the two-parent notification requirement when coupled with an adequate judicial bypass. In *Ohio v. Akron Center for Reproductive Health,* 497 U.S. 502 (1990), the Court upheld an Ohio law that generally prohibited abortions for unemancipated minors unless one parent had been notified or a court had ordered approval.

iii. **Information and waiting requirements.** *Casey* upheld a reasonable information requirement, coupled with a twenty-four hour waiting period, as not an undue burden on the abortion right, but made it plain that the decision was heavily influenced by the specific context and application of the Pennsylvania law. It is unlikely, but far from certain, that a state could require a woman to endure a barrage of antiabortion propaganda before obtaining an abortion. Similarly, even a twenty-four hour waiting period might constitute an undue burden in some other context.

Example: Suppose Montana has a single abortion provider, located in Missoula, in the northwestern corner of that large state. Suppose that Montana imposes an information requirement coupled with a twenty-four hour waiting period after provision of the information. Applied to a woman coming from Miles City, some 450 miles away, a twenty-four hour waiting period might well be an undue burden, and hence invalid.

iv. **Hospitalization requirements.** In *Akron v. Akron Center for Reproductive Health,* 462 U.S. 416 (1983), the Court invalidated a requirement that all abortions after the first trimester be performed in hospitals as not "reasonably designed to further [the] state interest . . . in health regulation," because the medical evidence showed that second trimester out-patient abortions could be safely performed.

e. **Publicly funded abortions.** While governments may not impose undue burdens on the obtaining of an abortion, they may prohibit the use of public funds to pay for abortions while permitting public funds to pay for childbirth expenses. Even though this has a sharply disparate impact upon pregnant women subsisting on welfare benefits, the Court has upheld the practice. The "Due Process Clauses generally confer no affirmative right to governmental aid, even where such aid may be necessary to secure life, liberty or property interests of which the government itself may not deprive the individual." *DeShaney v. Winnebago Dept. of Social Services,* 489 U.S. 189 (1989).

i. **Medically unnecessary abortions:** *Maher v. Roe,* 432 U.S. 464 (1977). A state regulation granted medical welfare benefits for childbirth but denied them for nontherapeutic (medically unnecessary) abortions. The Court (6-3) upheld the regulation against an equal protection challenge. The regulation did not impinge on the fundamental right to terminate an unwanted pregnancy because the state did not create the indigency that was the obstacle to obtaining an abortion. The state had no constitutional obligation to provide any medical welfare benefits. The state had not interfered with the indigent pregnant woman's right to an abortion; instead it had offered a financial inducement (which it need not offer) to childbirth. The indigent pregnant woman was no worse off after the state regulation than before; in neither situation was she very likely to obtain an abortion.

ii. **Medically necessary abortions:** *Harris v. McRae,* 448 U.S. 297 (1980). The so-called Hyde Amendment barred the use of federal Medicaid funds for abortions except when the pregnancy resulted from rape or incest, or when necessary to save the life of the pregnant woman. The Hyde Amendment thus prohibited some, but not all, medically necessary abortions. The Hyde Amendment was challenged under the Fifth Amendment's due process clause and the Court upheld its validity, 5 to 4: "[A]lthough government may not place obstacles in the path of a woman's exercise of her freedom of choice, it need not remove those not of its own creation. Indigency falls in the latter category. . . . [A]n indigent woman [has] . . . at least the same range of choice in deciding whether to obtain a medically necessary abortion as she would have had if Congress had chosen to subsidize no health care costs at all." By analogy, the Court noted that the fact that a state may not prohibit parents from educating their children in private schools does not mean that the state "has an affirmative constitutional obligation to ensure that all persons have the financial resources to . . . send their children to private schools." Since the Hyde Amendment did not interfere with the fundamental abortion right it was subjected to minimal scrutiny and upheld as rationally related to a legitimate state objective of discouraging "the purposeful termination of a potential life."

iii. **Use of public hospitals and medical staff:** *Webster v. Reproductive Health Services,* 492 U.S. 490 (1989). A Missouri statute prohibited "the use of public employees and facilities to perform or assist abortions not necessary to save the mother's life." The Court upheld the provision, reasoning as in *Maher* and *McRae* that "Missouri's refusal to allow public employees to perform abortions in public hospitals leaves a pregnant woman with the same choices as if the State had chosen not to operate any public hospitals at all." The Court also concluded that "private physicians and their patients" have no "constitutional right of access to public facilities for the performance of abortions." But the Court suggested the result might be different if a state had socialized medicine so that "all of its hospitals and physicians were publicly funded," or if the state barred from public hospitals a physician because he performed abortions privately.

f. Abortion counseling: *Rust v. Sullivan,* 500 U.S. 173 (1991). 7
ment of Health and Human Services adopted regulations
tioned receipt of federal funds for family planning ser·
recipient's agreement not to use the money to "provic
concerning the use of abortion as a method of family planr
referral for abortion as a method of family planning, encourage, μι֊
or advocate abortion as a method of family planning." The Court upheld
this so-called gag rule against a variety of challenges. With respect to
the due process claim that the gag rule infringed on the fundamental
abortion right the Court invoked the *Maher-McRae-Webster* principle that
there is no right to receive any particular service from the government
even when "such aid may be necessary to secure life, liberty, or property
interests of which the government itself may not deprive the individual."

g. Family relationships. The "privacy" right also protects a variety of family relationships from government interference. Once a particular family
relationship right has been identified as "fundamental," governmental
infringements of the right are subjected to strict scrutiny. The Court
occasionally uses "heightened scrutiny"—an ill-defined, deliberately
vague standard of review that is more searching than minimal scrutiny
but not as tough as strict scrutiny—when the Court identifies a right
that is important but perhaps not constitutionally fundamental.

   i. Zoning out the extended family: *Moore* **and** *Belle Terre.* Governments may adopt zoning regulations to achieve a variety of public
   purposes, one of which is limiting the occupancy density of residential structures. But governments may not subdivide the traditional
   extended family as a zoning classification, although they can
   use zoning to exclude or limit nontraditional family living
   arrangements.

   (a) *Village of Belle Terre v. Boraas,* 416 U.S. 1 (1974). Belle Terre
   restricted land use to one-family dwellings, and defined family
   to mean not more than two unrelated people living together.
   Expressly exempted from the ordinance were lodging, board-
   ing, fraternity, and multiple-dwelling houses. A landowner
   who had rented his house to six unrelated college students
   challenged the ordinance. The Court upheld the law, reasoning that its exclusion of three or more unrelated persons
   living together did not impinge upon any fundamental right.
   Minimal scrutiny was applied and the law was easily found
   to be rationally related to a legitimate municipal interest of
   preserving "zones . . . where family values, youth values,
   and the blessings of quiet seclusion and clean air make the
   areas a sanctuary for people."

   (b) *Moore v. City of East Cleveland,* 431 U.S. 494 (1977). East
   Cleveland adopted a zoning ordinance that limited occupancy

of any dwelling unit to a single family, and then defined the term "family" to include only a few categories of related persons. The definition was sufficiently narrow that it prohibited Moore from living with her son Dale, and her two grandsons, Dale, Jr., and his cousin John. The Court struck down the ordinance as violative of a fundamental privacy interest protected by substantive due process, but only a four Justice plurality agreed on the due process rationale. Justice Stevens supplied the fifth vote on the theory that the ordinance constituted "a taking of property without due process and without just compensation." The plurality concluded that minimal scrutiny was "inappropriate . . . [w]hen a city undertakes such intrusive regulation of the family," but *obscured the precise standard of review* it was using. **When "government intrudes on choices concerning family living arrangements, this Court must examine carefully the importance of the governmental interests advanced and the extent to which they are served by the challenged regulation."** Though the plurality did not attach the "fundamental" label to family living arrangements, it declared that "the Constitution protects the sanctity of the family precisely because the institution of the family is deeply rooted in this Nation's history and tradition," thus reciting the constitutional mantra of fundamental rights. Family, said the plurality, means more than the nuclear family. The "choice of relatives in this degree of kinship to live together may not lightly be denied by the State. [The] Constitution prevents East Cleveland from standardizing its children—and its adults—by forcing all to live in certain narrowly defined family patterns."

ii. **Child-rearing.** The Court has assimilated to the fundamental privacy right several specific claimed rights associated with raising one's children. The family value protected as fundamental by the Court is the functional, existing family, rather than genetic connections, although the Court is not indifferent to the claims of biological parents.

(a) *Pierce v. Society of Sisters,* 268 U.S. 510 (1925), discussed supra. Oregon's law requiring all children to attend public schools was invalidated as an unjustified interference "with the liberty of parents and guardians to direct the upbringing and education of children under their control."

(b) *Parham v. J.R.,* 442 U.S. 584 (1979). The Court upheld Georgia's practice of not requiring formal adversary hearings before parents commit their children to public mental institutions. Balancing the "individual, family, and social interests" at stake, the Court concluded that the informal Georgia admissions procedure was valid, given "the parents' traditional interests in and responsibility for the upbringing of their child" and a long-standing societal tradition of recognizing "the family as a unit with broad parental authority over minor children."

(c) *Quilloin v. Walcott,* 434 U.S. 246 (1978). Under Georgia law, if a biological father of a child born outside a marital relationship had not formally acknowledged his paternity, only the mother's consent was required for adoption. Quilloin had never formalized paternity of his eleven-year-old son. The mother consented to the boy's adoption by her husband, with whom she and her son were living. Quilloin sought to block the adoption but did not seek custody or visitation rights. A trial court concluded that it was in the best interests of the child to grant the adoption and a unanimous Court affirmed, rejecting Quilloin's contention that his status as the biological father conferred constitutionally fundamental rights. The Court readily agreed "that the relationship between parent and child is constitutionally protected," and opined that "the Due Process Clause would be offended '[i]f a State were to attempt to force the breakup of a natural family, over the objection of the parents and their children, without some showing of unfitness and for the sole reason that to do so was thought to be in the children's best interests.' " But "adoption in this case . . . give[s] full recognition to a family unit already in existence."

(d) *Stanley v. Illinois,* 405 U.S. 645 (1972). Joan and Peter Stanley lived together off and on for eighteen years, and had three children together. They never married each other. Joan Stanley died and Peter discovered that Illinois law automatically made children of unwed fathers and deceased mothers wards of the state. Peter maintained that Illinois deprived him of equal protection, because a married father in his situation could not be deprived of his children without the state proving his parental unfitness. The Court invoked the fundamental rights branch of equal protection (in which laws that impinge on "fundamental rights" are subjected to strict scrutiny; see Chapter 9, infra) and struck down Illinois' irrebuttable presumption of parental unfitness on the part of unwed fathers. At least where the natural father could establish an existing, functional relationship with his children his interest "in the companionship, care, custody, and management of his . . .

children" warranted heightened judicial scrutiny. Illinois had insufficient justification for its irrebuttable presumption that, as applied, would break up Peter Stanley's family. Decision "by presumption is always cheaper and easier than individualized determination. But when, as here, the procedure risks running roughshod over the important interests of both parent and child [it] cannot stand."

(e) *Michael H. v. Gerald D.,* 491 U.S. 110 (1989). In a California lawsuit, Michael H. sought to establish his paternity of and visitation rights with respect to Victoria, child of Carole D. and Gerald D., a married couple. Gerald D. was listed as the father of Victoria on her birth certificate but blood tests established a better than 98% probability that Michael H. was the father. Michael and Carole had carried on an adulterous affair and lived together when Victoria was an infant; at that time Michael had publicly claimed Victoria as his daughter. Later, Carole tired of Michael and lived with another man before finally resuming her marriage with the apparently tolerant and patient Gerald. California law presumes that a child born to a married woman living with her husband, who is neither impotent or sterile, is a child of the marriage. Because the presumption was rebuttable only under limited circumstances not available to Michael H. the California courts rejected Michael's claims. Michael contended that California had infringed his "constitutionally protected liberty interest in his relationship with Victoria." The Court upheld the California law, but only a four Justice plurality agreed on the rationale. The plurality, in an opinion by Justice Scalia, concluded that there was nothing in our traditions or conscience that recognized "the power of a natural father to assert parental rights over a child born into a woman's existing marriage with another man," particularly when that "extant marital union . . . wishes to embrace the child. . . . Since it is Michael's burden to establish that such a power . . . is so deeply imbedded within our traditions as to be a fundamental right, the lack of evidence alone might defeat his case." The historical evidence relied on by the Court proved the contrary—that our traditions have rejected claims of adulterous fathers to establish legally sanctioned relationships with their offspring born into another's marriage. "This is not the stuff of which fundamental rights are made."

(f) *Troxel v. Granville,* 120 S. Ct. 2054 (2000). Washington law permitted "any person" to obtain visitation rights with a child whenever such "visitation may serve the best interests of the child." A Washington court granted the Troxels visitation rights with their granddaughters over the objection of Granville, the girls' mother, who was conceded to be a fit, custodial parent. The Washington Supreme Court declared the law to be facially invalid. A four Justice plurality (O'Connor, Rehnquist, Ginsburg, and Breyer) ruled that the Washington law, as applied, violated Granville's due process right to make decisions concerning the care, custody, and control of her daughters because the Washington law permitted courts to disregard any and all desires of a fit, custodial parent regarding visitation. The plurality declined to decide whether substantive due process requires that nonparental visitation be premised upon a showing of harm or potential harm to the child without such visitation. Justices Souter and Thomas concurred in the judgment. Justice Thomas hinted that he regarded as unsettled the question of whether due process includes a substantive fundamental liberty interest in child-rearing but, in the absence of any direct challenge to the validity of the claim, explicitly adopted strict scrutiny as the appropriate standard of review. Justices Stevens, Scalia, and Kennedy dissented. Justices Stevens and Kennedy, in separate opinions, thought that the Washington law was not facially invalid and would have remanded the case. Both Stevens and Kennedy thought that the "best interests" standard might be valid in some circumstances and neither was convinced that a showing of harm or potential harm was necessary to support third party visitation. Justice Scalia rejected the entire notion that there was any judicially enforceable liberty interest of parents in child-rearing.

iii. **Right to marry.** The court has recognized that the right to marry is a fundamental right, but has developed that doctrine not only as part of substantive due process but also as a part of the "fundamental rights" branch of equal protection. (See Chapter 9, infra.) Its reasoning on the issues, though, partakes more of substantive due process than the equality of treatment concerns of equal protection.

(a) *Loving v. Virginia,* 388 U.S. 1 (1967). Virginia made interracial marriage a crime. The Lovings, a married couple consisting of a black woman and a white man, were convicted under the law. The Court upheld both their equal protection challenge (considered in Chapter 9, infra) and their substantive due process claim. "Marriage is one of the 'basic civil rights of man,' fundamental to our very existence and survival. . . . To deny this fundamental freedom on so unsupportable a basis as" race surely denies due process. Virginia's interest in barring interracial marriage—preserving white supremacy—was illegitimate. By implication, however, some infringements upon marriage might be justified, if narrowly drawn to achieve a compelling governmental interest.

(b) *Zablocki v. Redhail,* 434 U.S. 374 (1978). Wisconsin prohibited marriage by anyone not in compliance with valid court-ordered child support obligations. The Court invalidated the Wisconsin law under the fundamental rights prong of equal protection although Justice Stewart, concurring, called it "no more than substantive due process by another name." After reaffirming the fundamental status of the right to marry, the Court stated: "[W]e do not mean to suggest that every state regulation which relates in any way to the incidents of or prerequisites for marriage must be subjected to rigorous scrutiny. To the contrary, *reasonable regulations that do not significantly interfere with decisions to enter into the marital relationship may legitimately be imposed.*" But regulations that **"significantly interfere"** with the marriage right are subject to strict scrutiny. The Court found the law to be a significant interference with the right to marry and that Wisconsin's objectives—emphasizing the need for parental financial responsibility and "protecting the welfare of out-of-custody children"—were compelling, but concluded that "the means selected by the State for achieving these interests unnecessarily impinge on the right to marry," and so struck down the law.

(c) *Turner v. Safly,* 482 U.S. 78 (1987). The Court invalidated a prison regulation that permitted inmates to marry only when the prison warden found compelling reasons for marriage. The Court found the regulation to be a substantial interference with the right to marry and, although it acknowledged the state had legitimate security reasons to restrict inmate marriage, found the regulation at issue to be far more incursive than necessary. Once again, the state's means were not drawn narrowly enough.

(d) *Califano v. Jobst,* 434 U.S. 47 (1977). In this pre-*Zablocki* case the Court unanimously upheld the validity of a Social Security regulation that cut off benefits to a disabled dependent child of a covered wage earner upon marriage, unless the marital partner was independently entitled to benefits. The Court did not regard the regulation as a "substantial interference" with the right to marry, either in purpose or effect. As Justice Stevens argued in *Zablocki,* there is a substantial difference between a regulation that grants or denies public benefits on marital status (*Jobst*) and one that determines who may lawfully marry (*Zablocki*). The former is an "incidental" interference with the right to marry, triggering only minimal scrutiny; the latter is a substantial interference, triggering strict scrutiny.

h. **Consensual sexual behavior.** Based on the Court's solicitude for various aspects of sexual reproduction—contraception and abortion—and its concern for the voluntary association of marriage, one might think that the "privacy" right would be extended to include various forms of adult consensual sexual behavior. But that is not the case. At best, there is an uncertain and quite limited protection extended to sexual behavior that occurs outside marriage.

i. **Homosexual sex:** *Bowers v. Hardwick,* 478 U.S. 186 (1986). Georgia criminalized sodomy, defined as anal intercourse, fellatio, and cunnilingus, and punished the offense by imprisonment for one to twenty years. Hardwick was charged with committing the offense in his own bedroom with another male. The prosecutor dropped the charge before indictment and Hardwick brought suit in federal district court, challenging the validity of Georgia's sodomy law as applied to homosexual sex. The Court (5-4) upheld the law, finding that there was no fundamental right to engage in homosexual sex.

(a) **The Court's rationale.** The Court used three modes of constitutional reasoning to reach its decision.

- *Doctrine:* The Court parsed the relevant precedents and concluded that they failed to demonstrate any "connection between family, marriage, or procreation on the one hand and homosexual activity on the other. . . ."

- *History:* Applying the touchstones of fundamentality—is the claimed right "implicit in ordered liberty" or "deeply rooted" in national history and tradition—the Court concluded that, to the contrary, there was a long national history and tradition of suppression of homosexual behavior.

- *Prudential Concerns:* The Court asserted that it "is most vulnerable and comes nearest to illegitimacy when it deals with judge-made constitutional law having little or no cognizable roots in the language or design of the Constitution." Prudence counseled caution in expanding the categories of fundamental rights and, without a better case in history and tradition, the claimed right was thought better left in a minimally protected category. Similar concerns were evident as the Court rejected the claim that the right to engage in homosexual sodomy in the privacy of one's home should be recognized as fundamental. The Court said it was "unwilling to start down [the] road" toward immunizing "adultery, incest, and other sexual crimes" when committed in the home. Having disposed of the "fundamental right" claim, the Court applied minimal scrutiny and concluded that the law was rationally related to Georgia's legitimate objective of carrying into law a public sentiment "that homosexual sodomy is immoral and unacceptable."

(b) The dissents. The dissenters argued for recognition of an expansive fundamental right that "all individuals have in controlling the nature of their intimate associations with others." Justice Blackmun argued that the privacy right had two dimensions: a "decisional" dimension, protecting intimate choices, and a "spatial" one that protected certain places, notably one's home, from governmental intrusion. Blackmun contended that these two dimensions coalesced to produce "the right of an individual to conduct intimate relationships in the intimacy of his or her own home."

(c) Implications of *Bowers*. States may broadly proscribe homosexual conduct, although Justice Powell, concurring, indicated his reservations about the validity of lengthy prison sentences for homosexual sodomy. Government actions such as refusing to hire homosexual teachers or expelling homosexuals from the military are almost certainly subject to minimal scrutiny. *Romer v. Evans,* 517 U.S. 620 (1996), applied minimal scrutiny to strike down on equal protection grounds Colorado's constitutional prohibition of any anti-discrimination protections afforded gays or lesbians. (See Chapter 9, infra.)

ii. **Heterosexual sodomy.** The Georgia statute at issue in *Bowers v. Hardwick* criminalized sodomy in both its homosexual and heterosexual forms. Though the Court in *Bowers* did not address the issue, if both unmarried (*Eisenstadt*) and married (*Griswold*) persons may use contraceptives to engage in nonreproductive sex surely the state may not prohibit sodomy between consenting heterosexual adults, married or unmarried. If this conclusion is correct it raises the question of why Georgia can prohibit sodomy between homosexuals but not heterosexuals. Justice Stevens addressed this issue, dissenting in *Bowers,* and concluded that no distinction could be tolerated. The issue is discussed further in Chapter 9, section D.3.d.

iii. **Adultery.** Although undecided, it is not likely that the Court will recognize adultery as a fundamental right. *Griswold* emphasized the "sacred precincts of the marital bedroom," *Eisenstadt* was founded on the fundamental nature of the "decision whether to bear or beget a child," and so, too, are *Roe* and *Casey.* Lower federal courts and state courts have split on this issue, but the Court has never decided to review the matter.

iv. **Fornication.** This, too, is undecided but it is improbable that the Court would find fornication—sex between unmarried persons—a constitutionally protected fundamental right. *Eisenstadt* assures unmarried persons of their right to access to contraceptives but it is unlikely that there is any constitutional right to have the occasion to employ them.

i. **Personal appearance.** The Court has not decided whether there is a *general* fundamental right to be free of governmental interference in matters of personal appearance. The Court has rejected the claim as to the personal appearance of police officers, and there is a plethora of conflicting lower court decisions on school dress and appearance regulations.

   i. **Regulation of police officers' appearance: *Kelley v. Johnson,* 425 U.S. 238 (1976).** The Court upheld police regulations that controlled hair length and style, mustaches and sideburns, and prohibited beards and goatees save for medical reasons. The Court assumed for purposes of argument only that "the citizenry at large has some sort of 'liberty' interest . . . in matters of personal appearance," but concluded that the personal appearance of policemen was far removed from "basic matters of procreation, marriage, and family life," and that the regulations posed no substantial interference with any fundamental liberty interest protected by the due process clause. The Court applied minimal scrutiny and upheld the regulations as rationally related to a hypothesized governmental objective of instilling *esprit de corps* in the police department or furthering public recognition of police officers.

   ii. **Regulating the personal appearance of students.** The circuits are badly split on the standard of review to be used in assessing the validity of public school regulation of student appearance. Five circuits apply a modified minimal scrutiny test—reasonably related to important school objectives; three circuits apply "heightened scrutiny," requiring something more than a "reasonable" relationship between the regulations and the school objectives; two circuits believe that the issue is so insignificant that it does not even present a substantial federal question. The Court lets this splintered law continue, never having granted review of the issue. (See Tribe, at 1388 n.32.)

j. **Personal anonymity: Freedom from data collection.** Perhaps the most obvious application of a right of "privacy" is freedom from governmental accumulation of personal data about individuals. The Court, however, has not recognized a broad right of data privacy.

   i. **Data storage: *Whalen v. Roe,* 429 U.S. 589 (1977).** New York required physicians to report the details of all prescriptions written for specified legal drugs susceptible to abuse, particularly opiates and amphetamines. The state then stored this information, especially the names and addresses of the patients. The Court unanimously upheld the scheme against a privacy attack. The Court stated that privacy involved an interest in avoiding disclosure of personal matters and an interest in making certain important decisions affecting one's life. Neither interest was substantially implicated by the New York data collection and storage practice.

   ii. **Data storage: Abortion.** Recall that the Court in *Casey,* supra, upheld Pennsylvania's law requiring reporting and recording of information about abortions performed in Pennsylvania. Critical to the Court's decision, however, was that the identities of the women obtaining abortions was kept confidential and not made available even to the state.

k. **The right to die.** This "right" is so amorphous it doesn't really exist. The Court has hinted, but never held, that there is a right to die. It is probable, but *still undecided,* that **competent adults** possess a **liberty interest** protected by the due process clauses to **refuse governmentally mandated invasive medical procedures.**

   i. **Incompetent patients: *Cruzan v. Director, Missouri Dept. of Health,*** 497 U.S. 261 (1990). Nancy Cruzan, a single woman twenty-five years old, suffered injuries in an auto accident that left her in "a persistent vegetative state, . . . exhibit[ing] some motor reflexes but no indications of significant cognitive functions." For seven years she lay insensate in a hospital bed, curled into a fetal position. She was kept alive only by means of a gastronomy tube in her stomach, through which she received necessary nutrition and fluid. She had no chance of recovery. Her parents then decided that the gastronomy tube should be removed and Nancy permitted to die. Her medical caregivers were not willing to do so without a court order so directing them. The Cruzans sought and were denied such an order because the trial court was not persuaded that, as required by Missouri law, there was "clear and convincing" evidence that Nancy had expressed her desire, when competent, to refuse life-sustaining measures in her present condition. The Court upheld Missouri's proof requirement.

(a) **The Court's opinion.** The majority first opined, in dictum, that "the forced administration of life-sustaining medical treatment, and even of artificially-delivered food and water essential to life, would implicate a competent person's liberty interest." The Court then rejected the proposition that incompetent persons possess the same rights as competent persons, because incompetents, by definition, are not able to exercise their rights. The question to be decided was not the rights of competent adults but the rights of "a surrogate [to] act for the patient in electing to have hydration and nutrition withdrawn in such a way as to cause death." To evaluate this issue the Court balanced the state's interests and the interests of Nancy's surrogates, her parents. Missouri had a "substantial" interest in imposing a "clear and convincing" evidentiary requirement in order to safeguard incompetent patients against abuse and simply to "assert an unqualified interest in the preservation of human life." The Court weighed those interests "against the constitutionally protected interests of the individual," concluding that Missouri had validly sought to advance its interests by imposing the clear and convincing evidentiary requirement. The opinion was vague concerning the precise standard of review. It was certainly more than minimal scrutiny but possibly not quite strict scrutiny.

(b) **The concurrences.** Justices O'Connor and Scalia wrote separate concurrences.

- Justice O'Connor made clear her view that a competent adult's right to refuse "artificial provision of nutrition and hydration" was fundamental. O'Connor also intimated that governments may have a constitutional duty to "give effect to the decisions of a surrogate decisionmaker" when the delegation of decisional authority was made when the patient was competent.

- Justice Scalia argued that "the federal courts have no business in this field." Consistent with his wholesale rejection of substantive due process, Scalia declared his view that there were no due process limits on the power of governments "to prevent, by force if necessary, suicide—including suicide by refusing to take appropriate measures necessary to preserve one's life."

ii. **Competent patients.** *Cruzan* suggests, but did not hold, that competent patients have a fundamental liberty to refuse invasive, life-prolonging medical care. It is widely assumed that the Court would reach that decision if required to do so. This right is of most value when it constitutionally disappears—the moment one becomes a vegetable. Nancy Cruzan had the right to reject the gastronomy tube only until she went into the coma and it was inserted. From that comes this question: May a competent person express his medical care wishes while competent and enforce them against the state after lapsing into incompetency? There are two major aspects to this question.

(a) **Living wills.** One way a competent person can attempt to control his medical care is to execute a "living will," giving clear instructions as to the medical care to be given in various types of incompetency. Some states have given statutory effect to such wills, by providing that qualified wills are to be enforced and sometimes specifically providing an example of a qualifying will.

 # EXAMPLES AND ANALYSIS

Example: Suppose Nancy Cruzan had executed a living will before her auto accident, expressly stating her desire to refuse all measures to sustain life after lapsing into an irreversible coma. Under Missouri law, her living will would almost certainly be "clear and convincing" evidence of her wishes, sufficient to give legally enforceable effect to the living will. Some states have gone further and expressly directed courts to enforce qualifying living wills.

In the absence of such authorizing legislation, or in the face of prohibitory legislation, **are governments constitutionally obligated to observe living wills?**

Example: Suppose Nancy Cruzan had executed a living will before her auto accident, expressly stating her desire to refuse all measures to sustain life after lapsing into an irreversible coma, but Missouri had statutorily declared living wills invalid. Missouri's hypothetical law prevents competent adults from controlling their medical care after lapsing into incompetency. Absent proof that the hypothesized limitation is narrowly tailored to serve compelling state interests, Missouri would probably be required by the 14th Amendment's due process clause to honor Nancy's living will.

> **(b) Delegated decision (health care proxies).** Another way a competent person might address the problem of controlling medical care after lapsing into incompetency is to execute a **health care proxy, a durable power of attorney** by which a person designates someone else to make all health care decisions for him after he is no longer able to do so himself. The Court in *Cruzan* expressly avoided deciding "whether a State might be required to defer to the decision of a surrogate if competent and probative evidence establishes that the patient herself had expressed a desire that the decision to terminate life-sustaining treatment be made for her by that individual." The probable answer is that governments are so required, but are entitled to enact reasonable measures designed to ensure that the delegation is informed, reliable, accurate, and in accord with the patient's desires.

 # EXAMPLES AND ANALYSIS

Example: Jane Doe executed a durable power of attorney, effective upon her incompetency, giving her husband, Jack, the power to make all medical decisions for her, including the decision to cease all life-sustaining treatment. The state has prohibited anyone from exercising any powers as such an attorney-in-fact. Jane suffers serious injuries and is in an irreversible coma. May Jack nevertheless order the cessation of all life-sustaining treatment and successfully invoke the Constitution as a defense to any state prosecution of him for doing so? Probably. Though the *Cruzan* Court was not required to decide this issue, it is probably an aspect of the right of a competent adult to direct her medical care.

Example: Jane Doe executed a durable power of attorney, effective upon her incompetency, giving her husband, Jack, the power to make all medical decisions for her, including the decision to cease all life-sustaining treatment. The state has provided that before an attorney-in-fact directs the cessation of life-sustaining treatment he must prove to a court, *by clear and convincing evidence independent of the power of attorney itself,* that the cessation of life-sustenance would be the choice of the patient. Jane suffers serious injuries and is in an irreversible coma. Jack has no evidence, other than the executed power of attorney, concerning Jane's wishes. The state can probably enforce its evidentiary requirement. The state has a substantial interest in assuring that life is not ended before the patient so desires. The evidentiary requirement is fairly narrowly drawn to achieve that state interest.

iii.   **Suicide and assisted suicide:** *Washington v. Glucksberg*, 521 U.S. 702 (1997). Washington made it a crime to "cause" or "aid" a suicide. The Court upheld this prohibition, finding no denial of substantive due process. Neither suicide nor assistance in suicide is objectively deeply rooted in our national history and tradition. Putative fundamental rights must be "carefully" described, a process that means phrasing the claimed liberty interest no more broadly than the facts require. *Glucksberg* did not involve "a right to die," or "a liberty interest in determining the time and manner of one's death," as the Ninth Circuit had phrased the issue, but only the question of whether there is a fundamental "right to commit suicide which itself includes a right to assistance in doing so."

A companion case, ***Vacco v. Quill,*** 521 U.S. 793 (1997), held that New York's ban on assisted suicide did not violate equal protection. Since neither a fundamental right nor a suspect classification was involved the Court applied minimal scrutiny.

Justice O'Connor, joined in substantial part by Justices Breyer and Ginsburg, reserved judgment as to "whether a mentally competent person who is experiencing great suffering has a constitutionally cognizable interest in controlling the circumstances of his or her imminent death."

 # EXAMPLE AND ANALYSIS

Suppose Mary, a terminally ill cancer patient in great pain and in the last stages of her illness, persuades Jack Kevorkian, a physician, to assist her suicide. He does so even though the state makes his conduct a crime. May Kevorkian successfully invoke the Constitution as a defense to a criminal prosecution? After *Glucksberg*, probably not, although O'Connor, Breyer, and Ginsburg might disagree because of Mary's suffering and imminent death.

D. PROCEDURAL DUE PROCESS

1. Overview

This section deals with procedural due process, the other major function of the due process clauses. The due process clauses protect a person's "life, liberty, or property" from governmental invasion unless the government has used "due *process* of law"—employed adjudicative procedures that afford some sort of a hearing. Instinct may suggest that this is a guarantee of procedural regularity but it is, in fact, more limited than that.

a. **Substantive due process distinguished.** Procedural due process is concerned with two big issues.

- What are the *scope of the "life," "liberty," or "property" interests* to which "due process of law" attaches as a condition of their deprivation?

- Assuming that government action invades a protected life, liberty, or property interest, what are the *procedures due to the citizen* before the government may act?

Substantive due process, by contrast, is an attempt to identify substantive rights and to assess the government's justification for their infringement. The focus of procedural due process is to identify substantive rights—life, liberty, or property—*in order to assess whether the government's procedures for taking them away are constitutionally adequate.*

b. **Procedural regularity *per se* distinguished.** There is no general due process right to procedural regularity. *Constitutionally speaking, unless the government is depriving you of a **life, liberty, or property** interest it may use any procedure it wants, including **arbitrary and capricious** procedures.* (See Nowak & Rotunda, at 510; Van Alstyne, 62 Cornell L. Rev. 445.) Of course, Congress or state legislatures can and do enact legislation that requires the government to employ some modicum of procedural regularity. Professor Van Alstyne argues that while naked due process—procedural regularity—"is evidently not a free standing human interest . . . it is plausible [to] treat freedom from arbitrary adjudicative procedures as a substantive element of one's liberty." *Id.,* at 452, 487. The Court has not adopted Van Alstyne's position but California has adopted this position as part of its state constitutional law.

c. **Scope of discussion.** The procedural aspects of the due process clause cut across many areas of law study. Procedural due process is encountered in Civil Procedure, Conflicts of Law, Administrative Law, Criminal Procedure, and elsewhere. This discussion does not attempt to cover material that is dealt with in those courses. Instead, it focuses on the relatively narrow but important issue presented when a person asserts that his status as a government employee, licensee, or recipient of some governmental benefit may not be altered by the government without providing procedural due process. A court necessarily must first decide whether the status in question is a life, liberty, or property right to which due process attaches. If so, then the court must decide whether the pre-deprivation procedures constitute due process.

2.   Defining "Liberty" and "Property"

Over time, there have been three different approaches taken by the Court to the question of defining liberty or property interests protected by procedural due process. Aspects of each view continue to be observed by the Court, although the first view considered has been largely abandoned and the second has been much curtailed.

a.   Governmental benefits as privileges: Neither liberty nor property. The Court first used the common law to define liberty or property interests. Because there was no common law "property" right in government employment or continued receipt of a government benefit the protections of procedural due process were *not applicable* to deprivations of these interests. Thus, a person may have a right to due process if the government threatens to take away his car, but not if the government threatens to fire him. See *Bailey v. Richardson,* 182 F.2d 46 (D.C. Cir. 1950), aff'd by an equally divided Court, 341 U.S. 918 (1951). In essence, governmental employment and receipt of governmental benefits were treated as "privileges" that the government could suspend at its pleasure, rather than individual rights that may only be divested after affording the individual due process.

b.   Governmental benefits as entitlements: Either liberty or property. The "privileges—not rights" view was challenged as the social welfare state grew to ever larger proportions, making the social and economic significance of governmental employment and benefits ever more important. Statutory entitlements, or at least important ones, ought to be regarded as property interests to which procedural due process attaches, argued Professor Reich in 73 Yale L.J. 733 (1963). Seven years later the Court agreed with Reich and quickly formulated a doctrine that held, at its high-water mark, that any governmental benefit that was *essential* to a person's livelihood or simply an *important interest* was a form of liberty or property to which due process attached. The *importance of the interest* was determined as a matter of *federal law,* not state law.

   i.   *Goldberg v. Kelly,* 397 U.S. 254 (1970). The Court held that a welfare recipient was entitled to "an evidentiary hearing *before* the termination of benefits" because the "benefits are a matter of statutory entitlement for persons qualified to receive them" and their continued receipt was of the utmost importance to the affected individual. Elimination of the welfare benefits at issue would deprive the claimant "of the very means to live." The *Goldberg* principle was quickly extended to apply to claims made by government employees, licensees, students, prisoners, and debtors, to name a few.

ii. *Bell v. Burson,* 402 U.S. 535 (1971). Georgia suspended the vehicle registration and driver's license of any uninsured motorist who failed to post a security bond to cover the claimed damages in accidents to which he was a party. The Court invalidated the law because it failed to provide any form of pre-deprivation hearing. The Court said that due process attached because the licenses were "*essential* in the pursuit of a livelihood. Suspension . . . adjudicates *important interests* of the licensees."

iii. *Sniadach* **and** *Fuentes.* In *Sniadach v. Family Finance Corp.,* 395 U.S. 337 (1969), and *Fuentes v. Shevin,* 407 U.S. 67 (1972), the Court ruled that states could not allow creditors to use judicial process to attach or take the property of debtors before judgment without first providing a hearing to the debtor.

c. **State law defining property interests.** Even as the Court was developing the *Goldberg* doctrine it was also sowing the seeds of its retrenchment. Today, the issue of whether an interest is a "liberty" or "property" interest to which due process attaches is largely an **issue of state law.** The "importance" of the interest to the claimant is no longer the talisman for deciding whether due process attaches. Instead, the "sufficiency of the claim of entitlement [to a protected liberty or property interest] must be decided by reference to state law." *Bishop v. Wood,* 426 U.S. 341 (1976).

i. *Board of Regents v. Roth,* 408 U.S. 564 (1972). Roth was hired by a public university for a one-year term, with no tenure or other rights to continued employment. The university told Roth he would not be rehired, gave no explanation, and treated the decision as final. The Court rejected Roth's claim that the university's failure to give him either an explanation or a chance to contest it at some hearing violated due process. Roth had no liberty or property interest at stake: To "determine whether due process requirements apply in the first place, we must look not to the 'weight' but to the *nature* of the interest at stake. . . . [To] have a property interest in a [government] benefit, . . . [one] must have more than a unilateral expectation of it. He must . . . have a legitimate claim of entitlement to [it]. Property interests . . . are not created by the Constitution. Rather, they are created and . . . are defined by existing rules or understandings that stem from an independent source such as state law. . . .''

ii. *Perry v. Sindermann,* 408 U.S. 593 (1972). Like Roth, Sindermann, a professor at a public college, was not rehired when the fixed term of his contract expired. Unlike Roth, Sindermann claimed that the school had created a *de facto* tenure system by informing its faculty that the school "wishes each faculty member to feel that he has permanent tenure so long as his teaching services are satisfactory and as long as he displays a cooperative attitude." The Court concluded that Sindermann had raised a triable issue regarding his claimed property interest in continuing employment. Sindermann's lack of a formal contract right to continuing employment was no barrier: "A teacher . . . who has held his position for a number of years might be able to show from the circumstances of this service—and from other relevant facts—that he has a legitimate claim of entitlement to job tenure."

iii. *Bishop v. Wood,* 426 U.S. 341 (1976). Bishop, a city policeman, was dismissed without any hearing to determine the sufficiency of cause for his discharge. Bishop contended that, as a "permanent employee" of the city, he was entitled to a hearing because a city ordinance provided that permanent employees were entitled to be notified of deficient work before discharge and to receive written notice of discharge and the reasons for discharge, if requested. A trial judge, applying North Carolina law, concluded that Bishop held his post "at the will and pleasure of the city." Accordingly, Bishop had no property interest at stake. The Court affirmed, finding the trial court's reading of state law sufficiently "tenable . . . to foreclose our independent examination of the state law issue."

iv. **"Bitter with the sweet."** Many laws that create a "property" interest also establish procedures to be followed in depriving a person of the statutorily created property interest. If the procedures are insufficient to comply with procedural due process, is due process nevertheless satisfied because the "property" interest created by statute and to which due process attaches *includes and is limited by the statutory termination procedures?* This idea—that the scope of the statutory right to which due process attaches is bounded by the statutory procedures—has been termed the "bitter with the sweet" doctrine. It was rejected by a majority of the Court in *Cleveland Board of Education v. Loudermill,* 470 U.S. 532 (1985). Loudermill, a security guard for the Cleveland public schools, was fired when it was learned that he had lied on his job application by denying that he had ever been convicted of a felony. Under Ohio law, Loudermill was entitled to be fired for cause only and to an administrative review of his dismissal. The statutory procedures were followed but Loudermill contended that the procedures were insufficient to comport with due process. The Court agreed and rejected "the bitter with the sweet approach" as a misconception of due process. " 'Property' cannot be defined by the procedures provided for its deprivation any more than can life or liberty. . . . While the legislature may elect not to confer a property interest in [public] employment, it may not constitutionally authorize the deprivation of such an interest, once conferred, without appropriate procedural safeguards. . . . The categories of substance and procedure are distinct."

d. **State law defining liberty interests.** A similar, but not identical, analysis applies to the question of defining the liberty interests to which due process attaches. State law is the principal, but not quite exclusive, determinant of the liberty interests of which one may not be deprived without procedural due process. Under some narrow circumstances the Constitution may define such protected liberty interests. Not every governmental injury to an interest protected by state law implicates a "liberty" interest; *only government actions that alter one's legal status under state law implicate a liberty interest.*

   i. *Paul v. Davis,* 424 U.S. 693 (1976). After Davis was arrested for shoplifting, the police placed his name on a list of "active shoplifters" circulated to merchants in the Louisville, Kentucky area. Once the charges against Davis were dropped he brought a federal civil rights claim against the police, alleging that the circulation of his name had injured his reputation. Davis contended that before the police could validly deprive him of his "liberty" interest in his reputation they were required to afford him procedural due process. The Court rejected the claim. Adoption of Davis' argument, said the Court, would "result in every legally cognizable injury which may have been inflicted by a state official acting under 'color of law' establishing a violation of the Fourteenth Amendment." That would produce a vast constitutionalization of tort law, at least with respect to tort claims against governmental officials, and the Court was unwilling so to expand the role of constitutional law. Thus, "reputation alone, apart from some more tangible interests such as employment, is [neither] 'liberty' [nor] 'property' by itself sufficient to invoke the procedural protection of the Due Process Clause."

 # EXAMPLE AND ANALYSIS

Wisconsin law provided that whenever someone by "excessive drinking" exposes himself or his family "to want" or makes himself "dangerous to the peace," government officials could—without notice or hearing to the drinker—post the drinker's name in retail liquor stores and bars as a person to whom sales or gifts of liquor are forbidden for one year. Constantineau's name was so posted. The Court struck down the law as not in compliance with procedural due process. The Court in *Paul v. Davis* distinguished this case by noting that the name posting did more than cause reputational injury alone. It also deprived Constantineau "of a right previously held under state law—the right [to] obtain liquor in common with the rest of the citizenry." That added factor "significantly altered his status as a matter of state law. [I]t was that alteration of legal status which, combined with the injury resulting from the defamation, justified the invocation of procedural safeguards." *Wisconsin v. Constantineau,* 400 U.S. 433 (1971).

---

    ii.   *Vitek v. Jones,* 445 U.S. 480 (1980). Nebraska law provided that if a state physician finds that a prisoner is suffering from a "mental disease or defect" that cannot be treated adequately in prison the prisoner may be transferred to a mental hospital. Jones contended that before such a transfer he was entitled to procedural due process. The Court agreed, relying on two independent reasons.

- First, Nebraska's creation by statute and "official practice" of an " 'objective expectation' . . . that a prisoner would not be transferred" except under the prescribed circumstances "gave Jones a liberty interest that entitled him to the benefits of appropriate procedures in connection with determining the conditions that warranted his transfer to a mental hospital."

- Second, "independently of [Nebraska law], the transfer of a prisoner from a prison to a mental hospital must be accompanied by appropriate procedural protections." Confinement in a mental hospital, said the Court, is such a massive loss of liberty, even when the alternative is a prison, that due process attaches to the interest. If this has nothing to do with state law, it must be due to the Constitution. If so, it is because this interest—freedom from confinement to a mental hospital—is a liberty interest for other constitutional purposes.

3. Determining the Process That Is Due

The second part of procedural due process—after having determined that the government is depriving someone of a liberty or property interest—is to determine what procedures are required before that deprivation may occur. "The essence of due process is the requirement that 'a person in jeopardy of serious loss [be given] **notice of the case against him** and **opportunity**

to meet it.' *Mathews v. Eldridge,* 424 U.S. 319 (1976), quoting *Joint Anti-Fascist Refugee Comm. v. McGrath,* 341 U.S. 123, 171-172 (Frankfurter, J., concurring).

a. **Overview.** The Court's approach in statutory benefits cases is to employ a balancing test that requires a court to weigh "three distinct factors":

- The *"private interest that will be affected* by the official action,"

- Both "the *risk of an erroneous deprivation* of such interest through the procedures used, and the *probable value,* if any, of *additional or substitute procedural safeguards,"* and

- The *"Government's interest,* including the function involved and the fiscal and administrative burdens that the additional or substitute procedural requirement would entail." *Mathews v. Eldridge,* 424 U.S. 319 (1976).

In other contexts, such as criminal trials, a formal trial is required. In still others, exemplified by the short-lived *Goldberg v. Kelly* approach, a semiformal evidentiary hearing may be required. This section will discuss trials and evidentiary hearings briefly before turning to the *Mathews* balancing test and its application.

b. **Trial.** A formal trial is probably the acme of procedural due process.

  i. **Criminal trials.** The procedural requirements mandated by due process for a criminal trial are outside the scope of this outline.

  ii. **Civil trials.** Civil lawsuits raise similar issues, since governments are unable validly to deprive one private citizen of property in order to give it to another without first providing the elaborate process of civil litigation, including trial. The due process requirements for civil litigation are also outside the scope of this outline.

c. **Evidentiary hearings.** The next best thing to a trial is an evidentiary hearing. Such hearings may be functionally indistinguishable from a trial but also may be less formal and lack some of the procedural safeguards of trial. All evidentiary hearings will involve the introduction of documentary and oral evidence and most will involve the participation of counsel. The high-water mark of this approach was *Goldberg v. Kelly,* supra, which "held that a hearing closely approximating a judicial trial" was necessary before a welfare recipient's benefits could be terminated, even temporarily. That approach, at least as applied to statutory benefits cases, has now been discredited. The Court has characterized the use of evidentiary hearings "prior to adverse administrative action" as a "depart[ure] from the ordinary principle [that] something less than an evidentiary hearing is sufficient."

d. The modern balancing test: *Mathews v. Eldridge,* 424 U.S. 319 (1976). Eldridge had received disability benefits for years but on the basis of agency files on Eldridge, Eldridge's responses to questions about his condition, and reports from his doctor and psychiatric consultant, a government agency tentatively concluded that he was no longer disabled. The agency so informed Eldridge, gave him the reasons for the decision, and told him that he could submit a written response if he desired to do so. He did, disputing the conclusion that he was no longer disabled, but his benefits were terminated anyway. Eldridge was entitled to a post-termination evidentiary hearing and, if successful, would then be entitled to retroactive payments. Eldridge maintained that the pre-termination procedures were a denial of due process. The Court disagreed.

    i. The Court's opinion. The majority opinion was premised on the principle that "due process is *flexible* and calls for *such procedural protections as the particular situation demands.*" The Court adopted a test that requires courts to weigh three factors: (1) the private interest affected, (2) the risk of error in using the challenged procedures and the "probable value" of other or additional procedures, and (3) the public interest, including costs and burdens to the government. In applying this test the Court stated that "*substantial weight* must be given to the *good-faith judgments* of [governmental administrators] that the procedures they have provided assure fair consideration of the entitlement claims of individuals." The Court applied these factors to the case.

    (a) The private interest affected. Eldridge was contesting the validity only of the *pre-termination procedures* since he was entitled to an evidentiary hearing after termination of his disability benefits. Thus, the sole "private interest affected" was "in the uninterrupted receipt of [disability benefits] pending final administrative decision on [Eldridge's] claim." While this interest was "significant" given the "torpidity of the administrative review process and the typically modest resources of the physically disabled worker," the Court thought that "other potential sources of temporary income" were adequate. Thus, the Court adhered to "the ordinary principle [that] something less than an evidentiary hearing is sufficient prior to adverse administrative action."

    (b) The risk of error of current procedures and probable value of alternative procedures. The challenged procedures required a medical determination of physical disability. The Court thought that determination would "turn, in most cases, upon 'routine, standard, and unbiased medical reports by physician specialists,' " and thus believed that the risk of error was low and that there was little value in employing a pre-termination evidentiary hearing.

(c) **The public interest.** The public interest includes the "administrative burden" and "incremental cost" of additional procedures. The incremental cost includes not only the cost of providing pre-termination hearings but also "the expense of providing benefits to ineligible recipients pending decision." That cost does not occur in isolation. Since resources are finite, the cost of pre-termination hearings and expense of benefit payments to the ineligible would "likely come out of the pockets of the deserving." In short, there are no free lunches.

e. **Post-deprivation hearings and other remedies.** Due process can be satisfied by only a post-deprivation hearing. Sometimes, the availability of some other post-deprivation remedy (e.g., a civil suit for damages) is deemed sufficient to comport with due process. In general, if the deprivation is severe and there is a substantial risk of error in the governmental action a post-deprivation hearing or other remedy is not adequate. By contrast, when the government acts to prevent public harm by imposing a temporary deprivation of private rights until a post-deprivation hearing can occur, due process is satisfied.

 # EXAMPLES AND ANALYSIS

Example: Although *Bell v. Burson* held that a driver's license was a sufficient property interest to trigger due process, the government may temporarily suspend (without a hearing) the driver's license of a motorist refusing to submit to tests for intoxication when arresting officers suspect he is drunk. *Mackey v. Montrym,* 443 U.S. 1 (1979).

When the liberty or property interest at stake is minor and the government has a substantial interest in acting fast, a post-deprivation hearing or other remedy is likely to be adequate.

Example: Florida's common law permitted public school officials to administer corporal punishment to students. While corporal punishment implicated a liberty interest sufficient to require due process, the due process clause was satisfied by the availability of a post-spanking right to bring suit seeking damages for excessive, unjustified infliction of physical harm. *Ingraham v. Wright,* 430 U.S. 651 (1977).

The Court has been most apt to apply this rule—treating the possibility of post-deprivation suits for damages as compliance with due process—in the context of intentional acts of prison officials that inflict injury upon prisoners.

Example: A prisoner alleged that prison officials deliberately destroyed his personal effects, including legal papers, during a search of his cell. The Court concluded that due process was satisfied so long as there was a "meaningful post-deprivation remedy" available to the inmate. *Hudson v. Palmer*, 468 U.S. 517 (1984).

When prison officials negligently injure a prisoner the state need not provide any post-deprivation remedy.

Example: A prisoner suffered physical injuries when he slipped and fell on a stairway due to the presence of a pillow negligently left on the stairway by a sheriff's deputy. The state's sovereign immunity doctrine barred any claim for damages. Tough luck, said the Court in effect, since it ruled that due process was not violated. *Daniels v. Williams*, 474 U.S. 327 (1986).

REVIEW QUESTIONS AND ANSWERS

Question: The state of Allegro has concluded that the presence of E. coli bacteria in hamburgers poses a great danger to public health. Accordingly, Allegro has enacted legislation that bans the sale, possession, or consumption of ground beef. Wendy Donald, operator of a hamburger restaurant, challenges the validity of the law as a denial of her liberty interest without due process of law. Will Donald's challenge succeed?

Answer: No. If Donald's challenge had been made in the heyday of the *Lochner* era it might well have succeeded, but today the relevant test is whether there is any conceivable basis for Allegro to think that the legislation is rationally related to a legitimate state purpose. Given the well-known fact that hamburger does harbor E. coli bacteria, and that E. coli can cause serious illness or death, it is rational for Allegro to adopt a flat ban on ground beef. Of course, it would probably make better sense simply to require restaurants to cook hamburgers to a sufficiently high internal temperature to kill E. coli bacteria, but the courts will not second-guess the legislative choice so long as it is rationally related to legitimate state objectives.

Question: The state of Andante enacts legislation that prohibits the sale, dispensing, or use of intrauterine devices, contraceptives that operate by preventing fertilized eggs from implanting themselves in the uterine lining. The legislative history is replete with references to numerous medical studies that conclude that such IUDs greatly increase the risk of the user's contracting uterine or cervical cancer. Jane Doe and her doctor challenge the validity of the law as a denial of a liberty interest without due process of law. What result?

Answer: The law is probably valid. The law is not a total prohibition upon the use of contraceptives, but only prohibits one particular method, and does so on substantial health grounds. The law is probably subject to strict scrutiny, since it interferes with the right to obtain contraceptives (see *Griswold* and *Eisenstadt*), but it is narrowly tailored (by prohibiting only the contraceptive device that is believed to cause cancer) to achieve a compelling governmental purpose (safeguarding the health of Andante's women).

Question: Assume the facts of the preceding question. Suppose the state of Andante extends its ban on contraceptives to include birth control pills and condoms. With respect to birth control pills, Andante relies on controversial medical studies that indicate that use of birth control pills increases the risk of certain cancers, and with respect to condoms Andante relies on evidence that condoms are not 100% effective in preventing sexually transmitted disease. Will a challenge to the law succeed?

Answer: Yes. The prohibition is not narrowly tailored to the accomplishment of compelling state interests. While the desire to protect the health of women of childbearing age is likely a compelling interest, the means chosen are probably not sufficiently narrowly tailored because the evidence of the connection between the use of birth control pills and cancer is so controversial and disputed. The ban on condoms is even less narrowly tailored to a compelling state interest. The state interest in preventing the spread of sexually transmitted disease is likely compelling but a ban on condoms is perverse to the attainment of that end.

Question: The state of Regulus enacts legislation that requires a minor either to notify one parent of her intention to obtain an abortion or to obtain a judicial order permitting her to abort. The legislation requires courts to issue the order upon proof of either the minor's ability to make a "mature decision concerning abortion" or that an abortion would be in her best interests. Anne, a minor, challenges the validity of the law on due process grounds. Will her challenge succeed?

Answer: No. A minor's right to obtain an abortion is more limited than an adult's right. The Court has upheld laws imposing a one-parent notification requirement coupled with a judicial bypass procedure. See *Hodgson v. Minnesota*.

Question: The state of Antares enacts legislation that permits post-viability abortions only when (1) there is a reasonable medical belief that the fetus is defective or that continuation of the pregnancy would endanger the woman's life, and (2) the written consent of the woman's husband (if married) is obtained. Is the law valid under the due process clause?

Answer: No. After viability, states are generally free to impose any abortion restriction that is rationally related to a legitimate state interest. The first requirement surely meets that test, but the second requirement is invalid. The Court in *Hodgson v. Minnesota* implicitly determined that a two-parent notification requirement for a minor to obtain a previability abortion was not rationally related to a legitimate state objective. It is a legitimate state objective to preserve potential human life of fetuses after viability, and both requirements seem calculated to advance that goal simply by reducing the likely number of abortions. But the second requirement places the woman entirely at the mercy of her husband. She is unable to end even a life-threatening pregnancy unless her husband consents. It is not hard to imagine an angry, vindictive, and evil estranged husband refusing such consent. Under *Casey,* a state may not prohibit postviability abortions where needed to save a woman's life. The state may not delegate that power to a woman's husband.

Question: The state of Rigel enacts a law that makes it a crime for a parent to administer any corporal punishment to his or her child. Mrs. Paddel is convicted under the law because she applied two smacks of her open palm to the clothed buttocks of her five-year-old son, while seated on a bench in a shopping mall. She appeals on the ground that the law violates her liberty interest in child-rearing without due process of law. What result?

Answer: The law is probably invalid. The "privacy" right extends to protect a variety of specific rights associated with child-rearing. The Court has never addressed the issue of whether the child-rearing rights include the right to administer corporal punishment. *Pierce* identified as a protected liberty interest the right "of parents and guardians to direct the upbringing . . . of children under their control." That is probably sufficient to establish that, in general, parents possess a fundamental right to determine how best to discipline their unruly children. Rigel must justify the law as narrowly tailored to accomplish a compelling state interest. While it is surely a compelling interest to protect vulnerable children from physical or mental abuse by their parents, this law is not narrowly tailored to achieve that end. Violent beatings are as illegal as Mrs. Paddel's slaps on the bottom of her child. Corporal punishment may well be a poor, or even lamentable, child-rearing technique but so long as it is not excessive it is probably within the liberty interest of parents to rear their children without state interference. A more narrowly drawn law (e.g., one that prohibited "excessive" corporal punishment and that defined "excessive" objectively) might well be justified under strict scrutiny.

Question: The state of Aldebaran enacts legislation that automatically terminates spousal support obligations incurred as part of a divorce upon the remarriage of the person receiving spousal support benefits. Sydney's spousal support benefits are terminated upon Sydney's marriage. Sydney challenges the validity of the law. What result?

Answer: The law is probably valid. The law is only an incidental interference with the right to marry, and thus subject only to minimal scrutiny. Laws that grant or deny public benefits on the basis of marital status interfere far less with the fundamental right to marry than do laws that determine who may marry at all. Compare *Zablocki v. Redhail* with *Califano v. Jobst.* The law is rationally related to a state's legitimate interest in imposing spousal support obligations only as a way to avoid penury on the part of divorced spouses ill-equipped to fend for themselves financially. Though perhaps "politically incorrect" Aldebaran could rationally assume that a person who was once so dependant on a spouse as to merit spousal support upon divorce might well be financially taken care of by the new spouse. If the law were treated as a substantial interference with the right to marry, it would be valid only if Aldebaran could justify it under strict scrutiny.

Question: The state of Capella enacts legislation that requires men to have cleanshaven faces and women to have cleanshaven legs. Alice and Ted each challenge the validity of the law under due process. What result?

Answer: The law is probably invalid. The Court has rejected the contention that there is a fundamental right to choose one's personal appearance, at least as applied to such things as the decision whether or not to shave one's body hair. But that decision was in the context of an appearance regulation applicable to policemen. The Court expressly disclaimed any decision about whether the general public enjoyed such a right. On one hand, if the entire enterprise of substantive due process is regarded as faulty, or if the Court concluded that there was no fundamental right to regulate one's appearance, the Capella statute would be subject to minimal scrutiny. The law is rationally related to a particular view of human neatness and attractiveness, but is it a legitimate state interest to mandate a particular view of those issues? That is an open question, and related to the question of whether there is a fundamental "privacy" or "autonomy" interest in controlling one's personal appearance. If private sex with another consenting adult is not "fundamental"—as *Bowers* suggests—it is difficult to understand why the more frivolous concern with one's body hair should be fundamental. On the other hand, the idea of state regulation of public appearance is sufficiently authoritarian that it is difficult to understand how a country that claims to be a "free society" could tolerate such governmental regimentation of its citizens. Surely there is no historical tradition of such regimentation and, by implication, there must be a historical tradition of freedom from legal control of the public appearance of the general public. If, as this suggests, there is a fundamental right on the part of the general public to control one's appearance, Capella's law is invalid unless it can withstand strict scrutiny. That is unlikely; what conceivable *compelling* interest could the state have in hairless male faces and female legs?

Question: The state of Poplar has enacted legislation that prohibits suicide, and provides that the estates of persons who commit suicide are forfeited to the state. For purposes of the law, "estate" is defined to include all assets transferred by the person prior to death for less than a fair and equivalent consideration. George, a competent, adult, terminally ill cancer patient who alleges he wishes to take his own life, challenges the law in federal district court in an action seeking a declaratory judgment that the law violates his substantive due process rights. The court rules that George has standing and that the claim is sufficiently concrete to constitute a case or controversy, but waits for you (a law clerk) to advise it accurately on the due process issue. What advice should you give?

Answer: The law is probably invalid and the district court should so rule. Although the Court has never held that competent adults have a fundamental right to commit suicide it has intimated as much in *Cruzan*. On the other hand, there is a strong tradition (sometimes legal, sometimes social) discouraging suicide. Here, George does not wish to prevent the state from prohibiting others from assisting his suicide. George simply wishes to invalidate the state's collateral penalty (the forfeiture of his estate) upon his exercise of what he claims is his fundamental right. If he is correct that a competent adult has a fundamental right to commit suicide then Poplar must prove that its estate forfeiture is narrowly tailored to achieve a compelling state interest. That is almost impossible since the function of the law is to discourage suicide by making the would-be suicide realize that he will harm his loved ones by doing so. If only minimal scrutiny applies, the law is surely rationally related to a legitimate state goal of discouraging suicide. Thus, the answer hinges on whether the claimed right is fundamental.

Question: A statute of the state of Alligator provides that "all nontenured faculty members of any public university shall be employed at the will of the university, and may be terminated at any time with or without cause." Alligator State University, a public university, maintains a Faculty Handbook detailing the rights and responsibilities of faculty members that states that "nontenured faculty are expected to make regular progress toward tenure in six years and, unless advised to the contrary by their departmental chairman, may assume that they are making regular progress and will likely receive tenure in their sixth year of employment." Jean, a nontenured assistant professor of chemistry who had never been told anything adverse about her teaching or research, was summarily fired by Alligator State following her third year of teaching. She contends that the university violated due process by its failure to give her notice of the reasons for her firing and an adequate opportunity to respond. Is she correct?

Answer: Yes. The question of whether her interest in continuing employment is a "property" interest to which procedural due process attaches is determined by state law. Although the Alligator statute states that she is an employee at will (and thus has no property interest in continued employment) the Alligator State University Faculty Handbook contradicts that rule. Jean has more than a unilateral expectation of continued employment. Based on the Faculty Handbook and the lack of any adverse comment on her job performance Jean has reason to expect continued employment until at least her sixth year of employment. She is entitled to due process before termination. At the least, that means she must receive some notice of the charges and an opportunity to rebut them.

EXAM TIPS

- **Two Due Process Clauses.** The Fifth Amendment bars the federal government from denying due process and, by implication, equal protection. The 14th Amendment bars the states from denying due process.

- **Substantive Due Process.** This is a fertile exam area.

  - **Standard of Review.** Strict scrutiny applies only to infringements of **fundamental rights**—those implicit in "ordered liberty" or deeply rooted in our history and tradition. They may only be infringed if the government proves that it is necessary to do so to achieve a compelling interest. Infringements of "nonfundamental" rights are subject to minimal scrutiny—they are presumed valid and struck down only if the challenger proves that they are not rationally related to any legitimate state interest.

  - **Fundamental Rights.** The following rights are fundamental:

    — **Incorporated Rights.** Most of the important rights guaranteed by the Bill of Rights are incorporated into the 14th Amendment's due process clause.

    — **Contraceptive Use.**

    — **Abortion.**

    — **Family Relationships.**

    — **Right to Marry.**

  - **Possible Fundamental Rights.** The following claimed rights have never been found fundamental, but a good case can be made for each. Think through the case for and against each. Consider especially the outer limits of each.

    — **Right to Die.** Consider the differences between competent and incompetent persons, and to what extent governments must recognize the wishes of the incompetent patient expressed when competent.

    — **Right to Consensual, Adult Sex.** The Court has rejected such a right for homosexual sex. Consider heterosexual adultery, fornication, adult incest, or other possible pairings.

    — **Right to Personal Appearance.** No such right exists for police officers and, possibly, schoolchildren. What about the general population?

- **Definitely Not Fundamental Rights.** The Court has squarely rejected the following claims of fundamental rights:

  — **Economic Liberty.** Until the 1930s the Court sometimes voided laws on the ground that they infringed unduly and unjustifiably upon the private ordering of economic arrangements. "Economic substantive due process" is dead.

  — **Anonymity.** There is no fundamental right to be free of government collection and storage of personal information.

  — **Consensual Homosexual Sex.** The Court has rejected this claimed fundamental right.

- ■ **Procedural Due Process.** There is no **general right of procedural regularity**— procedural due process applies only when governments infringe **life, liberty or property.** This issue is typically raised on exams in the context of a denial or termination of some governmental benefit.

  - **What's "Property" or "Liberty"?** Property is defined according to the applicable state law. Liberty isn't infringed unless the government alters one's legal status under state law or invades an independent constitutionally recognized liberty interest.

  - **What Process Is Due?** At the least, a person is entitled to notice and an opportunity to be heard. Beyond that, the procedures required by due process depend on three factors:

    — The significance of the affected private interest,

    — The probable value of additional procedures in reducing the risk of error in decision, and

    — The public interest, including the costs and burdens imposed by more procedures.

9 EQUAL PROTECTION

CHAPTER OVERVIEW

This chapter deals with equal protection of the laws. The 14th Amendment provides that "No State shall . . . deny to any person within its jurisdiction the equal protection of the laws." The same principle applies to the federal government, via the due process clause of the Fifth Amendment. The most important points in this chapter follow.

- **Three Tiers of Scrutiny:** Courts use three levels of review to evaluate whether any given statutory classification is valid under equal protection.

  - **Minimal Scrutiny:** Classifications subject to minimal scrutiny are presumed to be valid. For a classification to be void, a challenger must prove that the classification is ***not rationally related to any conceivable legitimate state interest***. Any legitimate state interest, however hypothetical, will suffice. Minimal scrutiny is the "default review"—it *applies to all classifications* except those that are constitutionally suspicious. Minimal scrutiny is also called "*rationality*" or "*rational basis*" review.

  - **Strict Scrutiny:** Classifications subject to strict scrutiny are presumed invalid. For a classification to be valid, the government must prove that the classification is *necessary to accomplish a compelling governmental interest*. This generally means that the classification must be the least restrictive way to achieve the government's extremely important objective. This is a very difficult burden of proof to overcome. Strict scrutiny applies whenever a law employs a **suspect classification** or **substantially infringes upon a fundamental right.**

- **Intermediate Scrutiny:** Classifications subject to intermediate scrutiny are presumed invalid. For a classification to be valid, the government must prove that the classification is *substantially related to an important government interest*. This burden of proof is moderately difficult to overcome. Only the **actual purposes** for the classification matter. By contrast, under minimal scrutiny classifications are valid if they are rationally related to *hypothetical* purposes. Intermediate scrutiny is applied to classifications on the basis of *sex* or *illegitimate birth*.

■ **Suspect Classifications.** Classifications that intentionally discriminate against such a discrete and insular minority that the normal functions of representative government are unlikely to redress the situation are **suspect** and trigger **strict scrutiny.** In practice, only race, national origin, and alienage (in some circumstances) are suspect classifications.

- **Race and National Origin:** *All* such classifications are suspect, even those designed to benefit racial minorities.

- **Alienage:** Alienage classifications are generally suspect (and thus subject to strict scrutiny), but minimal scrutiny applies when:

— Congress or the President makes the classification, or

— The classification is designed to ensure that important governmental functions are performed by citizens.

"Enhanced minimal scrutiny" applies to classifications of aliens illegally present in the country.

■ **Fundamental Rights.** Classifications impinging on **fundamental rights** are subject to strict scrutiny. Fundamental rights are those rights that are "explicitly or implicitly guaranteed by the Constitution," *not* those that are "societally important." Here are the principal fundamental rights protected by equal protection:

- **Voting.** Classifications that *substantially interfere* with the implied constitutional right to vote are subjected to strict scrutiny.

- **Access to the Judicial Process.** There is no general right of access to courts but some monetary barriers to judicial process interfere so substantially with vital interests that strict scrutiny applies.

- **The Right of Interstate Mobility.** Classifications that substantially infringe this implied right are subjected to strict scrutiny.

A. OVERVIEW

1. Scope of the Equal Protection Clause

The 14th Amendment prohibits states from denying "any person . . . the equal protection of the laws."

a. **Applies only to governments.** The equal protection clause applies to *governments,* not private actions. Of course, much private behavior that would violate equal protection if performed by a government is prohibited by state or federal statutes.

   i. **States.** The 14th Amendment explicitly obligates *states* to provide equal protection of the laws.

   ii. **Federal government.** The federal government must also provide equal protection of the laws. In *Bolling v. Sharpe,* 347 U.S. 497 (1954), the Court concluded that the due process clause of the Fifth Amendment obliged the federal government to provide equal protection.

2. **Legislative Classifications**

   All laws classify and, by doing so, treat people differently. Two classes of people are created by any classification.

   Example: A state limits driving to those age sixteen or older. Two classes are created: those sixteen or over, who are eligible to drive, and those under sixteen, barred from the road.

   Legislative classifications are *presumed to be valid.* The Court has created a complex doctrine to evaluate when and how that presumption may be overcome. In general, classifications are invalid if proven they are (1) *utterly and totally irrational,* or (2) *unjustifiably discrimination* toward *specific categories of people,* or (3) adopted to further an *illegitimate governmental objective.* Courts use *three levels of review* to identify and strike down these categories of invalid classifications.

3. **Three Levels of Judicial Scrutiny**

   Since legislative classifications are *presumptively valid,* most are subjected to **minimal scrutiny.** Classifications that are constitutionally suspicious (e.g., by race) are subjected to **strict scrutiny.** Classifications that are not quite as constitutionally suspicious (e.g., by sex) are subjected to **intermediate scrutiny.** Since a classification's validity is progressively less likely as one goes from minimal to strict scrutiny, the doctrinal devices for sorting constitutionally suspicious classifications are almost as important as the levels of scrutiny.

   a. **Minimal scrutiny.** When minimal scrutiny applies the classification is presumed valid. It is struck down only if the challenger proves that the classification is ***not* rationally related to a legitimate state interest.** Most classifications are subject to minimal scrutiny. Higher scrutiny applies only when the classification is **suspect** (or nearly so) or **infringes on a fundamental right.**

      i. **"Enhanced" minimal scrutiny.** In rare circumstances the Court might apply an "enhanced" form of minimal scrutiny, in which the classification is invalid if it is not *substantially related* to a legitimate state interest. (See *Plyler v. Doe,* infra.)

b. **Strict scrutiny.** Classifications that are *suspect* or *infringe on a fundamental right* are subjected to strict scrutiny. Under strict scrutiny, a classification is presumed void unless the government proves that it is **necessary to achieve a compelling state interest.**

c. **Intermediate scrutiny.** Classifications by sex or illegitimacy are subject to intermediate scrutiny. Under intermediate scrutiny, a classification is presumed void unless the government proves that the classification is **substantially related to an important state interest.**

d. **"Sliding-scale" review: A rejected alternative.** Not everyone is happy with "tiered" review. Justice Stevens has frequently stated his view that a single standard should govern equal protection cases. Justice Thurgood Marshall advocated an infinitely variable "sliding-scale" form of review. Marshall argued that the degree of judicial review should depend upon "the constitutional and societal importance of the interest adversely affected and the recognized invidiousness of the basis upon which the particular classification is drawn." *San Antonio School District v. Rodriguez,* 411 U.S. 1 (1973) (Marshall, J., dissenting). The Court has never openly accepted "sliding-scale" review.

4. **Categorizing Classifications: Benign, Suspect, and Impinging on Fundamental Rights**

The level of judicial scrutiny used to evaluate a classification's validity depends on how that classification is categorized. **Suspect classifications** and those that **impinge on a fundamental right** are subjected to **strict scrutiny.** Classifications by sex or illegitimate birth are "quasi-suspect" and trigger **intermediate scrutiny.** All other classifications are presumptively benign and subject to **minimal scrutiny.**

a. **Suspect classifications.** Classifications that *intentionally* discriminate *in a constitutionally invidious (wrongful) manner* are suspect classifications. The classic example is a racial classification. The justification for treating some statutory classes as suspect is rooted in Justice Stone's "famous footnote 4" in *Carolene Products:* "There may be narrower scope for operation of the presumption of constitutionality when legislation . . . [is] directed at particular religions or national or racial minorities. . . . [P]rejudice against discrete and insular minorities may be a special condition, which tends seriously to curtail the operation of those political processes ordinarily to be relied upon to protect minorities, and which may call for a correspondingly more searching judicial inquiry." *United States v. Carolene Products Co.,* 304 U.S. 144, 152-153 n.4 (1938). To be suspect, a classification must be intentionally discriminatory, should be immutable, and have a history of purposeful inequality toward a group that has perennially been denied *access* to political power.

b.   **"Quasi-suspect" classifications.** There are two established "quasi-suspect" classifications—sex and illegitimate birth—that trigger intermediate scrutiny. These classifications are not as strongly presumed to be the product of invidious discrimination as are suspect classifications. But the Court thinks they are suspicious enough to subject them to review that is close to strict scrutiny. Some think that the entire concept of "quasi-suspect" classifications is dubious: If sex or illegitimacy classifications proceed from "prejudice against discrete and insular minorities" the classifications ought to be treated as suspect; if such classifications are not the product of such prejudice they ought to be subjected to minimal scrutiny.

c.   **Benign classifications.** All other classifications are benign, or nonsuspect, and trigger minimal scrutiny. The general presumption of constitutionality of legislation applies to such classifications.

d.   **Classifications impinging on fundamental rights.** Classifications that selectively impinge upon constitutionally fundamental rights are subjected to strict scrutiny. The principal examples are classifications that substantially restrict access to voting or interstate mobility, or that impose substantial obstacles to vindication of vital interests in the judicial process.

5.   **The Relationship of Classifications to Governmental Objectives**

a.   **Under- and over-inclusion explained.** Laws classify in order to achieve objectives, but the classification may not perfectly achieve the objective. Any law creates two classes: one consists of the people in the "statutory class" and the other consists of precisely those people necessary to achieve the objective (the "optimal class"). The statutory class may include *more* than is necessary in the classification to achieve the objective. If so, the law is **over-inclusive.** The classification may also include *less* than is necessary to achieve the objective. If so, the statute is **under-inclusive.**

EXAMPLES AND ANALYSIS

Example (Over-Inclusion): A curfew law, requiring all people under age eighteen to be off the streets between the hours of midnight and 6 A.M., presumably has as its objective the prevention of street crime by minors. The law is **over-inclusive:** the class of criminal minors (the optimal class) is completely included in the class of people under age eighteen (the statutory class), but many people under age eighteen are not part of the class of criminal minors.

Example (Under-Inclusion): A city ordinance bans streetcart vendors in a heavily visited "tourist quarter" of the city in order to alleviate sidewalk and street congestion. The law is **under-inclusive:** all streetcart vendors (the statutory class) contribute toward sidewalk and street congestion, but the class of people causing sidewalk and street congestion (the optimal class) surely includes many others as well. Cf. *New Orleans v. Dukes,* 427 U.S. 297 (1976).

A legislative classification may be simultaneously **over-inclusive** and **under-inclusive.**

Example: A law setting age sixteen as the minimum age for a driver's license serves the objective of limiting driver's licenses to safe drivers. The law is **under-inclusive** because the class of unsafe drivers (the optimal class) includes many people over the age of sixteen. The law is **over-inclusive** because the statutory class (people under age sixteen) includes some people who are perfectly safe drivers.

It is rare if not virtually impossible for a statutory class and an optimal class to coincide perfectly.

Example: Assume that a disease is transmitted *only* by blowing one's nose in public and that blowing one's nose in public *always* transmits the disease. A law prohibiting blowing one's nose in public creates a statutory class of public nose blowers that is perfectly congruent with the optimal class of people who transmit the disease. It is perfect; neither under-inclusive nor over-inclusive.

It is almost as rare for a statutory class and an optimal class to have no overlap at all.

Example: For the express purpose of limiting human consumption of animal fats, a state forbids the consumption of bottled mineral water. The optimal class (people who consume animal fats) and the statutory class (people who consume bottled mineral water) have absolutely no overlap. The classification is utterly irrational and absurd. The classification does *nothing* to achieve its objective.

> b. **Significance of under- and over-inclusion.** Over-inclusion and under-inclusion, by themselves, are not enough to invalidate laws as violations of equal protection. They are simply helpful tools in applying equal protection doctrine.
>
>> i. **Under-inclusion.** Under minimal scrutiny courts usually uphold under-inclusive classifications unless they are so wildly under-inclusive as to be irrational. Courts often state that legislatures are free to attack a problem in piecemeal fashion. Equal protection does *not* require "that all evils of the same genus be eradicated or none at all." *Railway Express Agency v. New York,* 336 U.S. 106

(1949). It is sometimes argued that under-inclusion may easily be used to attack a problem by singling out the politically weakest for unfavorable treatment. Courts address that issue by determining whether or not the classification is suspect.

ii. **Over-inclusion.** Over-inclusion, by itself, is not a violation of equal protection. Over-inclusive classifications burden more people than is necessary to accomplish legitimate public objectives. That virtually eliminates the possibility that the classification is designed to pick on the weak, but raises the question of whether laws imposing such "unfair burdens" ought to be scrutinized carefully. Courts apply minimal scrutiny to over-inclusive, but nonsuspect, classifications. (For more on over- and under-inclusion, see Tussman and tenBroek, 37 Cal. L. Rev. 341.)

B. MINIMAL SCRUTINY

1. The Test and Its Scope

Classifications subjected to minimal scrutiny are presumed valid. They are struck down only if the challenger proves that there is *no conceivable rational relationship* between the classification and *any legitimate state interest.* If government lawyers can dream up *any* plausible legitimate objective for the classification (whether or not the legislature actually had that objective in mind), and the classification serves to accomplish that objective *to any degree,* no matter how tiny, it is valid. To be invalid under minimal scrutiny a classification must have one of two traits: (1) *absolutely no conceivable legitimate purpose* or (2) be so *unconnected to any conceivable objective that it is absurd, utterly arbitrary, whimsical, or even perverse.* Very few laws fail minimal scrutiny. Minimal scrutiny is also called "rational basis" scrutiny, "mere rationality" review, or "deferential" review.

a. **Economic and social welfare legislation.** Virtually any classification that furthers legitimate economic or social welfare goals will be upheld under minimal scrutiny.

EXAMPLE AND ANALYSIS

Oklahoma barred opticians (the artisans who actually make eyeglasses) from making eyeglasses without a prescription from either an ophthalmologist (a physician specializing in the eye) or optometrist (a person with some eye-related medical training). But Oklahoma permitted drugstores and other sellers of ready-to-wear spectacles to dispense eyeglasses without a prescription. The Supreme Court reversed a federal trial judge's ruling that the discriminatory ban against opticians violated equal protection. So long as a legislature does not employ suspect classifications the Court will defer to its choice of classifications. A legislature "may take one step at a time, addressing itself to the phase of the problem that seems most acute to the [legislature] . . . [and] may select[ively] . . . apply a remedy . . . , neglecting the others. The prohibition of the Equal Protection Clause goes no further than the invidious discrimination." *Williamson v. Lee Optical Co.,* 348 U.S. 483 (1955).

---

2.   Means: What Is Not Rational?

Assuming a legitimate end (see section B.3, infra) almost any means are rational.

a.   **"One-step-at-a-time": Under-inclusion permissible.** Under-inclusive statutory classifications are generally permissible.

   i.   *Railway Express Agency v. New York,* 336 U.S. 106 (1949). New York City prohibited vehicles from carrying advertisements, but exempted "business delivery vehicles . . . engaged in the usual business . . . of the owner" carrying "advertisements of products sold by the owner of the truck." Railway Express, which carried paid advertisements on the sides of its 1900 trucks operating in New York City, was convicted of violating the law and appealed on equal protection grounds. The law's objective was to improve safety by reducing distractions to drivers and pedestrians. Railway Express attacked the law as so grossly under-inclusive as to be irrational, arguing "that the classification which the regulation makes has no relation to the traffic problem since a violation turns not on what kind of advertisements are carried on trucks but on whose trucks they are carried." The Court rejected that argument, hypothesizing that New York City "may well have concluded that those who advertised their own wares on their trucks do not present the same traffic problem in view of the nature or extent of the advertising which they use." Legislatures, said the Court, need not act to eliminate "all evils of the same genus . . . or none at all."

   (a)   **Justice Jackson's concurrence.** Jackson thought that under-inclusion ought to be viewed with some suspicion. "[T]here is no more effective practical guaranty against arbitrary and unreasonable government than to require that the . . . law . . . impose[d] upon a minority must be imposed generally. . . . [N]othing opens the door to arbitrary action so effectively as to allow . . . officials to pick and choose only a few to whom they will apply legislation and thus to escape the political retribution that might be visited upon them if larger numbers were affected." But Jackson was persuaded that it was reasonable for New York to ban vehicle advertising for hire while still permitting self-advertisement on vehicles.

ii. *New Orleans v. Dukes,* 427 U.S. 297 (1976). New Orleans banned all pushcart vendors in the French Quarter, but excepted vendors who had been doing so for eight or more years. Dukes, a vendor who had been in business for only two years, attacked the ban as a violation of equal protection. New Orleans declared its objective to be "to preserve the appearance and custom valued by the Quarter's residents and attractive to tourists." The Court upheld the law. "The legitimacy of that objective is obvious. . . . States are accorded wide latitude in the regulation of their local economies . . . [and] may implement their program step by step in such economic areas, adopting regulations that only partially ameliorate a perceived evil and deferring complete elimination of the evil to future regulations." It was thus permissible for New Orleans to conclude that the oldtimers permitted to continue vending in the French Quarter had "built up substantial reliance interests in continued operation" and were "part of the distinctive character and charm" of the French Quarter.

b. Rationally debatable over-inclusion permissible. Rational over-inclusion is also permissible.

i. *New York City Transit Authority v. Beazer,* 440 U.S. 568 (1979). The New York City Transit Authority excluded all methadone users from employment in order to assure job and passenger safety. Methadone is a drug used to help break addiction to opiates. The regulation was attacked as a violation of equal protection, specifically that it was so over-inclusive that the relationship between methadone use and safety was irrational. Evidence indicated that about 75% of people who have used methadone for a year or more are free from heroin or other illicit drug use. Nevertheless, the Court applied minimal scrutiny and upheld the law, finding that the " 'no drugs' policy now enforced by [the Transit Authority] is supported by the legitimate inference that so long as a treatment program (or other drug use) continues, a degree of uncertainty persists."

ii. *Massachusetts Board of Retirement v. Murgia,* 427 U.S. 307 (1976). Massachusetts required all uniformed state police officers to retire at age fifty. The Court rejected the idea that there was any fundamental right to public employment and the notion that classifications by age ought to be treated as suspect. Accordingly, the Court applied minimal scrutiny. The purpose of the mandatory retirement age was to assure a physically fit and vigorous cadre of police officers. Even though some (possibly many) officers over age fifty are fit and vigorous and some under fifty are not, the Court regarded the retirement age as a reasonable line, at least rational in relation to the goals of the regulation.

c. **Empirical linkage of means to ends not needed.** Under minimal scrutiny there is no need to prove by empirically verifiable evidence that the statutory means are in fact rationally related to the statute's objectives. It is enough to suppose, or hypothesize, such a connection.

    i. *Minnesota v. Clover Leaf Creamery,* 449 U.S. 456 (1981). Minnesota banned the sale of milk in plastic containers but permitted its sale in plastic coated paperboard cartons. The law was supposed to promote resource conservation, ease solid waste disposal problems, and conserve energy, all legitimate state interests. The law was attacked as not rationally related to those objectives because, in fact, the empirical evidence tended to show "that the probable consequences of the ban on plastic nonreturnable milk containers will be to deplete natural resources, exacerbate solid waste disposal problems, and waste energy." The Minnesota Supreme Court agreed, and struck down the law. The United States Supreme Court reversed. For the Court, Justice Brennan said that it did not matter that empirical evidence proved that the statute perversely served its purposes: "Where there was evidence before the legislature reasonably supporting the classification" the law would be upheld regardless of the strength of the empirical evidence "that the legislature was mistaken." Note that the "evidence before the legislature" was supposition and that the evidence of the legislature's mistake was empirically verifiable.

3. **Ends: What Is a Legitimate Public Purpose?**

a. **Deference to the legislative choice of objective.** So long as the legislative objective is not *prohibited by the Constitution* the legislature is free to formulate its own objectives. After all, it is the democratically elected body that represents the people.

    i. **Unwise is not illegitimate.** Courts routinely assert that they will not examine the wisdom of legislation. "States are not required to convince the courts of the correctness of their legislative judgments." *Minnesota v. Clover Leaf Creamery,* supra. "[T]he judiciary may not sit as a superlegislature to judge the wisdom or desirability of [legislation] . . . in areas that neither affect fundamental rights nor proceed along suspect lines." *New Orleans v. Dukes,* supra.

    ii. **Some objectives are illegitimate.** Under minimal scrutiny, judicial deference to legislative objectives is not total. Some objectives are illegitimate.

(a) *United States Dept. of Agriculture v. Moreno,* 413 U.S. 528 (1973). Federal law denied food stamps to any household containing an individual unrelated to any other member of the household. The Court applied minimal scrutiny but struck down the law. The "challenged statutory classification" was "clearly irrelevant" to the law's declared purposes—to raise nutrition levels of poor people and to strengthen the agricultural economy. The Court rejected as illegitimate a purpose gleaned from the legislative history: the law "was intended to prevent so-called 'hippies' and 'hippie communes' from participating in the food stamp program." Equal protection "must at the very least mean that a bare congressional desire to harm a politically unpopular group cannot constitute a *legitimate* governmental interest." The Court also concluded that the "unrelated persons" classification was not rationally related to the government's contention that the real objective of the law was to prevent fraud. In doing so, Justice Brennan, writing for the Court, refused "to accept as rational the Government's wholly unsubstantiated assumptions concerning the differences between 'related' and 'unrelated' households." Note that in *Clover Leaf Creamery* Justice Brennan, writing for the Court, was perfectly willing to defer to suppositional evidence before the legislature concerning the rationality of the statutory class, but that in *Moreno* he was unwilling to do so. Perhaps that inconsistency can be explained by the illegitimate purpose detected in *Moreno.*

(b) *Romer v. Evans,* 517 U.S. 620 (1996). Colorado voters amended their constitution to prohibit all Colorado governments from protecting homosexuals from public or private discrimination. Since homosexuality is not a suspect classification, the Court applied minimal scrutiny. Although Colorado claimed that its purpose was to respect its citizens' freedom of association and to conserve resources to fight other kinds of discrimination, the Court dismissed these purposes as so far removed from the amendment's sweeping effect as to be pretextual. Colorado's purpose, said the Court, was not legitimate—it was "a status-based . . . classification of persons undertaken for its own sake," designed to make homosexuals "unequal to everyone else . . . , a stranger to [Colorado's] laws." The nature of the amendment was the key factor in the Court's willingness to second-guess the state's motive. A total ban on government action protecting homosexuals against discrimination is an enormously broad civic disability to impose simply to conserve state resources and to honor freedom of association.

b. Determining the purpose of legislation. There are several ways courts can determine legislative objectives, or purposes.

- **Stated Purpose.** But sometimes the legislature fails to express a purpose.

- **Actual Purpose.** This can be revealed by the legislation itself, by legislative history, or by some other method.

- **Any Conceivable Purpose.** This includes anything that *might have been a purpose* had it actually occurred to the legislature, no matter whether real or not. Generally, *courts applying minimal scrutiny credit any conceivable purpose,* even after-the-fact conjecture, as the objective to which the statute is rationally related.

  i. *United States Railroad Retirement Board v. Fritz,* 449 U.S. 166 (1980). In 1974 Congress eliminated dual retirement benefits for some, but not all, railroad workers. The 1974 amendment denied dual benefits to unretired persons vested in both retirement plans unless they either (1) had worked in or had a "current connection" with the railroad industry in 1974, or (2) had completed twenty-five years of railroad service by 1974. In essence, unretired people not currently working in the railroad industry but with ten to twenty-five years of past service and presently vested retirement benefits were stripped of their railroad retirement pension benefits, while current railroad workers with vested benefits and unretired workers working elsewhere but with twenty-five years of service received their benefits. The benefit losers contended that the statutory distinction violated equal protection. The Court applied minimal scrutiny and upheld the law.

    (a) The Court's opinion. The majority stated that whenever the Court is applying minimal scrutiny "in cases involving social and economic benefits . . . the *plain language* of [the statute] marks the *beginning and end* of our inquiry." The Court hypothesized a congressional objective of protecting "the relative equities of employees and to provide benefits to career railroad employees," ignoring an explicit statement by Congress that its principal purpose "was to preserve the vested earned benefits of retirees who had already qualified for them." Since the classification was rationally related to the supposed objective, it passed minimal scrutiny. "Where . . . there are plausible reasons for Congress' action, our inquiry is at an end. It is . . . 'constitutionally irrelevant whether this reasoning in fact underlay the legislative decision.' "

(b) Brennan's dissent. Justice Brennan, dissenting, contended that "the *actual purposes* of Congress, rather than the post hoc justifications offered by government attorneys, must be the primary basis for analysis under the rational basis test." To Brennan, this meant that the Court should start with the explicitly stated purposes of legislation and look further only when the statute "is either irrelevant to or counter to that purpose." But even then "we must view any post hoc justifications proffered by Government attorneys with skepticism."

(c) Stevens's concurrence. Justice Stevens concurred in the judgment, but thought that the Court "must discover a correlation between the classification and *either* the *actual purpose* of the statute or a *legitimate purpose that we may reasonably presume to have motivated an impartial legislature.*"

ii. **Rationales for actual or conceivable purposes.** The argument for using actual purpose is that such a requirement would spur Congress to consider and state its purposes when legislating, a boon to public accountability and responsible legislating. The arguments against using actual purpose are (1) the difficulty of determining an *actual* purpose, and (2) the fear that such a quest would be undemocratic by giving the judiciary too much license to impute an impermissible or unrelated motive to legislation. Using any conceivable purpose, however, assumes the existence of an omniscient and invariably well-meaning legislature.

4. Some Legislation Is Void Under Minimal Scrutiny

Despite its deference to legislative judgment, the minimal scrutiny test does occasionally operate to invalidate legislation.

a. **Illegitimate purposes.** The Court occasionally identifies an impermissible purpose and invalidates the law on that ground.

i. **Desire to harm the politically unpopular.** Governments may not act simply "to harm a politically unpopular group." *United States Dept. of Agriculture v. Moreno,* supra. Nor may they enact "status-based . . . classifications" calculated to make an identified group "a stranger to its laws." *Romer v. Evans,* supra. The Court almost surely did not mean to describe *any* losing interest group when it used the term "politically unpopular group." The desire to harm hippies or homosexuals, *for the sake of harming them,* is different from the desire to harm opticians or consumers (*Williamson v. Lee*

Optical). In the latter case, the harm inflicted was incidental to a legitimate reason, rather than being the objective itself. Harming a group for the sole purpose of harming them is never legitimate. *Romer v. Evans,* supra.

ii. **Discrimination against newcomers and out of staters.** A state objective to discriminate purposefully against out of staters and newcomers is not legitimate. Often these statutes are invalidated under the commerce clause or Article IV's privileges and immunities clause. (See Chapter 6.) When the *only* purpose for a statutory classification is to discriminate against out of staters or newcomers its purpose is illegitimate under the equal protection clause as well.

   (a) *Zobel v. Williams,* 457 U.S. 55 (1982). Alaska decided to return to its citizens a large fiscal surplus. The amount refunded varied with the length of residence in Alaska. The Court thought that rewarding longevity of citizenship was "not a legitimate state purpose," because it interfered with the fundamental right of interstate mobility. Justice O'Connor concurred, but thought that the law should have been struck down as an unjustified interference with the privileges and immunities protected by Article IV, §2.

   (b) *Hooper v. Bernalillo County Assessor,* 472 U.S. 612 (1985). New Mexico granted a special tax exemption to Vietnam War veterans who were New Mexico residents as of a certain date. The exemption was not available to Vietnam War veterans who later became New Mexico residents. The law created " '*fixed, permanent distinctions* between . . . classes of concededly bona fide residents' based on when they arrived in the State."

   (c) *Metropolitan Life Insurance Co. v. Ward,* 470 U.S. 869 (1985). Alabama imposed much lower taxes on domestic insurance companies than on out-of-state companies liable to Alabama taxes. The Court invalidated the tax scheme, finding that "Alabama's aim to promote domestic industry is purely and completely discriminatory, designed only to favor domestic industry . . . , no matter what the cost to [outsiders, and] constitutes the very sort of parochial discrimination that the Equal Protection Clause was intended to prevent."

b. **Irrational and arbitrary legislation.** Even when the legislative objective is valid, the statute may be so arbitrary, or grossly at odds with its objective, as to fail minimal scrutiny.

   i. *Logan v. Zimmerman Brush Co.,* 455 U.S. 422 (1982). Illinois law prohibited discrimination against the handicapped, required an

administrative fact-finding hearing within 120 days of filing a claim
of discrimination, and extinguished the claim if a timely hearing
was not held. The purpose of the timely hearing rule was to expedite
dispute resolution. Through the state's negligence, a timely hearing
on Logan's claim was not held. As applied to Logan, the Court
invalidated the section destroying his claim. The Court called the
section "patently irrational." Terminating a claim because the state
acted negligently is not "a rational way of expediting the resolution
of disputes."

ii. *Allegheny Pittsburgh Coal Co. v. County Commission,* 488 U.S.
336 (1989). West Virginia's Constitution required that "taxation
shall be equal and uniform throughout the State, and all property
. . . shall be taxed in proportion to its value." A county assessor
nevertheless assessed newly purchased property at its market
value but did not increase assessments of property acquired
years earlier. The Court struck down the county assessor's
practice as not rationally related to the objective specified by
the West Virginia Constitution.

iii. *Nordlinger v. Hahn,* 505 U.S. 1 (1992). California's Constitution
requires that real property be assessed for taxation on the basis of
its purchase price, and sharply limits increases to such assessments.
Long time owners of real property have relatively low assessments
and taxes; new purchasers of nearly identical property have much
higher assessments and taxes. The Court applied minimal scrutiny
and upheld the law because it was rationally related to California's
objective of preserving neighborhood stability and protecting the
expectations of existing owners. The difference between *Nordlinger*
and *Allegheny Pittsburgh* lies in the different objectives of the state.
The classification in *Nordlinger* rationally served the state's objective; the practice in *Allegheny Pittsburgh* did not.

c. **"Enhanced" minimal scrutiny.** In some cases the Court purports to
apply minimal scrutiny and strikes down state laws, but in fact seems
to be applying a different test. Some say that the Court is really employing
"heightened" scrutiny—something more than minimal scrutiny—but
the Court often denies it is doing anything other than employing minimal
scrutiny. The trigger of "enhanced" minimal scrutiny is elusive. The
Court seems to apply a *gestalt* mode of reasoning—a montage of impres-
sions, hunches, and evaluations of state and individual interests. *Cleburne*
purports to apply minimal scrutiny and *Plyler* applies a unique test—
rationally related to a substantial state interest.

i. *City of Cleburne v. Cleburne Living Center,* 473 U.S. 432 (1985).
Cleburne Living Center was denied a special use permit needed
to operate a group home for the mentally retarded. The city's

zoning ordinance permitted hospitals, sanitariums, nursing or convalescent homes on the site, but excluded "hospitals for the feeble-minded" unless they received a special use permit. The Court reversed a lower court ruling that mental retardation was a "quasi-suspect" classification and explicitly stated that its standard of review was minimal scrutiny. The Court then ruled that denial of a special use permit violated equal protection. The city offered three objectives: (1) neighborhood fears of and hostility towards the mentally retarded, (2) the fact that the site was located in a "500 year flood plain," and (3) the size of the home and the number of occupants. The Court characterized the first objective as catering to "an irrational prejudice against the mentally retarded." While the other objectives were legitimate the Court regarded exclusion of the mentally retarded home, while simultaneously permitting other medical facilities, as so grossly under-inclusive as to be irrational. Justice Stevens concurred on the ground that the legislative objective was illegitimate. Justices Marshall, Brennan, and Blackmun concurred in the judgment but argued that the Cleburne zoning ordinance "surely would be valid under the traditional rational basis test applicable to economic and commercial regulation." Marshall noted that severe under-inclusion almost never results in invalidation of laws subject to minimal scrutiny, and contended that "something more than minimum rationality is at work here."

(a) **Critical analysis.** Since the Court tolerates extreme under-inclusion in minimal scrutiny cases, it is unclear why Cleburne's disfavorable treatment of the mentally retarded was less rational than New York's disfavorable treatment of ad-bearing trucks, or Oklahoma's disfavorable treatment of opticians. If Cleburne's objective was only to harm the mentally retarded, it had no *legitimate* objective. But the Court did not so hold. If Cleburne's other objectives were legitimate, perhaps the severity of the under-inclusion indicated to the Court that Cleburne's legitimate objectives were pretextual.

ii. *Plyler v. Doe,* 457 U.S. 202 (1982). A Texas statute denied free public education to children who were illegally present in the country. The Court held that the law violated equal protection.

(a) **The standard of review.** The Court, in an opinion by Justice Brennan, applied a unique version of minimal scrutiny in striking down the law. The Court required the classification to be *rationally related* to a *substantial,* rather than simply a legitimate, state interest and effectively shifted the burden of proof on this issue to Texas. The Court did *not* apply intermediate scrutiny, which would have obliged Texas to prove that its statutory classification was substantially related to an important state interest. The Court's justification for this "heightened," or just-a-bit-more-than-minimal scrutiny was that "certain forms of legislative classification, while not facially invidious, nonetheless give rise to recurring constitutional difficulties." Justice Blackmun, concurring, declared that "the State must offer something more than a rational basis for its classification" and noted that the Court's standard was a requirement that the statute "further some substantial goal of the State. . . . Since the statute fails to survive this level of scrutiny . . . there is no need to determine whether a more probing level of review would be appropriate." Justice Powell, concurring, noted that "[o]ur review . . . is properly heightened" and suggested that "[i]n these unique circumstances, the Court properly may require that the State's interests be substantial and that the means bear a 'fair and substantial relation' to these interests."

(b)   The rationale for "heightened" scrutiny. The Court required Texas to show that the provision at issue was *rationally related* to a *substantial* state interest or goal. In defending this heightened scrutiny Justice Brennan contended that "[o]nly when concerns sufficiently absolute and enduring can be clearly ascertained from the Constitution and our cases do we employ this standard to aid us in determining the rationality of the legislative choice." Brennan articulated two "sufficiently absolute and enduring" concerns that triggered heightened scrutiny in *Plyler:* (1) the fact that illegal status children acquire that status involuntarily, through the misconduct of their parents in entering and remaining illegally in the United States, and (2) "the importance of education . . . and the lasting impact of its deprivation on the life of the child." But the Court acknowledged that classification by illegal immigration status was legitimate, not suspect, and refused to characterize education as a fundamental right. Even so, the Court concluded that a legitimate classifying device that adversely affected a nonfundamental right must be subjected to "heightened" scrutiny. Texas's desire to devote its scarce educational resources to those legitimately residing in Texas was deemed an insufficiently substantial state interest. At bottom, the law failed because the Court considered it unwise: "In determining the rationality of [the Texas law], we . . . take into account its costs to the Nation and to the innocent children who are its victims. In light of these . . . costs," the

Court found the Texas statute irrational. Note that in *Clover Leaf Creamery,* supra, Justice Brennan, speaking for the Court, declared that "States are not required to convince the courts of the correctness of their legislative judgments" by empirical evidence.

C. MINIMAL SCRUTINY: SUMMATION

In applying minimal scrutiny keep the following points in mind:

- *Minimal Scrutiny Applies* unless the law involves a suspect or "quasi-suspect" classification or infringes a constitutionally fundamental right.

- *Any Conceivable Legitimate State Interest* will be hypothesized as the law's purpose. This is true even when the legislature has expressed a purpose. But occasionally courts insist on actual purpose.

- *The Rational Relationship of the Statutory Class to the Law's Purpose Need* ***Not*** *Be Proven Empirically.* So long as there is any conceivable basis to think that the law rationally serves its hypothesized purpose the Court will uphold it.

- *Be Aware of the Wild Card.* A particular classification, or combination of classification and objective, may sometimes trigger "enhanced" minimal scrutiny. This appears to occur under two conditions: (1) when the Court senses something not quite legitimate about the government's objective, but is unwilling to declare it illegitimate, or (2) when the Court thinks the classification is dubious, but is unwilling to call it suspect.

D. STRICT SCRUTINY AND SUSPECT CLASSIFICATIONS: RACE AND NATIONAL ORIGIN

Strict scrutiny is employed whenever the statutory classification is "suspect" or infringes upon a fundamental right. This section deals with the suspect classification prong, specifically as applied to racial classifications and their next of kin, ethnicity and national origin classifications.

1. Suspect Classifications

There are three suspect classifications—race, ethnicity or national origin, and lawfully resident alienage. All classifications by race or ethnicity trigger strict scrutiny; only *some* classifications on the basis of status as a lawfully resident alien trigger strict scrutiny.

a. Race. Racial classifications were the original problem that the equal protection clause was intended to address. The Court regards *all* racial classifications as suspect.

b. Ethnicity or national origin. Classifications by ethnicity or national origin are suspect. *Castenada v. Partida,* 430 U.S. 482 (1977).

c. **Lawfully resident aliens.** Some classifications that discriminate on the basis of one's status as a citizen or lawfully resident alien are suspect. In general, exclusions of lawfully resident aliens from voting or other participation in the "political community" are not suspect because states have a legitimate interest in limiting participation in the governance process to those who are truly within the political community. Also, the federal government has more constitutional power to regulate aliens, through its exclusive Article I, §8 powers over immigration and naturalization, than do the states. Thus, some regulations by states might trigger strict scrutiny while the same regulation imposed by the federal government would be subject to minimal scrutiny. (See section D.5, infra.)

d. **Wealth:** *Not* **a suspect classification.** For a period of time in the 1960s and 1970s the Court flirted with the idea of treating wealth classifications as suspect. The Court did take wealth classifications into account in finding some laws impeding access to voting or the judicial process violative of equal protection by infringing a fundamental right (see sections I.3 and I.5, infra) but eventually squarely rejected the idea of treating wealth classifications as suspect.

  i. *James v. Valtierra,* 402 U.S. 137 (1971). Article 34 of the California Constitution conditions development of any low-income public housing project upon voter approval in a referendum on the subject. The Court upheld the validity of Article 34 and refused to treat wealth classifications as suspect. Three Justices dissented, contending that Article 34 was "an explicit classification on the basis of poverty—a suspect classification which demands exacting judicial scrutiny."

  ii. *San Antonio Independent School District v. Rodriguez,* 411 U.S. 1 (1973). Texas financed its public schools through the local property tax, with the result that districts with an abundance of expensive property had greater resources for schools than districts with inexpensive property. The Court upheld the constitutionality of this system, again rejecting the invitation to treat wealth as a suspect classification.

2. Determining That a Classification Is Suspect

Because suspect classifications trigger strict scrutiny, the method by which the Court determines which classifications are suspect is of great importance.

a. **Invidious—wrongful—discrimination required.** Suspect classifications are classifications that immediately give rise to a presumption of invidious, or wrongful, discrimination. Discrimination *per se* is *not* suspect. Professors discriminate in grading; consumers discriminate in buying a new auto; people discriminate in finding a mate. It is only *wrongful* or *invidious* discrimination that is constitutionally significant. The Court has developed a calculus for determining when a statutory classification is presumptively invidiously discriminatory, and thus a suspect classification. This calculus is used sparingly. The Court is not quick to recognize new suspect classifications, probably because each new suspect classification presumptively invalidates a wide range of legislation. The Court is never eager to depart from its usual presumption that laws are constitutionally valid.

i. ***Carolene Products'* footnote four.** Justice Stone suggested the possibility that the following types of laws might "be subjected to more exacting judicial scrutiny":

- "[L]egislation which restricts those political processes which can obviously be expected to bring about repeal of undesirable legislation."

- "[S]tatutes directed at particular religions or national or racial minorities."

- Laws which are the product of "prejudice against discrete and insular minorities" and which tend "seriously to curtail the operation of those political processes ordinarily to be relied upon to protect minorities."

Stone's first concern was with the fairness of the democratic *process*, but the second and third concerns provide a partial basis for finding some legislative classifications to be suspect. In later years the Court has elaborated upon Stone's ideas by creating several factors to be used in assessing whether any given classification ought to be treated as suspect.

ii. **Immutable traits.** Legislation that classifies on the basis of an "immutable trait" is a candidate for suspect treatment. Immutable traits are those that cannot be changed and with which we are accidentally endowed, such as race or sex.

iii. **History of purposeful unequal treatment.** This factor is drawn partly from Stone's concern about prejudice, and partly from his concern for a fair process. When a particular group sharing an immutable trait has received purposefully unequal treatment for a long period, it is difficult to escape the conclusion that some prejudice is at the heart of that history. A history of purposeful unequal treatment and prejudice that blocks political redress of that treatment combine to render such classifications suspect.

iv. **Perennial lack of access to political power.** The mere lack of political power is not the issue. Nudists lack political power in

America, but that by itself does not make a law banning public nudity suspect. The issue is the perennial lack of political power coupled with a lack of any *access* to that power.

b. **Purposeful discrimination required.** In order for any particular legislative classification to be treated as suspect, it must be proven by the challenger that the law is *intentionally* discriminatory—its purpose is to employ the suspect criterion for classification. There are three ways to establish this.

    i. **Facially discriminatory.** If the suspect classification is on the face of the statute, it is facially discriminatory, as were the laws creating and enforcing racial segregation.

    ii. **Facially neutral, but applied discriminatorily.** If the law is facially neutral—classifies on some other basis than the suspect one—but is applied on a suspect basis it is treated as a suspect classification. The challenger has the burden of proving the suspect application of the law.

EXAMPLE AND ANALYSIS

A San Francisco ordinance forbade the operation of a laundry in anything but a brick or stone structure, except with the consent of the Board of Supervisors. Almost two-thirds of the 240 Chinese persons operating laundries were arrested for violation of the ordinance while eighty-odd laundries operated by Caucasians in wooden buildings were "left unmolested." The Court invalidated the ordinance because San Francisco had no justification for its invidiously discriminatory application of a facially neutral law. *Yick Wo v. Hopkins*, 118 U.S. 356 (1886).

    iii. **Product of a hidden discriminatory motive.** If a facially neutral classification can be proven by the challenger to be motivated, at least in part, by a suspect discriminatory motive, and that motive is not proven to have been irrelevant to the classification, it is treated as a suspect classification.

EXAMPLE AND ANALYSIS

By statute, the boundaries of Tuskegee, Alabama were redrawn from a square to an "uncouth twenty-eight sided figure." In the process about 99% of the black voters were eliminated from Tuskegee, while not a single white voter was removed. That was adequate proof of an unrebutted discriminatory motive, sufficient to trigger strict scrutiny. *Gomillion v. Lightfoot,* 364 U.S. 339 (1960).

---

   c. **Establishing purposeful discrimination.** Establishing *facial discrimination* is easy—it's either on the face of the law or it's not there. Establishing either discriminatory *application* or discriminatory *motive* is considerably more difficult. This subsection deals with these problems by examining racial classifications.

   i. **Facial discrimination:** *Strauder v. West Virginia,* 100 U.S. 303 (1879). Strauder, a black American, was convicted of murder by an all-white West Virginia jury. West Virginia law limited jury service to adult white males. The Court ruled that his conviction violated equal protection.

   ii. **Disparate impact not enough.** It is not enough to prove that a facially neutral law has a disproportionate racial impact.

      (a) *Washington v. Davis,* 426 U.S. 229 (1976). Applicants for the D.C. police force were required to take a qualifying examination and score at least forty out of eighty possible points. The test measured "verbal ability, vocabulary, reading and comprehension." Four times as many blacks as whites failed the test. The test was challenged as a violation of equal protection. The Court upheld its validity. The test was facially neutral and the challengers had failed to prove that the test was *purposefully* or *intentionally* discriminatory. The fact of its disparate impact, *by itself,* was not enough: "Disproportionate impact is not irrelevant, but . . . [s]tanding alone it does not trigger the rule that racial classifications are to be subjected to the strictest scrutiny." For that to occur there must be proof of *intentional discrimination:* either discriminatory application of the neutral law or an unrebutted discriminatory motivation to the law.

   iii. **Proving discriminatory intent.** There are a variety of evidentiary tools to prove discriminatory intent. The basic framework was explained by the Court in *Arlington Heights.*

      (a) *Arlington Heights v. Metropolitan Housing Development Corp.,* 429 U.S. 252 (1977). Housing Corporation requested Arlington Heights to rezone property to permit construction of low-income housing. Arlington Heights refused. Housing Corporation charged that the refusal was racially discriminatory and a violation of equal protection. The Court ruled that no equal protection violation had occurred because Housing Corporation had "simply failed to carry [its] burden of proving that discriminatory purpose was a *motivating factor* in [Arlington Heights'] decision." The Court opined that the determination of "whether discriminatory purpose was a motivating factor demands a sensitive inquiry into such circumstantial and direct evidence of intent as may be available." To do this the Court suggested the following items would be relevant:

- *Disparate impact* may "provide an important *starting point*" but rarely if ever will it be enough. **Example:** McCleskey, a black man, was convicted of murdering a white person and sentenced to death by a Georgia court. He challenged the death sentence as administered in a racially discriminatory manner. McCleskey's proof consisted of statistical evidence showing that defendants convicted of killing whites were four times more likely to receive a death sentence than defendants convicted of killing blacks. The Court concluded that McCleskey's evidence did "not demonstrate a constitutionally significant risk of racial bias affecting the Georgia capital-sentencing process." Moreover, McCleskey's statistical evidence of disparate impact did not "prove that the decision-makers in *his* case acted with discriminatory purpose." *McCleskey v. Kemp,* 481 U.S. 279 (1987). But note that sometimes the disparate impact is so pronounced, so overwhelming, that it produces "a clear pattern, unexplainable on grounds other than race." See *Gomillion v. Lightfoot,* supra.

- *Historical background* of the decision, particularly when there is a history of past intentional racial discrimination. **Example:** After *Brown v. Board of Education,* infra, Prince Edward County, Virginia, closed its public schools rather than desegregate them. The Court applied strict scrutiny and invalidated the closure because it was "for one reason . . . only: to ensure . . . that white and colored children . . . would not, under any circumstances, go to the same school." *Griffin v. County School Board,* 377 U.S. 218 (1964).

- "The *specific sequence of events* leading up to the challenged decision also may shed some light on the decisionmaker's purposes." **Example:** Suppose that the Washington, D.C., police force never used a written qualifying test for police applicants until significant numbers of blacks began to apply. The decision to begin testing at that point is relevant to whether there was intentional discrimination.

- *Departures from prior procedures* might indicate a racially biased decision. **Example:** Suppose that when Housing Corporation requested rezoning Arlington Heights changed the rules to require that all rezonings be approved by a voter referendum. That fact would be highly relevant to whether there was intentional discrimination.

- *Departures from prior substantive criteria for the decision* might also indicate an intentional discriminatory motive. **Example:** Suppose that Arlington Heights had always approved rezoning applications for multifamily constructions so long as the proposed density was less than a given maximum. If Arlington Heights denied rezoning to Housing Corporation even though its proposed density was less than the given maximum, that fact would be relevant to whether there was intentional discrimination.

- *Legislative or administrative history.* Legislators or administrators might leave a "smoking gun" in the legislative history, revealing a hidden intentionally discriminatory motive.

iv. **Discriminatory intent a "motivating factor."** It is *not necessary* that the challenger prove that intentional discrimination was the *sole reason* for the government action. It is sufficient that the challenger prove that such intentional discrimination was a *motivating factor* for the decision—simply *one of several motivations* for the governmental action. In *Arlington Heights* the Court stated that the rule of purposeful or intentional discrimination "does not require a plaintiff to prove that challenged action rested *solely* on racially discriminatory purposes. . . . [So long as] there is a proof that a discriminatory purpose has been a motivating factor in the decision, [minimal scrutiny] is no longer justified."

v. **Consequence of proving intentional discrimination as a "motivating factor": shifting burden of proof.** Once the challenger has proven that intentional discrimination was a "motivating factor" for the challenged action, the state has one last opportunity to avoid strict scrutiny. The state may negate the challenger's proof of an intentionally discriminatory motive if "by a preponderance of the evidence" the government can show "that it would have reached the same decision" if there had been no intentionally discriminatory motive. When the government meets this burden of proof, and thereby rebuts the challenger's proof of intentional discrimination, the governmental action is subjected to minimal scrutiny. *Strict scrutiny applies only if the challenger proves an intentionally discriminatory motive for facially neutral action and the government is unable to rebut that proof by showing that the action would have been taken anyway.* See *Mt. Healthy City School District Board of Education v. Doyle,* 429 U.S. 274 (1977) (proof that a teacher had been fired for exercising his free speech rights could be rebutted by proof that he would have been fired anyway).

3. Application and Effect of Strict Scrutiny

When strict scrutiny is applied its effect is almost always invalidation of the statute or action under consideration. Professor Gunther has characterized strict scrutiny as " 'strict' in theory and fatal in fact." (Gunther, 86 Harv. L. Rev. 1.)

a. **Racial classifications surviving strict scrutiny.** Strict scrutiny is not *always* fatal but there are very few instances in which the government is able to sustain its burden of proving that its challenged action is *necessary* to accomplish a *compelling government interest.*

    i. *Korematsu v. United States,* 323 U.S. 214 (1944). Fred Korematsu, an American of Japanese ancestry, was convicted of remaining at home in San Leandro, California, in violation of a 1942 military exclusion order that required all persons of Japanese ancestry to leave their homes and report for internment in guarded encampments in desolate parts of the American west. His conviction was upheld. The Court applied strict scrutiny since "legal restrictions which curtail the civil rights of a single racial group are immediately suspect." But the Court upheld the race-based exclusion on grounds of national emergency and reasonable military necessity. Justice Jackson, dissenting, argued that by accepting claimed military necessity as an adequate justification "we may as well say that any military order will be constitutional and have done with it." The Court's opinion, charged Jackson, "is a far more subtle blow to liberty than the . . . [exclusion] order itself. . . . [O]nce a judicial opinion rationalizes . . . the Constitution to show that the Constitution sanctions such an order, the Court for all time has validated the principle of racial discrimination. . . . The principle then lies about like a loaded weapon ready for the hand of any authority that can bring forward a plausible claim of an urgent need." Today, virtually everyone agrees that *Korematsu* was wrongly decided in that the government had neither adequately proven its compelling purpose for exclusion of Japanese-Americans from the West Coast nor established that this wholesale exclusion was necessary for any legitimate and compelling national security reasons the government might in fact have had. Fred Korematsu's conviction was vacated by a federal district court in 1984 after he proved that the United States had lied to the Court in 1944 in order to justify the exclusion order.

  ii. √ **To remedy past constitutional violations:** *Swann v. Charlotte-Mecklenburg Board of Education,* 402 U.S. 1 (1971), discussed in detail, infra. In prior litigation it had been determined that the Charlotte, North Carolina, schools had maintained an explicitly racially segregated school system in violation of the equal protection clause. When that has been determined, federal courts are free to order explicitly race-conscious remedies, such as race-based pupil placement and race-based busing.

  iii. **Prison security:** *Lee v. Washington,* 390 U.S. 333 (1968). In an opinion in which the Court invalidated Alabama's racially segregated prison system the Court reserved decision on the question whether racial separation of prisoners might be valid in instances of extreme racial tension or racial violence among prisoners.

  iv. **Vital statistics:** *Tancil v. Woolls,* 379 U.S. 19 (1964). The Court summarily affirmed, without opinion, a ruling that obtaining and recording racial information as part of the maintenance of vital statistics did not violate the equal protection clause.

  v. √ **Affirmative action:** *Adarand Constructors, Inc. v. Pena,* 515 U.S. 200 (1995), discussed in detail, infra. The Court concluded that "*all* racial classifications . . . must be analyzed by a reviewing court under strict scrutiny." The Court added some suggestive *dicta:* "The unhappy persistence of both the practice and the lingering effects of racial discrimination in this country is an unfortunate reality, and government is not disqualified from acting in response to it. [When] race-based action is necessary to further a compelling interest, such action is within constitutional constraints if it satisfies the 'narrow tailoring' test."

b. **Purportedly neutral suspect classifications.** When statutes use race as a classifying device it is futile for a government to contend that the law is neutral because the law applies equally to all races.

  i. √ *Loving v. Virginia,* 388 U.S. 1 (1967). Virginia prohibited interracial marriage. The Lovings, a married couple consisting of a black woman and white man, were convicted of violating the statute.

The Court applied strict scrutiny and struck down the law. Virginia contended that because the statute penalized blacks and whites equally for marrying one another the law was not racially discriminatory. The Court rejected this so-called equal application theory, ruling that racial classifications must "be subjected to the 'most rigid scrutiny.' " Justice Stewart concurred on the ground that "it is simply not possible for a state law to be valid under our Constitution which makes the criminality of an act depend upon the race of the actor."

ii. *Anderson v. Martin,* 375 U.S. 399 (1964). Louisiana's election law required that each candidate's race be designated on nomination papers and ballots. Louisiana defended the law against an equal protection challenge by arguing that it was race-neutral since it applied equally to everyone, no matter what race they might be. The Court rejected that argument, noting that the law "direct[ed] the citizen's attention to the single consideration of race or color" and thus violated the principle of *race-neutrality* or *color-blindness* that is at the heart of treating racial classifications as suspect. The Court applied strict scrutiny and voided the law.

c. **Race and the political process.** When governments take action that makes race relevant to the political process their actions are subjected to strict scrutiny. It is easy to employ strict scrutiny when race is explicitly made relevant. The harder job is to decide which race-neutral changes to the political process are so motivated by intentional racial discrimination that strict scrutiny must be employed in evaluating their validity.

i. *Reitman v. Mulkey,* 387 U.S. 369 (1967). California voters amended the state constitution by adding section 26, which prohibited the state from interfering with "the right of any person . . . to decline to sell, lease or rent [his real] property to such person or persons as he, in his absolute discretion, chooses." The Court subjected section 26 to strict scrutiny and invalidated it because it "was intended to authorize, and does authorize, racial discrimination in the housing market." The Court suggested that there was no "constitutional barrier to the *repeal of an existing law* prohibiting racial discriminations in housing." Similarly, California could "put in statutory form an existing policy of neutrality with respect to private discriminations." California had not simply repealed existing statutes that prohibited private racial discrimination, but had altered the *process* by which the state formulated its policies on private racial discrimination. Prior to adoption of section 26, proponents and opponents of state neutrality toward private racial discrimination were both able to obtain their desired outcome through the legislative process. After section 26, opponents of state neutrality were required to amend the state constitution to obtain their desired outcome. Alteration of the process *by itself* did not trigger strict scrutiny; it was the process alteration coupled with circumstantial evidence that the motive for doing so was to make "[t]he right to discriminate . . . one of the basic policies of the State" that triggered strict scrutiny. Note that *Reitman* expressly stated that "the State was not bound by the Federal Constitution to forbid [private racial discrimination]." But in the absence of an adequate justification California was forbidden from altering its political process specially to protect the right to practice private racial discrimination.

ii. *Hunter v. Erickson,* 393 U.S. 385 (1969). Akron, Ohio, voters amended the city charter to deprive the city council of power to adopt any ordinance addressing racial, religious, or ancestral discrimination in housing without approval of the voters through a referendum. The Court subjected the amendment to strict scrutiny because it (1) altered the political process by adding a unique obstacle to adoption of housing discrimination laws in Akron, (2) was motivated by a desire to insulate private racial discrimination from governmental action, and (3) had a disparate impact on racial minorities by deliberately disadvantaging them—"The majority needs no protection against discrimination."

iii. *Washington v. Seattle School District,* 458 U.S. 457 (1982). Shortly after the Seattle public schools began mandatory busing to produce "racial balance" in the schools Washington voters approved Initiative 350, which barred local school boards from requiring students to attend schools other than one of the two closest to their residence. Initiative 350 contained several exceptions to that pupil assignment rule, to address overcrowding, special educational needs, and to permit racial assignments when required by the Constitution. The Court applied strict scrutiny because "despite its facial neutrality there is little doubt that the initiative was effectively drawn for racial purposes." The Court elaborated: "[T]he political majority may . . . restructure the political process to place obstacles in the path of everyone seeking to secure the benefits of governmental action. But a different analysis is required when the State allocates governmental power non-neutrally, by explicitly using the *racial nature* of a decision to determine the decisionmaking process." Because Washington had failed to prove adequate justification for Initiative 350, the Court, 5 to 4, struck down the law. The dissenters argued that in fact no alteration of the political process had occurred, because the actions of the Seattle school district, as well as all other local school districts, were *always* subject to statewide legislative control. The dissenters also pointed out that the action that prompted Initiative 350—Seattle's adoption of race-based pupil assignment—was not *required* by the federal Constitution and could have been rescinded at any time by Seattle's school board.

iv. *Crawford v. Board of Education,* 458 U.S. 527 (1982). California courts ordered busing of students to achieve racial balance in public schools. These orders were *not* compelled by the federal Constitution, but were compelled by California's state constitution. California voters then amended the state constitution to provide that "state courts shall not order mandatory pupil assignment or transportation unless a federal court would do so to remedy a violation of the Equal Protection Clause." The Court, 8 to 1, found no violation of equal protection. Strict scrutiny was not applicable because the amendment did not "embody a racial classification, . . . distort[] the political process for racial reasons," nor did it "allocate[] governmental or judicial power on the basis of a discriminatory principle." Rather, it changed the substantive law of California on a race-neutral basis and did not alter the political process. Prior to the amendment advocates of busing were free to seek judicial orders to that effect under the state constitution; after the amendment advocates of busing were still free to do so, although their ability to obtain such orders was restricted by the substantive change to the state constitution. But, said the Court, "the mere repeal of race related legislation is [not] unconstitutional."

d. **Race and private biases.** The Court has sent mixed signals concerning its standard of review of government actions that cater to privately held and exercised racial biases. When governments openly embrace private racial prejudice as the basis for their action strict scrutiny will apply. When governments employ race-neutral criteria for actions that cater to private racial prejudice the Court is less willing to use strict scrutiny without additional proof of intentional racial discrimination.

i. **Open embrace of private bias:** *Palmore v. Sidoti,* 466 U.S. 429 (1984). A white divorced father sought custody of his three-year-old daughter from his white ex-wife after her marriage to a black man. A state judge ruled that the best interests of the child warranted the custody change, because "despite the strides that have been made in bettering [race] relations . . . it is inevitable that [the girl] will . . . suffer from . . . social stigmatization." The Court ruled that it was impermissible to take private racial bias into account in deciding what was in the best interests of the child: "The Constitution cannot control such prejudices but neither can it tolerate them. Private biases may be outside the reach of the law, but the law cannot, directly or indirectly, give them effect."

The Court, in essence, laid down a rule that open adoption of private racial prejudice by governments as the reason for some governmental action is *per se* invalid.

ii. **Facially neutral embrace of private bias:** *Palmer v. Thompson,* 403 U.S. 217 (1971). Jackson, Mississippi, closed its public swimming pools after a federal judge had ordered them to be desegregated. The Court upheld the validity of the closure. The closure, said the Court, affected all races equally and had been motivated by the city council's determination that operation of racially integrated swimming pools would be uneconomic, not out of an intent to discriminate on racial lines. Jackson's decision was not subject to strict scrutiny simply because one of the motives for it was "ideological opposition to racial integration." Perhaps additional proof of Jackson's intent to act in a racially discriminatory manner would have persuaded the Court to apply strict scrutiny, but even on the record before the Court it is apparent that the city council's belief that integrated swimming pools would be uneconomic is rooted in acceptance of private racial bias. *Palmore* undercuts *Palmer* but does not overrule it. *Palmer* is still good law insofar as a government makes a racially neutral decision within its area of presumptive competence. In such a case, the challenger must produce evidence that the government acted with the intent to discriminate.

e. **Official racial segregation.** Much of the modern law of equal protection pertaining to race has been developed in confronting the American practice of official racial segregation.

i. **Separate but equal:** *Plessy v. Ferguson,* 163 U.S. 537 (1896). Louisiana required railroads to provide "equal but separate accommodations for the white and colored races" and subjected passengers who used the wrong accommodations to criminal liability. Plessy refused to leave the "whites only" coach and was subsequently convicted under the law. The Court upheld his conviction. Even though "[t]he object of [equal protection] was undoubtedly to enforce the absolute equality of the two races before the law," this did not "abolish distinctions based on color," or operate "to enforce social, as distinguished from political, equality," nor did it require "commingling of the two races upon terms unsatisfactory to either." Louisiana's law was found "reasonable, . . . enacted in good faith for the promotion of the public good, and not for the annoyance or oppression of a particular class. . . . [Louisiana was] at liberty to act with reference to the established usages, customs, and traditions of the people, and with a view to the promotion of their comfort, and the preservation of the public peace and good order." The Court said it was an "assumption that the enforced separation of the two races stamps the colored race with a badge of inferiority. If this be so, it is . . . solely because the colored race chooses to put that construction upon it." *Plessy* established the doctrine of "separate but equal" as a reigning principle of equal protection law concerning racial classifications, and that principle was not overturned until *Brown v. Board of Education* in 1954.

ii. **Separate *and unequal:* the years from *Plessy* to *Brown*.** During the 56 years between *Plessy* and *Brown* the doctrine of separate but equal was undermined, as the Court found a variety of specific practices to be both separate *and* unequal.

(a) ***Missouri ex rel. Gaines v. Canada,*** 305 U.S. 337 (1938). Missouri law required racially separate education. The white university system included a law school; the black system did not. Missouri law authorized payment of reasonable tuition at out-of-state law schools to enable black students to attend law school. Gaines, a black man, wanted to attend the University of Missouri's law school, not one somewhere else. The Court found Missouri's scheme to be a violation of the "equal" prong of separate but equal. "The basic consideration is not . . . what sort of opportunities other states provide, or whether they are as good as those in Missouri, but . . . what opportunities Missouri itself furnishes to white students and denies to negroes solely upon the ground of color."

(b) ***Sweatt v. Painter,*** 339 U.S. 629 (1950). The University of Texas refused to admit Sweatt, a black, to its law school on the ground that a public "blacks-only" law school was available. The Court found Texas's refusal a denial of equal protection because the black institution was quantitatively and qualitatively inferior.

(c) ***McLaurin v. Oklahoma State Regents,*** 339 U.S. 637 (1950). The University of Oklahoma admitted McLaurin, a black, to its education school but made him sit in a special seat in a classroom reserved for blacks, gave him a special table in the library, and barred him from eating with white students in the cafeteria. While McLaurin enjoyed the same physical facilities as whites the Court found the arrangement unequal because it impaired and inhibited "his ability to study, to engage in discussions and exchange views with other students, and, in general, to learn his profession."

iii. **Separate is *not* equal: *Brown v. Board of Education (Brown I),*** 347 U.S. 483 (1954). The Court overturned *Plessy,* repudiating the separate but equal doctrine. The Court ruled that official racial segregation in public schools violated equal protection. "Separate educational facilities are inherently unequal." The Court admitted that history and original intentions were "inconclusive," but grounded its conclusion in the importance of education and its perception that racially segregated schools produced a "detrimental" and stigmatizing effect on racial minorities.

iv. *Brown II:* **early implementation of** *Brown I.* In *Brown II,* 349 U.S. 294 (1955), the Court was faced with the issue of what remedy *Brown I* required. If the essential rationale for *Brown I*'s repudiation of *Plessy* was the stigma of officially mandated racial segregation, a color-blind pupil assignment plan would presumably suffice as a remedy. But if *Brown I* was based on the belief that equality requires racial integration, a different remedy might be in order. The Court avoided a direct decision of these issues by remanding the cases to the trial courts with directions to use "equitable principles" in considering the many practical problems associated with "a transition to a racially nondiscriminatory school system." Lower courts were told "to take such proceedings and enter such orders and decrees . . . as are necessary and proper to admit . . . the parties to these cases . . . to public schools on a racially nondiscriminatory basis with *all deliberate speed.*" This direction produced a spate of later cases.

(a) √ **Closing the public schools invalidated:** *Griffin v. County School Board,* 377 U.S. 218 (1964). Prince Edward County, Virginia, opted to close its public schools rather than desegregate them. Blacks went without public education while whites attended private schools partially supported by state tuition grants and property tax credits. The Court found the closure to be a violation of equal protection. While there is no constitutional requirement that a state provide public education, the Court found that the closure was "for one reason . . . only: to ensure . . . that white and colored children . . . would not, under any circumstances, go to the same school."

(b) √ **"Freedom of choice" plan invalidated:** *Green v. County School Board,* 391 U.S. 430 (1968). A formerly segregated school district with two schools, approximately equal numbers of black and white students, and little residential segregation adopted a freedom of choice plan that permitted students to choose the school they wished to attend upon entering the system. After three years the formerly all-black school was still all-black and the formerly all-white school was about 85% white. The Court invalidated this plan because the movement toward a "unitary school system" was too slow—too deliberate, and with not enough speed. The "burden on a school board . . . is to come forward with a plan that promises realistically to work, and promises realistically to work *now.*"

v.   **Remedial power to dismantle segregation.** As *Brown I* slowly began to be implemented the Court was forced to confront ever larger questions concerning the power of federal courts to order remedial action designed to dismantle officially segregated school systems.

(a) ✓ *Swann v. Charlotte-Mecklenburg Board of Education,* 402 U.S. 1 (1971). Charlotte initially desegregated its public schools by adopting a court-approved geographic zoning plan coupled with "freedom of choice" transfers. This left over half the black students attending schools that were nearly 100% black. After *Green* the federal district court ordered racially gerrymandered districts and racially based busing of students. The Court upheld the trial court's order on four separate issues dealing with pupil assignment.

- *Racial Quotas:* The Court stated that a district judge *lacked power to order racial quotas,* but the trial judge had used "mathematical ratios [as] no more than a starting point in the process of shaping a remedy."

- *One-Race Schools:* A "small number of . . . virtually one-race schools . . . is not in and of itself the mark of [an officially segregated] system" but does impose on the school district "the burden of showing that [the one-race schools are] not the result of present or past discriminatory action on their part."

- *Racial Gerrymandering:* "Absent a constitutional violation there would be no basis for judicially ordering assignment of students on a racial basis." But Charlotte had violated the Constitution, and "[t]he objective is to dismantle the dual school system." Accordingly, "[a]s an *interim corrective measure*" racial gerrymandering was within "the broad remedial power of a court."

- *Busing for Racial Balance:* Given the past constitutional violations of Charlotte, "reasonable, feasible and workable" busing for racial reasons was a permissible remedy that a trial judge could employ to dismantle the segregated school system.

(b) √ *Milliken v. Bradley,* 418 U.S. 717 (1974). After a judicial finding that the Detroit schools had been unconstitutionally racially segregated a federal district court ordered fifty-three suburban school districts to participate in the desegregation of the Detroit public schools through interdistrict busing and other pupil assignment methods. The Court reversed the order, finding it beyond the court's equitable powers. The Supreme Court ruled that "the scope of the remedy is determined by the nature and extent of the constitutional violation." Because there was no proof that any of the suburban school districts had ever operated racially segregated schools in violation of the Constitution they were immune from the trial court's equitable power to remedy Detroit's violations of the Constitution. In short, trial courts have broad power to remedy past constitutional violations but no power to impose remedies on those who have not been proven to have violated the Constitution.

vi. √ **Northern segregation:** *Keyes v. School District No. 1,* 413 U.S. 189 (1973). *Brown I* did not consider the question of whether de facto racial segregation—occurring without legal compulsion—was a constitutional violation. *Keyes* was the first case in which the Court faced this issue. A federal district court concluded that Denver had deliberately maintained segregated schools in the Park Hill section through gerrymandered school zones but limited relief to the Park Hill section rather than systemwide. The Court reversed and remanded to the district court.

- *Prima Facie Case:* To make out a *prima facie* case of unconstitutional de facto segregation, the challengers must prove (1) the de facto segregation *and* (2) that the de facto segregation occurred through *intentional state action.* "[W]here no statutory dual system [of segregated schools] has ever existed, plaintiffs must prove not only that *segregated schooling exists* but also that it was *brought about or maintained by intentional state action.*"

- *Effect of Prima Facie Case:* Proof of a prima facie case *as to any part of a school system* "creates a presumption that other segregated schooling within the system is not adventitious." The school system has the "burden of proving that other segregated schools within the system are not also the result of intentionally segregative actions." To sustain that burden of proof, school officials must show either (1) that "*segregative intent was **not** among the factors that motivated their actions,*" or (2) "*that its past segregative acts did not create* *or contribute to the current segregated condition* of the core city schools.''

vii. **Unitary school systems: terminating court control of formerly segregated schools.** The Court has begun to confront the question of when the vestiges of past unlawful racial segregation have been so eliminated that federal judicial control of the schools must end.

(a) *Board of Education of Oklahoma City Public Schools v. Dowell,* 498 U.S. 237 (1991). Prior to 1954 Oklahoma City maintained a de jure racially segregated school system. In 1961 a lawsuit was brought to alter the system. In 1963 the district court ordered changes to the school system. In 1972 the court ordered system-wide busing for racial balance. In 1977, satisfied that Oklahoma City had achieved a unitary school system, the district court terminated the case and ended its jurisdiction. In 1984, responding to arguments that the pupil assignment scheme placed ''greater burdens on young black children'' the school board introduced a neighborhood school plan for grades K-4, coupled with an option to transfer from any school where the student is in the racial majority to any school in which the student would be part of a racial minority. The district court denied a motion to reopen the case and the Supreme Court upheld the dismissal.

- *Judicial Control Is "Transitional":* ''From the very first, federal supervision of local school systems was intended as a *temporary measure* to remedy past discrimination.'' Judicial control is part of the transition to a unitary system. ''[I]njunctions entered in school desegregation cases [are] not intended to operate in perpetuity.''

- *Judicial Control Ends When the Violation Is Remedied:* ''[A] federal court's regulatory control of [school] systems [may] not extend beyond the time required to remedy the effects of past intentional discrimination.'' Unitary status is achieved and judicial control should cease when (1) all ''vestiges of past discrimination'' have been removed and (2) the schools are in ''good faith compliance'' with any existing court orders.

(b) *Freeman v. Pitts,* 503 U.S. 467 (1992). The Court affirmed a district court's partial termination of judicial supervision of the De Kalb County, Georgia, schools. The district court concluded that De Kalb County's schools were unitary insofar as pupil assignment and physical facilities were concerned even though there was significant racial imbalance attributable to demographic changes since the court's initial remedial order, and so terminated its jurisdiction over pupil assignment and physical facilities. The Court ruled that partial termination of jurisdiction was appropriate and clarified the meaning of *Dowell*'s insistence on removal of all vestiges of past discrimination as a precondition to unitary status. "The vestiges of segregation that are the concern of the law in a school case . . . must . . . have a causal link to the de jure violation being remedied." But "resegregation [that] is a product not of state action but of private choices . . . does not have constitutional implications."

f. **Affirmative action.** *Strict scrutiny* applies to *all racial classifications* employed by governments—federal, state, or local. It does not matter that the classification is allegedly "benign." All racial classifications, including those undertaken by governments for purposes of "affirmative action"—voluntary provision of beneficial treatment to historically disadvantaged minorities—must surmount the hurdle of strict scrutiny.

   i. **States:** *Richmond v. J. A. Croson Co.,* 488 U.S. 469 (1989). Richmond, Virginia, adopted a "set-aside" program, by which general contractors on city construction projects were required to subcontract at least 30% of the contract amount to businesses owned and controlled by "Blacks, Spanish-speaking [persons], Orientals, Indians, Eskimos, or Aleuts." The Court applied strict scrutiny and voided the program.

   • *Strict scrutiny applies* no matter which race is "burdened or benefited by a particular [racial] classification." To do otherwise would "effectively assure[] that race will always be relevant to American life, and that the 'ultimate goal' of 'eliminat[ing]' entirely from governmental decisionmaking such irrelevant factors as a human being's race' . . . will never be achieved." Moreover, there is no principled way to distinguish "benign" racial discrimination from malignant racial discrimination. All racial discrimination is equally suspect.

   • *Richmond's plan failed strict scrutiny* for two reasons: (1) there was inadequate proof that Richmond's objective—overcoming past discrimination in the construction industry—was "compelling" and (2) the racial set-aside was not narrowly tailored to accomplish Richmond's objective, even assuming it to be compelling.

- *Richmond's objective was not compelling* because there was no proof of specific unlawful racial discrimination in which Richmond had played a part, even as minor a part as passive participation. Proof of amorphous "societal discrimination" was insufficient: "To accept Richmond's claim that past societal discrimination alone can serve as a basis for rigid racial preferences would . . . open the door to competing claims for 'remedial relief' for every disadvantaged group. The dream of a Nation of equal citizens in a society where race is irrelevant to personal opportunity and achievement would be lost in a mosaic of shifting preferences based on inherently unmeasurable claims of past wrongs."

- *Richmond's set-aside plan was not narrowly tailored* to accomplish its objective. There were a variety of race-neutral means available to Richmond to spur the award of public construction contracts to racial minorities. Moreover, "the 30% quota cannot be said to be narrowly-tailored to any goal, except perhaps outright racial balancing."

- *Richmond could act "to rectify the effects of identified discrimination"* within Richmond, so long as that discrimination is specifically identified and proven. But even then, a racial preference would have to surmount strict scrutiny.

ii. ✓ **Federal government: *Adarand Constructors, Inc. v. Pena,* 515 U.S. 200 (1995).** Racial preferences employed by the federal government are also subject to strict scrutiny. The Court ruled that strict scrutiny applied to a federal program that delivered advantages on federal contracts to "socially and economically disadvantaged individuals." Certain racial and ethnic groups were conclusively presumed to be socially disadvantaged and rebuttably presumed to be economically disadvantaged. Adarand, which lost out on a federal contract to a racial minority contractor even though it was the low bidder, charged that the preference given its rival violated equal protection. The Court applied strict scrutiny to the racially based preference system, restating the reasons for strict scrutiny of racial classifications:

- *There is no principled way to distinguish benign racial preferences from malign ones.*

- *Racial classifications create or maintain racial consciousness,*

- *The equal protection clause "protect[s] persons, not groups."* Evaluating racial classifications differently, depending on which racial group is burdened or benefited, is anathema to that principle.

Concurring, Justice Scalia stated his view that "government can never have a 'compelling interest' in discriminating on the basis of race in order to 'make up' for past racial discrimination in the opposite direction. Individuals who have been wronged by unlawful racial discrimination should be made whole; but under our Constitution there can be no such thing as either a creditor or debtor race."

Subjecting *all* racial preferences to strict scrutiny does not necessarily mean that affirmative action programs are unconstitutional. Some racial preferences undertaken for compelling reasons may survive strict scrutiny. Affirmative action programs that employ some nonsuspect criteria as the basis for preference may be subject to minimal scrutiny. In general, naked racial preferences are valid when they are employed to *make whole an individual victim of unlawful racial discrimination*. It is far less likely that any government can sustain its burden of overcoming strict scrutiny with respect to naked racial preferences that are employed to benefit entire groups in compensation for a societal history of past wrongs. After *Croson* and *Adarand* the use of racial preferences as a form of "reparations" is probably dead.

iii. ✓ **"Race as a factor":** *Regents of the University of California v. Bakke,* 438 U.S. 265 (1978). Before *Adarand* and *Croson* this was the leading case on race-based affirmative action. UC Davis's medical school admitted 100 persons each year into its entering class. Sixteen of those places were reserved exclusively for "Blacks, Chicanos, Asians, and American Indians" and admission decisions for those sixteen spots were considered separately from general admissions. UC Davis had no demonstrated history of unlawful racial discrimination in admissions. Bakke, a white man, had been rejected twice for admission to UC Davis's medical school although on both occasions the medical school had accepted minority applicants in its special admissions program with significantly poorer qualifications. The Court affirmed the California Supreme Court's determination that UC Davis's special admissions program was unlawful, but could not produce a majority opinion.

Four Justices (Burger, Rehnquist, Stewart, and Stevens) found the program to be a violation of Title VI of the 1964 Civil Rights Act, which bars racial discrimination by educational institutions receiving federal aid. Accordingly, they did not reach the constitutional issue.

Four Justices (Brennan, White, Marshall, and Blackmun) thought that the UC Davis program violated neither Title VI nor the Constitution. They read Title VI to forbid only those uses of race that would violate equal protection if employed by a state, and argued that some racial classifications ought to be subjected to something less than strict scrutiny.

Justice Powell effectively controlled the Court's decision. First, Powell concluded that an explicit racial preference (or quota, which UC Davis used) must be subjected to strict scrutiny and found that UC Davis had not proven sufficient justification for its racial quota. Powell conceded that UC Davis's goal of "attainment of a diverse student body" was a compelling interest but thought that UC Davis could easily have utilized more narrowly drawn means to achieve that end. To Powell, UC Davis's exclusive focus on race "would hinder rather than further attainment of genuine diversity." However, Powell thought that it was a permissible means to attaining diversity to "take race into account." Thus, for Powell *explicit racial quotas* were a forbidden means to a compelling end, but *use of race as a "factor"* was permissible. Powell asserted that treating race as a "plus" did not make race the determinative factor as did UC Davis's explicit racial quota.

(a) **The meaning of *Bakke* today.** *Bakke's* importance has been much diminished by *Adarand* and *Croson*. It may no longer be permissible to employ race as a "plus" factor in admissions to public schools and universities. In *Hopwood v. University of Texas,* 78 F.3d 932 (5th Cir. 1996), cert. denied, 518 U.S. 1033 (1996), the Fifth Circuit ruled that the University of Texas Law School "may not use race as a factor in law school admissions" but the Ninth Circuit reached the opposite conclusion in *Smith v. University of Washington,* 233 F.3d 1188 (9th Cir. 2000), cert. denied, 2001 U.S. LEXIS 4011.

iv. **Eliminating past unlawful discrimination.** It is permissible to use race explicitly if it is a necessary remedy for proven wrongful racial discrimination.

(a) **Ending official school segregation.** Recall that the Court approved the explicit use of race in order to dismantle segregated school systems. But even in this context, the Court limited the use of naked racial remedies to the specific constitutional violation: "[T]he scope of the remedy is determined by the nature and extent of the constitutional violation." *Milliken v. Bradley,* supra.

(b) **Employment discrimination—layoffs:** *Wygant v. Jackson Board of Education,* 476 U.S. 267 (1986). In 1969, when blacks constituted 4% of the teachers in the Jackson, Michigan, public schools, the NAACP complained that Jackson's schools were racially discriminatory in teacher hiring. Jackson settled the complaint by agreeing to take "affirmative steps" to hire minority teachers. In two years minority teachers composed nearly 9% of the work force but economic conditions mandated layoffs of some teachers. The school board and the teachers' union agreed that teachers would be dismissed in inverse order of seniority, except that the proportion of minority teachers dismissed would not exceed the total proportion of minority teachers in the work force prior to the layoffs. The use of this racial criterion resulted in the dismissal of some white teachers who had greater seniority than black teachers who were retained. The Court found the racially preferential layoff provision violated equal protection, but could not form a majority as to the reasons. The plurality opinion applied strict scrutiny, concluded that "societal discrimination alone is [not] sufficient to justify a racial classification," and noted that "the Court has insisted upon some showing of prior discrimination by the governmental unit involved before allowing limited use of racial classifications in order to remedy such discrimination." Even if Jackson had proven prior discrimination on its part in teacher *hiring,* the plurality concluded that racially preferential *firings* were not sufficiently necessary to the remedial goal to survive strict scrutiny.

(c) **Employment discrimination—hiring:** *Local 28, Sheet Metal Workers v. EEOC,* 478 U.S. 421 (1986). A federal district court determined that Local 28 had violated Title VII of the 1964 Civil Rights Act by racial discrimination in admitting new union members. The court ordered Local 28 to set aside a portion of its new admissions for racial minorities. The Supreme Court applied strict scrutiny and rejected the union's contention that racial preferences could not validly be extended to persons who were not individually identified victims of the union's past racial discrimination. Given the union's past unlawful discrimination in admission of new union members, the Court thought the quota was sufficiently narrowly tailored to the compelling governmental interest of remedying Local 28's past unlawful action. Critical to this conclusion was the fact that the remedial quota for new hiring "did not disadvantage *existing* union members."

(d) *United States v. Paradise,* **480 U.S. 92 (1987).** A federal district court determined that Alabama had violated equal protection by refusing to hire blacks for its state police force. Twelve years later Alabama had done little to alter the racial composition of its state police except at the entry level.

The district judge then ordered that 50% of all promotions be awarded to qualified black candidates. The order was challenged and upheld by the Supreme Court. In a plurality opinion the Court applied strict scrutiny. The government's interest in erasing continuing unlawful racial discrimination by Alabama was compelling. The means used—the racial promotion quota—was narrowly tailored to the objective. The plurality found the following factors as relevant to determining the closeness of that fit:

- The *"necessity for the relief."* The more needed the relief, the more likely it is narrowly tailored.

- The *"efficacy of alternative remedies."* The lack of efficacious alternatives made this remedy necessary. Adequate alternatives that do not use naked racial preferences would render the remedy unnecessary.

- The *"flexibility and duration of the relief, including the availability of waiver provisions."* Rigid, permanent racial hiring quotas are not narrowly tailored, but a temporary, transitional race-based remedy addressed to identified past unlawful behavior is acceptable.

- The *"relationship of the numerical goals to the relevant labor market."* If the racial hiring quota is unrealistic in relation to the labor market it is not narrowly drawn. Recall *Croson*—the Court thought that Richmond's 30% racial set-aside for public contracts bore no relationship to the proportion of contractors who were minority enterprises.

- The *"impact of the relief on the rights of third parties."* As suggested by *Wygant* and *Local 28,* racial quotas that take jobs away from people who presently hold them are not likely to be regarded as sufficiently necessary, but setting aside a portion of new jobs has a less obvious impact on third parties.

v. **Racially based voting districts.** The validity of electoral district boundaries is presumed, but when a challenger proves "that *race was the **predominant factor** motivating the legislature*" in drawing district boundaries that presumption is overcome. *Strict scrutiny* then applies and the government has the burden of proving sufficient justification for racially based districting.

(a) *Shaw v. Reno,* 509 U.S. 630 (1993). North Carolina created two "majority-minority" districts for the federal House of Representatives. Majority-minority districts are, as the name implies, districts in which a majority of the voters are of a racial minority. The districts were challenged as violative of equal protection and the Court concluded that the challenge stated a claim. When electoral district boundaries "cannot rationally be understood as anything other than an effort to separate voters into different districts on the basis of race, and that . . . separation lacks sufficient justification" equal protection is violated. Strict scrutiny applies once a "racial gerrymander" has been proven. The Court stated that no particular evidence was necessary to proof of a racial gerrymander but suggested that the following factors were useful indicators, though not constitutionally required:

- "Bizarre" boundaries, coupled with a concentration of voters by race.

- Disregard of "traditional districting principles, such as compactness, contiguity, and respect for political subdivisions," coupled with a concentration of voters by race.

(b) *Miller v. Johnson,* 515 U.S. 900 (1995). Georgia created three majority-black districts for the United States House of Representatives. The districts were challenged as racial gerrymanders invalid under the equal protection clause. The Court applied strict scrutiny and declared the districts unconstitutional. "The plaintiff's burden is to show, either through circumstantial evidence of a district's shape and demographics or more direct evidence going to legislative purpose, that race was the predominant factor motivating the legislature's decision to place a significant number of voters within or without a particular district. To make this showing, a plaintiff must prove that the legislature subordinated traditional race-neutral districting principles, including but not limited to compactness, contiguity, respect for political subdivisions or communities defined by actual shared interests, to racial considerations.''

(c) **Racial "vote-dilution":** *United Jewish Organizations v. Carey,* 430 U.S. 144 (1977). To comply with the Voting Rights Act, New York split the Hasidic Jewish community of the Williamsburgh section of Brooklyn into three separate districts, in order to accentuate the voting power of black voters. The Court upheld the validity of the districts, opining that "New York was entitled to consider racial factors in redistricting." The *Shaw* and *Miller* Courts regarded *UJO* as involving "vote dilution" produced by racial considerations among other factors, rather than resulting from race as the "predominant motivating factor." If *UJO* was not overruled *sub silentio* by *Shaw* and *Miller,* it was confined to its facts.

E.   STRICT SCRUTINY AND SUSPECT CLASSIFICATIONS: LAWFUL ALIENS

1.   Defining the Suspect Category

The Court has declared alienage to be a suspect category, but has qualified that conclusion so much that, in practice, it means that the only alienage classifications subject to strict scrutiny are those used by *states,* and then only with respect to matters that do not implicate a state's legitimate power "to preserve the basic conception of a political community."

a. **Alienage, not national origin.** Alienage classifications are those that use *noncitizenship* as the criterion. National origin classifications are broader in that they encompass citizens as well. Statutory classifications on the basis of national origin are subject to strict scrutiny and treated like racial classifications. (See *Hernandez v. Texas,* 347 U.S. 475 (1954); *Castaneda v. Partida,* 430 U.S. 482 (1977). Cf. *Korematsu v. United States,* supra.)

b. **Alienage means lawful resident aliens, not aliens abroad or aliens illegally present in the United States.** Laws that discriminate against nonresident alienage are not suspect. Laws that discriminate against aliens illegally present in the United States are not suspect, although they might trigger a form of "heightened" scrutiny. (See *Plyler v. Doe,* supra.)

c. **Alienage classifications by the federal government are not necessarily suspect.** The federal government has exclusive control over immigration and naturalization and thus enjoys broad authority to employ alienage as a statutory criterion.

Example: Congress limited Medicare eligibility to citizens and lawfully admitted aliens who had resided in the United States for at least five years. The Court applied minimal scrutiny in upholding the law, relying heavily upon Congress's plenary control over immigration. *Mathews v. Diaz,* 426 U.S. 67 (1976).

Even though Congress may use alienage as a classification device without triggering strict scrutiny, administrative agencies may offend the due process clause, rather than equal protection, by doing so.

Example: The Civil Service Commission barred aliens from most civil service jobs. The Court voided the broad exclusion as violative of due process but assumed that "if the Congress or the President had expressly imposed the citizenship requirement, it would be justified by the national interest in providing an incentive for aliens to become naturalized." *Hampton v. Mow Sun Wong,* 426 U.S. 88 (1976).

d. **Strict scrutiny does not apply to state alienage classifications that "preserve the basic conception of a political community."** States may use alienage as a classifying device without triggering strict scrutiny when they do so in order to "preserve the basic conception of a political community." *Sugarman v. Dougall,* 413 U.S. 634, 647 (1973). This *"political function"* exception to strict scrutiny permits states to deny the vote and close off important public offices to aliens. Applying this principle, the Court has upheld state requirements of citizenship to be a police officer, probation officer, or public schoolteacher. (See section E.3, infra.)

2. Strict Scrutiny Applied

The Court has applied strict scrutiny in striking down a state requirement of citizenship to receive public welfare benefits, practice law, obtain civil service employment, and serve as a notary public. The Court also used strict scrutiny to invalidate a state law denying college financial aid to those aliens who would not swear that they would apply for citizenship as soon they were eligible to do so.

a. **Public welfare benefits:** *Graham v. Richardson,* 403 U.S. 365 (1971). Pennsylvania restricted public assistance to citizens and Arizona limited such benefits to citizens and long-time lawfully resident aliens. The Court voided both laws. In doing so, the Court concluded that strict scrutiny applied to alienage classifications employed by states, characterizing "[a]liens as a class [as] a prime example of a 'discrete and insular' minority for whom such heightened judicial solicitude is appropriate." The Court made it clear in its opinion that states had far less reason to discriminate against aliens than does the federal government.

b. **Practice of law:** *In re Griffiths,* 413 U.S. 717 (1973). Connecticut, like most other states, limited law practice to American citizens. The Court applied strict scrutiny, stating that "to justify the use of [alienage], a State must show that its purpose or interest is both *constitutionally permissi-*

ble and *substantial,* and that its use of [alienage] is *'necessary* [to] the accomplishment' of its purpose or the safeguarding of its interest." Connecticut's interest in "high professional standards," protecting clients, and using lawyers as "officers of the Court" were legitimate but not substantial enough to support a blanket exclusion of all aliens from the bar.

c. **Civil service employment:** *Sugarman v. Dougall,* 413 U.S. 634 (1973). New York barred all aliens from employment in its "competitive classified civil service." The Court invalidated New York's flat ban, after having subjected it to strict scrutiny. The Court acknowledged New York's substantial interest in limiting public employment to those with an "undivided loyalty" to the state, and its equally substantial interest in defining its political community. The problem with New York's ban on civil service employment of aliens was that it was so indiscriminate—it was not fashioned narrowly enough to advance those interests in a permissible fashion. The exclusion was "neither narrowly confined nor precise in its application." It barred aliens from employment as janitors as well as from "formulation and execution of important state policy." It was the breadth of New York's flat ban that caused it to fail strict scrutiny. The Court was careful to suggest that a more selective prohibition of aliens from public employment would be valid. Just as states may confine voting to citizens they may **reserve for citizens alone** *"state elective or important nonelective executive, legislative and judicial positions"* **as well as offices involving** *"the formulation, execution, or review of broad public policy* . . . functions that go to the heart of representative government." As discussed in section E.3, infra, this dicta has become doctrine, spawning a "political function" exception with considerable breadth.

d. **Notaries public:** *Bernal v. Fainter,* 467 U.S. 216 (1984). Texas forbade aliens from becoming notary publics. The Court voided the ban, applying strict scrutiny because it concluded that the functions of a notary public were ministerial.

e. **Engineering:** *Examining Board v. Flores de Otero,* 426 U.S. 572 (1976). Puerto Rico restricted the practice of engineering by aliens. The Court applied strict scrutiny in invalidating the restrictions.

f. **College financial aid:** *Nyquist v. Mauclet,* 432 U.S. 1 (1977). New York limited public financial aid to resident alien college students to those aliens who affirmed that they would become citizens at the earliest opportunity to do so. By a 5 to 4 vote the Court invalidated the provision, even though it did not discriminate against all aliens but only those aliens who were unwilling to become American citizens. The Court stressed that the objective of encouraging naturalization was not a legitimate purpose for New York, since the subject of naturalization was an exclusively federal concern.

3. The "Political Function" Exception: Strict Scrutiny Does *Not* Apply

Recall that *Sugarman v. Dougall* suggested that states could legitimately deny aliens public employment in positions that involved discharge of a *political function.*

a. **Police officers:** *Foley v. Connelie,* 435 U.S. 291 (1978). New York required police officers to be American citizens. The Court upheld the requirement by invoking the political function exception and declining to apply strict scrutiny. Policing involved "a most fundamental obligation of government to its constituency." Because police officers are invested with "substantial discretionary powers" of a most powerful nature the Court found the police function appropriately included within the political function exception.

b. **Schoolteachers:** *Ambach v. Norwick,* 441 U.S. 68 (1979). New York refused to employ as public schoolteachers those aliens eligible for American citizenship who refused to become citizens. The Court found the political function exception applicable, applied minimal scrutiny, and upheld the restriction. Teaching school "constitutes a governmental function" sufficient to come within the exception because public schooling prepares children "for participation as citizens" and helps "preserv[e] the values on which our society rests." Teachers possess "wide discretion" over these matters and serve as "role model[s] . . . , exerting a subtle but important influence" over students' "perceptions and values." A teacher's "influence is crucial to the continued good health of a democracy." Even though this classification was virtually identical to the one voided in *Nyquist v. Mauclet,* supra, the Court perceived the objective of the schoolteacher restriction to be to assure inculcation of citizenship rather than simply encouragement of naturalization.

c. **Probation officers:** *Cabell v. Chavez-Salido,* 454 U.S. 432 (1982). California excluded aliens from serving as probation officers. The Court concluded that "peace officers," a California statutory classification that included probation officers, were endowed with enough of the "sovereign's powers to exercise coercive force" to be included within the political function exception. The Court applied minimal scrutiny and upheld the law.

4. Strict Scrutiny Does Not Apply to Federal Action

Because the federal government has exclusive control over immigration and naturalization it may discriminate against aliens in ways that would be forbidden to the states. Thus, Congress could validly deny Medicare benefits to lawfully resident aliens who had lived in the United States for less than five years. *Mathews v. Diaz,* 426 U.S. 67 (1976). But this power is not without constitutional limits. "[D]ue process requires that there be a legitimate basis for presuming that [an alienage classification] was actually intended to serve . . . an overriding national interest." In *Hampton v. Mow Sun Wong,* 426 U.S. 88 (1976), the Court indicated that such a basis would be presumed whenever the alienage classification was adopted expressly by Congress (in legislation), the President (in executive orders), or an agency that has direct responsibility for an overriding national interest.

Example: If the Central Intelligence Agency, on its own, excluded aliens from serving as CIA agents, the CIA's direct responsibility for safeguarding national security through espionage would give rise to a presumption that national security was the reason for its discriminatory rule.

5. Does the Court Really Use Strict Scrutiny for Alienage Classifications?

The Court says it uses strict scrutiny to evaluate the legitimacy of state alienage classifications that are not germane to preservation of the "basic political community," and eschews strict scrutiny with respect to federal alienage classifications. Some respected constitutional commentators claim that "the Court's decisions . . . would appear to be consistent if the Court were using an intermediate standard of review . . . which required the government to demonstrate that a citizenship classification bore a reasonable and substantial relationship to an important governmental interest." Nowak & Rotunda, at 742. The failure of most state alienage classifications inheres in the lack of a substantial *state* interest in such classifications, "[s]ince state and local governments have no interest in foreign affairs." Id. But when states act to preserve their basic political community they do have such an interest, and so their alienage classifications tend to be upheld. The federal government has a general and substantial interest in both foreign affairs and controlling immigration and naturalization. Those interests are sufficient to support most federal alienage classifications. However accurate and elegant this analysis may be, the Court continues to claim that it applies either minimal or strict scrutiny to alienage classifications, depending on which government is employing them and for what purposes.

F. INTERMEDIATE SCRUTINY: OVERVIEW

When intermediate scrutiny applies the burden of proof shifts to the government to establish that the statutory classification is *substantially related* to *important governmental objectives.*

1. Important Governmental Objectives

To apply intermediate scrutiny courts must assess the importance of the government's objectives. Courts typically do so by weighing the judicially perceived importance of the state interest against the burdens the statute imposes on the individual and society.

    a. Problematic approach. There are two major theoretical problems with this approach.

> • *Importance to the government* and *burdens imposed on the individual* are incommensurate values—they are not on the same scale. It is like comparing the temperature in Boston on the Fourth of July to the distance between Denver and Chicago.

> • Assessing the importance of governmental objectives is an essential role of legislatures, and the ineffable comparison of importance and burdens is fundamentally a legislative judgment.

    b. No hypothetical purposes. In applying intermediate scrutiny courts insist on identifying the *actual purposes* for the legislation and assessing the importance of those actual purposes. By contrast, under minimal scrutiny any conceivable purpose, however hypothetical, will suffice.

2. Means-Ends Fit: *Substantially* Related

The means employed—the specific statutory classification, regulation, or governmental practice at issue—must be *substantially related* to the actual purposes for the law or practice. This requires something more than a merely rational fit—the fit between statute and objective need not be perfect but must be reasonably snug. A heavy cotton sweater might be a rational, albeit unwise, choice of outerwear on a midwinter day with snow and wind in the forecast, but it is probably not *substantially* related to the objective of staying warm and dry.

    a. Other alternatives available? Although the Court does not expressly assess the presence of less burdensome alternatives when it examines the fit between means and ends, that factor plays a role in intermediate scrutiny. When intermediate scrutiny applies, sweeping generalizations by legislatures are more carefully examined.

G. INTERMEDIATE SCRUTINY: SEX

1. Introduction

Classifications by sex, although similar in some respects to racial classifications, do not trigger strict scrutiny. Instead the Court has created an *intermediate* tier of scrutiny for sex classifications. They do not enjoy the presumption of validity that accompanies minimal scrutiny, but it is easier for governments to justify their use. Governments must prove that sex classifications are *substantially related* to an *important state interest.*

    a. The peculiar nature of sex classifications. In almost every instance, racial classifications reflect racial prejudice. While many sex classifications reflect stereotypical thinking about sex roles, some are the product of real differences between men and women. Many differences are rooted in deeply held social attitudes, others are unique to our anatomical differences. This raises difficult questions. Is one type of difference more real than the other? How should we identify real differences and stereotypes?

 # EXAMPLE AND ANALYSIS

California made it a crime for a man to have sexual intercourse with a woman under the age of eighteen, but did not criminalize the woman's participation. A seventeen-year-old male, convicted of intercourse with a seventeen-year-old female, appealed on the grounds that the sex distinction in the penal statute violated equal protection. The Court applied intermediate scrutiny and upheld the law, finding that the sex distinction was substantially related to important California objectives. The Court noted that men and women "are not similarly situated with respect to the problems and the risks of sexual intercourse. Only women may become pregnant, and they suffer disproportionately the profound physical, emotional, and psychological consequences of sexual activity." For these reasons, California imposed criminal penalties on male participation in intercourse, hoping thereby to deter males from an act with such potentially devastating consequences to young women and with very little consequences to men. California assumed that the consequences of pregnancy were likely sufficient deterrence to most young women and thus chose not to impose criminal penalties on women. California also assumed that, generally speaking, males are more sexually aggressive than women and thus may need greater deterrence. To the Court, California's differential treatment of the same act—sexual intercourse—was justified by the different situation of young men and young women with respect to the consequences of sexual intercourse. The fact that only women can conceive and bear children may be a "real" biological difference, but the consequences of pregnancy are social. The Court treated both as "real" differences. *Michael M. v. Sonoma County Superior Court,* 450 U.S. 464 (1981).

   b.   Traditional judicial deference. Until *Reed v. Reed,* infra, the Court was uniformly deferential to legislative classifications by sex. Such classifications were subjected to minimal scrutiny and invariably upheld.

 # EXAMPLE AND ANALYSIS

Myra Bradwell had studied law and otherwise complied with Illinois's requirements for a license to practice law. Illinois refused to admit her to the bar on the sole ground that she was a woman. Bradwell contended that the practice of law was a privilege or immunity of national citizenship and that Illinois had violated the privileges and immunities clause of the 14th Amendment by denying her the opportunity to practice law. The Court rejected her claim. Justice Bradley, concurring, reflected the prevalent judicial attitude toward sex classifications. He declared that women were "unfit[] for many of the occupations of civil life" because of their "natural and proper timidity and delicacy," as well as "the divine ordinance . . . [and] the nature of things . . . [that ordains] the domestic sphere as that which properly belongs to the domain and functions of womanhood." A woman's place is in the home, and laws that enforce it are not only constitutional but part of "the law of the Creator," since the "paramount destiny and mission of woman is to fulfill the noble and benign offices of wife and mother." *Bradwell v. Illinois,* 83 U.S. 130 (1873).

---

2. The Development of Intermediate Scrutiny

a. ***Reed v. Reed,*** 404 U.S. 71 (1971). This was the first time that the Court invalidated a sex classification under the equal protection clause. Idaho law mandated that men should be preferred to women as court-appointed administrators of an intestate decedent's estate. The Court applied minimal scrutiny to the law but invalidated it anyway as irrational—"the very kind of arbitrary legislative choice forbidden by the Equal Protection Clause." The sex preference did further the objective of reducing the workload of courts by eliminating contests between men and women over the administration of such estates, but the Court thought that the means of doing so was completely arbitrary.

b. ***Frontiero v. Richardson,*** 411 U.S. 677 (1973). Federal law permitted a male member of the armed services automatically to claim his wife as a dependent, thus acquiring increased housing and medical benefits, but did not permit a female servicemember to do so unless she could demonstrate that her husband was in fact dependent on her for over half his support. The Court struck down the provision but could not muster a majority around any one standard of review.

c. ***Craig v. Boren,*** 429 U.S. 190 (1976). Oklahoma permitted females at age 18 to purchase and use 3.2% beer, but forbade males from doing so until age 21. The Court voided the sex distinction. In doing so it crafted a new standard of review—intermediate scrutiny. Oklahoma was required to justify its sex classification by proving that its objective—"the enhancement of traffic safety"—was *important* and that the means chosen to achieve that objective—the sex difference in the legal age to purchase 3.2% beer—was *substantially related* to accomplishment of the objective. The Court readily agreed that "the protection of public health and safety [is] an important function of state and local governments," but concluded that the sex difference for purchase of 3.2% beer did not "closely serve[] to achieve that objective" and was thus not substantially related to its accomplishment. The Court regarded Oklahoma's empirical evidence of the linkage between sex and drunk driving as inadequate, even though it showed that eighteen- to twenty-year-old males were arrested for drunken driving *eighteen times more frequently* than females in the same age group. The Court was more impressed by the fact that the same evidence showed that only 2% of males in the eighteen to twenty age cohort were arrested for drunken driving. As Justice Stevens put it in his concurrence, Oklahoma "visit[ed] the sins of the 2% on the 98%" of law-abiding males.

3.   Invidiously Discriminatory Purpose Required

For sex classifications to trigger intermediate scrutiny they must be shown to be invidiously discriminatory. This is generally, *but not always,* presumed when the statute facially discriminates on the basis of sex. But when statutes are facially neutral the challenger must prove that the neutral classification *purposefully discriminates by sex.* It is not enough to show that the neutral classification has a discriminatory *effect.*

   a.   **Neutral classification:** *Personnel Administrator v. Feeney,* 442 U.S. 256 (1979). Massachusetts provided that veterans were to be preferred over other similarly qualified applicants for jobs in the Massachusetts civil service. Feeney, a woman, challenged the validity of this preference as an equal protection violation and pointed to the fact that over 98% of Massachusetts veterans were men. The Court applied minimal scrutiny and upheld the rule. The classification was not sex-based because it was facially neutral as to sex, and was not intentionally designed to exclude women from the state civil service. The Court reasoned that the fact that the preference also operated to exclude large numbers of men as well as women blunted the claim of intentional sex discrimination. More importantly, the Court stated that proof of legislative awareness of a differential impact by sex was not enough to prove discriminatory intent. The challenger must prove that the facially neutral law was adopted ***because** of its sexually discriminatory impact,* not simply that it was adopted "in spite of" legislative knowledge of that impact.

   b.   **Neutral(?) classification:** *Geduldig v. Aiello,* 417 U.S. 484 (1974). California's disability insurance system excluded disabilities attendant to normal pregnancies and birth. The Court applied minimal scrutiny in rejecting an equal protection challenge to the provision. The distinction was not based on sex but on pregnancy, said the Court. Pregnant men and women were affected equally. Far more plausible was the Court's conclusion that California could legitimately decide which health risks it wished to insure against, and that exclusion of disabilities related to normal pregnancy and childbirth was rationally related to that legitimate objective. *Geduldig* drives home the point that facially neutral classifications must be proven to be *intentionally sexually discriminatory* in order to trigger intermediate scrutiny.

c. **Non-neutral but not invidious:** ***Parham v. Hughes,*** 441 U.S. 347 (1979). Georgia law permitted mothers of illegitimate children to sue for wrongful death of a child, but denied fathers that right. A plurality of the Court held that the law did not discriminate by sex because fathers were free to legitimate their children by formally acknowledging their paternity and it was unnecessary for mothers to make such an acknowledgment. "[T]he statutory classification does not discriminate against fathers as a class but instead distinguishes between fathers who have legitimated their children and those who have not."

4. **Application of Intermediate Scrutiny**

a. **Important state interests.** Sex classifications must serve *important* state interests or objectives.

i. **Must be *actual*, not hypothetical, purpose.** Governments are required to prove that the important state interest served by a sex classification was the "*actual purpose*" for the classification. When minimal scrutiny applies governments may assert any conceivable legitimate purpose for the statute, however hypothetical it may be. When intermediate scrutiny applies, however, governments must establish that the *actual purpose* of the statute is *important*.

 # EXAMPLES AND ANALYSIS

Example: Federal law provided for the payment of Social Security benefits to the wife (but not the husband) of a deceased wage earner with minor children. The government asserted that an important purpose for the rule was to "provide an income to women who were, because of economic discrimination, unable to provide for themselves" but the Court said that the statute and the legislative history showed that Congress's *actual purpose* was "to permit women to elect not to work and to devote themselves to the care of children." The law was irrational in relation to this legitimate purpose because it distinguished between men and women "when the sole question is whether a child should have the opportunity to receive the full-time attention of the only parent remaining to it." *Weinberger v. Weisenfeld,* 420 U.S. 636 (1975).

Example: The Mississippi University for Women, a public university, admitted only women to its nursing school. The restrictive admissions policy was challenged by a man as a violation of equal protection. The Court applied intermediate scrutiny and struck down the practice. Although Mississippi asserted that its sexually discriminatory policy substantially served an important state goal of compensating for discrimination against women in public education the Court held that "although the State recited a 'benign, compensatory purpose,' it failed to establish that the alleged objective is the *actual purpose* underlying the discriminatory classification." *Mississippi University for Women v. Hogan,* 458 U.S. 718 (1982).

  b. **"Substantially related" element.** A closer fit between classification and objective than "mere rationality" is required, but it is not necessary that the government prove that the classification is necessary to the accomplishment of the objective. The statutory means must bear a "fair and substantial relation" to the important objective. A rational but "unduly tenuous fit" with the important objective does not satisfy the "substantially related" element of intermediate scrutiny.

  c. **Intermediate review not satisfied**

  i. **Insufficiently important interest.** The lack of an *important* interest that was the *actual purpose* for the sex classification at issue will prove fatal under intermediate review.

EXAMPLES AND ANALYSIS

Example: Missouri paid worker's compensation death benefits to widows automatically but to widowers only if they could prove they were either economically dependent upon their deceased wives or were disabled. The Court said that Missouri's "claimed justification of administrative convenience fails" intermediate scrutiny because the objective—administrative convenience—was too insubstantial to support a sex-based distinction. *Wengler v. Druggists Mutual Insurance Co.,* 446 U.S. 142 (1980).

Example: The actual purpose and undoubted effect of Mississippi University for Women's policy of admitting only women to its nursing school was "to perpetuate the stereotyped view of nursing as an exclusively woman's job." The Court had little difficulty finding that objective less than important. *Mississippi University for Women v. Hogan,* 458 U.S. 718 (1982).

  ii. **Classification not "substantially related" to the important governmental interest.** When sex-based distinctions fail intermediate scrutiny they usually are found to be unsubstantially related to an important state interest.

EXAMPLES AND ANALYSIS

Example: Social Security survivor's benefits were automatically paid to widows of a deceased wage earner but paid to widowers only if the widower could show that he was receiving more than half his support from his wife at the time of her death. The government defended the distinction by arguing that Congress's important objective was to provide income maintenance for widows (a relatively more needy class than widowers) in order to compensate for "job discrimination against women." The Court rejected this argument, concluding that the *actual purpose* of Congress was to provide for dependent spouses, and did so by a presumption that women, but not men, were economically dependent on their spouses. The law's actual objective—to provide for dependent spouses—might have been important but the means selected for its accomplishment—using sex as a proxy for dependency in the case of women but not men—was not substantially related to that objective. It would be just as easy to make every widow, as well as widower, prove dependency. *Califano v. Goldfarb,* 430 U.S. 199 (1977).

Example: Alabama required only husbands to pay alimony and sought to justify it by arguing that the law provided "help for needy spouses, using sex as a proxy for need," and "compensate[d] women for past discrimination during marriage." The Court found the law insubstantially related to these objectives since Alabama already required individualized hearings at which it would be easy to determine which spouses were in fact needy and which had in fact been discriminated against during marriage. The use of sex as a proxy to achieve these goals was unnecessary and did little to advance Alabama's asserted goals. *Orr v. Orr,* 440 U.S. 268 (1979).

Example: Alabama sued J.E.B. for paternity and child support on behalf of T.B., the mother of the child in question. Alabama used nine of its ten peremptory challenges intentionally to remove all men from the jury. Alabama defended its action by asserting that the important state interest of a fair and impartial trial was substantially served by removal of men because they might be more sympathetic than women to the male defendant in a paternity action. The Court characterized this relationship as "the very stereotype the law condemns" and invalidated Alabama's intentional use of peremptory challenges on the basis of sex alone. *J.E.B. v. Alabama,* 511 U.S. 127 (1994).

---

    d. Intermediate review satisfied. Intermediate review is more easily satisfied than strict scrutiny. The Court has been particularly willing to do so when the sex classification at issue has as its purpose remedying past sex discrimination or when it reflects real differences between the sexes.

        i. Sex distinctions remedial of past discrimination. The Court is far more likely to accept justifications of sex distinctions when legislatures use them to remedy past sexual inequities, rather than adopting sex classifications as an "accidental by-product of a traditional way of thinking about females," or as a result of "archaic and overbroad generalizations" about women.

 # EXAMPLES AND ANALYSIS

Example: Federal law provided that Social Security benefits were to be based on the average monthly wage of the covered wage earner. In computing the average monthly wage women were permitted to exclude three more years of low wages than were men. The Court found that sexual distinction justified under intermediate scrutiny and upheld the provisions at issue. The purpose of the statute, said the Court, was "to compensate women for past economic discrimination." That objective was treated as important and the sex distinction was substantially related to its accomplishment. "[A]llowing women, who as such have been unfairly hindered from earning as much as men, to eliminate additional low-earning years from the calculation of their retirement benefits works directly to remedy some part of the effect of past discrimination." *Califano v. Webster,* 430 U.S. 313 (1977).

Example: Federal law required discharge of naval officers if they had not been promoted for nine years in the case of men and thirteen years in the case of women. The classification was examined under minimal scrutiny because the case preceded *Craig v. Boren, supra.* The Court upheld the law because it was not "premised on overbroad generalizations" or adopted merely for "administrative convenience." Instead, its purpose was "to provide women officers with 'fair and equitable career advancement' " opportunities. Since Navy regulations restricted female officers' opportunities for combat and sea duty, the traditional paths for promotion of line officers, the distinction was rationally related to this goal. It is likely the result would be the same under intermediate scrutiny, since the statutory distinction seems well-suited to an important goal. *Schlesinger v. Ballard,* 419 U.S. 498 (1975).

ii. **Sex distinctions based on real sex differences.** When sex classifications are bottomed on some "real" difference between the sexes, rather than reflecting stereotypical assumptions about the roles and capabilities of men and women, the Court is far more apt to find that such classifications are justified. Some "real" differences are rooted in biological differences between men and women, but some are rooted in societal patterns that are hardly immutable. The latter are especially difficult.

(a) **Real biological differences.** Only women can conceive and bear children. For the purpose of deciding which medical risks California wished to cover, this real difference was not thought particularly relevant in *Geduldig v. Aiello.* But in *Michael M. v. Superior Court,* where the Court upheld California's criminal prohibition on male (but not female) participation in sexual intercourse involving a young woman under age eighteen, the real difference of female conception was critical. The "real difference" was the perceived *consequences* of pregnancy. The Court regarded the social consequences of pregnancy and childbirth as just as real as the biological fact. Not everyone agrees.

(b) **Real societal differences.** Many of the sex classifications invalidated by the Court are rooted in "ancient canards about the proper role of women." But the Court upholds other sex classifications as justified by some societal difference between men and women that is so deeply entrenched as to amount to a "real difference." If the distinction between "ancient canards" and "real societal differences" seems elusive, it is because it is. Perhaps the best that can be done is to recognize that the Court will treat as "real differences" those societal differences that seem entirely extrinsic to the statutory classification involved, and that either cannot easily be modified by governmental action or that reflect a deeply felt and widely shared view of the roles of men and women.

 # EXAMPLES AND ANALYSIS

Example: A state excluded female prison guards in all-male prisons from positions in which they would come into the immediate physical presence of inmates. The Court upheld this exclusion as substantially related to the important state objectives of maintaining order in prisons and assuring the safety of prison guards. Women, said the Court, were inherently less able to maintain order in the "environment of violence and disorganization" that characterizes "a male, maximum-security, unclassified penitentiary," and were more likely to be assaulted by imprisoned "sex offenders" or "inmates deprived of a normal heterosexual environment." *Dothard v. Rawlinson,* 433 U.S. 321 (1977).

Example: By the Military Selective Service Act Congress required the registration of young men but not women in order to facilitate military conscription for combat duty. The Court applied intermediate scrutiny and upheld the provision. The important purpose of registration was to facilitate conscription of combat troops, surely an important objective. Because a different law excluded women from combat the sex-based registration distinction was held to be substantially related to that goal. The sex distinction at issue "realistically reflect[ed] the fact that the sexes are not similarly situated." The dissenters pointed out that the statutory bar of women from combat was hardly immutable, and that even given the combat bar and assuming its validity (a matter not at issue), the induction of women into the military would free men for combat service, a fact casting some doubt on the substantiality of the relationship of the sex-based registration system to the identified objective. The dissimilar situation of men and women was real enough, but the reality that produced it was another sex-based classification. *Rostker v. Goldberg,* 453 U.S. 57 (1981).

---

5.   Affirmative Action

In one sense, affirmative action pervades the Court's approach to sex classifications. When the actual purpose of a sex-based distinction is to remedy past invidious sex discrimination the Court accepts the importance of that goal and generally finds that the sex classification at issue substantially advances that goal. (See, e.g., *Califano v. Webster,* supra.) Unlike racial classifications, where for a time the Court toyed with the idea of subjecting so-called benign racial classifications to less than strict scrutiny, there has never been any suggestion that "benign" sexual classifications should be subjected to less than intermediate scrutiny. The *applicable standard of review for sex classifications undertaken for "affirmative action" is **intermediate scrutiny**.*

6.   Single-Sex Education: *United States v. Virginia,* 518 U.S. 515 (1996)

The Court ruled that the Virginia Military Institute, a public university, violated equal protection by its practice of restricting admission to men only. The Court applied intermediate scrutiny but characterized that standard as requiring the state to establish an "exceedingly persuasive justification" for sex discrimination. The majority did not believe that Virginia's actual objective was educational diversity. Instead, the Court characterized VMI's objective as educating citizen-soldiers and concluded that a male-only environment was not substantially related to that goal. Justice Scalia, dissenting, charged that the Court had covertly applied strict scrutiny to invalidate all ventures in public single-sex education.

   a.   **The significance of *United States v. Virginia.*** A large body of scholarly literature claims that single-sex education produces real benefits to both sexes, but with perhaps more pronounced benefits to girls and women. *United States v. Virginia* left open the possibility that single-sex public education might be substantially related to some important government objectives—perhaps increasing the self-esteem of students or improving the learning environment.

   Example: Suppose a public school district decides to offer, as an option to parents and schoolchildren, an all-girls elementary school and an all-boys elementary school. Is the objective of improving learning opportunities for girls sufficiently important to meet intermediate scrutiny? What if single-sex education delivers no benefits to boys or, even worse, reduces learning opportunities for boys?

H. INTERMEDIATE SCRUTINY: ILLEGITIMACY

1. Introduction

Statutes that classify on the basis of illegitimate birth are subjected to *intermediate scrutiny*. For such laws to be valid the state must prove that the classification is "substantially related to an important governmental objective." (See *Clark v. Jeter*, 486 U.S. 456 (1988).) Prior to 1968 statutes that discriminated on the basis of illegitimate birth were not regarded as offensive to equal protection. Minimal scrutiny applied to any such claims and the Court was willing to conclude that such laws were rationally related to legitimate state objectives. Between 1968, when the Court first invalidated such a law under minimal scrutiny, and 1988, when the Court finally adopted intermediate scrutiny for such classifications, the Court wavered between minimal scrutiny and some unspecified "heightened" scrutiny.

2. The Development of Intermediate Scrutiny

Initially the Court applied minimal scrutiny to void wrongful death statutes that employed illegitimacy as a classification. *Levy v. Louisiana*, 391 U.S. 68 (1968) found irrational a law that denied illegitimate children the right to sue for the wrongful death of their mother. *Glona v. American Guarantee & Liability Insurance Co.*, 391 U.S. 73 (1968), held that a law barring a mother from recovering damages for her illegitimate child's death was equally irrational.

In a series of cases in the 1970s the Court vacillated as to the standard to be used in evaluating restrictions on inheritance based on legitimate birth. See *Labine v. Vincent*, 401 U.S. 532 (1971) (minimal scrutiny); *Weber v. Aetna Casualty & Surety Co.*, 406 U.S. 164 (1972) ("stricter" scrutiny); *Trimble v. Gordon*, 430 U.S. 762 (1977) ("substantial relation" required); *Lalli v. Lalli*, 439 U.S. 259 (1978) (minimal scrutiny); *Califano v. Boles*, 443 U.S. 282 (1979) (minimal scrutiny).

Intermediate scrutiny finally arrived when the Court considered the issue of child support.

States typically provide that fathers are obligated to support their legitimate children but have no obligation to support their illegitimate children unless paternity has been established. Suits to establish paternity are barred if not brought within a specified period after birth of the child. Because legitimate children have an absolute right to paternal support and the inchoate support rights of illegitimate children may be terminated by elapse of the limitations period, the Court has been forced to confront the question of whether any given limitations period for paternity suits violates equal protection. In *Mills v. Habluetzel,* 456 U.S. 91 (1982), the Court invalidated a one-year limitations period on the grounds that it left illegitimate children with a support right that was no "more than illusory." In *Pickett v. Brown,* 462 U.S. 1 (1983), the Court struck down a two-year limitations period. Finally, in *Clark v. Jeter,* 486 U.S. 456 (1988), in voiding a six-year statute the Court expressly adopted intermediate scrutiny as the standard of review for classifications on the basis of illegitimacy.

Immigration may be a special case. In *Fiallo v. Bell,* 430 U.S. 787 (1977), the Court upheld an immigration preference that excluded the illegitimate children of fathers who were foreign nationals seeking their admission. Legitimate children and illegitimate children of mothers seeking their admission were given the preference. The Court upheld the law, primarily because it believed that exceptional judicial deference was due to congressional judgments in the field of immigration and naturalization. (See also section E.4, supra.)

3.   Why Intermediate Scrutiny?

The best justification for intermediate review of classifications on the basis of illegitimacy is that there is little the illegitimate child can do to overcome that status. While parents may marry and fathers may formally acknowledge their paternity in order to legitimize their illicit offspring, the child is unable to make them do these things. From a child's perspective, illegitimacy is well-nigh immutable. But the other attributes of suspicious (if not suspect) classifications are largely missing. As a class illegitimate children are not a "discrete and insular" minority, visible to all and subject to the kind of prejudice that walls them off from meaningful participation in the political process. Moreover, as traditional marriages and family relationships erode there is less and less stigma attached to illegitimacy. Do these factors warrant reconsideration of intermediate scrutiny? How, if at all, ought these factors be taken into account in applying intermediate scrutiny?

 # EXAMPLE AND ANALYSIS

A New Jersey program provided financial and other assistance to "families of the working poor," but limited that assistance to families "which consist of a household composed of two adults of the opposite sex ceremonially married to each other who have at least one minor child . . . of both, [or] the natural child of one and adopted by the other, or a child adopted by both." New Jersey contended that the classification denying assistance to families composed of unmarried adults and their illegitimate offspring was substantially related to its important state objective of encouraging the maintenance of legally and socially sanctioned family relationships. Put another way, New Jersey argued it had a "compelling state interest to refuse to subsidize a living unit which may lead to a state of anomie and which violates its laws against fornication and adultery." Without specifying the standard of review the Court invalidated the statute. The Court declared that "imposing disabilities on the illegitimate child is contrary to the basic concept of our system that legal burdens should bear some relationship to individual responsibility or wrongdoing." But the New Jersey statute did not single out illegitimate children for disfavored treatment so much as it singled out types of families. Is it an important state objective to protect only the traditional family unit "from dissolution due to the economic vicissitudes of modern life?" Or is New Jersey's objective rendered unimportant because increasing numbers of people reject traditional family arrangements? *New Jersey Welfare Rights Org. v. Cahill*, 411 U.S. 619 (1973).

I. FUNDAMENTAL RIGHTS: STRICT SCRUTINY REDUX

This aspect of equal protection, in which the court applies strict scrutiny to legislative classifications that infringe "fundamental" rights, is particularly controversial. The attempt to find fundamental rights in equal protection, rather than some other part of the Constitution like the Bill of Rights, has been criticized as an "empty idea." Westen, 95 Harv. L. Rev. 537; Cohen, 59 Tul. L. Rev. 884. The quest for fundamental rights textually unconnected to the Constitution has been repudiated by the Court (see *San Antonio Independent School District v. Rodriguez*, infra), but there still exists a large body of law that reflects earlier efforts in that direction.

1. Introduction: Another Trigger for Strict Scrutiny

Just as *suspect classifications* trigger strict scrutiny, so do classifications that *infringe upon fundamental rights*.

a. What rights are fundamental? In order for a right to "be regarded as fundamental for purposes of examination under the Equal Protection Clause" it must be *"explicitly or implicitly guaranteed by the Constitution."* *San Antonio Independent School District v. Rodriguez*, 411 U.S. 1 (1973). An interest is *not* fundamental simply because it is important to the affected individual, or is an "importan[t] . . . service performed by the State," or is "societally significan[t]."

Example: While housing and education are indisputably important interests, and perhaps even "fundamental" to life in our postindustrial age, they are not fundamental interests for purposes of the equal protection clause because they are not guaranteed, even implicitly, by the Constitution. (See *Rodriguez* (education), *Lindsey v. Normet*, 405 U.S. 56 (1972) (housing).)

  i. Explicit and independent constitutional rights. Rights that are explicitly guaranteed by the Constitution independently of the equal protection clause are fundamental rights for purposes of equal protection. Statutory classifications that infringe upon such rights are subject to strict scrutiny.

Example: A Chicago ordinance penalized as "disorderly conduct" any knowing picketing within 150 feet of a school while school was in session, but excepted from that rule "the peaceful picketing of any school involved in a labor dispute." Earl Mosley spent portions of his day carrying a picket sign, reading "Jones High School practices black discrimination. Jones High School has a black quota." He was concededly "always peaceful, orderly, and quiet." The Court held that Mosley's right of free speech, explicitly guaranteed by the First Amendment and incorporated into the 14th Amendment's due process clause, was infringed by Chicago's selective treatment of picketing—labor picketing was permitted; Mosley's political expression was not. The Court applied strict scrutiny; Chicago failed to justify its differential treatment of picketing as narrowly tailored to accomplish a compelling interest of the city. *Police Dept. of Chicago v. Mosley*, 408 U.S. 92 (1972).

ii. **Implicitly guaranteed constitutional rights.** There are three broad categories of implicitly guaranteed constitutional rights that make up most of the "fundamental rights" jurisprudence under equal protection, but these categories are not an exclusive catalogue of fundamental rights for equal protection purposes.

(a) **Voting.** The right to vote is not explicitly guaranteed by the Constitution. The Constitution assumes the existence of a voting electorate but largely leaves it up to the states to determine who may vote. The 15th Amendment (prohibiting racial barriers to voting), the 19th Amendment (prohibiting sexual barriers to voting), the 24th Amendment (prohibiting poll taxes in federal elections), and the 26th Amendment (prohibiting age barriers to voting for those aged eighteen or older) all circumscribe governmental power to limit the franchise. In addition, the Court has concluded that voting is a fundamental right for purposes of equal protection.

 # EXAMPLE AND ANALYSIS

In *Reynolds v. Sims*, 377 U.S. 533 (1964), the Court used strict scrutiny to conclude that legislative electoral districts apportioned on some basis other than population were violative of equal protection. In the course of that decision the Court observed that the right to vote "is a fundamental matter in a free and democratic society.

Especially since the right to [vote] . . . is preservative of other basic civil and political rights, any alleged infringement of the right of citizens to vote must be carefully and meticulously scrutinized.''

(b) **Access to courts.** The court has been less committed to the idea that there is a fundamental right of access to the judicial process. But depending on the context the Court regards access to the courts as fundamental. This is most true with respect to the criminal justice system.

Example: In *Griffin v. Illinois*, 351 U.S. 12 (1956), the Court held that a state must furnish an indigent criminal defendant a free trial transcript if necessary for "adequate and effective appellate review" of his conviction.

(c) **Right to travel.** Nowhere does the Constitution guarantee unimpeded mobility throughout the United States. Yet the Court has long treated the right of interstate travel as a fundamental right implicit in the concept of a single nation committed to the freedom of its citizens. (See, e.g., *Crandall v. Nevada*, 73 U.S. 35 (1867) (invalidating a Nevada exit tax on travelers leaving the state).) The most common modern application of this principle is with respect to durational residency requirements as a precondition to receipt of some governmental benefit.

 ## EXAMPLE AND ANALYSIS

In *Shapiro v. Thompson*, 394 U.S. 618 (1969), the Court applied strict scrutiny to invalidate state laws that imposed a one-year durational residency requirement as a precondition for eligibility to receive welfare benefits. The Court regarded as constitutionally impermissible any state objective of discouraging "the influx of poor families" from other states because it infringed upon the right of interstate mobility. More benign objectives, such as imposing durational residency requirements in order to facilitate budgeting for welfare assistance, were treated as insufficiently compelling to justify the classification.

(d) **Other fundamental rights.** Remember that *any right explicitly or implicitly guaranteed by the Constitution* is a "fundamental right" for purposes of equal protection. When legislative classifications selectively impinge upon fundamental rights the equal protection clause is implicated.

Example: In *Eisenstadt v. Baird*, supra, the Court struck down under the equal protection clause Massachusetts's prohibition of the distribution of contraceptives to unmarried people. The Court thought that the fundamental right of privacy protecting conception was infringed upon by the selective ban on contraceptive distribution.

b. **Claimed rights found not to be fundamental.** The Court has specifically rejected several claims of fundamental rights that are not to be found in the Constitution.

   i. **Education: *San Antonio Independent School District v. Rodriguez,* 411 U.S. 1 (1973).** Public schools in Texas were financed through property taxes levied by local school districts. Because districts with an abundance of expensive property had greater property tax revenues than districts with inexpensive property, per-pupil expenditures among school districts varied greatly. This disparity was challenged as a violation of equal protection. The challengers contended that strict scrutiny should apply because (1) education was said to be a fundamental right and (2) classifications by wealth were said to be suspect. The Court rejected both contentions, applied minimal scrutiny, and upheld the Texas school finance system. Education is undoubtedly important to society and affected individuals, and the provision of public education is surely an important function of government, but education is not "explicitly or implicitly guaranteed by the Constitution." The Court rejected Justice Marshall's dissenting position that fundamental rights ought to be determined by the degree "to which constitutionally guaranteed rights are dependent on interests not mentioned in the Constitution," but did suggest in dicta that a complete denial of public education to some portion of the population might present a stronger case for "judicial assistance."

   ii. **Housing: *Lindsey v. Normet,* 405 U.S. 56 (1972).** The Court applied minimal scrutiny to uphold Oregon's summary "wrongful detainer" statute permitting speedy eviction of tenants for nonpayment of rent. The Court specifically rejected the contention that there was a "fundamental interest" in "decent shelter" and "possession of one's home," sufficient to invoke strict scrutiny of governmental interference with this right. The Court acknowledged "the importance of decent, safe and sanitary housing" but, relying upon the absence of any constitutional guarantee to housing, concluded that "the Constitution does not provide judicial remedies for every social and economic ill."

iii. **Welfare benefits—the "necessities of life":** *Dandridge v. Williams,* 397 U.S. 471 (1970). Maryland provided Aid to Families with Dependent Children (AFDC) but imposed a maximum grant of $250 per month, regardless of family size or actual need. The Court applied minimal scrutiny and upheld the regulation. The Court rejected the claim that strict scrutiny ought to apply because Maryland's AFDC limit infringed upon "the most basic economic needs of impoverished human beings." There is no fundamental right to "minimum welfare," or an "absolute assurance that [basic needs] will be met . . . , free of any . . . effort, thrift, or foresight." Michelman, 83 Harv. L. Rev. 7.

2.   **Voting: Preclusions of the Franchise**

The 1787 Constitution permitted states to determine the qualifications of voters for both local and national elections. Today, four amendments (the 15th, 19th, 24th, and 26th) expressly limit state and federal power to deny the vote for reasons of race, sex, failure to pay a poll tax, or age (except with respect to minors). In addition, the Court has constructed an elaborate edifice of equal protection law limiting state interference with the "fundamental right to vote."

a. **Poll taxes.** The 24th Amendment, ratified in 1964, barred states from imposing poll taxes on voters in *federal* elections. *Harper v. Virginia Board of Elections*, 383 U.S. 663 (1966), involved an equal protection challenge to Virginia's $1.50 tax on voters in state elections. The Court applied strict scrutiny and struck it down. In an opinion by Justice Douglas, the Court admitted that the "right to vote in state elections is nowhere expressly mentioned" in the Constitution, but pronounced voting to be a "fundamental political right, because preservative of all rights." Oddly enough, the Court declared that it would "not stop to canvass the relation between voting and political expression." The Court found that Virginia had no justification for imposing a tax on voting: "[P]ayment of a fee as a measure of a voter's qualifications is [an] . . . irrelevant factor." In dissent, Justices Harlan and Stewart noted the long tradition of property qualifications to vote, based on the belief "that people with some property have a deeper stake in community affairs, and are consequently more responsible, more educated, more knowledgeable, more worthy of confidence, than those without means, and that the community and the Nation would be better managed if the franchise were restricted to such citizens." Justice Harlan observed that while even minimal property qualifications (such as Virginia's annual fee of $1.50) were "not in accord with current egalitarian notions" the equal protection clause does not "rigidly impose upon America an ideology of unrestrained egalitarianism." Justice Black also dissented, citing the long history of property qualifications for the vote and condemning the majority for employing "the old 'natural-law-due-process formula'" of *Lochner* to strike down Virginia's poll tax.

b. Special voter eligibility requirements. The Court has generally applied strict scrutiny to property qualifications for voting and found them to violate equal protection except when such qualifications are employed in less-than-general elections for governmental units organized for a limited, special purpose that affects only the property-qualified electors.

   i. School district elections: *Kramer v. Union Free School District,* 395 U.S. 621 (1969). New York law limited the franchise in school district elections to parents or guardians of children enrolled in the public schools and to owners or lessees of taxable real property within the district. Kramer, excluded from school district elections, claimed that his exclusion violated equal protection. The Court observed that "reasonable citizenship, age, and residency requirements" do not trigger strict scrutiny, but that selective restriction of the franchise to only *some* people who meet the *general* requirements of age, citizenship, and residency did trigger strict scrutiny. The Court thought that "[s]tatutes granting the franchise to residents on a selective basis always pose the danger of denying some citizens any effective voice in the governmental affairs which substantially affect their lives." The Court conceded without deciding that New York's goal of limiting the franchise in school district elections to those people "primarily interested [in or] affected" by school board decisions might be a compelling one, but struck down the law because it was not proven that "the exclusion of [Kramer and others like him] is necessary to achieve the articulated state goal." The Court seemed to think that *any* under-inclusion or over-inclusion was fatal to the validity of the law, thereby creating an impossibly high burden of proof. Justices Stewart, Black, and Harlan dissented, noting that the law did not infringe "upon a constitutionally protected right, [because] the Constitution . . . does not confer the right of suffrage upon any one." The dissenters also charged that the very classifications the majority conceded to be valid—age, citizenship, and residency—are just as over- or under-inclusive as the classification voided in *Kramer.*

   ii. General elections for special purposes. The Court has applied an approach similar to *Kramer* to general elections for special purposes.

      (a) *Cipriano v. Houma,* 395 U.S. 701 (1969). The Court struck down a Louisiana law that limited the vote to property owners in elections for the purpose of deciding whether to issue municipal utility bonds. Because the bonds would be repaid exclusively from utility revenues the Court thought that their issuance had no particular impact on property-owning taxpayers.

(b) *Phoenix v. Kolodziejski,* 399 U.S. 204 (1970). Arizona permitted only property-owning taxpayers to vote in elections considering issuance of general obligation bonds. General obligation bonds are repaid from all revenues of the issuing entity, which in practice means mostly property tax revenues. The Court invalidated the law, ruling that the differences between the interests of nonproperty owners and property owners were "not sufficiently substantial to justify excluding" nonproperty owners from the election. The Court thought that the interests of nonproperty owners in receiving services financed by the bonds were no different from the interests of property-owning taxpayers in paying for those services. By this reasoning, the recipient of a free lunch has the same interest in it as the person who picks up the check. Three Justices dissented.

iii. Special purpose elections for limited purpose governmental units. The Court has upheld the validity of property qualifications for voting in special purpose elections for limited purpose governmental units whose functions primarily affect the property-qualified electors.

(a) *Salyer Land Co. v. Tulare Lake Basin Water Storage District,* 410 U.S. 719 (1973). California law permitted only landowners within a water storage district to vote in district elections and allocated votes in proportion to the assessed value of the owner's land. Water storage districts maintain reservoirs and canals to provide water for farming and charge landowners for the costs of that effort in proportion to the benefits received. The Court applied minimal scrutiny and upheld the law. Strict scrutiny was inapplicable because of the district's "special limited purpose and . . . the disproportionate effect of its activities on landowners as a group." The voting scheme was rationally related to its legitimate objective of storing and distributing water for farming and passing on those costs to water users.

(b) *Ball v. James,* 451 U.S. 355 (1981). The Court extended the *Salyer* doctrine to uphold a "one acre-one vote" voting scheme for directors of a large water storage district in Arizona that sold hydroelectric power to several hundred thousand residents. The Court applied minimal scrutiny because the district was unable to "enact any laws governing the conduct of citizens, nor . . . administer . . . normal functions of government." The electrical generation business of the district created no governmental relationship between the district and nonvoting users of electricity. Their relationship was "essentially that between consumers and a business enterprise."

(c) *Quinn v. Millsap,* 491 U.S. 95 (1989). Applying minimal scrutiny, a unanimous Court invalidated a requirement that only property owners could be members of a board of freeholders possessing authority to propose reorganization plans for local government units. While the board of freeholders was of a sufficiently limited purpose to trigger only minimal scrutiny the Court agreed that the property requirement furthered no "defensible" governmental purpose.

c. **Durational residency requirements.** Durational residency requirements for voting are subject to strict scrutiny. Lengthy requirements—those longer than thirty to fifty days—are almost impossible to justify and thus virtually always invalid. *Dunn v. Blumstein,* 405 U.S. 330 (1972), is the leading case. Tennessee required voters to be residents of Tennessee for one year and of the county for three months. The Court applied strict scrutiny and invalidated the law. Tennessee offered three *compelling* interests: (1) limiting the franchise to bona fide residents, (2) the prevention of fraud, and (3) assuring that the franchise would be exercised by "knowledgeable voters." The Court acknowledged the legitimacy of using bona fide residence as a criterion for voter eligibility, but concluded that Tennessee had not proven that its durational residency requirement was *necessary* to accomplish this goal. Other, less restrictive means could have been employed by Tennessee to assure the state's objective of limiting the franchise to bona fide residents. The Court conceded the validity of the second interest but ruled that "30 days . . . [is] ample . . . [to] complete whatever administrative tasks are necessary to prevent fraud." With respect to "knowledgeable voters" the Court thought that the durational residency requirements were "much too crude" a means of assuring well-informed voters.

d. **Disenfranchising felons and the accused**

i. **Felons: *Richardson v. Ramirez,* 418 U.S. 24 (1974).** California denies the vote to convicted felons who have served their sentences and completed parole. The Supreme Court upheld the law. Strict scrutiny did not apply because §2 of the 14th Amendment made it quite clear that the framers of that amendment did not intend to forbid the disenfranchisement of convicted felons. Section 2 of the 14th Amendment provides for a reduction in congressional representation of states that deny the vote to adult male citizens "except for participation in rebellion, *or other crime.*" Based on that clause and the fact that disenfranchisement of felons was ubiquitous in 1868, when the 14th Amendment was proposed, the Court concluded "that those who framed and adopted the 14th Amendment could not have intended to prohibit" denial of the vote to convicted felons.

ii.   **Disenfranchising the accused by denial of absentee ballots.** The denial of absentee ballots to prisoners awaiting trial does not trigger strict scrutiny. Minimal scrutiny applies. *McDonald v. Board of Election Commissioners*, 394 U.S. 802 (1969), upheld a denial of absentee ballots to "unsentenced inmates awaiting trial."

In *O'Brien v. Skinner*, 414 U.S. 524 (1974), the Court applied minimal scrutiny but struck down as "wholly arbitrary" New York's practice of supplying absentee ballots to prisoners awaiting trial in a remote county while denying such ballots to prisoners awaiting trial in their home county. Justices Blackmun and Rehnquist dissented, noting that New York "need not have provided for *any* . . . absentee voting."

e.   **Party primary voter eligibility.** States commonly regulate party primaries. Many states conduct "closed" primary elections—in which voters may vote only in the primary of which they are registered. In order to conduct closed primaries it is necessary to impose some "cut-off" or "record" date in advance of the primary election to establish party affiliation for purposes of the primary election. These schemes have gradually become subjected to strict scrutiny. To the extent that they substantially interfere with a voter's or political party's First Amendment rights of speech or free association without adequate justification they are unconstitutional denials of equal protection.

i.   *Rosario v. Rockefeller,* 410 U.S. 752 (1973). The Court applied minimal scrutiny in upholding New York's rule that required voters to register in a party eight to eleven months prior to the primary election in order to participate in the primary. Unlike the durational residency requirements at issue in *Dunn* the durational party affiliation requirement did not absolutely foreclose voting—it simply foreclosed switching parties in order to vote in a primary. The rule was not arbitrary; rather, it furthered a legitimate purpose—preventing voters from one party from "poaching" on another's party primary with detrimental results to the second party's integrity.

Example: Suppose that the State of Mojave has a politically vulnerable incumbent Democratic United States Senator, Kelly, running unopposed in the Democratic primary. The Republican primary contest for the United States Senate nomination pits Warren, an attractive, extremely popular Governor, against Bruce, a political novice with a passionate following among a sizeable minority segment of Republicans and little appeal elsewhere. If large numbers of Mojave Democrats switch party affiliation in order to vote for Bruce (and thereby enhance Kelly's chances in the general election) the integrity of the primary system is damaged. Durational party affiliation requirements address this concern.

ii. *Kusper v. Pontikes,* 414 U.S. 51 (1973). Illinois barred voters from a party primary election if they had voted in a primary election of any other party during the preceding twenty-three months. The Court employed strict scrutiny to strike down the Illinois requirement. The Court thought that strict scrutiny was warranted because the Illinois bar "substantially restricts . . . freedom to change . . . political party affiliation" and thus interfered with a voter's First Amendment rights of free association.

iii. *Tashjian v. Republican Party,* 479 U.S. 208 (1986). Connecticut law required that all voters in a party primary be registered voters of that party. The law was challenged by Connecticut's Republican Party, which had adopted a party rule opening the Republican primary to independent voters. The Court again applied strict scrutiny because the law substantially interfered with the First Amendment associational rights of Republicans to decide for themselves who should vote in their primary.

iv. *California Democratic Party v. Jones,* 120 S. Ct. 2402 (2000). The Court voided California's "blanket primary" law, under which all voters, regardless of political party affiliation, were permitted to vote for a candidate of any party in primary elections, thus presenting the possibility that a Republican candidate in the general election might be nominated by Democratic voters, or a Democratic candidate might be nominated by Republican voters. The Court found this to be an infringement of the freedom of expression of political views that is at the core of political parties. The Court applied strict scrutiny and found the infringement of political expression unjustified.

3. **Voting: Burdens on Exercise of the Franchise**

a. **Vote dilution—"one person, one vote."** Equal protection requires that legislative representation be apportioned on the basis of voter population. Other apportionment schemes, such as apportionment on the basis of political boundaries without respect to population, are generally invalid dilutions of the right of each voter to have his vote count equally with others.

i. *Reynolds v. Sims,* 377 U.S. 533 (1964). This landmark case established the "one person, one vote" principle. The Court determined that Alabama's apportionment system for its legislature, which produced districts of widely varying population, interfered with the fundamental right to vote by diluting the right to vote. Some voters effectively counted more than others because they voted in a district with a small population, while voters in more populous districts possessed a proportionately weaker voice. This was held to be insufficiently justified and thus invalidated as a violation of equal protection. The Court's ruling in *Reynolds v. Sims* meant that seats in both houses of a bicameral legislature must be apportioned on the basis of voter population alone. "[T]he Equal Protection Clause requires that a State make an honest and good faith effort to construct districts, in both houses of its legislature, as nearly of equal population as is practicable. . . . [If] divergences from a strict population standard are based on legitimate considerations incident to the effectuation of a rational state policy, some deviations from the equal-population principle are constitutionally permissible."

(a) **Justice Harlan's dissent.** Justice Harlan charged that there was no historical evidence to suggest that the equal protection clause was ever intended to address state legislative apportionment. Moreover, Harlan noted that the Court's opinion destroyed long-recognized state power to account for a host of important factors in making apportionment decisions, such as "economic or other . . . group interests, . . . geographical considerations, . . . insur[ing] effective representation for sparsely settled areas, . . . availability of access of citizens to their representatives, . . . [political] theories of bicameralism, . . . an attempt to balance urban and rural power, [and] the preference of voters in a State. . . . [N]o principle of logic . . . or politics, still less any constitutional principle, . . . establishes . . . any of these exclusions."

ii. *Lucas v. Colorado General Assembly,* 377 U.S. 713 (1964). In this companion case to *Reynolds* the Court concluded that the fact that an apportionment scheme had been approved by the voters in a statewide plebiscite was irrelevant. Even if a state's voters voluntarily assent to vote dilution in order to achieve other objectives that they regard as more important, *and do so in an election in which everyone's vote is precisely equal,* the voters' preferences will be ignored by the Court.

iii. **Local governments and special entities.** In *Hadley v. Junior College District,* 397 U.S. 50 (1970), the Court ruled that the "one person, one vote" standard applied to all elections of persons performing governmental functions. But see *Salyer Land Co. v. Tulare Water District* and *Ball v. James,* considered supra.

iv. **Computing equal population apportionment.** The population base that must be apportioned equally is limited to the population of **potential qualified voters.** For apportionment purposes, a state need not count those who cannot vote; e.g., aliens, citizens under age eighteen, temporary residents. *Burns v. Richardson,* 384 U.S. 73, 91-92 (1966).

b. **Vote dilution: Implementing "one person, one vote."** In order to implement population-only apportionment the Court was required to address its impact in many different legislative areas—Congress, state legislatures, local governments, and other special governmental entities. The Court's doctrine varies with the governmental unit involved.

   i. **Congressional districts: permissible deviations from numerical equality**

      (a) *Wesberry v. Sanders,* 376 U.S. 1 (1964). The Court used Article I, §2, which provides that House Representatives shall be "chosen . . . by the People of the Several States," to impose the rule of equal population apportionment for House seats.

      (b) **Application of *Wesberry.*** As nearly as is practically possible, each House district within a state must have the same number of constituents. *Kirkpatrick v. Preisler,* 394 U.S. 526 (1969).

      Example: In the absence of proof that greater equality was not possible the Court voided an apportionment scheme with a maximum variation of *less than a percentage point. Karcher v. Daggett,* 462 U.S. 725 (1983).

   ii. **State legislatures: permissible deviations from numerical equality.** "One person, one vote" means quite another thing when the standard is applied to state legislative apportionment.

      (a) **Minor deviations: under 10%.** So long as the interdistrict population deviation is less than 10% the Court considers the deviation as *de minimus,* not even requiring any justification. *Gaffney v. Cummings,* 412 U.S. 735 (1973); *White v. Regester,* 412 U.S. 755 (1973).

      (b) **Larger deviations: legitimate justifications.** Interdistrict deviations of more than 10% are *valid if the state can show legitimate state considerations* that justify the greater deviation. Maintenance of the integrity of existing political units within a state, like counties, has been found to be such a legitimate state consideration.

Example: Virginia proposed an apportionment scheme for its legislature with interdistrict population deviations of as much as 16.4% from perfect equality. Virginia justified the large deviation by its objective of maintaining the integrity of the boundaries of existing political units. The Court agreed that this justification was a legitimate state consideration and upheld the plan. *Mahan v. Howell,* 410 U.S. 315 (1973).

Example: Wyoming sought to assure each county at least one representative in the legislature, and so proposed an apportionment scheme that contained one striking deviation: a district with a population of less than half the average district population. The Court upheld the plan. *Brown v. Thomson,* 462 U.S. 835 (1983).

iii. **Local governments: permissible deviations from numerical equality.** Apportionment of electors among electoral districts at the local government level is nominally subject to the same standards as applicable to the states. See *Avery v. Midland County,* 390 U.S. 474, 481 (1968); *Hadley v. Junior College District of Metropolitan Kansas City,* 397 U.S. 50 (1970). But the Court is far more willing to accept justifications for deviation from pure equality in local government electoral districts.

Example: A county's legislative districts deviated from pure equality by 12% in order to respect town boundaries within the county. The Court upheld the scheme, noting that local governments need more flexibility to govern and are often faced with apportionment of a far smaller base of qualified electors. *Abate v. Mundt,* 403 U.S. 182 (1973).

Very large deviations from pure equality in order to accommodate existing political boundaries are not justifiable, even though local governments have more freedom to deviate.

Example: New York City's method of electing the Board of Estimate, a city legislative body, produced nearly an 80% deviation from perfect equality in order to assure each borough at least one seat. The Court rejected this justification and invalidated the method. *Board of Estimate v. Morris,* 489 U.S. 688 (1989).

c. **Prohibiting write-in votes:** *Burdick v. Takushi,* 504 U.S. 428 (1992). Hawaii's prohibition of write-in voting was challenged as a denial of equal protection. The challenger argued that strict scrutiny should apply because the ban on write-in votes allegedly interfered with a voter's fundamental right of free expression. The Court ruled that when election laws impose "*severe*" burdens on voters' fundamental rights, strict scrutiny applies, "but when a state election law provision imposes only 'reasonable, nondiscriminatory restrictions' upon the First and Fourteenth Amendment rights of voters, 'the State's *important regulatory interests* are generally sufficient to justify' the restrictions." It probably did not help the challenger's case that he asserted Hawaii's law denied him the right to vote for "Donald Duck" as a protest.

4. Voting: Ballot Access

a. Introduction. States have broad authority to regulate elections. They may restrict access to the ballot by imposing *reasonable and nondiscriminatory* regulations on political parties and candidates. But when such regulations *unduly or severely interfere* with the fundamental rights of individuals to associate together in a political party or "to cast their votes effectively" the Court applies strict scrutiny, requiring the state to justify its ballot access regulations by proof the regulations are narrowly crafted to advance a compelling state interest.

i. Accommodation of competing interests. These rules represent the Court's attempt to accommodate two powerful competing interests.

- The *nature of democratic government* is "rule by successive temporary majorities." Tribe, at 1097. In order for democracy to function it is essential that the electoral system fairly enable those out of power to obtain it through the collected will of the voters. When those in power rig the system to keep themselves entrenched democracy is extinguished in favor of a corrupt political oligarchy. The courts are especially skeptical of government electoral regulations that substantially impede the ability of a person to *become a candidate, to associate with others in political parties for the advancement of common political purposes,* or *to cast his vote effectively.*

- Some *organization of elections is indispensable* to their occurrence. At the extreme, if everyone voted when they were individually so moved, for whatever person and office they desired, it would be impossible to canvass the *collective will of the people* in order to determine the "temporary majority" that ought to wield power for the moment. Thus, courts recognize that states are presumptively entitled to enact *reasonable and nondiscriminatory* electoral regulations that govern the *eligibility of candidates and voters* and *access to the ballot by political parties and their candidates.*

b. Regulations limiting political parties. State laws that *severely* restrict the ability of political parties to place those holding their views on the ballot are generally subjected to strict scrutiny because they interfere substantially with the fundamental rights of free political association and free exercise of the franchise. Strict scrutiny has a unique meaning here: While the state's objective must be *compelling,* the fit between the challenged electoral regulation and the compelling objective usually need not be the least restrictive, or most narrowly tailored, option open to the state. So long as the fit is *reasonable* and the result does not *effectively exclude from the ballot parties with significant support,* strict scrutiny is satisfied. Reasonable election regulations that do not impede fundamental rights severely are subject to minimal scrutiny.

i. Severe restrictions

(a) *Williams v. Rhodes,* 393 U.S. 23 (1968). Ohio law provided that any political party receiving at least 10% of the vote in a gubernatorial election automatically qualified for the next presidential election ballot. Other parties could obtain a place on the ballot only if they had created a complicated party structure, held a primary election in conformity with "detailed and rigorous standards," and filed a petition signed by voters "totalling 15 percent of the number of ballots cast in the last preceding gubernatorial election." Because these conditions to ballot access severely impeded minority parties from obtaining a spot on the ballot and worked to ensure an hegemony of the Democratic and Republican parties, the Court applied strict scrutiny. Ohio argued that the scheme advanced two compelling interests: (1) promotion of "a two-party system in order to encourage compromise and political stability," and (2) preventing such a proliferation of parties that the ballot would present voters "with a choice so confusing that the popular will could be frustrated." The Court rejected the first contention, noting that the Ohio system gave "a complete monopoly" to the two existing major parties. The Court dismissed the second claimed objective as "no more than 'theoretically imaginable.'"

(b) *Illinois State Board of Elections v. Socialist Workers Party,* 440 U.S. 173 (1979). Illinois required new parties and independent candidates seeking to qualify for a municipal ballot to file nominating petitions signed by voters representing at least 5% of the total vote cast in the municipality in the last election. As applied in 1977, the law required over 40% *more* signatures to qualify for the Chicago ballot than the Illinois statewide ballot. Because of the severe burden thus placed on associational and voting rights the Court applied strict scrutiny. The requirement was voided because Illinois had no adequate justification for its bizarre rule—the state's objectives could surely be accomplished by receipt of the fewer signatures needed for the statewide ballot.

ii. Reasonable restrictions

(a) *Jenness v. Fortson,* 403 U.S. 431 (1971). Georgia denied ballot access to independent candidates unless they paid a concededly valid filing fee and filed a nominating petition signed by voters representing at least 5% of the total registered voters at the last election. The Court thought this was an entirely different case from that presented in *Williams v. Rhodes.* Unlike Ohio's law, Georgia's system did not substantially interfere with associational or voting rights. Georgia had not attempted to "freeze[] the status quo" since independent voters with a modest amount of support could qualify for the ballot. The Court implicitly applied minimal scrutiny and upheld the law.

(b) *American Party of Texas v. White,* 415 U.S. 767 (1974). Under Texas law, "major" parties—those whose gubernatorial candidate had received at least 200,000 votes in the last gubernatorial election—could gain access to the ballot merely by nominating a candidate. "Minor" parties—those with less than 2% of the gubernatorial vote—were required to hold precinct, county, and state nominating conventions on primary day and present nominating petitions signed by voters totaling at least 1% of the vote at the last gubernatorial election. Petition signatories were required to affirm that they had not voted in any other party primary or otherwise participated in another party's nominating process. The Court applied strict scrutiny because these regulations severely interfered with associational and voting rights, but concluded that Texas had adequate justifications for the rules. The "vital state objectives" of Texas—preserving the integrity of the electoral process and avoiding voter confusion—could not be accomplished in any "less burdensome" fashion. Texas did not freeze the status quo; indeed, two of the plaintiffs had satisfied the requirements. Moreover, minor parties that had very modest appeal to the general electorate—barely 2% of the gubernatorial vote—could and would escape the requirements.

(c) *Munro v. Socialist Workers Party,* 479 U.S. 189 (1986). In order for minor parties to appear on the general election ballot, Washington required them to receive at least 1% of the vote in a primary election open to all voters, regardless of party affiliation. The Court applied minimal scrutiny and relied on both *Jenness* and *White* to uphold the requirement.

(d) *Storer v. Brown,* 415 U.S. 724 (1974). The Court upheld, under strict scrutiny, a California requirement that barred independent candidates from the ballot if they had a registered party affiliation within the preceding year. The provision was held to "further" California's compelling "interest in the stability of its political system."

iii. **Ballot access "gestalt":** *Anderson v. Celebrezze,* 460 U.S. 780 (1983). Ohio required John Anderson, an independent presidential candidate in 1980, to file nominating signatures of 5,000 voters by March 20 in order to appear on the November ballot. The Court struck down the provision by applying a "gestalt" analysis partly rooted in equal protection and partly in free speech. A court "must first consider the character and magnitude of the asserted injury to [First and 14th Amendment rights], then . . . identify and evaluate the precise interests put forward by the State as justifications for the burden imposed by its rule, . . . determine the legitimacy and strength of each of those interests, . . . [and] consider the extent to which those interests make it necessary to burden the plaintiff's rights. Only after weighing all these factors is the reviewing court in a position to decide whether the challenged provision is unconstitutional." In another place, however, the Court seemed to employ a form of intermediate review: "Although these rights of voters are fundamental, [the] state's *important* regulatory interests are generally sufficient to *justify reasonable, nondiscriminatory restrictions.*" Ohio's interests in political stability, treating candidates alike, and making certain that voters were well educated about presidential candidates were inadequate. Political stability amounted to "a desire to protect existing political parties from competition." Ohio's law did not treat candidates alike, since the names of the Democratic and Republican contenders would not be known until the midsummer nominating conventions. Finally, the Court thought it "unrealistic to suggest it takes seven months to inform the electorate about a particular candidate simply because he lacks a partisan label."

Justice Rehnquist, joined by Justices White, Powell, and O'Connor, dissented. They pointed out that "the Ohio filing deadline prevents [a] candidate such as Anderson from seeking a party nomination and then, finding that he is rejected by the party, bolting from the party to form an independent candidacy. This is precisely the same behavior that California sought to prevent by the disaffiliation statute this Court upheld in *Storer.*"

The *Anderson* test was applied in *Timmons v. Twin Cities Area New Party,* 520 U.S. 351 (1997), in which the Court upheld Minnesota's ban on "fusion" candidacies (where a person appears on the ballot as the candidate of more than one party) after concluding that the ban was not a severe restriction. Minnesota's "interests in avoiding voter confusion, promoting candidate competition . . . , preventing electoral distortions and ballot manipulations, and discouraging party splintering" were sufficient.

c. **Regulations limiting candidacy.** The Court has never held that political "candidacy [is] a fundamental right." Rather, regulations that impinge on political candidacy are subjected to strict scrutiny when "the challenged restriction *unfairly or unnecessarily burdens* the 'availability of political opportunity' " to the voters.

i. **Property ownership:** *Turner v. Fouche,* 396 U.S. 346 (1970). The Court struck down a Georgia constitutional provision that barred from service on county school boards any person who did not own real property in Georgia. The Court intimated that some "heightened" scrutiny applied to property qualifications for holding public office. The specific provision at issue was invalidated because it was poorly suited to any legitimate interest Georgia might have. The Court acknowledged that in some circumstances "a property qualification for office-holding could survive constitutional scrutiny."

ii. **Filing fees**

(a) *Lubin v. Panish,* 415 U.S. 709 (1974). California required candidates for public office to pay a filing fee in order to appear on the ballot. The Court invalidated the requirement as applied to an indigent seeking the office of county supervisor. The Court acknowledged California's compelling interest in eliminating frivolous candidacies and keeping the ballot to a manageable size but thought that a filing fee, at least "in the absence of reasonable alternative means of ballot access," was an "unfair" or "unnecessary" burden on the "continued availability of political opportunity."

(b) *Bullock v. Carter,* 405 U.S. 134 (1972). Texas financed its primary elections by charging filing fees of the candidates designed to defray the cost of the election. The result was filing fees that often amounted to thousands of dollars for each candidate. Texas defended the system by claiming that it was well suited to its purposes of financing primary elections and of limiting the ballot to serious candidates. The Court admitted the validity of Texas's goal of paying for primary elections but thought that the particular means chosen— making the candidates pay—unduly curbed "the prerogatives of voters" to make an unfettered political choice. The goal of confining the ballot to serious candidates was likewise valid but the method of doing so—high filing fees—was "extraordinarily ill-fitted" to that objective, because rich political dilettantes with no public following could qualify while poor candidates with a real constituency might be barred from the ballot. The Court did not ground its decision on wealth as a "suspect classification" but did recognize that such economic line-drawing unduly burdened voter choice.

iii. **Term limits and other regulations limiting the candidacy of incumbent office holders.** The Court has concluded that states lack authority to limit the term of service of their federal senators and representatives. State imposed *term limits on state legislators* and *other limitations on the candidacies of incumbents* are evaluated by the Court's usual standard for ballot access cases: "*insignificant interference[s]* with access to the ballot need only" meet minimal scrutiny, while "*substantial*" or "*severe*" impairments receive strict scrutiny.

(a) **State imposed term limits on federal legislators:** *United States Term Limits, Inc. v. Thornton,* 514 U.S. 779 (1995). Arkansas voters adopted a law that denied a ballot position for United States senators who have served two terms and United States representatives who have served three terms. The Court, 5 to 4, in an opinion by Justice Stevens, struck down the limits, but not on equal protection grounds. The Court concluded that the states had no power to add additional qualifications to hold a seat in Congress to those specified in the Constitution. The Court asserted that this result was compelled by the "fundamental principle of our representative democracy . . . 'that the people should choose whom they please to govern them.' " The Court added that states have no power to add qualifications because this power is not part of the states' reserved powers. In dissent, Justice Thomas pointed out that the federal government possesses only those powers delegated to it by the people through the Constitution, and the states retain all other powers not prohibited to them by the Constitution.

(b) **Other limits on incumbents' candidacies:** *Clements v. Fashing,* 457 U.S. 957 (1982). Section 19 of the Texas Constitution provides that identified public officeholders shall not "be eligible to the Legislature" until their current term of office has expired. Section 65 of the Texas Constitution provides that some, but not all, public officials must resign their current office in order to run for federal office or other state office. A four-Justice plurality of the Court applied minimal scrutiny and upheld these provisions. The "serve-your-term" provision of section 19 imposed a waiting period for running for the state legislature, "hardly a significant barrier to candidacy," and thus triggered only minimal scrutiny. Section 19 was rationally related to Texas's legitimate interest of preserving the integrity of public offices by ensuring that incumbents did not abandon their duties to further their personal political ambition. The "resign-to-run" provision of Section 65 posed even less of an interference with candidacy and was rationally related to the objective of ensuring an officeholder's unqualified attention to his duties. The fact that the provision was under-inclusive—it applied only to some officeholders and presumably Texas's objective extended to all public officials—was not a problem. Section 65 could be "upheld consistent with the 'one step at a time' approach" characteristic of minimal review.

5. **Access to the Judicial Process: Quasi-Fundamental Rights**

   a. **Introduction.** There is no "fundamental right of access" to the judicial process. Nowhere does the Constitution guarantee such a right, nor has the Court found such a right implicit in the Constitution. Nevertheless, the Court has subjected some state laws inhibiting access to the courts to an ill-defined "heightened" scrutiny. There is no single unifying principle to explain these cases, but some common threads can be identified.

      i. **Money as a barrier.** Although the Court has rejected the idea that wealth is a suspect classification triggering strict scrutiny, the Court has used the presence of money-based barriers to court access as a significant factor in applying heightened scrutiny to such money-based barriers.

      ii. **Civil v. criminal cases: "importance" of the right at issue.** Because the stakes are generally higher in criminal cases than civil ones the Court has tended to examine more skeptically state-imposed barriers to vindication of a criminal defendant's rights.

 # EXAMPLE AND ANALYSIS

In *Griffin v. Illinois*, 351 U.S. 12 (1956), the Court struck down a money barrier to appellate review of a criminal conviction as violative of equal protection and due process. By contrast, in *Ortwein v. Schwab*, 410 U.S. 656 (1973), the Court upheld a

$25 filing fee for appellate review of administrative decisions reducing welfare benefits of indigents. The difference seemed to lie in the perceived *importance* of the two rights—freedom from incarceration versus the relative amount of welfare benefits.

The Court has explicitly rejected the idea that the "fundamentality" of a claimed right depends on its "importance" but the relative importance of the right at issue in the judicial process is definitely a factor the Court considers in deciding upon the degree of scrutiny to be used in evaluating the validity of any given barrier to the courts.

iii. **Interrelationship with due process.** The "access to courts" cases typically raise both equal protection and due process issues. Any given state-imposed barrier to access may be thought of as applying with differential impact upon some people (raising an equal protection issue) or may be conceived as a denial of a procedural due process right of "opportunity to be heard." The cases are not readily assimilated to either provision, but seem to be grounded more in equal protection than due process.

b. **Criminal appeals.** There is no constitutional right to appeal a criminal conviction. See, e.g., *McKane v. Durston*, 153 U.S. 684 (1894). Nevertheless, the Court has found that, when a state does permit appeal of a conviction, some state-imposed barriers to appeal are invalid.

i. **Trial transcripts for indigents:** *Griffin v. Illinois,* 351 U.S. 12 (1956). In order to appeal a criminal conviction a trial transcript is essential. Illinois charged all convicted criminals (including indigents) for the cost of a trial transcript. Its purpose for doing so was to keep the costs of producing transcripts from burdening the taxpayers and to eliminate appeals by those who could or would not pay for a transcript. The Court thought that charging indigents for necessary trial transcripts was a denial of equal protection and due process. Apparently minimal scrutiny was applied. The Court stated that "the ability to pay [for a transcript] bears no rational relationship to . . . guilt or innocence" but ignored the fact that "ability to pay" was rationally related to Illinois's objectives. The Court simply concluded that charging indigents for trial transcripts was an impermissible discrimination "on account of their poverty."

(a) **Harlan's dissent.** Justice Harlan argued that equal protection was inapplicable. "All that Illinois has done is fail to alleviate the consequences of differences in economic circumstances that exist wholly apart from any state action. The Court['s] holding produces the anomalous result that a constitutional [requirement] to treat all persons equally means . . . that Illinois must give to some what it requires others to pay for. . . . [T]he real issue . . . is not whether Illinois *has* discriminated but whether it has a duty *to* discriminate." Harlan contended that "the basis" for the Court's ruling "is simply an unarticulated conclusion that it violates 'fundamental fairness' for a State which provides for appellate review [effectively to deny it to indigents.] That of course is the traditional language of due process." On the due process issue, Harlan was unpersuaded that a State could validly deny *any* appeal but could not condition appeal for reasons neither "arbitrary or capricious."

ii. **Appellate counsel.** The Court has concluded that states that provide for appeal of criminal convictions must provide appellate counsel to convicted indigents only with respect to the *first appeal, granted as a matter of statutory right.* States need not provide appellate counsel to indigents for discretionary appeals.

(a) **Appeals of right:** *Douglas v. California,* 372 U.S. 353 (1963). California required an indigent convict seeking appellate counsel to request the appellate court to review the record independently. Appellate counsel would be appointed only if the appeals court concluded that a lawyer "would be helpful to the defendant or the court." The Court held that this procedure violated both equal protection and due process. Without much indication of the standard of review the Court simply announced that California's prerequisite for a free lawyer amounted to "discrimination against the indigent." As for due process, the Court was similarly curt: "When an indigent is forced to run this gantlet of a preliminary showing of merit, the right to appeal does not comport with fair procedure."

The dissenters, led by Justice Harlan, stated that equal protection prohibits the states "from discriminating between 'rich' and 'poor' *as such* [but does not] prevent the State from adopting a law of general applicability that may affect the poor more harshly than the [rich]. Every financial exaction which the State imposes on a uniform basis is more easily satisfied by the well-to-do than by the indigent. [N]o one would dispute the constitutional power of the State to levy a uniform sales tax, to charge tuition at a state university, [or] to establish minimum bail for [crimes]. [T]he Equal Protection Clause does not impose on the States 'an affirmative duty to lift the handicaps flowing from economic circumstances.' " As in

Griffin, the dissenters argued that the real issue was whether California's procedure complied with due process. California denied "to no one the right to appeal," and ensured that "the indigent appellant receives . . . expert and conscientious legal appraisal of the merits of his case . . . , and whether or not he is assigned counsel, is guaranteed full consideration of his appeal."

(b) **Discretionary appeals:** *Ross v. Mofitt,* 417 U.S. 600 (1974). In *Ross* the Court refused to extend *Douglas* to discretionary appeals. Due process, which does not require *any appeal at all,* was not offended by a state's refusal "to provide counsel to indigent defendants at every stage of the way." Equal protection would be violated if "indigents are singled out by the State and denied meaningful access to the appellate system because of their poverty." But that was not the case where the state had already provided counsel for one appeal as of right. "The duty of the State . . . is not to duplicate the legal arsenal that may be privately retained by a criminal defendant, [but] only to assure the indigent defendant an *adequate opportunity* to present his claims fairly in the context of the State's appellate process." In short, the state is not required to supply indigents with the O.J. Simpson legal team.

c. **Civil litigation.** The Court has been much less willing to find that state-imposed obstacles to the civil justice system violate equal protection. In only three cases, one involving divorce, one a civil action to establish paternity, and one involving the validity of filing fees to appeal termination of parental rights, has the Court found access barriers violative of due process or equal protection.

   i. **Divorce:** *Boddie v. Connecticut,* 401 U.S. 371 (1971). Connecticut required persons seeking a divorce to pay filing fees of about $60 in order to commence the civil process of divorce. The Court invalidated this rule as applied to indigents, relying entirely upon due process. Writing for the Court, Justice Harlan concluded that "given the basic position of . . . marriage . . . in this society's hierarchy or values and the concomitant state monopolization of the means for legally dissolving this relationship, due process does prohibit a State from denying, solely because of inability to pay, access to its courts to individuals who seek judicial dissolution of their marriages."

   ii. **Paternity suits:** *Little v. Streater,* 452 U.S. 1 (1981). On due process grounds the Court followed *Boddie* and concluded that an indigent defendant in a paternity action was entitled to free blood grouping tests. The Court stressed the unique "exculpatory" power of such tests, "the State's prominent role in [the] litigation," and the "quasi-criminal" nature of the paternity proceeding.

iii. **Termination of parental rights:** *M.L.B. v. S.L.J.,* 519 U.S. 102 (1997). Mississippi required advance payment of fees to appeal civil judgments terminating parental rights. Because the right involved is of such fundamental importance and its loss is "severe and . . . irreversible," the Court, 6 to 3, ruled that the fee barrier violated both due process and equal protection.

iv. **Bankruptcy:** *United States v. Kras,* 409 U.S. 434 (1973). The Court upheld the federal Bankruptcy Act's requirement of a $50 filing fee to institute bankruptcy proceedings. Unlike *Boddie,* where the fundamental interest of marriage was implicated by the access barrier of a filing fee, the Bankruptcy Act provision infringed no fundamental right protected by substantive due process. Similarly, because the filing fee did not impinge upon any fundamental right for purposes of equal protection only minimal scrutiny was demanded.

v. **Judicial review of welfare reduction:** *Ortwein v. Schwab,* 410 U.S. 656 (1973). The Court upheld a $25 filing fee to obtain appellate review of an administrative decision to reduce welfare benefits. The right to receive any welfare benefits, much less any particular level of benefits, is not a fundamental right. Minimal scrutiny was applicable and the provision upheld. On the due process prong, the Court noted that due process does not require providing any appeal of a criminal conviction, and considered the agency hearing provided sufficient to comport with procedural due process.

6. **The Right of Interstate Mobility: The Right to Travel**

a. **Introduction.** Implicit in the concept of single nationhood is the idea that every person has the right to *move or travel within the United States.*

Example: Nevada imposed a $1 exit tax on travelers leaving the state. The Court voided the tax as an impermissible interference with an implied constitutional right to pass freely throughout the nation. "For all the great purposes for which the Federal Government was formed we are one people, with one common country [and] as members of the same community must have the right to pass and repass through every part of it without interruption." *Crandall v. Nevada,* 73 U.S. 35 (1868).

When states *discriminate substantially against new residents and in favor of long-time residents* the courts may apply strict scrutiny to evaluate such distinctions under equal protection. A shorthand way of expressing this concept is to say that otherwise legitimate state rules that *penalize* exercise of the right to travel are subject to strict scrutiny while rules that do *not* penalize travel, even though they may distinguish between new and old residents, are subjected only to minimal scrutiny. Of course, a rule that has as its *sole purpose* deterring immigration of new residents is invalid per se.

b. Durational residency requirements that penalize exercise of the right of interstate mobility

   i. What constitutes a penalty? The Court has suggested two criteria to determine when any given distinction between new and old residents is a "penalty": (1) whether the regulation at issue would "deter migration," and (2) the significance of the impact of the regulation on affected persons—the more "important" or *permanent* the impact the more likely the regulation will be treated as a penalty. Thus, durational residency requirements are penalties when imposed as a condition to receipt of certain welfare benefits (because the loss of benefits is both "important" and permanent) but identical durational residency requirements are not penalties when imposed as a condition to obtaining a divorce (because the wait, while "important," is not permanent).

   The factors that courts consider in evaluating whether any given distinction between newcomers and oldtimers is a "penalty" upon the right of interstate mobility follow:

   - *Deterring Migration:* Rules that are likely to deter migration are more apt to be considered penalties.

   - *"Importance" of the Interest Affected:* To the extent the rules in question infringe upon "important" interests they are more likely to be considered penalties. But note the curiosity that welfare benefits are seemingly more "important" than marital dissolution even though the latter, but not the former, is constitutionally fundamental.

   - *"Permanence" of the Deprivation:* Discriminatory rules against newcomers that produce permanent deprivations are more apt to be treated as penalties than rules producing only temporary deprivations.

   ii. Welfare benefits: *Shapiro v. Thompson,* 394 U.S. 618 (1969). Pennsylvania, Connecticut, and the District of Columbia, in common with most states, denied welfare assistance to persons who had not lived in the state for at least one year. The Court applied strict scrutiny and invalidated these durational residency requirements. Strict scrutiny was applied because the residency requirements "penalized" actual exercise of the fundamental right of interstate mobility and substantially deterred the future exercise of that right. The states sought to justify the residency requirement "as a protective device to preserve the fiscal integrity of state public assistance programs." However, the Court held that "the purpose of inhibiting migration by needy persons into the State is constitutionally impermissible." The states argued that the durational residency requirement also served other purposes, less invidious in nature: (1) to facilitate welfare budgeting, (2) provide an objective test of residency, (3) to reduce fraud, and (4) to encourage newcomers to enter the workforce. The Court used strict scrutiny to evaluate the relationship between the one-year residency rule and these objectives because it thought that the rule *penalized* the right of interstate mobility. The Court did not opine whether or not these objectives were compelling because it found that the durational residency rule was poorly fitted to the accomplishment of any of these state goals.

Chief Justice Warren and Justice Stewart dissented on the ground that, since Congress had authorized the states to impose durational residency requirements for receipt of welfare, the states had enhanced power to burden interstate mobility. Justice Harlan dissented on the ground that the Court's preoccupation with the "importance" of welfare benefits "creates an exception which threatens to swallow the standard equal protection rule. . . . [N]othing entitles this Court to pick out particular human activities, characterize them as 'fundamental,' and give them added protection under an unusually stringent equal protection test."

iii. **Public medical care: *Memorial Hospital v. Maricopa County,*** 415 U.S. 250 (1974). Arizona denied free nonemergency medical care to indigents who had resided in Arizona for less than a year. Relying on *Shapiro*, the Court invalidated this durational residency requirement. The majority regarded this waiting period for free nonemergency medical care to be a "penalty" because it deprived newcomers of a "basic necessity of life" and denied to "new residents the same right to vital government benefits and privileges . . . as are enjoyed by [long-time] residents."

iv. **Voting: *Dunn v. Blumstein,*** 405 U.S. 330 (1972). The Court applied strict scrutiny to evaluate the validity of Tennessee's one-year durational residency requirement to vote, because the requirement infringed upon both the fundamental right to vote and the fundamental right of interstate mobility. The waiting period "penalized" a newcomer's exercise of the mobility right.

v. **Welfare benefits reprise: *Saenz v. Roe,*** 526 U.S. 489 (1999). The Court struck down a California law that restricted welfare benefits of new residents of California, for the first year of their residency, to the levels provided by their former states of residence. The Court identified three different components to the right to travel: "[T]he right of a citizen of one state to enter and leave another state, the right to be treated as a welcome visitor rather than an unfriendly alien when temporarily present in [another] state, and, for those travelers who elect to become permanent residents, the right to be treated like other citizens of that state. What is at issue [here] is [the] third [aspect], the right of the newly arrived citizen to the same privileges and immunities enjoyed by other citizens of the same state. That right is [one of] 'the privileges or immunities of citizens of the United States' [protected by the 14th Amendment]. Since the right to travel embraces the citizen's right to be treated equally in her new state of residence, the discriminatory classification is itself a penalty." Chief Justice Rehnquist, joined by Justice Thomas, dissented: "I cannot see how the right to become a citizen of another State is a necessary 'component' of the right to travel. [A] person is no longer 'traveling' in any sense of the word when he finishes his journey to a State which he plans to make his home. [The] right to travel and the right to become a citizen are distinct, their relationship is not reciprocal, and one is not a 'component' of the other. [At] most, restrictions on an individual's right to become a citizen indirectly affect his calculus in deciding whether to exercise his right to travel in the first place, but such an attenuated and uncertain relationship is no ground for folding one right into the other. [Even] when redefining the right to travel in *Shapiro* and its progeny, the Court has 'always carefully distinguished between bona fide residence requirements [and] durational, fixed date, and fixed point residence requirements, which treat established residents differently based on the time they migrated into the State.' [If] States can require individuals to reside in-state for a year before exercising the right to educational benefits [or] the right to terminate a marriage, [then] States may surely do the same for the welfare benefits. [There] is no link between the need for an education or for a divorce and the length of residence, and yet States may use length of residence as an objective yardstick to channel their benefits to those whose intent to stay is legitimate."

Saenz grounds the right of migration in the 14th Amendment's privileges and immunities clause and may also call into question the legitimacy of any distinctions between new and old residents, however ephemeral or related to bona fide residency. An unanswered question is whether *Sosna*, which follows, is still good law.

vi. **Relationship to other doctrines.** The interstate mobility cases are related to several other constitutional doctrines.

- *Commerce Clause:* Some state restrictions on interstate mobility may also violate the dormant or negative commerce clause. In *Edwards v. California,* 314 U.S. 160 (1941), the Court used the commerce clause to void a California law prohibiting any person "bringing into the State any indigent person who is not a resident of the State."

- *Article IV, Section 2's Privilege and Immunities Clause:* Some state mobility restrictions may also violate Article IV's privileges and immunities clause. In *Zobel v. Williams,* supra, Justice O'Connor thought that Article IV's privileges and immunities clause deals with "just this type of discrimination," Alaska's disbursal of its surplus on length-of-residence criteria.

- *14th Amendment's Privileges or Immunities Clause:* Even though the *Slaughter-House Cases* limited the scope of this clause to federal privileges or immunities, some state mobility restrictions offend this guarantee. Examples include the Nevada exit tax voided in *Crandall v. Nevada,* supra, and *Saenz v. Roe.*

c. **Durational residency requirements that do not penalize exercise of the right of interstate mobility.** Many durational residency requirements are subject to minimal scrutiny because they are insubstantial interferences with interstate mobility—they do not *penalize* exercise of that right.

   i. **Divorce eligibility:** *Sosna v. Iowa,* 419 U.S. 393 (1975). Iowa required that a person reside in the state for a year before becoming eligible to commence a divorce action against a nonresident of Iowa. The Court effectively applied minimal scrutiny in upholding the requirement. Iowa's durational residency requirement did not totally foreclose divorce, but only delayed its availability. Of course, the same might be said of the durational residency requirements struck down in *Shapiro* or *Memorial Hospital.* Iowa did have weightier interests to justify its durational residency requirement; rather than mere "budgetary considerations or administrative convenience," Iowa wished to avoid "officious intermeddling in matters in which another State has a paramount interest, and [to minimize] the susceptibility of its own divorce decrees to collateral attack." But these interests were not labeled compelling; indeed, while the Court never precisely identified the standard of review it treated these interests as legitimate (perhaps as important) and regarded the one year waiting period as rationally related to Iowa's objectives. "Iowa may quite reasonably decide that it does not wish to become a divorce mill."

    ii. **Differential university tuition:** *Starns v. Malkerson,* 401 U.S. 985 (1971), affirming without opinion 326 F. Supp. 234 (D. Minn. 1970). Minnesota's public universities charged lower tuition rates for Minnesota residents than nonresidents and conditioned eligibility for resident rates on one year's residence in Minnesota. The Court summarily affirmed this scheme.

d. **Bona fide residency requirements.** States may *validly impose bona fide residency requirements.*

    i. *Martinez v. Bynum,* 461 U.S. 321 (1983). Texas law permitted local school districts to charge tuition to students who were not bona fide residents of the district. The Court applied minimal scrutiny and upheld the law. Minimal scrutiny was appropriate because a bona fide residency requirement "does not burden or penalize the constitutional right of interstate travel, for any person is free to move to a State and to establish residence there." The law was upheld because bona fide residence requirements further "the substantial state interest in assuring that services provided for its residents are enjoyed only by residents."

    ii. *McCarthy v. Philadelphia Civil Service Commission,* 424 U.S. 645 (1976). Philadelphia required its city employees to reside in Philadelphia. McCarthy, a Philadelphia firefighter, moved to New Jersey and was fired. The Court summarily upheld the regulation, explaining that *Shapiro* "did not question 'the validity [of] bona fide residence requirements.' "

REVIEW QUESTIONS AND ANSWERS

Question: The state of Tehama enacts legislation that requires all operators of motorcycles to wear helmets. Exempted from the requirement are all operators of mopeds and motorized scooters. Under Tehama law, mopeds and motor scooters are barred from freeways. Jane, who rides a large Harley-Davidson motorcycle, challenges the law as a violation of equal protection. What result?

Answer: The law is almost certainly valid. The law does not employ a suspect classification and does not infringe upon any constitutionally fundamental right. Accordingly, it is subject to minimal scrutiny—the law will be upheld if it is rationally related to any conceivable legitimate government interest. The Tehama legislature may well have thought that the lower power and speeds of motor scooters and mopeds, together with their absence from freeways, posed a lesser safety risk to their users. That judgment is very probably wrong, but it is not irrational for the Tehama legislature to act upon a misguided view. The Tehama law is under-inclusive—the law's objective is motorcyclist safety and it fails to include some motorcyclists exposed to the traffic and injury risks the law seeks to address. But under-inclusion is rarely fatal; the Court permits legislatures to take "one step at a time" in addressing the problems it perceives. Given the extreme deference to legislative judgment embodied in minimal scrutiny the Tehama law is probably valid.

Question: The state of Skagit adopted a "drug-free" workplace rule. Under the rule, no persons could be hired as Skagit state employees if they had ever used illegal drugs at any time in their lives. To implement the rule, Skagit conducted background checks of all job applicants by querying the comprehensive medical records of drug testing laboratories maintained in computerized data bases. If those records disclosed a positive result for any illegal drug at any time the applicant was rejected. Harry, a forty-two-year-old computer programmer, applied for a job with the Skagit Department of Social Services and was rejected because he had tested positive for marijuana when he was a seventeen-year-old high school senior and varsity athlete. Harry brings suit, arguing that Skagit denied him equal protection by its refusal to hire him. What result?

Answer: Skagit's refusal to hire Harry probably did not violate equal protection. Classification by prior drug usage is neither a suspect classification nor impinges upon a constitutionally fundamental right. There is no due process fundamental privacy right to keep sensitive medical information out of governmentally maintained or accessible data banks. (See *Whalen v. Roe.*) Accordingly, minimal scrutiny applies. Skagit's policy is designed to ensure that no state employee is a drug user, presumably to ensure a safe and efficient workplace. But the Skagit policy is extremely over-inclusive in two ways. First, it bars prior drug users from employment no matter how remote in time the prior drug use may be. Second, it bars prior drug users from employment in positions where safety and efficiency concerns may be minimal. In Harry's case, his prior drug use was twenty-five years ago when he was an adolescent. Even if he were a current user of marijuana, which a twenty-five-year-old positive test does little to establish, marijuana usage probably does not implicate any safety concerns, but may implicate efficiency concerns. Nonetheless, Skagit's use of old drug tests as a disqualification device is invalid only if use of such tests is *irrationally related* to a legitimate state interest. Skagit might rationally conclude that evidence of any past drug usage indicates a small degree of risk of future drug usage (present drug usage can be detected by a preemployment test) and that, even though the risk is small, it is one that Skagit can refuse to assume. While that disqualification device is over-inclusive—many people are barred from employment who are not current drug users nor likely to use drugs—over-inclusion is permissible so long as it is rational. See *New York City Transit Authority v. Beazer,* which upheld a flat and over-inclusive ban on employment of methadone users. However, the connection between risk of future drug use and present methadone use was much stronger in *Beazer* than the connection between old positive drug tests and future drug usage. This might be the rare case in which the over-inclusion is irrational but, given the high degree of legislative deference in minimal scrutiny, probably not.

Question: In order to promote neighborhood stability and to preserve the ability of current homeowners to remain in their homes, the State of Siskiyou enacted legislation granting an annual $500 property tax credit to all Siskiyou residents then owning taxable residential real property in Siskiyou. The law provided that the credit would be extinguished by any future transfer of the property. Jolene moved to Siskiyou a year after the law was enacted and bought a residence. She brings suit, charging that the tax credit (for which she is not eligible) violates equal protection. What result?

Answer: Jolene will not succeed. The law is subject to minimal scrutiny. It is rationally related to the legitimate state interest of promoting neighborhood stability and preserving the ability of present homeowners to remain in their homes. (See *Nordlinger v. Hahn.*)

Question: Assume that, in the prior question, Siskiyou enacted legislation that granted an annual $500 property tax credit to all Siskiyou residents as of that date who either then owned or later acquired residential real property in Siskiyou. The facts are otherwise as stated. What result?

Answer: Jolene will succeed. The law now establishes a *fixed* and *permanent* distinction between two classes of bona fide Siskiyou residents—owners of residential real property who were residents as of the date the law was enacted and owners of residential real property who later became Siskiyou residents. Such fixed, permanent distinctions between "oldtimers" to Siskiyou and "newcomers" to Siskiyou further an illegitimate objective—rewarding oldtimers but not newcomers. Since the illegitimate objective is detectable from the face of the law, it will not matter that the law might be rationally related to its goal of preserving existing home ownership and neighborhood stability. (See, e.g., *Hooper v. Bernalillo County Assessor.*)

Question: The state of Shasta enacts legislation that bars adult illegal aliens from receipt of unemployment compensation benefits. Arnold, a citizen of Canada illegally present in the United States and residing in Shasta, is laid off from his job and seeks unemployment compensation to which he would be entitled but for his status as an illegal alien. Under federal immigration law Arnold could not legally work in the United States. Arnold challenges the validity of the Shasta law as a denial of equal protection. What result?

Answer: Arnold will lose. *Illegal* alienage is not a suspect classification and there is no constitutionally fundamental right to receipt of unemployment compensation. Minimal scrutiny applies and the law is presumably rationally related to Shasta's legitimate state interest of deterring the employment of illegal aliens in violation of federal law. *De Canas v. Bica*, 424 U.S. 351 (1976), is squarely on point and so holds.

Question: Assume the facts stated in the prior question, except that Shasta has now enacted legislation that bars adult illegal aliens from receiving state-funded aid to dependent children. Arnold is father to three children, all citizens of Canada and illegally present in the United States. But for the Shasta legislation Arnold would be entitled to state-funded aid to dependent children. Arnold challenges his denial of such aid as a violation of equal protection. What result?

Answer: Although the Shasta legislation does not classify on a suspect basis or impinge upon a constitutionally fundamental right it is possible that the courts might apply "enhanced" minimal scrutiny. In *Plyler v. Doe*, the Court struck down Texas's denial of free public education to illegal alien children as not "rationally related to a *substantial* state interest." The Court thought that the relative innocence of children coupled with the importance of education warranted this heightened scrutiny. Here, it is possible that the denial of assistance to needy illegal alien children coupled with the "importance" of such assistance might trigger "enhanced" scrutiny. If so, it is an open question whether denial of state aid to dependent children is rationally related to a *substantial* state interest. In *Plyler*, the Court thought that the state's desire to save money was not a substantial interest. If *Plyler*'s "enhanced" test applies, Shasta's legislation may be invalid. Shasta's interest in saving money is not substantial, but its interest in deterring illegal immigration might be. *Plyler* stated that "States . . . have some authority to act with respect to illegal aliens, at least where such action mirrors federal objectives and furthers a legitimate state goal." Shasta's desire to deter illegal immigration certainly mirrors federal objectives, but it may do no more than that. Shasta probably has to have a substantial legitimate objective of its own, rather than having as its objective mimicry of federal law.

Question: The state of Cowlitz enacted legislation that makes possession of both powdered cocaine and crack cocaine a crime. Possession of one ounce of crack cocaine is punished by a prison term of one year. The legislative history of these provisions suggests that the Cowlitz legislature believed that crack cocaine was more addictive than powdered cocaine and that violence was more frequently associated with the distribution of crack cocaine than powdered cocaine. Several academic studies support this belief. About 80% of those charged by Cowlitz with possession of powdered cocaine are white. Over 95% of those charged by Cowlitz with possession of crack cocaine are black. Warren, a black man convicted of possession of crack cocaine and sentenced to a prison term of ten years, contends that the sentence imposed on him violates equal protection. What result?

Answer: Warren will probably lose. The Cowlitz law does not facially discriminate on the basis of race, but does have a disparate racial impact. Blacks are far more likely to receive a harsher punishment for substantially the same offense. In order for strict scrutiny to apply Warren must prove that a discriminatory racial purpose was a motivating factor in Cowlitz's decision to punish crack possession more harshly than possession of powdered cocaine. There does not appear to be much besides the statistical disparity to prove such a racially discriminatory motive. Even if Warren could prove that the Cowlitz legislature acted as it did because of the fact that blacks are the predominant users of crack cocaine, Cowlitz would then have the burden of proving that the disparate penalties would have been adopted even if there was no racially discriminatory motivation. It is likely that the apparently more harmful effects of crack cocaine would suffice to establish that Cowlitz would have punished crack possession more harshly even in the absence of racial motivations. Only if Warren proves that *purposeful* racial discrimination was a motivating factor *and* Cowlitz fails to rebut that proof would strict scrutiny apply. In the unlikely event that strict scrutiny applies the law would probably be voided, as it does not seem to be narrowly drawn to achieve a compelling state interest.

Question: For many years the state of Magnolia operated the University of Magnolia as a "whites-only" school and operated Magnolia State University as a "blacks-only" school. In 1963 the first black students were admitted to the University of Magnolia. The first white students were admitted to Magnolia State in 1968. Today, about 5% of the University of Magnolia's students are black and 95% are white; about 3% of Magnolia State's students are white and 97% are black. Magnolia's population of eighteen- to twenty-four-year-olds attending college anywhere is about 85% white and 15% black. Following revelations that the admissions office of the University of Magnolia had "steered" black applicants and inquiries to Magnolia State, Magnolia enacts legislation requiring the University of Magnolia, for each of the next five years, to reserve 10% of its spaces in the entering class for blacks. Sally, a white student denied admission to the University of Magnolia, challenges the validity of the plan as a denial of equal protection. What result?

Answer: Sally may lose. Strict scrutiny applies. The plan is void unless Magnolia can sustain its burden of proving that the racial classification is narrowly drawn to serve a compelling state interest. Magnolia has two arguably compelling state interests—increasing racial diversity and remedying past intentional and unlawful racial discrimination. The classification may not be narrowly drawn to achieve the first interest—there are probably methods to increase racial diversity that do not rely explicitly on race, such as, e.g., scholarship assistance, more recruiting among the black community, consideration of social background other than race in admissions. Moreover, racial diversity for its own sake may not be a compelling interest. The classification is far more likely to be treated as narrowly drawn to accomplish the second interest—the University of Magnolia appears to be continuing to practice illegal racial discrimination and imposition of a racial quota for a limited period of time may be necessary to redress this specific wrong-doing. Moreover, the quota is temporary, reasonably related to the relevant pool of students in Magnolia, and has relatively little impact on the rights of third parties. (Cf. *United States v. Paradise.*) Sally would be even less likely to prevail if Magnolia had acted in response to a judicial finding of intentional racial discrimination on Magnolia's part.

Question: Assume the same facts as the prior question except that the state of Magnolia also enacts legislation requiring Magnolia State University to set aside 10% of the spots in its entering class, for each of the next five years, for whites. Is this plan a denial of equal protection?

Answer: Yes. Strict scrutiny applies. The plan is invalid unless Magnolia can establish that the plan is necessary to the accomplishment of some compelling state interest. The only compelling state interest Magnolia can offer is that of ethnic diversity, yet there are other avenues open to Magnolia to encourage racial diversity at Magnolia State that do not employ racial classifications. Unlike the prior case, there is no evidence that Magnolia State University has been acting unlawfully by denying admission to white students. Without such evidence the plan cannot be upheld as necessary to achieve the compelling state interest in redressing specific unlawful racial discrimination.

Question: The state of Whatcom enacts legislation that requires Whatcom law enforcement agencies publicly to report the race of crime victims, criminal suspects, and those apprehended and charged with criminal offenses. Does the law violate equal protection?

Answer: Partially. While the law uses race as a classification it is neutral with respect to any particular race. Generally when race is used as a classifying device it is futile for a government to contend that the law is actually race-neutral because it applies equally to all races. (See, e.g., *Loving v. Virginia*.) Accordingly, strict scrutiny applies. But the Court has upheld the obtaining and recording of vital statistics by race. (See *Tancil v. Woolls*.) Whatcom's best grounds for defending the requirement that criminal suspects be identified by race is that the requirement is narrowly tailored to the compelling state interest of assuring public safety by providing the public with a complete description of criminal suspects at large. The other requirements—identifying crime victims and apprehended criminal suspects by race—"directs the citizen's attention to the single consideration of race or color" and thus offends the principle of official color-blindness. (Cf. *Anderson v. Martin*, in which the Court struck down a requirement that the race of political candidates be disclosed on ballots.)

Question: Because of a widespread public perception that racially based "affirmative action" plans are unjust, the state of Thurston amends its constitution to provide: "Except as required by federal law, no private or public employer or school may use race as a criterion for hiring, firing, promotion, admission, expulsion, or pupil assignment." The constitutional change has the effect of outlawing a variety of private racially preferential "affirmative action" plans. Does the change to the Thurston constitution violate the federal equal protection clause?

Answer: Probably not. The law does not classify by race and is not subject to strict scrutiny unless the challenger can prove that it was motivated by purposeful racial discrimination. The motivation was surely to eliminate racially based affirmative action plans but that motive was one based on color-blindness or racial neutrality—forbidding the use of race as a qualifying or disqualifying device. Unlike *Reitman v. Mulkey,* the change does not protect private racial discrimination—to the contrary, it forbids it. Nor does the constitutional change alter the political process by erecting a "unique obstacle" to adoption of remedies designed to eliminate unlawful racial discrimination—the change leaves unaffected any remedies required to vindicate equal protection. Rather, the change alters the substantive law of Thurston on a race-neutral basis and is probably subject only to minimal scrutiny. (See *Crawford v. Board of Education.*)

Question: The city of Modoc has maintained racially segregated public schools. The neighboring city of Tule has never operated its schools on a racially segregated basis. Modoc's school population is now 70% black, 20% Hispanic, and 10% non-Hispanic white. Tule's school population is 80% non-Hispanic white, 10% Hispanic, and 10% black. In a suit challenging the constitutional validity of Modoc's school system, the federal district judge issues an order requiring the merger of the Modoc and Tule school systems in order to produce better racial balance in both Modoc and Tule. The validity of the order is challenged on appeal. What result?

Answer: The order is invalid. Federal judges have broad equitable powers to remedy past constitutional violations of equal protection but have *no power* to impose remedies on persons who have not been proven to have violated the Constitution. Here, only Modoc has violated the equal protection clause. Tule has operated its school in compliance with equal protection. Tule cannot be forced to atone for the constitutional sins of Modoc. (See *Milliken v. Bradley.*)

Question: The state of Benton limited the receipt of welfare benefits to American citizens. George, a lawfully resident alien who would otherwise be entitled to welfare benefits, challenges the validity of Benton's action. What result?

Answer: George will prevail. Benton's welfare law classifies on the basis of alienage and is thus subject to strict scrutiny. On these facts, Benton has no justification for the exclusion of aliens from welfare benefits.

Question: Congress limited the receipt of welfare benefits to American citizens. George, a lawfully resident alien who would otherwise be entitled to welfare benefits, challenges the validity of this denial of welfare benefits. What result?

Answer: George will lose. Congress has exclusive power to regulate immigration and naturalization and may employ alienage as a classification device without triggering strict scrutiny. So long as the law is rationally related to immigration and naturalization it is valid. Congress might well have thought that the measure would encourage lawfully resident aliens to become American citizens. (See *Mathews v. Diaz.*)

Question: The state of Owyhee requires that public school guidance counselors be American citizens. Kate, a lawfully resident alien and highly qualified guidance counselor, challenges the validity of the rule. What result?

Answer: The answer depends on whether counseling public school students is a sufficiently "political function" that strict scrutiny does not apply. *Ambach v. Norwick* concluded that schoolteachers perform the political function of instructing children in national values and thus applied minimal scrutiny to a state alienage classification pertaining to schoolteachers. Guidance counselors, however, are far more involved in the mental health, social stability, and behavioral attributes of students than they are in the inculcation of political and social mores and values. The job is not likely to be treated as a political function. If it is not, Owyhee's classification is subject to strict scrutiny and will almost certainly be invalid. There does not appear to be any compelling justification for Owyhee's exclusion of Kate from a job for which she is highly qualified on the grounds of her alien status.

Question: The state of Kiowa has a policy of hiring only women for the jobs of "secretary" and "administrative assistant." Alan, a male applicant for a secretarial position, challenges the validity of the policy. What result?

Answer: The policy facially classifies on the basis of sex and is thus subject to intermediate scrutiny. While the actual purpose of this policy is not clear, it is highly likely that the objective of the policy is simply to perpetuate sexual stereotyping of jobs. If so, this is surely not an "important" state interest. (See *Mississippi University for Women v. Hogan*.)

Question: Responding to a number of behavioral and psychological studies that purport to prove that girls learn more and develop higher self-esteem in a single-sex school, the city of Algonquin operates two single-sex K-12 schools. The Susan Anthony School is all girls and the Theodore Roosevelt School is all boys. Enrollment at either school is voluntary and competitive. Is Algonquin's operation of these two schools constitutionally valid?

Answer: Possibly. The program is subject to intermediate scrutiny since it openly classifies on the basis of sex. Algonquin's actual purpose appears to be to foster learning and self-esteem of girls. That objective is surely important (if the studies are reliable) and the operation of the Anthony School is surely substantially related to that objective. But the Roosevelt School is bit more problematic. Operation of an all-boys school is not related to Algonquin's actual purpose of fostering learning by and self-esteem of girls. On the other hand, the operation of the Anthony School without the Roosevelt School would likely create sexual imbalance in the remaining schools. Moreover, there may be unstated benefits to boys from single-sex education. But since intermediate scrutiny requires courts to find that the means employed are substantially related to *actual purposes* it is possible that the Roosevelt School may be insufficiently related to Algonquin's purposes. But Algonquin might contend that the operation of the Anthony School and the Roosevelt School cannot be separated for analytical purposes because of the sexual imbalance resulting from operation of the Anthony School alone.

Question: In response to academic studies purporting to demonstrate that children are psychologically healthier if their mothers are actively involved in their rearing, the state of Sheridan enacts legislation that provides to mothers who provide fulltime personal care to their children a monthly stipend of $1000 for each child under the age of thirteen, provided that the mother has no other fulltime occupation. Fathers are eligible for the grant only if they are single and the relevant mother is not eligible to receive the grant. Tom, a Sheridan resident, is the father of and fulltime caregiver to twin nine-year-old boys and married to Ellen, a corporate executive who works seventy hours per work. Tom challenges his exclusion from the Sheridan grant program. What result?

Answer: The program may be valid. The Sheridan program is subject to intermediate scrutiny because it classifies on the basis of sex. Were Tom's and Ellen's sexes reversed, Tom would be eligible for the Sheridan grant. The program is valid only if Sheridan can prove that the denial of benefits to fathers like Tom is *substantially related* to an *important* state interest. Under intermediate scrutiny the *actual purpose* of the statute is critical. Here, the actual purpose seems to be to foster parental care of children, with a bias in favor of maternal care of children. If the academic studies are to be believed, this is probably an important state interest. Even if the academic studies are dismissed, this objective is at least legitimate. (Cf. *Weinberger v. Weisenfeld.*) Legislative reliance on the academic studies is probably enough to establish both the importance of the interest and the fact that this was the *actual interest.* The law is probably substantially related to that interest. Unlike *Weinberger v. Weisenfeld* the law does not support *only* maternal care—it provides support to fathers who care for their children when the mother is not eligible to receive the grant—but it does reflect a distinct bias in favor of maternal rather than paternal care. This question illustrates the instability of intermediate scrutiny—resolution depends on the importance of the state interest and that depends in part on whether a bias in favor of maternal care is an "outmoded stereotype" or a "real difference" between fathers and mothers.

Question: In order to protect the privacy of parents who give up their children for adoption and to foster harmony within families consisting in part of adopted children, the state of Shoshone enacts legislation denying to adopted children access to any public records that might enable them to learn the identity of their parents and prohibiting anyone from providing such information to any adopted child. Assume that over 90% of adopted children are born outside of marriage. Kay, an adult adoptee who now wishes to learn the identity of her mother, challenges the validity of the law. What result?

Answer: Kay will very probably lose. Intermediate scrutiny applies only if the law discriminates on the basis of illegitimacy; otherwise minimal scrutiny applies. The law is facially neutral on the subject of illegitimacy but does have a disproportionate effect on those of illegitimate birth. Thus, intermediate scrutiny will apply only if Kay can prove that Shoshone was motivated by a desire to discriminate on the basis of illegitimate birth and Shoshone cannot prove that it would have enacted the law anyway. There is no evidence that Shoshone acted with a discriminatory motive towards illegitimate children. Accordingly, minimal scrutiny applies—the law is surely rationally related to these legitimate objectives. Even if intermediate scrutiny applies (assume Kay can prove that Shoshone also wanted to protect illegitimate children later adopted from learning the "embarrassing fact of their illegitimate birth") the law may be valid. The other *actual* objectives of the law are fairly important and the law is surely closely and substantially connected to their accomplishment. Kay would be likely to prevail only if the sole reason Shoshone enacted the law was to spare illegitimate children knowledge of the "embarrassing fact of their illegitimate birth," since that actual purpose would hardly be important.

Question: The state of Cherokee enacts legislation limiting the franchise to all citizens of Cherokee over age eighteen who have paid income taxes to the state of Cherokee at any time during the year prior to an election. Larry, a thirty-four-year-old Cherokee citizen who has no income tax liability, challenges the validity of the Cherokee law. What result?

Answer: The law is invalid. It impinges upon voting, a constitutionally fundamental right, and thus is subject to strict scrutiny. It is valid only if Cherokee can prove that the restriction is narrowly tailored to serve a compelling interest. There is no compelling reason for limiting the franchise to Cherokee citizens who pay income taxes. (Cf. *Harper v. Virginia Board of Elections.*)

Question: The state of Nioka extends the franchise to Nioka residents who are lawfully resident aliens. Is this constitutionally permissible?

Answer: Yes. The Court has stated that "[t]he decision to include or exclude [aliens] involves choices about the nature of representation with which we have been shown no constitutionally founded reason to interfere." *Burns v. Richardson,* 384 U.S. 73, 91 (1966). States are free to *extend* the franchise; it is *restriction* of the franchise to a class of people smaller than bona fide residents who are age eighteen or over that is subjected to close judicial scrutiny.

Question: In order to encourage the development of its wine industry, the state of Chianti establishes the Chianti Wine Marketing Agency. The agency is empowered to levy a tax of $0.10 per ton on all producers of wine grapes and to expend the funds raised by the tax exclusively for the purpose of increasing demand for wines made from Chianti grapes. The agency has complete discretion how best to promote Chianti wines. The agency is composed of five directors elected by all Chianti growers of wine grapes. Each grower is entitled to one vote per ton of grapes. Lou, owner of a small vineyard that produces ten tons of grapes annually, challenges the validity of the electoral scheme by which the Chianti Wine Marketing Agency's directors are selected. What result?

Answer: The electoral scheme is valid. Strict scrutiny is usually applicable to franchise restrictions or to voting on other than a "one person, one vote" basis. Although the agency is a governmental unit and the voting scheme is both quite restrictive and apportions votes unequally, election schemes for limited purpose governmental units whose functions primarily affect the restricted electors are valid if they are rationally related to legitimate state purposes. Here, the agency is quite limited in purpose and its activities primarily affect wine grape growers and wineries. Since the tax is imposed on a tonnage basis it is rational to apportion votes on the same basis. (See, e.g., *Salyer Land Co.* and *Ball v. James.*)

Question: The state of Midorca limits its ballot for President to candidates representing political parties that have received at least 20% of the entire vote cast in Midorca for presidential candidates in the last presidential election. The presidential candidate of the Green Party, which received less than one-half of 1% of the Midorca presidential vote in the last election, challenges the validity of her exclusion from the Midorca ballot. What result?

Answer: The Midorca exclusion is subject to strict scrutiny since it severely interferes with the citizenry's right to cast votes effectively. Minor parties blossom and fail from time to time, but perform the critical function of transmitting to major parties important sentiments of voter alienation. Moreover, it takes time for minor parties to establish themselves as major parties and Midorca's rules prevent that from happening. Midorca's ballot access requirement frustrates these rights of the citizenry to choose a different path. The Midorca restrictions effectively exclude minor parties that may have significant support (but less than 20% in the last election). There is no compelling justification for such exclusion. (See *Williams v. Rhodes.*)

Question: The state of Cayuse imposes a $5.00 fee on every person who departs from any airport in Cayuse. Is the "departure fee" constitutionally valid?

Answer: Probably. It does not apply simply because a person is leaving the state. It applies to interstate and intrastate air travelers alike. Those who leave the state by other means are unaffected. The departure fee will be subjected to minimal scrutiny and is rationally related to the legitimate state objective of imposing a fee for the use of governmental services. (Compare to *Crandall v. Nevada.*)

EXAM TIPS

- **Make Sure Equal Protection Applies.** Equal protection applies when *any* government (state or federal) treats *entire groups of people* differently. If the government permits only licensed drivers without traffic convictions to operate autos it has divided the people into two classes. Equal protection applies.

  - **Classes, *Not Individuals.*** When the issue is whether a person is or is not *a member of a class* there is *no* equal protection issue. At most, there may be an issue of whether the government is required to provide due process in placing an individual in or out of a class. The question of whether Lucy is a licensed driver without any traffic convictions is *not* an equal protection issue. The question of whether the government may restrict auto operation to licensed drivers without any traffic convictions *is* an equal protection issue.

  - **State or Federal Government.** *State* action involving equal protection implicates the *14th Amendment*. *Federal* action involving equal protection principles is treated as an aspect of *substantive due process* under the *Fifth Amendment*. The *same standards* apply to both governments, but remember the different constitutional sources of the doctrine.

- **Determine the Right Level of Scrutiny.** Start from the presumption that minimal scrutiny applies, but check for indicators of more rigorous scrutiny. Suspect classifications and impingements of fundamental rights trigger *strict scrutiny;* classifications by sex or illegitimate birth trigger *intermediate scrutiny.*

  - **Strict Scrutiny.** When *strict scrutiny* applies the government has the burden of proving that the classification is necessary to accomplish a compelling state interest.

  - **Intermediate Scrutiny.** When *intermediate scrutiny* applies the government has the burden of proving that the classification is substantially related to an important state interest that is the actual purpose of the classification.

  - **Minimal Scrutiny.** When *minimal scrutiny* applies the challenger has the burden of proving that the classification is *not* rationally related to any conceivable legitimate state interest.

  - **Beware of "Enhanced Scrutiny."** Occasionally the Court employs unique "enhanced" minimal scrutiny, often based on the Court's reaction to the presence of a factual pastiche of "quasi-suspect" classifications or "quasi-fundamental" rights. (See, e.g., *Plyler v. Doe, Cleburne v. Cleburne Living Center,* and *Anderson v. Celebrezze.*) Some questions may give you an opportunity to apply "enhanced" scrutiny to a classification that has some, but not all, of the characteristics of suspect classifications.

■ **Suspect Classifications**

• *Race* **and** *National Origin.* When governments divide people into groups on the basis of *race* or *national origin* for the purpose of discriminating on that basis they have used a suspect classifications.

— **Intentional or Purposeful Discrimination.** Only those classifications that intentionally discriminate on racial or national origin grounds are suspect. Intentional discrimination is established if any of the following are present:

(1) The racial or national origin classification is facially open and obvious. Examples include racial segregation, racial preferences, and other racial distinctions.

(2) A facially neutral law is *applied* on the basis of racial or national origin. You must demonstrate that the government has acted *intentionally* to apply a neutral law only to members of a racial group. You need to rely on more than statistical evidence.

(3) A facially neutral law that produces results identifiable by race or national origin was adopted solely for the purpose of discriminating on the basis of race or national origin. Professors are always fond of testing on this. You need to analyze whether there is any evidence of racial *motivation.* If so, and the government cannot *rebut* this showing by proving that it would have adopted the law even without a racial motivation, the classification is suspect and strict scrutiny applies.

(4) **No Special Rules for Racial Preferences.** The same scrutiny applies to racial classifications that are intended to benefit racial minorities as to racial classifications designed to disadvantage racial minorities. Thus, racially preferential hiring programs or school admission programs are subject to strict scrutiny. Some racial preferences (but not many) will satisfy strict scrutiny. Racial preferences undertaken to remedy specific unlawful racial discrimination may satisfy strict scrutiny. This is a fertile exam topic.

• *Alienage:* **Sometimes a Suspect Classification.** Drawing lines on the basis of alienage, at least with respect to *lawful residents* of the nation, is suspect *unless:*

— A *state* does so in order to confine the performance of *political functions* to citizens, or

— *Congress* or the *President* do so.

Testing in this area is likely to focus on whether an alienage classification involves a political function.

- *Sex* and *Illegitimate Birth.* When governments divide people into groups on the basis of their sex or illegitimate birth for purposes of discriminating on that basis, *intermediate scrutiny* is triggered.

  - **Sex Classifications**

    — **Intentional Discrimination.** As with race, only those sex classifications that intentionally discriminate by sex trigger intermediate scrutiny. The same rules apply to sex classifications as racial classifications for determining whether a sex classification is intentionally discriminatory.

    — **No Special Rules for Sexual Preferences.** As with race, sex-based "affirmative action" programs are subjected to the same scrutiny as other forms of sex discrimination. But since the intermediate standard is more easily met than strict scrutiny, sex-based affirmative action plans are more easily justified than race-based plans.

    — **Be Aware of "Real" Sex Differences.** When a classification reflects a "real" sex difference (e.g., only women become pregnant) the intermediate standard is easily met. But when the classification reflects stereotypical assumptions about sex roles it will be hard to justify under intermediate scrutiny.

    — **Remember That Only Actual Purposes Count.** Unlike minimal scrutiny, where the government's objective may be *any conceivable* objective, no matter how hypothetical, intermediate scrutiny requires governments to prove the substantial relationship of the classification to the *actual purposes* of the classification.

  - **Illegitimacy.** The same rules apply for intermediate scrutiny of classifications by illegitimacy as for sex classifications. This problem usually comes up in the form of an intestacy statute restricting the right of illegitimate children to inherit. But it could come up in other contexts—a law denying child welfare benefits to illegitimate children, or a law denying to adopted children (mostly, but not entirely, born outside marriage) the right to learn the identities of their mothers.

- **Constitutionally Fundamental Rights.** When governments divide people in a way that impinges upon a constitutionally fundamental right, strict scrutiny applies. Constitutionally fundamental rights are those rights *explicitly* or *implicitly* guaranteed by the Constitution.

- **Voting.** Impairments of voting trigger strict scrutiny, but there are a number of exceptions to this rule.

  — **Limited Purpose Governmental Units.** When governments limit voting for "limited purpose" governmental units (e.g., an irrigation district) to those primarily affected, only minimal scrutiny applies. This is a *very narrow* exception.

  — **Write-in Votes.** Governments may ban write-in votes because there is no constitutionally fundamental right to write in your choice.

  — **Ballot Access Restrictions.** So long as governmental restrictions on access to the ballot are reasonable and do not severely impair the right of minor parties or candidates to get on the ballot strict scrutiny will *not* apply.

- **Access to the Judicial Process.** Strict scrutiny is largely confined to state laws that, as a practical matter, place indigents at a strong disadvantage in attempting directly to appeal a criminal conviction or vindicate some other equally important right.

- **Right of Interstate Mobility.** State laws or policies that impose permanent denials of some benefit to some residents of a state based on their recent arrival in the state, or which erect major obstacles to interstate movement, are subject to strict scrutiny. Congress, however, has substantially greater freedom to impose such barriers.

- **"Societally Important" Rights Are *Not* Fundamental.** Just because something is "societally important"—such as education or housing, or the "general necessities" of life—does *not* make it a constitutionally fundamental right.

STATE ACTION AND CONGRESSIONAL ENFORCEMENT OF CIVIL RIGHTS

CHAPTER OVERVIEW

This chapter examines the **state action** doctrine—the general rule that the Constitution limits *governments* only, and does *not* ordinarily limit *private action*—and the principal statutes Congress has enacted to limit the power of private persons to deny other persons their civil rights. The most important points in this chapter follow.

■ **State Action.** State action may be *express* or *implied*. Express state action is usually obvious; implied state action almost always involves *nominal private action* in which the state is so involved that it is treated as state action.

- **Public Function Doctrine:** State action is present when governments *delegate* to private persons functions that are indisputably governmental.

- **Inextricable Entanglement:** State action is present when governments are so "entwined" in private affairs that private actions produce *"symbiotic" benefits* to the governments or are directed by government officials.

- **State Coercion or Extreme Encouragement:** State action is present when governments *coerce* or *extraordinarily encourage* private persons to take specific actions.

- **Concerted or Joint Action:** State action is present when governments overtly act in concert with private actors.

- **Governmental Ratification of Private Action:** State action is present when governments ratify private action.

351

- **Licensing or Regulation *Not* Enough:** Mere licensing or regulation of private action is not sufficient to create state action.

■ **Congressional Enforcement of Civil Rights.** Congress has power to enforce the provisions of the 13th, 14th, and 15th Amendments.

- **13th Amendment:** Congress may regulate *private conduct* that it rationally determines is a *badge or incident* of slavery, but that power is probably limited to instances of invidious racial discrimination.

- Although the 13th Amendment is also *self-executing,* its scope is *very narrow* unless Congress enacts legislation to enforce it. By itself, the 13th Amendment only bars *actual slavery* or its near-equivalent, *peonage.*

■ **14th and 15th Amendments:** Congress may regulate *state action* that interferes with rights secured by the 14th and 15th Amendments, but the extent to which Congress can use these **"enforcement powers"** to regulate private racial discrimination is not clear. Through its **enforcement powers,** Congress:

- *Probably* is able to punish private action directed *at state officials and designed to interfere with their obligation to comply with the 14th Amendment,*

- *May* be able to prohibit private actions that are aimed at preventing others from exercising their constitutionally protected rights, but

- Almost certainly may *not* control private conduct that does not implicate constitutionally protected rights.

■ **Congressional Power to Alter the Substance of 14th and 15th Amendment Rights.** (This topic is addressed in Chapter 5.)

A. INTRODUCTION TO AND SCOPE OF THE STATE ACTION DOCTRINE

1. General Rule

a. Constitution limits governments, not private action. The Constitution is a charter for governance. It does not generally limit the power of individuals to act as they please. Statutes—ordinary laws—perform that function. For the *Constitution* to be triggered, a *government* must act. There must be **state action.**

i. State action required. State action is often obvious, but sometimes it is not clear whether the government has acted sufficiently to invoke the Constitution.

(a) Express action. When a government acts *expressly* the state action requirement is easily satisfied.

Example: The State of Hysteria enacts a law that bans all speech critical of the government. State action is obvious.

Example: The Governor of Hysteria, acting officially, issues an executive order banning all speech critical of the government. State action is equally obvious.

(b) **The conundrum of inaction as action.** A much more difficult question is to decide when, if at all, state *inaction*—failure to act—amounts to state action sufficient to trigger the Constitution. Generally, governments are under no obligation to take affirmative action, and *pure inaction* will not be considered state action.

 EXAMPLE AND ANALYSIS

Joshua DeShaney, a small boy in the custody of his father following divorce, was so severely beaten by his father that he suffered permanent brain damage, leaving him institutionalized for life. Through his mother, Joshua sought damages from the state of Wisconsin for its alleged deprivation of Joshua's liberty in violation of the due process clause. The essence of the claim was that Wisconsin social workers, having received and investigated reports of child abuse prior to Joshua's disabling injuries, should have acted to remove Joshua from the custody of his father. The Court rejected the claim that Wisconsin's *failure to act* was a form of state action. Like most other constitutional provisions, due process operates "as a limitation on the State's power to act, not as a guarantee of certain minimal levels of safety and security." Wisconsin had not acted to assume a special duty "of care and protection," as it would when it "takes a person into its custody and holds him there against his will." The Court noted that even though Joshua had no constitutional claim he was still entitled to pursue his tort remedies against Wisconsin and, of course, his criminal father. *DeShaney v. Winnebago County Dept. of Social Services,* 489 U.S. 189 (1989).

However, as discussed below, when state *inaction* is alloyed with *private action* in ways that unduly lend state power to the private action, the state action doctrine may be triggered. In general, *state action is present* when "there is a sufficiently close nexus between the State and the challenged action of the [private] entity so that the action of the latter may be fairly treated as that of the State itself." *Jackson v. Metropolitan Edison Co.,* 419 U.S. 345 (1971), discussed infra. This most commonly occurs when the government has *delegated* its power to a private person, or has become *inextricably entangled* with the private person, or has *coerced or extraordinarily encouraged* the private action. (See sections A.4 and A.5, infra.) But even the Court itself has acknowledged that "formulating an infallible test" of state action is "an impossible task." *Reitman v. Mulkey,* 387 U.S. 369, 378 (1967).

    ii. **The meaning of government.** Government, or the "state," is defined broadly to encompass all the many political subdivisions and instrumentalities of government. Thus, states include not only state governments but cities, counties, public agencies and public corporations. Similarly, the federal government consists of the government and all its many agencies, commissions, and other instrumentalities.

  b. **Exception to state action requirement: The 13th Amendment.** The principal instance in which the Constitution applies directly to private conduct, thus obviating the need for state action, is the 13th Amendment, which prohibits slavery. The 13th Amendment bars the private enslavement of persons every bit as much as it bans government from enslaving its citizens.

  c. **Valid statutes may limit private action.** To the extent governments act within the powers permitted to them, they are free to limit private action. Indeed, that is generally what statutes are about. When a government does so act, the question is always raised whether it has acted in conformity to the Constitution and, in the case of a state, whether it has complied with applicable federal statutory law and its own state constitution.

2. **Early Development of the State Action Doctrine**

  a. **The *Civil Rights Cases,*** 109 U.S. 3 (1883). The federal Civil Rights Act of 1875 prohibited private acts of racial discrimination in the operation of certain public accommodations. The validity of the Act was challenged on the ground that Congress had no source of authority to enact the statute. The Court agreed and invalidated the law, rejecting arguments that Congress had authority to act under the enforcement provisions of the 13th and 14th Amendments.

    i. **Fourteenth Amendment**

      (a) **State action required.** Section 5 of the 14th Amendment gives Congress power to enforce the substantive provisions of the Amendment, but the *14th Amendment limits government conduct only.* By their own terms, due process and equal protection only prohibit state action, and have no effect whatever on private action. The Court was thus required to consider whether Congress had power to make the substantive guarantees of the Amendment also applicable to private conduct.

      (b) **Section 5 enforcement power does not permit Congress to regulate private conduct.** The Court answered the question by concluding that since Congress only had power to "enforce" the 14th Amendment, it could not use that power to extend the scope of the substance of the Amendment to private conduct. The Court agreed that Congress had the power under section 5 to "correct[] any constitutional wrong committed by the States," but the Civil Rights Act did not do that; instead it operated directly upon private persons by laying "down rules for the conduct of individuals in society towards each [other], without referring in any manner to any supposed action of the State or its authorities." This construction of section 5 is *still good law.*

ii. **Thirteenth Amendment.** Section 2 of the 13th Amendment empowers Congress to enforce the substantive ban on slavery. The Court conceded that the 13th Amendment operates directly upon private conduct, and that Congress has power to regulate private conduct that imposes the "badges and incidents" of slavery upon people. However, the Court concluded that private racial discrimination in public accommodations had "nothing to do with slavery. . . . It would be running the slavery argument into the ground to make it apply to every act of [private] discrimination." This specific holding—that private racial discrimination is unrelated to the "badges or incidents of slavery"—is *no longer good law,* having been effectively overruled by *Jones v. Alfred H. Mayer Co.,* 392 U.S. 409 (1968), discussed infra.

iii. **Effect of the *Civil Rights Cases.*** Because of the *Civil Rights Cases,* Congress relied on its commerce power to enact the 1964 Civil Rights Act. In *Heart of Atlanta Motel* and *Katzenbach v. McClung,* the cases that upheld the legislation against a commerce clause challenge, only two Justices were willing to overturn the *Civil Rights Cases* and rely on §5 of the 14th Amendment.

3. Contemporary State Action Doctrine

The concept of when the state is "acting" has been broadened substantially from the *Civil Rights Cases,* which seems to suggest (but not to hold) that only explicit state action suffices. State action has been broadened considerably by the following notions of what constitutes state action.

- *Public Function Doctrine:* When governments *delegate* to private persons functions that are indisputably governmental, the resulting actions by the private party will be considered state action. (See section A.4, infra.)

- *State Coercion or Extreme Encouragement:* When governments either *coerce* or *extraordinarily encourage* private persons to take particular actions, the resulting actions will be treated as those of the state. (See sections A.5.b and A.5.c, infra.)

- *Inextricable Entanglement:* When governments so entwine themselves in private affairs that the private actions produce "symbiotic" benefits to the government or are directed by public officials, the nominally private actor will be considered a state actor. (See sections A.5.d and A.5.e, infra.)

4. The Public Function Doctrine

    a. Overview. The public function doctrine recognizes that private persons *exercising governmental powers* should be regarded as state actors. In its modern form the doctrine is limited to those instances when private actors are exercising powers *"traditionally exclusively reserved" to governments.*

 ## EXAMPLES AND ANALYSIS

Example: Texas law permitted private political parties to control who could vote in primary elections. When the Texas Democratic Party excluded blacks the Court found state action: Texas delegated its exclusively sovereign power over voting to the Democratic Party.

But the use of power of the sort that governments employ in common with private persons is not sufficient for state action.

Example: A customer of a publicly regulated but privately owned electrical utility claimed that it was a violation of due process for the utility to terminate service without first giving her notice and a hearing. The utility was claimed to be a state actor because it was performing a public function—providing an "essential public service" required by state law. Not so, said the Court. Because utility service was "not traditionally the exclusive prerogative of the State" the electrical utility was not performing a "public function" and was thus not a state actor. *Jackson v. Metropolitan Edison Co.,* 419 U.S. 345 (1974).

    b. Privately owned public places

        i. The company town: *Marsh v. Alabama,* 326 U.S. 501 (1946). Chickasaw, Alabama, was owned in its entirety by the Gulf Shipbuilding Corporation but otherwise had "all the characteristics of any other American town." Marsh, a Jehovah's Witness, distributed religious literature on the streets of the town without permission from Gulf Shipbuilding. She was arrested, convicted of criminal trespass, and appealed on First Amendment grounds. But was Gulf Shipbuilding a "state actor"? Private citizens are generally entitled to suppress unwanted religious and speech activity on their property and to summon the aid of the state to prosecute trespassers. Gulf Shipbuilding's ownership of *all* of Chickasaw made it different, said the Court. It was a state actor because the town, or at least its public spaces, was "built and operated primarily to benefit the public and [its] *operation is essentially a public function*. . . . [T]he town and its shopping district are accessible to and freely used by the public in general and there is nothing to distinguish them from any other town and shopping center except the fact that the title to the property belongs to a private corporation." It was not Gulf Shipbuilding's invocation of Alabama's criminal trespass law that triggered state action; rather, it was the profoundly public character of the town (voluntarily created by Gulf Shipbuilding) that transformed it from a private property owner to an agent of the state.

ii. **Shopping centers.** The broad sweep of *Marsh* might suggest that privately owned shopping centers fall within the public function doctrine but that conclusion, briefly adopted by the Court, has been repudiated.

(a) *Amalgamated Food Employees Union v. Logan Valley Plaza, Inc.,* 391 U.S. 308 (1968). The Court held that a privately owned shopping center was "the functional equivalent" of a town and that the actions of its owners in interfering with labor picketing were state action.

(b) *Lloyd Corp. v. Tanner,* 407 U.S. 551 (1972). The operators of a privately owned shopping center were not state actors when they excluded persons distributing antiwar literature from the center. *Logan Valley* was distinguished because the leaflet distribution in *Lloyd* "had no relation to any purpose [of] . . . the center."

(c) *Hudgens v. NLRB,* 424 U.S. 507 (1976). The Court overruled *Logan Valley* expressly, concluding that *Lloyd* had done so implicitly, and adopted the position taken by Justice Black, the author of *Marsh,* dissenting in *Logan Valley:* Privately owned shopping centers could be treated as public only "when that property has taken on *all* the attributes of a town."

(d) **State constitutions may differ.** Several state supreme courts, interpreting their state constitutions, have reached different results, finding that the guarantees of the state constitution (particularly free speech) extend to privately owned shopping centers.

iii.   **Senator Bacon's racist park.** The 1911 will of Senator Augustus Bacon devised to the city of Macon, Georgia, in trust, a parcel of real property, Baconsfield, so long as it was used as a park for whites only. The city was named trustee and a board of managers was created under the trust to administer Baconsfield. After it became clear that the city of Macon could not validly enforce the racial exclusion, the city began to admit blacks and the managers brought suit to remove the city as trustee. The city resigned as trustee and a state court appointed a private trustee to replace the city and continue the exclusion of non-whites from the park. In *Evans v. Newton,* 382 U.S. 296 (1966), the Supreme Court ruled that Baconsfield, even in the hands of a private trustee, could not be operated on a racially restrictive basis in conformity with the 14th Amendment. The constitutional requirement of equal protection applied for two independent reasons.

- *Private Trustee a Sham:* The record showed that the park continued to be operated and maintained by the city.

- *Public Function:* "The service rendered even by a private park of this character is municipal in nature. . . . A park . . . traditionally serves the community. Mass recreation through the use of parks is plainly in the public domain. . . . Like the streets of the company town in *[Marsh v. Alabama]* . . . the predominant character and purpose of this park are municipal." The case came back to the Court on a different issue in *Evans v. Abney,* 396 U.S. 435 (1970). (See section A.5.b.iii, infra.)

c.   **The white primary cases.** A series of cases involving the sordid attempts of the Democratic party to exclude blacks from its primary elections in Texas provide another illustration of the public function doctrine in action.

i.   **Direct state action:** *Nixon v. Herndon* **and** *Nixon v. Condon.* In *Nixon v. Herndon,* 273 U.S. 536 (1927), the Court voided a Texas statute that expressly barred blacks from voting in the Democratic party primary. The law was promptly revised to empower each party to prescribe the qualifications for voting in the party primary. When the Texas Democratic party adopted racially exclusive qualifications they were struck down in *Nixon v. Condon,* 286 U.S. 73

(1932), on the grounds that the Democratic party was wielding power expressly delegated to it by law.

ii. **No state action: *Grovey v. Townsend,*** 295 U.S. 45 (1935). The Democrats' next gambit was to adopt a party rule, entirely on their own, that forbade blacks from becoming members of the Democratic party. The Court found no state action (and thus no constitutional issue) because the Democratic party was not a state instrumentality—the rules for party membership were something with which Texas "need have no concern."

iii. ***Grovey* reversed: *Smith v. Allwright,*** 321 U.S. 649 (1944). The Court overruled *Grovey.* Conceding the party membership may be "no concern of a State," the Court ruled that when party membership "is also the essential qualification for voting in a primary to select nominees for a general election, the State makes the action of the party the action of the State." Texas's effective grant to the Democratic party of the power to establish voter qualifications "is delegation of a *state function* that may make the party's action the action of the State." Since Texas limited its general elections to candidates picked by party primaries it had involved itself sufficiently in the party primary process to make the Democratic party's actions the actions of Texas.

iv. **The ambiguous outer boundary of state action: *Terry v. Adams,*** 345 U.S. 461 (1953). Texas Democrats reacted to *Smith v. Allwright* by creating a voluntary club, the Jaybird Democratic Association, that held "pre-primaries" for their members. There were no legal or formal links between the Jaybirds and the Democratic party, but the winners of the Jaybird "pre-primaries" nearly always ran without opposition in the official Democratic primary. The Jaybirds frankly admitted that their *raison d'etre* was to exclude blacks from voting. By an 8 to 1 vote the Court found state action and invalidated the process as a violation of the 15th Amendment, but the Court could not muster a majority opinion. Four Justices, led by Justice Clark, thought that the record showed that the Jaybirds were the Democrats under another name. Thus, the *Allwright* holding governed. Three Justices, led by Justice Black, found state action in Texas's *inaction*—its failure to do anything other than regulate the electoral process from general election back to the point of the Jaybirds and wink at the Jaybirds' racist selection process. Speaking for himself, Justice Frankfurter found state action because state election officials participated in the Jaybird process. Justice Minton dissented, arguing that the Jaybirds' "straw vote" represented only the "concerted action" of private individuals and that "concerted action of individuals which is successful [does not] somehow become state action.''

d. **The modern requirement that private parties wield powers ''traditionally exclusively reserved to the state.''** The public function doctrine has been compressed to reach private action only when the private actor exercises powers ''traditionally exclusively reserved'' for governments. A quartet of modern cases illustrate the principle.

i. **Publicly regulated utilities:** *Jackson v. Metropolitan Edison Co.,* 419 U.S. 345 (1974). Jackson contended that a privately owned, publicly regulated power utility had violated due process by not affording her notice and hearing before terminating her electric service. She claimed the utility was a state actor because it provided an ''essential public service'' that the state required the utility to deliver. The Court found no state action because utility service is not a function ''traditionally exclusively reserved to the State.''

ii. **Sale of goods to enforce lien:** *Flagg Bros. v. Brooks,* 436 U.S. 149 (1978). When Brooks was evicted from her apartment she consented to the storage of her possessions in Flagg's warehouse. Brooks disputed the storage and moving charges and refused to pay them. Flagg threatened to sell the goods to enforce its warehouseman's lien in the stored goods. Brooks brought suit, claiming that a sale without prior notice and hearing violated due process. Brooks argued that state action was present because New York, by creating a warehouseman's lien, had delegated to Flagg a ''traditional function of civil government [—] the resolution of private disputes.'' Emphasizing that the public function doctrine requires delegation to a private actor of a power ''*exclusively* reserved'' to governments, the Court held that there was no state action involved and thus no occasion to consider due process. Brooks need not have consented to storage of her goods without a waiver by Flagg Brothers of its statutory lien. New York had not ''delegated to Flagg Brothers an exclusive prerogative of the sovereign'' because it had simply recognized ''the traditional place of private arrangements'' in resolving commercial disputes. Rather than delegating an exclusively sovereign power, the New York lien law acquiesced in a common private commercial practice—the sale of stored goods when the owner fails to claim them or refuses to pay for storage.

iii. **Nursing homes:** *Blum v. Yaretsky,* 457 U.S. 991 (1982). The Court held that the decision of private nursing home operators to discharge or transfer Medicaid patients to another facility was not state action, triggering possible due process rights of hearing prior to the discharge or transfer. No public function was performed by the nursing home operators because the decision to discharge or transfer a patient is not a function traditionally and exclusively exercised by the sovereign. (Other aspects of the case are discussed in sections A.5.b.iii and A.5.e.ii, infra.)

iv. **Private schools: *Rendell-Baker v. Kohn,*** 457 U.S. 830 (1982). The director of a private school for "students who have experienced difficulty completing public high schools" fired a teacher. The Court held this was not state action, even though virtually all of the school's students were referred to it by the state, almost all of the school's revenue was from public sources, and the school was heavily regulated by the state. Even though the school was performing a public service by educating maladjusted high school students it was not exercising the *exclusive prerogatives* of the state. (Other aspects of the case are discussed in section A.5, infra.)

5. **Commingling of Public and Private Power: State Involvement in Nominally Private Action**

a. **Overview.** There are several ways governmental power and private power can be so commingled that nominally private actions must be regarded as actions of the government.

- *Coercion:* When governments coerce private action, but do so short of actual regulation, the coerced private action is effectively state action. There are few cases of outright coercion, although *Shelley v. Kraemer,* infra, may be one.

- *Encouragement:* More often governments encourage private action rather than coerce it. When governmental encouragement of private action is extraordinary, unusual, or extreme it will result in changing the encouraged private action into state action. The prime example is *Reitman v. Mulkey,* infra.

- *"Symbiotic" Entanglement:* When governments become so entangled in the affairs of a private actor, and reap benefits from that entanglement, the resulting "symbiotic" relationship turns the actions of the private actor into state action. The classic example is *Burton v. Wilmington Parking Authority,* infra.

- *Concerted or Joint Action:* When governments overtly act in concert with private actors, the private action is treated as state action. See, e.g., *Lugar v. Edmondson Oil Co.,* infra.

- *Governmental Ratification of Private Action:* When governments ratify private action—adopt the private action as their own—the private action is transformed into state action. The peremptory challenge cases are prime examples. (See *Georgia v. McCollum,* infra.)

b.   When the state coerces private action

i.   Enforcement of racially restrictive covenants

(a)   *Shelley v. Kraemer,* 334 U.S. 1 (1948). Shelley, a black American, purchased a home in Missouri from a white seller. The property was burdened with a running real covenant that restricted occupancy to persons of "the Caucasian race," specifically excluding "people of the Negro or Mongolian race." Kraemer, owner of property "benefited" by the covenant, sued in state court to enforce the covenant by enjoining Shelley's occupancy of his new home. The Missouri court granted the requested relief. Shelley did not argue that the covenant itself was state action; rather, he contended that Missouri's *enforcement* of the covenant was state action subject to the 14th Amendment. The Court agreed: "[B]ut for the active intervention of the state courts, supported by the full panoply of state power, [Shelley] would have been free to occupy" his new home. State action was present because *both private parties—buyer and seller*—wished to proceed with the transaction. It was only the state, *through the injunction,* that frustrated private ordering. The state's injunction was distinctly coercive—the state said to the private parties: "You *must* obey the racially restrictive covenant." By contrast, had the seller declined to sell to Shelley in the first instance there would have been *no state action.* The decision not to sell (even if motivated by racial prejudice) would be an entirely private act. (But note that state or federal statutes prohibiting racial discrimination in housing might then apply.)

(b)   *Barrows v. Jackson,* 346 U.S. 249 (1953). Jackson entered into a racially restrictive ("whites only") real covenant with respect to her property, then violated the covenant by permitting non-whites to occupy the property. Barrows, a beneficiary of the covenant, sued Jackson for damages for breach of the covenant. The Court applied *Shelley* and concluded that delivery of damages via the state's judicial machinery constituted state action. State action was present because the damages remedy operated "to coerce [Jackson] . . . to observe a restrictive covenant that . . . [the state had no] right to enforce in equity. . . . [If] the State may thus punish [Jackson] for her failure to carry out her covenant, she is coerced to continue to use her property in a discriminatory manner. . . . [It is no longer Jackson's] voluntary choice but the State's choice that she observe her covenant or suffer damages." The Court observed that the coercive effect of the damages remedy would also manifest itself in either a refusal of prospective sellers to sell to non-whites or a sale at "a higher price to meet the damages which the seller may incur." As in *Shelley,* both private parties wished to transfer the property in violation of the covenant; only the coercive hand of the state's judicial system frustrated them.

ii. **The limits of *Shelley.*** In a series of post-*Shelley* cases, the Court has confined the potentially broad reach of *Shelley* to encompass only those instances when the state's judicial system operates to coerce willing private parties to refrain from their desired conduct. By contrast, when private parties invoke *constitutionally neutral rules of law* to achieve ends impermissible to the state itself there is no state action.

(a) *Evans v. Abney,* 396 U.S. 435 (1970). Following the Court's decision in *Evans v. Newton,* supra, that the operation of Senator Bacon's racially restrictive park in nominally private hands was state action and constitutionally infirm, the Georgia courts ruled that Senator Bacon's trust had failed because it was no longer possible to achieve his racially biased intent. Accordingly, the possibility of reverter in Baconsfield held by Bacon's heirs was activated. The Court, 6 to 2, affirmed this decision. "[T]he Georgia courts did no more than apply well-settled general principles of Georgia law to determine the meaning and effect of a Georgia will. . . . Senator Bacon's will . . . embod[ied] a preference for termination of the park rather than its integration. . . . [T]he Georgia court had no alternative under its relevant trust laws, which are long standing and neutral with regard to race, but to end the Baconsfield trust and return the property to the Senator's heirs."

(b) **The sit-in cases: *Bell v. Maryland,*** 378 U.S. 226 (1964). Prior to the Civil Rights Act of 1964 black Americans protested official and unofficial racial segregation in public accommodations by peacefully "sitting-in" at whites-only lunch counters and the like. Business proprietors often reacted by summoning the police, who arrested the demonstrators for criminal trespass. A series of cases presented to the Court the question of whether the private action of summoning the police to enforce the state's criminal trespass laws was state action. The Court reversed the convictions each time but always on grounds that avoided decision of the state action question. The closest it came to such a decision was in *Bell v. Maryland,* where the Court divided 3 to 3 on the point. Justice Black, joined by Justices Harlan and White, thought that *Shelley* was inapplicable since the state's racially neutral trespass law was not used to coerce two willing private parties to adhere to a racially discriminatory course of conduct. Even though the proprietors might be motivated by racial prejudice, or perhaps by nonracial motives, their decision to deny access to unwanted patrons was a private action. Justice Douglas, joined by Justices Warren and Goldberg, thought state action was present because the "corporation that owns this restaurant . . . thought 'it' could make more money by running a segregated restaurant." The connection between a profit motive for invoking a neutral trespass law and state action was not made clear by Douglas.

(c) **Private discretion:** *Blum v. Yaretsky,* 457 U.S. 991 (1982), discussed supra. Private nursing home operators decided to discharge or transfer certain Medicaid patients. The cost of caring for Medicaid patients is borne entirely by the state and federal governments. In addressing a claimed due process violation, the Court found no state action because "a State normally can be held responsible for a private decision only when it has exercised coercive power or has provided such significant encouragement, either overt or covert, that the choice must in law be deemed to be that of the State. . . . Mere approval of or acquiescence in the initiatives of a private party is not sufficient to justify holding the State responsible for those initiatives. . . ." Because the state had not coerced the transfer decision it was purely a matter of private discretion and thus private action.

c. **When the state unduly encourages private action.** The line between undue or unusual governmental encouragement of private action and ordinary public policy is thin indeed.

i. *Reitman v. Mulkey,* 387 U.S. 369 (1967). California's legislature enacted two laws barring racial discrimination in the sale or rental of housing. In 1964, a year after the second such law, California voters approved an initiative amending the state constitution to prohibit the state from abridging "the right of any person [to] decline to sell, lease or rent [real property] to such . . . persons as he, in his absolute discretion, chooses." Reitman refused to rent an apartment to the Mulkeys, who sued in the California courts, claiming that Reitman had violated the statutory prohibitions upon racial discrimination in housing. In defense Reitman asserted the invalidity of the laws under the state constitution. The Mulkeys countered by arguing that the state constitutional provision violated the 14th Amendment. The California Supreme Court agreed with the Mulkeys and the United States Supreme Court, 5 to 4, affirmed.

(a) **The Court's opinion.** Repeal of the statutes prohibiting racial discrimination would not be state action sufficient to trigger the equal protection clause, said the Court, since there is no affirmative obligation on the part of states to enact such laws at all. But the repeal-plus-constitutional-prohibition-upon-reenactment amounted to official state "authoriz[ation of] private racial discrimination in the housing market. . . . Those practicing racial discriminations need no longer rely on their personal choice. They could now invoke express constitutional authority, free from censure or interference of any kind from official sources."

(b) **The dissents.** Justice Harlan, joined by Justices Black, Clark, and Stewart, dissented. They regarded the state's action as a repeal of its antidiscrimination statutes (concededly valid) and contended that "[t]he fact that such repeal was also accompanied by a constitutional prohibition against future enactment of such laws by the California Legislature cannot . . . affect, from a federal constitutional standpoint, the validity of what California has done."

ii. **Limited scope of this strand of state action.** The degree of *encouragement* that the state must lend to private action in order to transmute private action into state action is quite high.

 ## Examples and Analysis

Example: In *Flagg Brothers v. Brooks* a private sale of stored goods to enforce a statutorily created lien for unpaid storage charges was found not to be state action. Brooks contended that the private sale "is properly attributable to the State because the State has authorized and encouraged it [by] enacting the lien law" but the Court's view was that "a State's mere acquiescence in a private action [does not] convert [ ] that action to that of the State. . . . New York has not compelled the sale . . . but has merely announced the circumstances under which its courts will not interfere with a private sale. . . . [T]he crux of [Brooks'] complaint is not that the State *has* acted, but that it has *refused* to act." *Flagg Bros. v. Brooks,* 436 U.S. 149 (1978).

Similarly, approval of private action by a state regulatory body is not necessarily sufficient encouragement or authorization to create state action.

Example: A customer argued that a publicly regulated utility's decision to terminate her service for nonpayment was state action because the state, through its regulatory process, had "specifically authorized and approved" the termination practice. The utility had filed and the state's Public Utilities Commission had approved a rate tariff that included the utility's right to terminate service for nonpayment. This was not sufficient encouragement or authorization because the PUC had not "order[ed] it," nor had it even investigated the termination procedure. "The nature of governmental regulation of private utilities is such that a utility may frequently be required by the state regulatory scheme to obtain approval for practices [other businesses] would be free to institute without any approval from a regulatory body." This was such a practice. Without some more specific governmental imprimatur upon the termination procedure, there was insufficient encouragement to create state action. *Jackson v. Metropolitan Edison Co.,* 419 U.S. 345 (1974).

A private actor's near total financial reliance on government does not amount to sufficient encouragement of the private actor's conduct to constitute state action.

Example: A private school that educated, at public expense, students who could not "adjust" to the public schools, was not a state actor. First, "the school's receipt of public funds does not make the discharge decisions acts of the State." Second, the extensive state regulation of the school was insufficient to create state action because "the decisions to discharge the [teachers] were not compelled or even influenced by any state regulation." *Rendell-Baker v. Kohn,* 457 U.S. 830 (1982).

---

d. **"Symbiotic" and other "entwined" public-private relationships.** When the state becomes so entangled or involved in the affairs of a private actor that it is difficult to separate their respective identities the private actor will be transformed into a state actor. This happens rarely; most such claims are rejected. For such state action to be present it is necessary to establish either an *extraordinary degree of interdependence,* the *intervention by the state in the specific decision challenged,* or some *necessarily joint action by private and public actors.* Mere regulation or provision of substantial funds to the private actor are not enough to create state action.

i. **Symbiotic relationships: when the state benefits from private action.** An unusually high degree of interdependence and commingling of private and public functions is necessary to establish a sufficiently "symbiotic" relationship to turn nominally private action into state action. *Burton v. Wilmington Parking Authority,* 365 U.S. 715 (1961), is the classic case. The city of Wilmington, Delaware, developed a public parking facility. As part of the project it entered into long term leases with a variety of commercial tenants, including the Eagle Coffee Shop. Eagle refused to serve Burton because of his race. Burton brought suit, contending that Eagle's action was effectively state action. The Court agreed. No single fact was dispositive but the following items each contributed to the ultimate conclusion that "[t]he State has so far insinuated itself into a position of interdependence with Eagle that it must be recognized as a joint participant in the challenged activity."

- *Public Character of the Building:* The entire structure was openly identified as a public building and was statutorily dedicated to "public uses." But this, by itself, does not mean that the acts of a private lessee or concessionaire in a public building are automatically state action.

- *Joint Operation:* Commercial tenants, such as Eagle, were an "indispensable part of the State's plan to operate its project as a self-sustaining unit." The Authority performed all "[u]pkeep and maintenance of the building" and "the restaurant operated as an integral part of a public building devoted to a public parking service." A privately owned cafeteria in the basement of a federal court house would be a similar operation.

- *Mutual Financial Benefits:* The Court thought the following were "indispensable elements in the financial success of a governmental agency": tax exemptions given Eagle to finance its construction of the restaurant improvements, reciprocal benefits from the proximity of the parking garage to the restaurant, and enhanced profits Eagle claimed to earn from practicing racial discrimination. The *totality* of these factors produced the conclusion that there was sufficient symbiosis, or interdependence, between Eagle and the state to warrant treating Eagle's racial discrimination as that of the state.

Justice Stewart concurred on the more straightforward ground that Delaware had authorized Eagle to discriminate by enacting a statute that expressly permitted "a restaurant to refuse to serve 'persons whose reception or entertainment . . . would be offensive to the major part of [its] customers.' "

By contrast, the fact that nearly all the revenue earned by a private actor comes from the state is insufficient to establish a symbiotic relationship. See *Blum v. Yaretsky* and *Rendell-Baker v. Kohn,* supra. To prove a symbiotic relationship the private actor must be more than a "contractor performing services for the government."

ii. **Licensing.** The actions of private licensees of the state are not, without more, state action. *Moose Lodge No. 107 v. Irvis,* 407 U.S. 163 (1972), involved a private club, the Moose Lodge, that restricted its membership to whites and refused to serve the black guests of its members. Irvis claimed that the club's racially discriminatory policy was state action because the club was licensed by the state to serve alcoholic beverages. The Court held that the mere licensing or regulation of a private actor, without more, did not turn private choices into state decisions. "[W]here the impetus for [racial] discrimination is private, the State must have 'significantly involved itself with invidious discriminations'" to trigger state action. Though Pennsylvania's liquor licensing and regulation system was "pervasive" there was nothing to show that Pennsylvania established or enforced "the membership or guest policies of the club that it licenses to serve liquor," nor did the licensing system grant to "club licensees a monopoly in the dispensing of liquor." The Court did find state action in Pennsylvania's regulation requiring club licensees to adhere to their own charters and bylaws. Because those documents mandated racial discrimination Irvis was entitled to an injunction preventing enforcement of that regulation.

iii. **Regulated and licensed private monopolies.** A private entity that is a publicly regulated and licensed monopoly is not a state actor simply by virtue of that fact. For state action to be present the state must specifically endorse the challenged private action in some way. In *Public Utilities Commission v. Pollak,* 343 U.S. 451 (1952), Capital Transit, a private entity regulated by the PUC, that provided bus service in the District of Columbia began playing amplified radio programs through loudspeakers in its vehicles. The PUC ordered an investigation into the practice to determine whether it was "consistent with public convenience, comfort and safety." Following a thorough investigation, including formal public hearings, the PUC concluded "that the public safety, comfort and convenience were not impaired" by amplified radio programming in the buses. Pollak and other passengers attacked the PUC's decision as violative of their constitutional rights of free speech and due process. The Court concluded that state action was present. It expressly stated that state action was **not produced** by the mere fact that Capital Transit was a publicly licensed and regulated monopoly. Instead, state action was created by the PUC's in-depth inquiry into and approval of the *very practice at issue.*

By contrast, in *Jackson v. Metropolitan Edison Co.* the Court rejected the claim that the mere monopoly status of a publicly regulated private electrical utility was sufficient to produce state action. See also *San Francisco Arts & Athletics, Inc. v. United States Olympic*

Committee, 483 U.S. 522 (1987) (no state action in the government's grant of exclusive use of the word "Olympic" in connection with athletic contests).

iv. **Necessarily joint action by private and public actors.** When private action is effective only with joint participation by the state, state action is present. *Lugar v. Edmondson Oil Co.,* 457 U.S. 922 (1982). Edmondson Oil sued Lugar in Virginia state court to collect a debt. In the course of that suit Edmondson Oil filed an ex parte petition seeking a prejudgment attachment of Lugar's assets. The court clerk issued the writ of attachment and it was executed by the sheriff. Although Lugar remained in possession of his assets he was effectively disabled from transferring or encumbering them. After the attachment was dismissed on substantive grounds, Lugar brought suit in federal court against Edmondson Oil, contending that the wrongful attachment had deprived him of his property without due process. No one disputed that the Virginia sheriff and court clerk engaged in state action, but Lugar did not sue them. The question was entirely whether Edmondson Oil, a private litigant, had engaged in state action by enlisting the aid of the courts to collect a debt. The Court, 5 to 4, found Edmondson Oil to be a state actor.

The majority reasoned that Virginia's procedure, which required "officers of the State [to] act jointly with a creditor in securing the property in dispute," placed Edmondson Oil in the position of being a state actor when it invoked that joint procedure. *Flagg Brothers* was distinguished because under the New York procedure at issue in *Flagg* no state participation of any kind was required for the creditor to act. The Court was careful to note that *"private misuse"* of Virginia's procedure would *not* be state action, but "the *procedural scheme created by the statute* obviously is the product of state action." Since that procedural scheme required joint participation of public and private actors to work, the private participation became state action. Four Justices dissented, arguing that it was "implausible" and "unjust" to hold that "a private citizen who did no more than commence a legal action of a kind traditionally initiated by private parties, thereby engaged in 'state action.' "

v. **"Entwinement":** *Brentwood Academy v. Tennessee Secondary School Athletic Association,* 121 S. Ct. 924 (2001). The TSSAA sanctioned Brentwood for a recruiting violation. Brentwood claimed that the TSSAA was a state actor and that the rule's enforcement was unconstitutional. The Court held that the TSSAA, a nominally private association composed of almost all the state's public high schools and some private high schools, was so entwined with the state that it was a state actor. "[T]o the extent of 84% of its membership, the Association is an organization of public schools represented by their officials acting in their official capacity. [The] public school officials . . . do not merely control but overwhelmingly perform all but the purely ministerial acts by which the Association exists and functions in practical terms. Only the 16% minority of private school memberships prevents this entwinement of the Association and the public school system from being total and their identities totally indistinguishable."

e.   **When the state has adopted or ratified private action as its own.** State action is also present when a government adopts or ratifies private action. The Court has ruled that a private party's use of its peremptory jury challenges in a racially discriminatory fashion is state action and violative of equal protection. The rationale is a mixture of state action theories. The state has delegated public power (some control of jury selection) to a private party, thus triggering the public function doctrine. The state is a joint participant with the private party in jury selection. Finally, the state adopts the private party's actions by seating a jury selected in part by a private party in a racially discriminatory fashion. (See *Edmonson v. Leesville Concrete Co.,* 500 U.S. 614 (1991) (civil actions) and *Georgia v. McCollum,* 505 U.S. 42 (1992) (defendants in criminal actions).)

6.   **State Action Theory**

a.   **Purposes of the state action doctrine.** The Constitution limits state action only for two different but related reasons.

   i.   **Preservation of individual liberty.** The Constitution constrains the way governments can act upon private individuals. The state action doctrine also ensures that private individuals are free to act as they choose, subject to such valid statutory limits that Congress or state governments may impose.

   ii.   **Preservation of separation of powers.** Because the Constitution only limits governmental action courts have no ability to invoke the Constitution to interfere with private actions. The state action doctrine thus confines the judiciary and leaves to democratically elected legislatures the important decision of how much (if at all), and for what purposes, individual liberty should be curtailed by legislative prohibitions.

b.   **Understanding state action doctrine.** The Court's doctrine has been frequently criticized as "a conceptual disaster area" (Black, 81 Harv. L. Rev. at 95), "chaos," lacking in "any general rule," and doctrinal "anarchy" (Tribe, at 1691). Perhaps. There are ways, however, to make sense of the Court's state action doctrine.

i. **What the Constitution is *not* about.** Tribe suggests that "if constitutional law is . . . a snapshot of the deepest norms by which we govern our political lives, . . . state action . . . is its negative." The frontier beyond state action "is what the Constitution is not about." Tribe, at 1720. Such observations, while useful to remind us of the *purposes* for a state action doctrine, do not by themselves describe any theory of state action, or explain the Court's doctrinal process.

ii. **Constitutional neutrality required.** Perhaps the most frequently suggested theory of state action is that governments are required to be "constitutionally neutral" in creating the rules of law that form the landscape upon which private action occurs.

 ## EXAMPLES AND ANALYSIS

Example: Missouri's background rule of law that required private parties to adhere to a racially biased real covenant even when they had no desire to do so was not constitutionally neutral because it coerced private parties to engage in behavior forbidden to a government. (See *Shelley v. Kraemer,* supra.)

Example: Georgia's background rule of law that terminated trusts when the trustor's intended purposes could not be accomplished was constitutionally neutral. It was indifferent to the private intentions expressed by the trustor, even when those intentions were racially biased. (See *Evans v. Abney,* supra.)

iii. **Ascertaining constitutional neutrality.** In order to determine whether the government's background rule is constitutionally neutral, a two-part inquiry must be made.

(a) **Locate the state's rule.** *First, look for a government rule that does what the challenger alleges.* If there is such a rule there is state action.

 ## EXAMPLES AND ANALYSIS

Example: Shelley contended that the state of Missouri denied him equal protection by barring him from moving into his new home because he was black. The government rule that did what he alleged was the injunction that barred him from occupying his home because of his race. Put another way, if one looked only at the relevant private actions there were no private barriers to Shelley's occupancy of his home—the seller was perfectly willing to sell and Kraemer could do nothing to bar Shelley without invoking the state. *Shelley v. Kraemer,* supra.

Example: Ms. Brooks, whose goods Flagg Brothers was about to sell to pay her storage debt, charged that she had been denied procedural due process by being deprived of her property without a prior hearing concerning the merits of her dispute with Flagg. The Court found *no governmental rule* that denied her due process. The New York statute merely announced New York's policy that it would do nothing to interfere with Flagg's sale, but did not require Flagg to deny a hearing to Brooks. The Court not only saw no affirmative obligation on the part of a state to prevent private parties from exercising traditional private remedies without affording their adversary a hearing, but also went a step further and held that a state could expressly immunize such private behavior. It was Flagg Brothers' decision to deny a hearing. Like Pontius Pilate, New York had nothing to do with the decision. *Flagg Brothers v. Brooks,* supra.

> **(b)   If there is no state rule, examine government involvement in the challenged private action.** If there is no state rule that inflicts the injury the plaintiff alleges, it is still possible to have state action if the government is so involved in the private decision that it bears responsibility for the decision.

 # EXAMPLES AND ANALYSIS

Example: Burton contended that he had been denied equal protection because he had been refused restaurant service on account of his race. Delaware did not mandate such discrimination by law. The Wilmington Parking Authority had failed to require its lessees *not* to discriminate by race but there is no constitutional obligation for it to do so. Thus, there was no government rule that did what Burton alleged. But the Wilmington Parking Authority was so deeply embroiled in the restaurant's behavior it was found to be responsible for Eagle's racial discrimination. *Burton v. Wilmington Parking Authority,* supra.

Example: Pollak and his fellow Capital Transit bus riders alleged that their free speech right *not to listen* to the radio was violated. The government had not compelled Capital Transit, its licensee, to play the radio. There was no state rule that inflicted the injury of which Pollak complained. But the PUC had investigated and held hearings about the advisability of the practice, ultimately concluding that it was in the public interest. That level of state involvement caused the separate identities of Capital Transit and the PUC to merge. *PUC v. Pollak,* supra.

Example: Catherine Jackson alleged that she was denied a liberty or property interest in continued electrical service by termination of her electrical supply without prior notice or hearing. There was no state rule requiring her private utility supplier to deny her notice or hearing before termination. Nor was there any significant government involvement in the private utility's decision to terminate service without prior notice. *Jackson v. Metropolitan Edison Co.,* supra.

This inquiry bears some similarities to the corporate law inquiry into "piercing the corporate veil"—ignoring a corporation's separate identity to hold its owners liable for the corporation's actions. In both cases the fundamental question is: When is there such a *unity of interest* between the two spheres (public-private or corporation-owner) that the *Constitution* (or, in corporate law, equity) demands that we ignore their separate existence, and treat them as one? There is no easy general answer. The best we can do, in either area of law, is list factors that are relevant to the answer and explain their relative importance and significance.

B.   CONGRESSIONAL ENFORCEMENT OF CIVIL RIGHTS

1.   Overview

The Constitution is not the only vehicle for protection of important human rights. As the state action doctrine reveals, the Constitution tolerates a wide range of private behavior. It is perfectly constitutional to engage in private action that is immoral, nasty, brutish, unwise, brilliant, pleasurable, ecstatic, useful, evil, boring, dangerous, and so on. By and large, the Constitution leaves to legislatures the responsibility of deciding what private behavior ought to be prohibited. Whenever Congress does so it must, of course, have some constitutional source of authority for acting. This section explores some of the federal legislation that is grounded upon the power given Congress to enforce the 13th, 14th and 15th Amendments, the principal constitutional vehicles for achieving the ultimate goal of a nation without racial consciousness. This enforcement power is contained in §2 of the 13th and 15th Amendments and in §5 of the 14th Amendment. There are two principal issues raised by this power. The first is discussed in this section; the second is discussed in Chapter 5, supra.

- *Congressional Power to Regulate Private Conduct:* May Congress use its enforcement power to regulate *private conduct?* The 13th Amendment forbids private as well as governmental conduct so Congress may certainly regulate private conduct to enforce the 13th Amendment. But the 14th and 15th Amendments only forbid governmental action, so congressional power to enforce those amendments is primarily limited to regulation of governments, *not private individuals.*

- *Congressional Power to Enforce the Rights Guaranteed by the Civil War Amendments.* This topic is covered in Chapter 5. Congress's power is solely *remedial.* Enforcement must be *congruent* with the constitutional injury remedied and *proportional* to that injury. Congress may *not* define for itself what constitutes a constitutional injury.

2.   Statutory Framework

There are many federal statutes that touch upon what might loosely be called "civil rights." Many of these are founded upon Congress's power to regulate interstate commerce. (See Chapter 4, supra.) We are not concerned with these; this section focuses on the variety of federal laws enacted under the enforcement power given Congress in the 13th, 14th, and 15th Amendments.

a.   Reconstruction era statutes designed to ensure racial equality. The Republican-dominated Congress of the Reconstruction years enacted a number of important pieces of civil rights legislation. Key portions of the civil rights acts of 1866, 1870, 1871, and 1875 survive and play important roles today in securing the equal treatment of people of all races.

i.   Civil remedies. The civil provisions of these Reconstruction era laws, as codified today, are as follows.

- **42 U.S.C. §1981:** *Equal Civil Status.* "All persons . . . shall have the same right . . . to make and enforce contracts, to sue, be parties, give evidence, and to the full and equal benefit of all laws . . . for the security of persons and property as is enjoyed by white citizens, and shall be subject to like punishments, . . . penalties, taxes, . . . and exactions of every kind, and to no other."

- **42 U.S.C. §1982:** *Equal Property Rights.* "All citizens . . . shall have the same right . . . as is enjoyed by white citizens . . . to inherit, purchase, lease, sell, hold, and convey real and personal property."

- **42 U.S.C. §1983:** *Deprivation of Rights Under "Color of Law."* "Every person who, under color of [law], . . . subjects, or causes to be subjected, any . . . person . . . to the deprivation of any rights, privileges or immunities secured by the Constitution or law, shall be liable to the party injured . . . for redress."

- **42 U.S.C. §1985(c):** *Private Conspiracies to Deprive Persons of Equal Protection.* If "two or more persons . . . conspire to go in disguise . . . for the purpose of depriving, either directly or indirectly, any person . . . of the equal protection of the laws, or of equal privileges and immunities under the laws; [the] party so injured" may recover damages from any of the conspirators.

- **42 U.S.C. §1988:** *Recovery of Attorneys' Fees.* Prevailing private parties in actions brought under these provisions may, in the court's discretion, recover "a reasonable attorney's fee."

ii.   **Criminal penalties.** The criminal provisions of these Reconstruction era laws, as codified today, are as follows.

- **18 U.S.C. §241:** *Private Conspiracies.* "If two or more persons conspire to injure, oppress, threaten, or intimidate any [person] in the free exercise or enjoyment of any right or privilege secured to him by the Constitution or [federal law], or because of his having exercised the same; or if two or more persons go in disguise . . . with intent to prevent or hinder his free exercise or enjoyment of any right or privilege so secured they shall be" fined or imprisoned or both.

- **18 U.S.C. §242:** *Deprivation of Rights Under "Color of Law."* "Whoever, under color of any law, . . . willfully subjects any [person] to the deprivation of any rights, privileges, or immunities secured or protected by the [Constitution or federal law], or to different punishments . . . , on account of such [person] being an alien, or by reason of his color, or race, than are prescribed for the punishment of citizens, shall be" fined or imprisoned or both.

b.   **Modern statutes designed to eliminate practices Congress regards as invidiously discriminatory.** Most of the modern statutes addressing invidious discrimination are grounded on congressional power under the commerce clause. Principal examples include the Civil Rights Act of 1964, especially Title II (public accommodations), Title VI (education), and Title VII (employment), Title VIII of the 1968 Civil Rights Act (fair housing), the Education Amendments of 1972 (Title IX, dealing with sex discrimination in federally funded educational programs), and the Age Discrimination Act of 1975. The principal civil rights statutes based upon congressional enforcement power under the Reconstruction amendments are summarized below.

i.   **Voting rights.** Although Congress enacted civil rights acts in 1957 and 1960 to expand remedies for racial discrimination in voting, the major such legislation is the Voting Rights Act of 1965, extended in 1970, 1975, and again in 1982. The key provisions of the Voting Rights Act are in §§2 and 5.

- **Section 2:** Section 2 tracks the language of the 15th Amendment by prohibiting states from enacting laws that "deny or abridge" the right to vote for racial reasons. In *Mobile v. Bolden,* 446 U.S. 55 (1980), the Court held that the 15th

Amendment only bars states from enacting voting laws that "purposefully" discriminate on racial grounds. In the 1982 extension §2 was altered to include state laws that "result" in such denials or abridgments.

- **Section 5:** Section 5 bars a variety of state voting practices, like literacy tests, and subjects certain jurisdictions to federal "preclearance" of any alterations in their laws affecting voting. Even though this "requirement that States come to Washington. . . . to beg federal authorities to approve . . . their laws . . . is reminiscent of the deeply resented practices used by the English crown in dealing with the American colonies" the Court held that Congress had power under §2 of the 15th Amendment to enact the legislation. *South Carolina v. Katzenbach,* 383 U.S. 301, 359 and n.2 (1966) (Black, J.). (See Chapter 5, supra.)

ii. **Civil Rights Act of 1968.** Following Martin Luther King's assassination Congress enacted this statute, a key provision of which added criminal penalties for the violent interference with civil rights.

- **18 U.S.C. §245:** *Violent Interference with Civil Rights.* This complex section imposes criminal penalties on anyone, "whether or not acting under color of law," who "by force or threat of force willfully [attempts to or does] injure, intimidate or interfere with" (1) any person exercising certain federally protected rights, (2) "any person on account of his race, color, religion, or national origin" because of their exercise of certain actions connected to federal power, (3) "during or incident to a riot or civil disorder, any person engaged in a business in commerce or affecting commerce," or (4) persons participating in, or affording others the opportunity to participate in, certain activities on a basis free of racial discrimination, or participating in lawful speech or assembly to protest such racial discrimination.

3. **Congressional Power to Regulate Private Conduct**

a. **Overview.** The 14th and 15th Amendments facially apply only to state governments, and the amendments grant Congress the power only to *enforce the provisions of those amendments.* From text alone, the enforcement provisions appear not to give Congress power to act upon private persons. That is too simple an answer to a complex issue, one that the Court has never definitively answered. Under the 14th or 15th Amendments Congress has *limited power* to regulate private conduct:

- *Congruent with State Action:* As discussed in section A, supra, some private action is treated as the state's. Congress can certainly regulate private action to the extent that it is a proxy for the state's action.

- *Private Action That Is Not State Action:* Though not entirely free from doubt, Congress *probably* is able to use its enforcement power to punish private action directed *at state officials and designed to interfere with their obligation to comply with the 14th Amendment.*

 # EXAMPLE AND ANALYSIS

Suppose private persons act to intimidate public school officials from carrying out their plans to comply with the 14th Amendment by racially integrating the public schools. Congress almost certainly has the power under §5 of the 14th Amendment to prohibit this conduct, consisting of private action *directed at state officials with the intent of interfering with their obligation to comply with the 14th Amendment.* (See *Brewer v. Hoxie School District No. 46,* 238 F.2d 91 (8th Cir. 1956).)

---

b. **Other sources of power to regulate private conduct.** The fact that Congress lacks much power to reach private conduct under the enforcement provisions of the 14th and 15th Amendments does not mean that Congress has no power to regulate private conduct. Congress may use at least the following sources of authority to regulate private action that falls within the scope of the authority invoked:

- *Article I, §8:* Through the commerce power, or other appropriate heads of regulatory authority in Article I, §8, Congress may regulate private behavior. Note that the public accommodations provisions of the 1964 Civil Rights Act are founded upon this source of authority. (See Chapter 4, supra.)

- *13th Amendment:* The 13th Amendment applies to private as well as public conduct. Congress's power to enforce this amendment thus extends to regulation of pertinent private conduct. (See section B.3.f, infra.)

- *Certain Implied Constitutional Rights:* There are a few implied constitutional rights that, like the 13th Amendment, operate upon private individuals as well as governments. These include the right to travel (*United States v. Guest,* infra), the right to be free of interference in elections (*Ex parte Yarbrough,* 110 U.S. 651 (1884); *United States v. Classic,* 313 U.S. 299 (1941)), and the right to petition Congress for redress of grievances (*United States v. Cruikshank,* 92 U.S. 542 (1875) (dicta)).

c. **Congressional enforcement power limited to state action.** In a series of cases the Court has held that Congress's power to enforce the 14th Amendment is limited to regulating state action.

i. *Civil Rights Cases,* 109 U.S. 3 (1883), discussed supra. The Court held that the enforcement provision of the 14th Amendment gave Congress no power to prohibit private acts of racial discrimination in the operation of "inns, public conveyances on land or water, theatres, and other places of public amusement." The Court concluded that, since the 14th Amendment itself only prohibited state action, Congress's enforcement power was limited to regulation of *state action.*

ii. *United States v. Harris,* 106 U.S. 629 (1883). The Court struck down §2 of the 1871 Civil Rights Act, which punished "private persons" for "conspiring to deprive anyone of the equal protection of the laws." The law exceeded the scope of Congress's power to enforce the 14th Amendment because it was "directed exclusively against the actions of private persons, without reference to [state action]."

iii. *United States v. Morrison,* 529 U.S. 598 (2000). The Court voided a portion of the Violence Against Women Act that provided a civil remedy to victims of "gender-motivated violence." The provision was "not aimed at proscribing discrimination by officials which the Fourteenth Amendment might not itself proscribe"; it was "directed not at any State or state actor, but at individuals who have committed criminal acts motivated by gender bias." The Court clarified *United States v. Guest,* 383 U.S. 745 (1966), in which the Court upheld an indictment of six private persons under 18 U.S.C. §241 for conspiracy to deprive other persons of their right to use public facilities without discrimination on the basis of race. The *Guest* Court thought the indictment contained "an express allegation of state involvement" with the conspiracy, so there was no need for it to decide the question of whether Congress could use its 14th Amendment enforcement power to prohibit purely private action interfering with the exercise of constitutional rights. Nevertheless, six Justices in *Guest,* in two separate concurrences, delivered dicta to the effect that Congress did possess such power. The Court in *Morrison* squarely repudiated that dicta. After *Morrison,* there is no doubt that Congress's enforcement power does not extend to purely private actions that interfere with other persons' exercise of their constitutional rights. Ordinary state criminal law is adequate to address that problem. In the event that states refuse to protect private persons in the exercise of their constitutional rights Congress would have power to legislate with respect to that *state* behavior.

iv. **The scope of 42 U.S.C. §1983.** The statute reaches private action taken under color of law. Although the statute refers to action taken under "custom, or usage of any State" the Court has held that a cause of action under §1983 "requires state involvement and [may not be founded upon] simply a practice that reflects long-standing social habit." *Adickes v. S.H. Kress & Co.,* 398 U.S. 144 (1970). The application of 42 U.S.C. §1983 was widened considerably by *Monroe v. Pape,* 365 U.S. 167 (1961), which permitted §1983 actions to be brought against state officers whose actions also violated state law, and by *Monell v. Department of Social Services,* 436 U.S. 658 (1978), which largely eliminated local governmental immunity from §1983 actions.

d. **The unique role of the 13th Amendment.** Unlike the 14th and 15th Amendments the 13th Amendment applies to private action. The result is that, under §2 of the 13th Amendment, Congress may regulate private behavior that reinforces the banned racial structures of slavery.

i. *Civil Rights Cases,* 109 U.S. 3 (1883), discussed supra. The Court concluded that §2 of the 13th Amendment granted Congress "power to pass all laws necessary and proper for abolishing all badges and incidents of slavery in the United States," but was of the opinion that private racial discrimination in public accommodations was not such a badge or incident.

ii. *Jones v. Alfred H. Mayer Co.,* 392 U.S. 409 (1968). Jones brought suit under 42 U.S.C. §1982, claiming that Mayer, a private entity, had refused to sell him a home solely on account of his race. The statute provides that "[a]ll citizens . . . shall have the same right [as] white citizens [to] purchase . . . real . . . property." The Court held that §1982 "bars *all* racial discrimination, private as well as public, in the sale or rental of property, and that the statute, thus construed, is a valid exercise of the power of Congress to enforce the 13th Amendment." The Court concluded that Congress had the power "rationally to determine what are the badges and the incidents of slavery," and that it was rational for Congress to conclude that private racial discrimination in the sale or rental of property was such a badge or incident.

iii. **Scope of amendment.** The 13th Amendment is *self-executing,* meaning that Congress need not act to prohibit slavery. But §2 permits Congress to act if it wishes.

(a) **Self-executing.** The scope of the Amendment *in the absence of congressional action is quite narrow.* The Court has found the 13th Amendment applicable without congressional action only to "peonage"—laws imprisoning people for breach of their promise to work for another. See *Pollock v. Williams,* 322 U.S. 4 (1944); *Bailey v. Alabama,* 219 U.S. 219 (1911). It is virtually certain that the Court would not find that the 13th Amendment, *by itself,* bars private racial discrimination in the sale or rental of property. Similarly, the Court has defined "slavery" itself quite narrowly. (See, e.g, *Memphis v. Greene,* 451 U.S. 100 (1981).)

(b) **Congressional action.** *Mayer* clearly establishes congressional power to reach private conduct that Congress rationally concludes is a "badge or incident" of slavery. But that does not mean that Congress has a virtually free rein to regulate anything it might think is related to the defunct system of race-based slavery. In a series of post-*Mayer* decisions the Court has intimated that congressional enforcement power under the 13th Amendment is limited to addressing racial issues.

REVIEW QUESTIONS AND ANSWERS

Question: The Gemini Company, a private corporation, acquires a large tract of ground in the state of Nez Perce, encompassing a mountainside and the vast glacial bowl at its base. In compliance with numerous state and federal requirements concerning every aspect of the project, Gemini constructed a ski resort, consisting of multiple runs and lifts on the mountain and a compact village at the foot of the runs. The resort became world-famous—the mountain was called Tehama and the unincorporated village was called Orion Village. The Gemini Company sold 999-year leasehold interests in about 60% of Orion Village's condominiums and houses, but owned all the other buildings and owned all the ground under the entire area. A small year-round community exists in Orion Village and a much larger transient community of skiers exists in winter. To preserve the remote character of the village, the Orion Company refused to permit any electronic cable connections to the village, thus shutting out television, telephone, and internet connections except by satellite link or radio. Bernie, a resident of Orion Village who is a computer, television and general communications junkie, sues the Gemini Company under 42 U.S.C. §1983, asserting that the Gemini Company has deprived him of his First and

14th Amendment rights of free speech. Bernie is joined in the suit as a plaintiff by Global Communications, a major vendor of television, telephone, and internet services. The Gemini Company moves for summary judgment on the sole ground that it has not been shown, on these facts, that Gemini Company acted "under color of law." What result?

Answer: The Gemini Company will probably lose. Resolution depends on whether Nez Perce has delegated to the Gemini Company the power to perform public functions. If Orion Village was "built and operated primarily to benefit the public" its operation is essentially a public function. But private owners of property generally open to the public are treated as state actors only when their "property has taken on *all* the attributes of a town." This case seems much more like Chickasaw, Alabama, the company town in *Marsh v. Alabama,* than the shopping center at issue in *Hudgens v. NLRB.* The fact that Nez Perce approved many aspects of the development is irrelevant.

Question: Ed, a practitioner of Zen Buddhism, purchased a small farm in the state of Germania from Bob, for the purpose of establishing a Zen retreat. Bob knew of Ed's intentions at the time he sold the farm to Ed and was also aware that the property was burdened by a running real covenant that restricted occupancy and ownership of the land to "Christians only." Zeke, owner of a farm benefited by the covenant, learned of Ed's intentions and sued to enjoin Ed's occupancy of the farm. A Germania trial court issued the requested injunction and it was upheld by the Germania Supreme Court. What arguments should Ed make to the United States Supreme Court and are they likely to succeed?

Answer: Ed should argue that Germania has coerced private action by its enforcement of a religious-restrictive real covenant at the behest of another private party. Even though the suit appears to be a private dispute between Zeke and Ed, the effect of Germania's enforcement of the covenant is to give to a private party (Zeke) the power to coerce compliance with the covenant. What at first appears to be a private dispute is revealed to be state coercion of both Bob and Ed, a willing seller and a willing buyer, who would ignore the covenant if left to themselves. Germania's enforcement of the covenant under these circumstances involves the commingling of private and public functions to coerce private persons to comply with a state-enforced norm. (See *Shelley v. Kraemer.*)

Question: The state of Garfield enacts legislation that immunizes people from civil or criminal liability if they use deadly violence against nocturnal intruders in their home. At 2 A.M. in her home Marty shoots and kills Ted, a burglar. The executor of Ted's estate sues Marty under 42 U.S.C. §1983, contending that Marty deprived Ted of his constitutional right to life except in accordance with due process. Marty seeks dismissal of the suit. What result?

Answer: Marty will prevail. The State of Garfield has not sufficiently encouraged Marty to use deadly force that her action will be treated as that of the state. The legislation itself is constitutionally neutral and there are no other factors suggesting extraordinary, unusual, or extreme encouragement. The decision to use deadly force was Marty's, not the state's. (See section A.5.c, supra.)

Question: The state of Grant leases an unused public building to Pyramid Corp., a private developer, who proposes to convert the building to studio and living spaces for artists. The lease requires Pyramid to pay to Grant a fixed annual rental and 10% of its net annual operating profits from the building. Pyramid converts the building but refuses to rent spaces to artists whose work Pyramid thinks is "indecent." Harry, an artist who paints nudes and who was denied space in the building, sues Pyramid under 42 U.S.C. §1983, contending that Pyramid acted under color of law to deny him his free expression rights. Pyramid moves to dismiss. What result?

Answer: Harry's suit will be dismissed. The entanglement between Grant and Pyramid with respect to this issue is minimal. While Pyramid's development has occurred under a lease from Grant and Grant shares in the profits from the venture there is neither an *extraordinary* degree of interdependence, any intervention by Grant in the *specific decision* at issue, nor any *necessarily* joint action by Pyramid and Grant. (See section A.5.d, supra.)

Question: The state of Fillmore permits private parties, when accompanied by a deputy sheriff, to enter private property to recover their property wrongfully held by another private party, but only after obtaining a "writ of entry" from a Fillmore court. A writ of entry may be obtained by filing a civil suit and requesting the clerk of the court to issue the writ of entry. Fillmore court clerks routinely issue the writs upon request. Miranda, a private party, sues Bill for recovery of Miranda's stereo that she claims she loaned to Bill and which he refuses to return. Miranda requests and obtains a writ of entry, then in company with a deputy sheriff, enters Bill's apartment through a window and removes her stereo. Later in the litigation, Bill proves that Miranda gave the stereo to him. Bill then sues Miranda under 42 U.S.C. §1983, contending that Miranda seized his property under color of law without affording him due process of law. Miranda moves to dismiss. What result?

Answer: Miranda's motion will be denied. Her private action was effective *only with joint participation* in the action by the State of Fillmore. Accordingly, her action and Fillmore's action are so connected and joined that Miranda's actions are treated as those of Fillmore. (See section A.5.d.iv, supra.)

Question: The city of Morgan long maintained racially segregated public facilities. In response to federal court orders Morgan announced that Morgan Central Park, formerly all-white, would be opened to all races. A group of "skinheads" then stalk Morgan officials, threatening them with violence unless they rescind the desegregation decision. The "skinheads" are then prosecuted under a federal law making it a crime for any person to interfere with a public official in the performance of official obligations of compliance with the equal protection clause. The defendants move to dismiss the indictment on the ground that Congress lacks power to enact the law. What result?

Answer: Congress has power under §5 of the 14th Amendment to prohibit private conduct that is directed at state officials with the intent of interfering with their obligation to comply with the equal protection clause. This is a necessary and proper adjunct to the power to enforce the constitutional requirement that states provide equal protection of the laws to their residents. (See B.3.c, supra.)

Question: Suppose that the skinheads in the preceding question threatened blacks who sought to use Morgan Central Park, and were prosecuted under a federal law making it a crime for a private person to interfere with another private person's attempt to exercise a right guaranteed against governments by the equal protection clause. What result if the skinheads move to dismiss the indictment?

Answer: The indictment will be dismissed. Congress lacks power under §5 of the 14th Amendment to prohibit private conduct that interferes with another private party's exercise of rights guaranteed against governments by equal protection. (See *United States v. Morrison*.) A state prosecution is appropriate.

Question: The Old Boys Club, a private club that owns a large tract of ground on which only members are permitted to hunt ducks, restricts its membership to male white Christians. Congress enacts legislation under §5 of the 14th Amendment that requires all social clubs to refrain from discriminating on the basis of sex, race, or religion. Is the law valid as applied to the Old Boys Club?

Answer: No. The action of Old Boys Club is purely private. However reprehensible the Old Boys' policy may be it does not infringe upon any *constitutionally protected* right.

Question: Congress enacts legislation that prohibits private schools from discriminating on the basis of race in the admission of students. Putting aside any of Congress' powers under Article I, §8, what is the best source of authority to support the validity of this law?

Answer: Section 2 of the 13th Amendment gives Congress power to enforce the ban on slavery. Since the substance of the 13th Amendment applies equally to governments and private parties, Congress may act to eradicate the "badges and incidents" of slavery as perpetuated by private parties. *Jones v. Alfred H. Mayer Co.,* section B.3.d, supra, upheld congressional power under the 13th Amendment to prohibit private racial discrimination in housing.

EXAM TIPS

- **State Action Issues Are Pervasive.** State action issues can crop up anywhere. The presence of state action is often obvious, but sometimes it is not. State action issues are easily inserted into questions that deal with other substantive matters, so stay alert for the presence of nonobvious state action.

  - **Nominally Private Actors as State Actors.** This is the usual state action issue. It comes in five forms:

    — *Public Function*—the state has expressly or impliedly delegated to a private actor the performance of functions that are traditionally the *exclusive* powers of the government.

    — *Inextricable Entanglement*—the connections between the state and the private actor involve either necessarily joint action, an extraordinary degree of interdependence, or intervention by the state in the specific action that is challenged.

    — *State Coercion or Encouragement*—the state has coerced private parties to act in the challenged manner or has provided extraordinary encouragement for them to do so.

    — *Joint Action*—the challenged private action could not have been effective without joint participation in the action by the state.

    — *State Ratification of the Private Action*—the state has acted to ratify, or adopt as its own act, the challenged private actions.

  - **An Analytical Checklist.** Ask yourself these questions:

    — *Is there a* **government rule** that does what the challenger alleges? Challengers allege that nominally private action violates the Constitution because it is actually the action of the state. If the government has a rule that mandates the private action state action is present.

    — *If there is no rule, is there sufficient government involvement in the challenged private action?* Here, the focus is upon the factors listed above. The doctrinal rules surrounding those factors are simply ways of expressing more precisely the circumstances under which we think there is such a *unity of interest* between state and private actors that the Constitution *ought* to apply.

- **Congressional Power Under the Reconstruction Amendments to Regulate Private Conduct**

  - **Remember that the 13th Amendment applies to private action.** Congress can act on private persons to prevent them from inflicting the "badges and incidents" of servitude on black Americans. The open question is how far this goes.

- **Remember that the 14th and 15th Amendments do not expressly apply to private actions.** These amendments operate only against governments. Professors may differ in their views of whether *Morrison* leaves open any opportunity for Congress to regulate private conduct. Pay attention to your professor's view on this point.

11   Free Expression
of Ideas

Chapter Overview

This chapter examines **free expression of ideas**—freedom of speech, association, assembly, the press, and the right to petition the government for redress of grievances. The most important points in this chapter follow.

- **Content-Based or Content-Neutral Speech Regulations:** Courts apply strict scrutiny to **content-based** speech regulations and lesser scrutiny to **content-neutral** regulations.

  - **Content-Based:** Regulation of the **communicative impact of speech**—what is said—is content based. A law forbidding political speech is content based.

    — **Viewpoint-Based:** Some content-based speech regulations discriminate on the basis of viewpoint. A law forbidding Marxist speech is viewpoint based.

  - **Content-Neutral:** Regulation of speech on some basis other than its communicative impact is content neutral. A law forbidding public speech at night is content neutral.

- **Judicial Review of Content-Based Regulations.** Content-based regulations are **presumptively invalid**—upheld only if the government proves that the regulation is **narrowly drawn** to accomplish a **compelling government interest.**

- **Exception: "Categorical Balancing":** Some speech categories, defined by their content, are so unrelated to the purposes of free speech that they are either unprotected or receive a lesser degree of protection.

  — **Unprotected Categories:** A government may freely regulate such speech, so long as it does **not suppress one particular viewpoint.** For example, while obscene speech may be banned, the state may not prohibit only obscene speech critical of the government. To determine if a category of speech is unprotected, courts balance the governmental interest in regulating the category and the value of the speech category in terms of the purposes of free speech. The following are unprotected categories of speech:

    (1) Incitement of Immediate and Likely Crime

    (2) Obscenity and Child Pornography

    (3) Face-to-Face Abuse Likely to Cause Violence

  — **"Limited Protection" Categories:** Some categories of speech receive only limited protection. Each of these categories has its own special rules for determining the validity of speech regulations within the category. The following speech categories receive limited protection:

    (1) Offensive to Captive or Sensitive Audiences

    (2) Defamation

    (3) Infliction of Emotional Distress

    (4) Invasion of Privacy

    (5) Commercial Speech

- ■ **Judicial Review of Content-Neutral Regulations**

  - **In General:** Content-neutral regulations of speech are valid if they are **narrowly tailored** to serve a **significant government interest** *and* **leave open ample alternative channels of communication.**

  - **Public Forum or Not:** Content-neutral regulations of the time, place, and manner of speech in a **public forum** must be **narrowly tailored** to serve a **significant government interest** *and* **leave open ample alternative channels of communication.** Content-neutral flat bans on speech in a **public forum** must be **narrowly drawn** to accomplish a **compelling government interest.**

    — **Public Fora:** Public fora are government property that is *either:*

      (1) Traditionally Open for Speech—e.g., parks, streets, and sidewalks; or

(2) Voluntarily dedicated by the government to all speech purposes—e.g., a community billboard open for notice posting. A public forum may not be closed to speech so long as it remains a public forum.

— **Limited Public Fora:** A "limited public forum" is government property:

(1) Voluntarily dedicated to **specific** speech purposes—e.g., a public school opened after hours for *student* speech purposes only. Limited public fora may be closed to speech purposes altogether. So long as they remain open to speech, they are open only for their limited purpose. For example, nonstudent speakers could be excluded from the school.

— **Nonpublic Forum:** The validity of content-neutral speech restrictions in a **nonpublic forum** depends on the severity of the restriction.

(1) **Severe Restriction:** When such restrictions are **so severe as to leave no alternative way to speak,** they are generally **presumed invalid** and subjected to **strict scrutiny.**

(2) **Nonsevere Restriction:** Insubstantial content-neutral restrictions need only be **rationally related** to a **legitimate government objective.**

• **Symbolic Conduct:** Nonverbal conduct that **intends to convey an idea** and that is **reasonably understood to convey that idea** is protected speech. Governments may restrict symbolic conduct if:

— The law furthers an **important** or **substantial** government interest,

— The government interest is **unrelated to the suppression of ideas,** and

— The speech restriction is **no greater than necessary** to further the government interest.

If the government interest is related to suppression of ideas the law still might be valid if it can pass **strict scrutiny.**

■ **Secondary Effects:** Speech regulations that are intended to address some effect of speech other than one produced by its communicative impact are treated as content-neutral.

■ **Money as Speech—Political Contributions and Expenditures:**

• **Expenditures:** Expenditures by political candidates from their own funds, or expenditures by individuals or organizations (including political parties) independent from a candidate may not be limited. In order to receive public funds, political candidates may be required to limit their total campaign expenditures.

- **Contributions:** Contributions to political candidates or organizations may be limited but contributions made in connection with ballot measures may not be limited.

- **Public Employees:** Governments may restrict the speech of public employees if justified by the government interest in efficiently delivering public services. Specifically:

  - **Partisan Political Activity** may be regulated.

  - **Criticism of Government** may be regulated only to the extent necessary to maintain an efficient workplace.

  - **Patronage** hiring, firing, or promotion is permissible *only* with respect to jobs for which party affiliation is an **appropriate** criterion to **ensure effective job performance.**

- **Restricted Environments:**

  - **Prisons and Military:** Regulations of the speech of prison inmates or military personnel are permissible so long as they are appropriate devices to secure some legitimate state objective. This is a very deferential standard of review.

  - **Schools:** Speech of elementary and secondary school students may be regulated to avoid disruption to school business and where it is related to the curriculum. Only curriculum related speech of university students may be regulated.

- **Government Sponsored Speech:** When governments pay or otherwise recruit people to deliver the *government's message,* the government can control the content of the message.

- **Freedom of Association:** When governments **substantially** restrict freedom of association the restriction is **presumptively void.** The restriction is valid *only* if the government proves it is the **least restrictive means** to accomplish **a compelling** government interest **unrelated to the suppression of ideas.**

- **Freedom from *Compelled* Speech or Association:** There is just as much right *not* to express ideas as there is a right to expression. Government compulsion of speech or association is **presumptively invalid**—upheld only if the government proves that the compulsion is the **least restrictive means** of achieving a **compelling governmental interest** unrelated to the forced expression of ideas.

- **Freedom of the Press:** In addition to free speech protection, the press may not be subjected to laws that apply only to the press on the basis of the content of speech.

■ **Overbreadth, Vagueness, and Prior Restraints: Procedural Restraints**

- **Overbreadth:** When laws **on their face** are **substantially overbroad**—most of their possible applications are invalid—they are facially invalid.

- **Vagueness:** A law is invalid if it is so vague that ordinary people cannot know in advance what speech is permitted.

- **Prior Restraints:** Speech may be restrained before it occurs only if absolutely necessary to achieve a most **super-compelling government interest**—such as national security.

A. INTRODUCTION

1. The Expression Rights of the First Amendment

Although the First Amendment never mentions "free expression of ideas," it protects that principle in several important ways.

    a. **The text of the First Amendment.** "Congress shall make no law . . . abridging the freedom of speech, or of the press, or the right of the people peaceably to assemble, and to petition the government for a redress of grievances."

    b. **The specific rights protected.** The First Amendment expressly protects **free speech, free press, peaceable assembly,** and the ability to **petition the government.** The Court has concluded that the First Amendment implicitly protects the right to **associate freely with others.**

    c. **Applicable to *all* governments.** Although the First Amendment speaks only of Congress, it applies to the entire federal government. The free expression guarantee is incorporated into the 14th Amendment's due process clause, thereby making it equally applicable to states and their subdivisions. State constitutions contain independent guarantees of free expression. Sometimes, the expression rights secured under a state's constitution are broader than under the federal Constitution.

2. Rationales for Free Expression

The free speech guarantee is not absolute. Some categories of speech are unprotected; others receive minimal protection, and still others are jealously protected. To make sense of this categorical approach it is necessary to understand the goals of a free expression guarantee. Some contend that free expression is valuable because it is a *means to an end;* others contend that free expression is an end in itself.

    a. **Free expression as a means to an end**

       i. **Self-governance.** The critical premise of democracy is that we govern ourselves. Free expression is indispensable to the free flow of ideas necessary for self-governance. We must be free to choose among all conceivable ideas. See Alexander Meiklejohn, Free Speech and Its Relation to Self-Government (1948).

ii. **The search for truth.** Free speech is necessary to determine the truth. In a famous dissent, Justice Holmes declared that "the theory of our Constitution" with respect to free speech is "that the best test of truth is the power of the thought to get itself accepted in the competition of the market." *Abrams v. United States,* 250 U.S. 616, 630 (1919). Some speech can never be verified as "true" and the marketplace of ideas may not always accurately filter the true from the false, but "[t]he critical question is not how well truth will advance absolutely in conditions of freedom but how well it will advance in conditions of freedom as compared with some alternative set of conditions." Greenawalt, 89 Colum. L. Rev. 135.

iii. **The development of moral virtue.** Our ability to make moral choices—to opt for good and to reject evil—requires that we be *free to choose.* Moral choice is not always easy or self-evident; humans must be free to think and speak since the process of moral deliberation often involves the expression of views, only to reconsider them when others reply or react to the expressed sentiments. Moral choice is valuable both to the individual and to the community. See John Milton, *Areopagitica* (1644).

iv. **Societal tolerance and self-restraint.** A society that guards and protects free speech cultivates the virtues of tolerance and self-restraint. Justice Holmes noted that free expression does not mean "free thought for those who agree with us but freedom for the thought we hate." *United States v. Schwimmer,* 279 U.S. 644, 655 (1929). (See Lee Bollinger, The Tolerant Society (1986).)

v. **Safety valve: letting off steam.** Thomas Emerson justified free expression on the grounds that "open discussion promotes greater cohesion in a society because people are more ready to accept decisions that go against them if they have a part in the decision-making process." Emerson, The System of Freedom of Expression, at 7. Free speech buys social peace.

vi. **Checking governmental abuse.** Free speech serves to "check the abuse of power by public officials" by providing to the citizenry the information needed to exercise their "veto power . . . when the decisions of [public] officials pass certain bounds." Blasi, 1977 Am. B. Found. Res. J. 527, 540.

b. **Free expression as an end in itself.** Some scholars contend that free expression is valuable in itself. Free speech "derives from the widely accepted premise . . . that the proper end of man is the realization of his character and potentialities as a human being." Emerson, 72 Yale

L.J. 879. Free "expression is an integral part of the development of ideas, of mental exploration and of the affirmation of self." Richards, 123 U. Pa. L. Rev. 62. At times the Court has edged toward embrace of this principle. In *Cohen v. California,* 403 U.S. 15 (1971), it upheld the right to wear a jacket in public inscribed with a vulgar and offensive (to some) epithet by noting that "no other approach would comport with the premise of individual dignity and choice upon which our political system rests." The main problem with this defense of free expression is that it fails to explain why expression deserves special protection, while many other self-fulfilling activities do not receive protection.

3. Governmental Action Impinging upon Expression

This subsection presents a brief overview of the doctrinal framework by which courts analyze free expression cases. The balance of the chapter explores in detail application of the analytical methods surveyed here.

a. The distinction between content-based regulation and content-neutral regulation. Free speech doctrine starts with a fundamental distinction between content-based and content-neutral regulations. Content-based laws regulate *the subject matter of speech*—they are aimed at the *communicative impact* of speech.

Example: During the Adams administration Congress enacted the Sedition Act of 1798, which punished "malicious . . . writings against [the] United States, [or] Congress, [or] the President, with intent [to] bring them [into] contempt or disrepute." The law punished only speech that delivered a particular message, speech that had a communicative impact. Although the Court never ruled on the validity of the Act, it is now universally agreed that the law was invalid.

Some content-based regulations are also **viewpoint-based**—they discriminate on the basis of the specific view expressed.

 EXAMPLE AND ANALYSIS

A Chicago ordinance barred picketing within 150 feet of a school while school was in session, but excepted picketing relating to labor disputes. Earl Mosley picketed Jones Commercial High School, carrying a sign declaring that the school was racially discriminatory. The Court invalidated the ordinance because it prohibited speech because of its content. Above "all else, the First Amendment means that government has no power to restrict expression because of its message, its ideas, its subject matter, or its content." *Police Department of Chicago v. Mosley,* 408 U.S. 92 (1972).

Some speech regulations have nothing to do with the content of the speech itself, but restrict speech regardless of its content. Such regulations are **content neutral.** Their purpose is to do something other than restrict the communicative impact of speech.

 # EXAMPLE AND ANALYSIS

A city ordinance forbade the use of any sound truck or any other device that emits "loud and raucous noises" on any public street. The regulation banned *all* loud and raucous speech, regardless of its content. The problem addressed was irritating noise, regardless of its content. (See *Kovacs v. Cooper,* 336 U.S. 77 (1949).)

i. **Content-based: Regulations aimed at the "communicative impact" of speech.** Content-based speech regulations are *presumptively invalid.* They are upheld only if the government proves that its content-based speech restriction is *narrowly tailored* to serve a *compelling governmental interest.* But the Court recognizes that some **categories of speech** are so unrelated to the purposes of the free speech guarantee that they are *unprotected* by the free speech clause. With respect to an unprotected category of speech governments are free to prohibit speech based on its content, provided that their method for doing so does not discriminate on the basis of the speaker's *viewpoint.*

    Example: Speech that incites the immediate commission of crime under circumstances where commission of the crime is likely to occur is unprotected, and may be prohibited by the government. See *Brandenburg v. Ohio,* 395 U.S. 444 (1969). While the government may prohibit threats of violence against the President it may not prohibit *only* such threats "that mention his policy on aid to inner cities." (See *R.A.V. v. St. Paul,* 505 U.S. 377 (1992).)

ii. **Content-neutral: Regulations aimed at the "noncommunicative impact" of speech.** Content-neutral speech restrictions are subject to more lenient scrutiny than content-based restrictions. In general, content-neutral regulations must survive an intermediate level of scrutiny. Governments must prove that such regulations of speech are *narrowly tailored to serve a significant government interest* and *leave open ample alternative channels of communication.*

b. Judicial review of content-based regulation: An overview. This subsection provides a quick summary of the process by which courts assess the validity of **content-based** speech restrictions.

i. First: Categorize the speech. The first step is to determine whether the restricted speech is *protected* or *unprotected* by the First Amendment. There are a variety of wholly unprotected speech categories and others that receive only *limited protection* by the First Amendment. These categories are discussed in detail in section C, infra. The reason for leaving entire categories of speech unprotected is that the category, *considered as a whole and without reference to any particular statement,* involves speech that is extremely remote from the central purposes for protecting free expression. The reason for a categorical approach, as opposed to a case-by-case approach, is that it is far easier to censor specific messages using a case-by-case approach.

ii. Test applicable to unprotected categories. Courts are extremely deferential toward government regulation of unprotected speech categories. In general, such regulation is valid unless the challenger can prove either that there is no rational relationship between the speech restriction and some legitimate government objective or that the regulation is *viewpoint based.*

(a) Viewpoint-based restrictions. A restrictions upon unprotected speech that is calculated to muzzle a particular viewpoint or to discriminate between viewpoints is an invalid viewpoint-based restriction. Governments may selectively prohibit unprotected speech if their reason for doing so "consists entirely of the very reason the entire class of speech is proscribable."

Example: A state "might choose to prohibit only that obscenity which is the most patently offensive in its prurience—i.e., that which involves the most lascivious displays of sexual activity. But it may not prohibit . . . only that obscenity which includes offensive political messages." *R.A.V. v. St. Paul,* 505 U.S. 377 (1992).

iii. Test applicable to protected categories. Restrictions upon protected categories of speech are presumed to be invalid. They are subjected to **strict scrutiny**—upheld only if the government can sustain the extremely high burden of proving that the regulation restricts speech only to the extent **necessary** to achieve a **compelling government interest.** The reasons for strict scrutiny are rooted in the following beliefs.

- *Counter Speech Suffices.* If the content of speech is unregulated, the harmful effects of any given speaker will be overcome by other speech. This is implicit in the marketplace of ideas as the best test of truth. The price of free speech is a certain amount of nonsense. The price is not too high so long as speech is sufficiently free to enable other speakers to denounce the nonsense. Freedom of speech implies a civic responsibility to speak out against stupid, wrongheaded speech.

- *Every Speaker Counts.* It is not an adequate defense of content-based speech restrictions to assert that *other speakers* remain free to deliver the suppressed speaker's message. Free speech is an *individual* guarantee. The idea that some speakers must be silenced in order to make room for other would-be speakers is repugnant to free expression.

- *Other Speech Opportunities Are Irrelevant.* It is not sufficient to argue that a given content-based speech restriction leaves the suppressed speaker free to deliver his message at some other time, or in some other place, or in some other way. Every speaker must be free of *content-based* restrictions on when, where, and how he speaks.

iv. **Consequences of the categorical approach.** The categorical approach to content-based speech restrictions forces courts to define abstractly speech that is unprotected because of its content. Abstract decision, in turn, minimizes the risk of suppressing only the unpopular viewpoint.

(a) **Abstract categorization.** By deciding whether entire categories of speech are protected or unprotected the Court necessarily proceeds along wholesale, abstract lines. The Court decides whether the **value** of a particular *type* of speech, in terms of its connection to the central purposes of the free speech guarantee, is greater than the social or individual harm it inflicts. This is a *"categorical balancing"* process—conducted at a general and abstracted level.

(b) **Reduced risk of suppression of only the unpopular message.** Categorical balancing avoids the problem of assessing whether a *particular message* is close enough to the core purposes of free speech to outweigh its social and individual harm. If balancing occurs at the level of particular messages the opportunity for censorship is magnified because the unpopularity of a specific message may color judgment.

Example and Analysis

Categorical balancing occurs when the Court concludes that the value of speech inciting immediate commission of crime is outweighed by its harm. Under the categorical balancing approach an identified member of a radical terrorist organization would be free to say on a radio show that "the United States government is an evil agent of Satan and ought to be blown up." Absent a categorical balancing approach, that statement would be weighed in isolation. Given today's concern about terrorism, a judge might well conclude that the statement is unprotected.

---

c. **Judicial review of content-neutral regulation: An overview.** Content-neutral speech restrictions are intended to control something other than the communicative impact of speech, but in doing so they have an incidental impact on speech. When that incidental impact is substantial courts ask whether the restriction is **reasonable, narrowly tailored to serve a significant government interest,** and **leaves open ample alternative channels of communication.** If these factors are not satisfied, the restriction is void even though content-neutral. Content-neutral restrictions upon speech can occur in a variety of contexts.

   i. **Symbolic conduct.** Speech is not always verbal. When people express ideas through their conduct—and that is intended and commonly understood—such symbolic conduct is protected. Governments may regulate symbolic conduct if the regulation furthers an *important* or *substantial* government interest, the government interest is *unrelated to the suppression of ideas*, and the speech restriction is *no greater than necessary* to further the government interest.

   ii. **Secondary effects.** When speech regulations are intended to control some side effect of speech that is not the product of the communicative impact of the speech the "secondary effects" doctrine holds that such regulations will be treated as content-neutral.

d. **Other regulatory contexts.** A recurring theme in speech regulation is the dual role of government. At times a government is a sovereign, a pure regulator of speech. At other times, the government acts like an ordinary private citizen, as when it is an employer, property owner, educator, or speaker itself. A variety of tests are used to separate the government as sovereign from the government as ordinary citizen. When the government acts like an ordinary citizen judicial scrutiny of its speech regulations is relaxed. See section E, infra. Regulation of the political process also poses special problems. See section G, infra.

e.   **Other expression rights.** Some expression rights are implicit in the free speech guarantee. The most important ones are freedom of association and the right *not* to speak. See section F, infra. Freedom of the press overlaps with speech and raises some unique issues. See section H, infra.

4.   **The Overbreadth, Vagueness, and Prior Restraint Doctrines**

These three doctrines invalidate speech restrictions because the *means* used to restrict speech are invalid even though the particular speech involved might be validly regulated by some other means. Prior restraint is peculiar to free speech law. Overbreadth and vagueness are not unique to free speech, but have special importance to free expression.

a.   **Overbreadth.** Statutes are overbroad when they prohibit actions that are constitutionally protected as well as actions that are *not* constitutionally protected. Governments may not "control or prevent activities constitutionally subject [to] regulation . . . by means which sweep *unnecessarily broadly* and thereby invade the area of protected freedoms." *NAACP v. Alabama,* 357 U.S. 449 (1958). When a statute *on its face*—considered in the abstract—is ***substantially overbroad*** it will be stricken in its entirety. A law is substantially overbroad "when the flaw is a substantial concern in the context of the statute as a whole." *Broadrick v. Oklahoma,* 413 U.S. 601 (1973).

 # EXAMPLE AND ANALYSIS

A law prohibiting all speech that "tends to excite public passion and encourage disorder" is enormously overbroad. While it proscribes speech that incites immediate lawless conduct (a category of constitutionally unprotected speech) it also prohibits a vast amount of constitutionally protected speech. Much political campaign speech, for example, tends to excite public passion and, perhaps, encourage disorder.

Overbreadth doctrine permits a person whose conduct is *not* constitutionally protected to escape punishment because the law under which he is prosecuted is an invalid *means* to regulate his unprotected speech.

b.   **Vagueness.** A law is void on its face if persons "of common intelligence must necessarily guess at its meaning and differ as to its application." *Connally v. General Construction Co.,* 269 U.S. 385, 391 (1926). Such laws violate due process.

EXAMPLE AND ANALYSIS

A law prohibiting all speech that "tends to excite public passion and encourage disorder" is also unconstitutionally vague. It fails to inform clearly what speech is prohibited. Reasonable people may differ as to whether the utterance "The President is a liar" is permitted or prohibited by the statute. If people cannot know in advance whether their conduct is legal or not, the law is vague and invalid.

---

      c. **Prior restraint.** Prior to 1695, English law prohibited the publication of *anything* without prior approval of the church and the state. When Americans established their own nation they meant, at a minimum, to outlaw such prior restraints on speech. Free speech means more than simply freedom from prior restraint upon speech, but prior restraints continue to be especially disfavored and presumptively invalid. As the name indicates, prior restraints consist of any kind of before-the-fact regulation of speech, such as licensing or permit requirements, censorship before publication, and injunctions or other prepublication bans. (See section B.3, infra.)

B. OVERBREADTH, VAGUENESS, AND PRIOR RESTRAINTS

1. Overbreadth

a. Overview

      i. **Definition.** An overbroad statute regulates constitutionally *unprotected* conduct by also regulating constitutionally *protected* conduct. Governments may not use "means which sweep *unnecessarily broadly* and thereby invade the area of protected freedoms" in order to control behavior legitimately susceptible to government control. *NAACP v. Alabama,* 357 U.S. 449 (1958). Only statutes that are *substantially overbroad* are voided for overbreadth. *Broadrick v. Oklahoma,* 413 U.S. 601 (1973).

      ii. **Importance.** Overbreadth doctrine is important for two reasons. First, it tests the validity of a statute *on its face* rather than as actually applied to the litigant before the court. Second, it permits speakers of constitutionally unprotected speech to challenge the validity of the law under which they are prosecuted on the grounds that the law is too sweeping rather than on the grounds that the speaker's speech is constitutionally protected. Successful overbreadth challenges permit the speaker of *unprotected* speech to go unpunished for speech for which they *could validly be punished* under a more narrowly drafted law. It is often said that this operates as a *de facto* exception to the normal standing rules, by permitting a party to assert others' claims, but that is not strictly correct. Rather, the unprotected speaker serves as a medium through which we can evaluate the validity of governmental *means* to control unprotected speech.

(a) **Facial validity at issue.** Because the overbroad statute controls constitutionally unprotected speech by also regulating protected speech, courts assume it has the effect of deterring law-abiding citizens from speaking in a manner prohibited by the law but protected by the First Amendment. Litigants who have violated the overbroad law by uttering constitutionally *unprotected* speech are permitted to challenge the law **on its face** rather than as actually applied to them. The usual judicial propensity to decide cases as narrowly as possible is suspended, and the courts consider the validity of the law in the abstract. If it is facially invalid the law is *totally invalid*. By contrast, when a law is voided *as applied* the law is only invalid in that *particular circumstance* and others indistinguishable from it.

 # EXAMPLE AND ANALYSIS

A law prohibits all speech that "tends to excite public passion and encourage disorder." If the law is invalid on its face it cannot constitutionally be applied to *anyone*. But if it is invalidated only as applied to a speaker who publicly denounces the President as a "morally bankrupt draft-dodger" the law remains valid if applied to a speaker who publicly threatens to kill the President.

(b) **Evaluating the means used to control unprotected speech.** Overbreadth doctrine permits a speaker of constitutionally *unprotected* speech to challenge a statute as facially overbroad. If successful, the law is void and may not be applied to anyone, including the challenger, a speaker of *unprotected* speech. It appears that the challenger is asserting the rights of other people—would-be speakers of constitutionally protected speech cowed into silence by the law—but that is not strictly the case. Even the speaker of constitutionally unprotected speech has the right to be free of laws that are catch-all proscriptions of speech—to be judged only by "a constitutionally valid rule of law." Monaghan, 1981 Sup. Ct. Rev. 1.

EXAMPLE AND ANALYSIS

Imagine an absurdly overbroad law: "No speech is permitted in public." Even the speaker urging an inflamed mob to riot is entitled to be free of such a law. The speaker is *not* free to urge the mob to riot, but does have the right to be prosecuted for that speech under a statute that more specifically and narrowly addresses the public's safety concerns. The facial overbreadth challenge vindicates the speaker's right to be free of an overbroad law, not the speaker's "right" to incite riot.

iii.   **Rationales for the overbreadth doctrine.** There are two major justifications for the overbreadth doctrine.

(a)   **Stops government intimidation of speech.** The overbroad law is apt to *chill* protected speech. A law-abiding person is not likely to violate the statute in order to assert his constitutionally guaranteed free speech right. A combination of respect for law—even invalid law—and the rational fear of prosecution combine to deter protected speech. Thus, even if governments do not enforce the overbroad law against protected speech the very presence of the law intimidates some unknown number of speakers from uttering some unknown amount of protected speech. Facial invalidation of overbroad laws checks this governmental abuse.

(b)   **Prevents selective enforcement against unpopular speakers.** The overbroad law also invites selective enforcement against certain speakers or certain viewpoints. Free speech is most threatened and of the most value when unpopular speech is at issue.

 EXAMPLE AND ANALYSIS

Imagine the existence of the following overbroad statute during the Vietnam War: "No person may publicly criticize a foreign government." It is easy to visualize prosecution of a pacifist for stating that "the South Vietnamese government is an evil, repressive and corrupt regime" and no prosecution of a military officer for stating that "Japan is a gutless hypocrite for its failure to help us defend against the communist menace in Vietnam."

Voiding overbroad statutes on their face reduces the opportunity of governments to engage in this sort of selective enforcement. (See Karst, 43 U. Chi. L. Rev. 38.)

b.   The requirement of *substantial* overbreadth. Only statutes that are *substantially* overbroad are voided for overbreadth. Substantial overbreadth has both a *quantitative* and a *qualitative* dimension.

- *Quantity of Overbreadth.* Only those statutes that proscribe a *significant amount of protected speech* have a sufficiently chilling effect upon protected speech to merit invalidation.

- *Quality of Overbreadth.* The Court has also suggested that the concerns behind overbreadth—intimidation and selective enforcement—become more attenuated when the *nature* of the overly broad speech restriction is such that it only proscribes speech that is peripheral to the central concerns of the free speech guarantee. Thus, laws that are overly broad attempts to **censor** speech—laws that "burden the advocacy of matters of public concern" are *most subject to overbreadth scrutiny.* Laws that merely **inhibit speech** and are *viewpoint-neutral* are of *next most concern.* **Remedial laws**—laws that seek to promote free speech values by regulating some speech (e.g., laws governing lobbying or political contributions)—are *least subject to overbreadth scrutiny.* (See Nowak & Rotunda, at 998.) Claims that state laws are overbroad can be eliminated if a state court construes the law narrowly enough.

i.   *Broadrick v. Oklahoma,* 413 U.S. 601 (1973). Oklahoma prohibited its civil servants from soliciting funds for political candidates and exhibiting bumper stickers or buttons endorsing political candidates. The Court, 5 to 4, rejected an overbreadth challenge and concluded that the law was not *substantially* overbroad. "[T]he overbreadth of a statute must not only be real, but substantial as well, *judged in relation to the statute's plainly legitimate sweep.*"

- *Quantity.* The bulk of the expression regulated by the law was constitutionally unprotected (e.g., the ban on solicitation of funds). Only a relatively minor amount of protected expression was banned. The risk of intimidation and selective enforcement was low and the forbidden but protected expression (e.g., display of buttons endorsing candidates) could be vindicated on a case-by-case, "as applied" basis.

- *Quality.* Oklahoma restricted partisan political activity by its civil servants in order to prevent political coercion of state workers and inhibit political bias in the performance of job duties. Oklahoma's interference with expression was remedial and thus subject to the least degree of overbreadth scrutiny.

ii.   ***Board of Airport Commissioners of Los Angeles v. Jews for Jesus, Inc.,*** 482 U.S. 569 (1987). The Los Angeles Airport Commission adopted a regulation that forbade "First Amendment activities within the Central Terminal Area at Los Angeles International Airport." The Court found the law facially invalid because of its substantial overbreadth. It "prohibits even talking or reading, or the wearing of campaign buttons or symbolic clothing." The law was quantitatively substantially overbroad.

iii.   ***Houston v. Hill,*** 482 U.S. 451 (1987). A Houston ordinance made it a crime to "assault, strike, or in any manner oppose, molest, abuse, or interrupt any policeman in the execution of his duty." Hill was convicted of violating the ordinance by shouting "Why don't you pick on somebody your own size?" at a policeman arresting Hill's friend. The Court decided that the ordinance was substantially overbroad, and thus facially invalid, because the law granted "unfettered discretion" to the police "to arrest individuals for words or conduct that annoy or offend them." The risk of selective enforcement was high and, though the Court did not say so explicitly, the law gave to police officers the power to exercise a censorship function by arresting the speaker who dares criticize perceived police misconduct. By striking the law as overbroad the Court avoided deciding the much harder question of whether Hill's speech could constitutionally be punished.

2.   **Vagueness**

a.   **Definition.** A law is unconstitutionally vague if persons "of common intelligence must necessarily guess at its meaning and differ as to its application." *Connally v. General Construction Co.,* 269 U.S. 385, 391 (1926). If a law does not provide "sufficiently definite warning as to the proscribed conduct when measured by common understanding and practices" it is unconstitutionally vague. *Jordan v. De George,* 341 U.S. 223 (1951). Vagueness is a subjective judgment, colored a great deal by judicial common sense.

 EXAMPLES AND ANALYSIS

Example: A city ordinance, as construed by the courts, prohibited noisemaking or other activity that would constitute an "actual or imminent interference with the 'peace or good order' of [a] school." The Court rejected a vagueness challenge, noting that "we think it is clear what the ordinance as a whole prohibits." *Grayned v. Rockford,* 408 U.S. 104 (1972).

Example: The Court invalidated a Massachusetts law making it a crime publicly to treat contemptuously the U.S. flag. The ban on contemptuous treatment of the flag did not "draw reasonably clear lines between the kinds of nonceremonial treatment that are criminal and those that are not." *Smith v. Goguen,* 415 U.S. 566 (1974).

---

    b. Effect of vagueness. Vague laws are usually, but not invariably, facially invalid. Vague laws burdening expression are almost always facially invalid. Three reasons justify this result. Vague laws are unfair, chill speech, and permit covert viewpoint-based enforcement.

    c. Aspect of due process. The vagueness doctrine applies to *all* laws, whether or not they involve expression. Vagueness is an aspect of the due process clauses. Vagueness has particular applicability to free expression because vague laws impinging upon expression chill protected speech. "Uncertain meanings inevitably lead citizens to steer far wider of the unlawful zone [than] if the boundaries of the forbidden areas were clearly marked." *Grayned v. Rockford,* supra at 109 and n.5, quoting *Speiser v. Randall,* 357 U.S. 513, 526 (1958).

    d. Connection with overbreadth. Vagueness and overbreadth are often, but not necessarily, linked.

    Example: A Cincinnati ordinance made it unlawful for three or more persons to assemble on public sidewalks and "conduct themselves in a manner annoying to persons passing by." The Court invalidated the law on its face. The law was "unconstitutionally vague because it subjects the exercise of the right of assembly to an unascertainable standard, and unconstitutionally broad because it authorizes the punishment of constitutionally protected conduct." *Coates v. Cincinnati,* 402 U.S. 611 (1971).

    A statute may be *precise* but *overbroad.* **Example:** Arkansas required public school teachers to declare annually every organization to which the teacher either belonged or contributed. The Court voided the law as an overbroad infringement of the First Amendment's association right. *Shelton v. Tucker,* 364 U.S. 479 (1960).

    A statute may be *vague* but *not overbroad.* **Example:** A law that prohibits "any public speech that is not protected by the federal or state constitutions" is not overbroad—it does not prohibit any protected speech—but it is surely vague. The ordinary person must necessarily guess about the boundaries of constitutionally protected speech.

However, if an apparently precise overbroad statute is not invalidated on its face but only as applied, it will become vague by reason of the limiting judicial construction. **Example:** A law that bans all outdoor speaking is not vague, but terribly overbroad. If courts invalidate it only as it is applied to protected speech, the law quickly resembles the law in the immediately prior example—it bans all outdoor speaking "that is not protected by the Constitution."

3. The Prior Restraint Doctrine

Prior restraints upon speech are among the most disfavored of speech restrictions. Prior restraints are presumptively void, but they are not invalid *per se.* Like overbreadth and vagueness, the prior restraint doctrine limits a *means* of controlling speech. A "prior restraint may be struck down even though the particular expression involved could validly be restricted through subsequent criminal punishment." Gunther, at 1203.

a. Overview and historical origins

i. What constitutes a prior restraint? A prior restraint is an *administrative or judicial order* that prohibits speech *before it occurs,* and does so on the *basis of its content.*

(a) **Administrative or judicial orders.** Judicial restraints in advance of speech are typically injunctions. **Example:** The United States government obtained a federal court injunction forbidding *The Progressive* magazine from publishing an article, based on publicly available sources, describing how to build and detonate a nuclear bomb. *United States v. The Progressive,* 467 F. Supp. 990 (W.D. Wis. 1979).

Administrative prior restraints are usually licensing requirements. **Example:** A city prohibited distribution of "literature of any kind" without a license. The Court voided the law on its face because there were no standards for denying a license. *Lovell v. Griffin,* 303 U.S. 444 (1938).

Punishments *after-the-fact* of speech are *not* prior restraints. **Example:** Alexander was convicted of violating federal obscenity laws and the Racketeer Influenced Corrupt Organizations Act (RICO). Under RICO, his entire business (consisting of more than a dozen stores and theaters selling sexually explicit but nonobscene material) was forfeited. Alexander contended that the forfeiture of the nonobscene books and films was a prior restraint. The Court disagreed. The forfeiture did not forbid Alexander "from engaging in any expressive activities in the future, nor does it require him to obtain prior approval for any expressive activities." *Alexander v. United States,* 509 U.S. 544 (1993).

(b)   Content-based prohibition. Only a *content-based* restriction on speech before it occurs is a prior restraint. Even if a judicial order bars speech in advance it is *not* a prior restraint if it is *content neutral* and its purpose and effect is not to suppress ideas but to advance legitimate state interests unrelated to the suppression of speech.

Example: A Florida court issued an injunction barring anti-abortion protesters from intruding upon a thirty-six foot zone extending outward from the property line of an abortion clinic into a public street and sidewalk. The Court upheld this aspect of the injunction, rejecting the contention that the injunction involved prior restraint of speech. The injunction was not issued to control expression but to control "prior unlawful conduct" on the part of the defendants. Had the injunction been issued "because of the content of petitioners' expression" it would have been treated as prior restraint. *Madsen v. Women's Health Center, Inc.,* 512 U.S. 753 (1994).

ii.   Types of prior restraints. There are two principal types of prior restraints.

- **Licensing** of speech before its utterance or publication usually raises the question of whether the licensing scheme operates to restrain speech prior to "an adequate [judicial] determination that it is not protected by the First Amendment." *Pittsburgh Press Co. v. Pittsburgh Commission on Human Relations,* 413 U.S. 376 (1973).

- **Injunctions** restraining speech from occurring at all raise the question of whether it is better "to punish the few who abuse rights of speech *after* they break the law than the throttle [them] beforehand. It is always difficult to know in advance what an individual will say." *Southeastern Promotions, Ltd. v. Conrad,* 420 U.S. 546, 559 (1975).

(a)   Licensing. The essence of licensing is the imposition of a requirement that speakers obtain the permission of the government before they speak. Licensing can be coupled with censorship, but does not necessarily involve censorship. The validity of licensing schemes depends upon the purpose for requiring speakers to obtain a prespeech permit to speak and upon the criteria established to determine when licenses will be issued or denied. (See section B.3.b, infra.)

(b) Injunctions. An injunction of speech before its occurrence is a powerful weapon, so powerful that it is especially disfavored. Only the most compelling reasons for enjoining protected speech will support the issuance of an injunction restraining speech in advance. (See sections B.3.c and B.3.d, infra.)

iii. The English licensing system. Until 1695, English law required publishers of written materials to obtain the permission of the Crown and the Church before publishing. Even though the English licensing system was nearly a century in its grave when the First Amendment was adopted, Americans intended the free speech guarantee to bar widespread prior restraint of speech.

b. Licensing restraints. Licensing schemes almost always employ some criteria to determine when a license to speak should be issued. If the criteria and procedures employed produce licenses for protected speech and deny them only for unprotected speech much of the reason for disfavoring prior restraints is eliminated.

i. Standardless licensing. When a license must be obtained in order to speak and there are no criteria for issuance of the license the danger to free speech is quite high.

- *Concealed Suppression of Speech:* The decision to grant or deny a license is more apt to occur outside public view, and thus escape public criticism or evaluation. A decision by an administrator is made without any of the procedural safeguards present in the judicial system.

- *Greater Chance of Content-Based or Viewpoint-Based Regulation:* Without licensing standards, the administrator charged with the decision to grant or deny licenses has freedom covertly to make that decision based on the content of the speech or the viewpoint of the speaker.

(a) *Lovell v. Griffin,* 303 U.S. 444 (1938). By city ordinance, Griffin, Georgia, prohibited the distribution of "literature of any kind" within the city "without first obtaining written permission from the City Manager." Lovell distributed religious tracts without applying for or receiving permission from the city manager. The Court reversed her conviction, finding that "the ordinance is void on its face." Its infirmity was rooted in the broad discretion vested in the city manager to curb speech of any kind and for any reason. The Court thought that the law's "character . . . strikes at the very foundation of the freedom of the press by subjecting it to license and censorship."

(b) *City of Lakewood v. Plain Dealer Publishing Co.,* 486 U.S. 750 (1988). A city ordinance gave the mayor standardless discretion to grant or deny permits for newsracks on city sidewalks. The Court found the ordinance facially invalid and explained why standardless licensing is always facially invalid. The "licensor's unfettered discretion [coerces] parties into censoring their own speech," and self-censorship cannot be challenged as applied because "it derives from the individual's own actions, not an abuse of government power."

(c) *Forsyth County v. The Nationalist Movement,* 505 U.S. 123 (1992). A Forsyth County ordinance imposed a fee of $1000 per day for a parade permit, and gave a county administrator discretion to increase the permit fee based on the expected expense of preserving the public peace in connection with the parade or demonstration. The Court found the ordinance facially invalid because there were no clear standards governing establishment of the permit fees. The administrator's discretion was so great that it was predictable that the size of the permit fee might well turn on the "listeners' reaction to speech," which "is not a content-neutral basis for regulation." The Court stated that speech "cannot be financially burdened, any more than it can be punished or banned, simply because it might offend a hostile mob." (See section C.4.b, infra.)

ii.   Licensing with standards. Licensing schemes that contain *clear standards* limiting the denial of licenses to circumstances where the speech could validly be punished after the fact are **facially valid,** although they still are susceptible to the constitutional challenges to the way they are applied.

(a) *Cox v. New Hampshire,* 312 U.S. 569 (1941). New Hampshire law required a permit for any "parade or procession" upon a public street. New Hampshire's Supreme Court construed the law to allow officials to condition issuance of permits only for "considerations of time, place and manner so as to conserve the public convenience." Without seeking or obtaining a permit, a religious group marched peaceably in Manchester, interfering with "normal sidewalk travel" but not breaching the peace. The Court affirmed the convictions of several marchers for marching without a permit, concluding that because the statute only permitted permit denials under circumstances where the speech could be constitutionally regulated or prohibited, there was no infirmity to the licensing scheme. "[T]he licensing board was not vested with arbitrary power or an unfettered discretion."

iii. **Licensing to restrain obscenity.** Licensing schemes designed to prevent publication of obscenity are a pervasive issue and have spawned a specialized body of law. Obscenity is not a protected category of speech, but a chronic problem is defining obscenity with sufficient precision to avoid overbreadth or vagueness problems. (See section C.2, infra.) Licensing schemes to prevent obscenity must confront the same definitional problem and are valid only if they incorporate certain procedural safeguards.

(a) *Freedman v. Maryland,* 380 U.S. 51 (1965). In the course of striking down Maryland's motion picture censorship statute, designed to prevent exhibition of obscene films, the Court identified the "procedural safeguards" necessary to "avoid[] constitutional infirmit[ies]" with a licensing scheme.

   • *Burden of Proof on the Censor:* "[T]he burden of proving that the film is unprotected expression must rest on the [censor]."

   • *Judicial Restraint Only:* "[W]hile the State may require advance submission of all films, . . . only a . . . judicial determination in an adversary proceeding . . . suffices to impose a valid final restraint." A government censor must, "within a specified brief period, either issue a license or go to court to restrain showing the film."

   • *Prompt Final Judicial Decision:* Any licensing "procedure must also assure a prompt final judicial decision, to minimize the deterrent effect of an interim and possibly erroneous denial of a license."

iv. **Facial and as-applied challenges to licensing**

(a) **Facial challenges.** When a **facial challenge** is made to a licensing scheme the speaker is *not required* to seek permission or to challenge the denial of permission in advance of actually speaking. Instead, the speaker can go ahead and speak and then raise the facial challenge to the licensing scheme as a defense. See *Lovell v. Griffin,* supra. If the law is facially void the speaker is exonerated; if the law is valid the speaker may be punished for failure to seek and obtain permission to speak.

(b) **As-applied challenges.** By contrast, when a licensing scheme is conceded to be facially valid and is challenged only **as applied** to the speaker, the prospective speaker must challenge the specific application before speaking. If the challenger speaks anyway, his conviction may be upheld even though the specific application is unconstitutional.

 # EXAMPLE AND ANALYSIS

Under a facially valid licensing law Poulos was denied a permit to hold religious services in a public park. He held the services anyway and in the subsequent criminal prosecution defended on the ground that the denial had been arbitrary and unlawful. The Court upheld his conviction, holding that he was obligated to seek judicial relief before the fact unless prompt judicial review of the administrative denial was not available. *Poulos v. New Hampshire,* 345 U.S. 395 (1953).

c. **Injunctions: In general.** Injunctions of speech "bear[] a heavy burden against [their] constitutional validity." When an injunction restrains speech by reason of its content it is invalid unless the government can prove that the restraint is no broader than absolutely necessary to achieving a state objective of the very first magnitude. Unlike licensing, injunctions do not present quite the same problem of stifling speech before an adequate judicial determination of whether the speech is protected. Once a court has reached a preliminary determination that the speech in question may be punished after the fact, what harm is there in preventing its occurrence? There are three answers.

   i. **The vice of injunctions.** Injunctions of unprotected speech are thought to be problematic for three debatable reasons.

      (a) **Chilled speech.** Injunctions chill speech, but if the only speech deterred is speech that may validly be punished after the fact, why should we care? Injunctions may not be this precise. While they may not be constitutionally overbroad, they might proscribe some protected speech in order to enjoin the unprotected speech. Also, even a precise injunction—one that enjoins *only* unprotected speech—might deter some protected speech that could be uttered without violating the injunction. For fear of violating the injunction, a speaker may stay well away from its edges.

      (b) **The collateral bar rule.** The collateral bar rule provides that a person who violates an injunction may be punished for the violation even if it turns out later that the injunction was invalid. The rule is generally applicable to all injunctions and has been upheld by the Court as applied to injunctions of speech. In *Walker v. Birmingham,* 388 U.S. 307 (1967), an Alabama court had enjoined a march and demonstration. After the march happened anyway the Alabama court imposed sanctions for contempt of the injunction. In doing so, it refused to hear the defense that the enjoined speech was constitutionally protected. The Supreme Court, 5 to 4, ruled that the Alabama courts had correctly relied on the general rule that injunctions must be obeyed until "reversed for error by orderly review." Even in speaking protected speech, persons are not "constitutionally free to ignore all the procedures of the law." When coupled with the collateral bar rule, injunctions have a strongly intimidating effect. Even if the injunction is in error, protected speech may not be uttered without suffering the collateral penalty of punishment for contempt of the injunction.

(c) **Loss of jury review.** The line between protected and unprotected speech is often a contestable factual judgment. When that judgment is made in advance by a judge there is no opportunity to assess the circumstances in which the speech actually occurs nor is there an opportunity for a jury to assess the facts. Injunctions are based on speculative harm; juries evaluate the real consequences of speech.

ii. **Validity of injunctive prior restraints.** Injunctions that are prior restraints of speech are invalid unless the government proves that the injunction is necessary to serve the very most compelling of governmental objectives.

(a) *Near v. Minnesota,* 283 U.S. 697 (1931). Minnesota law permitted prosecutors to seek abatement, as a public nuisance, of any "malicious, scandalous and defamatory newspaper." A Minneapolis prosecutor acted under the law and obtained an injunction permanently enjoining the publishers of the *Saturday Press* from publishing "a malicious, scandalous or defamatory newspaper." The *Saturday Press* had repeatedly charged "that a Jewish gangster was in control of gambling, bootlegging, and racketeering in Minneapolis and that law enforcing officers," particularly the chief of police, were involved in "illicit relations with gangsters" and "participation in graft." The Court struck down the Minnesota statute, noting that prior restraints were not absolutely prohibited but were valid "only in exceptional cases"—preservation of *national security* (e.g., forbidding "the publication of the sailing dates of [troop] transports"), preventing *obscenity,* and preventing *incitements of violence.*

(b) *New York Times v. United States (Pentagon Papers Case),* 403 U.S. 713 (1971). Over several days in June 1971 the *New York Times* and *Washington Post* published excerpts from a secret Defense Department study of the Vietnam War. The study, which quickly became known as the "Pentagon Papers," reviewed in great detail military operations and secret diplomatic initiatives concerning the Vietnam War. On June 15 the federal government filed suit and obtained a temporary restraining order preventing further publication of the papers. The T.R.O. remained in effect until June 30, when the Court ruled that the government had not overcome the "heavy presumption against [the] constitutional validity" of a prior restraint upon expression. The Justices could not agree on when national security reasons justified a prior restraint.

- Justices Black and Douglas thought that national security reasons were *never sufficient* to justify a prior restraint.

- Justice Brennan thought a prior restraint was justified only *during war,* and then only if the government has *"clearly"* proven that "publication must *inevitably, directly, and immediately* cause the occurrence of an event kindred to imperiling the safety of a transport already at sea."

- Justices Stewart and White thought a prior restraint was justified only if disclosure "will surely result in *direct, immediate, and irreparable damage.*"

- Justices Burger, Harlan, and Blackmun dissented, arguing that so long as the material the government seeks to suppress is "within the proper compass of the President's foreign relations power" and "the determination that disclosure would irreparably impair the national security" is made by the President it was improper for the judiciary to "redetermine for itself the probable impact of disclosure on the national security."

d. Injunctive restraints in the interest of a fair trial. A particularly nettlesome issue in prior restraint law is the question of the extent to which the details of an ongoing criminal prosecution may be published. Pitted against one another are two great constitutional ideals: free speech and a fair trial.

    i. The problem: free speech v. fair trial. Under some circumstances, press coverage of a criminal investigation and trial may endanger the defendant's right to a fair trial. The question then becomes whether a prior restraint on speech is justified in the interests of a fair trial. If so, some form of judicially imposed "gag order" results.

ii. **Limits on "gag orders."** The principal targets for fair trial gag orders are the press and the trial's participants.

(a) **Gag orders on the press:** *Nebraska Press Assn. v. Stuart,* 427 U.S. 539 (1976). Following a highly publicized mass murder in a small Nebraska town a Nebraska trial judge restrained the press from reporting confessions, incriminating statements, or other facts "strongly implicative" of the accused. The Court unanimously found the order was unconstitutional. In dicta, the Court suggested that three factors were useful in helping a trial judge determine when the harm of an unfair trial due to publicity was so probable as to justify restraints on the press.

- *Likelihood of an Unfair Trial:* The Court conceded that the trial judge "was justified in concluding that . . . intense and pervasive pre-trial publicity . . . might impair the defendant's right to a fair trial."

- *Lack of Adequate Alternatives:* The Court suggested that a prior restraint was justified only if there were *no other alternatives to a fair trial.* Among the alternatives mentioned by the Court were change of venue, trial postponement, juror sequestration, and gag orders on trial participants.

- *Probable Effect of Prior Restraint:* If a prior restraint is not likely to deliver much actual protection of an accused's right to a fair trial the restraint is surely unjustified. In this case the Court thought that the prior restraint would not likely have much effect on information already well known in the small Nebraska town of 850 people where the trial would be held and from whom the jury would be selected.

(b) **Gag orders on trial participants.** Prior restraints on trial participants—witnesses, lawyers, jurors, and the like—are probably subject to a lesser burden of justification in order to establish their validity. Partly because lawyers are officers of the court, the Court has concluded that governments bear a lesser burden of justification to impose an after-the-fact

> punishment on a lawyer for his possibly prejudicial extra-judicial statements that violated a state bar rule against such statements. *Gentile v. State Bar of Nevada,* 501 U.S. 1030 (1991). Jurors are routinely sequestered, a particularly strong form of restraint that is justified by the necessity (in highly publicized cases) of insulating jurors from extrajudicial "evidence." For much the same reason all jurors are routinely admonished not to talk about the case on which they are serving.

   iii. **Other barriers akin to prior restraints.** Generally, criminal proceedings may not be closed to the public. See *Richmond Newspapers, Inc. v. Virginia,* 448 U.S. 555 (1980). But this rule is not invariable, and to the extent that the public is barred from trials or other judicial proceedings an effective prior restraint occurs. This issue is discussed in section H, infra.

  e. **Injunctions that are *not* prior restraints.** An injunction that controls conduct and is content neutral as to speech is not a prior restraint. Such injunctions are valid if "the challenged provisions of the injunction burden no more speech than necessary to serve a significant government interest." *Madsen v. Women's Health Center,* 512 U.S. 753, 765 (1994). The governmental interest in "ensuring public safety and order, promoting the free flow of traffic . . . , protecting property rights, and protecting a woman's freedom to seek pregnancy-related services" are significant enough to support injunctions "to secure unimpeded physical access" to abortion clinics. *Schenck v. Pro-Choice Network of Western N.Y.,* 519 U.S. 357 (1997). In *Madsen* the Court upheld a "no-approach" zone extending 36 feet around an abortion clinic. In *Schenck* the Court upheld an injunction barring demonstrations within a "fixed buffer zone" of 15 feet of clinic entrances.

C. CONTENT-BASED REGULATION OF SPEECH

This section considers the categories that are either entirely unprotected by the First Amendment or that enjoy only limited protection. Governments are free to fashion content-based prohibitions on all or part of an *unprotected* category of speech, so long as the proscription on speech is *viewpoint neutral*—it does not single out a particular viewpoint and ban it for reasons unrelated to the reasons why the entire category of speech is unprotected.

 ## EXAMPLE AND ANALYSIS

The category of obscene speech is unprotected. A state might choose to prohibit only the most "lascivious displays of sexual activity" but may not prohibit "only that obscenity which includes . . . political messages" critical of the state. The former choice bans a subcategory of obscenity for the same reason all obscenity is unprotected—its lascivious display of sexuality—while the latter choice bans a subcategory of obscenity for reasons wholly unconnected to the reason all obscenity is unprotected. The former ban is viewpoint neutral; the latter is viewpoint based. (See *R.A.V. v. St. Paul*, 505 U.S. 377 (1992).)

---

1. **Inciting Immediate Lawlessness**

   a. **Introduction.** Speech that is *intended to incite "imminent lawless action"* **and** "*is likely to incite or produce* such action" is an unprotected category of speech. *Brandenburg v. Ohio*, 395 U.S. 444 (1969). It took fifty years and a great deal of judicial effort to reach this modern rule.

   b. **"Clear and present danger": Cases punishing speech as an attempt to accomplish prohibited conduct.** Many of the early cases punishing speech as an attempt to accomplish prohibited conduct were brought under the Espionage Act of 1917, a federal statute that made it a crime during war (1) to "make or convey false . . . statements with intent to interfere" with the military success of the United States or "to promote the success of its enemies," (2) intentionally to "cause or attempt to cause insubordination, disloyalty, mutiny, or refusal of duty, in the military or naval forces of the United States," or (3) intentionally to "obstruct the recruiting or enlistment service of the United States." In 1918, the Act was amended to prohibit statements intended to hinder the production of materials necessary to wage war against Germany.

      i. *Schenck v. United States,* 249 U.S. 47 (1919). Schenck and his fellow defendants were convicted of violating the Espionage Act of 1917 by distributing to prospective military conscripts and enlistees a handbill that denounced conscription as despotic and violative of the 13th Amendment, urged military recruits not "to submit to intimidation," and stated that "If you do not assert and support your rights, you are helping to deny or disparage rights which it is the solemn duty of all citizens and residents of the United States to retain." The Court upheld the convictions. For the Court, Justice Holmes stated that free speech did not extend to "words used [in] such circumstances and of such a nature as to create **a clear and present danger** that they will bring about the substantive evils that Congress has a right to prevent. It is a question of **proximity** and **degree.**" To illustrate the principle, Holmes asserted that "[t]he most stringent protection of free speech would not protect a man in falsely shouting fire in a theatre and causing a panic."

      ii. *Frohwerk v. United States,* 249 U.S. 204 (1919). Frohwerk and Gleeser were convicted under the Espionage Act of conspiring to cause insubordination, disloyalty, mutiny, or refusal of duty in U.S. military or naval forces. The conspiracy consisted of their publication of a series of articles in a German language newspaper, the *Missouri Staats Zeitung*. The articles were sharply critical of the American war effort in Europe, claiming American participation in World War I was orchestrated by "the great trusts," praising the spirit and strength of Germany, and expressing the view that illegal draft resistance was morally justified. The Court upheld the conviction. The paper's circulation was tiny, providing little evidence of a **clear and present danger** of harm posed by the speech. But "it was in quarters where a little breath would be enough to kindle a flame."

iii. *Debs v. United States,* 249 U.S. 211 (1919). Eugene Debs, the Socialist leader and frequent presidential candidate, was convicted under the Espionage Act for a speech made at a Socialist convention in Canton, Ohio. The speech was full of high praise for socialism and predictions of its ultimate success. Debs also intimated that three local Socialists jailed for aiding and abetting draft resistance were heroes to be admired and, perhaps, emulated: "You need to know that you are fit for something better than slavery and cannon fodder." The Court upheld Debs's conviction. So long as Debs "used words tending to obstruct . . . recruiting [and] meant that they should have that effect" he could be punished. If the **"natural tendency and reasonably probable effect"** of speech was to produce a substantive evil, the "clear and present danger" test was satisfied. This rule was really nothing more than a *"bad tendency"* test, prohibiting speech that *might* produce the substantive evil. "To put *[Debs]* in modern context, it is somewhat as though George McGovern had been sent to prison for his criticism of the [Vietnam] War." Kalven, 40 U. Chi. L. Rev. 235. President Harding later pardoned Debs.

iv. *Abrams v. United States,* 250 U.S. 616 (1919). Abrams and four others were convicted of violating the Espionage Act by reason of their distribution of a leaflet urging a general strike in order to frustrate American aid to the forces fighting against the Bolsheviks in Russia. The Court summarily affirmed the convictions on the strength of *Schenck* and *Frohwerk*.

(a) **Justice Holmes's dissent.** The only enduring part of the case is Justice Holmes's dissent. Holmes thought that the speakers had not spoken with the requisite intent—to frustrate the war against Germany—but added his view that the Court had applied the clear and present danger test improperly. Only speech that *"imminently threaten[s] immediate interference . . .*

with law" should be proscribed, argued Holmes, because the First Amendment protects "free trade in ideas—[the notion] that the best test of truth is the power of the thought to get itself accepted in the competition of the market."

v. **An alternative: The Learned Hand test of *Masses Publishing Co. v. Patten,*** 244 F. 535 (S.D.N.Y. 1917). District Judge Learned Hand enjoined the New York postmaster from refusing to mail the journal *The Masses,* having concluded that its contents did not constitute **"direct advocacy"** of illegal behavior. Speech that **expressly incites** lawbreaking was unprotected. By contrast, speech that was "political agitation"—the advocacy of ideas—was constitutionally protected.

c. **"Clear and present danger": Cases punishing speech alone as dangerous.** States went further than the federal Espionage Act and enacted laws that punished certain speech as inherently dangerous. These statutes, styled "criminal anarchy" or "criminal syndicalism" laws, typically punished the advocacy or even the "propriety" of "overthrowing" the government by "force or violence." Later, as the Cold War assumed prominence, the federal government began to prosecute communists under the federal version of these laws, the Smith Act.

i. *Gitlow v. United States,* 268 U.S. 652 (1925). Gitlow was convicted under New York's criminal anarchy statute for publishing a socialist manifesto that advocated the necessity of "revolutionary mass action" to destroy existing governments and replace them with a "revolutionary dictatorship of the proletariat." The Court upheld the conviction, holding that there was no need for the state to prove that the speaker intended to incite some *immediate* illegal act. Speech advocating distant violence—"ultimate revolution"—was constitutionally unprotected. "Such utterances, *by their very nature,* involve . . . immediate danger . . . because the effect of a given utterance cannot be accurately foreseen. . . . A single revolutionary spark may kindle a fire that, smouldering for a time, may burst into a sweeping and destructive conflagration." Holmes and Brandeis dissented on the grounds that there "was no *present danger* of an attempt to overthrow the government by force." Holmes charged that the defendants were punished for their ideas alone: "Every idea is an incitement."

ii. *Whitney v. California,* 274 U.S. 357 (1927). Anita Whitney, a niece of deceased Justice Stephen Field, was convicted under California's criminal syndicalism statute of knowingly becoming a member of an organization that advocates the use of "force and violence" to "effect[] political change." Whitney, a delegate to the organizational convention of the Communist Labor Party, personally opposed the advocacy of violence to achieve political change but remained a member of the Party even after her views were rejected. The Court upheld her conviction; it was enough that California had determined that mere membership in an organization advocating violent political change was a "danger to the public peace and the security of the State."

(a)   **Justice Brandeis's concurrence.** Brandeis, joined by Holmes, concurred in the result because there was sufficient evidence of a conspiracy "to commit present serious crimes." Brandeis and Holmes parted company with the majority's rationale, arguing that mere membership in an organization could not be punished unless that association "would produce, or is intended to produce, a *clear and imminent danger* of some substantive evil" that could legitimately be punished. In the course of defending this standard, Brandeis argued that free speech must be vigorously protected in order to create conditions for self-governance, and that only the clear presence of an "emergency" justified speech restrictions.

iii.   **The Smith Act and the varsity communists:** *Dennis v. United States,* 341 U.S. 494 (1951). The chief leaders of the American Communist Party were convicted of violating the Smith Act, which prohibited the knowing advocacy, or attempted advocacy, of the "duty, necessity, desirability, or propriety of overthrowing . . . any government in the United States by force or violence." The convictions were upheld. A four-Justice plurality concluded that speech could be prohibited as posing a clear and present danger of producing a substantive evil whenever "the **gravity** of the 'evil,' **discounted by its improbability,** justifies such invasion of free speech as is **necessary to avoid the danger.**" Given the size, cohesiveness, and fervent dedication of American communists to the goal of a violent overthrow of government, the Court concluded that the standard had been met with respect to the speech of the Party's leadership. Black and Douglas dissented. Black charged that the defendants were punished because "they agreed to assemble and to talk and publish certain ideas at a later date." Douglas dissented because there was no proof that the defendants had advocated anything but ideas—they merely "preached the creed with the hope that some day it would be acted upon."

iv.   **The Smith Act and the second-string communists:** *Yates* **and** *Scales*

(a)   *Yates.* Six years after *Dennis,* the Court in *Yates v. United States,* 354 U.S. 298 (1957), overturned the Smith Act convictions of several lesser communists. There had been no proof that the defendants advocated "*action* for the overthrow of government by force and violence. . . . [T]hose to whom the advocacy is addressed must be urged to *do* something, . . . rather than merely to *believe* in" something.

(b) ***Scales.*** In *Scales v. United States,* 367 U.S. 203 (1961), the Court upheld the Smith Act's prohibition of knowing membership in an "organization which advocates the overthrow of the Government of the United States by force or violence." Unlike *Yates,* in *Scales* there was specific proof of advocacy of violent political change—the *Scales* defendants had participated in small group meetings in which techniques for violent overthrow of the government were taught.

d. **The modern standard: *Brandenburg v. Ohio,*** 395 U.S. 444 (1969). Brandenburg, a Ku Klux Klan leader, was convicted under Ohio's criminal syndicalism statute for publicly stating: "We're not a revengent organization, but if our President, our Congress, our Supreme Court, continues to suppress the white, Caucasian race, it's possible that there might have to be some revengence taken." The speech was delivered to a television reporter at a Klan "rally," which consisted of about a dozen hooded people, some carrying firearms, gathered in front of a wooden cross in a lonely farmyard. The Court overturned the conviction, declaring that speech must be **"intended to incite imminent lawless action"** *and* **"likely to incite or produce such action"** to be constitutionally unprotected.

i. **The scope of *Brandenburg.*** One way to see the scope of the *Brandenburg* test is graphically.

	Imminent Danger	*Future Danger*
Express Advocacy of Crime	1	3
Discussion of Ideas	2	4

- The "bad tendency" test, exemplified by *Abrams* or *Gitlow,* punished speech identified in each of the four quadrants.

- The Holmes and Brandeis version of the clear and present danger test, exemplified by Holmes's dissent in *Abrams,* punished speech in quadrants 1 and 2.

- The *Dennis* and *Yates* test punished speech in quadrants 1 and 3.

- The *Brandenburg* test limits punishment to speech in quadrant 1 only.

ii.   The effect of *Brandenburg*. The *Brandenburg* test had at least the following effects.

- *Incitement:* The Learned Hand position in *Masses Publishing*—only speech *expressly inciting* crime could be punished—was adopted.

- *Imminent Harm:* The Holmes position—only speech posing an *immediate threat of harm* could be punished—was adopted.

- *Seriousness:* The question of the seriousness of the harm was left open by *Brandenburg*. The test makes no exception for speech inciting immediate commission of trivial harm nor provides for any relaxation of the imminence element with respect to extremely severe harm.

iii.   Applications of the *Brandenburg* principle

(a)   *Hess v. Indiana,* 414 U.S. 105 (1973). Following a campus antiwar demonstration punctuated by arrests of demonstrators, over 100 demonstrators blocking a street were pushed onto the curb and sidewalk by police. Hess then said "We'll take the fucking street later (or again)." For this he was convicted of disorderly conduct. The Court reversed, finding the *imminence* requirement unsatisfied. "At best, [the] statement could be taken as counsel for present moderation; at worst, it amounted to nothing more than advocacy of illegal action at some indefinite future time."

(b)   Pre-*Brandenburg*: *Bond* and *Watts*

- *Bond v. Floyd,* 385 U.S. 116 (1966). The Court ruled that the Georgia House of Representatives could not validly refuse to seat Julian Bond because of his opposition to the Vietnam War. Bond expressed admiration and respect for draft resisters, strong criticism of the American objectives in Vietnam, but stopped short of actual advocacy "that people should break laws." Compare to *Schenck, Frohwerk,* and *Debs.*

- *Watts v. United States,* 394 U.S. 705 (1969). Watts was convicted of willfully threatening to kill or injure the President after he addressed a small group of people during a public antiwar rally as follows: "I have got to go for my [draft] physical this Monday coming. I am not going. If they ever make me carry a rifle the first man I want to get in my sights is LBJ. [Nobody is] going to make me kill my black brothers." Although the Court agreed the law was facially valid, the Court held that Watts's remark did not constitute a "threat," but was protected "political hyperbole." It is not clear whether the Court classified the remark as hyperbole because Watts lacked any real intention of carrying out the threat, because the context of the statement suggested it was nothing more than exaggeration, or because there was no imminence to the threat.

2. Obscenity and Pornography

a. Introduction. Obscene speech is not protected by the First Amendment. Pornography—the nonobscene portrayal of sex in a fashion offensive to many—occupies a shadow category of limited protection. The continuing problem with obscenity is the difficulty of defining obscenity in a workable fashion—one that is neither overbroad nor vague and that adequately confines the discretion of triers of fact.

i. Obscenity. At present, speech is obscene if the following factors are proven.

(1) The " 'average person, applying **contemporary community standards,'** would find

- That the work, taken as a whole, **appeals to the prurient interest" in sex,** *and*

- That the speech "depicts or describes, in a **patently offensive way,** sexual conduct specifically defined" by the applicable law.

(2) A **reasonable person** would conclude that the "work, taken as a whole, **lacks serious literary, artistic, political, or scientific value.**" See *Miller v. California,* 413 U.S. 15 (1973), *Pope v. Illinois,* 481 U.S. 497 (1987), both discussed infra. In order to be punished for obscene speech or distribution of obscene material, the defendant must have known that the material was obscene. *Smith v. California,* infra.

ii. Pornography. The problem with pornography is developing usable criteria for filtering protected from unprotected pornography and providing a credible rationale for suppression or protection of pornography. Child pornography is unprotected; other pornography enjoys limited protection.

b.   Ousting obscenity from free speech

    i. *Roth v. United States,* 354 U.S. 476 (1957). In upholding Roth's conviction for mailing obscene material in violation of federal law the Court, per Justice Brennan, declared "that obscenity is not within the area of constitutionally protected speech or press." Justice Harlan dissented, contending that it was virtually impossible to define obscenity abstractly, as if it were "a peculiar *genus* of speech, . . . as distinct, recognizable, and classifiable as poison ivy is among other plants." But Harlan would have granted states wider discretion to suppress obscenity than the federal government, in part because "Congress has no substantive power over sexual morality."

    ii. **The rationales for suppressing obscenity.** The Court has embraced a number of rationales for banishing obscenity from the fold of protected speech.

        • *History and Intentions:* In *Roth* the Court concluded that "obscenity was outside the protection intended for speech. . . . All ideas having even the slightest redeeming social importance . . . [are protected, but] implicit in the history of the First Amendment is the rejection of obscenity as utterly without redeeming social importance."

        • *Link to Crime:* The Court sometimes defers to disputed legislative judgments that obscene speech inspires crime.

        • *Quality of Social and Moral Life:* The Court asserts that obscenity erodes moral standards and coarsens the social fabric of communities.

c.   The problem of defining obscenity

    i. **Justice Stewart: "I know it when I see it."** In a concurrence in *Jacobellis v. Ohio,* 378 U.S. 184 (1964), Justice Stewart penned his now-famous epigram in reference to "hard-core pornography," which Stewart thought was unprotected: "I know it when I see it, and the motion picture involved in this case is not that." This statement, combining subjectivity with judgment of each individual work, vividly illustrates the difficulty of attempting to define obscenity in the abstract. To paraphrase Harlan in *Roth,* if obscenity is a peculiar *genus* of speech it is, unlike poison ivy, not easy to identify characteristics that invariably describe it.

    ii. **The *Roth* definition.** In *Roth,* the Court defined obscenity as "material which deals with sex in a manner appealing to *prurient* interest." In a footnote the Court elaborated on the meaning of prurient: a morbid, lewd, lascivious longing, desire, or curiosity. In a later case, *Brockett v. Spokane Arcades, Inc.,* 472 U.S. 491 (1985), the Court said that material that sparked "normal, healthy" desires was not prurient, but if it appealed to a "shameful or morbid interest" in sex it was prurient. The problem, of course, is to recognize when a healthy sexual appetite becomes sufficiently debased to be shameful. I may know it when I see it, and you may know it when you see it, but are we seeing the same "it"?

iii. **The post-*Roth* morass.** For the seventeen years between *Roth* and *Miller* the Court tried unsuccessfully to refine its obscenity definition. No single position mustered a majority and the Court would simply issue terse *per curiam* reversals of obscenity convictions whenever five Justices, applying different standards, agreed that the material involved was not obscene. (See, e.g., *Redrup v. New York,* 386 U.S. 767 (1967).)

iv. ***Miller v. California,*** 413 U.S. 15 (1973). Miller conducted a mass mailing campaign to advertise his line of sexually explicit photo books, which presented in highly graphic detail virtually every conceivable form of sexual activity. Miller was convicted of violating California law by knowingly distributing obscene matter. The Court redefined obscenity and remanded the case for further proceedings in light of the new definition. Obscenity, said the Court, is limited "to works which depict or describe sexual conduct . . . specifically defined by the applicable . . . law." In determining whether any particular material is obscene the trier of fact must find that (1) the " 'average person, applying **contemporary community standards,'** would find that the work, taken as a whole, appeals to the prurient interest" in sex; and (2) the speech "depicts or describes, in a **patently offensive way,** sexual conduct specifically defined" by the applicable law; and (3) the "work, taken as a whole, **lacks serious literary, artistic, political, or scientific value."** Note that obscenity need not to be pictorial. *Kaplan v. California,* 413 U.S. 115 (1973).

(a) **Significance of *Miller*.** *Miller* signaled the Court's willingness to defer to state and local community judgments about the offensiveness, prurient appeal, or serious value of any given book, film, photograph, art exhibition, or the like. *Miller* and its progeny have produced a confined latitude for differing state and local judgments.

v. **Application of *Miller:* Limits on local community standards.** It is a paradox that while *local* community standards govern the factual issues of whether a work appeals to the prurient interest in sex and whether it depicts sex in a patently offensive manner, those standards are subject to judicial review.

(a) **Jenkins v. Georgia,** 418 U.S. 153 (1974). A film exhibitor was convicted of showing the movie *Carnal Knowledge* after a jury determined it was obscene. The Court reversed the conviction, finding that no jury could reasonably find the film to be obscene. The Court noted that while the film has "occasional scenes of nudity, . . . nudity alone is not enough to make material legally obscene. . . ." The Court found it significant that when sexual intercourse was depicted "the camera does not focus on the bodies of the actors . . . [and] [t]here is no exhibition of the actor's genitals, lewd or otherwise." Thus, local community standards of prurient appeal and offensiveness do not apply if those standards as applied in any given case are absurd to the judicial mind.

(b) **Smith v. United States,** 431 U.S. 291 (1977). Smith was convicted of mailing obscene material in violation of federal law. The material was sent from one place in Iowa to an adult who had requested it at another Iowa address at a time when Iowa did not bar the distribution of obscene matter to consenting adults. The Court upheld the conviction and ruled that in a federal prosecution the jury is entitled to apply "its own knowledge of community standards" and may ignore the state legislature's declarations of "what the community standards shall be" with respect to prurient appeal and offensiveness. A consequence of *Smith* is that the most localized community standard prevails. When that is coupled with the fact that the federal crime of mailing obscene matter may be prosecuted in any locale through which the material has passed, federal prosecutors are free to select the locale harboring the most restrictive community standards as the venue for prosecution. The practical result is a powerful incentive for publishers to conform to the most restrictive community standards of prurience and offensiveness anywhere in the nation.

(c) **Pope v. Illinois,** 481 U.S. 497 (1987). The Court ruled that *local* community standards do *not* govern the question of whether a work lacks serious literary, artistic, political or scientific value. The proper question is whether a *reasonable person* would find serious value in the work.

vi. **Application of *Miller*: Determining prurient appeal.** In *Miller* the Court suggested some "plain examples" of material with prurient appeal: "[p]atently offensive representations or descriptions of masturbation, excretory functions, . . . lewd exhibition of the genitals . . . [or] ultimate sexual acts, normal or perverted, actual or simulated." These examples are merely illustrative and do not exhaust the possibilities of prurient material.

(a) Pandering. In *Splawn v. California,* 431 U.S. 595 (1977), the Court reaffirmed its pre-*Miller* holding that "evidence of pandering to prurient interests [is] relevant in determining whether the material is obscene." *Ginzburg v. United States,* 383 U.S. 463 (1966). The Court in *Splawn* upheld a conviction for sale of obscene films where the jury had been instructed that they could convict even if the films did not have prurient appeal, so long as they found that the films were being offered and sold on the basis of their purported prurient appeal.

(b) Prurient appeal only to a target audience: *Ward* and *Mishkin*

- *Ward.* In *Ward v. Illinois,* 431 U.S. 767 (1977), the Court reaffirmed its pre-*Miller* holding that material with no prurient appeal to the average person, but with such appeal to a particular audience, could be suppressed. At issue in *Ward* was material that depicted and described sado-masochistic acts.

- *Mishkin v. New York,* 383 U.S. 502 (1966). Mishkin produced books depicting "sadomasochism, fetishism, and homosexuality." As a defense to an obscenity prosecution he maintained that since the books were apt to "disgust and sicken" the average person they lacked sufficient prurient appeal to be suppressed as obscenity. Nonsense, said the Court: Where "material is designed for and primarily disseminated to a clearly defined deviant sexual group, rather than the public at large, the prurient-appeal requirement . . . is satisfied if the dominant theme of the material taken as a whole appeals to the prurient interest in sex of the members of that group."

vii. **Application of *Miller:* Determining serious value of the work.** Local community standards do *not* govern the question of whether a particular work lacks serious literary, artistic, political, or scientific value. "The proper inquiry is . . . whether a reasonable person would find such value in the material, taken as a whole." *Pope v. Illinois,* supra.

Example: A Cincinnati art gallery and its officials were prosecuted for displaying an exhibit of Robert Mapplethorpe photographs containing explicit depictions of homoerotic and sadomasochistic acts. The jury acquitted the defendants after a trial featuring expert testimony concerning the artistic value of Mapplethorpe's photos.

d. Obscenity and consenting adults. There is no general protection for obscenity desired by consenting adults. One case, *Stanley v. Georgia,* infra, held that a person could not be prosecuted for possession of obscenity within his own home, but that case has been painted into a very small corner.

    i. Public exhibition unprotected: *Paris Adult Theatre I v. Slaton,* 413 U.S. 49 (1973). In this companion case to *Miller* the Court emphatically rejected the claim that "obscene, pornographic films acquire constitutional immunity simply because they are exhibited for consenting adults only." Legislatures may act on the "unprovable assumption" that public availability of obscenity, even when limited to consenting adults, has "a tendency to exert a corrupting and debasing impact leading to antisocial behavior." In so ruling, the Court expressly rejected the invitation to extend *Stanley v. Georgia,* infra, which held that simple possession of obscene material in one's home could not be punished.

    ii. Private possession protected: *Stanley v. Georgia,* 394 U.S. 557 (1969). In reversing Stanley's conviction for knowing possession of obscene matter, the Court concluded that the free expression guarantee barred a state from "making the private possession of obscene material a crime." The Court based its holding in part on privacy grounds, and in part on the belief that governments have no "right to control the moral content of a person's thoughts. . . . Whatever may be the power of the state to control public dissemination of ideas inimical to public morality, it cannot constitutionally premise legislation on the desirability of controlling a person's private thoughts." *Stanley* appeared to be a broad ruling that might undercut laws prohibiting the distribution of obscenity, but that notion was soon squelched.

    (a) No protection for distribution, transportation, or importation. In *United States v. Reidel,* 402 U.S. 351 (1971), the Court reversed a district court's dismissal of an indictment for mailing obscene material in violation of federal law. *Stanley* did not imply a right to obtain obscenity, but only protected "freedom of mind and thought and . . . the privacy of one's home." In *United States v. Orito,* 413 U.S. 139 (1973), the Court upheld the federal prohibition upon interstate transport of obscene materials as applied to transportation purely for private use. In *United States v. Twelve 200-Foot Reels,* 413 U.S. 123 (1973), the Court sustained the application of federal law to prevent the importation of obscene material for concededly personal use. After these cases, it was clear that obscenity remained a semi-contraband—unprotected save in the narrow sanctuary of personal use in one's home.

(b) No protection for child pornography: *Osborne v. Ohio,* 495 U.S. 103 (1990). The Court ruled that *Stanley* did not bar a prosecution for possession of obscene child pornography. Earlier, in *New York v. Ferber,* infra, the Court had ruled that even nonobscene child pornography was unprotected by the First Amendment. The Court's refusal to apply *Stanley* is strongly linked to the *Ferber* Court's belief that the creation of child pornography poses extreme dangers to children.

e. Children and ''nonobscene'' pornography. Governments may restrict minors' access to ''nonobscene'' pornography and governments may suppress adult access to ''nonobscene'' pornography that features children as subjects.

i. Child   pornography: Protecting   children   from   sexual exploitation

(a) *New York v. Ferber,* 458 U.S. 747 (1982). New York prohibited the distribution of material depicting children engaged in sexual conduct, whether or not the depictions meet the *Miller* test of obscenity. The Court unanimously upheld the validity of the law. Writing for the Court, Justice White declared that ''child pornography [is] a category of material outside the protection of the First Amendment.'' The Court reached this decision for four principal reasons.

- ''The prevention of sexual exploitation and abuse of children constitutes a government objective of surpassing importance. . . . [T]he use of children as subjects of pornographic materials is harmful to the physiological, emotional, and mental health of the [child].''

- ''[T]he distribution network for child pornography must be closed if the production of material which requires the sexual exploitation of children is to be effectively controlled.''

- ''The advertising and selling of child pornography provides an economic motive for and is thus an integral part of the production of such materials.''

- "The value of permitting live performances and photographic reproductions of children engaged in lewd sexual conduct is exceedingly modest, if not de minimus."

(b) **The definition of child pornography.** The majority in *Ferber* did not precisely define child pornography. They stated that there need *not* be proof of either prurient interest or patent offensiveness, and that the material need not be considered as a whole. The Court did not expressly decide whether child pornography that has some serious literary, artistic, political, or scientific value is protected speech. Only two concurring Justices would have expressly extended free speech protection to child pornography with serious value. By implication, child pornography is probably any depiction or description of children engaged in well-defined sexual conduct.

ii. Preventing children from access to pornography

(a) *Ginsberg v. New York,* 390 U.S. 629 (1968). The Court upheld a New York law defining obscenity in terms of the material's prurient appeal to minors. The object of the law was to deny to minors material that would not be obscene in the hands of adults. The Court reasoned that governments had greater power to control children than adults, the law aided parents in rearing their children, and the state had a greater interest in the moral welfare of children.

(b) *Butler v. Michigan,* 352 U.S. 380 (1957). Michigan made it an offense to make available to the general public "lewd" (but nonobscene) materials that would have a deleterious effect on minors. The Court voided the law, declaring that the state may not "reduce the adult population of Michigan to reading only what is fit for children."

f. Women and pornography. Various theorists have argued that nonobscene pornography that depicts women in degraded, humiliating, or abusive circumstances ought to be unprotected because of the harm such material inflicts upon women. Such pornography is claimed to be a means to encourage male subordination of women.

i. *American Booksellers Assn. v. Hudnut,* 771 F.2d 323 (7th Cir. 1985), summarily aff'd, 475 U.S. 1001 (1986). Indianapolis enacted an ordinance that prohibited pornography, defined as "the graphic sexually explicit subordination of women, whether in pictures or in words, that also includes one or more" of six specific depictions of women. Included in the forbidden depictions were the presentation of women as "sexual objects who enjoy pain or humiliation, . . . experience sexual pleasure in being raped, . . . [or] as sexual objects for domination, conquest, violation, exploitation, possession, or use, through postures or positions of servility or submission or display." Indianapolis defended the ordinance on the ground that "pornography influences attitudes, and the statute is a way to alter the socialization of men and women rather than to vindicate community standards of offensiveness." The Seventh Circuit struck down the law as viewpoint based: "Speech treating women in the approved way—in sexual encounters 'premised on equality'—is lawful no matter how sexually explicit. Speech treating women in the disapproved way—as submissive in matters sexual or as enjoying humiliation—is unlawful no matter how significant the literary, artistic, or political qualities of the work taken as a whole. The state may not ordain preferred viewpoints in this way. The Constitution forbids the state to declare one perspective right and silence opponents. . . . Any other answer leaves the government in control of all the institutions of culture, the great censor and director of which thoughts are good for us."

ii. **The Canadian view:** *Regina v. Butler,* [1992] 1 S.C.R. 452, 89 D.L.R. 4th 449 (1992). The Canadian Criminal Code makes it a crime to publish or distribute obscene material, defined in part as "any publication the dominant characteristic of which is the undue exploitation of sex." The Supreme Court of Canada ruled this provision was a justified infringement of the free expression guarantee contained in Canada's Charter of Rights and Freedoms. The Court explained that "undue exploitation" consisted in part of material depicting "women (and sometimes men) in positions of subordination, servile submission, or humiliation." Because this material "is harmful to society, particularly to women" its suppression was thought to be a justified invasion of free speech. This rationale is essentially the one urged upon and rejected by the *Hudnut* court.

g. **Prior restraints of obscenity.** The prior restraint doctrine was discussed in detail in section B, supra. Here is a brief summary of that doctrine as applied to obscenity.

i. **Licensing.** The Court permits licensing schemes designed to prevent the exhibition of obscene films but subjects them to two familiar doctrines—**vagueness** and the *Freedman v. Maryland* **procedural safeguards.** The Court has invalidated vague licensing schemes that sought to prevent exhibition of "sacrilegious" or "immoral" films. See *Burstyn v. Wilson,* 343 U.S. 945 (1952); *Com-*

mercial Pictures Corp. v. Regents, 346 U.S. 587 (1954). Recall also that the *Freedman* safeguards were developed in the context of a state licensing scheme designed to restrain obscenity.

ii.   **Injunctions.** Injunctions preventing the exhibition or publication of obscene material are permitted so long as (1) the state's definition of obscenity and method of determining what is obscene is "constitutionally acceptable," and (2) the injunction does not issue "until after a full adversary proceeding and a final judicial determination [that] the materials were constitutionally unprotected." *Paris Adult Theatre I v. Slaton,* supra. See also *Kingsley Books v. Brown,* 354 U.S. 436 (1957). Injunctions must be directed at a specific item of obscenity; the Court has voided a state statute authorizing judges to enjoin future violations of obscene movies after finding that the defendant had done so in the past, even though the state's definition of obscenity was constitutional. *Vance v. Universal Amusement Co.,* 445 U.S. 308 (1980).

iii.   **Seizures.** In general, material may not be seized as obscene without a prior finding in an adversarial proceeding that the material is constitutionally obscene. *Marcus v. Search Warrant,* 367 U.S. 717 (1961). This rule does not apply when the police seize a single copy of an allegedly obscene item for evidence purposes and leave the defendant with other copies of the same item. *Heller v. New York,* 413 U.S. 483 (1973).

3.   **Fighting Words**

a.   **Introduction.** Certain words—epithets and personal abuse—are thought to be so unrelated to the "exposition of ideas" and threatening to "the social interest in order and morality" that they receive no constitutional protection. This doctrine has been sharply limited. Virtually the only constitutionally unprotected words are those that are *directed at another individual, face to face,* and that are *likely to provoke a violent response.* It is nearly certain that the First Amendment protects words, however injurious, that are not directed to any particular individual.

b.   **The origins:** *Chaplinsky v. New Hampshire,* 315 U.S. 568 (1942). Chaplinsky was convicted of violating a New Hampshire law that prohibited the use of "any offensive, derisive, or annoying word to any other person . . . in [a] public place." Chaplinsky had been distributing religious literature and, according to bystanders, denouncing religion as a "racket." Bowering, the city marshal, told the bystanders that Chaplinsky's conduct was lawful but "warned Chaplinsky that the crowd was getting restless." After a later disturbance a traffic officer escorted Chaplinsky away from the scene, encountering Bowering, who repeated his earlier warning. Chaplinsky replied: "You are a God damned racketeer [and] a damned Fascist." The Court upheld the conviction, asserting that the Constitution does not protect "insulting or 'fighting' words— those which by their very utterance inflict injury or tend to incite an immediate breach of the peace." The reason offered was "that such utterances are no essential part of any exposition of ideas, and are of such slight social value as a step to truth that any benefit that may be derived from them is clearly outweighed by the social interest in order and morality."

c. **The *Chaplinsky* legacy: Never applied, freely limited.** In the sixty years since *Chaplinsky* the Court has never applied the doctrine. Instead, whenever it has been asked to do so it has either refused or limited the fighting words doctrine. As Professor Gunther has observed, "One must wonder about the strength of [a doctrine] that, while theoretically recognized, has for so long not been found apt in practice." Gunther, 24 Stan. Lawyer 41.

   i. *Street v. New York,* 394 U.S. 576 (1969). Following news that the black civil rights leader, James Meredith, had been shot in Mississippi by a sniper, Street, a black man, "took from his drawer a neatly folded, 48-star American flag which he formerly had displayed on national holidays," went to a nearby intersection and burned it in public, stating to the crowd that gathered: "We don't need no damn flag." When asked by a police officer whether he had burned the flag, Street replied, "Yes, that is my flag; I burned it. If they let that happen to Meredith we don't need an American flag." Street was convicted under a New York law making it a crime to "publicly mutilate, deface, defile, . . . or cast contempt upon" the flag because of "the possible tendency of [Street's] words to provoke violent reaction." The Court reversed the conviction, ruling that Street's "remarks were [not] so inherently inflammatory as to come within that small class of 'fighting words' which are 'likely to provoke the average person to retaliation, and thereby cause a breach of the peace.' "

   ii. *Cohen v. California,* 403 U.S. 15 (1971). In the corridor of a Los Angeles courthouse Cohen wore a jacket inscribed "Fuck the Draft." He was convicted of violating a California law prohibiting anyone from "maliciously and willfully" disturbing the peace of any person by "offensive conduct," a term interpreted by the California courts to mean "behavior which has a tendency to provoke *others* to acts of violence." California argued that the law, as interpreted, did no more than ban fighting words. Wrong, said Justice Harlan, writing for a 6 to 3 majority of the Court. "While [fuck] is not uncommonly employed in a personally provocative fashion, in this instance it was clearly not 'directed to the person of the hearer.' No individual . . . could reasonably have regarded the words on [Cohen's] jacket as a **direct personal insult.**''

iii. *Gooding v. Wilson,* 405 U.S. 518 (1972). Wilson was convicted under a Georgia law making it a misdemeanor to direct to another person "without provocation, . . . opprobrious words or abusive language, tending to cause a breach of the peace." Wilson and others had been blocking access to an Army induction center as part of an antiwar demonstration and refused to move. The police started to force them to move and Wilson said to a police officer: "White son of a bitch, I'll kill you. You son of a bitch, I'll choke you to death. You son of a bitch, if you ever put your hands on me again, I'll cut you all to pieces." The Court reversed the conviction, finding the Georgia statute overbroad and void on its face. Writing for the majority, Justice Brennan said the statute was overbroad because it was not "limited in application, as in *Chaplinsky,* to words that '**have a direct tendency to cause acts of violence by the person to whom, individually, the remark is addressed.**' '' The Court essentially gutted the alternative prong of *Chaplinsky*—words "which by their very utterance inflict injury"—and confined the fighting words doctrine to the narrow category of speech uttered directly to another and likely to provoke an immediate violent response.

iv. **The "mother-fucker" trilogy: *Rosenfeld, Lewis,* and *Brown*.** In three cases decided together the Court further emphasized the narrow scope of fighting words.

- *Rosenfeld v. New Jersey,* 408 U.S. 901 (1972). During the course of a public school board meeting with perhaps 110 adults and forty children in attendance, Rosenfeld used various permutations of "mother fucker" to describe the "teachers, the school board, the town, and his own country." He was convicted of uttering "indecent [and] offensive" language in a public place that was "likely to incite the hearer to an immediate breach of the peace or . . . affect the sensibilities of a hearer."

- *Lewis v. New Orleans,* 408 U.S. 913 (1972). Lewis cursed the police, who were arresting her son, as "god damn mother fuckers" and was convicted of using "obscene or opprobrious language" to a police officer on duty.

- *Brown v. Oklahoma,* 408 U.S. 914 (1972). Brown, a Black Panther, referred to police officers as "mother fucking fascist pig cops" and one particular officer as "that 'black mother fucking pig,' " resulting in his conviction of uttering "obscene or lascivious language . . . in any public place, or in the presence of females."

In all three cases the Court reversed the convictions and remanded for reconsideration in light of *Gooding v. Wilson*. Writing separately, Justice Powell spoke to the fighting words issue. In *Rosenfeld* the profanities were not fighting words because "the offensive words were not directed at a specific individual." In *Lewis,* the words would have been fighting words if "addressed by one citizen to another, face-to-face and in a hostile manner . . . [but] the situation may be different where such words are addressed to a police officer trained to exercise a higher degree of restraint than the average citizen." *Brown* combined both rationales—the words were not directed to any specific individual except the policeman.

   d.   Hate speech. Speech that is perceived to be harmful to ethnic or other minorities is often said to promote the subordination of minorities and thus ought to be unprotected. The case for suppressing nonobscene pornography that depicts women in a subordinate light (see section C.2.f supra) is one example. This section examines the arguments for suppressing ethnic slurs or other such hate speech.

   i.   *Chaplinsky:* Words that "inflict injury." When the Court in *Chaplinsky* said that the Constitution does not protect "insulting or 'fighting' words" it defined that category to include words "which by their very utterance inflict injury." Since racial slurs inflict emotional injury it might be thought obvious that hate speech is constitutionally unprotected. That conclusion ignores the fact that in the years since *Chaplinsky* the category of "fighting words" has been whittled down to encompass only words spoken to another person in a *face-to-face* encounter *and* which are of such a nature as to *trigger a violent response.* In short, the fighting words doctrine no longer includes words "which by their very utterance inflict injury."

   ii.   *R.A.V. v. St. Paul,* 505 U.S. 377 (1992). A teenager burned a cross on the lawn of a black family's home and was subsequently convicted of violating a St. Paul ordinance that prohibited the exhibition of symbols known by the exhibitor to "arouse[] anger, alarm or resentment in others on the basis of race, color, creed, religion, or gender. . . ." The Minnesota courts had construed the ordinance to apply only to *Chaplinsky's* definition of fighting words. The Court struck down the ordinance as facially invalid. The majority assumed, *but did not decide,* "that all of the expression reached by the ordinance is proscribable under the 'fighting words' doctrine." Even so, the law was "facially unconstitutional" because "it prohibits . . . speech solely on the basis of the subjects the speech addresses." *R.A.V.* created a new rule—*even within unprotected speech governments may not selectively prohibit speech on the basis of the viewpoint expressed.* Unprotected categories of expression may be selectively prohibited for the reason the entire category is unprotected but not for some content-based or viewpoint-based reason "unrelated to their distinctively proscribable content. Thus, the government may proscribe libel; but it may not make the further content discrimination of proscribing only libel critical of the government. . . . A State might . . . prohibit only that obscenity which is the most patently offensive in its prurience . . . [b]ut it may not prohibit . . . only that obscenity which includes offensive political messages." St. Paul's ordinance violated this principle because it applied only to fighting words that insult on the basis of race, color, creed, religion, or gender. Speakers remained free to hurl the nastiest of invective toward racists; only racists were prevented from using fighting words. St. Paul's ordinance banned "fighting words of whatever manner that communicate messages of racial, gender, or religious intolerance[,] . . . creat[ing] the possibility that the city is seeking to handicap the expression of particular ideas."

Four Justices concurred on the ground that the St. Paul ordinance, even as interpreted by the Minnesota courts, was unconstitutionally overbroad. The ordinance covered all speech within the *Chaplinsky* formulation of fighting words but the concurring Justices agreed that was too broad. The ordinance made "criminal expressive conduct that causes only hurt feelings, offense, or resentment." Such speech is protected by the First Amendment. The four concurring Justices squarely acknowledged that words that do no more than "inflict injury" are no longer part of the fighting words doctrine. The majority probably agreed with this but did not say so because they did not address the scope of the fighting words doctrine.

iii. **Hate crimes: *Dawson* and *Mitchell*.** Statutes often provide for enhanced penalties for crimes in which racial or other hatred is a motive. It is constitutionally permissible to punish criminal activity more severely when racial hatred is a motive than when it is absent. It is not constitutionally permissible to take racial hatred into account for punishment purposes when such hatred is unconnected to the crime or to other relevant considerations of punishment.

(a) *Dawson v. Delaware,* 503 U.S. 159 (1992). Dawson, a white man, murdered several white people. During Dawson's capital sentencing hearing Delaware introduced evidence of his membership in a racist organization, the Aryan Brotherhood. The Court ruled that this was an attempt to punish Dawson for his racist beliefs, since racial hatred had nothing to do with the crimes. In dicta, the Court indicated that Dawson's affiliation with an organization advocating racially motivated murder of other prison inmates might have been relevant to rebut mitigating evidence of Dawson's prior good behavior in prison.

(b) *Wisconsin v. Mitchell,* 508 U.S. 476 (1993). Angered by a scene in the movie *Mississippi Burning* depicting a white man beating a young black in prayer, Mitchell and several other black youths severely beat a white boy who happened by. Mitchell was convicted of aggravated battery, and his sentence was increased from two to seven years because the jury found that he had intentionally selected his victim by race. The Court unanimously reversed the Wisconsin Supreme Court's ruling that the sentencing enhancement violated the First Amendment. The statute was aimed entirely at *conduct* and not at speech or belief. As in any other criminal case, the motive for commission of the crime was relevant to determination of the punishment. Unlike *Dawson,* Mitchell's racial hatred—the motive for the crime—was directly relevant.

iv. **A discredited precedent:** *Beauharnais v. Illinois,* 343 U.S. 250 (1952). Beauharnais distributed a leaflet demanding that Chicago politicians "halt the further encroachment, harassment and invasion of white people, their property, neighborhoods and persons, by the Negro." The leaflet also referred to "the aggressions, rapes, robberies, knives, guns and marijuana of the negro." He was convicted of distributing material that "portrays depravity, criminality, unchastity, or lack of virtue of a class of citizens, of any race, color, creed or religion, which exposes the [portrayed class] to contempt, derision, or obloquy or which is productive of breach of the peace or riots." The Court (5-4) affirmed the conviction, relying almost entirely on the proposition that since speech "directed at an individual may be the object of criminal sanctions, we cannot deny to a State power to punish the same utterance directed at a defined group."

(a) **The decline of** *Beauharnais.* While *"Beauharnais* has never been overruled or formally limited in any way," *Smith v. Collin,* 436 U.S. 953 (1978) (Blackmun, J., dissenting), it has been eclipsed as good law for three reasons.

- *Defamation.* The Court in *Beauharnais* assumed that defamation of individuals was entirely unprotected by the Constitution. That is no longer true (see section C.5, *infra*). Since "group defamation" involves claims about entire categories of people, such claims are likely to be treated as if they were said of an individual "public figure," thus triggering some protection under the First Amendment. Also, claims made about individuals may be verified, but claims made about groups are evaluative opinions, thus taking them outside defamation.

 # EXAMPLE AND ANALYSIS

To say "President Bush uses marijuana" is to assert a specific factual claim capable of empirical verification. To say "Politicians use marijuana" is quite different. Some politicians may do so, but probably most do not. The question is whether marijuana usage "can appropriately be used to characterize the group. The fundamental issue is the nature of the group's identity, an issue that almost certainly ought to be characterized as one of evaluative opinion." Post, 32 Wm. & Mary L. Rev. 298.

- *Incitement of Illegal Conduct.* The Illinois courts construed the statute under which Beauharnais was convicted to prohibit only speech that had a "strong tendency [to] cause violence and disorder." That standard would not meet the *Brandenburg* test.

- *Fighting Words.* To the extent the *Beauharnais* Court implicitly relied on *Chaplinsky's* broad definition of "fighting words" that doctrine has been curtailed to reach only hostile speech delivered face to face and likely to trigger a violent reaction.

4. Offensive Speech

Offensive speech is speech that is reasonably likely to offend hearers or viewers but which lacks the violence-inducing character of fighting words. In general, offensive speech is *constitutionally protected*. But when such speech is directed toward an especially *sensitive* or *captive audience* it receives only limited protection.

a.   Punishing speech *because* it is offensive

i.   *Cohen v. California,* 403 U.S. 15 (1971), also discussed supra. Because Cohen publicly wore a jacket inscribed "Fuck the Draft" he was convicted of disturbing the peace by "offensive conduct [—] behavior which has a tendency to provoke *others* to acts of violence or to in turn disturb the peace." The Court reversed Cohen's conviction.

- The jacket was not obscene, and thus did not "give rise to the States' broader power to prohibit obscene expression."

- The jacket was not within the category of "fighting words." (See section C.3, supra.)

- The jacket's message was not inflicted on a captive audience since there was no proof that "substantial privacy interests" were "invaded in an essentially intolerable manner."

- California could not "excise, as 'offensive conduct,' one particular scurrilous epithet from the public discourse, . . . upon the theory . . . that the States, acting as guardians of public morality, may properly remove this offensive word from the public vocabulary." The "open debate" essential for self-governance requires toleration of some distasteful expression and it is impossible adequately to define "offensive" speech. "Surely the State has no right to cleanse public debate to the point where it is grammatically palatable to the most squeamish among us. . . . [O]ne man's vulgarity is another's lyric." Moreover, speech has an emotive as well as a cognitive aspect. Words that offend may be necessary to convey emotion and the "emotive function [of speech] . . . may often be the more important element of the overall message sought to be [communicated]."

b.   Offensive speech and the hostile audience.

Some speech may be so offensive that, while not "fighting words," it still might trigger a violent response. In general, the proper treatment of such speech is to control the audience, not suppress the speaker. Otherwise, the potentially violent heckler possesses a veto over speech with which he disagrees. Speech may be punished where there is

- An *imminent threat of violence,*

- The police have made *all reasonable efforts to protect the speaker,*

- The police have *requested that the speaker stop,* and

- The *speaker refuses to stop.*

i.   ***Terminiello v. Chicago,*** 337 U.S. 1 (1949). Terminiello spoke to an overflow crowd of 800 people in an auditorium. Outside, another 1,000 people protested Terminiello's speech by tossing stink bombs and breaking windows, in spite of the efforts of a "cordon of policemen" to maintain order. Inside, Terminiello condemned various political and racial groups and "goaded his opponents, referring to them as 'slimy scum,' 'snakes,' and 'bedbugs.'" Terminiello was convicted of disorderly conduct, defined to the jury as speech that "stirs the public to anger, invites dispute, brings about a condition of unrest, or creates a disturbance." The Court reversed the conviction. "A function of free speech . . . is to invite dispute . . . , induce[] a condition of unrest, create[] dissatisfaction with conditions as they are, or even stir[] people to anger."

ii.   ***Cantwell v. Connecticut,*** 310 U.S. 296 (1940). Jesse Cantwell, a Jehovah's Witness, sought converts by playing a phonograph record for the benefit of passers-by on the street. The record was sharply critical of Roman Catholicism. It offended enough people that Cantwell was charged and convicted of inciting a breach of the peace. The Court reversed the conviction. Cantwell played his record without any intent "to insult or affront the hearers." He did not threaten bodily harm to anyone, and his conduct evidenced "no truculent bearing, no intentional discourtesy, no personal abuse." While Cantwell's behavior "raised animosity . . . [it] raised no such clear and present menace to public peace and order as to render him liable to conviction." The Court's opinion rested on two somewhat contradictory premises: (1) speech may not be suppressed simply because it offends, unless (2) the speech is so offensive it creates a "clear and present danger of . . . immediate threat to public safety, peace, or order."

iii.   **Suppress the audience, not the speaker.** To avoid violence from a hostile audience, speech may be suppressed or punished only when all speech-protective alternatives have been exhausted.

(a)   ***Feiner v. New York,*** 340 U.S. 315 (1951). Feiner spoke to a crowd of about seventy-five people on a street corner in Syracuse, urging them to attend a meeting to be held that night. In the course of his remarks Feiner called President Truman a "bum," the mayor a "champagne-sipping bum" who "does not speak for the Negro people," and characterized the American Legion as "a Nazi Gestapo." The police responded to a complaint about Feiner's speech and, upon arrival, found Feiner exhorting blacks to "rise up in arms and fight for equal rights." One onlooker "threatened violence if the police did not act, [but others] appeared to be favoring [Feiner's] arguments." The police asked him to stop speaking in order "to break up the crowd" and "prevent it from resulting in a fight." After Feiner repeatedly ignored the police officer's requests, Feiner was arrested and subsequently convicted of disorderly conduct, consisting of his use of "offensive language" and refusal "to move on when ordered by the police" under circumstances "whereby a breach of the peace may be occasioned." The Court sustained the conviction, relying on *Cantwell's* dicta that speech can be muzzled when there is a "clear and present danger [to] public safety, peace, or order." Feiner, said the Court, passed "the bounds of argument or persuasion and [undertook] incitement to riot." Justice Black dissented, charging that there was no credible threat of disorder and asserting that, before stopping a speaker, the police "first must make all reasonable efforts to protect him." As seen below, *Feiner* has been eroded by subsequent cases.

(b) *Edwards v. South Carolina,* 372 U.S. 229 (1963). Nearly 200 young people, almost entirely black, walked to the public grounds of the South Carolina State House to protest racial discrimination. They paraded peacefully in front of about thirty police officers and several hundred onlookers. The crowd was not threatening in word or action. Nevertheless, after about forty minutes the police announced that the demonstrators would be arrested if they did not disperse within fifteen minutes. The demonstrators responded with patriotic songs, handclapping, and foot-stamping. They were arrested and convicted of breach of the peace. The Court reversed, finding that "there was no violence or threat of violence" on the part of the demonstrators or "any member of the crowd watching them."

(c) *Cox v. Louisiana,* 379 U.S. 536 (1965). Cox led a demonstration of about 2,000 black students protesting racial segregation and the previous arrest of twenty-three black students who had picketed stores maintaining segregated lunch counters. At the police chief's request Cox led his demonstrators to a specific street facing the courthouse and a crowd of whites across the street. As the demonstration neared its end Cox urged the students to eat lunch at the store lunch counters closed to blacks. Because the white onlookers were hostile to these sentiments the sheriff ordered the demonstrators to disperse. When they did not, the police broke up the demonstration with tear gas. Cox was convicted of breach of the peace. The Court unanimously reversed. As in *Edwards* the court concluded that there was no evidence of threatened violence by either the demonstrators or the onlookers.

(d) *Gregory v. Chicago,* 394 U.S. 111 (1969). Gregory led a group of eighty-five people to Chicago Mayor Daley's home in order to protest alleged segregation in the public schools. The demonstration began quietly but as a hostile crowd gathered the mood turned ugly. Rocks, eggs, and racial insults were hurled at the marchers. Gregory ignored police requests to leave and was arrested and convicted of disorderly conduct, consisting of "any improper noise, riot, disturbance, breach of the peace, or diversion tending to a breach of the peace." The Court overturned the conviction, calling it "a simple case."

(e) *Feiner:* **a dead husk?** Taken together, *Edwards, Cox,* and *Gregory* appear to gut *Feiner.* In *Gregory* the Court disregarded the Illinois Supreme Court's narrowing construction of the disorderly conduct ordinance because the jury had not been instructed in accordance with it, but that narrowing construction probably states the constitutional limits of police power to suppress speakers to avoid violence from a hostile audience. Speech may be punished where there is

- "An imminent threat of violence,"

- "The police have made all reasonable efforts to protect the demonstrators,"

- "The police have requested that the demonstration be stopped and explained the request, if . . . time [permits]," and

- "There is a refusal of the police request."

c. Offensive speech and sensitive or captive audiences. In contrast to the doctrine regarding suppression of offensive speech in the interest of catering to the hostile audience, the Court has shown a willingness to uphold regulation of "indecent" speech—speech that is lewd but not obscene—in order to protect sensitive or captive audiences, but has been unwilling to approve outright bans on such speech.

i. *Erznoznick v. Jacksonville,* 422 U.S. 205 (1975). A Jacksonville ordinance barred movie theaters with screens visible from public streets from exhibiting nudity. The Court declared the law to be facially invalid. Jacksonville defended the law on the ground that it simply protected unwilling viewers from offensive speech. The Court rejected that argument, stating that speech could be restricted on that basis only "when the speaker intrudes on the privacy of the home or the degree of captivity makes it impractical for the unwilling viewer or auditor to avoid exposure." The burden is generally upon the viewer to avert his eyes.

ii. *Young v. American Mini Theatres,* 427 U.S. 50 (1976). The Court upheld parts of a Detroit ordinance that confined movie theaters exhibiting "sexually explicit" but not obscene movies to limited portions of the city. Even though the ordinance was content based and regulated protected speech, the Court found it to be valid. In a plurality opinion, Justice Stevens argued that although nonobscene pornographic films could not be totally suppressed the "low value" of their content justified Detroit's "placing them in a different classification from other motion pictures." Justice Powell, who provided the fifth vote, concurred on the ground that the ordinance was an "innovative land-use regulation" that was viewpoint neutral within the category of "adult movies" and imposed no significant restrictions on "the viewing of these movies by those who desire to see them."

iii. *FCC v. Pacifica Foundation,* 438 U.S. 726 (1978). One weekday afternoon Pacifica's New York radio station broadcast a twelve minute monologue by George Carlin, a satirist, entitled "Filthy Words." Carlin expressed his feelings about the "seven words . . . you couldn't say on the public . . . airwaves, . . . ever." The seven magic words were repeated in various ways, to the amusement of Carlin's recorded audience but not to a man who had his radio tuned to the broadcast while driving with his young son. In response to the man's complaint the FCC issued a reprimand to the station and informed the station that patently offensive but nonobscene material should be confined "to times of day when children most likely would not be exposed." The Court upheld the FCC reprimand. In another plurality opinion, Justice Stevens rooted the FCC's power to restrict "patently offensive words dealing with sex and excretion" in their lesser value in the hierarchy of speech. But in addition to the asserted low value of terms like "shit, piss, [and] fuck" Stevens argued that radio audiences are a captive audience. "Because the broadcast audience is constantly tuning in and out, prior warnings cannot completely protect the listener or viewer from unexpected program content. To say that one may avoid further offense by turning off the radio when he hears indecent language is like saying that the remedy for an assault is to run away after the first blow." Justices Powell and Blackmun concurred, providing the necessary fourth and fifth votes, but refused to endorse Stevens's theory that some speech was of less value "and hence deserving of less [constitutional] protection."

iv. *Sable Communications, Inc. v. FCC,* 492 U.S. 115 (1989). In order to ban "sexually-oriented pre-recorded telephone messages"—

so-called dial-a-porn services—available to listeners who initiated the message by calling a "900" number, Congress amended the federal Communications Act by making it a crime to transmit obscene or indecent telephone messages. The Court voided the criminal prohibition of indecent messages. Unlike *Pacifica,* this involved a total ban on indecent messages. While the Court recognized the government's interest in shielding children from such messages, even when initiated by them, the Court was satisfied that there were less restrictive alternative methods to do so.

5. Defamation

a. Introduction. Common law defamation is speech asserting false facts impugning another's character. It is a strict liability tort—false statements of material facts about another person are defamatory without proof of any degree of culpability in their utterance. While truth is a defense the defendant has the burden of proving truth. Damages are frequently presumed. From the origins of the nation until 1964, when *New York Times v. Sullivan* was decided, defamatory speech was exiled from First Amendment protection. Since then some significant constitutional protection has been extended to defamatory speech, considerably altering the common law rules.

i. Summary of the First Amendment's protection of defamation

- *Public Figures.* Defamation of a **public figure** is protected unless the false statement of fact was made with **actual malice**—either *knowledge of its falsity* or *reckless indifference to its truth or falsity.* Some people are "public figures" for all purposes: *public officials* and people who are *famous or notorious* and *involved in public affairs.* Some people are "public figures" only for purposes of a specific issue: people who have *voluntarily entered a public controversy* or, very rarely, people who have been *involuntarily* thrust into such a controversy by the *actions of public officials* (such as a notorious criminal defendant).

- *Private Figures.* When a private figure is defamed as to a matter of "public interest" the First Amendment requires proof of *negligence* in order to recover actual damages, and *actual malice* must be proven in order to recover punitive damages. When a private figure is defamed as to a matter of *no public interest,* there is no First Amendment barrier to the recovery of either actual or punitive damages.

b. The origins: *New York Times v. Sullivan,* 376 U.S. 254 (1964). Sullivan, an elected commissioner of Montgomery, Alabama, charged with responsibility for supervising its police, sued the *Times* in state court for defamation. He alleged that a full-page advertisement published by the *Times,* entitled "Heed Their Rising Voices," falsely stated certain facts concerning the actions of the Montgomery police in connection with civil rights demonstrations. Following jury instructions in conformity with Alabama's common law of libel the jury returned a verdict awarding Sullivan $500,000 in damages. The Court reversed and announced unprecedented First Amendment restrictions on state laws concerning defamation. The free expression guarantee requires "a federal rule that prohibits a **public official** from recovering damages for a *defamatory falsehood relating to his official conduct* unless he proves that the statement was made with '**actual malice**'—that is, with **knowledge that it was false or with reckless disregard of whether it was false or not.**"

  i. **Rationale.** The Court emphasized the "profound national commitment to the principle that debate on public issues should be uninhibited, robust, and wide-open, and that it may well include vehement, caustic, and sometimes unpleasantly sharp attacks on government and public officials." Since erroneous statements are "inevitable in free debate, [they] must be protected [if] freedoms of expression are to have the 'breathing space' that they 'need [to] survive.'" The line the Court drew protected the negligent but not the knowing falsehood, representing its judgment that honest errors, or even sloppiness, are to be tolerated in public debate about the actions of governmental officials. Any other rule would choke off public discourse and strangle self-governance.

  ii. **Significance.** The *Sullivan* rule greatly altered the common law of defamation. *Sullivan* wrecked strict liability and the requirement that the defendant has the burden of proving truth. After *Sullivan* a *public official plaintiff* has the *burden of proving* that the defendant made the defamatory statement with *actual malice.*

c. **The *Sullivan* rule extended to public figures.** Two 1967 cases, *Curtis Publishing Co. v. Butts* and *Associated Press v. Walker,* decided together at 388 U.S. 130 (1967), extended the *Sullivan* rule to include defamation of **public figures** as well as of public officials. Butts, a well-known former football coach at the University of Georgia, claimed to have been defamed by an article in the *Saturday Evening Post* that asserted he had fixed a game. Walker, a prominent retired general, claimed that AP had defamed him by reporting that he had led a violent crowd in opposition to desegregation of the University of Mississippi. Both Walker and Butts were found to be public figures.

  i. **Public figure defined.** The Court in *Butts* and *Walker* suggested that public figures were those people who are "intimately involved in the resolution of important public questions or, by reason of their fame, shape events in areas of concern to society at large." Public figures are people who "assume special prominence in the resolution of public questions." *Gertz v. Robert Welch, Inc.,* 418 U.S. 323 (1974).

(a) **"Unlimited" public figure.** An "unlimited" public figure—a public figure for all times and purposes—is a person who "may achieve such pervasive fame or notoriety that he becomes a public figure for *all purposes and in all contexts."* More precisely, *"general fame or notoriety in the community* **and** *pervasive involvement in the affairs of society"* are needed to be an "unlimited" public figure. A defendant needs "clear evidence" to prove that the plaintiff is an "unlimited" public figure.

 # EXAMPLES AND ANALYSIS

Example: O.J. Simpson is an unlimited public figure. Through football, advertisements, and acting, he became a famous national television personality. By reason of his criminal trial he became nationally notorious.

Example: Jane Fonda is an unlimited public figure. Although occupying no public office, she has made herself a national political figure by reason of her voluntary involvement in numerous political controversies.

(b) **"Limited-purpose" public figures.** "More commonly, an individual voluntarily injects himself or is drawn into a particular public controversy and thereby becomes a public figure for a *limited range of issues."* To become a "limited-purpose" public figure a person must either "thrust himself into the vortex of the public issue, [or] engage the public's attention in an attempt to influence its outcome."

 # EXAMPLES AND ANALYSIS

Example: Russell Firestone divorced his Palm Beach socialite wife amid a highly publicized (in South Florida) court proceeding. *Time* magazine erroneously reported that the divorce was granted on grounds of adultery. When Mrs. Firestone sued *Time* for defamation the Court concluded she was not a public figure: apart from being a Palm Beach socialite, she had no *"especial prominence"* in public affairs, nor had she "thrust herself to the forefront of any particular public controversy *in order to influence the resolution of issues* involved in it." *Time, Inc. v. Firestone,* 424 U.S. 448 (1976).

Example: A New York news columnist expressed doubt that a female rape victim, never identified publicly, had actually been raped. In the ensuing controversy, the rape victim responded with outrage and public denials of the columnist's charge, though her identity remained unknown to the public. In her defamation suit against the columnist a New York state trial judge ruled that the plaintiff is a limited-purpose public figure for purposes of events relating to the rape complaint and its aftermath.

    (c) Involuntary limited-purpose public figure. The Court has suggested, but never held, that a person may, on "exceedingly rare" occasions, involuntarily become a public figure.

 ## Examples and Analysis

Example: Wolston was convicted of contempt for refusing to appear before a grand jury investigating Soviet espionage. The trial and conviction were highly publicized. Sixteen years later a book falsely identified Wolston as a Soviet agent. Wolston sued the publisher for libel and the Court ruled that Wolston was not a limited-purpose public figure because he had not grabbed "public [attention] in an attempt to influence the resolutions of the issues involved." A convicted criminal is not a limited-purpose public figure even for "comment on a limited range of issues relating to his conviction." *Wolston v. Reader's Digest Assn.,* 443 U.S. 157 (1979).

Example: Every month Senator Proxmire publicly bestowed the "Golden Fleece Award" to some recipient of federal money for purposes that Proxmire thought epitomized wasteful governmental spending. Professor Hutchinson received the award for his federally funded research into aggressive monkey behavior. Hutchinson was not a limited-purpose public figure. He had not sought public attention and had no public role with respect to federal spending. *Hutchinson v. Proxmire,* 443 U.S. 111 (1979).

---

   d. Private figures exempt from the *Sullivan* rule. To recover *compensatory damages* private figures need not prove actual malice but *must prove negligence.* To recover *punitive damages* private figures must prove *actual malice if the defamatory statements concern matters of **public concern,*** but not otherwise. To recover *anything* the private figure plaintiff must prove that statements on matters of *public concern* are false, a rule that reverses the common law rule requiring the defendant to prove truth as a defense.

i.   *Gertz v. Robert Welch, Inc.,* 418 U.S. 323 (1974). After Nuccio, a Chicago policeman, was convicted of murdering Nelson, Gertz represented Nelson's family in a civil suit against Nuccio. Gertz was an active and modestly well-known Chicago lawyer. *American Opinion,* the monthly magazine of the John Birch Society (published by Welch), ran an article that claimed Gertz "framed" Nuccio, had a criminal record, and long communist affiliations.

   (a)   **Not a public figure.** In Gertz's defamation suit against Welch, the Court ruled that Gertz was not a public figure. He had no public role in the Nuccio prosecution and never discussed the matter with the press.

   (b)   **Culpability standard: Compensatory damages.** Even though Gertz was a private figure the Court concluded that states could *not* make a person strictly liable for defamation. Even in defamation cases involving *private figures* the private figure plaintiff must prove that the defendant acted negligently in order to recover compensatory damages.

   (c)   **Culpability standard: Punitive damages.** Because the defamatory statements at issue in *Gertz* involved matters of *public interest* or *public concern,* the Court ruled that *punitive damages* could be recovered only if the plaintiff could prove that the defendant acted with *actual malice*—either knowledge of the falsehood or with reckless disregard for its truth or falsity.

   (d)   **Rationale.** The Court reasoned that since "there is no such thing as a false idea," and some errors are "inevitable in free debate," it is necessary to "protect some falsehood in order to protect speech that matters."

ii.   **Private figure plaintiffs must prove falsity:** *Philadelphia Newspapers, Inc. v. Hepps,* 475 U.S. 767 (1986). When a newspaper publishes "speech of public concern" a private figure plaintiff must prove that the speech is false. The Court justified the rule on the ground that newsworthy material might otherwise be suppressed out of fear of liability.

e.   **Private figures and statements of no public interest:** *Dun & Bradstreet v. Greenmoss Builders,* 472 U.S. 749 (1985). Dun & Bradstreet provides confidential reports to its subscribers concerning the creditworthiness of individuals and businesses. Dun & Bradstreet issued a false report that Greenmoss Builders had filed for bankruptcy. In the resulting defamation action the Court concluded that since the false report did *not involve any matter of* **public interest or concern** Greenmoss could recover *punitive damages without any proof of actual malice.*

f. **No special protection for opinions:** *Milkovich v. Lorain Journal Co.,* 497 U.S. 1 (1990). A newspaper columnist implied that Milkovich, a high school wrestling coach, lied under oath at an inquest concerning an altercation at a wrestling match. While the Court rejected the idea that opinions automatically receive constitutional protection, it did conclude that First Amendment protection extends to statements:

- Of *opinion,*

- That *relate to matters of public concern,* and

- That do *not* contain a *provable false factual connotation.*

6. **Invasion of Privacy and Intentional Infliction of Emotional Distress**

a. **Invasion of privacy—false light.** Individual privacy may be tortiously invaded when *material falsehoods* cast the person in a *false* and *offensive* light. As with defamation, the First Amendment limits the reach of this "civility" tort.

i. *Time, Inc. v. Hill,* 385 U.S. 374 (1967). The Hill family had been held hostage by escaped convicts who treated them nonviolently. Years later, *Life* magazine reported that a play, "The Desperate Hours," that depicted violence toward hostages was based on the Hill family's experience. The Court ruled that because the speech concerned matters of *public concern,* the Hills (conceded to be private figures) could not recover unless they proved that *Life* published with actual malice.

ii. **Effect of *Gertz* on *Hill:* No longer good law?** *Gertz* has implicitly overruled *Hill. Gertz* held that private figures could recover *compensatory damages* for defamation without proof of actual malice. The reasons for dispensing with actual malice in connection with defamation of private figures are equally applicable to "false light" invasion of privacy of private figures—both involve falsities inflicted upon people without the ability to reply in kind. The Court has not had occasion formally to declare that the *Gertz* standard applies to false light cases brought by private figures. In *Cantrell v. Forest City Publishing Co.,* 419 U.S. 245 (1974), the Court avoided this question because nobody had objected to the application of the actual malice standard to a false light case brought by a private figure. However, lower courts have done so. In *Wood v. Hustler Magazine,* 736 F.2d 1084 (5th Cir. 1984), *Hustler* published stolen nude photos of Wood that placed her in an offensive false light. The appeals court applied a negligence standard, ruling that *Hustler* had been negligent in failing to investigate whether the forged consent accompanying the photos was genuine.

b. Invasion of privacy—disclosure of true but highly personal information. Another tortious method of invading privacy is to disclose true but highly personal information. The Court has not decided the question of whether the First Amendment generally restricts such tort claims, but has ruled that disclosure of such facts is *constitutionally protected when the facts are obtained from public court records or proceedings.*

   i. *Cox Broadcasting Corp. v. Cohn,* 420 U.S. 469 (1975). After a television station released the name of a deceased rape victim, the victim's father sued for invasion of privacy. The Court ruled that "once true information is disclosed in public court documents open to public inspection, the press cannot be sanctioned for publishing it."

   ii. *Florida Star v. B.J.F.,* 491 U.S. 524 (1989). The Court held that Florida could not make a newspaper civilly liable for publishing the name of a rape victim that the newspaper had obtained from a public police report. Punishment of truthful information lawfully obtained "may lawfully be imposed, if at all, only when *narrowly tailored to a state interest of the highest order.*"

c. Intentional infliction of emotional distress. Since words can inflict emotional injury, the tort of intentional infliction of emotional distress may, in some jurisdictions, be premised upon speech alone and, in others, upon speech coupled with physical injury. The First Amendment limits this tort.

   i. *Hustler Magazine v. Falwell,* 485 U.S. 46 (1988). *Hustler,* a raunchy pornographic magazine, published a crude parody of a well-known liquor ad that featured celebrities speaking about the first time they had tried the liquor. Hustler's parody featured the name and picture of the nationally known minister and leader of the so-called Moral Majority, Jerry Falwell. In the ad parody Falwell was "quoted" as saying that his "first time" was a drunken liaison with his mother in an outhouse. Falwell sued for intentional infliction of emotional distress and prevailed at trial. The Court reversed, holding that even if *Hustler* intended to inflict emotional injury it could not be held liable. Political parody is essential for open public debate and such parody "is often based on exploration of unfortunate physical traits or politically embarrassing events—an exploration often calculated to injure the feelings of the subject of the portrayal." Nor could liability be premised on the "outrageousness" of the speech, because "outrageousness" has an inherent subjectivity that would invite punishment of speech "on the basis of the [jury's] dislike of a particular expression."

7. Invasion of Economic Interests: Copyright Infringement and Commercial Defamation

Recovery of damages for speech that wrongfully invades economic interests theoretically poses similar problems to speech that invades privacy and reputation interests. But there is little constitutional protection for such speech.

a. **Copyright infringement.** Federal copyright law protects the intellectual property of authors from exploitation by others. In *Harper & Row v. Nation Enterprises,* 471 U.S. 539 (1985), the Court concluded that *The Nation* magazine's publication of substantial portions of President Ford's unpublished memoirs without permission was *not constitutionally protected* even though the material was of public interest. The magazine's *"intended purpose"* was to steal the copyright holder's right of first publication.

b. **Commercial defamation.** Common law makes false disparagement of a product or service an actionable tort. The Court has never ruled on the question of whether such speech is entitled to any constitutional protection and, if so, whether the *Sullivan* or *Gertz* standards apply. In *Bose Corp. v. Consumers Union,* 466 U.S. 485 (1984), the Court accepted the lower court's use of the *actual malice* standard in a product disparagement case, but expressly reserved decision on whether actual malice was constitutionally required.

8. Commercial Speech

a. **Introduction and overview.** Commercial speech receives limited constitutional protection. Governments may freely regulate commercial speech that is either *misleading* or concerns *unlawful activity.* Governments may regulate truthful, accurate commercial speech concerning lawful activity if

- The government has a *substantial interest* in such regulation,

- The regulation *directly advances* the substantial governmental interest, and

- The regulation is *reasonably narrowly tailored* to achieve the objective.

b. **Limited protection for commercial speech**

   i. **The road to partial protection.** Initially, the Court held that the First Amendment imposed "no . . . restraint on government as respects purely commercial advertising." *Valentine v. Chrestensen,* 316 U.S. 52 (1942); *Breard v. Alexandria,* 341 U.S. 622 (1951). But in *Bigelow v. Virginia,* 421 U.S. 809 (1975), the Court voided a Virginia law that punished advertisement of abortions legal in New

York but illegal in Virginia. The advertisement "did more than simply propose a commercial transaction. It contained fact[s] . . . of clear 'public interest.' "

ii.   **The advent of protection:** *Virginia State Board of Pharmacy v. Virginia Citizens Consumer Council,* 425 U.S. 748 (1976). Virginia law made it professional misconduct for a pharmacist to advertise the price of prescription drugs. The Court ruled that the law violated free speech, holding for the first time that *exclusively commercial speech is entitled to some free expression protection.*

    (a)   **Rationale.** The Court found that there was a substantial "interest in the free flow of commercial information." Advertisers wish to communicate availability of and facts about their products and consumers wish to receive this information. Moreover, there is social value in this flow since much commercial speech contains matter of public interest. The state's justification for the ban—maintaining high professional standards—was undermined by the fact that alternative avenues were open to the state to achieve this goal.

iii.   **The problem of defining commercial speech.** Commercial speech is identified by its *content,* not just the intent of the speaker to make money.

 ## EXAMPLE AND ANALYSIS

A condom manufacturer distributed several informational pamphlets dealing with contraceptives and sexually transmitted disease. Even though the pamphlets contained "discussions of important public issues such as venereal disease and family planning" they were commercial speech because they were concededly advertisements and mentioned condoms by brand name. *Bolger v. Youngs Drug Products,* 463 U.S. 60 (1983).

iv.   **The current test.** There is no First Amendment protection for commercial speech that is either *misleading* or concerns *unlawful activity.* The First Amendment forbids governments from regulating accurate commercial speech concerning lawful activity unless the government can prove the following:

    •   The government has a *substantial interest* in such regulation,

    •   The regulation *directly advances* the substantial governmental interest, and

- The regulation is *reasonable: Narrowly tailored* to achieve the objective.

(a) ***Central Hudson Gas & Electric Corp. v. Public Service Commn.,*** 447 U.S. 557 (1980). Central Hudson successfully challenged a state PUC ban of all public utility advertising promoting the use of electricity. The Court announced and applied the current test, except that its last element was phrased to permit only commercial speech regulations that were "no more extensive than necessary to serve [the government's] interest." Since the use of electricity was lawful, advertisements promoting its use were within the umbrella of First Amendment protection. While the state's objective—resource conservation—was substantial and the advertising ban directly promoted that goal, the outright suppression of all promotion of electricity use was broader than necessary. Some promotional advertising might result in more efficient use of electricity. The state could have required such advertising to contain information about efficient electrical usage.

(b) ***44 Liquormart, Inc. v. Rhode Island,*** 517 U.S. 484 (1996). *Central Hudson* was questioned, but not overturned, by this successful challenge to Rhode Island's complete ban on advertising of liquor prices. A unanimous Court struck down the ban, but no majority could agree on a rationale. Rehnquist, O'Connor, Souter and Breyer thought the ban failed *Central Hudson*'s third prong—the ban was far more restrictive than necessary to achieve Rhode Island's goal of reducing liquor consumption. Stevens, Kennedy and Ginsburg would have applied strict scrutiny to all bans on truthful, nonmisleading commercial speech adopted for reasons unrelated to a fair market but, joined now by Souter, also thought that the ban failed both of *Central Hudson*'s second and third prongs. Thomas thought all bans on truthful price information are automatically void. Scalia dropped a hint that he might be willing to consider scrapping *Central Hudson*. Yet *Central Hudson* survived and is still good law—for now.

(c) **Direct advancement:** ***Metromedia, Coors Brewing and 44 Liquormart.*** So long as there is a *reasonable* or *rational* relationship between the substantial government objective and the commercial speech regulation the regulation "directly advances" the objective.

- *Metromedia, Inc. v. San Diego,* 435 U.S. 490 (1981). For aesthetic and traffic safety reasons San Diego banned all billboard advertising. The Court invalidated the ban as applied to *noncommercial* billboards, but upheld it as applied to *commercial* billboards. The Court said it was *"reasonable"* for the city to conclude that billboards presented "real and substantial" hazards to traffic safety. Finding that the city did not have "as an ulterior motive the suppression of speech" the regulation directly advanced the city's interest in aesthetics.

- *Rubin v. Coors Brewing Co.,* 514 U.S. 476 (1995). The Court voided a federal law prohibiting disclosure of the alcohol content of beer on labels. The prohibition did not "directly advance" the government's objective since brewers remained generally free to *advertise* the strength of their beers.

- *44 Liquormart.* A four-Justice plurality thought that Rhode Island's ban on all liquor price advertising was only "fortuitous[ly]" connected to Rhode Island's goal of reducing liquor consumption.

(d) **Narrow tailoring.** *44 Liquormart* created uncertainty about this standard. *Central Hudson* said governments are required to prove that their commercial speech regulations are the *least restrictive means* of accomplishing their substantial objectives. But *Board of Trustees of SUNY v. Fox,* 492 U.S. 469 (1989), held that they must only prove that the regulations are *reasonably narrowly tailored* to achieve the objective. The *Fox* Court concluded that commercial speech regulations are permissible means to achieve substantial government objectives if they are *"reasonable,"* with a *"scope . . . 'in proportion to the interest served,' "* or employ *"means narrowly tailored to achieve the desired objective."* But *44 Liquormart* found Rhode Island's price advertising ban wanting even though it might reasonably be thought to reduce liquor consumption.

v. **No discrimination against commercial speech.** Commercial speech may not be treated differently from similarly situated noncommercial speech absent proof of a peculiar harm inflicted by commercial speech. In *Cincinnati v. Discovery Network,* 507 U.S. 410 (1993), the Court invalidated a Cincinnati ordinance that, for aesthetic purposes, prohibited distribution of commercial handbills on public property. Cincinnati applied the ordinance to newsracks distributing real estate flyers and the like, but not to newspapers. The Court rejected Cincinnati's contention that every newsrack eliminated improved aesthetics, and thus the ordinance as applied was a reasonable fit. The Court ruled that Cincinnati must instead prove a reasonable fit between the city's objective—aesthetics—and the *differences* between newspaper racks and other newsracks. Cincinnati was unable to prove that newsracks housing real estate flyers were any more of an aesthetic blight than newsracks containing newspapers.

vi.   **Regulation of lawyer advertising and soliciting.** The general test for government regulation of commercial speech applies to advertising by regulated professionals. But since such advertising poses special problems some additional rules apply. States may impose reasonable disclosure requirements in order to ensure that advertising is not misleading. States may prohibit face-to-face client solicitation involving fraud, deception, or overbearing and oppressive behavior. States also may restrict mail solicitation of personal injury victims.

(a)   **Lawyer advertising generally protected**

In *Bates v. State Bar of Arizona*, 433 U.S. 350 (1977), the Court struck down an Arizona rule against lawyer advertising as applied to a newspaper advertisement by Bates, asking "Do You Need a Lawyer?" followed by a listing of fees for various routine uncontested matters. Arizona argued that prohibitions on lawyer advertising were justified in order to protect the quality of legal services, prevent unnecessary litigation, and keep fees down. The Court rejected all of these justifications but did not say what standard of review it was applying.

A series of later cases declared that absent some substantial interest a state may not ban truthful advertising by professionals. See *In re RMJ*, 455 U.S. 191 (1982); *Peel v. Attorney Registration and Disciplinary Commission of Illinois*, 496 U.S. 91 (1990); *Ibanez v. Florida Dept. of Business & Professional Regulation*, 512 U.S. 136 (1994).

(b)   **Mandated disclosure.** Lawyers may be compelled to disclose facts necessary to make their advertising not misleading, but the mandated disclosures may not be so voluminous as to preclude advertising true facts about the lawyer's credentials. *Zauderer v. Office of Disciplinary Counsel*, 471 U.S. 626 (1985), exemplifies the principle. Zauderer had advertised that in contingency cases, "if there is no recovery, no legal fees are owed," but did not mention that a client might incur liability for costs. The Court voided the state's advertising ban, but ruled that it could validly compel Zauderer to disclose the omitted fact if he chose to advertise his contingency arrangements.

(c) **Regulation of lawyers' solicitation.** When lawyers solicit clients in person they are subject to a great deal more regulation. Fraudulent, dishonest, overbearing, or deceitful solicitation may be barred altogether, even if no actual harm results. Personal solicitation of clients for "political" litigation is protected unless *actual harm* is proven by the state. Direct mail solicitation of clients cannot be barred altogether but can be regulated under the general test for commercial speech regulations.

- *Ohralik v. Ohio State Bar,* 436 U.S. 447 (1978). Ohralik directly solicited "two young accident victims at a time when they were especially incapable of making informed judgments or of assessing and protecting their own interests." Ohralik "solicited Carol McClintock in a hospital room where she lay in traction and sought out Wanda Lou Holbert on the day she came home from the hospital." He used "a concealed tape recorder . . . to insure . . . evidence of . . . oral assent to the representation." To cap it all, he "refused to withdraw" when requested to do so. The Court upheld discipline of Ohralik even with no showing of harm to the clients because of his extremely self-regarding conduct, but did *not* rule that states could bar *all* in-person solicitation.

- *In re Primus,* 436 U.S. 412 (1978). In a companion case to *Ohralik* the Court reversed discipline of an ACLU lawyer who had offered to represent a woman who had been sterilized in order to receive public medical assistance. Because the solicitation was not for private financial gain, and was on behalf of an organization that uses litigation as a form of political expression, the Court ruled that the state must prove *actual harm* before it could impose discipline.

- *Shapero v. Kentucky Bar Assn.,* 486 U.S. 466 (1988). The Court voided a prohibition on truthful, nondeceptive, direct mail solicitation of targeted clients. Unlike face-to-face solicitation, a letter involves no possibility of pressure tactics since it can always be thrown away by the recipient.

- *Florida Bar v. Went For It, Inc.*, 515 U.S. 618 (1995). In a decision limiting the scope of *Shapero* the Court, 5 to 4, upheld a Florida bar rule prohibiting direct mail solicitation of personal injury victims or their families within thirty days after the injury. The Court applied the basic *Central Hudson* test for commercial speech regulations. It found the state's interests— protecting "the privacy and tranquility of personal injury victims" and protecting the "flagging reputations of Florida lawyers"—to be substantial. The ban directly advanced the goal because there was ample evidence of the public distaste for such solicitations. The rule was narrowly tailored to the objective since it was limited in time and did not foreclose other advertising methods.

(d) Accountants' solicitation. The Court is less tolerant of state barriers to solicitation of clients by accountants, apparently on the theory that accountants are less likely than lawyers to engage in sharp and misleading practices. In *Edenfield v. Fane*, 507 U.S. 761 (1993), the Court invalidated a Florida ban on in-person or direct mail solicitation of clients by accountants. Florida could not prove that its regulation was *reasonably tailored* to serve a *substantial state interest*. Although the standard applied appears more lenient (and thus implies greater state power to control accountant solicitation) the Court stressed that accountancy clients are better able to fend for themselves.

vii. **Regulation of commercial speech promoting lawful vice.** In two cases involving advertising of legal gambling the Court applied the *Central Hudson* test but suggested in dicta that governments might partially prohibit commercial speech that advertises lawful "vice," on the theory that the governmental power to prohibit the advertised conduct implies a lesser power to prohibit some speech promoting the conduct. But the Court has never ruled that regulation of commercial speech promoting "lawful vice" should be given more lenient review than *Central Hudson* and a plurality in *44 Liquormart* has rejected *Posadas*.

(a) *Posadas de Puerto Rico Assoc. v. Tourism Co. of Puerto Rico,* 478 U.S. 328 (1986). Puerto Rico permitted certain forms of casino gambling but prohibited any casino advertising calculated to reach Puerto Ricans. The Court upheld the speech restriction. Puerto Rico had a substantial interest in discouraging gambling by Puerto Ricans, the regulation directly advanced that interest, and was narrowly tailored to its accomplishment. Puerto Rico had no practical alternative methods to discourage gambling by Puerto Ricans while simultaneously encouraging tourists to do so. In dicta, the Court observed that even though gambling was legal its promotion to Puerto Ricans could be prohibited because "the greater power to completely ban casino gambling necessarily includes the lesser power to ban advertising of casino gambling." This principle—that commercial speech can be banned simply because the underlying conduct might be banned—knows no boundaries. Taken literally it would remove virtually all constitutional protection for commercial speech. See also *United States v. Edge Broadcasting Co.,* 509 U.S. 418 (1993), in which the Court upheld the validity of a federal law that bars broadcast licensees from airing lottery advertising unless they are in a state that allows lotteries. The Court noted that Congress could "ban all radio or television lottery advertisements, even by stations in States that have legalized lotteries."

(b) Repudiation of the "lawful vice" exception. In *Rubin v. Coors Brewing Co.,* the Court refused to recognize an exception to *Central Hudson* for regulation of commercial advertising of beer. *44 Liquormart* appeared to repudiate the *Posadas* "lawful vice" exception and *Greater New Orleans Broadcasting Assn. v. United States,* 527 U.S. 173 (1999), did so explicitly. In *Greater New Orleans* the Court applied *Central Hudson* to void a federal law banning broadcasters from airing lottery results. In so doing, the Court repeated that the *Posadas* "greater-includes-the-lesser" rationale was defunct.

D. CONTENT-NEUTRAL REGULATIONS OF SPEECH

1. Overview

Content-neutral speech regulations restrict speech regardless of the "communicative impact" such speech has upon listeners. Deciding which regulations are actually content neutral is not always obvious. See section D.2, infra. Content-neutral speech restrictions receive more lenient judicial scrutiny than content-based restriction. For a content-neutral speech regulation to be valid, generally the government must prove that the regulation (1) is *"justified without reference to the content of the regulated speech,"* (2) *"promotes a substantial government interest that would be achieved less effectively absent the regulation,"* and (3) leaves open *"ample alternative channels"* of communication. See *Ward v. Rock Against Racism,* 491 U.S. 781 (1989). This intermediate level of scrutiny is also stated in slightly different form as follows: A "government regulation is sufficiently justified if it is [1] [*otherwise valid*]; if it [2] *furthers an important or substantial governmental interest*; if [3] the governmental interest is *unrelated to the suppression of free expression*; and if [4] the *incidental restriction on [free speech] is no greater than essential* to the furtherance of that interest." *United States v. O'Brien*, 391 U.S. 367 (1968). The *O'Brien* and *Ward* tests have converged in recent years, with *O'Brien* being the dominant test. Although courts do not commonly do so, the two tests can be merged into a single rule as follows: Content-neutral speech regulations must (1) further an important or substantial state interest that (2) is unrelated to suppression of ideas, (3) be no more speech restrictive than necessary to promote the interest most effectively, (4) at least leave open ample alternative channels of communication, and (5) otherwise be valid.

2. **Defining Content Neutrality**

   a. **Overview.** Some facially content-neutral speech regulations are treated as content based. Some facially content-based speech regulations are treated as content neutral. There are four common patterns.

   - *Facially Neutral, Neutrally Applied.* This is the classic content-neutral speech regulation; e.g., a law barring all amplified speech in public during the hours of midnight until 6 A.M.

   - *Facially Neutral but Applied on the Basis of the Communicative Impact of the Speech.* Such laws appear to be content neutral but are actually content based. (See section D.2.b, infra.)

   - *Facially Neutral but Motivated by a Desire to Suppress Speech on the Basis of Its Content.* Such laws appear to be content neutral but are not so intended. If there is good evidence of a motive to suppress speech on the basis of its content such laws will be treated as content based. (See section D.2.c, infra.)

   - *Facially **Content Based** but Motivated by a Desire to Control Noncommunicative "Secondary Effects" of Speech.* While such laws appear to be content based the Court treats them as content neutral so long as there is convincing evidence that the laws were intended only to control secondary effects of speech unrelated to communication. This doctrine has only been applied to laws restricting indecent but nonobscene speech. (See section D.2.d, infra.)

   b. **Facially content-neutral regulations whose application depends on the communicative impact of speech.** Content-neutral speech restrictions that are applied on the basis of the subject matter of the speech are content based.

Example: A city bans all public speaking in its parks from 11 P.M. to 6 A.M., but only applies the ban to political speech. When enforcement turns on the subject matter of the speech it becomes content based.

c.   **Facially content-neutral regulations motivated by a desire to suppress speech on the basis of its content.** When a government adopts a facially content-neutral speech regulation for the purpose of suppressing only certain speech it will be treated as a content-based regulation.

 ## EXAMPLE AND ANALYSIS

Eichman was charged with violation of a federal law making it a crime for anyone "knowingly" to mutilate, deface, defile, burn, or trample upon the U.S. flag. The government conceded that the forbidden acts were symbolic expression, but contended that the law should be upheld since it was content neutral—it did not "target expressive conduct on the basis of the content of its message." The Court rejected that argument. "Although [the law] contains no explicit content-based limitations, [it] is nevertheless clear that the Government's asserted *interest* is . . . concerned with the content of . . . expression." The Court treated the law as content based and invalidated it. *United States v. Eichman*, 496 U.S. 310 (1990).

d.   **Facially content-based regulations motivated by a desire to control noncommunicative "secondary effects" of speech.** Content-based speech regulations that are intended to control "secondary effects" of speech unrelated to the communicative impact of the speech are treated as content neutral. This doctrine arose in the context of and has been confined to regulations concerning nonobscene speech about sexuality, usually pornography.

 ## EXAMPLES AND ANALYSIS

Example: Renton, Washington, adopted a zoning ordinance that restricted "adult theaters"—those exhibiting nonobscene pornography—to locations in about 5% of Renton's total area. The ordinance plainly "treat[ed] theaters that specialize in adult films differently from other kinds of theaters." But since the ordinance was "aimed not at the *content* of [adult] films . . . but rather at the *secondary effects* of such theaters on the surrounding community" the Court regarded the ordinance as content neutral and upheld its validity after applying content-neutral analysis. *Renton v. Playtime*

Theatres, Inc., 475 U.S. 41 (1986). (See also *Young v. American Mini Theatres,* 427 U.S. 50 (1976), discussed supra.)

Example: The city of Erie adopted an ordinance banning public nudity and applied that ordinance to erotic dancers in a nightclub. Because such dancing is "expressive conduct" the Court applied *O'Brien.* Erie's objective was not related to the suppression of ideas because the city sought to "deter crime" and prevent other "deleterious effects" associated with the mere presence of nude dancing establishments. *City of Erie v. Pap's A.M.,* 120 S. Ct. 1382 (2000).

Laws that address the harmful "secondary effects" of speech must still satisfy the intermediate scrutiny applicable to content-neutral speech regulations.

EXAMPLE AND ANALYSIS

The Court voided a Mt. Ephraim, New Jersey, zoning ordinance that totally excluded vendors of nonobscene sexually oriented material. Mt. Ephraim argued that the ordinance was content neutral because it was intended to address the secondary effects of such speech—the social squalor and crime that coalesces around businesses catering to those unduly preoccupied with sex. The Court accepted this argument but applied content-neutral analysis to strike down the law. The ordinance severely restricted speech because it failed to "leave open adequate alternative channels of communication." *Schad v. Mt. Ephraim,* 452 U.S. 61 (1981).

The concept of "secondary effects of speech" refers to phenomena that result from the speech, but *which are **not** directly produced by the communicative impact of the speech.*

EXAMPLES AND ANALYSIS

Example: The Court voided a D.C. law barring display within 500 feet of any foreign embassy of any sign that might bring the foreign government into "public odium" or "public disrepute." The District of Columbia claimed that the law was content neutral since it was intended to address a secondary effect of such speech—the increased likelihood of crime or public disorder. The Court rejected the argument, and a plurality explained why: "Listeners' reactions to speech are not . . . 'secondary effects' [of speech]." Speech regulations "that focus on the direct impact of speech on its audience'' are content based. The Court applied content-based analysis and struck down the law. *Boos v. Barry,* 485 U.S. 312 (1988).

Example: The secondary effects of speech that Renton sought to control were crime and blight associated with the mere existence of "adult theaters." Renton's justification for regulating adult theaters had nothing to do with the content of the speech or the impact of the speech on viewers, but much to do with controlling crime that can empirically be demonstrated follows in the wake of such tawdry amusements. If Renton had justified its ordinance "by the city's desire to prevent the psychological damage it felt was associated with viewing adult movies," the ordinance would have been treated as content based.

---

3. **"Time, Place, and Manner" Restrictions**

Content-neutral regulations that restrict the "time, place, and manner" of speech must be *reasonable, effectively promote a substantial government interest,* and *leave open ample alternative channels of communication.*

a. **Effective promotion of a substantial interest.** The government need *not* employ the *least speech-restrictive* means of achieving its objective.

 # EXAMPLES AND ANALYSIS

Example: The National Park Service permitted demonstrators to erect "tent cities" in Lafayette Park and the Mall to illustrate homelessness, but refused to permit demonstrators to sleep in the tents. The Court assumed that the curbed activity was symbolic expression but upheld the refusal. It was content neutral (all camping was prohibited) and closely connected to "the Government's substantial interest in maintaining the parks [in] an attractive and intact condition" even though the Park Service might have had "less speech restrictive alternatives" open to it. *Clark v. Community for Creative Non-Violence,* 468 U.S. 288 (1983).

Example: To control noise levels, New York City required that events staged in Central Park's Bandshell use city technicians and sound systems. The court upheld this content-neutral requirement as narrowly tailored to its objective. "[S]o long as a regulation promotes a substantial governmental interest that would be achieved less effectively absent the regulation," the regulation is sufficiently narrowly tailored. Speech restrictions may *not* be *substantially overbroad* but they also need *not* be the *least speech-restrictive alternative* open to the government. *Ward v. Rock Against Racism,* 491 U.S. 781 (1989).

---

b. **Ample alternative channels of communication.** So long as the content-neutral speech regulation permits the speaker the opportunity to reach the same audience with the same message, the government has left open "ample alternative channels of communication."

 # EXAMPLES AND ANALYSIS

Example: In response to antiabortion pickets who congregated outside a physician's residence protesting his performance of abortions, a community enacted an ordinance prohibiting "focused picketing"—picketing that focuses upon and takes place outside any particular residence. The Court, 6 to 3, upheld the ordinance. It left open "ample alternative channels of communication" because the protesters were free to deliver their message by marching, door-to-door calls, unfocused picketing, leaflets, or mailings to neighbors of the physician. *Frisby v. Shultz,* 487 U.S. 474 (1988).

Example: To minimize "visual clutter," Ladue, Missouri prohibited homeowners from displaying *any* signs on their private property. Although content neutral, the Court unanimously found the law invalid because it failed to leave open ample alternative channels of communication—there was no "practical substitute" for a "yard or window sign" to reach the intended audience with the homeowner's message. *Ladue v. Gilleo,* 512 U.S. 43 (1994).

4. **Symbolic Conduct**

   a. **Overview.** Because the First Amendment protects free *expression,* not *just* free speech, some nonverbal conduct that is *symbolic* is also protected. Almost any action may be claimed to have some symbolic value. The government has a legitimate interest in regulating non-expressive conduct. This branch of free expression law seeks to reconcile these concerns.

      - First, a line is drawn between *symbolic conduct*—which is treated as speech—and ordinary, nonsymbolic conduct. Symbolic conduct is *intended to convey an idea* and *is reasonably understood by onlookers to convey that idea.*

      - Second, the Court has created a variation of the content-neutral test for review of symbolic conduct—one that tries to identify and invalidate regulations designed to *suppress ideas* while permitting *narrowly drawn* regulations that advance *important* or *substantial government interests.*

b. Early developments. The Court recognized that some symbolic conduct was protected speech when it struck down California's ban on display of a red flag "as a sign, symbol or emblem of opposition to organized government." *Stromberg v. California,* 283 U.S. 359 (1931). In *Brown v. Louisiana,* 383 U.S. 131 (1966), the Court reversed breach of the peace convictions based on the silent presence of young blacks in a whites-only public library, in protest of racial segregation. The Court declared that First Amendment "rights are not confined to verbal expression," but "embrace appropriate . . . . action" including "protest by silent and reproachful presence."

c. The *O'Brien* test. The modern standard of review for regulations restricting symbolic conduct was developed in *United States v. O'Brien.* Otherwise valid laws restricting symbolic conduct are valid if the following criteria are met.

- The law furthers an *important* or *substantial governmental interest,*

- The government interest is *unrelated to the suppression of ideas,* and

- The restriction on expression is *no greater than necessary* to further the government's interest.

If a regulation is related to the suppression of ideas it is *not* automatically void. As with all content-based speech restrictions it is valid only if the government proves that it is necessary to achieve a compelling government interest.

    i. *United States v. O'Brien,* 391 U.S. 367 (1968). O'Brien burned his draft registration card on the steps of a Boston courthouse and was convicted of violating a federal law that made it a crime knowingly to destroy a draft registration card. The Court concluded that even if O'Brien's conduct were speech the law "substantially furthers the smooth and proper functioning" of the draft registration system by assuring that a registrant's draft status could be immediately determined by inspecting the draft card that the registrant was required to carry at all times. The Court said that interest was unrelated to free expression and "perceive[d] no alternative means that would more precisely and narrowly assure the continuing availability of [draft cards] than [the law at issue]."

d. Flag burning and other flag obloquy. The contemptuous use of the American flag as a means for protest has generated much law. The Court has consistently voided all attempts to prohibit flag destruction or "misuse" because such attempts are *necessarily related to suppression of ideas.* By its nature, a flag is a *pure symbol*—its existence conveys a message of national identity. A national flag conveys that message *no matter how it is used.*

Example: An American flag used as a bedspread remains a symbol of the nation even while it assumes another role as bedspread. By contrast, a piece of plain brown cotton cloth is just a bedspread.

The fact that a flag cannot escape its symbolic role means that its public destruction is inherently a communicative event.

Example: If you publicly burn an American flag you cannot escape the fact that you are either expressing contempt or respect for it and the country it represents. It all depends on the context, but it must be one or the other. The flag that is burned on the public streets amid other protest expresses contempt. The ceremonial burning of a frayed flag is an expression of respect. Even if your professor impassively burns a small paper flag in the classroom to illustrate this principle one of these messages will be communicated.

   i. ***Spence v. Washington,*** 418 U.S. 405 (1974). In order to protest the Vietnam War Spence taped a large peace symbol onto his American flag, and hung the flag outside his window. Spence was convicted under Washington's flag misuse statute, which prohibited the exhibition of any U.S. flag to which had been attached any "design." Spence's adorned flag was speech because "[a]n intent to convey a particularized message was present, and in the surrounding circumstances the likelihood was great that the message would be understood by those who viewed it." The Court overturned Spence's conviction because Washington was unable to prove a credible governmental interest unrelated to the suppression of expression. Washington's claimed interest was to prevent deception— people might think that flags with designs implied governmental endorsement of the combined message. Ridiculous, snorted the Court, in a classic understatement: "There was no risk that [Spence's] acts would mislead viewers into assuming that the Government endorsed his viewpoint."

   ii. ***Texas v. Johnson,*** 491 U.S. 397 (1989). Johnson publicly burned an American flag as part of a political protest. Lest there be any doubt about the message, the protesters chanted "America, the red, white, and blue, we spit on you," while Johnson incinerated the flag. He was convicted of flag "desecration," defined as damaging the flag "in a way that the actor knows will seriously offend one or more persons likely to observe . . . his action." In a 5 to 4 vote, the Court reversed Johnson's conviction. As in *Spence,* the Court concluded that Texas had no interest in prohibiting flag burning that was unrelated to the suppression of ideas. Texas's asserted interest in protecting the flag "as a symbol of nationhood and national unity" was directly related to the suppression of ideas. Texas's claim that it was interested in preventing a breach of the peace was bogus. The majority recognized that the "purely symbolic" quality of the flag made any law prohibiting its destruction or "misuse" a content-based suppression of speech.

(a)   **The dissent.** The dissenters, led by Chief Justice Rehnquist, likened flag burning to "fighting words." They asserted that flag burning was "the equivalent of an inarticulate grunt or roar . . . indulged in not to express any particular idea, but to antagonize others." The dissenters did not confront the fact that flag burning antagonizes precisely because it conveys a powerful message, nor did they address the *Cohen v. California* principle that expression is protected as much for its emotive as its cognitive content.

iii.   *United States v. Eichman,* 496 U.S. 310 (1990). *Texas v. Johnson* sparked a political row. A constitutional amendment to overturn the decision was defeated in Congress, and the Flag Protection Act of 1989 was enacted instead. The Act made it a crime for anyone "knowingly" to mutilate, deface, defile, burn, or trample upon the U.S. flag. Eichman was charged with violation of the Act but a district judge dismissed the indictment. On appeal, the government conceded that the forbidden acts were symbolic expression, but contended that the law should be upheld since it was content neutral—it did not "target expressive conduct on the basis of the content of its message." The Court rejected that argument. "Although [the law] contains no explicit content-based limitations, [it] is nevertheless clear that the Government's asserted *interest* is . . . concerned with the content of . . . expression." The government asserted that the "physical integrity" of the flag must be protected in order "to preserve the flag's status as a symbol of our Nation and certain national ideals." Because the flag inherently has that status the Court recognized that the claimed government interest exists only to muzzle those who would like to deliver a contrary message. The Court treated the law as content based and invalidated it.

e.   **Nude dancing:** *Barnes v. Glen Theatre,* 501 U.S. 560 (1991). Indiana's public indecency law, as interpreted by the Indiana Supreme Court, prohibited nudity in places of public accommodation. The Kitty Kat Lounge, a South Bend saloon featuring nude dancing, sought to enjoin enforcement of the law. The Court, 5 to 4, upheld the law. Nude dancing was symbolic conduct, but "only marginally so." The Court applied the *O'Brien* test and concluded that regulation of public nudity furthers the substantial state interest of preserving Indiana's collective moral judgment that people ought not to appear "in the nude among strangers in public places." Indiana's interest in suppressing public nudity had everything to do with preserving this sense of public decorum and little to do with stifling public expressions of "eroticism" and sexuality. The law's restriction of this message was no broader than necessary to achieve the public interest at stake—nude dancers could deliver the same erotic message by employing the scantiest of clothing.

E. GOVERNMENT AS SOVEREIGN AND PROPRIETOR

1. Regulating Speech on Public Property: The Public Forum Doctrine

a. **Overview.** Public property is not uniform. Some public property—such as streets or parks—is open to everyone. Access to other public property—such as the Oval Office in the White House or a nuclear missile submarine—is restricted to a select few. The public forum doctrine reacts to these differences in the character of public property by permitting governments discretion to restrict speech on public property that is for good reason closed to the public, and forbidding undue restrictions upon speech in a **public forum**—a public place customarily or deliberately opened to the public.

b. **The general standards of review**

   i. *United States v. Grace,* 461 U.S. 171 (1983). A federal law prohibited anyone from displaying on the public sidewalks surrounding the Supreme Court building "any flag, banner, or device designed [to] bring into public notice any party, organization or movement." The Court voided the law. The Court explained the general rules governing speech restrictions in a **public forum.**

   - *Speech Regulation Short of Outright Prohibition.* Governments may enforce "reasonable time, place, and manner restrictions" if they are "content-neutral, . . . narrowly tailored to serve a significant government interest, and leave open ample alternative channels of communication."

   - *Absolute Prohibitions of Speech.* Governments may completely prohibit speech only if the prohibition is "narrowly drawn to accomplish a compelling governmental interest."

   - *Content-Based Regulation.* Content-based regulation is subject to strict scrutiny.

c. **Defining the public forum: A key issue.** Because the standard of review of restrictions upon speech in a public forum is so much stricter than when such regulations restrict speech in a nonpublic forum, identification of public fora is crucial to analysis. There are two ways in which public property can become a public forum.

- *Traditional Public Fora.* Some places are so traditionally endowed with unlimited public access that they are considered public fora. Streets, sidewalks, public parks, squares, and gathering places are the classic examples.

- *Deliberately Dedicated Public Fora.* Some places are not traditional public fora but, because the government has deliberately opened them to the public for speech purposes, they become public fora. These public fora can be either *unlimited public fora* (if the government has deliberately opened them to all speakers) or, more commonly, *limited public fora* (if the government has opened them for only certain limited speech purposes). A limited public forum is a public forum only with respect to the speech purposes for which it was opened.

i. **The traditional public forum.** The core rationale for the traditional public forum is that "streets and parks . . . have immemorially been held in trust for the use of the public and, time out of mind, have been used for purposes of assembly, communicating thought between citizens, and discussing public questions." *Hague v. CIO,* 307 U.S. 496 (1939). In short, the public has a "prescriptive easement" to speak in the parks, streets, squares, sidewalks, and other traditional public gathering places. Relying on this concept the Court struck down municipal laws prohibiting distribution of leaflets in the streets. *Schneider v. State,* 308 U.S. 147 (1939); *Jamison v. Texas,* 318 U.S. 413 (1943). In *Jamison* the Court squarely rejected the proposition that governments have "the power absolutely to prohibit the use of the streets for the communication of ideas."

ii. **The limited public forum: Opened for limited purposes only.** Whenever a government voluntarily dedicates public property to speech purposes it creates a public forum. These voluntarily created public fora are usually limited to some particular speech purpose. The same standard of review applies to the limited public forum as to the traditional public forum. There are, however, *two key differences* between the **limited public forum** and the **traditional public forum.**

- *Closure of the Forum.* A government may close a limited public forum to speech whenever it wishes, but until it does so it must comply with the speech standards governing public fora. **Example:** The federal government may open a military base for speech purposes, then decide to close it to public speech and operate it as a closed military post.

By contrast, a government may not close a traditional public forum to speech. **Example:** A city may not close a public park to speech and continue to operate it as a park. It can, however, convert the park to a prison and close the prison off to speech.

- *Limiting the Forum to its Dedicated Purpose.* A government may limit the speech uses of a limited public forum to the specific purposes for which it was voluntarily opened. **Example:** If a public school voluntarily opens its facilities to student groups for speech purposes, it may refuse an adult organization access to the facilities for speech purposes. The school created a limited public forum, limited to student usage for speech purposes.

  As the following cases demonstrate, a government may establish a limited public forum but its method of doing so must be viewpoint-neutral. If the limited forum is limited to speakers of a particular viewpoint a limited forum has been created in a manner that is presumptively invalid.

(a) **State fairs:** *Heffron v. International Society for Krishna Consciousness,* 452 U.S. 640 (1981). The Minnesota State Fair, which draws 100,000 people daily to its 125 acre site, prohibited distribution of printed material except from an officially licensed booth. Krishna solicitors challenged the ban, which the Court upheld. The Court ruled that the state fair "is a limited public forum in that it exists to provide a means for a great number of exhibitors temporarily to present their products or views [to] a large number of people in an efficient fashion." It was not voluntarily opened to the general speech free-for-all that characterizes city streets. The fair's prohibition was content neutral.

(b) **Public university facilities:** *Widmar v. Vincent,* 454 U.S. 263 (1981). By making its facilities available to student groups except those who wished to engage in "religious worship or religious teaching," a public university created a limited public forum. But the device for doing so was content based and thus subjected to strict scrutiny. The Court struck down the religious ban.

(c) **Public school facilities:** *Lamb's Chapel v. Center Moriches Union School District,* 508 U.S. 384 (1993). A public school created a limited public forum in its facilities by making them available after school hours for social, civic, and recreational uses but not for religious use. The Court invalidated the exclusion of religious users because the exclusion was viewpoint based and failed strict scrutiny.

(d) ***Rosenberger v. Rector and Visitors of the University of Virginia,*** 515 U.S. 819 (1995). The University of Virginia paid from the Student Activities Fund, generated by mandatory student contributions, the publication costs of student organizations advocating "particular positions or ideological viewpoints," but excluding religious organizations. The Court ruled that while the university thereby created a limited public forum in the fund it had impermissibly discriminated on the basis of viewpoint. The rule was invalidated.

iii. **Public property but not public fora.** A wide variety of public places have been held to be **nonpublic fora,** either because they lack the indicia of the traditional public forum or the government owner has not voluntarily dedicated the property to speech purposes. Nondiscriminatory speech restrictions in nonpublic fora are valid if they are *reasonable—rationally related to a legitimate state interest.*

(a) **Jail premises:** *Adderley v. Florida,* 385 U.S. 39 (1966). A crowd of 200 students gathered at a county jail to protest the arrest of several of their cohorts at a civil rights demonstration. The demonstrators blocked the jail entrance and driveway, areas normally used only by sheriff's deputies. The sheriff asked them to leave and warned them they would be arrested if they did not. Adderley and over 100 others were arrested and convicted of "malicious and mischievous trespass." The Court, 5 to 4, sustained the convictions. "The State, no less than a private owner of property, has power to preserve the property under its control for the use to which it is lawfully dedicated." The "part of the jail grounds" on which the demonstration occurred was "reserved for jail uses" and was not open to large public gatherings. It was neither a traditional nor dedicated public forum.

(b) **Advertising space of public transport:** *Lehman v. City of Shaker Heights,* 418 U.S. 298 (1974). A public transit system that offered advertising space on its vehicles refused to accept paid political advertising by a candidate for public office. The Court upheld the refusal. A plurality ruled that the advertising space was not a public forum. There was no traditional access right. The transit authority was free to refuse ads so long as it acted in a nondiscriminatory fashion. Closing of all political speech in a nonpublic forum was permissible; denying advertising space to only some political speakers would not be valid.

(c) Military bases: *Greer v. Spock,* 424 U.S. 828 (1976). Although the Fort Dix military reservation permitted civilian vehicular traffic and free civilian access to the unrestricted portions of the base, it prohibited "political speeches." Benjamin Spock, the 1972 People's Party presidential candidate, was denied permission to hold a meeting to discuss politics with servicemembers and their families. The Court, 6 to 2, sustained the prohibition. "[T]he business of . . . Fort Dix [is] to train soldiers, not to provide a public forum." Fort Dix's policy of permitting civilian access to portions of the base was not enough to demonstrate a voluntary opening of the base to political speech.

(d) Public school mail system: *Perry Education Assn. v. Perry Local Educators Assn.,* 460 U.S. 37 (1983). A public school district made its interschool mail system available to the teachers' union that was the collective bargaining agent for the teachers in the district, but denied access to the mail system to a rival union. The Court upheld the denial, having concluded that the school district had not voluntarily opened its mail system for speech purposes. Rather, the mail system had been made available to the collective bargaining agent simply to facilitate its obligation to represent all the teachers.

(e) Charity drive in public workplace: *Cornelius v. NAACP Legal Defense & Educational Fund,* 473 U.S. 788 (1985). By executive order, the federal government permitted only certain tax-exempt charitable organizations to participate in the CFC, a coordinated charity drive directed at federal employees during working hours. Legal and political advocacy groups were expressly barred. The Court upheld the order, concluding that the CFC was a nonpublic forum. There was no traditional access right. The government had opened its workplace to limited charitable solicitation *not* "to provide an open forum" but "to minimize the disruption to the workplace . . . by *lessening* the amount of expressive activity." The government's *intention* was critical—it *did not intend* to dedicate its property to speech purposes.

(f) *United States v. Kokinda,* 493 U.S. 807 (1990). In violation of a postal regulation a political advocacy group solicited contributions on a post office sidewalk. The sidewalk ran from a parking lot to the post office and was used solely by postal customers. It was not a public thoroughfare and so was not a traditional public forum even though it was open to the public. As in *Cornelius* the Court relied on the lack of proof of any governmental *intent* to open its sidewalk to speech purposes. Indeed, there was strong proof to the contrary. The Court applied nonpublic forum analysis and upheld the regulation as a reasonable content-neutral regulation of speech.

2.   Public Education

In balancing the free speech interests of students and the legitimate regulatory interests of public schools, the courts have used three principles:

- The older the student, the greater the speech interest,

- The closer the speech is to the business of the school, the greater the government interest in regulating it, and

- The further the speech is from the core of the First Amendment, the weaker the speech interest.

    a.   Elementary and secondary education. The idea that as students mature their speech interests increase is justified by the theory that younger students need behavioral instruction as much as cognitive instruction, and that such instruction necessarily involves some significant curbs on speech that would be impermissible in a less restrictive context. The deference with which the Court reviews school speech regulations decreases as the students become young adults.

        i.   Some protection of student speech: *Tinker v. Des Moines School District,* 393 U.S. 503 (1969). The Court struck down a public school regulation banning the wearing of armbands as applied to the wearing of a black armband in protest of the Vietnam War. The Court treated this symbolic conduct as "pure speech" and concluded that the regulation discriminated on the basis of the speaker's viewpoint. While the Court recognized that students do not leave their free speech rights "at the schoolhouse gate," the Court also observed that otherwise constitutionally protected student speech might lose its protection when it "materially and substantially interfere[s] with the requirements of appropriate discipline in the operation of the school."

        ii.   But not much protection. When student speech touches upon subjects of "low value"—far removed from the core First Amendment values of self-governance—or when the speech is directly germane to the curriculum, the Court defers to the *reasonable* judgments of school administrators.

(a) *Bethel School Dist. No. 403 v. Fraser,* 478 U.S. 675 (1986). Before a high school assembly of about 600 students, Fraser delivered a nominating speech for another student's bid for a student office. The speech was laden with sexual innuendo, which delighted some students and bewildered others. The school disciplined Fraser for his speech. The Court upheld the discipline, reasoning that Fraser's "vulgar and lewd . . . sexually explicit monologue" was "wholly inconsistent with the 'fundamental values' of public school education" and "unrelated to any political viewpoint." The twin messages of *Fraser* are that *nonpolitical speech* and *educationally inappropriate speech* that occurs *in school* may be regulated to prevent "undermin[ing] the school's basic educational mission."

(b) *Hazelwood School District v. Kuhlmeier,* 484 U.S. 260 (1988). A high school principal censored the school newspaper, run by students in connection with a journalism course, by excluding a story on student pregnancy and the impact of parental divorce on some of the school's students. The Court upheld the censorship. First, it concluded that student speech that is "supervised by faculty members and designed to impart particular knowledge or skills to student participants and audiences" is "part of the school curriculum." Second, the free speech guarantee permits educators to exercise "editorial control over the style and content of student speech in school-sponsored expressive activities so long as their actions are *reasonably related to legitimate pedagogical concerns.*" The fact that the articles concerned issues of public importance did not matter. The Court said that Tinker requires schools to tolerate *nondisruptive student political speech* but not "affirmatively to promote particular student speech." Since the newspaper was a school sponsored expressive activity, apparently even "high value" quasi-political speech could be suppressed.

(c) **Summary.** *Fraser* and *Kuhlmeier,* taken together, suggest that the ability of school administrators to control *nonpolitical* student speech may be quite broad. *Fraser* indicated that inculcation of "fundamental values" (e.g., civility, self-restraint, a sense of public decorum) are "legitimate pedagogical concerns." *Kuhlmeier* extends judicial deference of student speech regulation to "school sponsored expressive activities." Moreover, *Kuhlmeier* limits *Tinker* to nondisruptive student expression occurring outside of "school sponsored expressive activities," implying that even political speech can be regulated in school sponsored activities.

 # Example and Analysis

A public high school cheerleading group, performing at a high school football game held in a municipal stadium, employs sexual innuendo in words and gestures. School officials remove the offending cheerleaders from the squad. The sanction is valid. Cheerleading is a school-sponsored expressive activity. The judgment of the administrators that the sexual innuendo was inconsistent with the school's fundamental values is valid so long as it is reasonable.

---

   iii. **Banning books in the public school library:** *Board of Education, Island Trees Union Free School District v. Pico,* 457 U.S. 853 (1982). The validity of book banning in public school libraries turns on the motivation for the ban. After consultation with a committee of parents and teachers, the school board removed from the school library nine books, including works by Kurt Vonnegut, Desmond Morris, and Eldridge Cleaver. A federal district court granted summary judgment to the school board, but the Court of Appeals reversed and remanded for a trial on the merits. The Supreme Court affirmed. The issue to be decided at trial was the *motivation* of the school board. If the board was motivated by the desire "to deny [students] access to ideas with which [the school board] disagreed, and if this intent was the *decisive factor* in [the school board's] decision, then [the school board has] exercised [its] discretion in violation of the Constitution." But if the school board removed the books because of a good faith belief that they were vulgar or otherwise educationally unsuitable they would not have violated the Constitution. Suppression of ideas violates free speech, but limiting the school library to educationally suitable materials does not. This fine line turns on the evidence adduced at trial.

b. **University education.** University students enjoy far greater speech rights than their younger counterparts. Outside of "curricular speech"—speech in the classroom or in connection with coursework—student speech is as protected as nonstudent speech.

   i. *Healy v. James,* 408 U.S. 169 (1972). A public university refused to recognize Students for a Democratic Society (SDS) as a campus organization because it was a radical group advocating "violence and disruption." The Court remanded a case challenging the refusal, instructing the lower courts that "the mere expression of [such] repugnant . . . views . . . would not justify the denial of First Amendment rights."

ii.   *Papish v. Board of Curators of the University of Missouri,* 410 U.S. 667 (1973). A public university expelled a student for distributing on campus a newspaper depicting a policeman raping the Statue of Liberty and employing vulgar language. The Court reversed, reasoning that the university had expelled the student because of the content of his speech, and noting that the university could not prohibit expression "in the absence of any disruption of campus order or interference with the rights of others."

iii.   *Doe v. University of Michigan,* 721 F. Supp. 852 (E.D. Mich. 1989). A district judge struck down the University of Michigan's student speech code that barred student speech "stigmatizing" a person on account of race, religion, sex, or sexual orientation, under circumstances where the "reasonably foreseeable effect" of such speech might be to interfere with another's "academic efforts."

3.   Public Employment

a.   **Overview.** Unless prohibited by statute, private employers may freely adopt speech rules. Many employers do so for reasons they think are germane to employment. Public employers have the same employer interest that private employers have, but they are also governments.

The idea that a government may condition public employment upon a surrender of free speech rights has been rejected. *Perry v. Sindermann,* 408 U.S. 593 (1972) (discussed in Chapter 8) observed that even though a person has no right to "a valuable government benefit," and even though the benefit can be denied "for any number of reasons," the benefit *cannot* be denied by infringing upon constitutional liberties—"especially . . . freedom of speech."

But some restrictions on the speech rights of public employees are valid. Differing rules apply in each context, but the general theme is judicial *balancing* of the *legitimate reasons the government may have for suppressing expression* and the *value of the speech in terms of the core concerns of the free expression guarantee.*

b.   **Restrictions on speech critical of government policy.** Most private employers have little patience with an employee openly critical of company policy. When the government is the employer, however, the First Amendment demands that the government show more patience. If the critical speech relates to a matter of *public concern* the speech may be regulated only if the *government interest in efficiently delivering public services* outweighs the *employee's interest in speaking.* Both interests must be evaluated in context.

 EXAMPLE AND ANALYSIS

If a Drug Enforcement Administration agent openly advocates the legalization of drugs and opines that "crack usage does no harm to anyone," the statements are surely matters of public concern. The government's interest in punishing such speech is much higher than if a federally employed wildlife biologist makes the same comments. The biologist probably could not be punished for such comments but the DEA agent could. Cf. *Rankin v. McPherson,* infra.

   i.   *Pickering v. Board of Education,* 391 U.S. 563 (1968). The Court held that the dismissal of a public schoolteacher for public statements about the school district's need for more revenue from a proposed new tax violated the teacher's free speech rights. The statements related to a matter of public concern. In balancing "the interests of the teacher, as a citizen, in commenting upon matters of public concern and the interest of the State, as an employer, in promoting the efficiency of the public services it performs through its employees" the Court concluded that the teacher's statements, though "critical of his ultimate employer," had not been proven "to have in any way either impeded the teacher's proper performance of his daily duties in the classroom or to have interfered with the regular operation of the school generally." The Court observed that where the "teacher's public statements are so without foundation as to call into question his fitness [to teach] . . . the statements would merely be evidence of the teacher's general competence, or lack thereof, and not an independent basis for dismissal."

   ii.   *Connick v. Meyers,* 461 U.S. 138 (1983). The Court upheld the dismissal of Meyers, an assistant district attorney, for circulating a questionnaire among the other district attorneys soliciting their views on a variety of workplace issues, including whether they felt pressured to work in political campaigns. The Court concluded that the inquiry regarding coerced political work was barely a "matter of public concern," and upheld Meyers's dismissal because Connick's judgment that the "questionnaire was an act of insubordination which interfered with working relationships" was reasonable given the "close working relationships . . . essential" in a prosecutor's office. The First Amendment did "not require that Connick tolerate action which he reasonably believed would disrupt the office [and] destroy working relations."

iii. ***Rankin v. McPherson,*** 483 U.S. 378 (1987). McPherson, a clerical employee in a county constable's office, was fired for remarking to her coworker after an assassination attempt on the President, "If they go for him again, I hope they get him." The Court, 5 to 4, held that the speech related to a matter of public concern and that McPherson's dismissal violated the First Amendment. Because the remark was made in "the course of a conversation addressing the policies of the President's administration" it was related to matters of public concern. Its "inappropriate or controversial character" was deemed "irrelevant to the question whether it deals with a matter of public concern." There was no proof that the remark had interfered with the efficient functioning of the office and thus the free speech interests of the employee were the weightier in the balance.

c. **Restrictions on partisan political activity.** In the interest of efficiency, avoiding partisan bias in the administration of government services, and avoiding coercion of public employees, both the federal government and some states forbid certain partisan political activities on the part of government workers.

i. ***United Public Workers v. Mitchell,*** 330 U.S. 75 (1947). The federal Hatch Act prohibits federal civil servants from taking "an active part in political management or in a political campaign." The Court upheld the application of this prohibition to a production worker in the U.S. Mint who "was a ward executive . . . of a political party and was politically active on election day as a worker at the polls." Within "reasonable limits," said the Court, Congress could proscribe the political activities of its employees.

ii. ***United States Civil Service Commission v. National Assn. of Letter Carriers,*** 413 U.S. 548 (1973). The Court again upheld the Hatch Act and reaffirmed *Mitchell*, stating that "the problem . . . is to . . . balance" the speech interests of the employee and the "obviously important [government] interests sought to be served by [the] Hatch Act." As close to the core of free speech as active politicking may be, the government's interest was found to be heavier. By the Hatch Act the government sought to achieve three different, but equally important, objectives:

- Unbiased administration of the law, both in actual fact and in appearance,

- Prevent the recruitment of government workers into "a powerful, invincible, and perhaps corrupt political machine," and

- "[M]ake sure that Government employees [are] free from pressure [to] vote in a certain way or perform political chores in order to curry favor with their superiors rather than to act out of their own beliefs."

    iii. *Broadrick v. Oklahoma,* 413 U.S. 601 (1973). The Court upheld an Oklahoma law, typical of laws in all fifty states, patterned after the Hatch Act and applicable to state civil servants.

  d. Patronage. Conditioning public employment on affiliation with the winning political party is a classic American tradition, but taken too far it violates the First Amendment. Political party affiliation may be used as the criterion for *hiring, dismissal, or promotion decisions* **only** where party affiliation is an *appropriate* criterion to ensure *effective job performance.* The burden of proof is upon the government to establish that party affiliation is appropriately employed in connection with any particular job, and must do so by showing that the patronage practice at issue is *"narrowly tailored to further vital governmental interests."*

 # EXAMPLE AND ANALYSIS

Football coaches at public universities formulate policy, but their political affiliation is irrelevant to effective job performance. By contrast, publicly employed election-day poll watchers do not make policy, but the practice of selecting such people from the ranks of the contending political parties is relevant to the performance of the job. See *Branti v. Finkel,* infra.

    i. *Elrod v. Burns,* 427 U.S. 347 (1976). Elrod, a Democrat, became sheriff of Cook County, Illinois, and promptly discharged Burns, a process server, solely because Burns was a Republican. The Court concluded that patronage dismissals may be justified by "the need for political loyalty of employees" in order to implement the policies resulting from the electorate's decision, but that interest was "inadequate to validate patronage wholesale. *Limiting patronage dismissals to policymaking positions is sufficient to achieve this governmental end."* The Court suggested that patronage dismissals must be shown to be "the least restrictive alternative" to accomplishment of the legitimate government end.

ii. *Branti v. Finkel*, 445 U.S. 507 (1980). The Court held, 6 to 3, that the First Amendment voided the discharge of two assistant public defenders solely because of their Republican party affiliation. "[T]he ultimate inquiry is not whether the label 'policymaker' or 'confidential' fits a particular position; rather, **the question is whether the hiring authority can demonstrate that party affiliation is an** *appropriate requirement* **for the** *effective performance* **of the public office involved.**"

iii. *Rutan v. Republican Party of Illinois*, 497 U.S. 62 (1990). The Court concluded that the First Amendment limited the making of *promotion* decisions, as well as *hiring* or *dismissal* decisions, on the basis of party affiliations. In rejecting the application of patronage to promotion decisions for jobs where party affiliation was irrelevant to job performance, the Court stated that in order for governments to justify patronage practices as appropriate to job performance they must prove that the practice at issue is *"narrowly tailored to further vital governmental interests."* Four Justices (Scalia, Rehnquist, O'Connor, and Kennedy) dissented, arguing that *Elrod* and *Branti* should be overruled and condemning the majority's use of the "strict-scrutiny standard" as without "support in our cases."

e. **Loyalty oaths.** Government employers sometimes require employees to affirm their loyalty as a condition to employment. These loyalty oaths may infringe free speech or free association rights of public employees. Such oaths are *valid* so long as they are **not vague** and do **not:**

- Require the disclaimer of present or past *political views,*

- Require the disclaimer of present or past *association* with "subversive" organizations, except to the extent the disclaimer relates to *knowing participation in illegal activities* or *knowing membership coupled with the* **specific intent** *to further the illegal aims of the organization,* or

- Require the disclaimer of *speech protected by the First Amendment.*

i. *Elfbrandt v. Russell*, 384 U.S. 11 (1966). Arizona required public employees to swear, in effect, that they were not members, and would not become members, of the Communist Party or any other organization that the employee knows has as one of its purposes the overthrow of government. Elfbrandt, a prospective schoolteacher, refused to take the oath and the Court held the oath to be invalid. The Court adapted its holding in *Scales v. United States* (see section C.1, supra) to this situation. The oath was invalid since it was not limited to a disclaimer of *knowing* membership in an organization committed to governmental overthrow *coupled with the **specific intent** of furthering the organization's unlawful objectives.*

ii. **Subsequent cases.** After *Elfbrandt,* the Court used the vagueness and overbreadth doctrines to strike down laws that sought to disqualify from public employment those with "subversive" associates or who indulged in "subversive" speech. In *Keyishian v. Board of Regents,* 385 U.S. 589 (1967), the Court voided a New York law prohibiting public schoolteachers and administrators from knowing membership in any organization that advocates the violent overthrow of government. The lack of a specific intent requirement was fatal. In *United States v. Robel,* 389 U.S. 258 (1967), the Court voided a federal law barring employment in any defense facility of knowing members of certain Communist-related organizations. The Court found the law to be overbroad, primarily due to the lack of any specific intent requirement.

f. **Confidential information.** Governments may hobble the speech of employees in order to protect confidential information entrusted to them. *Snepp v. United States,* 444 U.S. 507 (1980), is the foremost case. Snepp, a former CIA agent, published a book about CIA activities in Vietnam. His employment agreement with the CIA obligated him to refrain from publishing anything about the CIA without its prior approval. Snepp neither sought nor obtained prior approval from the CIA. The Court upheld an injunction requiring Snepp to submit future writings to the CIA for prepublication review and an order imposing a constructive trust upon Snepp's book proceeds in favor of the government. The Court reasoned that "the CIA could . . . protect substantial government interests by imposing reasonable restrictions on [speech] that in other contexts might be protected by the First Amendment. The Government has a compelling interest in protecting both the secrecy of information important to our national security and the appearance of confidentiality so essential to the effective operation of [the CIA]. The [employment] agreement . . . is a reasonable means for protecting this vital interest." Three Justices dissented, arguing that since the government conceded that Snepp's book contained no classified, confidential, nonpublic information it had suffered no injury.

g. **Independent contractors protected.** Governments have no more ability to restrict the speech of their independent contractors than their employees. *O'Hare Truck Service, Inc. v. City of Northlake,* 518 U.S. 712 (1996), extended to independent contractors the protection against patronage discharge afforded public employees under *Elrod v. Burns* and *Branti v. Finkel.* (See section E.3.d, supra.) *Board of County Commissioners v. Umbehr,* 518 U.S. 668 (1996), extended to independent contractors the interest-balancing test of *Pickering v. Board of Education.* (See section E.3.b, supra.)

4. Public Sponsorship of Speech

    a. Overview. Governments may sponsor speech they like and decline to sponsor speech they dislike, but governments may not withhold some unrelated benefit from private speakers who use their own resources to say things the government dislikes. Governments may subsidize speech but they may not penalize those who utter disfavored speech.

 ## EXAMPLES AND ANALYSIS

Example: California denied a property tax exemption to veterans who refused to state that they did not favor the forcible overthrow of the government. The denied benefit—the tax exemption—was unrelated to the private speech. The Court held that this was an unconstitutional penalty imposed on free expression. *Speiser v. Randall,* 357 U.S. 513 (1958).

Example: Federal law grants a subsidy to charities by making donations to them tax deductible to the donor, thus encouraging such donations. Federal law denies that subsidy to charities that engage in lobbying by making donations to such charities nondeductible. This disparate treatment was upheld by the Court as a legitimate refusal by Congress to "pay for lobbying out of public moneys." Congress is not required to "subsidize lobbying." The nondeductibility rule was not a penalty because it neither foreclosed a charity's ability to obtain tax deductible donations to support its nonlobbying work nor did it "deny any independent benefit" to a charity that engages in lobbying. *Regan v. Taxation with Representation of Washington,* 461 U.S. 540 (1983).

    b. Subsidies that promote *government* speech. A government may subsidize its *own speech* on the basis of content or even viewpoint. In *Rust v. Sullivan,* 500 U.S. 173 (1991), the Court upheld federal agency regulations that conditioned receipt of federal funds for Title X family planning projects on the recipient's agreement not to use the money to "encourage, promote, or advocate" abortion in the operation of a Title X project. Recipients were free to use their own resources to promote abortion in any other non-Title X project they might operate. Free speech was allegedly infringed because the "gag rule" suppressed a particular idea, but the Court said this was not so because the "Government can fund a program to encourage certain activities it believes to be in the public interest, without at the same time funding an alternate program which seeks to deal with the problem in another way." The government is "simply insisting that public funds be spent for the purposes for which they were authorized."

c. **Subsidies that promote *private* speech.** A government may *not* subsidize *private speech* in a way that is viewpoint based. In *Rosenberger v. Rector and Visitors of the University of Virginia*, 515 U.S. 819 (1995), the Court voided a public university's viewpoint-based subsidy of student publications. The University of Virginia used mandatory student fees to pay the printing costs of publications of student organizations but refused to subsidize any religious publications. The Court distinguished *Rust* by noting that when "the government disburses public funds to private entities to convey a governmental message, it may . . . ensure that its message is neither garbled nor distorted by the grantee. [But] viewpoint-based restrictions are [not] proper when the University does not itself speak or subsidize transmittal of a message it favors but instead expends funds to encourage a diversity of views from private speakers." In *Legal Services Corporation v. Velasquez*, 121 S. Ct. 1043 (2001), the Court struck down a federal law that barred federally funded legal services lawyers from "litigation, lobbying, or rule-making involving an effort to reform a federal or state welfare system" or litigation involving "an effort to amend or otherwise challenge existing law." Unlike in *Rust*, the speech regulated was not the government's. The legal services program was "designed to facilitate private speech, not to promote a governmental message. . . . The lawyer is not the government's speaker." The regulations were viewpoint discriminatory by discouraging challenges to the status quo.

5. **Special Cases: Prisons and the Military**

a. **Overview.** There are some settings controlled by governments where the government has a legitimate and enhanced interest in regulating behavior. Prisons and the military are the clearest examples. Prisons are designed to punish and segregate dangerous predators from decent society. The military's function is to defend the nation by combining unquestioning obedience with extraordinary self-sacrifice. To perform these specialized functions considerable regulation of individual behavior is required. While free speech rights are not surrendered upon entrance to one of these settings, the range of protected speech diminishes. The courts are quite *deferential to governmental judgments concerning the necessity of curbing speech.* The burden of proof lies with the individual to prove by clear and substantial evidence that the speech restrictions are inappropriate to the accomplishment of legitimate state objectives.

b. **Prisons.** Governments may restrict prisoner speech unless the affected prisoner proves by *"substantial evidence"* that the speech restriction was *unrelated* to *"proper penological objectives"* or *preservation of prison security and order.* In essence, this is an extremely deferential version of rational basis scrutiny.

i. **The general standard of review:** *Jones v. North Carolina Prisoners'*

Union, 433 U.S. 119 (1977). North Carolina prohibited prisoners from soliciting others to form a "prisoners' union," meeting to discuss the union, or sending or receiving mail concerning the union. The Court upheld this content-based speech restriction. The burden of proof was on the prisoners "conclusively" to establish by "substantial evidence" that the speech restrictions were unrelated to North Carolina's objectives of preventing friction among union and nonunion inmates and between guards and inmates. "[C]ourts should ordinarily defer to [the] expert judgment [of prison officials] in such matters." The two dissenters claimed that it was a deviation from free speech precedent to defer "to the judgment of [prison] officials simply because their judgment was 'rational.'"

ii. **Applications of the standard.** In *Turner v. Safley,* 482 U.S. 78 (1987), the Court applied deferential review to uphold a general prohibition on correspondence between inmates of different penal institutions. In *Bell v. Wolfish,* 441 U.S. 520 (1979), the Court upheld a prohibition upon inmates receiving hardcover books except directly from publishers, distributors, or bookstores, because the regulation was rationally related to security concerns. In *Thornburgh v. Abbott,* 490 U.S. 401 (1989), the Court upheld a broader such regulation on the ground that it was reasonably related to legitimate penological interests. In *Pell v. Procunier,* 417 U.S. 817 (1974), the Court upheld a prison regulation prohibiting face-to-face interviews with the press as rationally related to legitimate concerns of preventing inmates from becoming celebrities.

c. **Military.** In reviewing restrictions upon the speech of service members, the Court is almost as deferential to the judgment of military officials as it is with respect to prison officials. So long as the speech restriction is rationally related to the maintenance of the military as "an effective military force" it is valid.

i. *Parker v. Levy,* 417 U.S. 733 (1974). During the Vietnam War and while on active duty Levy, an Army captain, publicly stated to enlisted men his belief that the United States was wrong in fighting the Vietnam War and urged them to refuse to perform their orders to serve in Vietnam. Because of this speech Levy was convicted by court martial of violating two sections of the Uniform Code of Military Justice. The Court upheld the conviction. "[T]he military is, by necessity, a specialized society apart from civilian society. . . . While members of the military are not excluded from the protection granted by the First Amendment, the different character of the military community and of the military mission requires a different application of those protections." In short, speech may be restricted in the military, so long as the speech restriction is reasonably related to the effective accomplishment of the military mission.

    ii. *Brown v. Glines,* 444 U.S. 348 (1980). The Court upheld an Air Force regulation that prohibited distribution of any written material on an Air Force base without the base commander's permission. In order to ensure morale, discipline, and military readiness, said the Court, the base commander "must have authority over the distribution of materials that could affect adversely these essential attributes of an effective military force." The Court deferred to the apparently reasonable judgment of the military commander.

F. IMPLICIT EXPRESSION RIGHTS

1. Overview

The right to speak freely implies certain rights that are not expressly mentioned in the First Amendment. The right to choose one's associations is an aspect of free speech because certain associational choices are expressive. The right to express oneself implies a corollary negative freedom—the right to be free of coerced speech or association.

2. Freedom of Association

    a. **Overview.** The Court has inferred the existence of a right to associate as a necessary corollary to both the right to speak freely and the right to assemble peaceably. The Court has also treated some associational choices as part of the fundamental liberties protected by due process and equal protection.

        i. **Scope.** People select their associates for different reasons and in different contexts. Some associational choices are wholly lacking in expressive content; others are at the heart of expression.

 ## EXAMPLE AND ANALYSIS

By choosing to eat in a fast-food restaurant one also selects some momentary associates. That associational choice has next to nothing to do with expression. If the government prohibits fast-food restaurants, the fast-food dinner's associational rights are surely not impaired significantly. By contrast, if a person chooses to join an organization supporting abortion the individual has made an associational choice that is suffused with expression. The government surely infringes associational rights if it makes it a crime to belong to an organization supporting abortion.

While freedom of association is an implied First Amendment right there are aspects of freedom of association that have more to do with the fundamental liberties protected by substantive due process or equal protection than by free expression.

EXAMPLE AND ANALYSIS

The choice of a marital partner is a highly personal subjective judgment. It has little if anything to do with free speech, and almost everything to do with the realization of one's happiness. A law requiring prospective marital partners to obtain governmental permission to marry would violate due process and equal protection. (See Chapter 8, section C.3, supra.)

Some associational choices are so far removed from either expression or fundamental liberties protected by either due process or equal protection that they receive little or no judicial protection from legislative invasion.

EXAMPLES AND ANALYSIS

Example: The choice to affiliate in a labor union or a trade organization is an associational choice motivated almost entirely by economic concerns. As a result, the deferential standard of review would probably be employed by courts in evaluating legislative restrictions upon this choice.

Example: The City of Dallas limited the use of certain dance halls to persons between the ages of fourteen and eighteen. The Court unanimously agreed that the ordinance did not violate any associational rights, whether grounded in fundamental liberties or as an aspect of free expression. *Dallas v. Stanglin,* 490 U.S. 19 (1989).

      ii. **Standard of review.** When governments *substantially* restrict freedom of association the restriction is *presumptively void.* The restriction is valid *only* if the government proves it is the *least restrictive means* to accomplish a *compelling* government interest *unrelated to the suppression of ideas.*

      iii. **Origins.** The modern development of free association is of recent vintage. In *NAACP v. Alabama,* 357 U.S. 449 (1958), the Court invalidated an Alabama demand that the NAACP reveal the names and addresses of its members. The Court treated the demand as "a *substantial restraint* upon the exercise by [the NAACP's] members of their right to freedom of association." Accordingly, the Court required Alabama to prove that it had a *compelling interest* to require disclosure. Alabama's only asserted interest was to determine whether the NAACP "was conducting intrastate business in violation of the Alabama foreign corporation registration statute." That interest was hardly compelling and, in any case, could be accomplished in a far less restrictive fashion than demanding the NAACP's membership roster.

b.   Litigation as an associational right

    i.   Political or constitutional litigation. Some litigation is inherently expressive.

        (a)   *NAACP v. Button,* 371 U.S. 415 (1963). Virginia prohibited "improper solicitation of . . . legal . . . business." Virginia applied that prohibition to the NAACP's practice of explaining to parents and children the legal steps necessary to accomplish school desegregation in the wake of *Brown,* then distributing forms authorizing the NAACP to represent the signer in desegregation suits. The Court, 6 to 3, held that the NAACP's actions were "modes of expression and association protected by the [First Amendment]." Because the litigation was intended to achieve "equality of treatment for the members of the Negro community" it was deemed by the Court be "a form of political expression. . . . [L]itigation may well be the sole practicable avenue open to a minority to petition for redress of grievances."

        (b)   *In re Primus,* 436 U.S. 412 (1978). The Court struck down state bar disciplinary action taken against a lawyer who, on behalf of the ACLU, solicited a woman whose constitutional rights had arguably been violated to determine whether she wished the ACLU to represent her in litigation.

    ii.   Nonpolitical litigation. Litigation that is not inherently expressive also may involve associational freedom. The Court has struck down state restrictions on union assistance to union members designed to ensure members' awareness of their legal rights and to ensure competent legal representation. The leading case is *Brotherhood of Railroad Trainmen v. Virginia,* 377 U.S. 1 (1964). Relying on Virginia's prohibition of improper legal solicitation Virginia enjoined the Brotherhood from advising its members to obtain legal advice before settling their personal injury claims. The Court reversed the injunction, reasoning that Virginia had not proven "any appreciable public interest" in curbing the associational rights of the Brotherhood's members "to advise one another." See also *United Mine Workers v. Illinois Bar Assn.,* 389 U.S. 217 (1967), *United Transportation Union v. State Bar of Michigan,* 401 U.S. 576 (1971).

c.   **Political boycott as an associational right.** Boycotts undertaken for purposes of political expression, but which are *not designed to coerce behavior,* are a protected form of expression. This is a *very narrow* category. The "coercive" political boycott is not protected, but the line between "coercion" and "communication" is elusive. Boycotts undertaken primarily for economic purposes are not protected.

   i.   *NAACP v. Claiborne Hardware Co.,* 458 U.S. 886 (1982). The NAACP organized a boycott of white businesses in order to dramatize claims of racial discrimination. The state courts ruled that the boycott was unlawful, rejected a First Amendment defense, and found the NAACP and certain boycott organizers liable for tortious interference with economic advantage. The Court reversed. Because the boycott was intended to express political views and a boycott necessarily involves association to achieve its ends, the state could "not award compensation for the consequences of nonviolent, protected activity."

   ii.   *International Longshoremen's Assn. v. Allied International,* 456 U.S. 212 (1982). To protest the Soviet Union's invasion of Afghanistan, the longshoremen's union refused to handle cargoes coming from or going to the Soviet Union. The Court ruled that the boycott was not a form of protected expression, despite its apparent political nature, because it was "conduct designed not to communicate but to coerce."

d.   **Intimate and commercial association.** Not every aspect of freedom of association is rooted in the expression values of the First Amendment. "Intimate" association—such as marriage, family, and choice of one close friends—is protected because it is considered to be a fundamental liberty. But once a person's associational choices slide from the intimate to the commercial, associational protection ceases.

   i.   *Roberts v. United States Jaycees,* 468 U.S. 609 (1984). Pursuant to a Minnesota law prohibiting sex discrimination in places of public accommodation the Jaycees, a national civic organization that limited voting membership to men between the ages of eighteen and thirty-five, was ordered to admit women as full voting members. The Court rejected the Jaycees' claim that the Minnesota law violated their members' freedom of association, but employed two different ways of reaching that conclusion.

(a) **Intimate association.** The Court noted that associational "choices to enter into and maintain certain intimate human relationships" were a form of "freedom of association [that] receives protection as a fundamental element of personal liberty." Protected intimate associations can be identified by their "relative smallness, a high degree of selectivity in decisions to begin and maintain the affiliation, and seclusion from others." Membership in the Jaycees did not involve intimate association, because it was "neither small nor selective," nor was it at all secluded.

(b) **Expressive association.** The Court conceded that membership in the Jaycees was also a form of expression, because the Jaycees engaged in various forms of protected expression. But that right was not absolute. Infringement of expressive association is "*justified* by regulations adopted to *serve compelling state interests, unrelated to the suppression of ideas,* that *cannot be achieved through means significantly less restrictive of associational freedoms.*" The Court found that standard to be satisfied because Minnesota had a compelling interest in eradicating sex discrimination in public accommodations, an interest not related to the suppression of any idea, and the obligation to admit women as full voting members did not impose "any serious burden on the male members' freedom of expressive association."

(c) **O'Connor's concurrence.** Justice O'Connor had a different view of the expressive association issue. She contended that *commercial association* enjoyed only "minimal constitutional protection." In her view, only an "association engaged exclusively in protected expression enjoys First Amendment protection of both the content of its message and the choice of its members." Would it make a difference to the outcome of *Roberts* if the principal belief of the Jaycees was the idea that "a woman's place is in the home"? In the majority view, it probably would. In O'Connor's view, it would make a difference only if these hypothetical Jaycees were no longer a commercial association, but one devoted exclusively to expressing this particular view of women.

ii. **The scope of *Roberts.*** In *Board of Directors of Rotary Intl. v. Rotary Club of Duarte,* 481 U.S. 537 (1987), the Court unanimously upheld the application of California's sex discrimination law to the Duarte Rotary Club, a civic organization. Admission of women would not "affect in any significant way the existing members' ability to carry out their various [expressive] purposes."

e. **Expressive association.** The Court clarified the nature of expressive associations and emphasized their constitutional significance in *Boy Scouts of America v. Dale,* 120 S. Ct. 2446 (2000). After the Boy Scouts revoked James Dale's membership as an assistant scoutmaster, the New Jersey Supreme Court concluded that the Boy Scouts had violated New Jersey law prohibiting discrimination on the basis of sexual orientation in places of public accommodations. The Supreme Court, 5 to 4, reversed, finding that New Jersey had unjustifiably infringed the Boy Scouts' right of expressive association. The majority ruled that an association is "expressive" whenever it engages in expressive activity, not just when the association is for the *purpose* of expressing a particular message. On that basis, the majority concluded that the Boy Scouts' practice of using adults to inculcate its value system to youngsters was expressive activity sufficient to make the Scouts an expressive association. The expressive association right is infringed, said the majority, whenever the state's forcible inclusion of an unwanted member significantly affects the group's ability to advocate public or private viewpoints. The Boy Scouts asserted that homosexuality was inconsistent with its inculcation of moral purity, and the Court accepted the idea that forced inclusion of a homosexual member would significantly undercut the Scouts' ability to convey its message that homosexuality and moral purity were incompatible. The Court applied strict scrutiny and found that, although New Jersey had a compelling interest in eliminating discrimination against sexual minorities, the method of accomplishing the objective—forcible inclusion of gay scouts and scoutmasters—was, unlike *Roberts* or *Duarte,* a serious burden on the Scouts' freedom of expressive association.

Four dissenters (Stevens, Souter, Ginsburg, and Breyer) argued that the moral values the Scouts seek to inculcate did not include antipathy to homosexuals, and that thus the New Jersey law did not pose any significant obstacle to the Scouts' ability to inculcate their proclaimed moral values.

3. **The Right to Be Free of *Compelled* Speech, Disclosure, or Association**

a. **Overview.** The mirror image of the right of free expression is the right **not** to express ideas. Just as government control of the content of expression is presumptively invalid, so is government compulsion of specified expression. As with other content-based speech regulation, governmental compulsion to speak, disclose, or associate may be justified if the government can prove that the compulsion is the *least restrictive means* to accomplish a *compelling government interest* that is unrelated to the forced expression of ideas.

b. **Freedom from compelled speech.** The right **not** to express ideas is at its strongest when the government seeks to compel the expression of a belief or point of view.

i. **The flag salute cases:** *West Virginia State Board of Education v. Barnette,* 319 U.S. 624 (1943). The Court struck down a state law requiring all public school students to salute and pledge allegiance to the flag of the United States. The Court stated that only the most "immediate and urgent grounds" could justify an "involuntary affirmation . . . of a belief. . . . [If] there is any fixed star in our constitutional constellation, it is that no official, high or petty, can prescribe what shall be orthodox in politics, nationalism, religion, or other matters of opinion or force citizens to confess by word or act their faith therein. If there are any circumstances which permit an exception, they do not now occur to us." By this strong denunciation of compelled speech the Court overruled *Minersville School District v. Gobitis,* 310 U.S. 586 (1940), which had upheld a forced flag salute.

ii. **The license plate motto—"Live free or die":** *Wooley v. Maynard,* 430 U.S. 705 (1977). The Court held that New Hampshire could not prosecute a New Hampshire motorist who covered the state motto—"Live Free or Die"—on his passenger vehicle license plates because the motto was repugnant to his moral, political, and religious beliefs. The state's justifications for infringing upon "the right to refrain from speaking at all" were insufficient. The state's interest in facilitating distinction between passenger vehicles and all others was hardly a compelling interest and, in any case, could be achieved by "less drastic means." New Hampshire's interest in promoting "appreciation of history, individualism, and state pride" was "not ideologically neutral." Rather, New Hampshire desired to compel its residents to convey a particular message.

iii. **The unwanted petitioners in the shopping center:** *PruneYard Shopping Center v. Robins,* 447 U.S. 74 (1980). The PruneYard, a privately owned shopping center, expelled several high school students who were soliciting signatures opposing a United Nations resolution against Zionism. The California Supreme Court ruled that the California Constitution protects reasonable expression "in shopping centers even when the centers are privately owned." The PruneYard contended that the California rule compelled it to use its property to express views that it did not wish to express. The Court rejected the contention. California had a compelling interest—ensuring that the public could speak freely in places generally open to the public. California did not dictate the message and the PruneYard remained free to "disavow any connection with the message." In short, the compulsion was not to speak but to open for *public speech purposes* a privately owned space to which the public was invited.

iv. **The forced enclosure in the utility bill:** *P.G. & E. v. Public Utilities Commission,* 475 U.S. 1 (1986). The California Public Utilities Commission (PUC) ordered PG&E to insert into its billing envelopes a flyer prepared by utility critics. The Court agreed that the PUC's order violated PG&E's free speech rights. "Compelled access . . . both penalizes . . . expression . . . and forces speakers to alter their speech to conform with an agenda they do not set." The PUC's order was viewpoint discriminatory.

v.   **The unwanted St. Patrick's Day marchers:** *Hurley v. Irish-American Gay, Lesbian and Bisexual Group of Boston,* 515 U.S. 557 (1995). Massachusetts required private citizens who organized an annual St. Patrick's Day parade to include as marchers GLIB, a group who wished to advertise their homosexuality. The Court held that the law, as applied to the St. Patrick's Day parade, was a violation of free expression. "Parades are . . . a form of expression," said the Court, and the parade organizers were entitled "not to propound a particular point of view." That choice was "beyond the government's power to control." The parade was not a mere conduit for other's speech, like the shopping center in *PruneYard*, but was itself a thematic message. The forced inclusion of GLIB would compel the parade to express a state-mandated message.

vi. **Forced contributions to distasteful views:** *Abood v. Detroit Board of Education,* 431 U.S. 209 (1977). Michigan law authorized "agency shop" collective bargaining for public employees. In an agency shop, a union representing all workers in a workplace is entitled to withhold a "service charge" from the paychecks of nonunion members equal to union dues collected from union members. Abood, a nonunion public schoolteacher, asserted that the agency shop practice violated his First Amendment rights because he did not believe in collective bargaining and because the union used his money to advocate political positions with which he disagreed. The Court rejected the former contention but accepted the latter. The agency or union shop arrangement distributes the cost of collective bargaining among all who benefit, even those who prefer to do without those benefits. But forced support for repugnant ideological causes is just another form of compelled speech. See also *Keller v. State Bar of California,* 496 U.S. 1 (1990), in which *Abood* was applied to mandatory bar dues.

Abood and *Keller* were found inapplicable to a mandatory student activity fee used to fund a *viewpoint-neutral* program facilitating student extracurricular speech. *Board of Regents of the University of Wisconsin v. Southworth,* 120 S. Ct. 1346 (2000).

c. **Freedom from compelled disclosure.** The First Amendment is violated by forced disclosure of information that substantially interferes with associational or expression rights, without sufficient justification for disclosure.

   i. **Membership lists.** In *NAACP v. Alabama,* 357 U.S. 449 (1958), the Court ruled that in order to determine whether the NAACP was required to qualify as a foreign corporation, Alabama's demand that the NAACP reveal the names and addresses of its members was "a *substantial restraint* upon the exercise by [the NAACP's] members of their right to freedom of association." The Court required Alabama to prove that it had a *compelling interest* to require disclosure. Alabama's interest was not compelling and it could be accomplished in a far less restrictive fashion than forced disclosure.

   ii. **Authorship of political messages.** Prohibition of anonymous political literature is subject to strict scrutiny. There is no reason to think people are too stupid to evaluate the messages on their content alone. There are less restrictive ways to address fraud or libel. Finally, anonymous political pamphleteering has a long and honorable tradition in American life, the Federalist Papers being the most notable example.

      (a) *Talley v. California,* 362 U.S. 60 (1960). Los Angeles prohibited the distribution of any flyers or handbills unless the name and address of the author appeared on its face. The Court invalidated the ordinance, reasoning "that identification and fear of reprisal might deter perfectly peaceful discussions of public matters of importance." Los Angeles said it was interested in identifying "those responsible for fraud, false advertising, and libel," but the Court thought that justification insufficient.

      (b) *McIntyre v. Ohio Elections Commission,* 514 U.S. 334 (1995). Ohio prohibited the distribution of anonymous literature "designed to influence voters in an election." Because the law burdened "core political speech" the Court applied "exacting scrutiny"—the law could be upheld only if Ohio proved it was "narrowly tailored to serve an overriding state interest." The Court concluded that neither interest advanced by Ohio—ensuring that the electorate possesses all "relevant information" and "preventing fraud and libel"—was sufficiently "overriding" to justify the restriction.

   iii. **Disclosure of political contributions.** While disclosure of the source of political contributions implicates expression rights, the government has a stronger interest in such disclosure. Absent proof by the challenger of a substantial interference with expression and an insubstantial state interest in disclosure, forced disclosure of the source of political contributions is valid. In *Buckley v. Valeo,* 424 U.S. 1 (1976), the Court upheld a requirement that every political candidate or political committee maintain records of the names and addresses of contributors of $10 or more and to disclose those records to the Federal Election Commission. The government advanced three justifications—provision of information to the electorate, deterrence of actual corruption and the appearance of corruption, and detection of violation of valid contribution limits. The Court found that disclosure directly served these "substantial government interests." Forced disclosure would be invalid where disclosure posed a "serious . . . threat to the exercise of [expression]" and the government interest in the particular disclosure was "insubstantial." But in *Brown v. Socialist Workers '74 Campaign Committee,* 459 U.S. 87 (1982), the Court struck down an Ohio disclosure law as applied to the Socialist Workers Party, "a minor political party which has historically been the object of harassment by government officials and private parties," because it had proven a "reasonable probability of threats, harassment, or reprisals" sufficient to establish that disclosure posed a severe threat to the exercise of associational and speech rights.

iv. **Compelled disclosure of public employees' or licensees' views.** Governments have some legitimate reasons for precise inquiries into the associations or beliefs of public employees and licensees. But since such inquiries raise the possibility of government reprisal against employees or licensees on the basis of their associations or opinions the Court has sharply limited these inquiries. If a mandated disclosure *substantially interferes* with expression it is valid only if the government proves that the disclosure is the *least restrictive means* to accomplish a *legitimate state interest.*

(a) **General rule:** *Shelton v. Tucker,* 364 U.S. 479 (1960). As a condition of employment, Arkansas required every public school teacher annually to disclose every organization to which the teacher belonged or to which he "regularly contributed" during the preceding five years. The Court, 5 to 4, invalidated the law. The mandated disclosure "impair[ed] . . . free association" and did so in a wildly overbroad manner. The Court hinted that Arkansas could validly inquire into a teacher's "relationships [that] . . . bear[] upon the teacher's occupational competence or fitness" but ruled that even such a "legitimate and substantial . . . purpose cannot be pursued by means that broadly stifle fundamental personal liberties when the end can be more narrowly achieved." Arkansas didn't come close to selecting the least restrictive means to accomplish whatever legitimate goals it may have had.

(b)   The bar admission cases. Initially the Court upheld the validity of inquiries into past associations and beliefs in connection with applications for admission to the bar, but in a trio of 1971 cases it sharply limited such inquiries. In *Baird v. State Bar,* 401 U.S. 1 (1971), the Court (5-3) ruled that the Arizona bar had violated the First Amendment when it refused to process Baird's application because she would not answer whether she had ever been a member of the Communist Party or any other organization advocating the violent overthrow of government. Four Justices thought that inquiry into "an individual's beliefs and associations" could only be undertaken upon proof that "the inquiry is necessary to protect a legitimate state interest." *In re Stolar,* 401 U.S. 23 (1971), invalidated Ohio's denial of bar admission to Stolar because he would not divulge all of his prior associations and whether he had ever been a member of an organization advocating the violent overthrow of government. But in *Law Students Civil Rights Research Council v. Wadmond,* 401 U.S. 154 (1971), the Court upheld the New York bar's requirement that applicants disclose whether they had ever been a knowing member of an organization advocating the violent overthrow of government.

v.   Compelled answers to legislative investigations. In order for any legislature to make informed decisions it must obtain information on the issues it considers. Accordingly, legislatures have considerable authority to "compel a private individual to appear . . . and give testimony needed to enable it efficiently to exercise [its legitimate] legislative functions." *McGrain v. Daugherty,* 273 U.S. 135 (1927). But that power is not unlimited. Witnesses may invoke their privilege against self-incrimination and legislative investigations must confine themselves to subjects of possible legislation. Investigations that intrude upon expression rights are valid only if the government proves that there is a *substantial relation* between the information sought and a subject of *overriding and compelling* state interest.

(a)   *Barenblatt v. United States,* 360 U.S. 109 (1959). Barenblatt, a Vassar College instructor, was subpoenaed to testify before the House Un-American Activities Committee, which was investigating an alleged communist presence in American education. Barenblatt refused to answer questions concerning his past or present membership in the Communist Party and was convicted of contempt of Congress. The Court upheld the conviction. Even though Congress was investigating "the theoretical classroom discussion of communism" rather than "advocacy of or preparation for [violent] overthrow" of government the "strict requirements of a prosecution [for such advocacy] are not the measure of the permissible scope of a congressional investigation into 'overthrow,' for of necessity the investigatory process must proceed step by step."

    (b) *Gibson v. Florida Legislative Investigating Committee,* 372 U.S. 539 (1963). Gibson, the president of the Miami branch of the NAACP, refused to tell a Florida legislative committee investigating communist infiltration into various organizations whether fourteen specific alleged communists were members of the NAACP. Gibson was convicted of contempt and the Court reversed. Since the inquiry intruded upon associational rights Florida was required to "show a substantial relation between the information sought and a subject of overriding and compelling state interest." The Court distinguished *Barenblatt* because that case involved inquiry into the witness's own communist affiliation. By contrast, the Florida investigation demanded of Gibson that he disclose membership information about the NAACP. Without proof of a "substantial connection between the Miami branch of the N.A.A.C.P. and Communist *activities*" the demanded disclosure was constitutionally unjustified.

   d. **Freedom from compelled association.** Just as there is a freedom from compelled speech or compelled disclosure there is also a freedom from compelled association. Governmental attempts to compel either *intimate association* or *expressive association* are invalid unless they are the *least restrictive means* to accomplish some *compelling state interest* that is *unrelated to the suppression of ideas.*

4. **Are There Free Expression Access Rights to Private Property?**

   a. **Overview.** In general, the Constitution does ***not*** command owners of private property to make their property accessible to others for speech purposes. The usual rationale is that there is a risk that the speech will be attributable to the property owner.

   b. **Access to privately owned "public spaces."** In the exceedingly rare circumstance where a private owner of property controls an entire town, the private owner of the town performs "public functions" and thus may not exclude speech from the streets and other public fora within the town except to the extent the government may do so. The private owner is treated as a state actor, and his conduct is analyzed as if he were the government. See *Marsh v. Alabama,* 326 U.S. 501 (1946), discussed in Chapter 10, supra. The "public function" analysis of *Marsh v. Alabama* does not extend to private shopping centers. But some states have reached a contrary judgment under their state constitutional guarantees of free speech. The net result is that citizens of some states *do have such a right of access* under their *state constitution,* but nobody has such a right of access under the federal Constitution. Initially, in *Amalgamated Food Employees v. Logan Valley Plaza,* 391 U.S. 308 (1968), the Court treated the shopping center as the "functional equivalent" of the company town in *Marsh v. Alabama,* by ruling that a state's trespass law could not be applied to enjoin nonviolent labor picketing of a store in a privately owned shopping center. In *Lloyd Corp. v. Tanner,* 407 U.S. 551 (1972), the Court ruled that a private shopping center could ban the distribution of antiwar leaflets. Antiwar leafleting was wholly unrelated to the center's commercial purposes and there were ample alternatives means to deliver the same message to the same audience. Finally, in *Hudgens v. NLRB,* 424 U.S. 507 (1976), the Court expressly overruled *Logan Valley.* However, several states have ruled that the free speech guarantee contained in the state constitution requires private shopping center owners to permit public speech access to the center. In such states, private shopping center owners may regulate speech in their shopping centers only to the extent the government could do so. *PruneYard Shopping Center v. Robins,* 447 U.S. 74 (1980), held that such forced access does not generally violate the shopping center owner's federal free speech right to be free from compelled speech or association because the speech is not likely to be attributed to the property owner.

c. **Access to the broadcast media.** Broadcasters pose unusual problems. We accept the principle of public control of the airwaves, if only to prevent the chaos that would result from simultaneous broadcasting of two signals on the same frequency. Broadcasters are government licensees although their facilities and businesses are generally privately owned. Since there are many more potential broadcasters than available frequencies, the government is inevitably placed in the position of rationing a speech medium. From all of this the Court has concluded that broadcasters may be compelled to air certain speech.

i. **The "fairness doctrine."** The FCC's "fairness doctrine," which required broadcasters to provide a right of reply to political editorials or attacks on identified persons or groups, was rescinded by the FCC in 1987. Since then, a plethora of divergent political views have developed on radio and television, suggesting that the "fairness doctrine" may have chilled speech. But the "fairness doctrine" was upheld as constitutional in *Red Lion Broadcasting v.*

FCC, 395 U.S. 367 (1969). The Court reasoned that the scarcity of broadcast frequencies leads to the rule that "the licensee has no constitutional right [to] monopolize a radio frequency to the exclusion of his fellow citizens. There is nothing in the First Amendment which prevents the Government from requiring a licensee to share his frequency with others and to conduct himself as [a] fiduciary with obligations to present those views and voices which are representative of his community and which would otherwise, by necessity, be barred from the airwaves."

ii. **Broadcast editorializing.** Two issues are raised—must broadcasters accept unwanted editorializing, and may publicly funded broadcasters be barred from editorializing?

    (a) **Access rights:** *CBS v. Democratic National Committee,* 412 U.S. 94 (1973). The Court held that the First Amendment did not require broadcasters to sell advertising time to political advertisers. The Court thought that the fairness doctrine's objective of ensuring a fair sampling of representative viewpoints would not be advanced by forcing broadcasters to air all the political advertising requested of them, since well-heeled advertisers could overwhelm the airwaves.

    (b) **Bans on broadcast editorializing:** *FCC v. League of Women Voters,* 468 U.S. 364 (1984). The Court struck down a federal law that prohibited publicly funded noncommercial broadcasters from engaging in "editorializing." The Court conceded that the law was designed to achieve the same objective as the fairness doctrine, but distinguished *Red Lion* on the ground that the fairness doctrine opened the microphone to more speakers while the editorializing ban closed the microphone to its operator.

iii. **A right of access for office seekers:** *CBS v. FCC,* 453 U.S. 367 (1981). Federal law authorized the FCC to penalize broadcasters who fail to "allow reasonable access," by purchase or otherwise, to "a legally qualified candidate for Federal elective office on behalf of his candidacy." CBS refused to sell thirty minutes of air time to the Carter reelection campaign and the FCC concluded that CBS had failed to provide "reasonable access." The Court upheld the law.

d. **Access to cable television.** Cable television does not pose the same scarcity problems as the broadcast medium. The technology of cable transmission permits a virtually unlimited number of signals to be disseminated. Accordingly, the Court does not apply the same relaxed scrutiny to governmentally mandated access to privately owned cable systems.

A 1992 federal law required privately owned cable transmission systems to carry, free of charge, local broadcast television signals. Turner Broadcasting challenged the validity of these "must carry" provisions. In *Turner Broadcasting System v. FCC* (*Turner I*), 512 U.S. 622 (1994), the Court treated the "must carry" provisions as content neutral and applied the intermediate scrutiny standard of *O'Brien*. For a plurality of four, Justice Kennedy remanded on the question of whether the "must carry" provisions were no more restrictive than necessary to achieve the government's significant objective, unrelated to the suppression of ideas, of "protect[ing] the viability of broadcast television." In *Turner Broadcasting System v. FCC* (*Turner II*), 520 U.S. 180 (1997), the Court upheld the "must-carry" provisions as a direct and effective method to ensure the economic vitality of over-the-air television broadcasters and as no more burdensome than necessary to accomplish that objective.

e.   **Access to newspapers.** The arguments for mandated access to the broadcast medium have been squarely rejected in the context of newspapers. This is partly due to the fact that, alone among speakers, the press enjoys special constitutional protection and partly due to the fact that newspaper publication is not subject to the same allocation problem that applies to scarce broadcast frequencies. *Miami Herald Publishing Co. v. Tornillo*, 418 U.S. 241 (1974), is the leading case. Florida law required newspapers that printed any attacks on the character or record of a candidate for public office to make equivalent space available to the candidate, free of charge, to reply to the attack. The Court unanimously struck down the law. The Court regarded the law as content based, subjected it to strict scrutiny, and found it to be an impermissible governmental directive to the press telling the press what it must print, as repugnant to the First Amendment as a law prohibiting the press from speaking.

f.   **Access to other people's mail:** *P.G. & E. v. Public Utilities Commission,* 475 U.S. 1 (1986). The California Public Utilities Commission (PUC) concluded that the "extra space" in the monthly billing envelopes of PG&E, a gas and electric utility, belonged to the ratepayers. The "extra space" consisted of the difference between the weight of the bill and the maximum weight that could be mailed for the same price as the bill alone. The PUC ordered PG&E to insert into its billing envelopes a flyer prepared by a band of utility critics. The Court agreed that the PUC's order violated PG&E's free speech rights. "Compelled access . . . both penalizes . . . expression . . . and forces speakers to alter their speech to conform with an agenda they do not set." Moreover, the PUC's order was viewpoint-discriminatory since it granted the "extra space" only to PG&E's critics.

G. FREE EXPRESSION AND THE POLITICAL PROCESS

1. Money As Speech: Political Contributions and Expenditures

In our populous and technologically advanced society it is virtually impossible to communicate political messages without the use of money. Speech may be free, but it is not cheap. Accordingly, the expenditure of money to deliver political speech is generally protected. But since there is a risk that contributions of money used to fuel political speech may corrupt public officials, or give the appearance of corruption, the Court has upheld some limits on contributions.

a. Overview. The Court has created the following doctrinal rules dealing with money as speech.

 i. Expenditure regulations. Governments may *not* limit the amount of money a *political candidate spends from his or her own funds.* Governments may *not* limit the amount of money that either *individuals* or *organizations independent of a political candidate (including political parties) may spend on behalf of a candidate.* But governments *may* restrict the total expenditures of a political candidate *as a condition to receipt of public funds.* Corporations are treated like persons, but some corporate expenditures on political speech may be limited.

 ii. Contribution regulations. Governments *may* impose limits on the amount that may be contributed to *political candidates or political action committees.* Governments may *not* limit contributions made in connection with *ballot measures.*

 iii. Corporate political spending. Corporations occupy a tenuous middle ground. Although they are generally free to spend money on politics they may be prohibited from spending from their *general treasury* unless they are nonprofit corporations.

b. Regulations of political contributions and expenditures

 i. General principles: *Buckley v. Valeo,* 424 U.S. 1 (1976). The Federal Election Campaign Act limited both contributions to political candidates and campaigns and expenditures by or on behalf of political candidates. The Court upheld the contribution limits but struck down the expenditure limits. The Act was designed to "suppress communication" by limiting the *extent* of speech. Unlike content-neutral restrictions that restrict only *where, when,* and *how* speech may be uttered, expenditure limits control how *much* may be said. The idea that *governments* may muzzle speakers by saying, in essence, "Your time is up; shut up," is anathema to the free expression guarantee. Applying this principle, the Court reasoned that contributions and expenditures presented quite different speech issues.

(a) **Rationale for *contribution* limits.** Political contributions may be limited for three reasons:

- Contributions convey a diffuse rather than a specific message—rather than speech itself, contributions merely aid a candidate's speech,

- Contribution limits do not substantially impair a candidate's ability to raise money, since the candidate simply has to appeal to a wider base of supporters,

- There is a "weighty" public interest in curbing political corruption by restricting the ability of persons to buy influence with or access to public officeholders, and the limits on contributions to political candidates were narrowly tailored to that objective.

(b) **Rationale for protecting *expenditures*.** By contrast, expenditures are directly and specifically related to the expression of political messages. Only the most compelling government interest might justify measures indispensable to achieving such an interest. The Act's expenditure limits failed this test for two reasons:

- Expenditure limits were poor means to root out political corruption. The amount of money a candidate spends has little relation to his susceptibility to corruption, especially given contribution limits.

- The claimed governmental interest in "equalizing the relative ability of individuals and groups to influence the outcome of elections" was **illegitimate,** because *"the concept that the government may restrict the speech of some elements of our society in order to enhance the relative voice of others is wholly foreign to the First Amendment."*

ii. **Post-*Buckley* contribution limits.** *Buckley v. Valeo* upheld federal contribution limits to or on behalf of political candidates but did not deal with state limits, contributions to independent political action committees, or in connection with ballot measures.

(a) **To political action committees: *California Medical Assn. v. FEC,*** 453 U.S. 182 (1981). The Court upheld a federal limitation upon contributions by individuals or associations to "multi-candidate" political action committees.

(b) **In connection with ballot measures: *Citizens Against Rent Control v. Berkeley,*** 454 U.S. 290 (1981). A Berkeley, California ordinance limited contributions to committees supporting or opposing ballot measures. The Court invalidated the ordinance because it posed a "significant restraint" upon free association and free speech and the interest in limiting contributions to curb corruption was totally inapplicable to *ballot measures.*

(c) **State contribution limits:** *Nixon v. Shrink Missouri Government PAC,* 120 S. Ct. 897 (2000). The Court extended *Buckley* to uphold state limits on contributions, but three Justices urged that *Buckley* be overruled. Justice Kennedy claimed that *Buckley* had forced political speech "underground, as contributors and candidates devise ever more elaborate methods of avoiding contribution limits. . . . Soft money may be contributed to political parties in unlimited amounts" and is used to fund issue advocacy advertisements that attack the opponent without ever calling for a candidate's election or defeat. Kennedy thought *Buckley* immunized this system from political change because "[s]oft money must be raised to attack the problem of soft money." He would overrule *Buckley* to permit Congress start all over from ground zero. By contrast, Justices Scalia and Thomas would overrule *Buckley* and subject contribution limits to strict scrutiny.

iii. **Post-*Buckley* expenditure limits.** *Buckley* struck down expenditure limits, leaving individuals and candidates free to spend whatever they desire on behalf of a candidate from their own funds. *Buckley* upheld the practice of conditioning receipt of federal funds for political campaigns upon compliance with total campaign expenditures. *Buckley* did not address the question of expenditures by independent political action committees or expenditures in connection with ballot measures.

(a) **Expenditure limits on political action committees and other independent spenders:** *FEC v. NCPAC,* 470 U.S. 480 (1985). The Court voided a federal law barring independent political action committees from spending more than $1,000 in support of any presidential candidate. The Court reasoned that, as in the case of expenditures by individuals or the candidate (from personal funds), there was an insufficient risk of corruption to justify the limitation.

(b) **Expenditure limits on political parties:** *Colorado Republican Federal Campaign Committee v. FEC,* 518 U.S. 604 (1996). In a plurality opinion by Breyer, O'Connor, and Souter, the Court voided federal limits on expenditures of a political party that were made independently of the party's candidate. Four Justices (Rehnquist, Scalia, Kennedy, and Thomas) would have ruled limits on political party spending to be facially invalid, regardless of whether such expenditures were coordinated with or independent of a candidate.

(c) Prohibitions on paid circulators of petitions to qualify ballot measures: ***Meyer v. Grant,*** **486 U.S. 414 (1988).** Colorado prohibited the use of paid circulators to gather citizen signatures necessary to qualify proposed state constitutional amendments for the ballot. The Court struck down the law. Speech was substantially burdened because the law restricted "access to the most effective, fundamental, and perhaps economical avenue of political discourse, direct one-on-one communication." The Court rejected Colorado's argument that the statute was "justified by its interest in making sure that an initiative has sufficient grass roots support to be placed on the ballot, or by its interest in protecting the integrity of the initiative process."

c. **Corporate political spending.** Although corporations are generally free to spend for political purposes some special rules apply to corporations. Corporations have less freedom to spend for political purposes than do individuals, candidates, or political action committees.

   i. *First National Bank of Boston v. Bellotti,* 435 U.S. 765 (1978). Massachusetts prohibited corporations from spending money to influence the outcome of ballot measures other than those "materially affecting . . . the property, business, or assets of the corporation." The Court voided the law. The statute curbed speech "at the heart of the First Amendment's protection," speech that is "indispensable to decisionmaking in a democracy." Massachusetts could prevail only by showing a compelling state interest to which the law was narrowly linked. Massachusetts argued that corporations are "wealthy and powerful and their views may drown out other points of view." The Court rejected that justification because it is obnoxious to the First Amendment to contend that some speakers must be muzzled in order to permit others to speak. The state's argument also assumed that the people were nitwits—too stupid to evaluate the political messages of corporations.

   ii. *Austin v. Michigan Chamber of Commerce,* 494 U.S. 652 (1990). Michigan prohibited corporations from spending funds *from their general treasury* on behalf of or in opposition to candidates for public office, but permitted such expenditures from segregated funds used solely for political purposes. The Court upheld the restriction on the ground that the law was narrowly tailored to advance Michigan's compelling interest in limiting the "distorting effects" on the political process of "immense aggregations of wealth that are accumulated with the help of the corporate form and that have little or no correlation to the public's support for the corporation's political ideas.'' The majority distinguished *FEC v. Massachusetts Citizens for Life,* 479 U.S. 238 (1986), which had struck down a virtually identical restriction as applied to a nonprofit corporation formed for the sole purpose of political advocacy, on the ground that its funds were the product of the appeal of its political views, not the result of economic success unrelated to political views.

(a)   **The dissents.** Justices Scalia, Kennedy, and O'Connor dissented. Scalia accused the majority of combining two wrong ideas—that speech can be squelched on the basis of the speaker's wealth or corporate status—to produce an ''Orwellian'' result. The majority gave to the state power to suppress speech simply because it thinks too much (or any) speech from one quarter is evil. To Scalia, the implications to free speech were alarming. The majority relied on the ''proposition [that] expenditures must 'reflect actual public support for the political ideas espoused.' '' By that reasoning, it should be permissible to curb the political spending of the AFL-CIO, or Ross Perot, or Hollywood moguls, because their wealth does not reflect ''actual public support'' for the positions they espouse. Kennedy argued that the Michigan law should be struck down because it was ''overinclusive [—] it covers all groups which use the corporate form, including all nonprofit corporations'' and because it wrongly ''assumes that the government has a legitimate interest in equalizing the relative influence of speakers.''

iii.   **Corporate solicitation.** In *Federal Election Commission v. National Right to Work Committee,* 459 U.S. 197 (1982), the Court upheld a federal law prohibiting political action committees controlled by corporations from soliciting funds from other than the shareholders of members of the corporation. The Court agreed that the solicitation was expression but concluded that the federal government had proven that the prohibition was narrowly tailored to serve the government's compelling interest of preventing ''substantial aggregations of [corporate] wealth'' from being converted into ''political warchests'' and to ''protect individuals who have paid money into a corporation or union for purposes other than the support of candidates to whom they may be opposed.''

2.   Election Regulation

a.   **Overview.** Government regulation of elections raises a variety of constitutional issues. Restrictions on ballot access and certain voter registration requirements were considered in Chapter 9 in sections I.2, 3, and 4.

This section examines two issues: (1) the conflict between government regulation of the form of party primaries and the freedom of association rights of party members, and (2) government attempts to regulate the substance of speech in political campaigns.

b.   Associational rights of members of political parties. Because states control the elections process, including party primaries, and political parties have a heightened interest in who may vote in a party primary election, the interests of political parties and states can diverge. Some objectives of political parties are constitutionally illegitimate, as was the desire of Texas Democrats to close their party primaries to all but white voters. (See Chapter 10, section A.4.c.) But generally the Court has required states to conform their regulation of party primaries to the associational preferences of political parties, on the theory that representative democracy depends on permitting people to band together to promote candidates who espouse their political views.

   i.   *Democratic Party of United States v. Wisconsin ex rel. La Follette,* 450 U.S. 107 (1981). The Court voided a state law that required Democratic convention delegates to vote in accord with the results of Wisconsin's open primary, in which members of all parties could vote for Democratic presidential candidates, because this was a "substantial intrusion" into the associational freedom of Democrats.

   ii.   *Tashjian v. Republican Party,* 479 U.S. 208 (1986). The Court applied strict scrutiny to void a Connecticut requirement that all voters in a party primary be registered voters of that party. Republicans wished to permit anybody to vote in their party and that associational choice was presumptively entitled to be honored.

   iii.   *Eu v. San Francisco Democratic Committee,* 489 U.S. 214 (1989). The Court applied strict scrutiny to void a California law that prohibited political parties from taking any position with respect to candidates for nomination by that party for a partisan elective office. If political parties wish to express a preference about their own rival candidates in a party primary election they are presumptively free to do so.

   iv.   *California Democratic Party v. Jones,* 120 S. Ct. 2402 (2000). California required political parties to select their nominees using a "blanket primary," in which voters of all parties are free to choose among candidates of all parties for each office. As a result a party's nominee for each office is the candidate with the most votes among all candidates of the same party seeking the office, regardless of whether those votes were cast by party members. Republicans could thus be nominated by Democratic voters and Democrats nominated by Republicans. The Court applied strict scrutiny and voided this arrangement as a violation of freedom of association. None of California's asserted interests were compelling. Dampening partisanship in selection of candidates and making the vote more "effective" for minority party voters were simply euphemisms for violating associational freedom, and the remaining objectives—promoting fairness, privacy, choice, and voter participation—were simply not compelling because they were either not implicated by the legislation or the blanket primary operated perversely (e.g., by reducing fairness and choice). The Court expressly reserved judgment on the question of whether open primaries are constitutionally valid.

c. **Regulations of campaign speech.** In the interest of ensuring fair elections governments sometimes seek to prohibit certain corrupt practices that can influence electoral outcomes—such things as vote-buying or lying to the electorate. Although the government's objective is admirable, perhaps even urgent, the effect on protected speech can be profound. Such laws will be upheld only when they are precisely tailored to achieve a compelling government interest.

    i. **Vote-buying:** *Brown v. Hartlage,* 456 U.S. 46 (1982). Kentucky's Corrupt Practices Act prohibited a political candidate from "giving, or promising to give, anything of value to a voter in exchange for his vote or support." Brown promised the voters that, if elected, he would reduce the salary of the office that he sought to occupy. A Kentucky judge ruled the election void on the ground that Brown had violated the Corrupt Practices Act. The Court reversed. The law might validly be applied to secret vote buying, but not to promises "made openly, subject to the comment and criticism of . . . political opponent[s] and to the scrutiny of the voters." Kentucky had no valid interest in curbing speech that is the legitimate subject of campaign debate, much less a compelling interest.

    ii. **False or misleading campaign speech.** When states prohibit false or deceptive campaign speech they implicate some of the same speech concerns present in defamation cases. Even though false political speech undermines the integrity of the political process and saps voter confidence in the statements of any candidate, it is necessary to protect some of this useless speech in order to ensure that legitimate political speech is not chilled. The Court has implicitly recognized this by dicta in *Brown v. Hartlage,* and by making the *Sullivan* rule apply to defamation suits by political candidates against newspapers covering their campaign speech. See, e.g., *Monitor Patriot Co. v. Roy,* 401 U.S. 265 (1971); *Ocala Star-Banner Co. v. Damron,* 401 U.S. 295 (1971).

H. FREEDOM OF THE PRESS

1. Overview

The First Amendment protects freedom of the press as well as free speech. Since the press uses speech as its stock in trade, the explicit guarantee of a free press raises some free expression issues peculiar to the press.

a. Issues presented. The free press clause raises the following major issues, and the law concerning the free press clause mediates the tensions present in these issues.

   i. Special role for the press? The fact that the Constitution twice bestows protection to the press—via the free speech clause as well as the free press guarantee—seems to imply that some degree of special press protection was intended. The founding generation expected the press to perform a unique role of investigation, criticism, and reporting upon public affairs, functions critical to democratic self-governance.

   ii. May the press be restrained from publishing? While prior restraints of *any speech* are presumptively invalid, prior restraints of the press may be especially suspect.

   iii. May the press refuse governmental demands for information? The press may desire to shield its sources in the interest of fuller reporting, but the government may also have some legitimate reasons for demanding information from the press.

   iv. Is the press immune from liability for breaching a confidence? Sometimes the press may think that the public need to know justifies breaching its promise of confidentiality given to a source. To what extent, if at all, does the Constitution protect this breach of trust?

   v. May the press demand access to governmental information and proceedings? If a key function of the press is to expose government actions to the light of public accountability the press must have some right of access to the workings of government. But governments also have legitimate reasons to preserve secrecy.

2. Special Role for the Press?

a. In general. The press does have a special role in reporting to the public upon the activities of government. But that does not mean that the press enjoys an exemption from laws that are generally applicable to everyone. It does mean that the press may not be singled out for unfavorable treatment and it also means that the press enjoys the same right of access to government actions and proceedings that is possessed by the public. The latter issue is discussed in section H.6, infra.

b. **Picking on the press: Government may not treat the press uniquely unfavorably.** When governments subject the press, or a segment of the press, to unique treatment based on the *content of speech* or that *"threatens to suppress the expression of particular ideas or viewpoints"* the regulations are "constitutionally suspect." Such regulations are valid only when the government proves that they are *"necessary to achieve an overriding governmental interest."*

   i.   *Minneapolis Star & Tribune Co. v. Minnesota Commr. of Revenue,* 460 U.S. 575 (1983). Minnesota imposed a sales tax on all retail sales but exempted sales of newspapers and other publications. Minnesota then imposed a use tax on ink and paper used, but exempted from the use tax the first $100,000 worth of ink and paper used annually by a publisher. The effect was to impose the use tax on only 14 of the 388 newspapers in Minnesota. The *Minneapolis Star & Tribune,* the major daily in Minneapolis, paid two-thirds of the entire revenue Minnesota raised by the tax. The Court applied strict scrutiny because the tax "singled out the press for special treatment." The Court rejected Minnesota's contention that the tax was justified as a revenue raising measure because Minnesota could easily have raised revenue by imposing the general sales tax on all retail sales. Justice Rehnquist dissented on the ground that the Minnesota use tax system was in fact more beneficial to the *Star & Tribune* than would have been a generally applicable sales tax.

   ii. *Arkansas Writers' Project, Inc. v. Ragland,* 481 U.S. 221 (1987). Arkansas exempted from its sales tax all newspapers and "religious, professional, trade and sports journals" but no other magazines. The Court struck down the law because "a magazine's tax status depends entirely on its *content.*"

   iii. *Leathers v. Medlock,* 499 U.S. 439 (1991). Arkansas extended its sales tax to cable television services but exempted sales of newspapers, magazines, and satellite broadcast services. The Court upheld the tax scheme because the tax did not threaten "to suppress the expression of particular ideas or viewpoints." Unlike *Ragland* the tax did not discriminate on the basis of the content of particular publications. Rather, the Arkansas tax system distinguished between two different media. "The danger from a tax scheme that targets a small number of speakers is . . . censorship; a tax on a small number of speakers runs the risk of affecting only a limited range of views. The risk is similar to that from content-based regulation: it will distort the market for ideas." None of these dangers were present in a tax on an entire medium.

    iv. *Simon & Schuster, Inc. v. New York State Crime Victims Board,* 502 U.S. 105 (1991). A New York statute confiscated any income earned by a person "accused or convicted of a crime" from books or other publications concerning the crime, and provided that such proceeds be held in trust to satisfy civil judgments obtained against the accused or convicted criminal by his victims. The Court struck down the law. A "statute is presumptively inconsistent with the First Amendment if it imposes a financial burden on speakers because of the content of their speech." While New York's interest in facilitating compensation to crime victims was a compelling interest, New York had "little if any interest in limiting such compensation to the proceeds of the wrongdoer's speech about crime." The law was not sufficiently narrowly tailored to achieve New York's compelling interest in victim compensation. Not only did the law apply to "accused" persons; it also reached *any* book in which the author admitted to a crime, thus including such authors as Thoreau or Saint Augustine.

3. Prior Restraints

Prior restraints of the press are presumptively invalid. (See discussion in section B.3, *supra*.)

4. May the Press Refuse Governmental Demands for Information?

The general answer is "no." Reporters may be required to testify about criminal activity that they have witnessed. Publishers sued for defamation may be required to reveal details of their editorial processes.

    a. The "reporter's privilege." No such privilege is created by the Constitution. Some states have enacted statutes that provide such protection, but those "shield laws" are not enforceable in the federal courts exercising jurisdiction over federal questions.

        i. Criminal investigations: *Branzburg v. Hayes,* 408 U.S. 665 (1972). Branzburg, a reporter, had written several articles about drug activities. He was subpoenaed to testify before a grand jury about the drug transactions he had witnessed. Branzburg refused to testify; the Court rejected his claim of constitutional privilege. "[T]he Constitution does not . . . exempt the newsman from performing the citizen's normal duty of appearing and furnishing information relevant to the grand jury's task." The strong public interest in investigating crime outweighs the press interest in protecting its sources. The Court left open the question of whether there might be some constitutional shield with respect to administrative or legislative investigations.

ii. **Civil suits:** *Herbert v. Lando,* 441 U.S. 153 (1979). The Court refused to fashion a constitutional shield to protect publishers from inquiry into their editorial processes in the context of civil defamation actions but did not squarely reject all claims to a reporter's privilege in civil cases.

iii. **State shield laws.** Several states have enacted shield laws, providing a statutory reporter's privilege. These laws potentially conflict with federal and state constitutional guarantees of a fair trial. When a shield law would operate to deprive a criminal defendant of access to potentially exculpatory evidence, several courts have ruled that the shield law must yield to the constitutionally secured guarantee of a fair trial. See, e.g., *In re Farber,* 78 N.J. 259, 394 A.2d 330 (1978). This rule has been criticized on the ground that many other evidentiary privileges (e.g., attorney-client, spousal, physician-patient) have long been regarded as enforceable without violating a criminal defendant's fair trial right. See Nowak & Rotunda, at 1051.

b. **Search warrants.** Newspapers enjoy no constitutional immunity from search of their premises for evidence of crime when the search is conducted under a warrant based on probable cause. The Privacy Protection Act, a federal statute enacted in response to the *Zurcher* case, limits the power of federal or state officials to obtain evidence from the news media by search warrant unless the media itself is believed to be the criminal or there is a reasonable basis to believe that the evidence would be destroyed if sought by subpoena. See 42 U.S.C. §2000aa.

i. *Zurcher v. Stanford Daily,* 436 U.S. 547 (1978). The *Stanford Daily,* a student newspaper, published photos of a violent encounter on campus between student demonstrators and the police. The police obtained a warrant to search the *Daily* for negatives, film, and prints that might aid the police to identify the demonstrators who had assaulted the police. After the search, which proved to be fruitless, the *Daily* sought damages for what it contended was a search that violated the First Amendment. The Court rejected the contention, reasoning that so long as the Fourth Amendment is satisfied, the First Amendment does not impose any requirement that law enforcement officials proceed by subpoena instead of search warrant.

5. **Is the Press Immune from Liability for Breaching a Confidence?**

The press enjoys no immunity from generally applicable laws that subject persons to liability for breach of explicit promises of confidentiality.

a.   *Cohen v. Cowles Media Co.,* 501 U.S. 663 (1991). Pursuant to an explicit promise of confidentiality Cohen, a political campaign worker, provided reporters of the *Minneapolis Star* with information about the past criminal activities of a political candidate. The information was accurate but its significance was highly exaggerated. The *Star* then wrote stories that revealed Cohen's name, resulting in his dismissal. Cohen sought and obtained damages on a promissory estoppel theory. The Court rejected the *Star's* claim that the First Amendment insulated it from liability, reasoning that Cohen's claim was founded on a content-neutral principle of contract law.

6.   **May the Press Demand Access to Governmental Information and Proceedings?**

The press enjoys a limited right of access to the judicial process. In general, the press may not be excluded from criminal trials or preliminary hearings in criminal cases. Only if there is some *overriding public interest* (such as preserving a defendant's fair trial right) may the press be excluded. But the press enjoys no *general right* of access to governmental information and nonjudicial government proceedings.

a.   **Right of access to criminal trials.** The press and public have a right of access to criminal trials that may be overcome only if the government proves that the exclusion is *narrowly tailored* to serve a *compelling governmental interest.*

   i.   *Richmond Newspapers v. Virginia,* 448 U.S. 555 (1980). The Court held that, unless there is "an overriding interest articulated in findings, the trial of a criminal case must be open to the public." A plurality said this guarantee was found to be "implicit in . . . the First Amendment" because the rights guaranteed by the First Amendment "share a common core purpose of assuring freedom of communication on matters relating to the functioning of government." Access to the press was especially important, given the media role of "functioning as surrogates for the public." Concurring, Justice Stevens said the right announced was a general right to the "acquisition of newsworthy matter." Justice Brennan, joined by Marshall, also concurred, arguing that the right was grounded in a structural role of the First Amendment—a constitutional commitment not only to wide-open public debate but also to a process making that debate a fully informed one. Restraints on "access to governmental information [must be] dictated by the nature of the information and countervailing interests in security or confidentiality."

   ii.   **Scope of the *Richmond Newspapers* access right**

      (a)   *Globe Newspaper Co. v. Superior Court,* 457 U.S. 596 (1982). Massachusetts law required exclusion of the press and public from a courtroom during testimony by a minor allegedly the victim of a sex crime. The Court struck down the law, having concluded that Massachusetts had not proven that denial of access "is necessitated by a compelling governmental interest, and is narrowly tailored to serve that interest." The Court ruled that the state's inflexible closure rule was not narrowly tailored to achieving the state's compelling interest of protecting the minor victims of sex crimes from further trauma.

(b) ***Press-Enterprise Co. v. Superior Court (Press-Enterprise I),*** 464 U.S. 501 (1984). The Court extended *Richmond Newspapers* to voir dire of the jury pool in a criminal trial involving the rape and murder of a teenager.

(c) ***Press-Enterprise Co. v. Superior Court (Press-Enterprise II),*** 478 U.S. 1 (1986). The Court extended *Richmond Newspapers* to transcripts of a preliminary hearing in a criminal case, over the objections of the judge, prosecutor, and the defendant, all of whom thought that public access to the transcripts would endanger a fair trial. The Court treated a preliminary hearing, at which the court decides whether there is sufficient evidence against the accused to warrant a trial, as the constitutional equivalent of a criminal trial.

b. **Right of access to jails.** There is no right to interview inmates, but there is a right to access to prisons on the same controlled conditions available to the general public.

i. ***Pell v. Procunier,*** 417 U.S. 817 (1974). California barred the press from face-to-face interviews with prison inmates. The Court upheld the validity of the prohibition, reasoning that the regulation did not abridge free expression since it did "not deny the press access to sources of information available to members of general public." The Court rejected the contention "that the Constitution imposes upon government the affirmative duty to make available to journalists sources of information not available to members of the public generally." Even though this was a pre-*Richmond Newspapers* case, this principle has not been disturbed by *Richmond Newspapers* and its progeny. The access rights of the press recognized in *Richmond Newspapers, Globe,* and the *Press-Enterprise* cases are coextensive with the access rights of the general public. A companion case, *Saxbe v. Washington Post,* 417 U.S. 843 (1974), upheld a federal prison regulation virtually identical to California's policy at issue in *Pell.*

ii. ***Houchins v. KQED, Inc.,*** 438 U.S. 1 (1978). A San Francisco public television station was denied access to the "Greystone" portion of the Santa Rita county prison for purposes of filming prison conditions. The sheriff instituted monthly tours of Santa Rita, limited to twenty-five participants including press representatives, but barred cameras or recorders and did not include Greystone on the tour. The Court concluded that the sheriff could exclude the press from Greystone but could not bar cameras and recorders and must provide more frequent tours. But since the Court agreed that the First Amendment does not "guarantee the press any basic right of access superior to that of the public generally," it may be that the sheriff was free to close off Santa Rita entirely—to public and press alike.

REVIEW QUESTIONS AND ANSWERS

Question: By statute, the state of Alcatraz prohibits the publication of any photograph that depicts "naked male or female genitalia, or naked female breasts." The statute defines publication to include the "printing or developing of photos." Gary, a photographer with no artistic reputation, takes extremely explicit photographs of two persons engaged in sexual intercourse and displays the photos in his shop window. He is convicted of violating the Alcatraz statute. What is his best argument on appeal and is it likely to succeed?

Answer: Gary's best argument is to attack the facial validity of the law as substantially overbroad. The law is probably valid as applied to him, since it is likely that the photos will satisfy the constitutional definition of obscenity under the *Miller* test—the average person, applying contemporary community standards, would find that the photos appeal to the prurient interest in sex; the photos are probably patently offensive; and the photos probably lack serious artistic value. But the law *on its face* bars a wide variety of nude photos that are constitutionally protected—medical photos, anthropological photos, artistic photos, perhaps even some political photos. Since this flaw may be "a substantial concern in the context of the statute as a whole" the law may be found to be substantially overbroad and thus invalid on its face.

Question: Congress prohibits the posting of any "indecent" material on the Internet unless it has first been approved by the federal Internet Licensing Board. The law directs the board to approve all indecent speech unless the government has proven that the indecent speech is also obscene under the *Miller* definition, but provides that the determination of the board is final. Joan, a novelist who participates in an Internet writers' discussion group where she posts excerpts from her racy novels, challenges the validity of the law. What are her best arguments and are they likely to succeed?

Answer: Joan's best argument is the contention that the preposting approval system is an invalid prior restraint. It is a licensing scheme that subjects indecent speech to approval before posting and, as such, is a prior restraint. It is invalid because it lacks the necessary procedural safeguards that must accompany licensing systems. The government censors do have the burden of proving that the speech may be punished after the fact as obscene, but there is no opportunity provided for a judicial determination of that crucial issue. Another good argument is that only "indecent" speech must obtain prior approval and the term "indecent" is unconstitutionally vague. It is surely vague—a reasonable person is left guessing as to what speech is decent and what speech is not—and the consequence of guessing wrong is to incur liability for posting "indecent" but "nonobscene" speech without first obtaining the Licensing Board's approval.

Question: The city of Laurel, a large city with a racially diverse population, has experienced three riots in the past year. Each has occurred following a widely publicized incident of alleged police abuse of an African-American motorist. Two days after the fourth such incident—in which Officer Carter shot and killed Bill Barton, a black teenager—a well-known black separatist, Albert, spoke at a public rally in the predominantly black portion of Laurel. Albert spoke to the crowd as follows: "Don't take this racist abuse from scum like Carter. Defend yourselves. Take control of your neighborhood. Keep the racist cops out. Whites want to kill you just like Barton, so be prepared for self-defense. Sometimes you've got to stand up and be counted—let them know who you are and what you're mad about. Then those white folks will notice you." At this point Albert was arrested by a riot squad of police and charged with inciting a riot. Following Albert's arrest the crowd grew angry and a riot broke out within an hour of the arrest. Albert was convicted of inciting a riot and has appealed on free speech grounds. What result?

Answer: Albert's conviction should be overturned. While his speech was certainly intended to inflame passions it does not seem to be speech deliberately calculated to incite immediate lawlessness. While there was certainly a heightened danger that the crowd under these circumstances might be susceptible to invitations to riot, Albert's speech was not a direct call for immediate lawless action. Indeed, Albert counseled self-defense and his only invitation to lawless action was the advice to "keep the racist cops out" of the neighborhood. At most, this was advocacy of future lawlessness in the form of interfering with lawful police patrols. The fact that a riot broke out is of some relevance to the question of whether Albert's speech was likely to produce immediate riot, but Albert's speech was not intended to produce that action. Indeed, the most likely cause of the riot was the police action of arresting Albert.

Question: The state of Coronado has long operated a university open only to men, the Coronado Military College. As a result of a highly publicized lawsuit in which it was determined that CMC's admission policy violated the equal protection guarantee, Wendy was admitted to CMC. Dick, a male CMC student, was sufficiently angered by Wendy's presence at CMC that he chalked "Go Home, Bitch" on the sidewalks and surreptitiously posted flyers around the campus that contained the same statement. Wendy encountered these flyers and chalked messages daily. After several weeks Dick was apprehended, chalk in hand, by the campus police. He was expelled for violating a campus regulation prohibiting a student from "abusing another student by words or statements that inflict injury, contempt, or obloquy." Dick seeks an order reinstating him as a CMC student because he contends his expulsion violated his free speech rights. What result?

Answer: Dick will probably prevail. His statements certainly come within the regulation but the question is whether CMC may punish such speech. Dick's speech did not constitute fighting words—it was not delivered face to face under circumstances where an immediate violent response might reasonably be anticipated. Dick's comments were surely directed at Wendy but the anonymous, cowardly delivery takes them out of the fighting words doctrine. The mere fact that the words inflict emotional injury is not enough. Such words are not "fighting words." Though crude and offensive, Dick's sentiments are germane to an issue of public concern. Thus, CMC cannot validly defend on the ground that the expulsion serves the interest of vindicating Wendy's emotional well-being. The proper remedy, which is outside law's purview, is complete ostracism of Dick.

Question: The state of Lobo prohibits distribution of obscene material, defined in accord with the *Miller* standard. Los Locos, a city in Lobo with a reputation as a "wide-open town," tolerates the open display and sale of obscene material. Gerald, owner of a book and magazine store, displayed for sale a magazine with a sexually graphic and explicit cover depicting the President of the United States copulating with an animal. Gerald was arrested and convicted under Lobo's obscenity statute. He appeals. What result?

Answer: Gerald's conviction should be reversed on appeal. Although the Lobo statute appears to be constitutionally valid its application to Gerald is invalid. Even though obscene speech may be entirely prohibited (as Lobo has done) the law may not be selectively applied in a viewpoint-discriminatory fashion. (See *R.A.V. v. St. Paul.*) Los Locos tolerates open flouting of Lobo's obscenity law and has applied it only to the case of obscene speech that expresses contempt toward the President. The obscenity law, as applied, discriminates on the basis of a viewpoint that has nothing to do with the underlying reasons for treating the category of obscene speech as proscribable speech. In effect, Gerald was convicted for distributing literature contemptuous of the President.

Question: Allen, who describes himself as a "beatnik poet," likes to recite his poetry in public. He traveled to Corsage, a community composed overwhelmingly of adherents to a religious sect that advocates chaste morality above all else. In a public park in Corsage, before a small crowd of curious onlookers, Allen recited one of his poems exalting sexual gratification. After several verses the crowd was visibly angry and one large, beefy man approached Allen, demanding that he stop speaking "before I punch your lights out." An unarmed policeman, who had been overhearing the exchange, stepped in and grabbed the beefy man, declaring to the crowd: "This is a public park and this man has the right to recite his poem. Lay off him." The policeman warned the beefy man not to threaten Allen again. Allen resumed speaking and the crowd began to get larger. The beefy man returned with two dozen friends, all carrying axe handles. They surrounded Allen, glaring at him. The policeman radioed for help. The police dispatcher replied that none was available due to a hostage crisis in another part of the city. The policeman warned the crowd to leave Allen alone, and demanded that the axe handle carriers leave the park. They refused and one responded, "We're going to pound that bastard into a pulp." The policeman then asked Allen to stop. Allen continued speaking. The policeman then removed but did not arrest Allen. He was released as soon as the crowd had dispersed. In a civil suit, Allen seeks damages for violation of his constitutional rights. What result?

Answer: Allen will lose. While speech that offends the audience is entitled to constitutional protection, such speech may be suppressed where there is an imminent threat of violence, the police have made all reasonable efforts to protect the speaker, the police have asked the speaker to stop, and the speaker has refused to do so. Those elements are all present in this case.

Question: The Cleanlife Center, a drug rehabilitation organization, purchased a building in Roy's neighborhood and sought zoning changes to permit it to operate a drug rehab center at the location. Roy opposed the change and went from door to door, explaining to residents the Cleanlife Center's intentions and advising them when and where the zoning hearing would take place. Roy urged residents to show up and oppose the zoning change. A local television station learned of the controversy and interviewed the president of Cleanlife, who said of Roy, "We're a threat to him because he deals drugs." The reporter then sought out Roy for an interview. Roy refused to talk to the reporter, stating that he craved privacy. The reporter did no further investigation. The television station aired a broadcast in which Roy was mentioned by name as a "neighborhood activist and alleged drug dealer" opposed to the zoning change. Roy has never used or sold illegal drugs. Roy sued the television station for defamation, seeking punitive and compensatory damages. What constitutional issues, if any, are raised?

Answer: Is Roy a public figure? If so, he can only recover by proving that the television station acted with actual malice—it either knew the charge was false or was recklessly indifferent to its truth or falsity. He is certainly not an unlimited public figure, and is probably not a limited-purpose public figure. Though he injected himself into a public controversy he did so in a way that was not calculated to invite public attention, but his involvement was definitely for the purpose of influencing the resolution of a public issue—the rezoning. The same might be said of Gertz, the lawyer who was held not to be a public figure in *Gertz v. Robert Welch, Inc.* If he is not a public figure, but the issue is one of public concern, Roy can recover compensatory damages upon showing that the television station was negligent in airing its false charge, but will be required to prove actual malice to recover punitive damages. The issue is certainly one of public interest and concern, involving both the public policy issue of rezoning and the social policy issue of drug rehabilitation. If Roy is a private figure (likely) and the issue is only of private concern (not likely) Roy can recover both punitive and compensatory damages upon showing that the station was negligent. The station will not be able to assert any constitutional immunity because it qualified its statement by calling Roy an "alleged" drug dealer. The statement connotes some factual basis for the assertion, and the station aired the charge on the uncorroborated claim of Roy's adversary. It is a question of fact whether the station met an ordinary duty of care, was negligent, or acted with actual malice.

Question: Jane, an unknown tennis fan, went to the U.S. Open. While watching a match she ate her lunch, a portion of which was a ripe and juicy peach. Unknown to her, a camera crew working for David, a late-night television humorist, recorded the event. For the following two weeks David broadcast the image of Jane eating the peach, referring to Jane as a "seductive temptress" and asking Jane to identify herself. David then broadcast her picture on the Times Square "Jumbotron," a large outdoor television screen, asking her to call an 800 number. Jane sued David for invasion of her privacy and David defends by invoking the First Amendment. What constitutional protection, if any, does David's speech receive?

Answer: Since Jane is not a public figure and David's speech does not involve a matter of public concern it receives very little constitutional protection. David's best argument is to invoke the cases holding that, absent a compelling government interest, liability can not be imposed on a speaker who repeats true but embarrassing information obtained from publicly available court records and similar sources. But this alone does not insulate David. His references to Jane as a seductive temptress, while intended as humor, cast Jane in a false light. *Gertz* implicitly overruled *Hill,* thus subjecting David to false light privacy liability if he acted negligently in so characterizing Jane. Since he knew nothing about her, he was probably negligent.

Question: Congress proposes legislation that would slash the defense budget, primarily by eliminating major weapons procurement programs. A national debate ensues concerning the wisdom of this proposal. During that debate it becomes clear that the legislation would cause closure of a plant in the city of Texada operated by Armament Corporation, a major weapons producer. Armament is the overwhelming source of employment in Texada. Armament displays on billboards in Texada, a city that bans commercial billboard advertising, the following message: "Don't let *your* guard down. Tell Congress to keep the nation's guard up. Armament Corporation." The Texada city attorney charges Armament with violation of the billboard law. What is Armament's best defense and will it succeed?

Answer: Armament's best defense is that the billboard does not constitute commercial speech and thus is both permitted under the Texada statute and entitled to the full protection of the free speech clause. The commercial billboard ban is valid under *Metromedia.* Because the billboard message is undoubtedly an advertisement, identifies Armament by name, and was intended to produce public pressure against legislation inimical to its commercial interests, it is probably commercial speech despite the public interest of the message. Its content also suggests by innuendo that Texada citizens should protect their own economic interests by protesting proposed legislation against Armament's economic interest. (See *Bolger v. Youngs Drug Products Corp.*)

Question: Acting on evidence that tobacco use imposes enormous health costs, Congress passes a bill, signed into law by the President, that prohibits all advertising of tobacco products in any medium. The law is promptly challenged by the tobacco industry. Assess its constitutional validity.

Answer: The prohibition is entirely of commercial speech. The government has a substantial interest in decreasing the use of tobacco in order to ameliorate the costs to public health imposed by tobacco usage. The regulation directly advances those interests because advertising is a principal method of spurring demand for tobacco products. The regulation need not be the least restrictive means of achieving the government objective. The government need only prove that an absolute prohibition on tobacco advertising is a reasonably narrowly tailored means of achieving the government's objective, a means with a scope in proportion to the objective. But a flat ban on advertising is probably too restrictive to achieve the governmental objective of reducing the costs associated with tobacco use. See *44 Liquormart v. Rhode Island.*

Question: In order to preserve "respect for law and the appearance of impartiality in judicial decision," Congress enacts legislation that forbids picketing or demonstrations of any kind on the public sidewalks adjoining the United States Supreme Court during the Court's term (October through June). On Christmas Day Bob carries a sign in front of the Supreme Court protesting the Court's rulings on public displays of Christmas symbols. Only the Justices' law clerks and a few security guards are in the building. Bob is convicted of violating the law and appeals his conviction. What result?

Answer: Bob will prevail. The law is a content-neutral regulation of speech in a traditional public forum—the public sidewalks. While the law seeks only to regulate the time, place, and manner of speech it is probably not narrowly tailored to serve a significant government interest. First, while maintaining respect for law is surely a significant government interest, it is not at all certain that forbidding citizen protest of the Supreme Court is calculated to achieve that end. It may well serve the *appearance* of respect but probably has little to do with actual respect. Maintaining the "appearance of judicial impartiality" is a more problematic objective. Even assuming that it is a significant government objective, there is little reason to think that the presence of picketers will cause doubts to emerge on that score. In any case, a ban on protest speech outside the Court for the Court's term may be sufficiently close to a total prohibition to invoke strict scrutiny, under which the government would be required to prove that the ban was narrowly tailored to serve a compelling government interest. Neither of these interests seems compelling, and the ban is surely not very narrowly tailored. A ban on picketing when the Court is in session (approximately one or two weeks, on average, each month during the term) would be more narrowly tailored. Finally, the ban may not leave open *ample* alternatives for protesters to convey their message to the Court *and* to visitors to the Court. Cf. *United States v. Grace,* in which the Court struck down a total ban of demonstrations around the Court.

Question: The south side of a federal courthouse opens onto a large sunny plaza divided by steps that descend to a public sidewalk some distance away. The plaza itself is a favorite lunchtime gathering spot in good weather. Visitors to the courthouse typically enter from the steps dividing the plaza. During a highly publicized trial, knots of demonstrators chanting "Guilty, Guilty, He's so guilty" gathered in the plaza under the windows of the courtroom on the eighth floor. The demonstrators were informed by U.S. Marshals that the area was closed to public demonstrations of any kind. They ignored the Marshals' request to leave and were arrested for violation of the "no demonstrations" rule. On constitutional grounds they have moved to dismiss the indictment. Please rule on the motion.

Answer: The motion should be denied. The portion of the plaza on which they gathered is not a public forum. While it may be open to the public for casual gatherings, as for lunch, it has not been voluntarily dedicated to speech purposes. It is not a traditional public forum. Plaza spaces surrounding courthouses do not perform the same public recreational functions as parks and are not devoted to public passage or gathering in the manner of streets or sidewalks. Since the plaza area is not a public forum the government may impose reasonable nondiscriminatory content-neutral speech restrictions. Here, the restriction is content neutral—no demonstrations of any kind—and is reasonable—it is designed to protect the tranquility of court business and avoid unfair influence upon jurors.

Question: During a very dry, hot summer, the city of Alhambra banned all outdoor fires, except for those in fireproof containers (e.g., barbecues). A presidential candidate visited Alhambra that summer and was greeted by a band of protesters who burned his effigy on a large bonfire in a public square where he was speaking. Tom, one of the protesters, was arrested and convicted of violating the ban on outdoor fires. On appeal, he argues that the conviction was unconstitutional. What result?

Answer: Tom will probably lose. Tom's conduct is certainly symbolic—he intended to express contempt for the presidential candidate and his action would undoubtedly be so interpreted by onlookers. But Alhambra's ban on outdoor fires is not related to the suppression of ideas and furthers the substantial objective of preventing out-of-control fires in a dry, hot season. The speech restriction produced by the fire ban is not much—surely no greater than necessary to achieve the important goal of fire prevention. However, if Tom can prove that Alhambra has enforced the ban only to restrict political speech (or, even worse, speech critical of *this* presidential candidate) he will prevail.

Question: Based on an exhaustive study that purportedly proved that bumper stickers increase traffic accidents, the state of Cornucopia banned the display of any bumper sticker on motor vehicles, but exempted parking stickers or other permits. George, who drives a car with a sticker that says "Register Communists, Not Guns" and his wife, Mary, who drives a car with a sticker that consists of a pink triangle against a black background, each receive traffic citations for the display of their respective stickers. Each challenges the validity of the law. What result?

Answer: In George's case the law is a content-neutral restriction of speech but fails to leave open ample alternative channels of communication to other drivers. In Mary's case, the law impinges upon symbolic conduct—her expression of affinity with homosexuals. Whether under *O'Brien* or *Ward,* the law should be void as applied to George and Mary. Cornucopia's interest in traffic safety is an important or substantial interest, there is no evidence that Cornucopia's interest is related to the suppression of ideas, but the restriction may be broader than necessary to address the traffic safety problem.

Question: Clancy, a New York City policeman assigned to the drug squad in a section of Manhattan noted for widespread drug usage and drug dealing, gave a long interview to a *New York Times* reporter. The subsequent story, entitled "Confessions of a Drug Cop," quoted Clancy as saying: I give up; there's nothing that can be done to stop drugs. Too many people want to use them and there's too much money to be made in dealing. We can't stop it. It's time to legalize drugs. What I do is a waste of time and money.

Clancy's supervisor read the article and initiated an internal inquiry into Clancy's fitness to remain part of the drug squad. After interviews with Clancy's fellow officers, Clancy himself, and review of relevant records, the inquiry recommended that Clancy be removed from the drug squad and reassigned to a desk job. Clancy contends that the demotion violates his free speech rights. What result?

Answer: Clancy will lose. His remarks surely relate to a matter of public concern—the difficult issue of drug policy. Thus, he may be punished for his speech only if the government interest in the efficient performance of police duties outweighs Clancy's interest in informing the public of his views on drug policy. This is a close call. Both the government's interest in making sure that its police officers are efficient enforcers of the current drug laws and Clancy's interest in telling the public his opinion that the current laws cannot be enforced are important. In this case, Clancy's remarks do call into question his ability to enforce energetically the laws he believes to be unenforceable. He was not demoted for that speech, however. Instead, the police department used his speech as evidence sufficient to trigger a broader inquiry into his suitability for the drug squad. The police department's conduct comports with the Court's dicta in *Pickering* that a public employee's statements might be used as evidence of incompetence so long as they did not constitute an "independent basis for dismissal."

Question: Amanda, a public high school student, represented her school in an interschool speech and debate tournament. As an impromptu speaker she was given a topic—"What are the proper limits to free speech?"—and was asked to speak about it ten minutes later. Her speech on the topic was delivered to an audience of several judges, one or two fellow competitors, and her speech coach. Amanda asserted that there were no real boundaries to free speech, and to illustrate her contention, she repeated a lewd and vulgar joke circulating among her peers at school. The speech coach and one judge were offended by the joke; another judge thought that the joke was a brilliant illustration of her point. Amanda was suspended from the speech and debate team as a result. Is the suspension valid under the First and 14th Amendments? What is Amanda's best argument?

Answer: The suspension is probably valid but surely stupid. *Kuhlmeier* (section E(2), supra) suggests that while *Tinker* holds that schools must tolerate nondisruptive political expression of their students they need not "affirmatively . . . promote student speech." Since Amanda's speech occurred in the context of a "school sponsored expressive activity" her suspension from the team is valid if reasonably related to a legitimate pedagogical concern. Based on *Fraser,* it is possible that the repetition of a lewd joke, even to illustrate her legitimate point, is so inconsistent with the school's fundamental values that suspension is reasonable. Amanda's best argument is that she intended the entire speech to make a political point about the futility of speech regulation. If so, it may be that her speech, even though part of a school sponsored expressive activity, is the sort of nondisruptive personal political expression that *Tinker* found was protected free speech.

Question: Beta Beta Beta is a college fraternity. Its objectives are to instill pride, responsibility, self-esteem, character, self-reliance, and self-discipline in African-American college students, and to foster an independent and self-reliant black community separate and apart from white society. It limits membership to black males. Beta Beta Beta has a chapter at Canopus State University, a predominantly white public university in the state of Canopus. The CSU chapter of Beta Beta Beta, which consists of sixty students living together in a very large fraternity house, accepts as members virtually every black male CSU student who applies for membership. Over 90% of the African-American males enrolled at CSU are members of Beta Beta Beta. Following a complaint by a white male who was told he would not even be considered for membership in Beta Beta Beta, the Canopus Human Rights Commission rules that the Canopus Civil Rights Act, which bars racial discrimination in public accommodations, applies to fraternities. Is the application of the Act to the CSU chapter of Beta Beta Beta constitutionally valid?

Answer: Probably not. Beta Beta Beta is probably not an intimate association. Though relatively small (sixty people) and secluded from nonmembers, the Court's idea of intimate association is probably limited to family relationships. If it is an intimate association Canopus may not validly apply its Civil Rights Act to the fraternity without the strongest possible justification. It is more likely that Beta Beta Beta is an expressive association. The fraternity advocates a self-reliant black community separated from white society, an objective that presumably may be better fostered by a monoracial environment. Whether intimate or expressive, Canopus has the burden of overcoming its burden of justifying its infringement of Beta Beta Beta's intimate or expressive associational rights. While eliminating racial discrimination is surely a compelling goal of the state, that goal is not unrelated to the suppression of Beta's idea of racial separation. Cf. *Boy Scouts v. Dale.*

Question: Van Buren University, a public university in the state of Van Buren, imposes a $50 fee each semester upon Van Buren students. The fee is called the "Student Activities Fee" and is paid to the Van Buren Student Association (VBSA), which disburses funds from it to various student organizations. Among the organizations receiving funds are the Van Buren Animal Rights Caucus, the Van Buren Committee for Universal Health Care, and the Students for Socialism. All three of these organizations devote most of their efforts to political lobbying. Erika, a VBU student, challenges the constitutional validity of the $50 fee as applied to her, alleging that she is opposed to the purposes of each of the three named student organizations. What result?

Answer: Erika will lose unless the VBSA selects fund recipients on the basis of their viewpoint. Collection of the fee for the ultimate purpose of supporting political expression places Erika in the position of compelled expression of views with which she disagrees. But the forced expression—through her compelled contributions—may be upheld if Van Buren proves that the mandatory student fee is disbursed by VBSA on a viewpoint-neutral basis. See *Board of Regents v. Southworth,* section F(3)(6).

Question: In order to ensure that the electorate may contact candidates for political office, the state of Hornblower requires all candidates for public office to disclose their residence address and residence telephone number in a document available to the public. Gillian, a candidate for public office, invokes the First and 14th Amendments in a suit to enjoin enforcement of that requirement. What result?

Answer: Gillian should prevail. The requirement is a substantial interference with Gillian's right *not* to speak, by requiring her to disclose confidential information about herself. The requirement may be upheld if it is necessary to achieve a compelling state interest. Hornblower's interest in ensuring that the electorate can contact candidates for public office is important—probably compelling. But that interest can be achieved by less restrictive means—for example, Hornblower could require candidates for public office to disclose an address and telephone number at which the candidate may be reached, or a message left for the candidate, during normal business hours.

Question: As an environmental measure, the state of Oregano exempts from its sales tax all newspapers that make the full text of the newspaper available on the day of publication on the World Wide Web. Of the 400 newspapers published in Oregano about 200, including the *Daily Rant,* Oregano's largest daily, fail to publish online. The *Daily Rant* challenges the validity of the law. What result?

Answer: The challenge will probably fail. There is no indication that the exemption was based on the content of the *Rant.* However, the *Minneapolis Star* case casts some doubt on this conclusion. There, a use tax that applied to only fourteen of 388 newspapers was subjected to strict scrutiny because it "singled out the press." This exemption is much more diffuse in its effect, but does subject the state's largest daily to the tax. Oregano's asserted interest has nothing to do with the content of speech and may well be a compelling interest. The means of accomplishing this interest is narrowly drawn to that end, since it encourages electronic publication. *Ragland* lends some support since *Ragland* treated *Minneapolis Star* as a case turning upon the content-based nature of the use tax. There is little evidence that this exemption is content based. While the call is close, the law is valid.

Question: The state of Spinna permits only state officials to witness executions. Prison officials refuse to permit a television station to televise an execution. The station claims that its First Amendment rights have been violated. What result?

Answer: The station will lose. The press has no more right of access to executions than the public, and the public has no constitutional right of access to executions.

EXAM TIPS

- **Make Sure Expression Is Involved.** Don't deal with expression issues unless they are there.

  - If a statute regulates conduct that *might* be symbolic conduct, don't spend all your time discussing an esoteric symbolism. Get to the heart of the problem.

  - Remember the *flip side of expression*—compelled speech, disclosure, or association. Free expression is involved when governments compel expression.

  - Don't forget the *money = speech* equation in the context of political expenditures.

- **Distinguish between *Content-Based* and *Content-Neutral* Regulations.** Once expression is involved, your analysis will be quite different if the regulation is content based as opposed to content neutral.

- **Content-Based**. Check to see if the law at issue regulates a *category of speech* that is either *unprotected* or receives *limited protection*.

  — **Unprotected Categories.** Be sure the law only regulates speech within the *unprotected category*. If it regulates too much speech outside the category it is probably *overbroad*. Check to see if the law regulates within the category on the basis of *viewpoint*. Even unprotected speech can't be regulated on a viewpoint-discriminatory basis.

  — **Limited Protection Categories.** Be sure to identify the right doctrinal test that fits your limited protection category.

- **Content-Neutral.** Make sure it's really content neutral. For example, if the law is applied on the basis of content, or if the *"secondary effects"* of speech it addresses are the listeners' reactions, it's not content neutral.

■ **Don't Forget *Overbreadth*.** Focus on the facts to assess whether the law is challenged facially or as applied. If not clear, can the law be challenged facially? If so, overbreadth may be an issue.

■ **Don't Forget *Vagueness*.** *Any* law might be too vague, but don't raise this unless it is really a problem. Ask yourself if *you* would know what is forbidden by the law.

■ **Don't Forget the *Prior Restraint* Doctrine.** If the law licenses speech or enjoins speech, special scrutiny is warranted.

■ **Crossover Questions.** Remember that free expression problems can also raise equal protection or due process issues.

THE RELIGION CLAUSES

CHAPTER OVERVIEW

This chapter examines the two **religion clauses** of the First Amendment—the **establishment clause,** which prevents governments from establishing religions, and the **free exercise clause,** which prevents governments from interfering with religious beliefs. The most important points in this chapter follow.

- **Core Purposes of the Religion Clauses:** Both religion clauses secure **freedom of religion.** They apply equally to the federal and the state governments.

  - **Establishment Clause:** Governments may not create an **official state church** or a **de facto state church by excessive support, endorse** or **coerce** religion or nonbelief, or **prefer one religion to another.**

  - **Free Exercise Clause:** Governments may not interfere with **religious belief,** and must provide *limited* **accommodation to religious practices.**

- **The Establishment Clause:** There are two approaches to the establishment clause: **neutrality** and **accommodation.**

  - **Neutrality:** Under the current version of the *Lemon* test, government assistance to religion violates the establishment clause if *either* of the following elements are *not* satisfied:

    — **Secular Purpose:** The purpose of the governmental action must be to further a **secular objective.**

    — **Neutral Effect:** The primary effect of the governmental action must **neither advance nor inhibit religion,** but a variety of factors influence resolution of this element.

- **Accomodation:** The accommodation approach has modified *Lemon*. In this view, government involvement with religion violates the establishment clause if any of the following three factors are present:

  — **Discrimination between religions,**

  — **Endorsement** of religion, or

  — **Coercion** of religious belief or nonbelief.

- **Which Approach to Use?** The modified *Lemon* test dominates, but the **accommodation** approach has both influenced *Lemon* (especially the **neutral effects** prong) and supplanted *Lemon* in some areas (particularly public displays of religious imagery).

- **Financial Aid:** The modified *Lemon* test is used. **Direct aid** to religious institutions is generally void. **Indirect aid** is usually valid when part of a general, secular aid plan.

- **Religion and the Public Schools:** A combination of the *Lemon* test, endorsement, and coercion tests is used to evaluate religion in the public schools. Religious instruction and school-sponsored prayer are not permitted, but spontaneous student-initiated prayer is probably permissible. Governments may provide equal access to religious users of public facilities and, sometimes, must do so to afford free exercise of religion.

- **No Preferences:** Governments may not prefer one religion to any other, whether openly or covertly.

- **Religious-Based Exemptions from Law:** Religious institutions may be included in general exemptions given to secular institutions but when designed only to aid religion (and not required by the free exercise clause) they are probably void.

- **Delegations of Public Power to Religious Institutions are not permitted.**

- **Public Ceremonies or Displays of Religious Imagery:** Governments may neither **endorse** religion nor **coerce** religious belief by religious ceremony or display of religious imagery.

- **Government Inquiry into Religious Belief:** Governments may not inquire into religious beliefs but can assess whether religious beliefs are sincerely held.

■ **The Free Exercise Clause:** The free exercise clause absolutely bars governments from interfering with **religious belief. Minimal scrutiny** applies to governmental interference with **religious conduct** by **laws generally applicable to everyone. Strict scrutiny** applies to governmental interference with religious conduct that is **deliberately intended to suppress only religious conduct,** where such interference is coupled with an **infringement of another**

constitutional right, or arises in the narrow context of individualized assessment of eligibility for government benefits.

- **Minimal Scrutiny:** Laws generally applicable to everyone that burden religious practice or conduct are presumptively valid. They are void only if the challenger proves that they are not rationally related to a legitimate objective.

- **Strict Scrutiny:** The following types of governmental action are presumed to be invalid, and will be upheld only if the government proves that the action is essential to the achievement of some compelling government interest.

  — **Purposeful Interference with Religious Practice.**

  — **Individualized Denials of Government Benefits.**

  — **Burdens on Religious Conduct *and* Other Constitutional Rights.**

A. INTRODUCTION AND OVERVIEW

1. The Two Religion Clauses

Both religion clauses are in the First Amendment. The **establishment clause** provides that "Congress shall make no law *respecting an establishment of religion.*" The **free exercise clause** provides that "Congress shall make no law . . . *prohibiting the free exercise*" of religion. They apply to *any* action of the federal government.

2. Incorporated into 14th Amendment Due Process

Both religion clauses have been incorporated into the 14th Amendment's due process clause and so *apply with equal force to the states and the federal government.* The free exercise clause was first applied to the states in *Cantwell v. Connecticut,* 310 U.S. 296 (1940), and the establishment clause was first applied to the states in *Everson v. Board of Education,* 330 U.S. 1 (1947).

3. Purposes and Functions

The religion clauses were intended to work together to secure religious autonomy. The national government may neither establish religions nor interfere with individual religious beliefs. But these dual purposes both *overlap* and *conflict.* The Court has tried to reinforce the overlap and mediate the conflict.

   a. **Overlap.** Barring state religions preserves individual freedom of choice in religious belief. Barring governmental interference in religious belief keeps the government away from the entire institution of religion. When the religion clauses overlap doctrine developed under either clause is readily portable to the other.

EXAMPLE AND ANALYSIS

State law required that all retail businesses close on Sundays. The laws were challenged as violations of both religion clauses. An establishment clause issue was presented by the state's selection of Sunday as a uniform day of rest. A free exercise clause issue was presented by the economic penalty imposed on persons whose religious beliefs required them to close on Saturdays. The Court treated the clauses as overlapping but concluded that there was a secular purpose behind the law sufficient to justify it under both clauses. (See *McGowan v. Maryland,* 366 U.S. 420 (1961); *Braunfeld v. Brown,* 366 U.S. 599 (1961).)

---

b.   Conflict. The problem of conflict between the two religion clauses is more difficult.

EXAMPLES AND ANALYSIS

Example: The federal government employs chaplains in the armed forces. Is this a forbidden establishment of religion? Would the government's refusal to provide a chaplain be an invalid interference with the free exercise rights of the individual service member? (See *Abington School District v. Schempp,* 307 U.S. 203, 309 (1963) (Stewart, J., dissenting) (suggesting that the failure to provide a chaplain might violate free exercise).)

Example: Virtually all state and local governments exempt church property from taxation that generally applies to all real property. Is that exemption a prohibited establishment of religion? Would the refusal to exempt church property be an impermissible interference with the free exercise of religious belief? In *Walz v. Tax Commission,* 397 U.S. 664 (1970), the Court upheld a tax exemption for charities (including churches) as not an establishment of religion.

---

i.   Possible solutions. There are two imperfect "solutions" to the problem of conflict between the two religion clauses. The first is skewed toward avoiding establishments of religion at the expense of free exercise values. The second is biased toward preserving free exercise of religion at the expense of tolerating greater government involvement in religion.

(a)   Strict separation. This view, *never adopted by the Court,* holds that religion may never be used by government "as a basis for classification, . . . whether . . . the conferring of rights . . . or the imposition of . . . obligations." Kurland, 29 U. Chi. L. Rev. 5. This would also bar governmental accommodations of religion.

Example: Strict neutrality would mean no military chaplains, no property tax exemptions for churches, and no religious exemptions from compulsory military service.

(b) Accommodation permitted. This view, *which represents what the Court actually does,* holds that some governmental accommodations of religion are permitted but not required, some are prohibited because of the establishment clause, and some are required because of the free exercise clause. The difficulty is deciding which accommodations fall into which classification. This view does not eliminate conflict between the clauses—it does require the Court to mediate it.

EXAMPLE AND ANALYSIS

The Court's role may be visualized by imagining the establishment and free exercise clauses as opposite poles of a spectrum:

Establishment ------------- 1 -------------2------------ 3 ------------4 ------------ Free Exercise

The Court's establishment clause cases define a zone of *impermissible accommodation* and its free exercise cases define a zone of *required accommodation.* Everything in the middle is neither required nor forbidden, but the size of the middle can be expanded or contracted by the Court. Points 1 through 4 are arbitrary graphic indicators of where the limits of required and impermissible accommodations might be set. Currently the free exercise limits are nearer to point 4 than anywhere else, and the establishment limits, *depending on the issue,* vary from something close to point 1 to point 3. The materials that follow will help you gain a sense of where the Court actually sets these limits in each issue and why it does so.

B. THE ESTABLISHMENT CLAUSE

1. Overview

a. Doctrinal tension. The principal problem with the establishment clause is the fact that the Court oscillates between two different—and often contradictory—approaches to establishment clause cases. Keep both approaches in mind.

i.   **Neutrality.** This has been the Court's dominant approach and is embodied in the original *Lemon* test, which, as modified, is the reigning doctrinal test for determining when government action is a forbidden establishment. By this approach governments may not purposefully or inadvertently provide substantial assistance to religion or become excessively involved in religious affairs. This is **not** *absolute* separation—the Court recognizes that churches, like everyone else, are entitled to such public services as police and fire protection.

ii. **Accommodation.** The other approach is toleration of governmental aid to religion, provided that such aid:

- Does *not discriminate among religions,*

- Is not so significant as to constitute a governmental *endorsement* of religion, or

- Does not *coerce* religious belief or nonbelief.

This approach has modified *Lemon* and is often applied in addition to, and sometimes is substituted for, the *Lemon* test.

b. **Original purpose.** The establishment clause was the product of at least three different conceptions of its purpose.

i.   **Protect the church.** Roger Williams argued that a ban on state establishments of religion was needed to *protect religion* from the "worldly corruptions" of the secular state.

ii. **Protect the state.** Thomas Jefferson claimed that the establishment prohibition was necessary to *protect the secular state* from religious "depredations and incursions." A "wall of separation between Church and State" was needed.

iii. **Protect both church and state.** James Madison believed that separation of religion and government would *protect both church and state* by enabling each to fulfill its functions. No religious sect could dominate religious thought via government aid. No religion could dominate secular life through a capture of government. No religious sect could be bullied by government. Diffusion of power and separation of functions were Madison's themes.

c. **The development of neutrality**

i.   **The basic principles.** In *Everson v. Board of Education,* 330 U.S. 1 (1947), discussed in section B.2, infra, the Court stated in dicta a very broad conception of strict separation. The establishment clause "means at least this: Neither a State nor the Federal Government can set up a church. Neither can . . . aid one religion, aid all religions, or prefer one religion over another. Neither can force nor influence a person to go to or to remain away from church against his will or force him to profess a belief or disbelief in any religion. . . . No tax . . . can be levied to support any religious activities . . . Neither . . . government can . . . participate in the affairs of any religious organizations . . . and vice versa." These are very broad principles of "strict separation." The Court has preferred to apply a less strict version of neutrality. The alternative approach—accommodation—rejects the proposition that governments may not aid religion or that there can be no involvement between religion and government.

ii. **The original *Lemon* test.** Despite erosion by the **endorsement** and **coercion** tests, the *Lemon* test is still the dominant doctrinal test to determine whether a law violates the establishment clause. Derived from *Lemon v. Kurtzman,* 403 U.S. 602 (1971), discussed in section B.2, infra, the original *Lemon* test provided that a law violates the establishment clause if the challenger proves that the law:

- Lacks a *secular purpose, or*

- Lacks a *neutral primary effect*—it *either advances or inhibits religion, or*

- Produces an *excessive government entanglement with religion.*

iii. **The modified *Lemon* test.** After years of attack and erosion the Court in *Agostini v. Felton,* 521 U.S. 203 (1997), restated the *Lemon* test to hold that a law is an impermissible establishment of religion if the law:

- Lacks a *secular purpose,* **or**

- Lacks a *neutral primary effect.*

Laws lack a neutral primary effect if they (1) produce **government indoctrination or endorsement,** or (2) **classify by reference to religion,** or (3) create an **excessive entanglement** between government and religion. The modified *Lemon* test generally permits government aid to religion so long as it furthers a secular purpose and does not prefer one religion to another.

(a) **Secular purpose.** This requires courts to assess legislative motives. The Court does not accept at face value a stated secular purpose, but evaluates whether the *actual purpose* of the law is secular. A secular purpose need *not* be the *exclusive* purpose of the law.

EXAMPLES AND ANALYSIS

Example: Kentucky law required that the Ten Commandments be posted in public school classrooms, with a statement that the secular effect of the Ten Commandments may be seen in the common law. Because the Ten Commandments are a "sacred text" and the posting was unrelated to the curriculum, the Court concluded that the law had "no secular legislative purpose" but was "plainly religious." *Stone v. Graham,* 449 U.S. 39 (1980).

Example: Louisiana law required public school teachers who teach evolution also to teach "creation science." Louisiana declared its purpose to be to "protect academic freedom." The Court concluded that the law restricted rather than advanced academic freedom, and so rejected the stated purpose. Because creation science "embodies the religious belief that a supernatural creator was responsible for the creation of humankind" the Court ruled that Louisiana was motivated by a "preeminent religious purpose." *Edwards v. Aguillard,* 482 U.S. 578 (1987).

> **(b) Neutral effect.** The Court is satisfied that a law has a *neutral primary effect* if the religious impact of the law is *"remote, indirect and incidental."* Tribe, at 1215.

 EXAMPLES AND ANALYSIS

Example: Minnesota permitted taxpayers to deduct from income up to $700 of the "tuition, textbooks, and transportation" costs incurred in educating their children in elementary or secondary schools. The secular purpose of the law was to encourage education of children. Because the deduction was available to all parents, regardless of whether their children were attending public or private schools, the law had a neutral effect despite the fact that the vast majority of the deductions were claimed by parents of children enrolled in religious schools. The broad availability of the deduction was "an important index of secular effect." *Mueller v. Allen,* 463 U.S. 388 (1983).

Example: New York assisted low-income educationally deprived children by providing additional teaching of reading and arithmetic in both public and private schools. As part of the program New York supplied public school teachers to teach remedial reading and arithmetic in parochial schools. The Court upheld the validity of the aid, declaring that aid that "is allocated on the basis of neutral, secular criteria that neither favor nor disfavor religion, and is made available to both religious and secular beneficiaries on a nondiscriminatory basis, [is] less likely to have the effect of advancing religion." *Agostini v. Felton,* 521 U.S. 203 (1997).

A law may also violate the establishment clause if its primary effect is to *inhibit* rather than *favor* religion.

d. **The development of the accommodation approach.** From the nation's beginning both the states and the federal government have provided assistance to religion. While for a time some states maintained an established church, that practice is long dead and now clearly forbidden by the incorporation of the establishment clause into the 14th Amendment. Based on this history some Justices contend that the establishment clause flatly forbids two things only: (1) establishment of a national religion, and (2) preference among religious sects. The accommodation approach tolerates nonpreferential aid to religion, unless it is either *coercive* or represents a governmental *endorsement* of religion. Strong adherents to accommodation reject the endorsement test as reflecting "an unjustified hostility toward religion." See *Allegheny County v. Greater Pittsburgh ACLU,* 492 U.S. 573 (1989) (Kennedy, J., dissenting and concurring). To these Justices, nondiscriminatory aid to religion is permitted so long as it is neither *coercive* nor provides **direct** *benefits to religion so large as to create a de facto established church.*

i. **The "endorsement" test.** "The Establishment Clause prohibits government from making adherence to a religion relevant in any way to a person's standing in the political community. . . . [G]overnment endorsement . . . of religion . . . sends a message to nonadherents that they are outsiders, not full members of the political community, and . . . to adherents that they are insiders, favored members of the political community. Disapproval sends the opposite message." *Lynch v. Donnelly,* 465 U.S. 668 (1984) (O'Connor, J., concurring). To determine if endorsement exists courts must determine whether

- The government *intends* to convey a message of endorsement or disapproval of religion, *and*

- The *"objective meaning"* of the government's statement in the community was to endorse or disapprove religion.

Example: During December, a community displays a crèche scene in a public park, together with a Christmas tree, a display of Santa and his reindeer, a menorah, and an explanation of Kwanzaa. The intended message appears to be acknowledgment of various holidays and an objective viewer would so construe it. There is no endorsement or disapproval of religion.

Endorsement is often used as a gloss upon *Lemon*—to assess more precisely the purpose and effects prongs of *Lemon*. Perhaps for this reason, the "strong" adherents to accommodation reject the endorsement test.

ii. **The "coercion" test.** "The coercion that was a hallmark of historical establishments of religion was *coercion of religious orthodoxy* and of *financial support [of an official state church] by force of law and threat of penalty.*" *Lee v. Weisman,* 505 U.S. 577 (1992) (Scalia, J., dissenting). Coercion of religious orthodoxy necessarily involves government *preference* for one set of religious beliefs over others. Coerced financial support for an official state religion, via taxation and spending, also involves the same sort of preferential treatment among religious beliefs. Under *Lemon,* the establishment clause may be violated without coercion. For "strong" accommodationists, coercion is essential to an establishment clause violation.

e. **Relationship of the *Lemon* test and the *endorsement* and *coercion* tests.** The *Lemon* test, either originally or as modified, and the *endorsement* and *coercion* tests are not necessarily contradictory. Examination of governmental purpose, effect, and entanglement may produce the same results as testing for endorsement or coercion.

 # EXAMPLE AND ANALYSIS

In company with secular symbols of the December holiday season, Pawtucket, Rhode Island displayed a crèche. The Court applied *Lemon* and upheld the validity of the display, having concluded that Pawtucket had a secular purpose for the display. Justice O'Connor, concurring, applied *Lemon*'s purpose and effect prongs to help determine whether Pawtucket's crèche display constituted a forbidden endorsement. *Lynch v. Donnelly,* 465 U.S. 668 (1984).

But because the *Lemon* test and the *endorsement* and *coercion* tests apply different criteria to determine prohibited establishments of religion they may well produce different results.

 # EXAMPLE AND ANALYSIS

A city government erects a sign outside city hall declaring "Worship this Week at the Church of Your Choice!" Under the *Lemon* test the sign is probably invalid. While the city may have a secular purpose—perhaps church attendance reduces social disorder—the primary effect of the sign is to aid religion. The endorsement test would also invalidate the sign. But the sign would survive the coercion test—it does not impose any religious orthodoxy backed by the mailed fist of the state. Note that the "strong" adherents to accommodation would only apply the coercion test to this example.

Finally, the endorsement approach has influenced *Lemon*'s effects prong by prompting the Court to restate it in *Agostini* as a prohibition against endorsement, preferential aid, or excessive entanglement.

f.   **Relationship to free speech.** Government discrimination against speech on the basis of its religious content is subject to strict scrutiny. (See Chapter 11, supra.) But governments sometimes seek to justify such discrimination on the grounds that it is required by the establishment clause. The free speech issue cannot be resolved without also resolving the establishment clause issue.

 # EXAMPLES AND ANALYSIS

Example: A public university that opened its facilities to student groups sought to close them to religious student groups, and defended its conduct on the grounds that it was compelled to do so by the establishment clause. The Court ruled that the establishment clause did not require that the university close its doors to religious students. *Widmar v. Vincent,* 454 U.S. 263 (1981).

Example: The University of Virginia's Student Activities Fund paid the expenses of student organizations but refused to pay the printing expenses for a religious student publication. Virginia argued that its refusal was justified on establishment clause grounds. The Court disagreed. Applying a pure religion-neutral approach and eschewing any reliance on *Lemon,* the Court found that the establishment clause did not prohibit aid on a religion-neutral basis. *Rosenberger v. Rector and Visitors of the University of Virginia,* 515 U.S. 819 (1995).

2.   **Financial Aid to Religious Institutions**

The provision of governmental financial aid to religious institutions has been an especially contentious subject.

a.   **Overview.** The neutrality approach to the establishment clause developed in this area—*Lemon v. Kurtzman* involved aid to religious schools—and continues to play an important role. However, the ascendancy of the accommodation approach has begun to manifest itself in this area, culminating in *Agostini*'s modified version of *Lemon,* which will make aid more readily available.

b. Transport to and from school: *Everson v. New Jersey,* 330 U.S. 1 (1947). New Jersey permitted local school boards to reimburse parents of children in private schools for the cost of school bus transportation to and from school. Most of the private schools were Roman Catholic. The Court, 5 to 4, upheld the practice. New Jersey had done nothing more than "help parents get their children, regardless of their religion, safely and expeditiously to and from accredited schools." In *Lemon* terms, New Jersey's purpose was secular, the effect of the practice was primarily to enhance the safety and educational well-being of schoolchildren, and government involvement with religious institutions was nonexistent.

c. Instructional assistance. This aid typically is in the form of supplying teachers, supplying teaching materials, or supplying money to pay teachers or buy materials.

   i. Supplying teachers to religious schools. In *Agostini v. Felton,* 521 U.S. 203 (1997), the Court upheld this practice under certain conditions. New York assisted educationally deprived children by providing remedial instruction in reading and arithmetic in both public and private schools. As part of the program New York supplied public school teachers to teach these subjects in parochial schools and barred those teachers from participating in any religious activities or instruction at the schools. The Court disavowed two earlier cases on the same point, *Grand Rapids School District v. Ball,* 473 U.S. 373 (1985), and *Aguilar v. Felton,* 473 U.S. 402 (1985), as "no longer good law" and declared that aid that "is allocated on the basis of neutral, secular criteria that neither favor nor disfavor religion, and is made available to both religious and secular beneficiaries on a nondiscriminatory basis, [is] less likely to have the effect of advancing religion."

   ii. Supplying instructional materials to religious schools. In *Mitchell v. Helms,* 120 S. Ct. 2530 (2000), the Court sustained the validity of a federal program by which library and media materials and computer hardware and software were loaned to public and private schools to implement "secular, neutral, and nonideological programs." The aid complied with the *Agostini* version of *Lemon.* A plurality thought that there was no government indoctrination so long as aid is either broadly distributed to secular as well as religious recipients or results from private choice. The Court overruled *Meek v. Pittenger,* 421 U.S. 349 (1975), and *Wolman v. Walter,* 433 U.S. 229 (1977), to the extent they were inconsistent with *Mitchell.* Both cases had voided loans of secular instructional materials to religious schools and their students.

iii.   **Salary and instructional material reimbursements to religious schools or teachers.** Direct financial aid to religious schools or teachers in religious schools, typically in the form of reimbursement for or supplements to teacher salaries, is generally invalid. The validity of other reimbursements to religious schools depends on the degree to which it is tied to specific secular purposes. But all of these cases predate *Agostini*.

(a)   *Lemon v. Kurtzman,* 403 U.S. 602 (1971). Rhode Island paid a 15% salary supplement directly to certain religious school teachers of secular subjects. Pennsylvania reimbursed religious schools for a portion of the cost of teachers and instructional materials in secular subjects. The Court voided both programs. The Court accepted the claimed secular purpose of the programs, avoided decision whether their primary effect was neutral toward religion, but concluded that the administration of both programs involved excessive entanglement between religion and government.

(b)   *Levitt v. Committee for Public Education,* 413 U.S. 472 (1973). A state grant to all private schools of a lump sum per pupil in order to reimburse such schools for services mandated by state law, such as testing and record keeping, was struck down. Even though the unrestricted grants were keyed to the per-pupil cost of providing the mandated services the effect of a direct grant of money was an impermissible advancement of religion.

(c)   *Wolman v. Walter,* 433 U.S. 229 (1977). The Court upheld an Ohio program providing funds directly to religious schools, but limited to reimbursement of the costs of distributing, administering, and scoring state-prepared standardized tests necessary to assess the academic performance of religious school students. Unlike *Levitt,* the funds were tied to this specific benign state objective.

(d)   *Committee for Public Education v. Regan,* 444 U.S. 646 (1980). Without reversing *Levitt* the Court upheld, 5 to 4, state reimbursement of the expenses of religious schools incurred in administering standardized tests, collecting and reporting student attendance data, and reporting statistical information about the school. Unlike *Levitt,* this program tied reimbursement directly to the state-mandated services, thus avoiding the possibility of unrestricted grants aiding the avowedly religious functions of the recipient.

d.   **Noninstructional assistance to religious school students.** In *Zobrest v. Catalina Foothills School District,* 509 U.S. 1 (1993), the Court sustained government provision of noninstructional assistance to religious school students. Pursuant to a program by which public school districts paid the cost of a sign-language interpreter for deaf students, no matter what school they attended, an Arizona school district hired a signer for Zobrest, a student at a Roman Catholic high school. The Court upheld the practice since it was part of a program that provided benefits without reference to religion and there was virtually no benefit received by the religious school itself.

e.   **Tuition assistance and tax benefits to parents of children in religious schools.** The validity of governmental aid provided directly to parents of schoolchildren depends on its neutrality toward religion. Aid that is available to all parents is valid. Aid that is limited to parents of children in religious schools is invalid.

   i.   **Aid limited to private school parents: *Nyquist* and *Sloan*.** In *Committee for Public Education v. Nyquist,* 413 U.S. 756 (1973), and *Sloan v. Lemon,* 413 U.S. 825 (1973), the Court struck down measures by which New York and Pennsylvania sought to reimburse parents of private schoolchildren for a portion of their tuition costs. The New York program at issue in *Nyquist* involved a carefully crafted combination of grants to low-income families and tax credits to middle-income families that were graduated to provide effective reimbursement of 50% of tuition costs. Pennsylvania's system was a cruder version of grants and tax deductions. Both programs were *limited to parents of private school children* and in each case the overwhelming proportion of private school students were enrolled in religious schools. Applying the *Lemon* test the Court found that both programs had the primary effect of advancing religion.

   ii. **Aid to all parents: *Mueller v. Allen,* 463 U.S. 388 (1983).** Under its state income tax law, Minnesota permitted anyone to deduct from their taxable income up to $700 of expenses incurred in providing tuition, textbooks (other than religious texts) and transportation for their children attending either public or private elementary or secondary schools. The Court applied *Lemon* and upheld the plan. The law furthered the secular purpose of aiding the education of all young Minnesotans. The law had a neutral effect toward religion—it was facially neutral with respect to religion and any aid to religion was both attenuated and the product of the independent decision of parents. The dissenters argued that because most of the deductions were claimed by parents of children in religious schools the plan's primary effect was to advance religion.

   Because the "primary effect" prong of *Lemon* was satisfied by facial neutrality toward religion, *Mueller* suggests that laws furthering a secimals purpose while indirectly delivering substantial benefits to all religions through parental benefits are valid.

EXAMPLE AND ANALYSIS

A state adopts a voucher plan by which it gives parents of all schoolchildren a "voucher" redeemable at any school, public or private, in exchange for a specified portion of the cost of their child's education. In essence, the plan permits parents to specify which school will receive state funds. While religious schools will receive direct aid from the state the decision to grant that aid rests entirely with parents—private citizens. The plan furthers the secular purpose of increasing educational choice and fostering innovation. It is facially neutral and presents no entanglement with religion. But the size of the aid might be constitutionally significant.

---

f. **Public scholarships for religious study:** *Witters v. Washington Department of Services for the Blind,* 474 U.S. 481 (1986). The Court unanimously sustained a Washington law granting scholarships to handicapped students, as applied to a scholarship given a blind student who used the funds to pay tuition at a Christian college where he was preparing for the ministry. The majority applied *Lemon* and concluded that Washington had a secular purpose—helping handicapped students achieve self-sufficiency—and that the scholarship was neutral in its effect since the aid was received by the *student,* not the religious college. As in *Mueller,* aid to private persons that ends up in religious institutions has a *neutral effect* because the private person, *not the state,* makes the choice of delivering it to a religious institution.

g. **Aid to higher education.** Government aid delivered directly to religious colleges and universities (except, perhaps, "pervasively sectarian" schools such as seminaries) is more constitutionally acceptable than aid to sectarian elementary and secondary schools. This is because the Court thinks college "students are less impressionable and less susceptible to religious indoctrination" than younger students and thus "there is less likelihood than in primary and secondary schools that religion will permeate . . . secular education." *Tilton v. Richardson,* 403 U.S. 672 (1971). As a result, the Court has upheld, after applying *Lemon:*

   * Federal aid to religious colleges to finance construction of buildings used entirely for secular purposes. *Tilton v. Richardson,* 403 U.S. 672 (1971).

- A state law permitting the issuance of the state's tax-exempt bonds to finance construction of buildings used for secular purposes by church-related colleges. *Hunt v. McNair,* 413 U.S. 734 (1973).

- A state program providing all private colleges (including church colleges) a per-pupil cash grant equal to 15% of the state's per-pupil expenditures in its public university system. The grant could only be spent on secular purposes. This requirement was enforced by mandated accounting and reporting. *Roemer v. Maryland Board of Public Works,* 426 U.S. 736 (1976).

  h. **Grants to religious groups for secular purposes—the Adolescent Family Life Act:** *Bowen v. Kendrick,* 487 U.S. 589 (1988). The Adolescent Family Life Act provided federal funds to a variety of public and private organizations, including religious institutions, to counsel adolescents concerning sexual relations and pregnancy. The Court applied *Lemon* and found the Act to be *facially* valid. Congress's secular purpose was to eliminate or reduce the social and economic problems associated with teenage sexuality. The effect of grants to religious institutions to further that purpose was neutral because the services provided were "not religious in character" nor did they involve the furtherance of sectarian dogma. The fact of overlap between the government's secular goals and religious principles concerning teenage sexuality was not enough to produce a conclusion that the "primary effect" of the Act was to advance religion. Government monitoring of the services provided under the Act by religious institutions was too insignificant to trigger the entanglement prong of *Lemon.*

3. **Religion in the Public Schools**

   By a series of rulings the Court has virtually, but not quite entirely, banished religious symbolism and observance from the public schools.

   a. **Religious instruction.** Public schools may not provide religious instruction. Public schools may release some students from school before the usual time in order to permit those students to receive instruction away from school. *Zorach v. Clauson,* 343 U.S. 306 (1952). Public schools may not release students for religious instruction given on school premises. *McCollum v. Board of Education,* 333 U.S. 203 (1948).

   b. **Prayer, Bible readings, and other invocations of God.** Except for the possible exception of the Pledge of Allegiance ("one nation, under God") and voluntary, spontaneous, student-sponsored and composed prayer, public schools may not invoke God or conduct prayer or Bible readings.

      i. **Voluntary state-composed prayer:** *Engel v. Vitale,* 370 U.S. 421 (1962). New York composed the following nondenominational prayer and recommended, but did not require, that students recite it each morning: "Almighty God, we acknowledge our dependence upon Thee, and beg Thy blessings upon us, our parents, our teachers and our Country." Wherever implemented, objectors were excused from the daily recital. The Court struck down the prayer, primarily on the ground that "it is no part of the business of government to compose official prayers for . . . the people to recite as part of a religious program carried on by government."

ii. **Voluntary Bible readings:** *Abington School District v. Schempp,* 374 U.S. 203 (1963). The Court invalidated a state requirement that ten verses of the Bible be read aloud at the beginning of each public school day. The law had a religious purpose and a distinctly religious effect.

iii. **Voluntary silent prayer:** *Wallace v. Jaffree,* 472 U.S. 38 (1985). Alabama authorized its public schools to devote one minute at the start of each day "for meditation or voluntary prayer." The Court found the law to be an establishment of religion because Alabama's *motive* in enacting the law was "to return voluntary prayer" to the public schools.

iv. **Prayer at school functions.** *Lee v. Weisman,* 505 U.S. 577 (1992), involved a bland, ecumenical prayer at a public school graduation. The Court thought that the practice "subtly coerced" unwilling students to participate in or observe the prayer. The four dissenters, led by Scalia, argued that "subtle coercive pressure" exerted by one's peers is not the sort of coercion that is barred by the establishment clause. The dissenters construed the establishment clause to bar "coercion of religious orthodoxy" or forced financial support of a state church, not the social "compulsion" implicit in quiet acquiescence to a vaguely theistic graduation benediction.

In *Santa Fe Independent School District v. Doe,* 120 S. Ct. 2266 (2000), the Court extended *Lee v. Weisman* to strike down as facially invalid a school district policy, never implemented, that permitted students to vote on whether to have a student speaker "solemnize" high school football games and, if so, to select the student speaker. The Court regarded the policy as designed to perpetuate prayer at the opening of football games, thought the student vote and the football game forum made the speech officially sanctioned rather than private, and concluded that the policy would both constitute endorsement of religion and coercion of those students (such as band members) required to attend football games. Chief Justice Rehnquist, joined by Justices Scalia and Thomas, dissented, arguing that it was premature to rule on the facial validity of the policy.

v. **Posting the Ten Commandments:** *Stone v. Graham,* 449 U.S. 39 (1980). Because the Kentucky legislature concluded that "the Ten Commandments have had a significant secular impact on the development of secular [law in] the Western World," Kentucky required the posting of the Ten Commandments in every public school classroom. The Court invalidated the law on the ground that it lacked any actual secular purpose, despite the Kentucky legislature's finding.

c. **Curriculum modification for a religious purpose.** Governments may not mandate curriculum modifications in public schools for a religious purpose.

i. **Ban on teaching evolution:** *Epperson v. Arkansas,* 393 U.S. 97 (1968). Arkansas prohibited its public schools and universities from teaching "the theory that man evolved from other species of life." The Court struck down the law on the ground that it was motivated by a desire to and had the effect of conforming "a particular segment" of the curriculum to "the religious views of some of its citizens."

ii. **If evolution is taught, creation science too:** *Edwards v. Aguillard,* 482 U.S. 578 (1987). For the purpose of enhancing academic freedom, Louisiana enacted legislation that required public schools to teach creation science if they taught evolution. Even though the legislative history was bereft of any indication that Louisiana's legislature had been motivated by a religious purpose, the Court ruled the legislature's "preeminent purpose . . . was clearly to advance the religious viewpoint that a supernatural being created humankind." The Court found evidence of this religious motive partly in the fact that the statute was poorly suited to its stated objective—academic freedom—and partly in the Court's belief that the statute was rooted in the "same historic and contemporaneous antagonisms" between religion and evolution that were present in *Epperson.* Rehnquist and Scalia dissented, arguing that there was no *evidence* of a religious motive, only the Court's *assumption* that hidden religious objectives motivated the law.

4. **Sunday Closing Laws and Other Laws for Sabbath Observance**

Sunday closing laws and laws that mandate accommodations to sabbath observance seemingly present problems of endorsement or preferential aid to religion. The Court has refused to treat Sunday closing laws as forbidden establishments of religion but has struck down a law mandating that employers honor their employees' Sabbath. The former was seen to advance secular goals; the latter was regarded as designed to advance and protect a particular religious practice.

    a. **Sunday closing laws:** *McGowan v. Maryland,* 366 U.S. 420 (1961). In four companion cases the Court upheld the validity of state laws requiring business closures on Sunday. Even though Sunday is the Christian Sabbath the Court regarded the closure laws as furthering the secular goal of providing "a uniform day of rest for all citizens."

    b. **Mandating employer observance of employees' Sabbath:** *Estate of Thornton v. Caldor, Inc.,* 472 U.S. 703 (1985). When Connecticut revised its Sunday closing law by permitting some businesses to open on Sunday it also prohibited employers from forcing an employee to work on the employee's Sabbath or dismissing the employee for his refusal to do so. The Court invalidated the law because it lacked any purpose other than protecting religious observance and practice: (1) the Connecticut law focused exclusively on religion and was not simply one aspect of a state attempt to reach the broader, and secular, goal of limiting invidious discrimination in employment; (2) the law *mandated* observance of religious practice rather than simply *permitting* such observance unimpeded by the state; (3) the law absolutely preferred religious to secular interests; and (4) the burden of Sunday work was shifted to other employees who could not claim a religious reason for refusing to work on Sundays.

5. Religion-Based Exemptions from Law

Religion-based exemptions from law are permissible if they are part of a broader secular objective of the state or if they simply *permit* religious practices free of government control.

    a. **Property tax exemptions:** *Walz v. Tax Commission,* 397 U.S. 664 (1970). The Court upheld the common practice of exempting churches from the property tax. The exemption for churches was part of a broader exemption of property owned by nonprofit public-benefit corporations thought to be "beneficial and stabilizing influences in community life." The Court found this to be a sufficiently secular purpose. It also found the nation's "unbroken practice of . . . exemption" of church properties from taxation to be "significant" and "not something to be lightly cast aside."

    b. **Exemption from employment discrimination law:** *Corporation of Presiding Bishop v. Amos,* 483 U.S. 327 (1987). Title VII of the Civil Rights Act forbids employment discrimination on the basis of religion, but exempts churches from that ban. Mayson, a janitor at a Mormon church gymnasium, was discharged from his employment because he was a lapsed Mormon. Mayson contended that the statutory exemption violated the establishment clause. Applying *Lemon,* the Court disagreed. A secular purpose need not be "unrelated to religion." The governmental purpose is valid so long as the government has not acted "with the intent of promoting a *particular* point of view in religious matters."

The effect prong of *Lemon* was satisfied because the exemption merely permitted *churches* to advance religion. For "a law to have forbidden 'effects' . . . the *government itself* [must have] advanced religion through its own activities and influence."

c. **Sales tax exemptions:** *Texas Monthly v. Bullock,* 489 U.S. 1 (1989). Texas exempted religious periodicals and books from its otherwise applicable sales tax. In a plurality opinion by Brennan the Court struck down the exemption, relying primarily on the fact that the exemption was not available to any nonreligious publications. The benefits accorded religion were not part of a wider package of benefits aimed at furthering secular goals. By limiting the tax exemption to religious publications Texas had sought to advance only religious purposes. Scalia, joined by Rehnquist and Kennedy, dissented. The dissenters argued that *Walz* controlled and that, in any case, religion-neutral state accommodation of religion generally rather than accommodation of a single sect ought not implicate the establishment clause.

6. **Governmental Preference for One Sect**

Adherents to neutrality and accommodation agree that governmental preference for one sect violates the establishment clause. Rarely does a government brazenly prefer one religion to another. These problems usually arise in the form of "religious gerrymandering"—the creation of an ostensibly neutral law that in practice favors or disfavors a single sect.

a. **Selective conscientious objection:** *Gillette v. United States,* 401 U.S. 437 (1971). The federal military conscription law exempted persons who, because of their "religious training and belief," were opposed to "war in any form." Gillette claimed that, in accordance with Catholic doctrine, he was opposed to "unjust" wars and that Congress's failure to exempt him from the draft constituted an impermissible establishment of religion in the form of a governmental preference for religions, like the Quakers, that reject all war. The Court upheld the law. The law was not discriminatory on its face and the burden thus fell on Gillette to prove that there was no "neutral, secular basis for the lines the government has drawn." The Court accepted the government's argument that extending the exemption to selective conscientious objectors would jeopardize the fairness of the exemption by injecting much subjectivity and uncertainty into its administration.

b. **Charitable contributions:** *Larson v. Valente,* 456 U.S. 228 (1982). Minnesota regulated charitable solicitation but exempted religious organizations that solicit at least half of their contributions from members. The Unification Church (the "Moonies") challenged the law and the Court invalidated it. The law was couched in terms entirely unrelated to any religious sect but the law was intentionally discriminatory. The proof could be gleaned from the incredibly honest statement of one Minnesota legislator, who asked his colleagues during debate "why we're so hot to regulate the Moonies, anyway?" Intentional discrimination on the basis of religious belief is invalid.

c. **Drawing school district boundaries:** *Board of Education of Kiryas Joel Village v. Grumet,* 512 U.S. 687 (1994). A Hasidic Jewish sect that vigorously rejects assimilation into the mainstream culture created a community, Kiryas Joel, in Orange County, New York. Kiryas Joel is entirely populated by the Hasidic sect. Adherents to the religion educate their children in parochial schools. Federal and state law requires public schools to provide special educational services to handicapped children. Hasidic residents of Kiryas Joel, however, preferred to do without such education rather than enroll their handicapped children in the public schools providing such services. New York responded to this fact by authorizing Kiryas Joel to create its own public school district. Kiryas Joel did so, but confined its public schooling to the provision of special educational services to handicapped children. All the handicapped children enrolled in the Kiryas Joel system were Hasidic. The Court invalidated the New York legislation authorizing the Kiryas Joel school system because it was "tantamount to an allocation of political power on a religious criterion." The boundaries of the district were carefully drawn to include all Hasidim but exclude nonmembers of the sect. The benefit received by the Hasidim of Kiryas Joel was not provided equally to other religions.

i. **Kennedy's concurrence.** Justice Kennedy expressed a three-part test for acceptable accommodations of religion: (1) the state seeks "to alleviate a specific and identifiable burden" on religious practices, (2) the accommodation does "not impose or increase any burden" on non-members of the accommodated religion, and (3) there is no evidence the state has denied other religions the same benefit "under analogous circumstances."

ii. **Dissent.** Justices Scalia, Rehnquist, and Thomas dissented. In their view, New York had simply accommodated the deeply held and unusual religious beliefs and practices of the Kiryas Joel Hasidim. Rather than favoring the Hasidic residents of Kiryas Joel, New York had responded to the cultural insularity of the sect by accommodating their desire to remain apart from the mainstream. The dissenters also argued that New York had a secular purpose—to spare children the emotional trauma of education in an environment where they would be treated as an object of curiosity and ridicule.

7. **Involving Religion in Government**

Delegation of public power to religious institutions is forbidden. In *Larkin v. Grendel's Den,* 459 U.S. 116 (1982), the Court struck down a Massachusetts law that granted to religious institutions an absolute veto of liquor license applications for sites located within 500 feet of the religious institution. The law fused government and religion by delegating public power to churches. There was no assurance that a religious institution would exercise its delegated public power on a secular basis. The delegation was an endorsement by government of religious decision-making on issues of public policy.

8. **Government Ceremonies and Displays of Religious Imagery**

Government displays of religious imagery and public ceremonies involving prayer or other invocations of religion are valid if they do not involve *endorsement* or *coercion*. This means that the validity of the practice depends upon the message the government intends to deliver and the message an objective observer would perceive. If the message is too clearly religious it is likely an endorsement and so a forbidden establishment of religion. If the message is sufficiently drained of sectarian dogma to make it generic or blended with enough secular imagery to make the religious message incoherent it is valid.

a. **Legislative prayer: *Marsh v. Chambers,*** 463 U.S. 783 (1983). The Court upheld the Nebraska legislature's practice of opening each day with a prayer offered by a chaplain employed by the state. The Court eschewed *Lemon* and relied instead upon the lengthy American history of legislative prayer. Given this "unambiguous and unbroken history of more than 200 years," legislative prayer was treated as a "tolerable acknowledgement of beliefs widely held among the people of this country." In a sense it was a **"ceremonial deism,"** like the motto "In God We Trust" that is imprinted on the nation's currency and coinage. Justices Brennan and Marshall dissented, arguing that *Lemon* should be applied to strike down the practice.

b. **Government displays of religious imagery.** The Court has upheld government display of crèches, menorahs, crosses, and other religious imagery where the circumstances are such that the government is not reasonably seen to have endorsed the religious message implicit in the imagery.

i. **Crèche: *Lynch v. Donnelly,*** 465 U.S. 668 (1984). Each December Pawtucket, Rhode Island, displayed a crèche in a public park. The crèche was surrounded with an eclectic mixture of secular imagery, including lights, a Christmas tree, Santa and his reindeer, candy-striped poles, a banner reading "Seasons Greetings," and even images of a clown, an elephant, and a teddy bear. The Court applied *Lemon,* concluded that Pawtucket had a secular purpose for the display—to celebrate the Christmas holiday season—and upheld the validity of the entire ensemble. A moment's reflection on the nature of Christmas in America ("only *x* more shopping days . . .") will confirm the Court's judgment that Christmas is largely a secular holiday.

ii. **Crèches and menorahs:** *Allegheny County v. Greater Pittsburgh ACLU,* 492 U.S. 573 (1989). Shifting majorities of a divided Court invalidated the display of a crèche by itself in the central public space of a county courthouse, but upheld the display of a menorah accompanied by a Christmas tree and sign saluting liberty. The Court effectively abandoned the *Lemon* test and substituted the endorsement test for purposes of evaluating the legitimacy of government displays of religious imagery. Four Justices (Rehnquist, Scalia, Kennedy, and White) would have upheld both displays because the displays were not coercive. Three Justices (Brennan, Marshall, and Stevens) would have voided both displays. Blackmun and O'Connor, the pivotal votes, found the undiluted message of the crèche to be the birth of Christ, and that was an endorsement of Christianity. The menorah was permissible because Blackmun found its religious symbolism was diluted by the Christmas tree and sign saluting liberty, and he was joined in the result by the four accommodationists. O'Connor thought the menorah's message was religious but concluded that the Christmas tree and the sign diluted the overall message to one of "pluralism and freedom to choose one's own beliefs."

c. **Private displays of religious imagery on public property.** The display of religious imagery on public property by private speakers is valid so long as observers would understand the display to be the speech of a private party, *not* the state.

i. *Capitol Square Review and Advisory Board v. Pinette,* 515 U.S. 753 (1995). An Ohio government agency denied the Ku Klux Klan permission to erect an unattended Latin Cross in the public square in front of Ohio's capitol building but, after a federal court enjoined Ohio from refusing permission, a cross was displayed with a sign disclaiming government involvement. Although Ohio conceded that the square was a public forum and that its denial was based on the content of the image, it defended the denial by claiming that the establishment clause prohibited the display. The Court found no establishment clause problem with the intended display of a cross. For a four-Justice plurality, Justice Scalia concluded that while the establishment clause prohibited *government* endorsements of religion it did not forbid "the government's neutral treatment of *private* religious expression." Justices O'Connor, Souter, and Breyer concurred on the ground that the establishment clause was not violated so long as the government posted a sign disclaiming its endorsement of the message conveyed by the cross.

9.   Government Inquiry into Religious Beliefs

The establishment clause and free exercise clauses together disable governments from inquiring into religious beliefs.

a.   **Internal church affairs.** The establishment clause precludes courts from "resolving church property disputes on the basis of religious doctrine or practice." *Jones v. Wolf,* 443 U.S. 595 (1979). In *Jones,* a church had acquired property in the name of the "Vineville Presbyterian Church." A majority of the congregation left the national Presbyterian Church, which body declared the minority to be the "true congregation." In a suit for a judicial declaration to determine ownership of the church property the Court ruled that secular courts may only apply secular "neutral principles . . . of trust and property law" to resolve such intrachurch disputes. But even those "neutral principles" are of no help when resolution of them depends on a construction of theological doctrine.

 ## EXAMPLE AND ANALYSIS

When a local church joined a national church it transferred its property in trust to the national church "until" the national church abandoned church doctrine existing at the time the local church had joined. The Court held that secular courts could not determine whether the condition triggering termination of the trust had occurred because its resolution was dependent on construction of church dogma. *Presbyterian Church v. Mary Elizabeth Blue Hull Church,* 393 U.S. 440 (1969).

b.   **"Truth" v. "sincerity" of religious beliefs.** The establishment and free exercise clauses bar courts from examining the truth of religious beliefs but do permit inquiry into whether any given set of beliefs is sincerely held. This is a fine and difficult distinction to make.

i.   *United States v. Ballard,* 322 U.S. 78 (1944). Ballard was prosecuted for mail fraud in connection with his solicitation of money for the "I Am" movement, a cult that claimed to be divine messengers of a deity, "Saint Germain," and endowed by that deity with supernatural powers to cure disease. The Court ruled that the religion clauses barred a jury from determining the truth or falsity of Ballard's beliefs.

ii. **The conscientious objector cases.** In a series of Vietnam War era cases the Court upheld the validity of a statutory exemption from military conscription that applied only to those who opposed all war on religious grounds. Application of the statute necessarily required some judicial determination of whether the individual claims to the exemption were sincerely held or offered only for the expedient purpose of avoiding military service. (See section C.2.j, infra.)

C. THE FREE EXERCISE CLAUSE

1. Overview

The free exercise clause forbids governments from infringing upon religious *beliefs*. It would be redundant if that was its sole function, as religious beliefs are a form of expression protected by free speech. The free exercise clause also provides some limited protection for religious *practices*. Free exercise claimants often seek exemption on religious grounds from obligations generally imposed. The free exercise clause is incorporated into the 14th Amendment's due process clause and applies to the states.

a. Distinction between belief and conduct

i. *Reynolds v. United States,* 98 U.S. 145 (1879). Congress outlawed the practice of polygamy, then a tenet of the Mormon religion. The Court upheld Reynolds's conviction under the law, ruling that while the free exercise clause prevented Congress from interference "with mere religious belief" it could interfere with religious practices.

ii. *Cantwell v. Connecticut,* 310 U.S. 296 (1940). Cantwell, a Jehovah's Witness, was convicted of breach of the peace resulting from playing an anti-Catholic phonograph record to anyone who would listen. The Court reversed the conviction, stating that the free exercise clause protected "freedom to believe and freedom to act." Freedom of religious belief is "absolute" but religious conduct may be regulated so long as the regulations do not unduly "infringe the protected freedom." Some regulation of religious conduct is permitted; some is forbidden. The problem, of course, is drawing a sensible line.

b. The problem: Government action that impinges on conduct inextricably related to religious belief. Rarely do governments prohibit or regulate mere *belief*. Governments do regulate conduct bound up in religious belief. Regulation of religious conduct takes two forms.

i. **Forbidding or burdening conduct required by religious belief**

EXAMPLE AND ANALYSIS

The City of Hialeah, Florida, outlawed the ritual slaughter of animals. The central sacramental rite of the Santeria religion is the ritual slaughter of an animal. The law banned conduct essential to religious belief. Because the city had acted for the sole purpose of suppressing the Santerians' sacramental rite the Court found the law invalid under the free exercise clause. *Church of the Lukumi Babalu Aye v. City of Hialeah*, 508 U.S. 520 (1993).

> ### ii. Compelling or encouraging conduct prohibited by religious belief
>
> **Example:** Wisconsin required that children be educated until age 16, thus compelling the Old Order Amish to violate their religious belief that education past age fourteen was improper. The Court voided the requirement as to the Amish, partly because it also infringed the parents' due process rights to raise their children without undue government interference. *Wisconsin v. Yoder,* 406 U.S. 205 (1972).

c. **The Court's guiding principles.** The Court's doctrine must be divided into two periods—before *Employment Division v. Smith*, 494 U.S. 872 (1990), and after *Smith*. Before *Smith* the Court relied on *Sherbert v. Verner,* 374 U.S. 398 (1963), and *Wisconsin v. Yoder,* 406 U.S. 205 (1972), to apply strict scrutiny to laws that substantially burdened religious conduct. The Court in *Smith* ruled that minimal scrutiny applies to most such laws.

> i. **Before *Smith:* Strict scrutiny.** From the early 1960s until *Smith* the Court applied strict scrutiny to laws that *substantially* impinged upon religious conduct. Deliberate interference with religious conduct was presumptively invalid and upheld only if the government proved that the interference was necessary to the achievement of a compelling government interest. When governments unintentionally imposed ''substantial'' burdens on religious conduct the regulations were presumed to be invalid and upheld only if the government could prove a ''compelling'' objective that would be impaired by exempting religious conduct.

 EXAMPLES AND ANALYSIS

Example: A state denied unemployment benefits to a Seventh Day Adventist who refused to work on Saturdays. The Court found that the denial substantially interfered with religious conduct and concluded that the state had failed to establish a compelling objective that would be impaired by providing a religious exemption. *Sherbert v. Verner,* 374 U.S. 398 (1963).

Example: An Old Order Amish carpenter refused to pay social security taxes because his religious beliefs obligated him to eschew government assistance in caring for the elderly. The Court upheld the validity of social security taxation upon the Amish carpenter because mandatory participation in social security was found "indispensable" to the "fiscal vitality" of social security. The government's refusal to provide a religious exemption from social security taxation was "essential to accomplish an overriding governmental interest." *United States v. Lee,* 455 U.S. 252 (1982).

---

ii.   **After *Smith:* two levels of scrutiny.** *Smith* introduced two levels of review—strict and minimal scrutiny.

(a)   **Purposeful interference: Strict scrutiny.** Strict scrutiny is triggered when governments regulate conduct "only when . . . engaged in for religious reasons, or only because of the religious belief that [it] display[s]." Such regulations are presumptively void—upheld only if the government proves they are necessary to some compelling government objective.

 # Example and Analysis

If a state were to prohibit the possession or use of wine for religious sacramental purposes, strict scrutiny would apply. It is virtually impossible that the government could justify such a purposefully inhibitory regulation of religious conduct. "It would doubtless be unconstitutional . . . to ban the casting of 'statues that are to be used for worship purposes.' " *Employment Division v. Smith,* 494 U.S. 872 (1990).

(b)   **Generally applicable but burdensome laws: Minimal scrutiny.** Minimal scrutiny applies to "generally applicable law[s] that require (or forbid) the performance of an act that [one's] religious belief forbids (or requires)." Such laws are presumptively valid. They are void only if the challenger proves that they are not rationally related to a legitimate state objective.

Example: Suppose that a state were to prohibit all use or possession of alcoholic beverages by anyone under any circumstances. The law would be subject to minimal scrutiny because it does not single out the sacramental use of wine for prohibition.

(c) **Exceptions to minimal scrutiny.** There are two important exceptions to minimal scrutiny.

- **Individualized Assessment of Eligibility for Government Benefits:** *Denial of benefits as a result of an individualized assessment of eligibility and on a basis infringing religious conduct remains subject to strict scrutiny.*

Example: If a state were to deny unemployment compensation to a person who refused to work on their sabbath, strict scrutiny would apply. The regulation that produces the denial requires an individualized assessment of eligibility—has the person refused suitable work?

- **"Hybrid" or Multiple Rights:** *Generally applicable laws that burden religious conduct **and some other constitutional right,** such as free speech or the right to privacy, remain subject to strict scrutiny.*

Example: While Wisconsin's compulsory education law at issue in *Yoder* was generally applicable, it also burdened the parents' privacy right to determine how best to raise their children. Strict scrutiny applies because the law implicates free exercise and another constitutional right. See *Wisconsin v. Yoder,* 406 U.S. 205 (1972).

(d) **The Religious Freedom Restoration Act.** In reaction to *Smith* Congress enacted the Religious Freedom Restoration Act, Pub. L. No. 103-141, codified at 42 U.S.C. §2000bb. RFRA provides that the federal and state governments may not "substantially burden" religious conduct, even by "a rule of general applicability," unless the government proves that the burden "is the least restrictive means of furthering . . . a compelling governmental interest." In *City of Boerne v. Flores,* 521 U.S. 507 (1997), the Court voided RFRA as beyond congressional power. See Chapter 5, section E.

2. **Before *Smith:* Development of Strict Scrutiny**

a. **The road to strict scrutiny.** The Court went from a position that the free exercise clause did not bar regulation of religious conduct to a position that substantial burdens upon religious conduct were presumptively void.

       i. **No scrutiny:** *Reynolds v. United States,* 98 U.S. 145 (1879). The Court upheld Reynolds's conviction under a federal law barring polygamy, despite his religious belief in the practice, because the Court was of the opinion that the free exercise clause does not bar regulation of religious conduct. (See also *Jacobson v. Massachusetts,* 197 U.S. 11 (1905), upholding compulsory smallpox vaccinations of religious objectors.)

       ii. **Some scrutiny:** *Braunfeld v. Brown,* 366 U.S. 599 (1961). An orthodox Jew challenged Pennsylvania's Sunday closing law as a violation of his free exercise rights because he was compelled by law to close on Sunday and compelled by his religion to close on Saturday. The Court upheld the law, ruling that generally applicable laws that impose an "indirect burden on religious observance" are valid "unless the State may accomplish its purposes by means which do not impose such a burden." Pennsylvania's objective of a uniform "family day of rest" would be undermined by religious exemptions. From *Reynolds* to *Braunfeld* the Court moved from the position that regulation of religious conduct is *always valid* to a position that such regulation is *valid unless there is a less burdensome means to achieve the state's objective.*

       iii. **Strict scrutiny:** *Sherbert v. Verner,* 374 U.S. 398 (1963). South Carolina denied unemployment benefits to Sherbert, a Seventh Day Adventist, because she had refused "suitable work when offered." She refused to work on her sabbath, Saturday. The Court found that the denial substantially interfered with her religious conduct by denying her valuable benefits available to other discharged employees and concluded that the state had not proven a *compelling* objective for the denial that would be impaired by a religious exemption.

   b. **Applications of strict scrutiny to *vindicate* free exercise claims.** In the twenty-seven years between *Sherbert* and *Smith* the Court applied strict scrutiny to strike down laws burdening religious conduct. In *Wisconsin v. Yoder,* 406 U.S. 205 (1972), the Court applied strict scrutiny and struck down Wisconsin's compulsory education law. The law imposed a substantial burden on the Amish and the secular goal of the state—fostering a more educated population—would not be substantially undermined by granting a religious exemption to the Amish.

    In reliance upon *Sherbert* the Court has consistently required religious exemptions from regulations that would otherwise deny unemployment compensation. See *Thomas v. Review Board,* 450 U.S. 707 (1981) (denial of unemployment benefits to a person who, for religious reasons, quit his job in a munitions factory) (void); *Hobbie v. Unemployment Appeals Commission of Florida,* 480 U.S. 136 (1987) (same); *Frazee v. Employment*

Security Dept., 489 U.S. 829 (1989) (denial of unemployment benefits to a "generic" Christian who refused Sunday work void).

    c. **Applications of strict scrutiny that *denied* free exercise claims.** In the heyday of *Sherbert* the Court occasionally applied strict scrutiny but found that the government had met its high burden of proving its justification for burdening religious conduct.

        i. **Social security taxes: *United States v. Lee,*** 455 U.S. 252 (1982). Lee, an Amish farmer and carpenter, refused to pay social security taxes because "the Amish believe it sinful not to provide for their own elderly." The Court applied strict scrutiny but upheld the validity of social security taxation because mandatory participation in social security was found "indispensable" to the "fiscal vitality" of social security. Denial of a religious exemption from social security taxation was "essential to accomplish an overriding governmental interest."

        ii. **Tax-exempt status: *Bob Jones University v. United States,*** 461 U.S. 574 (1983). Based on religious belief, Bob Jones University practices racial discrimination. On free exercise grounds, the university challenged the IRS's denial to it of tax-exempt status. The Court applied strict scrutiny but concluded that the government's interest in eliminating racial discrimination in education was compelling and that the religious burden imposed—denial of tax-exempt status—was essential to the achievement of this objective.

    d. **Applications of minimal scrutiny.** During the *Sherbert* era the Court applied minimal scrutiny when government action was not a substantial burden on religious conduct or when governments regulated religious conduct in special institutional contexts, such as prisons or the military.

        i. **Denial of veterans' benefits to conscientious objectors: *Johnson v. Robison,*** 415 U.S. 361 (1974). Federal law made veterans' benefits available to veterans of the armed forces but not to conscientious objectors who had performed mandatory service in lieu of military service. The Court rejected a free exercise challenge to this statutory scheme. The Court applied minimal scrutiny because the law imposed only an "incidental burden" on religious conduct and the government's "substantial interest in raising and supporting armies" was "clearly sufficient" to uphold the legislation.

        ii. **Military: *Goldman v. Weinberger,*** 475 U.S. 503 (1986). Goldman, an Air Force officer and orthodox Jew, was disciplined for wearing a yarmulke in violation of military uniform regulations. The Court applied a version of minimal scrutiny—courts "must give great deference to the professional judgment of military authorities" in deciding whether "military needs" justify a burden on religious conduct—and upheld the validity of the discipline.

iii. **Prison:** *O'Lone v. Estate of Shabazz,* 482 U.S. 342 (1987). Islamic prison inmates challenged the validity of prison regulations that prevented them from observing a Friday midday religious service. The Court, 5 to 4, applied a "reasonableness" standard and upheld the regulations. The Court specifically rejected the contention that prison officials were under a burden to prove the absence of less restrictive alternative means to achieve the prison's objectives.

iv. **Logging an Indian sacred site on public land:** *Lyng v. Northwest Indian Cemetery Protection Assn.,* 485 U.S. 439 (1988). The U.S. Forest Service planned to build a road through an area regarded as sacred by several Indian tribes and permit logging in the area. A free exercise challenge was rejected. The Court applied minimal scrutiny because the government action, while imposing a substantial burden on religious conduct, was neither *coercive* nor a *penalty.* Citizens simply may not "veto . . . public programs that do not prohibit the free exercise of religion."

3. *Smith* and Its Aftermath

The Court's opinion in *Smith* severely restricted the scope of strict scrutiny upon governmental regulation of religious conduct.

a. *Employment Division v. Smith,* 494 U.S. 872 (1990). Smith, employed by a drug rehabilitation clinic, was fired because he used peyote, an illegal drug, as part of a sacramental rite of the Native American Church. Oregon denied him unemployment compensation because his discharge was for good cause. Smith claimed Oregon's refusal to provide him unemployment benefits was a denial of his 14th Amendment due process right to free exercise of religion. The Court disagreed. Oregon's prohibition of peyote applied to everyone and under all circumstances—it was not directed to the sacramental use of peyote. *"[T]he right of free exercise does not relieve an individual of the obligation to comply with a 'valid and neutral law of general applicability' "* on the ground that the law compels conduct his religion forbids or forbids conduct that his religion compels. Such laws are valid if they are rationally related to any legitimate state interest.

i. **Exceptions to minimal scrutiny.** Of the four exceptions to the *Smith* rule, two are implicit in the rule.

(a) **Laws intentionally burdensome of religious conduct.** When governments act deliberately to burden religious conduct the law is not truly of general applicability and so subject to strict scrutiny. A law forbidding the use of wine in sacramental religious rites is subject to strict scrutiny.

(b) **Laws not truly generally applicable.** When governments enact a law of general applicability but riddle it with enough exemptions that it effectively applies only to religious conduct it is treated identically to laws intentionally burdensome of religious conduct. A law forbidding the use of wine by anyone but exempting from the law all uses except the use of wine in ritual ceremonies would be subject to strict scrutiny since the effective impact of the law would be almost entirely upon religious conduct.

(c) **Individualized assessment of benefit eligibility.** Strict scrutiny applies when governments deny government benefits after an individualized assessment of eligibility and the reason for denial pinches religious conduct.

(d) **Laws burdening religious conduct and another constitutional right.** Laws that burden both religious conduct and some other constitutional right are subject to strict scrutiny.

b. **Application of *Smith***

   i. **Ritual animal sacrifice: *Church of the Lukumi Babalu Aye v. City of Hialeah,*** 508 U.S. 520 (1993). Hialeah, Florida, is home to a number of practitioners of the Santeria religion, the central sacramental rite of which is the ritual slaughter of animals. Hialeah outlawed the ritual slaughter of animals but exempted from the ban almost all conceivable ritual killings of animals except religious ones. The Court applied strict scrutiny because it was evident that Hialeah had acted for the sole purpose of suppressing the Santerians' sacramental rite. The city was unable to prove sufficient justification and the Court struck down the law.

c. **Statutory response: The Religious Freedom Restoration Act.** Congress responded to *Smith* by enacting the Religious Freedom Restoration Act ("RFRA"), which prohibited any government from imposing a substantial burden on a "person's exercise of religion" unless the government could prove that the burden "is the least restrictive means" of furthering a "compelling government interest." As to states RFRA was voided in *City of Boerne v. Flores,* 521 U.S. 507 (1997). See Chapter 5.E, supra.

4. **The Meaning of Religion**

   The Court has never adequately defined religion.

   a. **Conventional definition.** The 19th century Court was willing to define religion in terms of theistic beliefs, conventional forms of observance, and conformity to "the enlightened sentiments of mankind."

   Example: The Court upheld the revocation of the Mormon Church's status as a religious corporation because the Court concluded that one of its religious tenets at the time, polygamy, was a "pretense" when viewed by "the enlightened sentiments of mankind." *Late Corporation of the Church of Jesus Christ of Latter-Day Saints v. United States,* 136 U.S. 1 (1890).

b. **Functional definition.** The twentieth century's embrace of moral relativism produced a parallel shift in the Court's approach to the meaning of religion. Beliefs that are not "acceptable, logical, consistent, or comprehensible" may still be religious so long as they are sincerely held. But the Court has drawn an outer line to this functional approach. Deeply held personal philosophic positions are not religious, but how is one to tell the difference? As Thomas Paine, the American revolutionary pamphleteer, stated: "My mind is my own church." The Court may not have gone quite that far, but sincerely held beliefs about man's nature and his place in the cosmos that are central to a person's life are religious beliefs, whether or not they are theistic or even shared by others. (See Tribe, at 1180-1183.) The Court frequently relies on reasoning by analogy to compare exotic claims of religion to more conventional ones.

c. **Conscientious objection: A case study.** The federal military conscription law exempted those who objected to all war because of their "religious training or belief." The statute defined that phrase as a "belief in relation to a Supreme Being involving duties superior to those arising from any human relation" but excluding "essentially political, sociological, or philosophical views or a personal moral code." The Court's interpretation of this statute provides some glimpse into the Court's view of the meaning of religion.

   i. *United States v. Seeger,* 380 U.S. 163 (1965). The Court interpreted the exemption broadly, finding that a person has a "belief in relation to a Supreme Being" if his beliefs are "sincere and meaningful" and occupy "a place in [his] life . . . parallel to that filled by the orthodox belief in God of one who clearly qualifies for the exemption."

   ii. *Welsh v. United States,* 398 U.S. 333 (1970). A plurality of the Court extended the scope of the statutory exemption to include those with deeply held opposition to war founded "upon moral, ethical, or religious principle."

REVIEW QUESTIONS AND ANSWERS

Question: In order to foster an appreciation of art by schoolchildren and to enrich their education, the state of Matisse adopts an Art Enhancement Program. Under the program, art teachers employed by the state travel from school to school in buses converted into mobile art studios. They are scheduled to appear at each school once weekly. Private schools are also included in the program. As a result the mobile art vans appear once weekly at religious schools in Matisse. At all schools the students come from their classrooms to the art vans, accompanied by their home room teacher. Art instruction, however, is the exclusive responsibility of the state employed art teachers. For safety reasons, the vans park as close to the schools as possible, preferably on the school grounds and away from streets. There are 2,000 public schools and 600 religious schools located in Matisse. Is the Art Enhancement Program constitutionally permissible?

Answer: Almost certainly. After *Agostini v. Felton,* the program surely has a secular purpose, and its primary effect appears to be neutral. The aid does not involve government indoctrination in religion, is nonpreferential to religion, and presents no excessive entanglement problems.

Question: In order to stimulate competition in the provision of elementary and secondary education, and to increase parental and student educational choices, the State of Mackenzie enacts legislation that grants to the parent of each school-age child an annual $4,000 voucher. The voucher may be tendered to any school in Mackenzie, public or private, at which the child enrolls and that school will receive $4,000 from Mackenzie for each voucher surrendered to Mackenzie, to-gether with proof of the child's enrollment. Mackenzie's voucher plan does not exclude religious schools. After its implementation, over 75% of Mackenzie students enrolled in public schools. Of the remaining 25% about half were enrolled in religious schools. Is the voucher plan constitutionally valid?

Answer: Probably. Under *Lemon,* Mackenzie has acted for a secular purpose; the primary effect of the voucher plan may be neutral with respect to religion, and it does not entangle the government and religion. The principal issue is the plan's effect. Mackenzie's aid undoubtedly will be used, in part, to advance openly religious objectives of religious schools. But this does not seem to be the *primary* effect of the program. Mackenzie's aid is formally direct (the state sends a check directly to each school) but Mackenzie does not decide who gets aid—that decision is made entirely by parents and children. The size of the aid ($4,000) may encourage attendance at religious schools. The fact that religious aid is part of a general, secular assistance plan and the aid arrives at the religious institution through the independent decisions of private citizens supports its validity. See *Mueller v. Allen.* Mackenzie's voucher plan is clearly valid under the accommodation approach—it does not discriminate among religions, does not endorse religion (it endorses choice) and does not coerce religious belief or nonbelief. *Agostini*'s modified *Lemon* test would add further support to this conclusion.

Question: Despite explicit instructions from the school not to do so, Jean, the valedictorian of her public high school graduating class, opened her valedictory address at her graduation ceremony with a lengthy prayer, invoking the "blessings of God upon this Christian nation." Herbert, a graduating student, was so incensed that he walked out of the graduation. Herbert later sued Jean and the school district under 42 U.S.C. §1983 for violating his constitutional rights. Jean and the school district move to dismiss Herbert's claim. What result?

Answer: Herbert has probably failed to state a cause of action. The question is whether Jean's prayer constitutes a governmental endorsement of religion. That depends on what message the school *intended* to convey and what message a reasonable observer would receive. The school district certainly had no intention of endorsing religion—it had instructed Jean not to pray. Would a reasonable observer read into Jean's prayer governmental endorsement? A valedictory is the student's turn to speak—no reasonable person would think that valedictory remarks are those of the school. Jean's prayer was wholly student initiated.

Question: The state of Topaz enacted legislation that required public schools that offer sex education to students to teach the "moral virtue of sexual abstinence prior to marriage." The Topaz legislature acted because it believed that promiscuous sexuality contributes to the increase of sexually transmitted disease, and that births of children outside marriage are socially undesirable. About 60% of the population of Topaz belongs to fundamentalist sects that embrace sexual abstinence before marriage as a tenet of their faith. Is the legislation constitutionally valid?

Answer: The law is valid on its face but might be void as applied. There is no evidence that Topaz acted for religious purposes, or that the primary effect of the requirement will be to advance religion. The fact that the government endorses a position that happens also to be an article of religious faith is not dispositive. If there were no secular reason for doing so the endorsement would surely violate the establishment clause, but governments are not disabled from pursuing policies for secular reasons that may also be desired by religious adherents. The fact that a majority of Topaz residents embrace this position as an article of religious faith should be irrelevant. Absent evidence that Topaz acted for religious reasons the law is valid. But if the law is implemented by teaching fundamentalist religious dogma as the reason for abstinence it is invalid as applied.

Question: After intense lobbying by fundamentalist ministers, the state of Topaz amended the legislation described in the preceding question by requiring public schools that offer sex education to students to teach the doctrine that "abortion is immoral under all circumstances." Is the legislation constitutionally valid?

Answer: Probably not. There is some evidence that Topaz might have acted for religious purposes, by responding to religious lobbying. Religious people are surely not barred from lobbying their representatives, but the state may act only for secular purposes. Here, one of Topaz's secular objectives—discouraging out-of-wedlock births—is served not at all by this amendment. The other objective—discouraging sexual promiscuity—is served poorly by the requirement. Even though there are secular moral objections to abortion, the state's motivation is suspect and the amendment probably violates the establishment clause. (See *Edwards v. Aguillard*.)

Question: The state of Orchid exempts from property taxation all property owned by charitable organizations devoted to charitable purposes. Orchid amends the exemption to exclude from the exemption any church that is "under the ultimate control of a foreign entity." During the debate over the amendment, the sponsor of the amendment stated on the floor of the Orchid legislature that "the law is designed to deprive the Pope of Orchid's help." Is the legislation valid under the First and 14th Amendments?

Answer: Probably not. Although the amendment is facially neutral between religions it has the clear effect of denying the tax exemption to the Roman Catholic church and probably not very many, if any, other religious institutions. The sponsor's statement is probably fatal to the legislation. (See *Larson v. Valente*.) A general tax exemption for charitable organizations, including churches, is valid. (See *Walz v. Tax Commission*.)

Question: A small communal sect in the city of Floribunda follows the teachings of Dorobba, a mystical monk reputed to live somewhere in the Andes Mountains. The central sacramental rite of the Dorobbans is the outdoor lighting of a fire in a large ceramic bowl and the burning of "greenwood" sticks, which produce an extremely smelly and smoky fire. Dorobbans chant a mantra while walking around the fire. Acting on complaints from neighbors of the Dorobbans the Floribunda city council enacts an ordinance that bans "all outdoor fires emitting smoke visible more than 10 feet from the fire source, but excepting therefrom any and all outdoor barbecues, campfires, refuse disposal fires, accidental fires, or fires conducted by governments." The Dorobbans challenge the validity of the ordinance. What is their best argument and will it succeed?

Answer: The Dorobbans' best argument is that the ordinance violates the free exercise clause, made applicable to Floribunda through the due process clause of the 14th Amendment. The Dorobbans should contend that the ordinance is subject to strict scrutiny for two reasons. First, the ordinance is not generally applicable—it is so riddled with exceptions that in fact it applies only to their sacramental rite. Second, the actual effect of the ordinance coupled with evidence that Floribunda acted in response to neighbors' complaints strongly suggests that Floribunda acted with the deliberate intent of circumscribing the Dorobbans' religious practices. These arguments will succeed. (See *Church of the Lukumi Babalu Aye v. Hialeah*.) Under strict scrutiny the ordinance is presumed to be void unless Floribunda can prove that the burden placed on the Dorobbans' religious practice is essential to the accomplishment of some compelling objective. There is no evidence of any facts suggesting that Floribunda could sustain its burden of proof. The ordinance is invalid.

Question: In order to ensure "civic tranquility" and to alleviate parking problems the city of Greenwich has for many years prohibited "musical instruction or concerts in private residences." Marta, a recent Greenwich resident, is a musician who also believes that music is the sole connection between man and God and that only through the performance of music can man realize his place in the cosmos. Over time, Marta has collected a small circle of followers who share her beliefs. They come individually to her home for musical instruction and, once weekly, they gather for a concert. The city of Greenwich prosecutes Marta for violation of the ordinance. Does Marta have a good constitutional defense to the prosecution? If not, does she have any other line of defense that is likely to be successful?

Answer: Marta does not have a constitutional defense. Her beliefs are sufficient to constitute a religion—they are evidently sincerely held and occupy a place in her life analogous to more conventional religious beliefs. The courts will not inquire into the validity of her beliefs. See *United States v. Ballard*. But even though her religious practice is severely burdened by the ordinance the ordinance is generally applicable to all. It is thus subject to minimal scrutiny—it is presumed valid unless Marta can prove it has no rational connection to a legitimate state interest. Although the Greenwich ordinance is not very well suited to its objectives it will probably survive such weak judicial scrutiny. (See *Employment Division v. Smith*.)

EXAM TIPS

- **Establishment Clause:** Doctrine is unstable because the Court can't agree on a uniform theory of the establishment clause. Especially here, you need to provide an answer on both levels: *theory* and *doctrine*.

  - **Theory:** The Court is divided between *neutrality* and *accommodation*.

  - **Doctrine:**

    — *Lemon* is the core of the neutral approach, but its meaning has been altered from within by accommodationists:

      (1) *Any plausible actual secular purpose* will do.

      (2) Only effects *directly produced by government* count.

      (3) *Fusion* of state and church, or *delegation of public power* to religion, is *excessive entanglement*. Lesser entanglements are excessive when they involve too much scrutiny of religion, or too much symbolic interconnection, or endorsement or coercion of religious belief.

    — *Endorsement* is the operative test for public displays or uses of religious imagery, but it plays a lesser role under *Lemon*'s third prong.

— *Coercion* is embraced by both neutralists and accommodationists. Any government action that coerces beliefs—one way or another—is invalid.

— *General nonpreferential aid to religion* has not been accepted as valid by a majority of the Court.

- **Crossover Questions:** Watch for factual settings that combine both public forum/free speech principles and establishment clause principles. If the government infringes religious speech in a public forum it must justify the infringement under free speech doctrine by proving that the infringement is compelled by the establishment clause.

■ **Free Exercise:** The Court views the free exercise clause to protect religious *belief* but not religious *conduct or practice* unless the government has acted *deliberately* to restrict or heavily burden religious conduct.

- **Doctrine:** Free exercise claims are subject to either *strict scrutiny* or *minimal scrutiny.*

— **Strict Scrutiny** applies to all burdens on *religious belief* and, with two exceptions, only to *intentional* burdens on *religious practice.*

  (1) Intentional burdens occur when the law is focused *exclusively* on religious practice or has such a strongly focused *effect* that intentional motive is inferred.

  (2) Strict scrutiny applies to *individualized denial of benefits* cases where the basis for denial impinges on religious conduct.

  (3) Strict scrutiny applies to laws that burden both religious practice *and some other constitutional right*.

— **Minimal Scrutiny:** Burdens on religious practice that are produced by laws *generally applicable to everyone* are valid if they are rationally related to any conceivable legitimate government interest.

ECONOMIC RIGHTS: THE TAKINGS CLAUSE AND THE CONTRACTS CLAUSE

CHAPTER OVERVIEW

This chapter examines two significant protections of economic rights—the takings clause and the contracts clause. The most important points in this chapter follow.

- **Takings Clause:** No government may take private property *except for **public use**,* and then only if **just compensation** is paid. The takings clause applies to both tangible and intangible property and to any governmental action—legislative, executive, and judicial.

  - **Public Use:** The public use requirement is satisfied if a taking of private property is **rationally related** to any *conceivable* **public purpose.**

  - **Regulatory Takings:** Government regulations may be a de facto taking if the regulations are sufficiently destructive of property rights. Courts use three per se rules and a multi-factor balancing test to determine if a regulation is a taking.

    — **Nuisance Regulations Are *Not* Takings.** If a regulation simply abates a common law nuisance it is not a taking, regardless of what other effects it may have. It is not a taking, per se.

    — **Permanent Physical Occupations of Private Property Are Takings Per Se.** Regulations that produce permanent physical occupations of property are takings per se.

    — **Destruction of All Economically Viable Uses.** Regulations that bar the property owner from all economically viable uses of the property are takings per se.

— **Balancing.** Regulations that interfere with property rights must **substantially advance** a **legitimate state interest** in order not to be treated as a taking. In assessing this relationship, courts examine the following factors:

(1)   **Whether the Public Benefits Produced by the Regulation Are Greater Than the Private Costs Imposed.**

(2)   **Whether the Regulations Leave the Property Owner with a "Reasonable Return" on His Investment.**

(3)   **Whether the Regulations are Arbitrary.**

— **Conditions as Takings.** Governments may not attach conditions to building permits that would themselves be takings unless the government proves two conditions:

(1)   **"Essential Nexus":** The condition advances the government's legitimate reason for restricting the owner's development in the first place.

(2)   **"Rough Proportionality":** The extent of the conditions imposed are "roughly proportional" to the impact of the proposed development.

■   **Contracts Clause:** The contracts clause prohibits states from *unreasonable* impairments of contractual obligations. Sliding scale scrutiny applies—the *more severe* the impairment the *closer the scrutiny.* Different rules apply to impairments of *public* and *private* contracts.

•   **Private Contracts:**

— "Incidental" impairments trigger minimal scrutiny.

— Is there a **"substantial impairment"** of some contractual relationship?

— If so, the **burden of proof falls on the state to justify the impairment,** by showing all of the following:

(1)   A **significant, legitimate public purpose.**

(2)   The impairment's **character** is appropriate to the public purpose.

(3)   The impairment is **reasonable.** Courts defer to legislative judgment as to the necessity and reasonableness of the law.

•   **Severe Impairments of Private Contracts.** When governments **severely impair** private contracts courts will **carefully examine** the **nature and purpose** of the law.

(1) Severe impairments occur when **express terms** of a private contract are **nullified** and an **unexpected and potentially disabling** liability is imposed.

(2) Severe impairments are **presumed invalid.** To be upheld, the state must prove that they are **necessary** to meet an **important general social problem.** Laws that permanently impair contracts in order to benefit a "narrow class" rather than "to protect a broad societal interest" are especially suspect.

- **Public Contracts:** When states unilaterally modify their own contracts courts will **not defer** to the legislative assessment of reasonableness and necessity. The state must prove that the impairment was **necessary** and **reasonable.**

(1) **Necessity.** To be necessary, it must be **essential**—there must be **no less impairing alternative** available to the state to achieve its public objectives.

(2) **Reasonable.** The impairment must be prompted by radically altered circumstances of an unforeseeable nature.

A. INTRODUCTION AND OVERVIEW

1. The Constitutional Role in Protecting Economic Rights

The Framers considered economic rights to be just as much a part of constitutional liberty as noneconomic rights. The principal devices to protect property rights were the Fifth Amendment's *takings clause*—which bars governments from taking private property for public use without payment—and the *contracts clause* of Article I, §10—which bars states from impairing contractual obligations. By judicial construction, however, these barriers to governmental invasion of economic interests have been much reduced.

2. Relationship to Economic Substantive Due Process

The due process clauses bar governments from depriving persons of property without due process of law. The Court adopted and then discarded a *substantive* component to due process that protected preexisting economic arrangements valid under the common law from unreasonable interference by governments. (See Chapter 8.) The Court applies minimal scrutiny to economic claims asserted under due process or equal protection, but more vigorous scrutiny is applied to claims that the takings or contracts clause has been violated.

B. THE TAKINGS CLAUSE

1. Overview

The Fifth Amendment's takings clause provides that "private property [shall not] be taken for public use without just compensation." The takings clause applies to the states as well as the federal government, via incorporation into the 14th Amendment's due process clause. (See *Chicago, Burlington & Quincy Ry. v. Chicago,* 166 U.S. 226 (1897).)

a. **Purpose.** The takings clause has two purposes:

  i. **No forced redistributions of property.** The central purpose of the takings clause is to *prevent forcible redistributions of property.* The just compensation requirement operates to make sure that when governmental power is used to take private property the public pays for it.

  ii. **No takings for private benefit.** The public use requirement was intended to prevent even *fully compensated* takings if the purpose is simply to force a transfer of property from one private person to another. The idea is that *governmental compulsion should be used only for public benefit.*

b. **Scope of discussion.** There are two major constitutional issues raised by the takings clause:

  • Is a proven or acknowledged taking for *public use?*

  • Is a *regulation* of property so extensive that it *amounts to a de facto taking* of property?

Most takings for public use are straightforward—the government admits it is taking private property and the only issue is the amount of compensation. Although there is a large body of law dealing with "just compensation" as an independent issue it is not usually studied in the usual constitutional law course. By contrast, the point at which *regulations become takings* is a source of great controversy.

c. **Applies to tangible and intangible property: *Ruckelshaus v. Monsanto Co.,*** 467 U.S. 986 (1984). The takings clause protects both tangible and intangible property. Federal law required public disclosure of certain proprietary trade secrets. The Court ruled that the forced disclosure constituted a taking for which compensation must be paid.

d. **Applies to all branches of government.** The takings clause applies to *all* actions of governments—whether undertaken by the *legislature,* the *executive,* or the *judiciary.* (See *Hughes v. Washington,* 389 U.S. 290 (1967).) But judicial takings frequently escape meaningful scrutiny. See Thompson, 76 Va. L. Rev. 1449 (1990).

2. **The Public Use Requirement**

Private property may be taken *only* for **public use.** This is true *even if just compensation is paid.* But this requirement has virtually been eliminated by the Court's extreme deference to legislative judgments about what constitutes public use. So long as takings are *rationally related* to any ***conceivable** public purpose* the public use requirement is satisfied.

a. *Berman v. Parker,* 348 U.S. 26 (1954). Congress enacted a Redevelopment Act for the District of Columbia, under which private "slum" properties were taken (and paid for) and later transferred to private developers. A unanimous Court declared a public use to be anything that the legislature might reasonably think is conducive to "the public welfare." Later, in *Midkiff,* the Court characterized *Berman* as ruling that "[t]he 'public use' requirement is . . . coterminous with the scope of a sovereign's police powers."

b. *Hawaii Housing Authority v. Midkiff,* 465 U.S. 1097 (1984). Hawaii enacted a Land Reform Act that was designed to break up the oligopoly of fee ownership of land in Hawaii. On Oahu, the most urbanized island, only twenty-two landowners owned 72.5% of the fee titles to land. The Act created the Hawaii Housing Authority, which was empowered to seize the fee titles when enough tenants in any given "development tract" asked the HHA to do so. After the fee titles were taken and paid for the HHA was authorized to sell title to the tenants and to lend the tenants up to 90% of the purchase price. In effect, the Act used Hawaii's sovereign power to transfer ownership of land from landlords to tenants. The Court held that the public use requirement was satisfied, because the takings were "rationally related to a conceivable public purpose"—reduction of "the perceived social and economic evils of a land oligarchy traceable to [the Hawaiian] monarchs."

3. Regulatory Takings: How Much Regulation of Property Is Too Much?

The principal constitutional problem of takings is defining the point at which government regulation of property is so extensive that it amounts to a *de facto* taking, even though the government denies that it is taking the property. There is no general answer to this question. The Court applies three "bright-line" rules and several balancing tests to assess whether a regulation is a de facto taking. (See section B.3.b, infra.)

a. **The Court's early approach:** *Pennsylvania Coal Co. v. Mahon,* 260 U.S. 393 (1922). Pennsylvania's Kohler Act prohibited underground mining of coal that would cause the subsidence of any residence except where the owner of the coal also owned the surface. Mahon, owner of a surface residence threatened with subsidence, sought to restrain the Pennsylvania Coal Company from further underground mining. Pennsylvania Coal Company had conveyed the surface property by a deed expressly reserving the right to mine coal underground, and under which the surface owner assumed all risk of such mining and waived any claims for damages resulting from underground coal mining. Justice Holmes delivered the Court's opinion striking down the Kohler Act.

"[W]hile property may be regulated to a certain extent, if regulation goes too far it will be recognized as a taking." The Kohler Act went "too far" because it made "it commercially impracticable to mine . . . coal," a condition that had "very nearly the same effect for constitutional purposes as appropriating or destroying" the right to mine coal. Although the Court admitted that the Kohler Act was the product of "a strong public desire to improve the public condition" the means of improving the public condition—destruction of the "previously existing" right to mine coal—required Pennsylvania to pay for its seizure of these rights. Justice Brandeis dissented. (See section B.3.c, infra.)

b.   **The modern Court's functional framework.** Two "bright-line" rules identify when a taking *has* occurred; the other rule identifies when a taking has *not* occurred. If the "bright-line" rules do not resolve the issue, the Court employs one or more balancing tests.

   i.   **The "bright-line" rules**

   (a)   **Nuisance abatement: no taking.** When governments regulate property to *abate common law nuisances* there is *no taking.* (See section B.3.c, infra.)

   (b)   **Permanent physical occupation: taking.** When government regulations produce a *permanent physical occupation* of private property, a *taking has occurred.* (See section B.3.d, infra.)

   (c)   **No economically viable use: taking.** When government regulations leave the owner with *no economically viable use* of his property, a *taking has occurred.* (See section B.3.e, infra.)

   ii.   **The balancing tests**

   (a)   *Public benefit v. private costs.* If the bright line rules provide no answer, regulations are valid if they *substantially advance* a *legitimate state objective.* In making this assessment courts weigh the public benefits produced by the regulations against the harms imposed on the property owner. Only if the harms outweigh the benefits will the regulations constitute a taking. (See section B.3.f, infra.)

   (b)   **Conditions on building permits.** When governments attach conditions to building permits that would be takings if imposed alone, the conditions are takings unless the government can prove both of the following:

   • The condition is *substantially related* to the *state's objective in restricting development.*

- The nature and scope of the condition are *roughly proportional* to the impact of the proposed development.

(See section B.3.g, infra.)

c. **Nuisance abatement.** It is *no taking* when a government regulates property to prohibit private or public nuisances, even if the regulations prohibit *all* economically viable use. The property never included the right to inflict nuisances, and so the government has taken nothing by prohibiting the use of property to inflict nuisances.

  i. **Justice Brandeis's dissent in *Mahon*.** Justice Brandeis dissented in *Pennsylvania Coal Company v. Mahon*, 260 U.S. 393 (1922), arguing that the Kohler Act did not take property because it simply prevented the public nuisance of residences collapsing because of underground coal mining.

  ii. **Noxious uses: *Miller v. Schoene*,** 276 U.S. 272 (1928). In order to protect the destruction of apples by "cedar rust" fungus, Virginia enacted legislation that mandated the uncompensated destruction of red cedar trees that help spread the disease. The Court upheld the validity of the law on the theory that Virginia was forced to choose which property—cedar trees or apple trees—were to be preserved. The Court thought that Virginia's judgment that apple orchards were of far greater economic and social utility than ornamental cedar trees was "not unreasonable." Though the Court did not expressly decide whether the cedar trees were a nuisance, it deferred to Virginia's legislative declaration that cedar trees harboring cedar rust were, in effect, a public nuisance.

  iii. **The current doctrine: *Lucas v. South Carolina Coastal Council*,** 505 U.S. 1003 (1992). After Lucas paid nearly a million dollars to acquire two beachfront lots on which he intended to construct homes, South Carolina enacted legislation that prohibited any development of the lots. South Carolina's objective was to prevent further development of ecologically fragile barrier islands. The South Carolina Supreme Court ruled that the legislation was not a taking. The United States Supreme Court reversed, having concluded that the law denied all economically viable use of the lots. The Court remanded the case to determine whether the law simply abated a private or public nuisance. Governments may regulate property without creating a taking so long as the regulations "do no more than duplicate the result [obtainable by private parties] . . . under the State's law of private nuisance, or by the State under its complementary power to abate [public] nuisances." Such regulations, even when they forbid the *only* economically viable use of the property, do not "proscribe a productive use that was previously permissible under relevant property and nuisance principles." On remand, the South Carolina Supreme Court ruled that the uses prohibited by the law were not common law nuisances.

(a) **Regulation of "noxious" use not enough.** Regulations that aim to preclude "noxious uses" of property, but which are *not nuisances,* are not within the bright-line rule of per se validity. Mere recitation of a government objective to "prevent harm" rather than to confer public benefits at the expense of the affected property owner is *not sufficient* to trigger per se validity because "the distinction between 'harm-preventing' and 'benefit-conferring' is . . . in the eye of the beholder." South Carolina's regulation might equally prevent ecological harm or confer the public benefit of ecological preservation. If the objective is something less than stopping a common-law nuisance the per se nuisance rule does not apply.

d. **Permanent physical occupation.** When governments cause a *permanent physical occupation* of all or a part of private property they have taken that property. The burden of proving permanent physical occupation is on the property owner.

i. **The general rule:** *Loretto v. Teleprompter Manhattan CATV Corp.,* 458 U.S. 419 (1982). New York law provided that landlords must permit cable television operators to install cable facilities on their property and, by regulation, fixed $1 as the compensation for such forced installations. Loretto, owner of an apartment house burdened by Teleprompter's cable installation, claimed that Teleprompter's installation pursuant to the New York law was an uncompensated taking of her property. The Court agreed, concluding that a "permanent physical occupation authorized by government is a taking without regard to the public interests that it may serve."

(a) *Permanent* **occupation required.** *Temporary* physical occupations of private property do not trigger the per se takings rule. Whether or not such occupations are takings depends on application of the balancing tests. (See section B.3.f, *infra.*)

ii. **Personal property.** Permanent physical occupation of personal property occurs when governments confiscate personal property. In *Webb's Fabulous Pharmacies v. Beckwith,* 449 U.S. 155 (1980), the Court held that government appropriation of the interest earned on private funds deposited into court in an interpleader case was a taking. In *Hodel v. Irving,* 481 U.S. 704 (1987), and *Babbitt v. Youpee,* 519 U.S. 234 (1997) the Court voided a federal law that barred inheritance or device of certain property by providing for escheat of the property. "Such a complete abrogation of the rights of descent and devise [cannot] be upheld."

iii.   **Constructive occupation.** In rare cases, the Court will find government action to be a taking on the ground that it constitutes a constructive permanent physical occupation. **Example:** Government aircraft continually took off and landed over Causby's land. The Court found that the landowner could not use his land for any purpose due to the frequency and altitude of government overflights. The resulting loss to the landowner was "as complete as if the United States had entered upon the surface of the land and taken exclusive possession of it." *United States v. Causby,* 328 U.S. 256 (1946).

This principle is not freely applied. **Example:** Rent control ordinances authorize tenants physically to occupy the landlord's property at a price below what the landlord regards as sufficient inducement to permit the tenant to occupy his property. The Court has consistently held that the permanent physical occupation requirement is not implicated by these statutes because the initial decision of a landlord to deliver occupation of the property to the tenant is not compelled by the state. *Yee v. City of Escondido,* 503 U.S. 519 (1992); *FCC v. Florida Power Corp.,* 480 U.S. 245 (1987).

e.   **Destruction of all economically viable use.** Government regulations that destroy all economically viable use of private property, and are not abatements of public or private nuisances, are takings per se. The property owner has the burden of proving that the regulations at issue destroy all economically viable use of the property.

i.   **Total destruction:** *Lucas v. South Carolina Coastal Council,* 505 U.S. 1003 (1992), discussed supra. The Court squarely endorsed the rule that a taking occurs when government "regulation denies all economically beneficial or productive use of land," except when the regulations do no more than abate common-law nuisances. Such regulations are so extreme that they cast doubt on the usual assumption that government regulation of property is for the advantage of everyone, including affected property owners. Moreover, there is good reason to think that such regulations may be adopted as a cheap way for governments to achieve public benefits by imposing the costs of such benefits *entirely* upon affected property owners.

ii.   **Partial destruction or "conceptual severance": in general.** The Court in *Lucas* did not define the extent of the "property" to be examined to determine whether it has been stripped of all economically viable use.

Example: A government adopts a zoning law that designates some land as "wilderness," a category that precludes any commercial, agricultural, industrial, or residential use. Farmer Bob has a 100 acre dairy farm, 90 acres of which are pasture land upon which he runs his dairy herd. The zoning law designates Farmer Bob's 90 acres of pasture as "wilderness." Has Farmer Bob suffered a total economic deprivation of 90 acres, or has he suffered a significant diminution of the value of the entire 100 acres? The *Lucas* Court avoided answering this question.

The fact that this issue is unresolved means that there will continue to be arguments about the precise scope of the "property" interest affected by regulation.

iii. **Partial destruction: specific applications.** The problem of partial destruction (or conceptual severance, as it is often called) is illustrated by the Court's two cases involving restrictions on underground coal mining in order to support the surface.

   (a) *Pennsylvania Coal Co. v. Mahon,* 260 U.S. 393 (1922), discussed supra. The Court voided Pennsylvania's Kohler Act because it prevented underground coal miners from reaping the only economically viable use of their coal—removal for sale as fuel. The Court regarded limits on the removal of *any* coal as absolutely destructive of the property interest in the coal required to be left in place to support the surface.

   (b) *Keystone Bituminous Coal Assn. v. De Benedictis,* 480 U.S. 470 (1987). The Court found a modern version of the Kohler Act not to be a taking. The Subsidence Act required sufficient coal to be left in place to support the surface. The Court distinguished the Subsidence Act from the Kohler Act on two grounds:

   - The Kohler Act required owners of underground coal to leave it in place to support surface residences owned by others. It sacrificed the "private economic interests of coal companies" to benefit the "private interests of the surface owners." By contrast, the Subsidence Act sacrificed the private economic interests of coal owners for the "public interest" in surface support. The Court did not explain why that made any difference.

   - The 27 million tons of coal that the Subsidence Act forced miners to leave in place to support the surface did "not constitute a separate segment of property for takings law purposes." Because the 27 million tons was only a small fraction of the total amount of coal that could be removed the miners had "not come close to . . . proving that they have been denied the economically viable use of [their] property."

f. **Balancing public benefits and private costs.** When the per se or "bright-line" rules fail to answer the question, the Court applies a balancing test. Regulations are not takings if they *substantially advance a legitimate state objective*. But in order to determine whether this test has been satisfied the following conditions must exist:

- *Public benefits of the regulation must be greater than the private costs thereby imposed.*

- *The regulation may **not** be arbitrary.*

- *The regulation must leave the property owner with uses that permit the owner to earn a "reasonable return" on his investment.*

i. **Landmark preservation: *Penn Central Transportation Co. v. New York City*,** 438 U.S. 104 (1978). New York City designated Penn Central's Grand Central Terminal an architectural landmark, thus subjecting any proposed architectural changes to advance approval by New York City's Landmarks Preservation Commission. Penn Central's proposal to build a fifty-five story slab sided office tower above Grand Central Terminal was rejected by the Commission. Penn Central claimed that the Commission's refusal to permit the development constituted a taking. The Court ruled that the landmark regulations were not a taking. Justice Brennan, writing for the Court, asserted that the balancing test was an "essentially ad hoc, factual inquir[y]." Since the regulations did not fit within any of the per se rules the Court tried to determine whether the landmarks law substantially advanced a legitimate government interest. The public benefits of landmark preservation may be considerable and widely dispersed, but the burden of supplying those benefits was concentrated upon Penn Central. No matter, said Brennan, for the landmark designation was not arbitrary; Penn Central was still left with all its preexisting uses of the Terminal and could earn a "reasonable return" on its "investment-backed expectations." Moreover, the landmarks law permitted Penn Central to transfer a portion of its "development rights" in the airspace above the terminal to other properties it owned, thus increasing the intensity of permitted development of those other properties. This, said the Court, "mitigate[d] whatever financial burdens the law has imposed on [Penn Central]."

    ii. **Forced access for speech:** *PruneYard Shopping Center v. Robins,* 447 U.S. 74 (1980). The owner of a large shopping center open to the public refused to permit private persons to collect petition signatures. After the California Supreme Court ruled that the California Constitution's free speech guarantee protected the signature gathering, the shopping center owner contended that California had taken his property by forcing him to tolerate the unwanted speech activity. The Court unanimously rejected the contention. Even though California had interfered with the owner's right to exclude others there was no "permanent physical occupation" because the owner had *not* sought to exclude the public. California had a legitimate interest in protecting the public's free speech rights. Forcing an owner of a shopping center open to the public to tolerate reasonable exercise of free speech substantially advanced that goal in a way that did not impose unreasonable burdens on the property owner.

    iii. **Surface support:** *Keystone Bituminous Coal Assn. v. De Benedictis,* 480 U.S. 470 (1987), discussed supra. The Court refused to consider the coal required to be left in place as a separate piece of property. Thus, the Court saw no physical occupation and no total economic destruction of the property. The Court focused on the diminution of value to the entire coal mining enterprise produced by Pennsylvania's requirement that 27 million tons of coal be left in place. Since that diminution in value was not so large as to deprive the coal miners of a reasonable return on their investment there was no taking.

  g. **Conditions on building permits.** One of the most active areas of regulatory takings has been the problem of conditions attached to building permits. If the condition, by itself, would be a taking, is it saved by virtue of its attachment to a building permit? Put another way, if the state may deny a building permit without effecting a taking, may it condition the grant of a building permit on the property owner's consenting to what would otherwise be an uncompensated taking?

  Example: The city of Draco refuses to grant Jane a building permit to enlarge her home unless she creates two public parking spaces on her property. The condition—turning over a portion of her property for public parking—is clearly a taking if imposed outright. More facts are needed to determine whether it is a taking when attached as a condition to the grant of a building permit.

    i. **General rule.** Under the "unconstitutional conditions" doctrine a government may not require persons to surrender their property without compensation "in exchange for a discretionary benefit conferred by the government where the property sought has *little* *or no relationship to the benefit." Dolan v. City of Tigard,* 512 U.S. 374 (1994). That general standard consists of two components:

- An **"essential nexus"** between the legitimate state interest and the condition, by which the condition advances the state's reason for limiting development in the first place, and

- **"Rough Proportionality"** between the condition imposed and the impact of the development upon the state's legitimate interest.

Example: "Essential Nexus." The City of Draco imposes a building moratorium in order to prevent increased demand on its already scarce municipal water supply. Jane wished to increase the size of her home to accommodate her infant twins. Draco refuses to grant a building permit to Jane unless she creates two parking spaces on her property dedicated for public use. The condition—donation of two public parking spaces—bears no connection whatever to the reason Draco has imposed a building moratorium—to reduce demand on its scarce water supply.

Example: "Rough Proportionality." Suppose instead that the City of Draco refused to grant Jane a building permit unless she installed roof guttering piped to a cistern located on her property, which cistern must be dedicated to public use and connected to the municipal water supply. Now the condition imposed—donation of a cistern collection system dedicated to public use—is closely connected to the reason Draco has imposed a building moratorium—scarce water. It passes the "essential nexus" test. Whether it passes rough proportionality depends on whether the water collected by the cistern system is "roughly proportional" to the impact of Jane's development on the municipal water supply. If the cistern will collect and funnel to the municipal water supply an amount of water that is roughly proportional to the increased demand on the water supply that might be fairly attributable to her larger house, the rough proportionality test is satisfied.

The government has the burden of proving each of these elements.

ii.   **"Essential Nexus":** *Nollan v. California Coastal Commission,* 483 U.S. 825 (1987). Nollan wished to demolish his small, dilapidated beachfront cottage and replace it with a larger structure in keeping with the neighborhood. The California Coastal Commission refused to grant him a development permit unless he recorded an easement permitting the public to cross his beachfront in order to enable the public to move more easily between two public beach areas to the north and south of Nollan's property. Nollan contended the condition was a taking. The Court agreed. Were it imposed in isolation, the condition would be a taking because it amounted to a permanent physical occupation, a direct interference with the right to exclude others from one's property. The reason that the California Coastal Commission restricted development in the first place was to preserve "the public's ability to see the beach" from the roadway. The condition imposed—a public right-of-way along the beach itself—was in no way related to the reason the Coastal Commission restricted development. That *"essential nexus"* was lacking, and so the condition was held to be a taking.

iii. **"Rough proportionality":** *Dolan v. City of Tigard,* 512 U.S. 374 (1994). Florence Dolan wished to expand her plumbing and electric supply store in Tigard, Oregon, a suburb of Portland. The city refused to grant her a building permit unless she donated about 10% of her property to the city for two purposes—enhanced flood control regarding the creek adjoining her property and construction of a pedestrian and bicycle pathway along the creekside. Dolan contended that the conditions imposed constituted a taking. The Court agreed.

   (a) **Essential nexus.** The essential nexus element was satisfied because Tigard proved that its reason for restricting development in the first place was to prevent flooding and to reduce traffic congestion in the central business district. The conditions were related to that objective.

   (b) **The flood control condition.** While Tigard had proved that Dolan's development would increase runoff and thus exacerbate flooding, Tigard had failed to prove that there was any reason to require Dolan to donate a portion of her property to the public for floodplain purposes rather than simply restrict its use to floodplain purposes. Tigard "has never said why a public greenway, as opposed to a private one, was required in the interest of flood control." There was nothing proportional, rough or otherwise, between the impact of Dolan's development and the requirement that title to the floodplain be turned over to the public.

   (c) **The pedestrian and bicycle path.** The Court accepted Tigard's contention that Dolan's development would "increase traffic on the streets" but concluded that the city had "not met its burden of demonstrating that the additional number of vehicle and bicycle trips generated by the . . . development reasonably relate to the city's requirement for a dedication of the pedestrian/bicycle pathway easement."

h. Remedies. Several remedies apply once a regulation has been found to be a taking.

- **Injunctive and Declaratory Relief.** Future enforcement of the regulation will be enjoined or the regulation will be declared invalid. If the government wishes to proceed with the regulatory scheme, it must openly exercise its power of eminent domain and pay just compensation for its taking of property.

- **Damages.** Injunctive and declaratory relief provide no redress for the time period during which the regulation (which was a taking) was in place. For a long time the Court refused to provide a damages remedy for this "interim taking" of property, but that is no longer the case. The property owner is entitled to damages for the loss of his property during the period a regulatory taking was in effect.

C. THE CONTRACTS CLAUSE

1. Overview

The contracts clause provides that "No State shall . . . pass any . . . Law impairing the Obligation of Contracts." Article I, §10.

a. Original purpose. The contracts clause was intended to prevent the states from altering the economic consequences produced by private, voluntary contracts. Specifically, it was intended to prevent states from enacting laws relieving debtors of their contractual obligations and thereby depriving creditors of their contractual rights.

b. Modern doctrine. By virtue of judicial interpretation, the contracts clause today should read "No state may *unreasonably* impair the obligation of contracts." In general, the *more severe the impairment* the *closer the scrutiny* of the law's *nature and purposes*. Application of this principle depends on whether the contract is *public* or *private*.

i. Public contracts. When a state unilaterally modifies its *own* contract to benefit itself, its self-interested action is inherently suspect. Such contractual abrogations are valid only if the state proves that they are:

- *Reasonable* in terms of the scope of the contractual impairment, and

- There are *no less impairing means available* to accomplish the state's legitimate objectives.

ii. **Private contracts.** When a state impairs private contracts the level of judicial review depends on the severity of the impairment.

(a) **Severe impairments.** If a state "severely impairs" private contracts the impairment is valid only if the state can prove that it is:

- *Temporary,*

- *Reasonable in scope,* and

- *Directly related* to a *compelling,* or *emergency,* objective of the state.

(b) **Substantial impairments.** If a state's impairment of private contracts is not severe, but still "substantial," the impairment is valid if the state can prove:

- The state has a *legitimate* and *significant* public purpose for the impairment, and

- The impairment is based on *reasonable conditions* and is of a *character appropriate* to the public purpose.

Courts "defer to [the] legislative judgment as to the necessity and reasonableness of a particular measure."

(c) **Incidental impairments.** If a state impairs a private contract by a law that declares "a generally applicable rule of conduct" the contractual impairment is "incidental" and the law is subject to minimal scrutiny.

2. Early Development of the Contracts Clause

During the first half of the nineteenth century the Court acted vigorously to protect vested contract rights.

a. Public contracts: *Fletcher* and *Dartmouth College*

i. *Fletcher v. Peck,* 10 U.S. 87 (1810). A corrupt Georgia legislature was bribed to convey to land speculators Georgia's "Yazoo" lands (present-day Alabama and Mississippi) for pennies per acre. After public outcry a more virtuous legislature rescinded the Yazoo grant. The Court held that Georgia's grant, once made, was a public contract that could not be impaired by the action of the later legislature.

ii. *Trustees of Dartmouth College v. Woodward,* 17 U.S. 518 (1819). The New Hampshire legislature revoked Dartmouth College's royal charter, transforming it from a private to a public institution. The

Court held that the contracts clause barred New Hampshire from abrogating the public contract implicit in Dartmouth's charter.

b. **Private contracts:** *Sturges v. Crowninshield,* 17 U.S. 122 (1819). New York enacted legislation that ended imprisonment for nonpayment of debt by discharging unpaid debts upon the debtor's surrender of his property. The Court struck down the law because it erased the debtor's preexisting contractual obligations.

3. Early Balancing of Public and Private Interests

As early as 1827, the Court began to alter its contract clause doctrine. By the end of the nineteenth century the Court had created a number of exceptions to its early strict doctrine.

a. **Public contracts**

i. **Economic impairment:** *Charles River Bridge v. Warren Bridge,* 36 U.S. 420 (1837). In 1785 Massachusetts had granted to the Charles River Bridge Co. the right to construct and operate a toll bridge across the Charles River. In 1828 Massachusetts chartered another company to construct a competing toll-free bridge. The Court rejected the Charles River Bridge Company's contention that Massachusetts had impaired its charter. Massachusetts had never promised "not to establish a free bridge at the place where the Warren bridge is erected," nor had it promised an exclusive franchise to the Charles River Bridge Co. Massachusetts may have destroyed the economic value of the Charles River Bridge Company's charter but it had not impaired the legal rights granted under it.

ii. **The police power:** *Stone v. Mississippi,* 101 U.S. 814 (1880). Mississippi granted to a private party the right to run a lottery for twenty-five years. A later legislature made lotteries illegal. The Court found no breach of the contracts clause: The "legislature cannot bargain away the police power."

b. **Private contracts**

i. **Bankruptcy:** *Ogden v. Saunders,* 25 U.S. 213 (1827). New York enacted a bankruptcy law that permitted discharge of a debtor's contractual obligations, but only with respect to obligations entered into after the effective date of the law. The Court, 4 to 3, upheld this law, reasoning that the law in effect at the time a contract is formed is the "law of the contract" and thus the law does not impair the obligation of such contracts. Chief Justice Marshall dissented, arguing that the clause made no distinction between prospective or retrospective impairments, and that the clause protects a natural law right to enter into contracts from state invasion.

It was the only time in his career as Chief Justice that Marshall was in the minority in a constitutional case.

4. Modern Doctrine

In the 20th century the Court has generally deferred to legislative judgments of a public interest sufficient to justify impairments of contractual obligations. The two exceptions are *public contracts* and *severe impairments of private contracts*.

a.   **Deference to the legislature.** Modern contract clause doctrine concerning private contracts originated in *Home Building & Loan Assn. v. Blaisdell*.

  i.   **Mortgage moratorium:** *Home Building & Loan Assn. v. Blaisdell,* 290 U.S. 398 (1934). In 1933, during the Great Depression, Minnesota enacted legislation that declared an economic emergency existed and, for the period of the emergency but not after May 1935, authorized courts to postpone mortgage sales and extend the postsale redemption period. The Court, 5 to 4, upheld the validity of the law.

  (a)   **The Court's opinion.** Minnesota's mortgage moratorium was valid because it was a "reasonable and appropriate" exercise of the police power to address a legitimate public emergency. Though phrased like minimal scrutiny the Court's application of this test was more demanding.

  - *Directly related to a public emergency.* Although "[e]mergency does not create [or] increase . . . power" the Court thought that the existence of an emergency was relevant to the question of whether it was "addressed to a legitimate end"—preventing another downward turn in the spiral of economic and social depression by keeping Minnesotans in their homes instead of on the streets.

  - *Reasonable in scope.* The moratorium was a "reasonable and appropriate" way to achieve Minnesota's legitimate objective.

    - The moratorium was for the general "protection of a basic interest of society," not for the "mere advantage of particular individuals."

    - The "character [of] the relief afforded" was a moratorium on enforcement of the mortgage, not outright cancellation of the mortgage.

    - The moratorium was "temporary"—"limited to the exigency which called it forth."

(b) **The dissent.** The dissenters, led by Justice Sutherland, charged that the Minnesota statute did just what the Framers specifically intended the contracts clause to prohibit. The law produced "a material and injurious change in the obligation," not merely "a modification of the remedy."

ii. **"Windfall" profits:** *Energy Reserves Group v. Kansas Power & Light,* 459 U.S. 400 (1983). Kansas Power agreed to purchase natural gas from Energy Reserves under a contract that provided that the price would be the highest price permitted by any government regulation. Kansas enacted a law that barred such price increases. The Court upheld the Kansas law, restating the doctrinal test as follows:

- Is there a *"substantial impairment* of [a] contractual relationship?"

- If so, the *burden of proof falls on the state to justify the impairment,* by showing all of the following:

  — A *"significant and legitimate public purpose behind the regulation,"*

  — The impairment "is based upon *reasonable conditions* and is of a *character appropriate to the public purpose."* Courts should "defer to legislative judgment as to the necessity and reasonableness of a particular measure."

b. **"Stricter" scrutiny.** The Court does not apply deferential scrutiny to *public contracts*—those to which a state is a party—and to *severe impairments of private contracts.*

i. **Public contracts:** *United States Trust Co. v. New Jersey,* 431 U.S. 1 (1977). In 1962 New York and New Jersey, acting together through the Port Authority, borrowed millions of dollars from the investing public on the strength of a promise that the Port Authority would not use its revenues to subsidize rail transit. In 1974 New York and New Jersey decided that rail subsidies were needed to "discourag[e] automobile use and improv[e] mass transit." Each state enacted a law that repealed the promise. The Court struck down the repeal as violative of the contracts clause. "[D]eference to a legislative assessment of reasonableness and necessity is not appropriate [when] the State's self-interest is at stake." The repeal was neither necessary nor reasonable.

- **Necessity.** The repeal was not necessary because there were "less impairing" means to achieve the public objectives of resource conservation and improved rail transit. Total repeal was not proven to be *"essential."*

- **Reasonableness.** The repeal was not reasonable because it was not in response to unforeseen changes that might have caused the promise "to have a substantially different impact . . . than when it was adopted." Total repeal would be reasonable only under radically altered circumstances of an unforeseeable nature.

ii.   **Severe impairments of private contracts:** *Allied Structural Steel Co. v. Spannaus,* 438 U.S. 234 (1978). Minnesota enacted a "pension protection" law that required certain employers with pension plans who either terminate the plan or cease doing business in Minnesota to (1) provide pensions to all employees with at least ten years' service and (2) make a lump-sum payment in an amount sufficient to provide the required pensions. Allied's pension plan stipulated that Allied could amend or terminate the plan at any time for any reason. Thus, pensions were payable only to employees on reaching age sixty-five *if* Allied was still in business *and* the pension plan still existed. Allied ceased doing business in Minnesota and the state demanded $185,000 under its pension protection law. The Court voided Minnesota's law as violative of the contracts clause.

(a)   **The Court's rationale.** As a general matter the "severity of the impairment measures the height of the hurdle the state legislation must clear." *Severe impairments* require *"careful examination of the nature and purpose* of the state legislation." Minnesota's law severely impaired Allied's prior pension contract because it "nullifie[d] express terms of [Allied's] contractual obligations and impose[d] a completely unexpected liability in potentially disabling amounts." The law was invalid because Minnesota failed to prove that the severe impairment "was *necessary* to meet an *important general social problem.*" The extraordinarily narrow focus of the law indicated that it was designed to benefit a "narrow class" rather than "to protect a broad societal interest." Unlike *Blaisdell,* there was *no emergency* and the impairment was *not temporary* but *permanent.*

c.   **Incidental impairment: No scrutiny.** If impairment of private contractual obligations is an incidental by-product of a law declaring "a generally applicable rule of conduct" that is not directed at contractual obligations, the law is presumed valid. Only if the challenger can prove that the law has a strongly disproportionate effect on private contractual obligations and that the law does not advance a "broad societal interest" will the law be subjected to contracts clause scrutiny.

i. *Exxon Corp. v. Eagerton,* 462 U.S. 176 (1983). Alabama increased its severance tax on oil and gas and prohibited the pass-through of the increase to purchasers of the oil and gas. Exxon contended that the law impaired its contractual right to pass through to the customer all such tax increases. The Court held that Alabama's law was generally applicable and designed to achieve broad societal benefits. The law's effect on pass-through contracts was incidental and not designed to impair private contracts. The Court did not explain what effect, other than impairing pass-through contracts, the law was designed to achieve.

REVIEW QUESTIONS AND ANSWERS

Question: The state of Tohoku enacts a law that provides that, after the sale of the first 1,000 copies of any copyrighted work, anyone is free to publish or reproduce the work. Bill, a creator of computer software, asserts that the law is a taking. Is he right? In answering, ignore the possibility that Tohoku's law might be preempted by federal statute.

Answer: Bill is correct. Intangible property is entitled to protection under the takings clause. The law is a permanent dispossession of the intangible copyright, analytically identical to a permanent physical occupation of land. Because the law comes within the per se rule of permanent dispossession, it is automatically ruled to be a taking for which compensation is required.

Question: The state of Aoshima enacts a law that prohibits construction upon and all agricultural uses of "Fragile Habitat Zones" identified by the statute. Gloria owns a 320-acre cattle ranch that she has recently subdivided into 32 ten-acre single family residential homesteads, each worth about $100,000. A Fragile Habitat Zone includes about 200 acres of Gloria's ranch, taking in eighteen lots in their entirety, excluding twelve others, and evenly dividing the remaining two. Gloria contends that the Aoshima law is a taking. Is she correct?

Answer: Yes, in part. The result turns on whether each lot is a separate piece of property. According to *Lucas* each fee title is a separate piece of property. Since she has subdivided the ranch into thirty-two separate fee titles she has created thirty-two separate pieces of property. The restriction with respect to the eighteen lots entirely in the Fragile Habitat Zone deprives Gloria of all economically viable use of those eighteen lots. The law is a taking as to them. The law has no effect on the twelve lots outside the zone, and so there is no taking. The two lots evenly divided by the zone are reduced in value, but the Court appears to repudiate the idea of "conceptual severance"—dividing one piece of property into two portions using the regulatory impact as the dividing line. A taking has occurred only if the reduction is so severe that all economic use is lost or if the diminution is so serious as to deprive Gloria of any reasonable return on her investment in these two properties.

Question: Megawatt Power acquired a large tract of land, zoned for industrial use only, for purposes of constructing a nuclear power plant on the site. A known earthquake fault slices through the tract. After Megawatt announced its plans, the State of Morioka enacted legislation that forbids the construction of any nuclear reactor or other industrial facility on or in immediate proximity to a known earthquake fault. Megawatt contends that the construction ban is a taking of its property, and produces uncontroverted evidence that due to the construction ban the parcel no longer has any economic value. Will Megawatt succeed?

Answer: No. Morioka may act to abate or prevent the occurrence of private or public nuisances. Preventing construction of a nuclear facility on a seismically risky location is well within the power to prevent nuisances, although the precise issue of whether nuclear reactors on earthquake faults are a nuisance will be determined under Morioka law. If Morioka has acted solely to prevent a nuisance its regulation is not a taking, even though the regulation destroys all economic value. Megawatt never had any property right to create or maintain a nuisance so nothing has been taken from it.

Question: By statute, the state of Murasaki forbids any destruction of "historic monuments," as designated by Murasaki's Historical Preservation Commission. George lives in a valuable old log cabin that Murasaki's Historical Preservation Commission has designated a historical monument. He claims that the law, as applied to him, is a taking. Is George correct?

Answer: No. The law is not a taking per se—it is neither a permanent dispossession nor does it eliminate all economically viable use. The law is also not simply a regulation of common law nuisance. Thus, its validity depends on whether the law substantially advances legitimate state interests. Historical preservation is surely legitimate. The law advances that interest while still leaving George with his rights to exclusive possession, use, and transfer of the cabin. Its existing residential purposes are valuable, so it is not likely that the diminution in value produced by the regulation interferes with George's "investment-backed expectations" and the regulation leaves George with a reasonable return on that investment.

Question: Harry purchased a carefully restored 18th century house located in Charlesfort, a historic city on the eastern coast of the United States. In order to ensure the safety of structures Charlesfort requires that a permit be obtained to build or alter any residential structure. Harry applied for a building permit to renovate the kitchen, which dates from the 1950s. Charlesfort refused to grant the permit unless Harry would grant to the public an easement of right of way into a limited and defined portion of his front garden, from which perspective the public could view his historic home more easily than from the street. Harry claimed that Charlesfort's action constituted a taking. Is he correct?

Answer: Yes. The condition imposed by Charlesfort does not advance the government's legitimate reason for restricting the owner's development in the first place.

Charlesfort requires building permits to ensure that structures are safe, not to ensure that the public gets better views of historic structures. As in *Nollan,* there is no *essential nexus* between the condition imposed and the governmental objective inherent in building permits.

Question: Suppose Charlesfort had enacted an ordinance designating its historic structures as "historical landmarks," and requiring that any alterations to historical landmarks must be approved by the Charlesfort Historical Review Board before a building permit for the alterations may issue. Would it be a taking if the Board refused to approve Harry's alterations unless he used exterior finish materials that matched the existing 18th century architectural details of the house?

Answer: No. The condition imposed—match the existing 18th century architectural details—squarely advances Charlesfort's reasons for limiting alterations of historical residences in the first place. Moreover, the extent of the conditions imposed are "roughly proportional" to the impact of the proposed development—they relate directly to the possibility that the alterations might compromise its character as a historical landmark.

Question: The state of Akita enacts a law that imposes a 100% tax on all copyright royalty income earned by Akita taxpayers. Julie, a successful author whose income is composed almost entirely of royalties, claims that the law is a taking for which she has received no compensation. Is she correct?

Answer: Possibly. Intangible property is equally entitled to the protection of the takings clause. While governments have wide latitude to tax, they may not use taxation to violate other individual rights, like free speech or the right to compensation for takings. The problem, of course, is that a tax is by nature a taking. The usual answer to this dilemma is to assert that the taxpayer is fully compensated for whatever "taking" has occurred by the governmental benefits conferred upon him funded by everyone's taxes. But surely some taxes may be so pointed and confiscatory that they operate to sacrifice the few for the benefit of the public. Under such conditions a taking has arguably occurred. Here, Julie is permanently dispossessed of her intangible property. Moreover, the tax has effectively destroyed all the economic value in her copyrights. If the doctrinal principles mean anything, this kind of pointed and confiscatory tax ought to be treated as a taking.

Question: In order to provide more money to local public schools in dire financial straits produced by years of financial neglect the state of Koyama enacts legislation by which it lowers the rate of interest one percentage point on all its existing public debt. Mary, who owns a Koyama bond bearing interest at a stated rate of 10% per year, claims that Koyama's unilateral reduction of the interest rate to 9% per year is a violation of the contracts clause. Is she correct?

Answer: Yes. Courts will not defer to legislative judgments of the necessity or reasonableness of impairments to public obligations. Koyama must prove that its unilateral reduction of the interest rates on its public debt is the least impairing alternative available to it to achieve its objective of providing more money to local schools. It will surely be unable to do that—Koyama could raise taxes or curtail other spending. Moreover, the circumstances that prompt the impairment—the financial condition of local schools—is not the product of radically altered unforeseeable circumstances.

Question: Acting on the belief that the tobacco industry has promoted human suffering and death, the state of Murata enacts legislation that requires that all tobacco manufacturers or wholesalers located in Murata ("covered companies") refund the purchase price of all tobacco products ever purchased from them, or in lieu of such obligation to pay to the Murata Tobacco Abatement Agency an amount equal to 50% of a covered company's total sales from tobacco products for the past ten years. Any such payment in lieu must be held by the Agency in trust for the "victims of tobacco use." Nick Teen, Inc., a tobacco wholesaler located in Murata, asserts that the law violates the contract clause. Is it correct?

Answer: Yes. The law is a severe impairment of the contractual obligation arising from the sale of tobacco products. It nullifies the express terms of a private contract for the sale of tobacco and simultaneously imposes an unexpected and potentially disabling liability. Since severe impairments are presumed invalid Murata must prove that the law is necessary to meet an important general social problem. Moreover, this law benefits a narrow class—tobacco users—and does so by means of a severe and permanent impairment. There are far less impairing means available to Murata to discourage the use of tobacco.

Question: Acting in response to a severe and general housing shortage, the state of Nagano enacts a law that freezes rents at current levels for one year. Landlord asserts that the law violates the contracts clause, at least as applied to his leases that call for rents to increase $10 each month during the life of the lease. Is he correct?

Answer: No. The law may substantially impair the escalator clause of his leases but Nagano will be able to sustain its burden of proving that it has a significant and legitimate public purpose for the law, the impairment's character is appropriate to the public purpose, and the impairment is reasonable under the conditions. Courts will defer to legislative judgments as to the necessity and reasonableness of the law. Here, Nagano acted in response to a severe and general housing shortage and impaired private obligations temporarily and only in order directly to address the problem.

EXAM TIPS

- **Takings:** Almost always, regulatory takings problems involve some restrictions on land use—typically zoning or environmental restrictions. The general rule is that a regulation must *substantially advance a legitimate state interest*.

  - **The Per Se Rules.** Check to see if any of the *per se* rules apply.

    - **Partial Takings—"Conceptual Severance":** Regulations that destroy all economic value to part of a single property are not within the per se rule if a reasonable return can be earned on the *entire property*. Regulations that destroy *all economic use of the entire property* are takings per se.

    - **Permanent Dispossession:** Regulations that permanently oust the owner from exclusive possession (even from the tiniest portion) are takings per se.

    - **Nuisance:** Regulations that abate or prevent nuisances under preexisting common law are not takings.

  - **The Public Use Requirement:** Although no taking can occur except for a public use the courts will defer to the legislative judgment unless its judgment is so irrational that the purpose of the taking has no relationship to any conceivable public purpose. Don't waste time discussing this point in depth.

  - **Intangible Property:** While exam questions usually involve restrictions on real property, don't forget that the takings clause applies equally to intangible property; e.g., intellectual property, money, contract or reputation rights.

- **Contract Clause:** Check to see if the state is modifying its own contracts (to make the deal better for the state at the expense of the other party) or if the law severely impairs private contracts (by expressly modifying the terms of private contracts and imposing a crushing liability). If either is true, the law is subject to stricter scrutiny.

  - **Stricter Scrutiny:** The state must prove that the impairment is both *necessary* and *reasonable*.

  - **Usual Review:** Usually, the state need only prove that it has a *significant* and *legitimate* purpose. In these cases, the necessity and reasonableness of the measure will be accepted unless the legislative judgment is irrational.

- **Incidental Impairments:** The contracts clause does not apply to "generally applicable rules of conduct" that impair private contracts as an unintended and incidental byproduct, unless the challenger proves that the effects of the law are primarily to impair private contracts and that the law produces no broad societal benefits.

EXAM ESSAY QUESTIONS

These essay questions are intended to provide you with examples of typical examination essay questions. They contain multiple issues from various areas of constitutional law. As with most examinations, you need to spot all the issues, then deal with them accurately (by applying the appropriate doctrinal tests) and convincingly (by using the facts to bolster your argument). The discussion following each question is not a model answer, but a guide to help you in spotting the issues, organizing your own answer, and seeing how facts may be used to bolster your analysis.

Question: Congress enacts legislation that establishes a ''Border Commission,'' charged with the responsibility of ''determining how the nation's borders might be better policed to prevent illegal entry into the United States.'' The Border Commission is also authorized to promulgate regulations binding upon all federal agencies, including the Border Patrol and the Immigration and Naturalization Service, whenever the Border Commission determines that its regulation is ''reasonably necessary to improve the security of the nation's borders.'' Under the statute, the Border Commission consists of two federal judges to be appointed by the Chief Justice of the United States and to serve at his pleasure, the Chairman of the House Subcommittee on National Security, the Chairman of the Senate Subcommittee on Internal Affairs, and three members appointed by the President to serve at his pleasure. The Border Commission promulgates a regulation requiring that every alien admitted to the United States be issued an ''Entry Permit,'' which must be carried at all times, and requiring the arrest and immediate expulsion of any alien apprehended without possession of an Entry Permit. Three plaintiffs file suit in federal district court, challenging the validity of the regulation: (1) Amnesty International, an association of people devoted to the elimination of torture and imprisonment or persecution of people on account of their political beliefs; (2) Mark, a citizen of Ireland, residing lawfully in the United States and in possession of an ''Entry Permit''; and (3) George, a citizen of Canada and member of Amnesty International, apprehended in the United States without an Entry Permit and facing deportation solely for that reason. Please assess the likely disposition of their claims.

Answer: The threshold issue is **standing.** Amnesty International's only claim to standing is by virtue of either third-party standing or the associational standing doctrine. Both will fail.

Third-party Standing. There is no indication that Amnesty International has such a special relationship with George (or any other third party) that Amnesty International can be safely entrusted with the responsibility of vindicating George's (or anybody else's) claim. Moreover, it is not impossible for George to press his own claim (he has done so) and presumably other ''Georges'' will press their claims on their own. The only appreciable risk that third party claims will be lost lies in the possibility that some lawfully resident aliens may shy away from challenging the validity of the regulation for fear of retribution. But to the extent that such aliens are lawful residents the fear is unfounded.

Associational Standing. There is no direct injury to Amnesty International. Nor can Amnesty International succeed in claiming that it is representing its members. The basic problem is that AI cannot show that its members would have standing to sue independently. A member of an organization devoted to the elimination of political persecution is not, by that fact, personally injured by the regulation. Nor is the interest asserted—invalidity of the regulation and freedom from possessing an ''Entry Permit''—germane to AI's purposes.

Mark. Mark's claim to standing depends on whether he has been personally injured in fact. He faces no threat of deportation, so his only injury is in the requirement that he keep his Entry Permit in his possession at all times. This is not much of an injury but any injury will suffice, so long as it is individualized and actual. His injury, while minor, is real and personal. Mark's injury is surely caused by the regulation and the injury may be redressed by an injunction forbidding the Border Commission from enforcing the regulation. Mark's claim is ripe since the injury—required possession of an Entry Permit—is ongoing.

George. George surely has standing. George's injury is clear—he faces deportation solely because of his failure to have an Entry

Permit in his possession. His injury is caused by the regulation and it may be redressed by an injunction.

The **merits** of the claims involve four major issues: (1) whether the composition of the Border Commission complies with the Constitution's rules concerning appointment of federal officials, (2) whether the required service of federal judges on the Border Commission is an impermissible encroachment upon the judiciary, (3) whether the removal provisions of the law are valid, and (4) whether Congress has impermissibly delegated its legislative power to the Border Commission.

Appointment. The Border Commissioners are clearly federal officials—they exercise "significant authority pursuant to the laws of the United States." They are probably "inferior" officers—the scope of their duties is limited and their authority, though extremely powerful within their sphere of jurisdiction, is similarly limited. Thus, Congress probably may specify their appointment by the President, the Courts of law, or executive departments. If so, the members appointed by the President are certainly validly appointed. The validity of the appointment of two federal judges by the Chief Justice is less clear—the Chief Justice is not, by himself, a "court of law." The ex officio appointment of two members of Congress—chairmen of specified subcommittees—is invalid. Congress has no power to appoint executive officers itself, and the specification of certain congressional officers to the Commission is surely such an appointment.

Encroachment on the Judiciary. One aspect of the general separation of powers test is the idea that no branch may be forced to undertake tasks that are "incongruous" with its constitutional tasks or that would substantially impede the performance of its constitutional duties. Although the Court in *Mistretta* upheld the validity of federal judges serving on the Sentencing Commission there was a far closer connection between the work of that Commission and the judiciary than there is between border security and the judiciary. It is probably incongruous for federal judges to be making regulations governing border security and thus constitutionally impermissible for them to serve on the Border Commission. In the early years of the nation the Court implied that it was impermissible to force judges to serve as commissioners determining the validity of pension claims by Revolutionary War veterans.

Removal. The three members appointed by the President are removable by him. That is valid. The President, however, has no ability to remove either of the two federal judges or the two congressional members. Since the Border Commissioners probably are "inferior" officers, Congress may restrict the President's ability to remove Commissioners but may not do so in a manner that "impede[s] the President's ability to perform his constitutional duty." Here, the President has no ability either to appoint or remove a majority of the Commission, a body charged with grave responsibility to promulgate regulations bearing upon the President's power and duty to enforce the laws governing admission to the United States. The lack of *any* ability on the President's part to remove the Commissioners is an impediment of his ability to perform his constitutional duty.

Delegation. The nondelegation doctrine is comatose but this might be an occasion for its revival. Congress told the Border Commission to determine how better to prevent illegal entry into the nation and gave it the power to promulgate any regulation it found to be "reasonably necessary" to attain that goal. Congress may have declared a policy but it hasn't specified *any* factual circumstances that trigger the policy.

Question: A newly enacted federal statute reads, in its entirety: "No government, private person, or any other entity, may exhibit the Confederate battle flag in public, except for exhibitions by museums and for any other historical purposes only. Violators are subject to a fine of not more than $10,000, or imprisonment for up to five years, or both; except for governments, which are subject to a fine of no more than 10% of the violator's total revenue for the full fiscal year immediately prior to the year of the violation." The sponsors of the bill argued during congressional debate on the measure that it was needed because the Confederate battle flag had become the symbol of racial bigotry. All hearings and debate were focused on that issue. The validity of the law is challenged by the state of Mississippi, which by statute incorporates the Confederate battle flag into its state flag; by the state of Alabama, which by executive order makes it a practice to fly the Confederate battle flag at state buildings; and by Harry, as a defense to the charge of violating the law by flying the Confederate battle flag at a Ku Klux Klan rally that resulted in a riot. Please assess the claims asserted.

Answer: The Mississippi and Alabama Claims. Mississippi's first argument should be statutory—that the law prohibits the exhibition of the Confederate battle flag only as a discrete "flag-in-itself," not as a symbol appearing in another flag, Mississippi's state flag. Courts should adhere to the rule that if constitutional issues can be avoided by plausible statutory construction, they should be. But if this is not a plausible construction, the constitutional problems must be addressed. On that score, Alabama's and Mississippi's claims are identical.

Congressional Power to Enact the Law. The first issue is the source of Congress's power to enact the law.

Interstate Commerce. It might be argued that the power to regulate interstate commerce extends this far, but congressional power to regulate commerce extends only to activities that "substantially affect" interstate commerce. Perhaps the public exhibition of the Confederate battle flag inflames racial sensibilities, which acts upon interstate commerce by creating friction among the people, taking their minds off commercial activities. But this is far-fetched. Moreover, Congress made no factual finding that exhibition of the Confederate battle flag was related to commerce, substantially or otherwise. That fact frees the courts to make their own determination of the substantiality of the connection to interstate commerce, and the connection is so tenuous that it is likely insufficient to support congressional action under its commerce power. See *Lopez* and *Morrison*.

Even if the public display of the Confederate battle flag is substantially related to interstate commerce, principles of state autonomy—whether implicit in the commerce clause or a product of the Tenth Amendment's structural truism—probably bar Congress from forbidding the states to exhibit the Confederate battle flag. Here, Mississippi's and Alabama's claims diverge.

Mississippi may assert that the federal law forces it to alter its official state flag to conform to congressional demands or to forfeit 10% of its total revenue, an astoundingly large fine. As in *New York v. United States,* this may well constitute a command to the state to legislate in a particular way on an issue unique to governance or sovereignty. But *New York v. United States* suggested that this doctrine applied only to legislation that affected only the states, and not private persons. Here, the law applies to everyone, but the penalties applicable to the states are different and unique.

Alabama will argue that *Printz* bars the federal government from issuing commands to the executive branch of state government. Alabama officials must exercise their discretion in conformity to a federally prescribed standard, making them conscripts into the federal service though politically accountable for those actions only to a state electorate.

Section 5 of the 14th Amendment. The United States might argue that Congress acted to protect equal protection. Although the Supreme Court has never addressed the issue of whether a state's official display of the Confederate battle flag is a violation of equal protection, the United States might argue that Congress is simply providing a remedy for violations of equal protection in advance. This argument depends upon whether the federal ban is congruent with and proportional to the claimed equal protection injury. The United States would argue that the message conveyed by the Confederate flag is intended to be one of racial animosity and is commonly so understood. Governments may not validly make racial distinctions unless they prove that the racial distinction is necessary to achieve a compelling public objective. On this view, the federal law simply eliminates any possibility that a state could justify the practice. The states might counter that the exhibition of a flag is purely symbolic and that the message is as much one of heritage as racism. Thus, the exhibition of a Confederate flag is like a disparate impact case. The burden is on the plaintiffs to prove that the exhibition was an intentional act of racial discrimination. Generally, governments are free to speak however they wish and any injury inflicted is not constitutionally cognizable. The emotional distress of seeing the Confederate flag is akin to the nonredressable emotional distress suffered by a witness to a public display of nonobscene pornography. On that view, it will be difficult for the United States to sustain its burden of proof and the outright ban is thus neither congruent nor proportional.

Section 2 of the 13th Amendment. Congress may act reasonably to prohibit the "badges and incidents" of slavery. The Confederate battle flag might well be a symbolic "badge" of slavery, and if so, it is because of the message it sends, a fact that implicates the free speech clause.

The Free Speech Clause. Even if Congress has a source of authority to enact the law, the law may be a forbidden infringement of free speech. The degree to which state governments are protected by the free speech guarantee is unsettled. Resolution of this issue may depend on the perceived purposes of the free speech clause. If free speech is an end in itself, presumably state governments are equally entitled to assert it to expand the range of protected expression. If free speech is a means to an end, then the scope of state protection under free speech probably depends on the degree to which the state speech relates to the perceived end. But to the extent that self-governance is the goal of free speech, the 14th Amendment limits state self-governance. Valid congressional action under the 14th Amendment's enforcement power may supersede any latent protection of state speech provided by the 14th Amendment.

Harry's Claim. Harry may raise the same commerce clause objections to the validity of the statute invoked by the states, except that state autonomy principles do not apply. As applied to Harry, Congress is unable to use its enforcement power under §5 of the 14th Amendment as authority for the law. Equal protection only applies to state action, and Harry's conduct is not state action. See *United States v. Morrison.*

Through §2 of the 13th Amendment, Congress may regulate private conduct that perpetuates the "badges and incidents" of slavery. Congress has great leeway to identify racially based practices that constitute such badges and incidents. Perhaps public display of the Confederate battle flag is such a badge or incident, but if so it is because of the message conveyed by the Confederate battle flag— white supremacy. While that conclusion supports congressional power to enact the law, it raises an independent question of the validity of the law under the free speech clause.

The flag ban is a prohibition of symbolic conduct. Public display of the Confederate battle flag is intended to convey one or more of a variety of messages—white supremacy, respect for Southern valor, or personal heritage—and is likely to be so understood. However it is not self-evident whether display of a Confederate flag is meant to convey white supremacy or personal heritage. Nor is it easy to be sure what is meant. Still, most viewers of the Confederate flag see it as a message—perhaps an amalgam of Southern pride, white racial supremacy, and honor of heritage. Even though the message is mixed, the Confederate flag communicates ideas. Accordingly, the law regulates symbolic conduct and is subject to the *O'Brien* test.

The law may not be otherwise valid, if it is beyond congressional power to enact. See above. But if Congress has authority to enact the law, it may still violate one or more of the remaining *O'Brien* tests. The objective of the law—to dampen racial hostility—is surely important. But the regulation employed—banning most public displays of the Confederate flag—is related to the suppression of ideas. Sponsors of the legislation openly urged its adoption to curb expressions of racial bigotry. Secondly, the law excepts displays that are solely historical, thus effectively focusing more on the display that is intended to express white supremacy or personal heritage. While not as sharply viewpoint discriminatory as the ordinance at issue in *RAV v. St. Paul,* the law is viewpoint discriminatory. These two facts—evidence of a viewpoint-discriminatory motive and use of a viewpoint-discriminatory ban in the law itself—

prove that the regulation is intended to suppress ideas. Even if the Confederate flag is thought to be a "fighting symbol," the use of a viewpoint-discriminatory ban is invalid under *RAV*. Moreover, under *O'Brien*, the ban is far broader than necessary to curb expression of racial hostility. The law forbids a descendant of Robert E. Lee from displaying a Confederate battle flag on General Lee's birthday, while also forbidding the Ku Klux Klan to display the same flag to promote racial hatred.

For Harry's defense to succeed, however, he probably must prove that the law is facially invalid. He might be validly punished for his display under *Brandenburg* (the flag might have incited the riot) but his defense is good if he can prove that the law is substantially overbroad. Given the broad range of messages conveyed by the Confederate battle flag, and the narrow set of circumstances under which mere display of the flag might constitutionally be forbidden, the law is surely substantially overbroad and thus facially invalid.

Question: Island County, Maine, consists of a small archipelago of islands. The majority of its inhabitants are followers of Lifo, an ascetic monk who teaches that all animal life is sacred. By ordinance, Island County forbids anyone from eating animal flesh, or using any product made in whole or part from dead animals. To preserve the tranquility of Island County waters for humans and animals, another Island County ordinance forbids anyone from operating motorized "jetskis" in Island County navigable waters. Federal law governs certain safety devices and operating features of jetskis, and requires users of jetskis to observe the rules of navigation, but does not mention state law. There are no jetski manufacturers located in Island County, though there is one manufacturer in Maine, responsible for less than one-tenth of one percent of the jetskis in use in Maine. Jake, a New Yorker visiting Island County, spends a day careening around on his jetski, followed by a sumptuous barbecue of grilled meats. He is arrested and charged with violation of both ordinances. He moves to quash the indictment on constitutional grounds. Please identify and evaluate Jake's claims.

Answer: The "Dead Animal" Ordinance. There are four possible arguments. The least plausible ones are based on the dormant commerce clause, substantive due process and equal protection. The best argument (and it is not very good) is based on the establishment clause, incorporated into the 14th Amendment's due process clause.

Dormant Commerce Clause. The law is facially neutral toward interstate commerce, since it bars all use of animal products. There is no indication of any motive to discriminate against interstate commerce or of any significant discriminatory effect. But the law bans a very large number of goods containing animal byproducts. Jake must prove that this burden on interstate commerce is clearly excessive in relation to the local benefits obtained. The local benefits are improvements to human health and preservation of animal life. These benefits are not illusory, though they may not be enormous. The actual burden of Island County's ordinance is probably not large. This contention is likely to fail.

Substantive Due Process. A variety of constitutionally unenumerated "privacy" or "autonomy" rights have been deemed to be protected by the due process clause. Governments may not infringe these fundamental rights unless it is necessary to do so to achieve a compelling state objective. The problem is that fundamental rights, so far, have all involved aspects of human sexuality, marriage, family, and the manner of one's death. To decide whether there is a fundamental right to eat animal flesh a court must decide whether this practice is so deeply rooted in our history and traditions that it is implicit in the concept of liberty. From a normative perspective, one might wonder whether this judgment is properly for the judiciary. From a doctrinal perspective, the task is to canvass the evidence bearing on the point. Americans have always been predominantly carnivores, though perhaps less so over time. But regulation of food offered for sale is legitimate, at least when undertaken for the purpose of preserving public health and safety. This issue is not obviously resolved by using the doctrinal criteria. Perhaps the susceptibility of the issue to resolution along lines of personal preference or notions of social morality suggest that the legislature might be the better forum for resolution. Doctrinally, one can argue the point effectively either way.

If eating meat is a fundamental right, then Island County must prove a compelling objective—preserving human health and safety? or, preserving animal life?—and that the law is necessary to accomplishment of that objective. Preservation of human health and safety may be compelling, but is an absolute ban on meat necessary to that goal? Even if there is empirical evidence that vegetarians outlive carnivores, that may not establish the necessity of forcing carnivores to alter their habits. Preservation of animal life, however noble, is not likely a compelling state objective. But if it is, the ban may well be necessary to accomplishment of the objective, since humans are among the most voracious of predators.

Equal Protection. Since the ordinance classifies by eating habits, it does not employ suspect criteria. Nor does the law infringe upon a fundamental right—one explicitly or implicitly protected by the

Constitution. Unless the right to eat meat is part of the penumbral shadow of "quasi-suspect" classifications or "quasi-fundamental" rights, the law is presumptively valid. The law does not pick on a politically vulnerable minority with a history of purposefully invidious discriminatory treatment. Nor is the right to eat meat connected in any way to the vindication or enjoyment of other constitutional rights. Unless Jake can prove that the law is not rationally related to any legitimate state goal his equal protection claim is not meritorious. Banning meat consumption is a rational method of improving human health and preserving animal life, both of which are legitimate possible objectives of the law.

Establishment Clause. The establishment clause, through the 14th Amendment's due process clause, forbids Island County from establishments of religion. Under the modified *Lemon* test, Island County must establish that there is a secular purpose for the law and that the primary effect of the law is neither to advance nor inhibit religion. The secular purpose is easy—preserve animal life and improve human health. While the law is facially neutral about religion, it compels all people to observe the fundamental tenet of Lifo. That effect is part of a general rule of conduct, though, and there is no automatic reason why Island County cannot adopt laws that happen to coincide with religious views. The effect is highly coercive, but the conduct coerced is not exclusively religious.

The ''No Jetskis'' Ordinance. Jake has three plausible arguments. None is likely to succeed. He also has several implausible arguments that are probably not worth advancing.

Preemption. The federal law regulating jetskis might impliedly preempt state law on the subject. Since the federal law doesn't mention state law there is almost certainly no express preemption of the Island County ordinance. The federal law does not appear to regulate jetski usage so extensively as to occupy the field of regulation of permissible watercraft in navigable waters. The federal interest in regulating navigable watercraft may be pervasive, but it is not apparent from the facts. Nor is there any indication of conflict preemption. Jake should examine the federal law with great care to construct the best possible preemption argument.

The Dormant Commerce Clause. The ban on jetskis is facially neutral with respect to interstate commerce, and arguably has no discriminatory effect. All jetskis are imported into Maine, but Island County bans them all, making no exception for local jetskis. This may not be a deliberate discriminatory effect, but the attempt by Island County to wall itself off from interstate traffic in jetskis does impose substantial burdens on interstate commerce. The local objective is to preserve the tranquility of Island County's waters. That legitimate objective may be impossible to obtain if jetskis, which emit a particularly loud and high-pitched whine, are permitted to operate. If so, the discrimination doctrine would be satisfied, as the ordinance would be the least discriminatory alternative open to Island County to achieve its objective. If this level of necessity is present, then the burden on interstate commerce is not clearly excessive in relation to those local benefits.

Establishment Clause. The ordinance has a secular purpose. Its primary effect is to preserve tranquility of Island County waters. That effect may promote the tenets of Lifo, the County's predominant religion, but produces so many other effects that are unrelated to religion that it is probable the "primary effect" of the ordinance is neither to advance nor inhibit religion. There is no excessive entanglement. The ordinance does not expressly endorse Lifo religious tenets, but it does do so by implication. That level of endorsement seems at least as diluted as the Pawtucket crèche in *Lynch v. Donnelly.* There is no coercion to observe Lifo religious tenets. One could still destroy animal life without using a jetski. Jake will not succeed with this argument.

Substantive Due Process. The first question is whether the asserted fundamental right is to jetski usage (as Justices Scalia and Rehnquist would frame it) or to water recreation (as Justice Brennan might have put it). It is highly unlikely that jetski usage is a fundamental right—a practice deeply rooted in our history or traditions. Nor is it likely that there is a fundamental right to recreation. Many recreational pursuits—from hang gliding to bicycle riding to hiking—are susceptible to regulation or prohibition. If there is a fundamental right it might be difficult for Island County to establish that its objective is compelling.

Equal Protection. This argument is a near-certain failure. The law does not employ a suspect classification nor does it infringe a fundamental right. It is surely rationally related to a legitimate state interest.

GLOSSARY

Abstention. Prudential doctrines that require federal courts to abstain from exercising their jurisdiction, generally in order to allow state courts freedom to decide. See Chapter 2.

Accommodation. As used in the context of the **establishment clause,** this describes an interpretational approach to that clause designed to prevent governments from coercing religious belief or nonbelief, or preferring one religion to another, or providing such significant aid to religion as to create a *de facto* state church. See Chapter 12.

Actual malice. A term of art describing the culpability standard constitutionally required to be proven in order to recover damages for defamation of public figures and in certain other cases. To prove **actual malice** a defamation plaintiff must show that the defendant knowingly uttered a falsehood or spoke with reckless disregard of truth or falsity. See Chapter 11.

"Adequate and independent state grounds" doctrine. A judicial doctrine, possibly constitutionally required, that bars the Supreme Court from reviewing cases that have been decided by state courts on state law grounds that are both adequate for the decision and independent of federal law. See Chapter 2.

Advisory opinions. The doctrine, derived from the **"case or controversy"** requirement, that federal courts may not decide issues outside of the context of a real, live dispute between truly adversarial parties. See Chapter 2.

Appointment power. The power of the President to appoint **principal officers** of the United States, subject to Senate confirmation. See Chapter 7.

"As applied" challenge. Statutes are generally challenged, and their validity determined, as they are actually **applied** to specific circumstances raised by a particular litigant. When a statute is voided **as applied,** its validity in other circumstances is left undisturbed. See also **facial challenge.**

Articles of commerce. Any item that can be bought and sold, thus becoming the subject of a commercial transaction. See Chapter 4.

Bicameralism. The constitutional requirement that federal legislation may only be enacted by the vote of both houses of Congress. See Chapter 7.

"Case or controversy" requirement. The phrase in Article III that limits federal jurisdiction to "cases" or "controversies." From this phrase are derived a number of doctrines limiting federal jurisdiction. See Chapter 2.

Categorical balancing. The process by which courts determine which categories of speech deserve either limited or no constitutional protection. Entirely unprotected categories are sometimes referred to as **"no value speech."** Speech categories receiving limited protection are sometimes referred to as **"low value speech."** Fully protected speech is sometimes referred to as **"high value speech."** See Chapter 11.

Certiorari. The writ granted by the Supreme Court to enable review of a case from another court. This is the most common way in which a case is heard by the Supreme Court. When the Court grants a petition for certiorari it agrees to review specified issues in the case. When the Court denies a petition for certiorari it refuses to hear the case; the other court's judgment stands. Denials of certiorari have no value as precedent. See Chapter 2.

Collateral bar rule. This doctrine holds that a person who violates an injunction may be punished for that violation, even if the injunction itself later turns out to be invalid. The collateral obligation to obey a court order until and unless it is reversed is independent of the grounds for issuing the injunction. See Chapter 11.

Commerce. (1) Mercantile exchange; the buying and selling of **articles of commerce."** (2) Often used as a shorthand way of describing the *"interstate, foreign and Indian"* commerce that Congress is empowered to regulate.

Commerce power. This is the shorthand expression for Congress's power, expressed in Article I, §8, to regulate interstate commerce, commerce with foreign nations, and commerce with the Indian tribes. See Chapter 4.

"Commerce-prohibiting" technique. A device used by Congress to exercise its **commerce power,** consisting of regulating the interstate movement of some article of commerce. See Chapter 4.

Conditional spending. A device used by Congress to spend federal money, but only if certain conditions are met by the recipient. The nature of the conditions can be constitutionally problematic. See Chapter 5.

Content-based regulation. A regulation that restricts speech based on the subject matter of the speech or its communicative impact on the listener. Some **content-based regulations** are also **viewpoint based.** See Chapter 11.

Content-neutral regulation. A regulation that restricts speech regardless of its subject matter or communicative impact. The classic example is a regulation that restricts only the time, place, or manner of speaking. See Chapter 11.

Cumulative effect doctrine. A judicially created doctrine, sometimes called the "aggregation principle," that the "cumulative effect" of an entire class of activities is the relevant effect when determining whether the class of activities has a *substantial effect* on interstate commerce. See Chapter 4.

Delegation doctrine. See **Nondelegation doctrine.**

Disparate impact. The term given to the result of **legislative classifications** that are facially neutral but that, nevertheless, have a disproportional effect on suspect lines, usually race. See Chapter 9.

Dormant commerce clause. A judicially implied role for the commerce clause, limiting state power to regulate interstate, foreign, or Indian commerce. See Chapter 6.

"Enhanced" minimal scrutiny. An uncommon variant of minimal scrutiny, sometimes expressed as a requirement that a **legislative classification** must be "rationally related to a *substantial* state interest." The triggers for enhanced minimal scrutiny are vague and ill-defined, but seem be the Court's assessment of some classifications as "quasi-suspect," but not "quasi-suspect" enough to trigger intermediate scrutiny. See Chapter 9.

Enumerated powers. This is a fundamental constitutional principle—the idea that the federal government possesses only certain powers that are specified, or "enumerated," in the Constitution.

Enumerated rights. Certain rights of the people, which governments may not infringe without exceptional justification, have been specified, or "enumerated," in the Constitution.

Equal footing doctrine. A judicial doctrine that the Constitution requires every new state to be admitted on equal terms with all existing states.

Establishment clause. This clause in the First Amendment forbids governments from creating establishments of religion. There are two principal approaches to interpretation of this clause—**neutrality** and **accommodation.** See Chapter 12.

Executive agreement. As distinguished from a **treaty,** this is an agreement between the United States and another nation made entirely by the President, without Senate confirmation. Such agreements are limited to matters wholly within the President's unilateral powers.

Executive immunity. A judicially created immunity from suit for members of the executive branch. The President is absolutely immune from civil suits seeking damages resulting from his official acts. Other executive officers enjoy **qualified immunity.** See Chapter 7.

Executive privilege. An evidentiary privilege that, with sufficient justification proven to a court, can be invoked by the President to preserve the confidentiality of executive communications. See Chapter 7.

Expressive association. Voluntary associations that are entered into for the purpose of expressing some message are **expressive associations,** entitled to some protection under the First Amendment. See Chapter 11.

Facial challenge, or Facial validity. Statutes may be challenged on their **face** or **as applied. A facial challenge** contends that the statute has so many unconstitutional applications that it is absolutely void. See **overbreadth.**

Federalism. A fundamental constitutional principle—the division of governmental power between a national government of **enumerated powers** and state governments with general powers.

Free exercise clause. This clause in the First Amendment bars governments from abridging free exercise of religion. In practice, this bars governments from interfering with religious belief or intentional interference with religious conduct. See Chapter 12.

Fundamental rights. This term is used in several different contexts, with different meaning in each. (1) For equal protection purposes, it is those rights explicitly or implicitly guaranteed by the Constitution. (2) For **substantive due process** purposes, it is those rights that are deeply rooted in our history and traditions, whether or not enumerated. (3) For Article IV **privileges and immunities** purposes, it is those rights that are essential to national unity and harmony.

General welfare. Congress may *spend,* but may not *regulate,* for the **general welfare.** The **general welfare** is effectively whatever Congress says it is. See Chapter 5.

Heightened scrutiny. This term has two meanings: (1) a loose description of all levels of judicial scrutiny more exacting that minimal scrutiny, and (2) another term for **"enhanced" minimal scrutiny.**

"High value" speech. A term sometimes used to describe speech that is fully protected by the First Amendment. See **categorical balancing.** See Chapter 11.

Incorporation doctrine. This judicial doctrine "incorporates" most of the Bill of Rights guarantees into the 14th Amendment's due process clause, thus making them applicable to the states as well as the federal government. See Chapter 8.

Inferior officer. Any executive officer of the United States other than one exercising extremely high level responsibility. See Chapter 7.

Intermediate scrutiny. A judicial test used mostly to review **legislative classifications** by sex or illegitimate birth. Under intermediate scrutiny **legislative classifications** are presumptively invalid unless the government proves that the classification is substantially related to an important state interest. See Chapter 11.

Intimate association. Voluntary associations characterized by their smallness, selectivity, and seclusion are treated as **intimate associations** and protected both by freedom of association and the privacy component of **substantive due process.** See Chapters 8 and 11.

Invidious discrimination. Constitutionally wrongful discrimination. A **legislative classification** is invidiously discriminatory when it classifies by an immutable trait that reflects irrational prejudice that has long been used to deny the targeted class any access to the political process. Invidious discrimination is the talisman to determine which **legislative classifications** are subject to **strict scrutiny.** See Chapter 11.

Judicial review. A fundamental concept—the power of courts to invalidate legislation and executive action on the ground of unconstitutionality. Judicial review is implied in the Constitution. See Chapter 2.

Just compensation. The Fifth Amendment's takings clause requires that all government takings of private property be accomplished by payment of **just compensation**—fair market value—to the affected property owner. See Chapter 13.

Justiciability. The idea that some issues possess characteristics that make judicial decision of the issue imprudent or constitutionally improper. See Chapter 2.

Legislative act. Action taken by a legislator or his aides that is germane to the process of legislation. Legislators and their aides possess **legislative immunity** only for legislative acts. See Chapter 7.

Legislative classification. The statutory division of people or things into two different classes, as by a law that sets sixteen as the minimum age to drive. One class consists of those under sixteen; the other class is of those over sixteen. Legislative classifications always relate in some way to a **statutory objective.** See Chapter 11.

Legislative immunity. An immunity from suit based on **legislative acts** for members of Congress and their aides. See Chapter 7.

Legislative veto. A device, now declared unconstitutional, by which Congress seeks to control the exercise of executive discretion bestowed by legislation. See Chapter 7.

Level of scrutiny. A reference to one of the three principal judicial tests used to evaluate laws or **legislative classifications**—(1) **minimal scrutiny,** (2) **intermediate scrutiny,** or (3) **strict scrutiny.** See also **tiered scrutiny.**

Limited public forum. A **public forum** that has been voluntarily created by a government, but only for limited speech purposes. See Chapter 11.

Line-item veto. A device, the constitutionality of which is unresolved, to give the President statutory authority to veto specific single items of tax or appropriations bills. See Chapter 7.

"Low value" speech. A term sometimes used to describe speech that receives only limited constitutional protection. See **categorical balancing.** See Chapter 11.

Market-participation doctrine. A judicially created doctrine by which states acting as market participants (like businesses) are excepted from the **dormant commerce clause.** See Chapter 6.

Minimal scrutiny. The basic (or "default") judicial test for legislation. Under minimal scrutiny, laws or **legislative classifications** are presumed valid, and struck down only if the challenger proves that they are not rationally related to any conceivable legitimate purpose. See Chapters 8 and 9.

Mootness. A judicially created doctrine that avoids decision of cases where events have rendered decision unnecessary—**standing** in a time frame. See Chapter 2.

Necessary and proper clause. The last clause of Article I, §8, which gives Congress power to select any rational or reasonable means it desires to carry out its legitimate legislative powers. See Chapter 3.

Negative commerce clause. Another name for the **dormant commerce clause.**

Neutrality. As used in the context of the **establishment clause,** this describes an interpretational approach to that clause designed to keep governments neutral on matters of religion by barring governmental endorsements of religious belief or disbelief, or government preferences of one religion to another, or government actions intended only to aid religion, or that have that as its primary effect, or that involve excessive entanglement of government and religion. See Chapter 12.

Nondelegation doctrine. The idea, implicit in **separation of powers,** that Congress may not delegate its legislative power to somebody else. In practice, Congress may empower agencies to make rules that have the force of law so long as Congress gives agencies an intelligible standard by which to know when to apply a congressionally declared policy. See Chapter 7.

Noninterpretivism. A philosophy of constitutional "interpretation" that espouses the manufacture of constitutional law by methods other than interpretation. Adherents often claim that it is impossible to "interpret" the Constitution, or that other values matter more. See Chapters 8 and 9.

Nonpublic forum. Public property that is neither traditionally open for speech nor voluntarily dedicated to speech purposes; e.g., a nuclear submarine in active naval service. See Chapter 11.

"No value" speech. A term sometimes used to describe speech categories that are constitutionally unprotected, save for **viewpoint-based** regulations. See **categorical balancing.** See Chapter 11.

Optimal class. The class of people or things that includes everyone or everything necessary to achieve the law's objective, and no more. A perfect fit between the **legislative classification** and the **statutory objective.** See Chapter 9.

Overbreadth. A concept used to determine whether a law is susceptible to a **facial challenge.** A law that, on its face, appears to have more unconstitutional applications than valid ones is overbroad. Only substantially overbroad laws are void on their face. See Chapter 11.

Over-inclusion. A **legislative classification** that includes more people or things within the class than is necessary to achieve the **statutory objective.** See Chapter 9.

Pocket veto. The death of a bill that results from the President's failure to either sign or veto a bill presented to him within ten days of a significant recess or adjournment of Congress. See Chapter 7.

Police power. A freely used, poorly defined term. States possess a general police power—the power to do anything reasonably related to protecting public health, safety, morals, or convenience. The federal government's "police power" is limited to those things reasonably related to accomplishment of its **enumerated powers.**

"Political function" doctrine. A judicial doctrine that exempts from **strict scrutiny** those **legislative classifications** that preclude lawfully resident aliens from performing certain public jobs that are "political functions." See Chapter 9.

"Political question" doctrine. A branch of **justiciability,** by which certain issues are deemed incapable of judicial resolution, either because the Constitution commits decision of the issue to some other branch of government or because there are very strong **prudential** reasons for a judicial refusal to decide. See Chapter 2.

Poll tax. A tax levied on the right to vote. Poll taxes on federal elections are barred by the 24th Amendment. Poll taxes in state elections violate equal protection absent some extraordinary justification. See Chapter 9.

Preemption. A logical corollary to the **supremacy clause,** this doctrine holds that federal statutes preempt, or displace, state law on the same subject whenever Congress so intends. There are a variety of ways to detect congressional intent. See Chapter 3.

Presentment. The constitutional requirement that bills be presented to the President for signature or veto. See Chapter 7.

Principal officer. Those executive officers of the United States, below the President and Vice President, who exercise the highest levels of responsibility. See Chapter 7.

Prior restraint. Any administrative or judicial act forbidding speech in advance of its occurrence. **Prior restraints** usually come in the form of injunctions or the requirement that a license to speak be obtained before speaking. See Chapter 11.

Privileges and immunities. A term used twice in the Constitution, but with different substance. (1) The P & I clause in Article IV, §2, protects natural persons from state discrimination on account of their out-of-state status, but only with respect to matters fundamental to the nation's unity. (2) The P & I clause in the 14th Amendment bars states from infringing those few rights that are attributable to federal citizenship. See Chapters 6 and 9.

Procedural due process. The requirement that, when any government infringes life, liberty, or property, it must do so *only* by a procedure that provides the affected person some notice and opportunity to be heard before the decision is made. See Chapter 8.

Process federalism. The emerging judicial doctrine that seeks to protect **state autonomy** by requiring Congress to act only in certain ways when it curtails the independent governance ability of the states. See Chapter 4.

Protective principle. A principle used in defining the limits of Congress's **commerce power,** by which the courts permit Congress to regulate intrastate matters that substantially affect interstate commerce. See Chapter 4.

Prudential. (1) A mode of reasoning about the Constitution that relies on practical considerations. (2) A term used to describe nonconstitutional doctrines of the Supreme Court. See, e.g., **abstention.** See generally Chapters 1, 2, and 7.

Public figure. In the constitutional law of defamation, a **public figure** is someone who has assumed special prominence in the resolution of public questions. See Chapter 11.

Public forum. Public property that is either traditionally open to speech (e.g., streets, sidewalks, and parks) or has been voluntarily dedicated by the government to speech purposes, either generally or for only limited purposes. The latter is a **limited public forum.** See Chapter 11.

Public use. The takings clause of the Fifth Amendment requires that all government takings of private property must be for a **public use.** The requirement is satisfied if there is any conceivable public purpose for the taking. See Chapter 13.

Pullman **abstention.** A judicial doctrine that requires federal courts to stay exercise of their jurisdiction where a federal constitutional issue turns on an undecided issue of state law, in order to permit the state courts to decide the state law issue. See Chapter 2.

Qualified immunity. Executive officers other than the President are immune from suit based on their official acts taken in good faith.

"Quasi-suspect" classifications. A loose term, never precisely defined by the Court, that describes **legislative classifications** subject to "enhanced" minimal scrutiny or intermediate scrutiny. See Chapter 9.

Rational basis review. Another name for **minimal scrutiny.**

Recess appointment. The power of the President to appoint persons to offices requiring Senate confirmation (e.g., federal judges and **principal officers**) without such confirmation if the Senate is in recess at the time of the appointment. Such appointments expire at the end of the next Senate session if not sooner confirmed. John Rutledge was appointed Chief Justice by President Washington as a recess appointment, but the Senate never confirmed his appointment. See Chapter 7.

Regulatory taking. When a government regulates property so extensively that the property owner is unable to possess it, or derive a fair economic return from its use, the property has constructively been taken by the government. Such *de facto* takings are referred to as **regulatory takings** and are subject to all the constitutional obligations imposed by the takings clause—primarily **public use** and **just compensation.** See Chapter 13.

Removal power. The implied power of the President to remove executive officials. See Chapter 8.

Reporter's privilege. This is an evidentiary privilege, created by some state statutes, that enables a news reporter to preserve the confidentiality of news sources. There is no constitutionally required **reporter's privilege.** See Chapter 11.

Retroactive legislation. Any law that alters the legal consequences of past actions is **retroactive legislation.** The due process clauses limit governmental ability to impose **retroactive legislation.** See Chapter 14.

Ripeness. The judicial doctrine, derived from the **case or controversy** requirement, that federal courts may not decide cases where the facts are sufficiently in flux that there may not be any need to decide the issues presented—a suit started too soon, before any damage has been done. See Chapter 2.

Secondary effects of speech. Effects produced by speech that are unrelated to the communicative impact of speech are **secondary effects.** Government regulation of speech to control **secondary effects** is treated as a **content-neutral regulation** rather than as a **content-based regulation.** See Chapter 11.

Separation of powers. The constitutional principle that the powers of the federal government are divided among the three branches of government—executive, legislative, and judicial. See Chapter 7.

Speech and debate clause. The clause from which is derived **legislative immunity.** See Chapter 7.

Standing. A judicial doctrine, consisting of a constitutional core and a **prudential** veneer, that requires federal courts to refuse to decide cases where the plaintiff lacks a sufficient stake in the dispute presented. The constitutional core is derived from **separation of powers** and the **case or controversy** requirement. See Chapter 2.

State autonomy. The principle that guides constitutional interpretation in order to preserve the states' ability to govern themselves independently of the federal government. A necessary corollary of **federalism,** this principle appears throughout Chapters 2 through 6, but especially in Chapters 2 and 4.

Statutory class. The actual class or classes created by a **legislative classification.** See Chapter 9.

Statutory objective. The reason for a **legislative classification.** It may be actual or imaginary, depending on the applicable judicial test, or **level of scrutiny.** See Chapter 9.

Strict scrutiny. The most stringent judicial test, or **level of scrutiny,** used only when the law or **legislative classification** has some constitutionally suspicious trait. Under strict scrutiny, a law is presumptively invalid unless the government proves it is necessary to achieve a compelling government purpose. See Chapters 8, 9, 10, 11, and 12.

Sovereign immunity. (1) The general principle, derived from English law, that governments are immune from suit without their consent. (2) The judicial doctrine, derived from the Eleventh Amendment, that states are immune from suit in federal court unless they consent or Congress validly abrogates their immunity. See Chapter 2.

Substantive due process. The judicial doctrine that certain **fundamental rights** are so inherent in "liberty" that governments may not infringe them without the exceptionally strong justification necessary to survive **strict scrutiny.** Unjustified infringements are a "substantive" denial of due process. See Chapter 8.

Supremacy clause. The clause in Article VI that makes federal law supreme and binding upon the states, regardless of anything to the contrary in state law. See Chapter 3.

Suspect classifications. Those **legislative classifications** that divide people or things by criteria that are presumptively the product of **invidious discrimination.**

Symbolic conduct. Nonverbal conduct that is intended to communicate a message and reasonably likely to be so interpreted. See Chapter 11.

"take care" clause. The clause in Article II that obligates the President to enforce law. Implicit in that obligation is some discretion to decide how best to enforce the law. See Chapter 7.

Tiered scrutiny. A description of the judicial practice of using different tests of increasing difficulty to evaluate the constitutional legitimacy of legislation and executive action. See **level of scrutiny.**

Treaty. An agreement between two or more nations, legally binding all parties. The President may negotiate treaties but they are not binding until and unless the Senate has ratified them. See also **executive agreement.** See Chapters 5 and 7.

Ultra vires. The Latin term to describe the attempted exercise of unauthorized power. As used here, it refers to congressional legislation that is beyond Congress's **enumerated powers,** quite apart from the separate question of whether it invades any **enumerated rights.**

Undue burden. The term coined in abortion law to describe constitutionally illegitimate governmental impediments to an abortion. See Chapter 8.

Under-inclusion. A **legislative classification** that includes fewer people or things within the class than is necessary to achieve the **statutory objective.** See Chapter 9.

Unenumerated foreign affairs power. A judicially implied exclusively federal power. Although the Constitution gives discrete bits of pieces of power to conduct foreign affairs to the President and to Congress, or shared between them, the Constitution is silent about the existence of any general foreign affairs power. See Chapters 5 and 7.

Unenumerated rights. A description of constitutionally protected **fundamental rights** that have little if any connection with the Constitution's text. See **substantive due process** and Chapters 8 and 9.

Vagueness. When laws are so vague that ordinary people cannot determine what conduct is prohibited they violate due process. See Chapter 11.

Viewpoint-based regulation. A regulation that restricts speech on the basis of the particular viewpoint expressed. **Viewpoint-based regulations** are a subcategory of **content-based regulations.** See Chapter 11.

War power. (1) Most commonly, the power of Congress to declare war and the power of the President to conduct war. (2) A congressional legislative power, limited to those means reasonably related to conducting warfare. See Chapter 7.

War Powers Resolution. A federal statute designed to define more precisely the circumstances under which the President may (and may not) unilaterally commit American armed forces to hostilities. See Chapter 7.

***Younger* abstention.** A judicial doctrine that requires federal courts to dismiss cases challenging the validity of pending state criminal prosecutions or civil actions in state court that implicate important state interests. A few exceptions apply. See Chapter 2.

Table of Cases

Table of Statutes

Index